MISSING BEAUTY

MISSING BEAUTY

A TRUE STORY OF MURDER AND OBSESSION

TERESA CARPENTER

W.W. NORTON & COMPANY

NEW YORK   LONDON

Published simultaneously in Canada by Penguin Books Canada Ltd.,
2801 John Street, Markham, Ontario L3R 1B4.
Printed in the United States of America.
The text of this book is composed in Avanta, with
display type set in Perpetua Black and Perpetua Italic.
Composition and manufacturing by The Haddon Craftsmen, Inc.
Typography by Adele Grodstein and Margaret Wagner.
Art by Adele Grodstein.

First Edition

Library of Congress Cataloging-in-Publication Data
Carpenter, Teresa.
Missing beauty: a true story of murder and obsession/Teresa Carpenter.
p. cm.
1. Murder—Massachusetts—Case studies. I. Title.
HV6533.M4C37 1988
364.1 '523'097447—dc 19 87-37110

ISBN 0-393-02569-1

W. W. Norton & Company, Inc.
500 Fifth Avenue, New York, N. Y. 10110
W. W. Norton & Company Ltd.
37 Great Russell Street, London WC1B 3NU

1 2 3 4 5 6 7 8 9 0

FOR STEVEN

One thing is certain; that when one thinks to touch the mountain top, one must reckon with its unfathomable gorges.

The Blue Angel
HEINRICH MANN

A hundred years from now histories will be written from the stubs of Exxon bills.

Lancelot
WALKER PERCY

CONTENTS

9

10   *Contents*

SOURCES

This account contains no fictitious characters. No names have been changed. The author has drawn upon nearly four hundred interviews as well as police reports and court records, books, periodicals, and personal observation.

MISSING BEAUTY

THE INTRUSION

SANDY RIDGE CIRCLE is a finger of road which curls through a high woodland into a cul-de-sac. From its terminus one can look out upon a stretch of marsh bounded by a pair of peaks. On one side stands Moose Hill, a tiny Eden of forest and wildlife. On the other is Rattlesnake Hill, a stack of rocky outcroppings which colonial superstition, fraught with visions of perdition, imagined to be crawling with serpents.

Between these peaks lies the town of Sharon, a resolutely civilized bedroom community of professionals who commute thirty-five minutes each morning to Boston and retreat each evening to their split-level homes with bay windows and redwood decks. Among these commuters was Professor William H. J. Douglas, whose moss green ranch house sat on the edge of the wilderness at 38 Sandy Ridge Circle.

The Douglas family seemed in most respects unremarkable. Nancy, the professor's wife, worked at a nursing home in Norwood, some five miles away. From the time the family moved to the neighborhood, in the summer of 1978, Nancy Douglas customarily set off for work after dinner and returned in the morning before light. In the late afternoon she emerged, still wearing her nurse's uniform, to chauffeur her three adolescent children to classes and athletic events. Pamela took flute and piano lessons. She showed no particular talent for either of these instruments, but it pleased her father to hear her play. Billy and Johnny participated in a seasonal cycle of ice hockey, basketball, and baseball. The Douglas boys were game but not gifted athletes. This lack of promise, too, seemed lost on their father, who bought them the most expensive equipment available.

Professor Douglas himself was the only one who seemed slightly out of step with the ordinariness of this domain. The professor was thought to be an important scientist. This reputation was due in large part to the hesitant accounts of his ability which Nancy Douglas rendered to her few close friends. She did not give the particulars of his work, only veiled intimations of its eminence. As she told it sometimes, he was trying to find a cure for cancer; at others, a solution to the riddle of crib death. As one might expect of such a dedicated man, William Douglas was rarely home. He spent sixteen-hour days in his laboratory at Tufts University School of Medicine, in downtown Boston. Often he would stay the night so as not to leave an experiment unattended. During 1982 these professional demands called him away so often that he was rarely seen. By early 1983 the most conspicuous thing about Professor Douglas was his absence.

ON THE EVENING of March 19, 1983, however, William Douglas was at home. He retired before midnight to the master bedroom on the second floor. That room normally served as a sort of den strewn with quilted sleeping bags in which the children would wrap themselves to watch television. This night, it was occupied by no one but Professor Douglas.

For some weeks Nancy Douglas had taken to sleeping on a couch in Johnny's room. Johnny, obliging this odd usurpation by his mother, had retreated to the living room, where he slept on a red futon. Pammy was asleep in her own room, off the second-floor hall. Billy was staying over at the house of a friend.

Shortly after midnight the doorbell rang. William Douglas made his way down the hallway and a short flight of stairs to answer it. Standing before him in the chill of the New England spring night were two men. One, in his midfifties, had thinning gray hair and a grin that in no way reflected the gravity of the situation. He hung back slightly behind a younger man whom Douglas recognized as State Trooper Paul Landry.

"Dr. Douglas," said Landry with a trace of deference. He was at the doorway of an educated man. "This is Detective Lieutenant James Sharkey."

The older man nodded. Landry then withdrew a search warrant and handed it to Douglas, who accepted it calmly.

"I have told you all I know, and that's all I can do," he replied. Then, hesitating, he added, "Why don't you come in."

Events on the porch of 38 Sandy Ridge Circle had been unfolding as in a dream. But as soon as William Douglas stepped inside and turned on the light, the full scope of this intrusion became apparent. Following on the heels of Landry and Sharkey came two more state troopers, as well as a chemist and a photographer. When Nancy Douglas, clad in a short white bathrobe, emerged from the second-floor hallway, her foyer was filled with invaders.

Lieutenant Sharkey moved in quickly on Nancy and enveloped her in solicitude. "We are sorry for the inconvenience, Mrs. Douglas, but . . . it is beyond our control." Nancy said she understood. Sharkey beckoned to the chemist, who withdrew from an evidence bag a large blue man's shirt spattered with small rusty stains. The detective asked whether she recognized this shirt.

"It looks like a shirt that Bill might have owned," Nancy Douglas offered.

Sharkey turned the shirt inside out to show her the armpits, which had been mended with a blue thread. Did she know whose work that was?

"Yes," she replied softly. "That looks like my sewing."

"Could you please show me where the thread was that you sewed this with?" Sharkey requested.

Nancy went to the bureau in the dining room and from the top drawer removed a spool of blue thread. It was clearly too dark to match the stitching in the armpits.

"Is there any other thread that you could possibly have used to sew this shirt?" Sharkey pressed.

Nancy padded mutely to the master bedroom and returned with another spool, which appeared to be a better match. Sharkey explained solicitously to Mrs. Douglas that her husband was a suspect in the disappearance of a young woman. She began trembling violently, and the detective took her hand to comfort her. Could she, Nancy asked, wake her children and take them to her father's, or anywhere to get them out of the way of the search? Of course, Sharkey replied. He would have liked to press her further, but she had already begun rousing her sleeping brood.

As troopers and technicians fanned out over the house, Lieutenant Sharkey asked William Douglas if he would please take a seat at the kitchen table. Douglas obliged, settling his bulk into a leatherette banquette. Trooper Landry, at that moment, entered the room and, drawing close to the professor, presented a two-and-a-half-pound sledgehammer, slightly worn, the head blunted on both ends. The investigators studied Douglas's face for some change of expression. There was none.

"Have you ever seen this before?" Landry asked.

"No," Douglas replied. "It is not mine."

Sharkey took out a pad of paper. "I'd appreciate it if you'd speak slowly, Doctor," he said amiably. "I like to get it all down precisely." Douglas nodded and got a pad and pen of his own.

"Dr. Douglas," Sharkey began. "I must tell you that you are a suspect in the disappearance of Nadine Benedict."

Far from appearing shaken by this news, Douglas responded as genially as if Sharkey had invoked the name of an old and mutual friend.

"You mean Robin," he corrected.

Sharkey removed from his wallet a card imprinted with the Miranda warnings and read them aloud. "I understand," said Douglas a little testily. "I am not altogether uneducated."

At his interrogator's urging, Douglas explained that he had done undergraduate work at the State University of New York at Plattsburgh and received his master's and doctorate in biomedical sciences at Brown University, in Providence, Rhode Island. This recitation was interrupted by Trooper Landry, who entered without announcement, carrying a package of brown trash bags. He had found them in the professor's blue Toyota Starlet. What, Landry asked, had these been used for?

It was clear from the nervous glances exchanged between Landry and Sharkey that something of enormous importance was riding upon this discovery. Douglas, nevertheless, replied evenly, "I have never seen those bags before."

"Dr. Douglas," said Sharkey, drawing the professor back to his narrative, "would you please tell me exactly what happened on the day Robin disappeared?"

Douglas seemed eager to oblige.

"We'll start with that Saturday," he began. "She called me in the morning around eleven o'clock. She told me she was calling from Despina's Pizza, which is on Mass. Ave. She said she was going to give her car to a working girl named Pam. Now, I thought that was rather unusual because Robin didn't like Pam. Secondly, she didn't give her car to anyone. . . .

"Then she called back in the afternoon, about three-thirty or roughly around then. She said she would be over by around six-thirty and drop off the slides. This is the artwork she does for me, and she was going to pick up additional work. I said fine."

"Oh," Douglas had a thought. He was intent upon being precise. "Then she called back and said she was having a fight with her boyfriend and that . . . would it be all right for her to come later. I said yes."

Douglas explained how Robin said she was coming at eight-thirty, then called and said she couldn't make it until nine. About every half an hour after that she called to say she would be delayed.

"Were you at home all this time?" Sharkey asked.

"I was home all night," Douglas replied. "Probably from four or five in the afternoon. . . . The reason I was alone is that my wife was in New Hampshire and the kids were either at basketball or babysitting or with friends. . . . I did go out . . . for a walk. Robin said she was coming at ten-thirty, but ten-thirty came and went. She didn't show up until about a half hour after that. She came about eleven. She came by car, and she parked in the driveway and walked in the front door."

"How was she dressed at the time?" Sharkey asked.

"I noticed she had slacks on and a blouse. And shoes. No hat. I don't honestly remember the colors of what she had on. When she came in, we sat down on the couch out there and I said something kidding about her being late, and she said something about J.R. and her having a fight. J.R. is her boyfriend, and she had told me about him in the past.

"We looked at the slides, and she left the two slides that she had made. Let me get them and show them to you." Douglas repaired to the master bedroom and returned with a large catalog of 35-mm slides. He showed Sharkey two black-and-white exposures, which he described as "cells." The detective nodded.

"Then I drew [on] an eight-and-one-half-by-eleven sheet of paper what I wanted her to do. You see"—Douglas demonstrated on his note pad—"I would draw them out in a rough sketch, and she would draw them out in the artistic drawings which would finally be made into a slide after I approved them. She was going to draw five figures for me. . . .

"After I received the slides and we discussed the drawings, that was it. I asked her what she was going to do now, and she said she was going to Joe's in Charlestown. She told me he had called her answering service and that he was a 'good date.' Then she left around midnight. . . . She left here anywhere between seven and eight minutes past midnight to quarter past midnight. This would be, naturally . . . early Sunday morning."

Douglas, all this while, had been sitting with his back to the kitchen door. Sharkey had arranged it that way so that Landry could signal him unobtrusively should he discover anything of value. What Landry and the other two troopers were uncovering in the rooms beyond was, in fact, so astonishing that Landry appeared in the doorway trying to convey the extent of it in an ecstatic pantomime. From the closet and bureau of the master bedroom, he had uncovered a peculiar trove of artifacts, among them a pair of coded address books, a pair of pink panties, and phone bills addressed to a Robin Benedict. Landry selected one item which he deemed particularly suspicious, a Panasonic beeper, and took it to the kitchen, where he thrust it in front of William Douglas. For the first time, the professor lost his composure.

"Shit," he exclaimed. "I have no idea of how that beeper got into my closet. You know . . . that reporter, Sheila Murphy, called and said, 'Boy, Dr. Douglas, someone is trying to do a number on you,' and she is right. She is a reporter for the *Herald*, and she must know something that I don't."

Trooper Landry now handed Douglas a bluish black purse which he had found in the bedroom closet.

"This is Robin's pocketbook," Douglas replied blankly. "It certainly looks like it with contraceptives inside."

"Dr. Douglas," said Sharkey. "Don't you think it is fair to say or at least surmise that this is a bit incriminating?"

"It's unbelievable," Douglas muttered. "Things don't look good. I don't know how that got in the house."

The state chemist Ronald Kaufman called Sharkey into the living room to show him something in the hallway closet, a blue windbreaker. Kaufman had tested it with chemicals sensitive to human blood, and it was giving positive readings. Sharkey took the coat to the kitchen. "This yours?" he asked Douglas.

"Well," the professor regarded it thoughtfully. "It looks like mine and I would say it was mine, but I don't know. Could I try it on?"

Douglas pulled on the jacket and zippered it up the front. The fit was nearly perfect. "It looks like mine, but I'm not going to say it was mine."

Sharkey, who had remained civil—even courtly—in the face of these discoveries, drew the interrogation to a blunt close. "If you killed Robin," he abjured, "would you please be gentlemanly enough to tell us where the body is so that she could have a decent Christian burial? If you have any principles, morals, or scruples—or any concern whatsoever for your wife and children—you will do the right thing and lead us to her remains."

Douglas replied quietly, "I didn't kill her, and everything I told you is the truth. I only wish I could help you more."

As Sharkey continued his questioning of Douglas, the troopers searching the master-bedroom closet came upon a brown camera bag stuffed with papers and mementos. Wedged among them was a Xerox copy of a newspaper article from the *Boston Herald*. It was dated Tuesday, March 15, of the week before. It was accompanied by the photo of an oval-faced girl with large dark eyes. The eyes were cast askance, flirtatious and full of promise. The story read as follows:

Distraught Dad Hunts Daughter
BY SHELLY MURPHY

A DISTRAUGHT Methuen father yesterday launched a search for his 21-year-old daughter, who disappeared without a trace 10 days ago. . . . [T]he search followed the discovery by police of a blood-stained jacket, believed to be the missing girl's, in a dumpster in Mansfield.

The jacket, the author elaborated, was found in a plastic bag, along with a bloodied man's shirt and a two-and-a-half-pound hammer. Her disappearance was purportedly "shrouded in mystery."

Police sources working on the case said the missing girl is a prostitute, and was at the home of Dr. William Douglas of 28 Sandy Road, Sharon the night before she was reported missing.

Douglas, 41 said last night she had come to his home March 5 to deliver graphic art work she had designed for manuscripts he was preparing. . . .

The blood-stained corduroy jacket found on Rte 95 in Mansfield, next to Sharon, was identified as Benedict's yesterday by her live-in boyfriend of 1 1/2 years, Clarence "J.R." Rogers—described by police sources working on the case as a pimp.

Something unmistakably odd had happened at 38 Sandy Ridge Circle. The belongings of a girl—apparently an artist, possibly a prostitute, probably dead—had found their way into the clutter of an ordinary suburban closet. They had, furthermore, lain there unconcealed. Had Nancy Douglas not noticed these things while cleaning? Sharkey and Landry would have liked to inquire but, by now, Nancy Douglas and her children had fled into the night. Only William Douglas remained, and from this night forward he would be the principal suspect in the presumed murder of Robin Benedict.

If the professor was aware of the furies at his back, he betrayed no anxiety. He had become so calm, in fact, that he asked if he might take a nap. Incredulous, the investigators watched him amble down the hall toward the master bedroom and climb into bed. Was he trying to demonstrate that his conscience was clear? Had he been overcome by some terrible, private knowledge? His behavior gave no clue. While investigators carted their discoveries to cruisers parked in the cul-de-sac, Dr. William Douglas simply turned his back to the bustle in the hallway and fell asleep.

I
THE
PLAYERS

BILL

WHEN William Henry James Douglas took up the serious study of biology in 1967, it was an unruly discipline. Even its most ardent practitioners would tell you that it was more of an art than a science. A certain amount of unpredictability was naturally to be expected in the very "science of life." The science which required the observation of thousands of creatures, each with its own diseases, peculiarities of reproduction, and distinct temperament. These eccentricities remained, nonetheless, a continual affront to the scientific impulse to measure and generalize.

A certain breed of biologist—the anatomist—historically met this challenge by reducing life to ever smaller particles, hoping to discover in the infinitesimal recesses of cells something that was ultimately controllable. Well into the twentieth century, however, the resolving power of conventional microscopes remained limited by the wavelength of light, and one could peer into those constellations only so far before the details became hazy. The interior components of cells, invisible to the naked eye, hovered out of sight like distant stars.

Then, in 1946, a revolution occurred well beyond the notice of the ordinary man. A concentrated beam of electrons broke through the light barrier and brought the subcellular world into focus. The electron microscope, however, was a rare and expensive item. For twenty years after its invention, its use was limited to a few privileged enclaves of research. Occasionally a school would be fortunate enough to come into possession of a second-hand instrument. In the early sixties, Brown University, in Providence, Rhode Island, acquired an old RCA training model. It was a clumsy contraption that took up most of a room in the basement of Partridge Hall, a three-story Victorian mansion which served as the head-quarters of the Department of Anatomy and Biology. To align its con-densers and lenses, one had to take a rubber mallet and strike the columns, causing them to vibrate noisily. This haphazard process often produced nothing. But sometimes, miraculously, a nucleus emerged. Projected to the size of the floor of the room, it beckoned the observer to enter it and embark upon that long-awaited journey into the interior of matter.

It was during this exhilarating period of discovery that William Doug-las came to Brown as a graduate student. He was from upstate New York, an awkward country boy whose credulous round face scarcely made him appear bright, let alone gifted. His high, childlike voice did not demand that he be taken seriously. Yet he learned to play that unwieldy old RCA like a Stradivarius. He mastered the difficult technique of cutting tissue into thin sections and mounting it on slides. And when the outlines of membranes were still too indistinct to be observed, he developed methods of staining them with heavy metals to make them more vivid.

Douglas's technical innovations were not in themselves earthshaking, but they facilitated bigger developments. On balance, they were signifi-cant enough to propel their innovator into a tributary of the revolution. The staining techniques he had developed as a graduate student came to the attention of a scientific society called the Tissue Culture Association (TCA), an international organization of biologists which, since the early forties, had been experimenting with extracting cells from the organs of living creatures and growing them artificially—in vitro. This process made it possible to cultivate thousands of identical cells, allowing researchers far more control over the outcome of experiments than they had ever enjoyed using live animals. These cultured cells, as it happened, also grew in a very thin layer, which made them ideal for viewing under the electron micro-scope. Tissue culturing therefore emerged as a companion skill to electron microscopy.

In the early seventies the TCA was preparing to forge a permanent union between the two techniques. The widow of an oil magnate named W. Alton Jones deeded to the society a piece of wilderness which the family owned in Lake Placid, New York. Upon this tract the society was to establish a center that would do honor to her late husband's name by promoting the culture of plant and animals cells, "the basic building blocks of life."

Even as construction on the W. Alton Jones Cell Science Center was begun outside of Lake Placid, William Douglas's application was receiv-ing admiring scrutiny from the TCA's board of governors. In 1971 the young Ph.D. was invited to take over as director of the center's electron microscope facility. During the next seven years Douglas applied his expertise in microscopy to cell culture.

Cells became his singular passion. With almost religious devotion he perfected techniques for isolating them from their interlocking systems and scrutinizing them with greater and greater particularity. The cells which he succeeded most brilliantly in culturing were from the human lung. These Type Twos, as they were called, secreted a waxy substance known as surfactant, which allows the lungs to inflate and deflate. It was the lack of that substance in premature infants that often caused cerebral palsy or other neurological damage. Earlier attempts had been made to culture the Type Twos, but no one had been able to come up with just the right growing surface, or substrate, that would mimic the conditions of a human body. He made an extract of actual lung tissue and coated a glass surface, a maneuver which essentially fooled the cells into dividing naturally.

Douglas's culturing techniques were admirable in their simplicity, and they won him many admirers. Among them was Dr. Karen Hitchcock, a cell biologist from Tufts University in Boston. An earthy, likable woman in her late thirties, Hitchcock was involved professionally with a number of collaborators from other campuses, including a research group in Pawtuxet, Rhode Island, which, like Alton Jones, was studying ways to stimulate the production of surfactant. During the midseventies, Hitchcock learned that William Douglas had developed a culture system that she might use, and so she prevailed upon a colleague to arrange an introduction. During the months that followed, Hitchcock and Douglas corresponded and swapped specimens. Gradually, with the studious detachment of scientists, they became friends.

When, in the fall of 1977, Karen Hitchcock was made chairman of the Tufts Department of Anatomy and Biology, she put in motion an ambitious set of plans which she hoped would invigorate the sleepy department. Hitchcock hoped to attract scientists who were doing similar kinds of work so that she could build what she called "focused research groups," nuclei of investigators doing related work and building upon each other's findings. One of those units, of course, would be devoted to study of the lung, and, she felt, it would be an impressive coup if she could recruit Douglas. His expertise in cell culture would be useful, but he had another skill that was nearly as valuable. At Alton Jones, Douglas had displayed an ability to sense trends in research. He had shown himself a masterful grantsman, and that excited Hitchcock, who wanted to enrich her department not only with more federal money but with grants from industry and private foundations as well. The chairman set about wooing him to her faculty.

Tufts University, whose main campus was in Medford, some five miles north of Boston, was a small institution of fewer than five thousand students. It had the misfortune to labor in the shadow of Harvard, which sometimes obscured the fact that it had a commendable medical school of its own. During the late seventies, Tufts's president, the esteemed nutritionist Jean Mayer, was putting into effect a master plan to expand the medical campus in downtown Boston. This included expanding the veterinary school and adding the Human Nutrition Center. These were exciting times at Tufts, a fact which Karen Hitchcock pointed out to Bill Douglas when she offered him an associate professorship and a lab of his own. He accepted quickly. Perhaps a little too quickly for a man of his apparent distinction.

Hitchcock, however, did not scrutinize her good fortune too carefully. She was delighted with her catch and made no bones about it. Her pride in William Douglas was so obvious that he was referred to by those less graced by the chairman's favor as the "jewel of the department." Even skeptics, however, had to admit that Douglas was a credit to the institution. He had brought with him an impressive dowry of grants. Among them were two large federal projects funded by the National Institutes of Health—one to study his lung cells and another to culture and characterize cells of the human prostate. The latter presented a rich area of research and one of pressing clinical importance, since medical literature suggested that 40 percent of all men over the age of sixty contracted prostatic cancer. After arriving in Boston, Douglas picked up two more prostate projects. He became a consultant to the Tufts Center for Nutrition and Aging, an agency of the Department of Agriculture, which was hoping to culture and characterize cancerous prostatic cells. He also entered into a collaboration with Dr. Peter Offner, an elderly investigator from the state labs who was studying the effects of male hormones on the sex glands.

While it was usual for his colleagues to be working on only one or two projects at a time, Douglas's agenda swelled to six, then eight. His lab, which brought in $300,000 to $400,000 a year, became the richest in the department. It occupied five rooms, which opened off a labyrinth of pastel hallways in the Medical and Veterinary Building, also known as M&V. A convivial clamor emanated from that complex for most of the day and sometimes much of the night. The high spirits which resonated throughout the lab were never, however, allowed to obscure a clearly defined hierarchy.

At the bottom of the pecking order were the dishwashers and bottle washers, mostly work-study students who collected their $1.50 an hour and disappeared at the end of the semester. Sometimes one or another would impress his personality upon the lab with a feat of roguery or incompetence. But for the most part they were beneath notice. Slightly higher on the scale of life was the graduate student. His position was usually awkward since he had not yet been inducted into the fraternity of science. Yet a graduate student who went on to do good research would reflect credit upon the lab which spawned him, so he did not merit total disregard. Occupying the next echelon was a staff of four technicians who ran the day-to-day operation of the lab, monitoring experiments and ordering supplies. They did not enjoy the prestige of a doctorate, but they were so indispensable that they mingled easily with the top echelon of the research personnel, the postdoctoral candidates. These were young scientists who had been attracted to the lab by its reputation in cell culture. At any one time you could find three to five of them at 530 M&V. Most labs had only enough research money to support one. The postdocs were investigators-in-training who were honing their in vitro skills and would someday go on to head labs of their own. As the young apostles of cell culture, they commanded respect.

They in turn deferred to William Douglas. The Man, as he was known, was an odd fellow whose physique seemed out of character with his reputation. While his shoulders were thin, almost frail, his ballooning girth made him look like a great penguin. His voice was unexpectedly high and childlike. He dressed carelessly, his shirts ripped under the armpits, shirttails hanging out, wearing the same drab brown sport coat day in, day out. His recessed chin, wide eyes, and thin upper lip made him appear simple. There was a naïve, unlived quality about him.

Every morning at six-thirty sharp, Douglas swayed heavily through the halls, stopping at 530 M&V to open the lab. He proceeded through a small foyer, which had become a secretary's station, to his own office. Unlocking that, he would trip over a lump in the gray carpeting that covered his office floor. It was one of those things he would make a mental note to fix, but never did. Although Douglas had chosen this little warren on the periphery of the lab to afford himself some solitude for writing, it did not reflect a quiet mind. His desk, which extended five feet across one wall, was swamped by a welter of abstracts and monographs. More documents were crammed into a horizontal filing cabinet which covered nine feet of another wall. The overflow lay in stacks on the floor. It looked, in the words of one assistant, like "an explosion in a paper factory."

Douglas demanded a copy of every document that came into his office.

He apparently filed these according to some personal system, because if someone came to him seeking advice on the structure of fetal rat lungs, for example, he would disappear into his office and emerge minutes later with a journal article on the subject. To the casual observer, Douglas's schedule seemed as disorderly as his surroundings. He was forever running off to meetings, papers flying out of a bulging brown briefcase. No record was kept of how many committees he had joined since coming to Tufts. He was, however, a member of eight scientific societies, all of which had annual and regional meetings. He made several trips a year to Washington, D.C., to review grants for prospective lung research funded by the National Institutes of Health and the Veterans Administration. At least once a year he flew out to Ardmore, Oklahoma, to do some microscopy consulting for a private biomedical research outfit called the Noble Foundation. And he traveled now and again to Germany, where Tufts had an exchange program with a university in Hanover.

Douglas seemed to enjoy the chaos of his own existence. It was visible proof of his importance, something about which he seemed to need constant reassurance. He was impressed by rank and was flattered by the attention of those whom he considered senior. To superiors such as Karen Hitchcock, he was not simply deferential but obsequious. Hitchcock would later say that she never saw Bill Douglas angry. When he was upset, all the expression drained from his face. The only hint of his feelings was a clenching of the teeth.

Whatever anger Douglas had pent up in dealing with those above him, he vented upon inferiors. He was given to occasional fits of rage which kept the lab on edge. Late one afternoon the technicians were working in the tissue culture room, a sterile chamber equipped with a filtering system that wheezed like a great hair dryer. To drown out the droning, one of the graduate students had brought a radio, which he set on the back of a sink. Douglas's office lay on the other side of a cinder block wall and, safe in the conviction that he could not hear, one of the work-study students turned up the volume. A couple of dishwashers began to jitterbug. This caper came to an abrupt halt when Douglas stormed in, threw a book at the wall, and screeched, "There'll be no more radio in this lab."

Incidents like that kept the lab off balance. The slightest trace of irritation in his voice inspired fear. And during those times the lab personnel tiptoed out of their way to avoid giving offense. One of those who became skillful at detecting and defusing Douglas's moods was the chief technician, Jane Aghajanian. A slender, efficient woman in her midthirties, Aghajanian not only handled the logistics of the lab, ordering supplies and equipment, but practically ran the federal mucous project. That was an almost unheard-of responsibility for a technician. She was hired shortly after Douglas's own arrival at Tufts, and her seniority afforded her some immunity to his temper. Douglas also relied upon her to brief him each morning at seven-fifteen sharp on the status of the projects. Aghajanian was not a manipulative woman by nature, but she had learned to play what she called "the Man's game." That meant never challenging him. Douglas could not bear to be questioned about anything. Certainly not about a point of science. Not even about anything as trivial as a petty cash voucher. So Aghajanian learned to let the little stuff slide. She gave him strictly the essentials and didn't bother him with things like squabbles in the lab. She also learned to say yes even if it eventually meant no. By the time the truth dawned on him, he wouldn't be sure whom to punish. By observing those rules, she stayed in Douglas's good graces and stayed in the running to be his "right-hand man."

This was an ephemeral distinction that during Douglas's early days at Tufts was passed from one assistant to another, depending upon who was in favor at the moment. Aghajanian often enjoyed the inside track because she had her fingers on the lab's levers. At other times the imperial favor passed to Dr. Ronald Sanders, a testy postdoc with heavy spectacles and a thick mustache. Douglas had brought him from Lake Placid to work on the Type Twos. Sanders was an excellent scientist who possessed an expertise in biochemistry that Douglas lacked. This made him indispensable to the lung project. Sanders, however, was not much of a politician. Though not without ambition, he found himself temperamentally unsuited to flattery. Since he came the closest of anyone to being Douglas's peer, he found it difficult to refrain from challenging him on points of science. The necessity to exercise tact made him irritable. That resentment deepened in time, particularly as Douglas reminded him, as he occasionally did, that Sanders had ridden to Tufts on his coattails.

Dr. Stanley Spilman was an altogether different case. Of all the postdocs drawn to Tufts by Douglas's reputation, Spilman was the most in awe. They had met in June of 1976 when Spilman, who had been working on a graduate degree at the University of California at Riverside, made a pilgrimage to Lake Placid to take Douglas's cell culture seminar. Douglas had made a national name for himself teaching this class. It was attended not only by postgrads such as Spilman but also by midcareer scientists from all over the country. That summer Spilman came to idolize Douglas. He was later to admit that he was taken not so much by the man as by his prestige. When, four years later, he applied for and got a position in Douglas's laboratory at Tufts, he expressed his gratitude in unctuous accolades. To anyone who would listen, he extolled Douglas as a "renowned scientist," praise which might flow credibly from the pen of a biographer but sounded silly coming from Spilman.

Spilman cut a comical figure in the eye of his colleagues. He was a short, wiry fellow whose thinning red hair was combed far over from one side. He smoked unfiltered Camels, drank rotgut bourbon, and spoke in a very authoritative tone of projects in the "go mode." The militarese which laced his conversation was a holdover from his Air Force days. He had reportedly worked in a missile silo somewhere in the Southwest. His own accounts of that period were so outlandish as to raise doubts as to their authenticity. His lab mates liked to tell about the time when he explained quite earnestly that the only way to stop a missile once it had left the silo was to station marksmen in a circle to shoot it down. Spilman's lab colleagues tended to find his exaggerations and fawning ridiculous. Douglas, however, took a liking to Spilman. In the version of events that Spilman consistently presented him, there were no problems—everything was in the "go mode." As a reward, Douglas installed Spilman as his permanent aide-de-camp.

Isolated as he was from his underlings, Douglas was often fearful that they were gossiping about him. If he saw a group of technicians together chatting he would sidle casually into their vicinity to eavesdrop. All conversation would, of course, stop cold, and the technicians learned to save their conversation until lunchtime. Then over plates of Mongolian stew in nearby Chinatown, they would pick over Douglas's eccentricities. Sometimes they discussed how he couldn't seem to think on his feet. Sometimes they laughed about his insistence upon the multiple copies. He required one technician, usually a dutiful dark-haired girl named Joanne Sateriale, to spend much of the day in apparently needless Xeroxing. And there was his habit of making lists. He tried to impose some order upon his haphazard schedule by making detailed notes of things to do. The yellow legal sheets on which he scribbled these reminders were eventually churned under the jumble of papers on his desk, thus adding to the clutter. The more obsessively he tried to control his belongings, the more they ran riot. At one point he had taken to taping his initials—WHJD— on everything from reference books down to his scissors. Every time the techs ran across one of these items, it provoked a fit of giggling since, as someone had observed, they sounded like the call letters of an FM station.

The words "WHJD BOSTON, 530 on your dial!" became a private joke that ran around the office, out of earshot of Bill Douglas. It did not surface until an impious graduate student showed up at a lab cookout one spring wearing a sweatshirt imprinted with the slogan. There was an uneasy silence while the lab waited to see what effect it achieved upon the Man. He stared blankly for a few moments; then his face brightened with delight. He had clearly taken the gag for a tribute. "I think," he said, "that we should have them printed up for the entire lab!"

There was something touching in Douglas's intermittent attempts to portray himself as a fun boss. It was as though he really wanted to be one of the boys but just didn't know how. He never seemed at ease at lab parties. Late each Friday afternoon, someone would yell "pizza" and the lab would order in six kind of pies. Douglas would chip in money, not only for his own share but enough to cover the work-study and graduate students who were generally scraping by. Then, as the party got going, he would disappear without taking any of the food. There were always generous leftovers, and the techs, hoping to nibble on them during the coming week, stored them in the laboratory refrigerator. When they returned on Monday, the pizza had disappeared.

It didn't take much detective work to conclude that Bill Douglas was a closet eater. He was there in the evenings long after the postdocs had gone. He would even come in on weekends and work sixteen-hour days, spending most of that time alone. Traces of habitation, like the missing pizza, gave clues to how he spent those hours. Now and then a postdoc would come in at night to check on an experiment and hear easy-listening music wafting from Douglas's office. He had apparently borrowed the radio from the culture room, hoping to return it before it was discovered. It was difficult to conjure up the image of Douglas crooning to Barry Manilow while penning observations on the progress of mucous cells. There was apparently some vein of sensuality that ran hidden beneath his awkward self-importance. And it was only late at night and in the early hours of the morning that Douglas could enjoy his pleasures in private.

BILL DOUGLAS never spoke much about his personal life. He seemed to have cultivated no close friends in whom he might confide. Ron Sanders, who had known him since their time at Lake Placid, never got beyond professional formalities. Once, during an outing to Whiteface Mountain, the two of them were caught on a ski lift. Suspended over the silent grandeur of the Adirondacks, a more introspective man might have been moved to share a few private thoughts. Douglas, however, chattered on incessantly about science.

Neither could Karen Hitchcock, with all of her hearty goodwill, penetrate his preoccupation with work. She had met his wife and three children, who since coming to Boston had been ensconced in rural Norfolk County, but she knew them only slightly. Nancy Douglas showed up at departmental affairs only when her presence was strictly required. On those occasions she might have gone unnoticed had it not been for her size. Whereas her husband's bulk was concentrated around his middle, Nancy's was spread more evenly over a mannish frame. Although her face was plump and round, there was nothing soft about it. Her eyes were small and recessed, utterly without emotion, which gave her an unfortunate porcine stare.

Nancy did not try to soften her inhospitable countenance with pleasantries. On the occasions she did appear at office functions, she hardly said a word. In the beginning Douglas's colleagues suspected that the cause of Nancy's timidity was the fact that she was only a nurse and might therefore feel insecure about making conversation with her husband's professional friends. Yet the wife of one of the technicians was also a nurse, and Nancy didn't seem to have much to say to her either. If Nancy mixed rarely, she entertained even less. Once in 1980, Bill Douglas invited the lab people to his home for a Christmas party. Bill had shown enthusiasm for this gathering, drawing a detailed map which gave not only significant natural landmarks between Boston and his cul-de-sac but also the precise mileage between them. When guests arrived at the house on Sandy Ridge Circle, they were a little surprised to find it so unassuming. Although the Douglases had been living there for two years, the interior was conspicuously plain, the walls unadorned, the floors bare. The Douglases, however, had laid in a generous spread of cold cuts. Bill played the genial host, filling glasses and urging Pammy to play the piano for the guests. The only limitation on Bill Douglas's spirits that night seemed the silent figure of his wife patrolling the perimeter of the gathering. Her presence served as a reminder that the Douglas household, this display of hospitality notwithstanding, did not welcome casual visitors. Nancy was clearly jealous of her domain and maintained a dogged vigilance to keep her family's privacy safe from intrusion. Christmas 1980 was one of the few times that anyone could recall being invited to the Douglas home.

What little was known of Bill Douglas's background resulted from the fact that Lake Placid was not only the spot in which Douglas had done some of his major work as a scientist; it was also the town in which he had been born and raised. Dr. Douglas's colleagues at Alton Jones therefore had neighbors who had once known the eminent cell culturist as little Billy Douglas. So it was that the stories of Douglas's youth and boyhood found their way out of the gossip mill of that tiny resort community and into that of academe. Predicated as it was upon this erratic intelligence, Douglas's history was awkward and incomplete.

What could be said for certain was that he had come from humble roots. His father, William Douglas, Sr., hailed from Saranac Lake, a resort town and the haunt of such nineteenth-century intellectuals as Oliver

Wendell Holmes and Ralph Waldo Emerson. Its splendid, healthful air also made it a retreat for urban consumptives, who made pilgrimages to its world-renowned tuberculosis sanatorium.

During the late 1930s, Billy Douglas, Sr., worked as a plumber for one of the lodges. Douglas was a tiny, nervous man who walked with a limp. He remained unmarried until his late thirties, when he left Florida and returned with a bride, the former Eleanor Wintz. Eleanor was a stout, blond German woman who spoke in broken English. She was also slightly older than Billy. Neither of these attributes apparently endeared her to her husband's family, whose members never understood why he had to go outside the North Country to find a wife. But Eleanor gradually won her in-laws' approval by virtue of fastidious housekeeping. Two years after her marriage, she gave birth to a son. She was forty-one at the time, and the doctor advised her not to have another child.

Little William Henry James Douglas—named for his father and an uncle—became the focus of his parents' doting. Everything the child did was wonderful. Every day when Billy Douglas would go into work, he would bring new stories about "the little man." Although Eleanor occasionally hired out as a domestic, she spent most days tending the child. He was a good little boy, who did everything his mother asked of him and ate everything she laid before him, usually generous German servings of meat, rice, and potatoes.

When the boy was five, the Douglases moved to nearby Lake Placid, where Billy Douglas, Sr., got a better job at the Lake Placid Club. Founded in 1895 by Dr. Mavil Dewey, creator of the Dewey decimal system, the club was a retreat for rich New Yorkers. Jews and blacks were not welcomed. Neither were consumptives from nearby Saranac Lake. If the resort was a bastion of bigotry, it was also a a marvel of self-sufficiency. Guests never had to leave the grounds. The main hotel was serviced by its own carpenter shop, meat market, buttery, and even a "piggery." Billy Douglas, Sr., was hired to work in the plumbing shop, which alone employed eight to ten men. The club exercised a paternal solicitude over its retainers and so provided the Douglases with an apartment on the second floor of a two-story frame house which it owned on the outskirts of the golf course. They lived there for the next ten years in relative comfort.

William Douglas would later reflect reverently on his boyhood in Lake Placid, referring to it as God's place. During the period of his boyhood and youth, however, he endured considerable misery there. Since the turn of the century, when the Lake Placid Club introduced winter sports to the North American continent, the character of this little resort town had been determined by athletes. Civic affairs were dominated by families like the Pelkeys and Beaneys, whose sons engaged in avid pursuit of the regional sport, hockey. Passion for the game lent the town a masculine temperament which took pride in its own decency and was, at the same time, as intolerant of weaklings as the Lake Placid Club was of consumptives.

Little Billy Douglas was not destined to become an athlete. He admired the strapping sons of the North Country and often tagged around behind them like a puppy. But he was a plump, timid mama's boy whose good manners invited abuse. Once, when he was about seven, a couple of older boys caught him on the golf course and beat him badly. For weeks after that, he had nightmares from which he awakened screaming, having just suffered imaginary abuse at the hands of a phantom bully. His mother was beside herself with worry. Not being an assertive woman and not quite sure what powers could be invoked to stop the persecution of her son, she sought out the advice of a neighbor, Mrs. Nellie Cobane, who instructed her to report the beating at once to the elementary school principal.

Mrs. Cobane was a compassionate woman who recognized that Billy Douglas was a very lonely little boy. From the time his parents brought him to Lake Placid, she went out of her way to be kind to him. Each morning before school, he would wander down the block to the Cobanes' gray bungalow and sit while Nellie read stories to her own children. Nellie never had him pegged for a brilliant child, but he was sweetly receptive to learning. And he showed a precocious curiosity about the natural world. Nellie's husband, Orville, ran the ski room at the club. He was also a professional guide, who would sometimes take Billy on excursions into the mountains to hunt and to fish and to capture frogs in the streams.

Billy Douglas's fascination with biology revealed itself under the gentle tutelage of the Cobanes. This proclivity was apparently lost on his mother, who, when her son was still small, became a Christian Scientist. She insisted that young Billy accompany her to meetings. Billy Douglas, Sr., however, made it clear that he disapproved of his wife's new faith and tried quietly to discourage it. Of the two, he had the better appreciation of his son's potential and resolved that the little man would go to college. When the boy was a sophomore in high school, Billy, Sr., got a job at the Plattsburgh Air Force Base, some ten miles northeast of Lake Placid on the shores of Lake Champlain. The family moved to Plattsburgh, which was also a site of the State University of New York.

DURING the early fifties, SUNY Plattsburgh was a quiet little campus idylling in the congenial torpor of the Eisenhower era. Although only a state teachers' college, it had certain affectations of a private school. This was because the dean of students was an ex-Navy commander who believed that decorum built character. On Wednesdays and Sundays all students dressed for dinner and were served by student waiters. The administration forbade liquor and imposed a curfew upon women—a largely gratuitous precaution since the male population was temporarily depleted by the Korean War.

When Bill Douglas enrolled in the fall of 1958, the campus had started to come alive. Servicemen returning on the GI bill cheerfully flouted liquor regulations and contrived schemes to spirit women out of the dorms past curfew. A mark of their success was the profusion of supine couples nestled among the firs of Rugar's Woods. During his freshman year, at least, Bill Douglas was not at liberty to indulge in these escapades. He was still living at home with his parents at a trailer court on Cornelia Street, near the southern outskirts of town. It was an incommodious arrangement. The little trailer was only eight by forty feet. His parents shared what passed as the "master bedroom" at the far end. Bill slept in a cramped berth that opened off the hall. He hadn't the privacy required by a young man entering college. It was not until the following year that he found a refuge on campus with the brothers of Pi Alpha Nu.

PAN was not a prestige fraternity. Athletes and scholars ended up at Theta Kappa Beta and Delta Kappa Delta. Pledge time for Pi Alpha Nu reaped a harvest of good-natured misfits. PAN liked to think of itself as a "social fraternity," which meant it did a lot of drinking. Every night the brothers would convene at a hole-in-the-wall called Meron's, where they quickly escalated from beer to a concoction of Southern Comfort and bourbon, appropriately named the Panic. They would then pile into a 1946 Ford dubbed Boris and careen drunkenly through the environs of Plattsburgh.

The fraternity house was a small two-story Cape Cod that stood under the sentence of a demolition order. Pi Alpha Nu, in fact, got to use it for only one year before it was leveled in a campus-wide renewal program. After Bill Douglas pledged that fall, he took to spending most evenings at the cottage before returning to the trailer on Cornelia Street. Bill was more studious than most of the brothers, but he came to enjoy boozing. This served to expand his girth, which had been increasing steadily from the time he was twelve. Though not obese, he but had a pillowy softness which gave him the appearance of a big baby. The brothers regarded him as a sort of mascot, and he joined in the fun by ridiculing his own bulk. The degree to which his appearance actually bothered him was clear a few months into his sophomore year when he announced that he intended to lose weight.

Bill Douglas attacked his fat with such ferocity that it inspired awe among his more dissolute brothers. They would wander in at night—having just crashed Boris through a fence on the edge of Rugar's Woods—and find him wheezing furiously through a set of sit-ups. He bent his entire will to remaking his body. For days he consumed nothing but vitamins. Someone then slipped him a tip about protein, and he began eating nothing but eggs. Poached, scrambled, hardboiled, deviled. No one documented exactly how much weight Douglas lost, but the transformation was dramatic. His midriff shrank into a taut, muscular torso. His face lost its baby fat, becoming nearly gaunt. His eyes seemed to reveal for the first time the intelligence of an adult.

Before this metamorphosis, Bill had never dated anyone steadily. He could usually scare up a date to a frat party—from the pool of drab, slightly overweight nursing students—but these never developed into serious relationships. It was shortly after losing weight that he met a country girl from the Champlain Valley. If slightly stout, Bill's new girlfriend had a pert face. She had a steady fellow back home, but she wanted to experience a little of life before settling down to marry. Since she was a devout Christian, the life she intended to experience presumably excluded defilements of the flesh.

Bill's girl had never known him in his earlier incarnation, so even years later she remembered him as trim and—because he was an upperclassman—sophisticated. Although she had a fiancé in the wings, she developed "quite a crush" on him. Bill, she knew, was living with his family, and she thought it was odd that he never took her home to meet them. In the spring of 1961, a few months after they had met, Bill's father died of a heart attack.

Outwardly, Bill showed no signs of grief. But his girlfriend discerned through his offhanded comments that things were not well at home. His father's death had apparently sent his mother into decline. One night, a few months after the funeral, Bill took his girl out to the trailor to meet her. As they entered the trailor, the girl was shocked to discover sitting at one end of the couch a plump, little gray-haired woman who appeared dazed and incoherent. Eleanor Douglas drooled slightly and ran her fingers compulsively over the edge of a washcloth. More disturbing, she kept repeating in high broken English, "Is that you, Bill? Is that you, Bill? Is that you?"

Bill's girl thought she might get a bit closer to him by ingratiating herself with Mrs. Douglas. This wasn't the case. Bill seemed "rough" toward his mother. On succeeding visits, as the girlfriend sat talking to the old woman, Bill would sit down at the kitchen table and begin to read aloud from his textbooks, in effect assaulting his mother, who had a spiritual aversion to science, with his own apparent passion for it. When her high keening "Is that you, Bill? Is that you?" got too much for him, he would snap at her to keep quiet.

Bill and his girl were pinned. And, as was the custom, the men of Pi Alpha Nu dressed up in their gray blazers and serenaded her beneath her dorm window. No sooner were they engaged to be engaged, however, than Bill announced inexplicably that he wanted to date others, and their pre-engagement dissolved. These "others" Bill dated were not considerably more worldly than his recently forsaken love. No one can ever remember seeing him with a woman in Rugar's Woods. Once when his mother was out of town, he did allow a fraternity brother to bring his fiancée to the trailer for a tryst, but there is no indication that he ever took the same liberties. As one of his fraternity brothers later wrote, "Bill was never very attractive to women. The girls he dated tended to be shy, gentle creatures. He treated them with great respect approaching awe."

Among these unassuming creatures was Nancy Boulton.

Nancy was a nursing student and, like Bill's earlier love, a small-town girl. She had grown up in the village of West Warwick, Rhode Island, a community nestled among textile and chemical factories in the otherwise rural Pawtuxet Valley. Her grandfather was a lace dyer. Her father, John, was a Navy airman. In 1943, when hundreds of acres of the Pawtuxet Valley were being seeded into victory gardens, John Boulton married Lois Graemiger, a young woman who worked at the Warwick Chemical Company. Nancy was born the following year, followed soon afterward by Barbara and Steven.

When, at the age of thirty-three, Lois Boulton died of cancer, her husband moved his three children to Smithtown, Long Island, in New York State, to be closer to his brother's family. To all appearances, Nancy, a plain big-boned girl of fifteen, had accepted the death of her mother stoically. In the Boulton family, hardships were borne in silence. Whatever social life she enjoyed as a high school student seemed to revolve around Future Homemakers of America. After graduating from high school in 1962, she enrolled in the nursing program at SUNY Plattsburgh.

Nancy was such a private person that she never confided in friends the details of her meeting with Bill Douglas. Their courtship proceeded fairly rapidly, however, for they were married in August 1963, two months after Bill's graduation from Plattsburgh. The wedding took place at the St. James Episcopal church near Smithtown. Nancy wore a long organza gown trimmed with alençon lace and carried her mother's prayer book covered with white roses. Afterward the bridal party and about one hundred guests repaired to the Masonic Temple in Smithtown for a reception, during which at least one of Bill's fraternity brothers passed out drunk on the floor.

The newlyweds took a wedding trip through upstate New York before settling in Castleton-on-Hudson, where Bill had secured a position teaching biology at the high school. He later recalled the three years spent here as the happiest years of his marriage. He and Nancy had money and freedom. They went on trips to the mountains and the sea. They bought a little red convertible. Yet Bill Douglas was unhappy teaching. He had expected the students to be more disciplined, more eager to learn. He would come home at night and start snacking to ease his frustration. The snacking turned to binging. The pounds returned, and with them disappeared the trim, taut young man who scarcely three years earlier had struck his country love as a dashing sophisticate.

Once in 1966, after Douglas had been married for three years, he telephoned to tell his former girlfriend how well his life was going. He told her he had been teaching high school but had received an award from the National Science Foundation for a year of academic study at Yale. He was changing the direction of his career from teaching to research. This upbeat news notwithstanding, he sounded wistful, as if he would like to see her. When she broke the news that she had been married for a year, he cut the conversation short and never called again.

During the year the Douglases spent in New Haven, Nancy became pregnant. She was over five months gone when they moved to Providence, where Bill was scheduled to begin graduate work at Brown. They rented a pleasant, modern apartment in a subsidized complex called University Heights. It was situated on a bluff overlooking a shopping center by the same name. In the gulf between the apartments and stores ran an alley lined with dumpsters. These were ostensibly for use by the center, but in fact served as trash bins for the tenants of University Heights. At night, graduate students made furtive forays into the alley to dump things that had outlived their usefulness: refrigerator boxes when they moved in; old mattresses when they moved out. The University Heights dumpsters caught the debris of transition, the make-do belongings of those who were moving on to what they hoped were better times.

NANCY'S baby came on December 12. The following morning, Bill Douglas went up and down the corridors of Partridge Hall sticking squares of blue paper on the doors to notify his colleagues that he had a new son. In the months to follow, Nancy would show up at the department with

little Billy in a stroller. Both parents were unabashedly proud of him.
Seventeen months later, Nancy gave birth to Pamela. Bill's colleagues
later surmised that it must have been hard on Nancy to be pregnant so
much of the time, especially with Bill spending sixteen-hour days master-
ing the intricacies of the electron microscope in the basement of Partridge
Hall. Nancy, however, seemed to bear her maternity with equanimity. She
seemed to want no more from life than to watch her babies play in the
large, sunny courtyard of University Heights.

What little socializing Bill and Nancy did was with those who had
children. Among them were Jim and Izola Hogan, a black couple from
Georgia. Jim was one of the first minority students that Brown University
had recruited during the late sixties, when it was feeling pressure to fill
racial quotas. He was treated with scrupulous courtesy at Partridge Hall,
but it was clear that he was part of a social experiment and most of his
fellow students regarded him with skepticism. Douglas, something of an
odd duck himself, befriended Hogan. Jim and Izola, who lived only a few
doors down at University Heights, had four children, who played with the
two little Douglases. Even Nancy, who did not seem to feel the need for
friends, warmed up to Izola, a registered nurse. Sometimes when they
were in the courtyard tending their children, Nancy would confide in Izola
her plans to go back and finish her own nursing degree. She had put
everything on the back burner until Bill got on his feet.

There were limits, however, to how far Nancy would reveal herself. Her
essential character seemed locked inside a forbidding primness. Once Jim
and Izola gave a party for two or three other couples, including the
Douglases. Late in the evening Izola put on a comedy album. It was risqué
but appropriate, Izola figured, for adults. She gradually sensed that Nancy
was becoming uncomfortable. Finally, without a word, the Douglases got
up, put on their wraps, and left.

Among his Partridge Hall peers Bill did not seem so prudish. After
working until ten or eleven o'clock, Bill and a fellow named Hank Holden
would often tag along with a handful of others to a student bar called the
Graduate Center for a couple of beers. They were not conspicuously
macho men, but now and again someone would let fly an oath. On one
of these occasions, Hank asked Bill if it bothered him. Douglas shook his
head and replied, "The only thing that offends me is . . . obscenity when
my wife is around."

Hank Holden also had a wife and infant son, with whom he lived on
the Connecticut border in Westerly. He had an hour's commute each
day. Since Hank, like Bill, often worked late at Partridge Hall, he had a
standing dinner invitation at the Douglases'. Nancy would whip up a

frugal meal of potato pancakes. The Holdens, in return, sometimes invited the Douglases and their babies to Westerly for weekend beach parties. Hank, Bill, and two or three others would wade into a cove which fronted the Holden property to catch blue crabs. Then they would haul their catch back to shore for a midnight cookout. It was on those occasions that Bill displayed the full range of his gargantuan appetite. Beer, sweet corn, crabs, smoked eel, potato chips, all disappeared indiscriminately down his gullet. Far from discouraging her husband's appetite, Nancy seemed to condone it, even to encourage it. His feats of consumption became the subject of amused gossip. This was not lost on Bill, who was once again trying to lose weight. After consulting with a university physician who put him on a strict diet of mushrooms and peas, he dropped fifteen pounds. But he put it back on in one weekend of beer drinking. Now, in his late twenties, he seemed unable to summon the willpower which had allowed him to transform himself so admirably some eight years earlier. This weakness apparently filled him with shame.

On the day the Douglases moved out of their apartment at University Heights, a contingent from Partridge Hall—secretly fearing that Bill might suffer a heart attack—offered to help them. One of the volunteers found Bill in the basement going through a box of equipment. He withdrew a wet suit and held it up for his friend to see. "Would you believe that's mine?" he asked ruefully. "The day I was married I weighed 175 pounds. You should have seen my wedding pictures. Look at me now."

WHEN Douglas left Brown in the spring of 1970, he had been hoping to go straight to Alton Jones, but snags in funding and construction delayed the opening of the center for many months. Douglas spent one more restless year teaching at Edinboro, a small college in western Pennsylvania, before Alton Jones finally gave him the nod. In the spring of 1971, he packed up his family, which now included baby Johnny, and moved them to Lake Placid.

To return wrapped in eminence to the scene of early humiliations was no doubt satisfying to Douglas. The new Cell Science Center, sitting astride a high wooded ridge north of town, was the showpiece of the community. Its lobby, dominated by an enormous fireplace, opened onto an atrium designed to accommodate a twenty-foot avocado tree. The communal areas were flanked by two wings of laboratories. From his office at the center of this complex, Douglas could look down figuratively, if not literally, upon the golf course of the Lake Placid Club and reassess his old tormentors with contempt.

The fraternity of town athletes which had excluded him as a boy now welcomed him as the father of a pair of potential hockey players. Billy was just old enough to start playing with the Lake Placid Termites, first level of Pee Wee League. Douglas, hoping no doubt that his son would turn out to be a better-coordinated specimen than himself, outfitted Billy with the most expensive equipment he could find. When Johnny turned four, he too was steered onto the ice.

The Douglas boys stayed in hockey long after it became clear that they were not going to be particularly good athletes. But Pee Wee sports, no matter how badly played, were believed to build character. The association, accordingly, relied upon fathers to staff the league and recruited Douglas as an assistant hockey coach. He cut a rather ridiculous figure on the ice, and on those occasions when he announced games, his high, womanish voice provoked laughter in the arena. But he was a good sport and reliable. Every fourth Tuesday of every month, he attended youth commission meetings upstairs at the American Legion Hall. Afterward, when the men made their way downstairs to the bar, Douglas would have a polite drink, then excuse himself so that he could get home to Nancy and the kids in their little tract home on Hurley Avenue.

His position at the Cell Science Center required a certain amount of socializing. Every summer he hosted a cocktail party at the Howard Johnson motel for his summer students. There was some hobnobbing with visiting members of the Tissue Culture Association. The president of the TCA was a Canadian anatomist named Sergey Fedoroff, who had been particularly impressed with Douglas's work at Brown and had taken an active hand in getting the young scientist his job as director of the electron microscope facility. Fedoroff dropped into Lake Placid occasionally to keep an eye on things, and when he did, he sometimes visited the Douglases.

Nancy endured these professional evenings, as she did every personal trauma, stoically. She seemed more at ease in the company of other hockey parents, particularly the town barber, Roger Smart, and his girlfriend, Carol Stanclift, who had three boys of her own by a previous marriage. They were all Pee Wees. Her oldest was a close friend of Billy Douglas. Roger and Carol would generally take Bill and Nancy to Newman's Opera House, a drafty barn of a restaurant that catered to locals. It wasn't rough or noisy, which was good since Bill and Nancy couldn't tolerate rowdiness. They had an aversion to the small working-class bars that lay along Main Street. Once a couple of other hockey fathers tried to lure him to the Handlebar, a dive notorious for its clientele of brawling loggers. Douglas flinched and shook his head saying, "I don't know if I can go in there."

If he was timid, Douglas was also tight with money and didn't see the point in paying for drinks at the counter when you could get a bottle, go home, and enjoy it. He and Nancy sometimes invited the Pee Wee parents over to Hurley Avenue to play pinochle or poker. Bill didn't handle himself too well once he got to drinking. He lost track of his cards, and his bets were more than they should have been. Still, no one ever saw him get mean drunk, just silly. No one could recall ever seeing him angry, during seven years he spent at Lake Placid. If he got upset over a bad call in hockey, his face grew red, but he never raised his voice.

Ironically, it was Nancy, the more silent of the two, who was given to outbursts. Not that she was as strident as those hockey mothers whose maternal solicitude took the form of angry tirades. But if one of her Termites took a bad call, she shouted abuse at the referees. Those who had an opportunity to peer, however shallowly, into her domestic life saw that she was the one who ran the Douglas household. Bill was blessed with intelligence, but Nancy had the sterner stuff. When Johnny was scarcely out of diapers, Nancy decided it was her turn to go back to school. During that period, the Douglas home often suffered from lack of attention. Nancy rarely had time to cook, and the family came to rely upon take-out food, usually hamburgers. The Douglases apparently accepted the disarray as temporary, assuming it would subside as soon as Nancy got her degree. Looking forward to that time, the Douglases bought a lot in an exclusive new subdivision and made plans to build a house in which they would live out the rest of their lives in the North Country. But this was not to be. By 1977 Bill Douglas found himself in growing disfavor at Alton Jones.

His difficulties stemmed from a feud with the center's director, Dr. Paul Chapple. It was unusual for anyone not to get along with Chapple, a likable, easygoing fellow. In Douglas's contemptuous opinion, however, the director was more a public relations man than a scientist. The normal procedure would have been for Douglas to take whatever grievances he had against Chapple to the board of directors. Disregarding protocol, however, he wrote a letter directly to the Jones family's attorney charging that Chapple was neglecting and mismanaging the center. The Jones family was shocked to learn of rancor among its scientists, who were supposed to be occupied with loftier goals. They demanded an accounting from the Tissue Culture Association, which required that Sergey Fedoroff fly to Lake Placid to assess the damage. Had Douglas gone through Fedoroff to begin with, the problems, which seemed minor enough, might have been mediated quietly. But Douglas's letter was the first bite of the apple in Eden. The Joneses grew increasingly suspicious of the center and wanted a larger role in running it. The Tissue Culture Association, however, did not want to relinquish its prerogatives. Senior scientists, worried that the center might not have money to continue operating, were quietly updating their résumés. It was in the midst of this upheaval that Douglas received the offer from Karen Hitchcock that presented a graceful exit. As the author of discord, Douglas knew he had no future in Lake Placid. In the summer of 1978 he left, under a cloud, for Massachusetts.

THE DOUGLASES, who by all accounts had been very happy in Lake Placid, had truly been cast out of Eden. Accordingly, Bill and Nancy hoped to recapture the missing beauty and solitude of the Adirondacks in the environs of Boston. On its face, at least, Sharon, lying ten miles southwest of the city, seemed ideal. The town sat on a highland ringed by small hills. During the nineteenth century it called itself "the healthiest town east of the Rockies," rivaling Saranac Lake as a retreat for consumptives. Sharon was virtually free from lung disease. The air, supposedly, contained a high concentration of ozone, a condensed form of oxygen that smelled vaguely of chlorine. The odor notwithstanding, Sharon became popular as a health retreat. Patients flocked to a sanitorium on the summit of Moose Hill, where, bundled in furs, they spent the night on open verandas breathing wintry air. During the 1920s those fleeing the sweltering Boston summer could take a trolley to the shores of Massapoag, a 400-acre lake fed by a network of ponds. From there the wealthy caught a steamer to the great Massapoag Lake House, which boasted one hundred rooms, billiards, livery stables, and tennis courts. Those of lesser means summered in the cottages along Beach Street.

By the late seventies the Lake House had been converted to a community center. Lake Massapoag and its surrounding marshlands had become a nature preserve. The rail replaced the trolley and brought with it an influx of commuters who moved into subdivisions that were snaking into the hills. One of these, Beaverbrook Colony, appealed to Bill and Nancy Douglas. It didn't feel like a suburb. It was within easy walking distance of a town which had a *real* main street. They could run for supplies to the Bradlee's shopping center on Route 119. On days when Nancy had no time to cook, they could run out to the Burger King at Cobb's Corner, a crossroads jammed with tiny shops, in nearby Canton. Bill could take the commuter railroad into Boston from a modern brick station at Route 128. If he needed to travel out of town, he could take a bus to Logan Airport from Foxboro Plaza, a ten-minute drive to the south. There one bought a ticket at the knitting shop. Most of life out in Sharon was conducted on this same, human scale.

At Beaverbrook Colony the Douglases found a split-level for an afford-able $56,000 on a cul-de-sac called Sandy Ridge Circle. It was private and spacious with three large bedrooms on the second level and a recreation room in the basement. No sooner had Bill Douglas seen it than he began making plans to build an indoor pool in the back. As he was not very good in carrying through on home improvement, this project never got under way.

A month after moving to Sharon, Nancy Douglas got a job at the Ellis Nursing Home, in Norwood. Ellis was a pleasant brick complex, and every day at 10:55 P.M., Nancy reported for work in the Cherrywood Wing wearing her white uniform, white nylons, white shoes, nursing cap, school pin, and name tag. The administrators of Ellis were extremely satisfied with Nurse Douglas, rating her "excellent" on all points, from "technical skills" to "sensitivity." Nancy, in turn, liked Ellis and, although earning less than $10,000 a year, was happy to have found work that left her days free to tend the children.

Nancy was also pleased to be closer to her family in West Warwick, now only about a forty-five-minute drive. About half an hour beyond that was Narragansett, where she and the kids could vacation in the family camper at Scarborough Beach. Bill would come down to join them when-ever his increasingly hectic schedule permitted. They found the Rhode Island beach resort so congenial that they bought an undeveloped lot there. It was not beachfront property, but if one stood on the property's eastern boundary one could almost see beyond a low retaining wall to the sea. Here they planned to retire.

Beneath the surface contentment of their new life, however, the Doug-lases were troubled. Billy, who was ten when they moved to Boston, was having difficulty adjusting. For one thing, Sharon's hockey program wasn't as organized as the one he had known in Lake Placid. The practice rink was located far out of town, and he would have to be up by four in the morning to be on the ice by six. He began having trouble in school, showing no interest in studying, and getting into fights.

His mother and father tried to ease the transition by arranging for him to spend holidays with Craig Stanclift. Bill Douglas drove eight hours to Lake Placid to take Billy to Craig's tenth birthday party. He drove back the same night because he had to be at work at five in the morning. Still, Billy did not seem to adjust. His parents even considered putting him in a private school. When colleagues would ask Bill how his children were doing, he would answer sadly, "Still problems with the Kid."

"Billy the Kid," as he became known to lab members, seemed always to be upset about something, and his father's response was to buy him something, in the hope of placating him. Once when Douglas had promised to spend time with Billy and this engagement was preempted by a visit from a Dutch scientist, Douglas wondered aloud to a grad student "how much it was going to cost" to get himself out of hot water. Douglas spoke of his oldest son with a mixture of concern and admiration: "That Billy, he's all boy." He seemed to enjoy better rapport with his other two children.

Pammy was his own little darling, and he made touching gestures of tenderness toward her. Once when she had a part in a school play, he had an assistant go out and buy her a bouquet of bright perennials. But he seemed particularly close to John, who was developing into a gangly preteen with buck teeth. Douglas would often say, "You're doin' good, John. Right, John?" as if to reassure himself that this was indeed true. As his responsibilities increased and Douglas spent less and less time at home, he seemed less inclined to talk about his children. He did confide to a colleague that once, while Nancy was working the graveyard shift at Ellis, Johnny crept into the master bedroom and crawled into bed. "There was a thunderstorm," he explained. "Johnny was just feeling lonely." But something in the terseness of this utterance suggested that the loneliness at Sandy Ridge Circle went far beyond little Johnny Douglas.

BY THE SPRING of 1982 Karen Hitchcock's dreams of a research empire were bearing fruit. She and Douglas had conceived of something called the Cell Culture Research Unit, which would be a sort of mecca for scientists hoping to learn the most advanced techniques of cell culture. Someday, they hoped, it would even operate autonomously of the university in its own facility, the William H. J. Douglas Research Building, perhaps. The first phase of this expanding scheme grew out of a rather odd grant that Douglas had received from the New England Anti-Vivisection Society.

Douglas first became involved with the society in the fall of 1980 when he was invited to a conference sponsored by the Cosmetic, Toiletry and Fragrance Association in Washington, D.C. The association and its members, which included such giants as Revlon, Bristol-Myers, and Avon, were reeling from recent public outrage over something called the Draize test. This procedure, named after a former FDA bureaucrat, was used by cosmetic companies to measure the toxicity of shampoo, hair spray, and eye shadow. It required strapping unanesthetized albino rabbits in a metal harness and planting potentially irritating substances into their lower eyelids. If the lids became swollen, the iris inflamed, or the cornea ulcerated, the products were declared unsafe for humans.

The Draize test was hideously cruel, and a coalition of animal rights groups had in the summer of 1979 targeted Revlon for a national boycott. Revlon was no worse an offender than Avon or Bristol-Myers, but it had the largest sales and as the industry leader was in a position to reform testing across the board. In its first eighteen months, the coalition bought a share of Revlon stock and debated the company president at the annual stockholders meeting. In May of 1980 a contingent of protesters dressed in bunny costumes marched outside of Revlon's New York headquarters. That same spring the coalition took out a full-page ad in the *New York Times.* It featured a large white rabbit with its eyes plastered shut. Underneath, ran the question "How many rabbits does Revlon blind for beauty's sake?"

In the wake of this bad press, Revlon gave $750,000 to Rockefeller University, in New York, to fund research into alternatives to animal testing. The CTF itself offered another $2,000,000 as seed money to develop a center for alternatives at some yet-unnamed institution. Hoping to define more precisely what this center should do, the association organized the Washington conference. It was here that William Douglas met a prominent animal rights activist named Henry Spira.

Spira was leader of the Draize coalition and mastermind of the campaign that had brought Revlon to its knees. A stout, grizzled man in his midfifties, he was a New York City schoolteacher who had spent his life agitating for various radical causes. At the top of the list was anitvivisection work because, he reasoned, animals, of all disenfranchised creatures, had the least power to defend themselves.

The animal rights movement consisted of hundreds of self-righteous, autonomous, and frequently warring factions. The only thing that united these fractious elements was hatred for the scientific establishment, which they perceived as a bloodthirsty fiend stuffing its maw with puppies and kittens. Scientists, in turn, dismissed animal rights activists as hysterics. Henry Spira was sufficiently pragmatic to see that no real progress could be made without enlisting the goodwill of the adversary. Not all researchers were happy experimenting upon animals. One could never be sure if an animal was infected with parasites or eating the wrong kind of food. Any rogue variable could queer the results. With the Draize test, for instance, the tortured animal's stress reaction sometimes rendered the results worthless. Beyond that, lab animals were costly and researchers had a natural incentive to consider less expensive alternatives. Some investigators were already looking into the possibility of using the membranes of chicken eggs. Others were experimenting with animal placentas. But the work that William Douglas was doing in cell culture seemed the most promising to date.

For at least nine years before the Washington conference, Douglas had hung on the outskirts of the animal rights debate. Whenever he went to Saskatoon, Canada, to visit Sergey Fedoroff, the subject turned to the morality of animal experimentation. Fedoroff, who had some radical notions for a man of science, was trying to draft a code of ethics that required researchers to acknowledge the "symbiotic relationship between men and animals." Before sacrificing any creature, Fedoroff felt, the scientist must carefully think through the justification for it. On these occasions, Douglas refused to be lured into discussions of ethics. Whatever sympathy he felt for the animal rights movement stemmed not from compassion for animals but rather from a cold, scientific distaste for them. He could not help seeing those wretched, writhing creatures as inferior to a single cell which he could nurture to divide to the end of its natural life, producing hundreds of identical sister cells with properties he was looking for.

Douglas had made it clear to his colleagues at the Washington conference that he was there purely out of scientific curiosity. But Spira, a pragmatist, recognized him as someone the movement could use. Spira knew enough about researchers to know that their intellectual interest often followed funding. In the weeks after the Washington conference, he visited Tufts, where he began educating Douglas on the politics of animal rights. Individual societies had coffers swollen with bequests from wealthy animal lovers. Cosmetics companies were pumping money into research. Even the federal government was beginning to fund it. The two men began laying the groundwork for a collaboration.

At Spira's urging, Douglas drew up a proposal for research on an alternative to the Draize test. The plan called for obtaining human corneas from an eye bank. From each cornea, Douglas figured, he could grow enough cells for least fifty experiments. This would be much cheaper than using rabbits. More important, however, the tissues had the advantage of being human, and researchers would not have to extrapolate results from animal tests. Spira began shopping this proposal around the animal rights circuit. At the top of his list was the New England Anti-Vivisection Society.

NEAVS, as it was known, was among the preeminent animal rights groups in the country. In social prestige it had no peer. Formed in the late 1800s by seventeen Brahmins, the society was run like a private club. In its early days, details of its meetings at a drawing room on Park Street were recounted slavishly by the *Transcript,* Boston's aristocratic daily. Those accounts usually ended with "tea was served." This decorum fell by the wayside, however, when it came to the society's central objective, which was to "expose and oppose secret or painful experiments upon living animals, lunatics, paupers or criminals." Members radicalized by these tenets stormed prisons and private laboratories to bring atrocities to light.

During the 1930s, the mantle of leadership fell upon the Honorable George R. Farnum, a Boston barrister and former U.S. Assistant Attorney General. Farnum increased the society's treasury by finessing bequests from dowagers. He also infused NEAVS with a philosophy based loosely upon the teachings of Dr. Albert Schweitzer, who abhorred vivisection and urged a "reverence for life." The society took this as its battle cry and as the name of its monthly publication. *Reverence for Life* became a vehicle for Farnum's long, brooding essays, whose preoccupation with "living tissue" approached religious fervor.

After Farnum died, in 1971, NEAVS continued getting richer, but it lost its fire. During the sixties and seventies, under the leadership of one John O'Neill, it did little more than run ads soliciting still more funds. For more than a decade NEAVS slumbered on its riches like a drowsy old tabby. It began stirring once again in 1981 with the election of Robert Ford.

Judge Ford sat on the probate bench in Norfolk County. A gaunt, white-haired man, he could easily have passed for a Brahmin. He was, in fact, the son of a Quincy leather broker. As "Ford" was a sufficiently fungible name to obscure his ethnic roots, he enjoyed the social mobility of an "Irish Yankee." The judge was not a sentimental man, certainly not a conspicuous animal lover. As the former law partner of the recently deceased John O'Neill, however, he was the logical fiduciary for the society's millions.

Like most of its sister organizations, NEAVS had a history of antagonism toward medical colleges, particularly Harvard, which had lobbied to defeat legislation prohibiting the seizure of pound animals for scientific research. In early 1980s Harvard revealed that a young scientist named John Darsee had falsified data on a grant from the National Heart, Lung, and Blood Institute. Judge Ford took considerable public satisfaction in this humiliation, publicly assailing the university for waiting nearly six months to make this fraud public. "For Harvard to exhibit a bunker mentality," he chastened, "is truly ironic when one considers its aggressive role in live animal experimentation."

Privately, however, Ford felt that the society could profit from an alliance with an academic institution. Funding research might be not only productive but also prestigious. When Henry Spira offered the prospect of purchasing credibility in the person of so eminent a scientist as Dr. William Douglas, the society sprang for it, offering Douglas a grant for

$200,000. On April 8, 1981, Judge Ford himself visited the medical school to preside over a solemn ceremony, during which he presented Douglas with a check for the first installment of $100,000. NEAVS trumpeted this occasion as "An Historical Moment." "Never before," gushed an editorial in *Reverence for Life,* "has an animal rights organization joined forces with a medical research institution to develop an alternative to the use of animals in experimentation and product testing."

For their part, Karen Hitchcock and William Douglas were flattered to be in league with NEAVS—particularly with Judge Ford, upon whom Douglas seemed determined to make a good impression. When the judge was scheduled to make his first visit to the lab, Douglas wanted to be sure there was visible evidence of his commitment to animal rights. Some months earlier, a colleague from Johns Hopkins had sent him the full-page *New York Times* ad with the famous bunny photo, and he had taped it to the door of the laboratory incubator. With passing weeks it became yellowed and stained with culture media. One Saturday morning Ron Sanders and other members of the lab came in for a volunteer cleanup project. Sanders saw the tattered bunny fluttering on the incubator door and ripped it down. Three weeks later, on the eve of Ford's visit, Douglas strolled by the incubator and noticed the bunny missing. He went into a rage, storming down the hall, pounding his hand into his fist, swearing revenge upon the person who took the clipping. That afternoon, he called in the lab personnel one by one to interrogate them. No one would blow the whistle on Sanders, but the bunny furor subsided only when someone thought to order a back issue from the *New York Times.*

When, a few days later, Judge Ford arrived on the scene, Douglas led him through the lab as he would a visiting potentate, introducing him to Dr. Stanley Spilman, in whose hands this important project had been placed. Douglas also steered Ford by the desk of Jane Aghajanian, who, he said, had been designated "principal technician." This, in fact, was not true. Aghajanian had nothing to do with the grant. The day-to-day work was being done by a technician named Diane Romeo. On the occasion of that visit by Judge Ford and later ones by Henry Spira, Douglas saw to it that Romeo was safely hidden. That left Aghajanian having to extemporize upon a project she knew little about.

This arrangement understandably irked Diane Romeo, an ambitious young woman in her midtwenties. She had come to Tufts in the summer of 1981 from a much smaller lab in Amherst and was looking forward to more responsibility. She was pleased to be assigned, shortly after her arrival, to the Draize grant. It was obviously a high-priority project, and she enjoyed being at the center of the action. But Douglas seemed to arrange things so that she never received any credit.

One day a photographer came to the lab to take her picture with Douglas and Spilman. It was to appear in a newsletter called *In Touch*, the official publication of a society of ethical vegetarians headquartered in New York City. The Millennium Guild, as it was called, was also funding Douglas. Spira had taken the Draize proposal to the guild's president, an elderly animal lover named Pegeen Fitzgerald. Miss Fitzgerald hosted a radio show on New York's WOR from her apartment on Central Park South. At Spira's urging, Fitzgerald had given Douglas about $5,000 in seed money. This carried with it the promise of another $250,-000 to $500,000 if he actually succeeded in finding a nonanimal replacement for the Draize test. Fitzgerald also invited Douglas to sit on the editorial board of the guild's quarterly newsletter. And in the spring of 1982 he contributed a brief article summarizing the preliminary results which he and Spilman were getting with their corneal cell cultures. The piece, scheduled to appear in May, was to be accompanied by the photo of Douglas and Spilman with Diane Romeo positioned prominently between them at a microscope.

Romeo was excited about the prospect of seeing her name and photo in print. She had told her parents and had gotten them all excited about it. Douglas gave her a copy of the galleys to read for corrections, and everything seemed fine. Then one day he called her into his office and showed her the final publication. She was stunned. In the caption where her name had been, it now read "Jane Aghajanian." Flustered, Romeo muttered, "It must have been a typo, Bill. No problem." But she knew this was no mistake. When Romeo managed to get a peek at the grant, she saw that Douglas had substituted Aghajanian's name for her own on the proposal. Being the more senior of the two, Aghajanian would command a higher salary. The surplus could be used any way Douglas wanted. It was an old investigator's trick to increase the overall dollar figure of a grant.

The way Douglas was behaving toward the NEAVS project was causing Aghajanian to worry too. Whenever he received federal grants, his spending was subject a set of strict guidelines. With the NEAVS money, however, he was under no obligation to account. Judge Ford, flush with enthusiasm for this alliance, had written Tufts a letter specifying that William Douglas was to be given carte blanche in spending those funds. This was a worrisome development from Aghajanian's perspective since Douglas tended to bend the rules a little with research money. Technically, every expense should be charged scrupulously to the grant on which the research was being done. But Douglas's habit was to lump the dollars into one big pot. He would then buy equipment for one project that could be used for another. You could argue that, managed this way, his projects all fertilized one another, making his research all the richer. He was, after all, in the unusual position of having many grants. It was possible to reason that the rules that applied to other investigators at Tufts did not apply to Douglas.

DOUGLAS'S colleagues, meanwhile, were finding all of the ballyhoo over the NEAVS grant rather ludicrous. It wasn't seemly for a man of science to allow himself to be recruited by a special-interest group. This contempt, which manifested itself in caustic asides at faculty meetings, was indicative of a new climate in the department. By Douglas's third year at Tufts, he found himself being edged out by a handful of newer faculty members known as the Harvard clique. For the most part they had migrated to Tufts from Harvard, where they had been denied tenure. While acknowledging Douglas's work as technically superb, these young men also considered it to be lacking in intellectual content. Proof of this charge seemed to be its diversity. A serious researcher generally found a specialty like heart or lung work and stuck with it for his entire career. Since Douglas's specialty was his culturing technique, he was called in to serve as co-investigator on projects that ran the gamut from lungs to prostate. He was like a plumber whose services were required by many contractors. The Harvard clique dismissed him a "technician"—worse yet, an "entrepreneur."

Even Karen Hitchcock, who was offended by intellectual snobbery, had to admit that Douglas didn't ask "the big questions." He was inclined to ask *how* a cell produced surfactant, but not *why.* The "why" queries were often unanswerable, but the theoretician who asked them had a lifetime of work ahead of him. His grants were renewed endlessly. Douglas, however, developed techniques, and his projects all had a predictable end point. Hitchcock suspected that Douglas, who had turned forty in the fall of 1981, knew he was bumping up against the limits of his own abilities as a scientist. There was something a little desperate in the way he pinned his hopes on new funding sources. Hitchcock, looking back on these events many harrowing months later, thought she knew what accounted for it. Douglas was struggling to find himself some niche in medical history. If he had a future, it lay in turning his entrepreneurial genius to founding an institution that would immortalize his culturing techniques.

In pursuit of that goal, Douglas had suffered a setback. He had proposed to the Cosmetic, Toiletry and Fragrance Association that it establish its proposed alternatives center at Tufts—and bring its $2 million in

seed money along with it. The Tufts proposal was one of the three
finalists, but in the end the CTF chose Johns Hopkins University, in
Baltimore, site of the first successful attempt at cell culture. Douglas
seemed to rebound admirably from this disappointment and devoted
himself to his brainchild, the Cell Culture Research Unit. During the
early months of 1982, much of his energy went to developing the unit's
first formal class—a week-long summer seminar funded by the New England Anti-Vivisection Society.

II

That spring William Douglas's behavior grew noticeably odder. He had
seemed irritable since the preceding October when grant deadline played
havoc with everyone's nerves. Virtually every investigator in the department waited until the last minute to have his or her proposals typed, so
there was a bottleneck at the secretaries' desks. Douglas was visibly frustrated with poor Joanne Sateriale, who did her best to keep up with the
avalanche of Xeroxing but kept falling behind. A mild hysteria spread
through 530 M&V. Diane Romeo wrote an old school chum, "It has been
one of those days . . . corner tears. The worst part is it's only lunchtime.
. . . Bill, Dr. Douglas, is furious and holding back a torrent of emotion
that will be unleashed as soon as the grant season is over. Beware the wrath
of WHJD . . . for it is mighty and furious—"

Douglas began arriving at the lab well past his customary hour of 6:30
A.M. Sometimes he would call in with excuses. Once he called at eleven
to say that his Pinto had been totaled on the expressway. Only three weeks
earlier, he had remarked to a grad student that the car was nearly shot
and he needed a new one. When Douglas finally got to the lab that
afternoon, everyone was solicitous. One tech inquired, "How are you
feeling?" He replied blankly, "Okay. Why?" A few weeks later he showed
up driving a new blue Toyota Starlet.

One Thursday afternoon in June, Diane Romeo had gone to the Bank
of Boston one block west of the medical school, on Kneeland Street, to
cash a check. She had returned to the lab and was removing her coat when
Douglas walked in, pale and shaken.

"What happened, Bill?" she inquired.

"I was just mugged," he replied.

"In the middle of the day?" Romeo was incredulous. "Where were you
mugged?"

Douglas explained that he was coming out of the bank when a pair of black youths pushed him into a phone booth and stole his wallet. Romeo had just come from Kneeland Street and hadn't witnessed any disturbance. She found the story a little odd. Three weeks later Douglas claimed he had been mugged again. It finally became apparent that he was invoking these disasters whenever he had missed a meeting or needed to account for an absence.

Around this time, Douglas bought a cheap blue upholstered couch, which he stashed under a table in his office. Douglas took pains to explain that this was to allow him "to take naps" during the day. Sometimes he shut himself away in his office in the late afternoon with instructions to screen his calls. One morning, however, Diane Romeo came into the lab early. Needing something from Douglas's office, she retrieved the special key from a secretary's desk. As she was inserting it in the lock she heard a stirring inside. The door finally opened and there stood Douglas, drowsy and disheveled.

Romeo stammered, "Bill, I didn't know you slept here."

"I had to stay last night," he replied.

When Jane Aghajanian arrived at the office of a morning, she would find lists of things to do left on her desk or chair. Among these were an increasing number of requests for petty cash. Normally, the lab withdrew only about $10 a month from the bursar. Now it was pushing upward of $200 a week. Douglas seemed to be taking cabs everywhere, particularly to "meetings" near Beacon Hill. This was an easy walk from the medical school, but, Douglas explained offhandedly, he had "almost gotten mugged once going across the Common."

While going through the receipts one morning, Aghajanian found two items that struck her as curious. Both were from the Carl Martin Pharmacy, at the end of the block from the medical school. The lab had a standing account with Carl Martin for supplies such as cotton and thermometers. But the receipts in question were for items Jane had never heard of. One was for "fluid collection adapters"; the other was for several gross of "biological fluid collection units." Aghajanian mused over this for a moment until she saw scrawled at the bottom of one receipt the word "RAMSES."

"What the heck is this?" she said to herself. Then calling Ron Sanders aside, she pointed at the receipt.

"He's charged safes to the grant," she whispered.

Sanders stared uncomprehendingly. He had never heard the term "safes."

"Condoms!" Aghajanian clarified.

Neither could think of any experiment the lab was currently running that required prophylactics. Certainly not by the gross. Douglas, however, was involved in so many projects with so many outside collaborators that the "biological collection units" could well be legitimate. Aghajanian set her doubts aside and put the payment through.

The increase in petty-cash requests was drawing heat from the bursar's office downstairs. Each time Aghajanian sent a work-study student down with another handful, the bursar groused, "This is not a bank, honey." Finally, accounting sent up an emissary, Mr. Richard Wong, to look into the matter. Mr. Wong, unfortunately, was relatively new and uncertain of his position in dealing with scientific investigators. When he undertook with extreme deference to question Douglas about what seemed like a lot of taxi rides, Douglas exploded.

"Don't you know how much money I bring into this university every year!"

That outburst sent Mr. Wong fleeing downstairs in retreat. For the present, at least, the matter was closed.

KAREN HITCHCOCK noticed something was strange when Douglas started missing meetings. He was on scores of committees and had no doubt spread himself too thin, but she had never noticed him being derelict. It was also apparent to her that he was losing weight. One day she stopped him in the hallway to ask about it. He had had pains around his heart, he explained, and his doctor had put him on a strict diet. He was embarrassed that his clothes were growing loose and that was why he had taken to working at night. Hitchcock accepted this. She took a generally laissez-faire attitude toward the day-to-day operation of the department and if Bill could get the work done, that was all that mattered. As a biologist, however, she knew the dangers of losing weight too quickly and warned him, "You'd better be careful."

Douglas's metamorphosis dawned gradually upon the lab. One day Ron Sanders whispered to Jane Aghajanian, "I think he's using Grecian Formula. Is it me, or is it true?" Aghajanian, who in her three years with Douglas had failed to notice any hint of personal vanity in him, was eager to check this out. She visited his office on a pretext and glanced surreptitiously at his scalp, but she couldn't tell for sure. What she did notice was that he had gotten a new arm stretcher, which he kept stored behind the blue chair. He had also taken to squeezing a hard rubber ball to build up his hand muscles. One afternoon in May a faculty member came back to the department bearing the most incongruous account to date. She had seen Douglas in a jogging suit. He was standing, as if to catch his breath, on the edge of the Combat Zone.

THE COMBAT ZONE was Boston's red-light district. Scarcely four blocks square, it was bordered on the south by the low brick buildings of Tufts's Boston campus and to the north by the retail district dominated by Jordan Marsh and Filene's. It extended east to Chinatown and west to Tremont Street. Prostitutes routinely ignored this western frontier, strolling past it to Park Square and on to the Public Gardens, a spacious meadow bounded to the north by exclusive Beacon Hill and to the west by the Ritz-Carlton. In theory, at least, most of the street element in Boston was confined to an irregular rectangle bisected by Lower Washington Street.

Boston's vice had not always been so neatly circumscribed. Up until the early sixties, it was more widely dispersed throughout the metropolitan area. During World War II, when the city was a port of call, sailors flocked to the top of Washington Street to revel at Scollay Square, a quarter teeming with honky-tonks, tattoo parlors, gin mills, and flophouses. Although the Watch and Ward society routinely excoriated Scollay as a "sinkhole of depravity," the pleasures it afforded were largely innocent. Hookers hung out farther south on the edge of the Roxbury ghetto. The corner of Massachusetts and Columbus avenues was the gathering place for black prostitutes seeking to flag down white hunters cruising through what one Boston jurist termed "the crossroads of hell."

During the fifties, the sailors moved farther down Washington Street to the theater district, where vaudeville had passed out of fashion, leaving magnificent empty halls with Beaux Arts facades and Florentine interiors. These shells were converted to rock and roll clubs, which drew headliner entertainment. They also attracted cycling gangs from the suburbs whose frequent brawls with the military gave Lower Washington Street the designation "Combat Zone."

Despite occasional violence, the Zone was still a place where couples might go unmolested of a Saturday night. Its character did not change until the early sixties when the U.S. Supreme Court liberalized pornography laws. Stores selling X-rated books began springing up in respectable areas of the city. One porn peddler even set up shop on Beacon Hill. In the face of this outrage, the city fathers set to work on a plan to keep vice from contaminating the neighborhoods. The solution they arrived at ran counter to conventional wisdom. Most American cities were adopting dispersion ordinances to keep smut peddlers separated and their influence presumably diluted. Boston, however, ordered them confined to a special "adult entertainment district."

The city fathers never intended to legalize prostitution, but in fact Lower Washington Street had effectively been zoned for a new kind of combat. Among pimps who traveled with their stables up and down the Eastern Seaboard, Boston got the reputation as a "sweet city." Bail was only five dollars and, after taking a bust, a girl could be back on the street in a couple of hours. When forced busing was enacted in the fall of 1974, every spare man on the Boston police force was sent to control rioting in the South End and Charlestown. After that, a working girl scarcely had to worry about being arrested at all.

The Combat Zone became a little city within a city. It had its own leaders, its own laws. It even had its own publicist, hired by the "business community," who spread a gospel that lust could be cute. Information issued from the Zone in press releases. The average customer was purportedly an electrical engineer, an IBM salesman, or an ad executive. The preferred commodity was reportedly fellatio. Some girls had become such specialists in oral sex that they never bothered with actual intercourse. One hooker chirped in an interview with a national magazine, "It seems to me that guys aren't getting much head at home in Boston." Strippers became local, and even national, celebrities. Princess Cheyenne, prima donna of the Naked i, was touted by *Playboy* as "a stripper and coed who stems from a social-register family. . . . In Boston, even the Combat Zone has class."

This boosterism came to an abrupt end after the Harvard-Yale game of 1976. Harvard's starting cornerback, Andy Papuolo, was enjoying a boozy postgame revel with six companions in the Zone when a fight broke out and Papuolo was stabbed through the heart by a reputed pimp. Vice didn't seem so cute anymore. Particularly not after the police department released the results of an internal investigation revealing incompetence and corruption in District One, whose command covered the Combat Zone. Police had been caught leaking confidential law enforcement memos to the New England crime family headed by Gennaro Angiulo. A detachment from District One actually provided an escort for the funeral cortege of Angiulo's mother. The report also explained that Zone prostitutes, used to plying their trade without interference from police, were becoming more aggressive and, in many cases, larcenous. They often traveled in packs, encircling a prospective john and forcing him into an alleyway. A couple of girls would manipulate him sexually while a third haggled over a price. Then the girls would fan out in a screen around the poor, fluttering moth while one of their number brought him to climax. These encounters might have left the client feeling he had gotten his money's worth, except that the girls usually made off with his wallet.

These incidents, combined with the Papuolo affair, caused the entertainment district experiment to be pronounced a failure. The Suffolk County District Attorney's Office charged that the Zone had created "an illusion of license," and launched a crusade to eliminate it. So many uniformed police were dispatched to Lower Washington Street that it took on the appearance of an occupied sector. Bail was raised to $150. The city passed a disorderly-persons ordinance so broad that a girl had only to be seen stopping traffic to be arrested. Pimps moved their stables to sweeter cities. By the spring of 1982, a dolorous lethargy had settled over the Combat Zone. It was like a sick creature waiting to be finished off by predators. Chinatown was looking to acquire land on the east. Tufts was hoping to expand from the south. And it was there in the shadow of a doomed Sodom that Bill Douglas was seen on a weekday afternoon, seemingly oblivious to the gloom around him, breathless from jogging.

ABOUT this time, Douglas began showing solicitude over a graduate student. She was, he said, working for an MIT colleague who could no longer pay her. In March or April he told Jane Aghajanian, "We're going to pick up her salary at $1,000 a month." Aghajanian found this strange. To begin with, it was a great deal to pay a graduate student. But beyond that, Douglas had made provisions for her to receive overtime. Aghajanian could not remember Douglas ever paying anyone overtime. Odder still, he had put the name Robin Benedict on a list of people who were so important that he could be interrupted at meetings if they called. Graduate students simply did not enjoy that kind of priority.

Could Douglas be having an affair with her? Ron Sanders did not think that was likely. He could not conceive of Douglas as a womanizer. In fact, he had always struck Sanders as rather sexless. He did not engage in any of the usual male banter and had never shown interest in any of the women in the lab. There had been only a hint of an episode with an older graduate student. She had had the indiscretion to mention that she was receiving harassing phone calls, and she thought these might have come from Bill. Word of this got back to Douglas, and he fired her. He did, however, throw in several months' severance pay, which was quite irregular.

The lab knew, from certain gossip that had circulated at Alton Jones, that things were not quite right between the Douglases. Nancy had suffered a miscarriage in Lake Placid. When that happened, Douglas had taken off a week of work to care for her. But after that there seemed to be a strain between them. In many ways, Douglas seemed abnormally dependent upon his wife, often calling her several times a day. He didn't appear to be able to make a decision without consulting her. Yet he never mentioned her name in conversation.

He did, however, allude periodically to Robin Benedict.

One rainy night that spring, Douglas gave a lecture in Connecticut to which he took a couple of lab members as guests. Among these was a grad student named Lance Kisby, a slender, sandy-haired fellow, who was engaged to Diane Romeo. Lance's charm and high spirits gained him entry to circles above his own station. He already held a Ph.D. in pediatric dentistry, which gave him standing to mingle with postdoctoral candidates and even banter with Douglas. Kisby, who had switched to biomedical sciences hoping to get through this second doctorate as quickly as possible, had presented to Douglas a simple, straightforward project for culturing tooth cells called odontoblasts. Those cells could then be used to test dental products for toxic substances. Douglas was intrigued, for although the culture seemed simple, it had never been done before. He agreed to serve as Kisby's adviser, and since the young man stood to be the first graduate student to get a degree under his aegis, Douglas felt a special kinship with him.

During the drive back to Boston, Douglas turned to Kisby and asked, "Lance, do you think it would be good to take my kids to see the *Rocky Horror Picture Show?*" This suggestion took Kisby aback. The *Rocky Horror Picture Show* was a punk musical which was shown every Friday and Saturday night at the Exeter Theater, about ten blocks from the medical school. The film had a loyal youth following who saw the film again and again. Sometimes as many as a thousand *Rocky Horror* loyalists, clad in fishnet stockings and garter belts, waited in line for two hours outside the Exeter for their weekly fix. *Rocky Horror*'s appeal was that it invited participation. As the film rolled, a troupe of transvestite mimes on the apron of the stage urged the audience to act out familiar scenes. These frolics included such things as throwing toast and squirting water pistols at the screen.

"No, Bill," Lance finally replied to Douglas query. "It's a little on the far-out side."

A few days later, Douglas brought up the subject again, regaling Kisby with how he had seen it with a "graduate student friend from MIT" and how they had had a "fun time."

"You know," Douglas continued, oblivious to his listener's bewilderment, "we ought to make a lab party out of it and go to see the *Rocky Horror Picture Show.*"

The idea of William Douglas, status conscious as he was, having a "graduate student friend" was almost as ludicrous as the notion of him squirting water pistols at the screen of the Exeter. The student, Kisby guessed, must be Robin Benedict. This conjecture seemed to be supported by other occurrences. Jane Aghajanian caught a glimpse of a floral bouquet on Douglas's desk. The next time she looked, it was gone. In the same spot, Ron Sanders found a textbook entitled *Lung Development:*

Biological and Clinical Perspectives. It was lying open to a page upon which someone had written:

> May our friendship grow more wonderful as time goes on.
>   Let's keep it strong as we help each other to achieve all that we've talked about.
>   We can [the writer crossed out "can" and inserted "will"] do it!
>
> Friends always,
Robin

Sanders showed the inscription to Aghajanian. It left no doubt in their minds that Douglas was engaged in some kind of dalliance with the mysterious Miss Benedict. But during the summer of 1982 she remained a phantom.

THE NEAVS summer course went off as scheduled. On July 19, eighteen doctoral scientists and six postgraduate researchers arrived at Tufts, where they were welcomed by Professor William Douglas and Vice-President Robert Levy. The class was introduced with pomp and enthusiasm to its patron, Judge Robert Ford. For the next five days the students performed lab exercises and listened to lectures from morning until night. Among the speakers was Douglas's old grad school chum Hank Holden, who had gone to work as a research scientist for Pfizer Pharmaceuticals in Groton, Connecticut. Douglas took him to lunch at a Chinese restaurant on the edge of the Combat Zone.

Reflecting upon these events months later, Holden could not recall anything peculiar about Douglas, except perhaps that he had lost a lot of weight. But others—notably Ron Sanders and Jane Aghajanian—noticed an uncommon air of distraction in him. During the entire five days of classes, Douglas gave only two one-hour lectures. Other than that, he was scarcely around. That was curious, considering that the future of the embryonic Cell Culture Research Unit was at stake. Most of the burden fell on Sanders and Aghajanian. And although the departing summer class of 1982 evaluated the seminar as "excellent," it left Douglas's two underlings exhausted.

Aghajanian took a short vacation to refresh herself. Then she settled down to catch up on the bookkeeping that had accumulated during the hectic weeks before the summer course. Every month the accounting department at the main campus in Medford sent the lab a printout of expenses incurred on various grants. Since the computer operators frequently fouled up the figures, it was necessary to go over them line by line to see if they matched the amounts on the invoices. No sooner had Aghajanian started scanning the sheets than she could tell something was wrong. Travel expenses, marked by a special numerical code at the side of the column, were far out of proportion to the amounts usually allowed. Aghajanian felt she should confide this to someone, so she took the printouts to Sanders, whose senior position in the lab gave him access to accounting documents. He had no idea what to make of them. When could Douglas possibly have done all of this traveling?

At first, they accused each other of losing the paperwork. Realizing this was ridiculous, Sanders tried to catch Douglas on the run to ask him about the charges. Douglas waved him off saying he would get back to him. Several weeks passed and nothing happened. Sanders finally finessed a complete set of invoices out of the accounting department downstairs. Many of these, Aghajanian had never seen before. Douglas had been circumventing her and taking the invoices to the front office for Karen Hitchcock's signature.

Normally when Douglas went out of town, he would let Aghajanian or Sanders know where he could be reached. He was scrupulous about giving a forwarding contact. But most of these trips suggested by the invoices had been taken on weekends when no one would miss him and when he would not be obligated to leave a forwarding number. There were trips that Douglas had supposedly taken to Atlanta, Memphis, Chicago, and Dallas. There were trips for Miss Robin Benedict to Washington, D.C., where she was to have attended a training session at the Image Analysis Lab of the National Institutes of Health. She had apparently been sent on another ten-day training trip to Chicago to take another course in image analysis. One might send a postdoc to these kinds of seminars, but hardly a graduate student.

Douglas had requested reimbursement for a number of nights at the Chalet Best Western in Lyon, Illinois. Sanders reviewed the dates.

6/26	William Douglas	$103.95
7/16	William Douglas	103.95
8/5–8/6	William Douglas	207.90
8/14–8/16	William Douglas	311.85
8/17–8/27	Robin Benedict	1,039.50
8/27–8/31	William Douglas	519.75
9/18	William Douglas	2,390.85

Their stays did not overlap. According to the paperwork, Benedict had checked out discreetly on August 27, just as Douglas was checking in. Sanders wrote a letter to the Chalet asking that these dates be verified.

He got a reply from the management saying they had reviewed all guest registrations between May 1 and September 24, 1982, and found no record of either a William Douglas or a Robin Benedict.

From what Sanders and Aghajanian could see, there was about $7,000 to $8,000 in questionable expenses. But embezzlement was a serious charge to bring against a man. For the next several weeks, they investigated quietly, looking for more proof that would support their suspicions. They carefully checked the documents against Sanders's office calendar for inconsistencies. At last they found two separate vouchers with Douglas's signature showing him to be in Atlanta and Chicago on the same day.

"That's it," Aghajanian said. "Show me no more."

They were not sure whom, if anyone, they should tell. Douglas still enjoyed the favor of Karen Hitchcock, and they were afraid to confide to her what they had found. Aghajanian, particularly, could not afford to lose her job. She was going through a divorce and had a little boy to consider. The more she pondered this predicament, the angrier she became at Douglas. He had known about the troubles she was having in her personal life. Beyond her own worries, she was angry at him for having betrayed the lab. To Aghajanian and Sanders, and to others who over the years had passed in and out of the pastel labyrinth, 530 M&V was more than five rooms equipped with incubators and glass tubing. It was an affiliation they took pride in, a sanctuary where they practiced a vocation. Aghajanian and Sanders had kept house carefully. Often they would sit and compare suppliers' catalogs to get the best deal on a piece of equipment. They were inclined, Aghajanian used to joke, to "squeeze a dollar 'til the eagle squawked." In squandering those coveted dollars on condoms and cab rides, Douglas had been mocking them all.

As weeks passed, it became clear to Aghajanian that she could not stay. Each time she saw Douglas, she felt like a hypocrite for not confronting him with what she knew. How much is your job worth? she asked herself. Can you afford to keep it if it means losing your integrity? The strain finally became too great, and she began sending out résumés. Around the end of September, she found a job at a private research outfit in Wellesley and composed a letter of resignation. This was the hardest thing of all. To get out gracefully, she had to lie. Her problem was mainly financial, she wrote. She was afraid her estranged husband was going to move out of state and discontinue child support, which was completely untrue. When she presented the letter to Douglas, he was unusually gracious. He did not betray the slightest hint of concern about her leaving. There would always be a place for her, he promised, if she decided to come back.

For Sanders, leaving was not such a simple matter. He was a scientist in his own right, one of the young apostles who had been nurtured by Douglas and who had now grown to maturity at Tufts. He had been made an assistant professor. He had grants of his own. His roots were deeper than those of technicians like Aghajanian and Romeo, who could find comparable jobs elsewhere. Unpleasant as the coming months were likely to be, Sanders felt he had no choice but to stay put and try to ride out the storm.

ALTHOUGH Sanders and Aghajanian had told no one else in the lab what they knew, others had suspicions. Diane Romeo for one. Resentful at having received no recognition for the work she did on the NEAVS project, she also had doubts about Stanley Spilman. She did not particularly trust him. She felt he was too caught up in playing politics to manage the Draize project properly.

For some time, too, there had been rumors circulating through the lab that Spilman did not actually have his doctorate. If that was so, there could be serious repercussions, since he had been represented on certain government grants as having a Ph.D. That was fraud. No one had dared make an issue of it. If you fell out with Spilman, there was no appeal, because he was Douglas's favorite. Romeo was fearful that if a scandal broke over Spilman's credentials, she, as his technician, would receive some of the taint. She quietly found another job, and her fiancé, Lance Kisby, also began easing himself out of 530 M&V. Lance shut down his research on the odontoblasts, freezing his cells in liquid nitrogen, and contrived to look busy so that Douglas would not suspect anything. Douglas seemed oblivious to the fact that the lab was dying, defection by defection.

Romeo and Aghajanian both left around Labor Day. The lab held a farewell party for them at the European Restaurant, near the medical school. Douglas did not attend. During the course of this forlorn affair, Aghajanian pulled Romeo aside and whispered to her, "Come over to my house tonight so that we can talk." That evening Romeo went out to the bungalow in Milton. There Aghajanian and Sanders showed her the incriminating documents, thus drawing her into their circle of confidence.

The question remained—who else should they tell?

Aghajanian asked the attorney who was handling her divorce what he thought she should do. He advised, "Appeal to the highest law possible." The highest law Aghajanian could think of was her next-door neighbor, Gerry Kirby, who was an assistant district attorney in Norfolk County. But when she showed him the invoices, he said it was out of his jurisdiction.

Tufts was in neighboring Suffolk. She could see that he was a very busy man, so she didn't bother him further.

The next logical candidate was Judge Ford. What higher authority was there, after all, than a judge, particularly one who knew all the persons involved? As most of the questionable expenses seemed to have shown up on the NEAVS grant, Judge Ford was possibly an injured party and certain, therefore, to be concerned.

At Aghajanian's request, her attorney invited Judge Ford to a meeting in his office on October 8. There Aghajanian and Sanders presented him with the most damning evidence from their stack of invoices. Ford appeared shaken. Douglas, he said, had once mentioned a Robin Benedict, explaining that she was a black graduate student at MIT, but Ford had never met her. There was certainly no reason why she should be running up these kinds of expenses. The judge gathered up the materials and said he would take care of things.

Sanders had faith that Judge Ford, if anyone, would get to the bottom of this mess. But weeks passed, and they did not hear from him. The potential for scandal had apparently mortified the judge. The man who would criticize Harvard for failing to come forward with details on the Darsee fraud was put in a position of revealing moral turpitude in his own ranks. Given the possibility that the William Douglas affair could be dealt with quietly, Judge Ford slipped into the "Bunker mentality" he found so reprehensible in others.

Finally, Aghajanian and Sanders heard through the grapevine that the judge had passed the documents on to a friend who was a Tufts trustee. From there they had found their way through the administrative maze, ending up on the desk of Executive Vice-President Steven Manos. No more eager than Ford for a scandal to break, Manos summoned the university's internal auditor, a tall, silver-haired gentleman named Richard Thorngren, and instructed him to begin a discreet investigation. Thorngren took the documents back to his office and began sorting through them to see what he could learn. Within two weeks he had found questionable expenses that far exceeded the $10,000 which Sanders and Aghajanian had uncovered. In a memo to Manos, Thorngren reported that a preliminary check revealed numerous petty-cash vouchers for packages delivered from the New England Medical Center to the Newton Wellesley Hospital by the Yellow Cab of Belmont. A quick check with the company, however, established that Yellow Cabs did not even operate between those locations. Thorngren examined the bills that Douglas had submitted for stays at the Chalet Best Western Motel in Lyon, Illinois, and discovered that they were not of the type normally issued by that establishment. Douglas appeared to have dummied up a letterhead of his own using the hotel's logo and large typewriter script. The forgery had been so sloppily executed that it even contained a misspelling: "Convient [*sic*] to Chicago, Ill."

As for Miss Benedict, she had submitted thirty-two meal receipts indicating that while staying at the Chalet in Lyon she had eaten breakfast, lunch, and dinner every day for a week at a Howard Johnson. Thorngren might have accepted this if the HoJo had been next door, but it was three miles away. Benedict, furthermore, had been issued TWA tickets for travel to New York and Washington, D.C. She had been reimbursed for those expenses, but then the tickets were canceled and she received the refunds too. Although Douglas had styled Benedict as a graduate student at MIT, Thorngren had checked with the institute, which was unable to locate her on any of its rosters of students or employees.

Douglas had to be confronted with the evidence, but this raised a question of protocol. Neither Manos nor Thorngren knew him personally. The auditor had only seen his name on the payroll. At length it was decided that Manos should be the one to do it, if only to emphasize to Douglas how serious the situation was. When the vice-president called the professor's home in Sharon, he got Nancy Douglas, who said her husband was in Washington, D.C. Something in his voice must have conveyed the urgency of the situation, because when Douglas called back, he seemed to suspect something. He showed up at Manos's office on Thursday, October 28, carrying a brown briefcase, which he took pains to place near Manos's desk. Manos discovered only many months later that the open case contained a cassette recorder and that Douglas had succeeded in taping their entire conversation.

"*DID YOU* have any trouble finding the place or have you been out to the Medford campus?" Manos inquired. He was struggling to strike a genial tone. Douglas mumbled monosyllabic replies. He seemed not defensive but subdued, like a child that realizes it is about to receive some inevitable but unspecified punishment.

Manos cleared his throat nervously and said, "I did try, when I chatted with you for a couple of minutes [by phone] to indicate why I was calling. There has been some question about activities on the grant. Do you have any reaction to that?"

"Well, coming from the vice-president of the university . . ." Douglas's voice trailed off.

"Let me. . . Perhaps I can help by being specific . . ." This was painful.

"There's obviously not an easy way to try . . . and deal with. . . . There have been a number of plane trips. . . . Were these plane trips all necessitated by the grant?"

There was a long silence. Douglas finally replied, "I don't know how to explain that."

With gentle prodding from Manos, Douglas revealed that he was reluctant to talk about the matter until he could get in to see a university psychiatrist. "I'm not trying to be uncooperative," he assured Manos. "But I'm having some problems."

"I understand," Manos replied. "And obviously, so am I . . . Let me frame something and it's free of charge. If you think that it's not a helpful approach, say that and then we'll forget the statement. . . . Okay?" He chose his words carefully. "I'd like to be able to agree with you that there were many charges that you were reimbursed for that really weren't necessary. . . . Is that something that we can agree on?"

"Would you say that once again? I'm really not being uncooperative— but you'd like to agree with me that there are problems?"

Douglas refused to be pinned down. Manos gave a heavy sigh.

"Let me. . . . I don't want to get too far out in front of ourselves. . . . Obviously, given the situation, the university is, one, in a difficult situation and, two, wants to resolve the situation as gracefully as possible."

Manos then laid out a plan wherein if Douglas acknowledged that the expenditures were not, as he put it, "necessary" and subsequently made restitution, he would try to see that the matter was handled as quietly as possible.

"Do you have a reaction to what I've discussed?" he asked.

"I can say I have an overall reaction to the way you're handling this," Douglas replied. "I'm very surprised by how graceful you are. You've been very kind. I appreciate it. I don't know what would have happened if you would have started yelling. . . . I appreciate [it] even though I'm sure you have no reason to smile at me. I appreciate your creating appearances. . . . Nothing that you've said surprises me."

SO INTENT was Manos upon secrecy that he did not even notify Karen Hitchcock. But rumors filtered back to her. Stung at being left out of the deliberations, she seized the initiative and called Dr. Henry Banks, dean of the medical school, who confirmed that Douglas was indeed under investigation. She then called Manos, who, though apparently not pleased that she had been told about this matter, gave her a status report from the executive committee of the board of trustees. Members, he said, were of three minds on how to deal with the problem. One faction favored contacting the district attorney of Suffolk County and asking him to prosecute. The second advised an extensive internal inquiry. In either case, the publicity would be painful. The third option, which Manos favored, was to elicit from Douglas a quiet resignation with a promise to pay back the money.

Karen Hitchcock, widely acknowledged as Douglas's patron and protector, was now disturbed by the conciliatory attitude the university was taking toward him. To be sure, it was a tricky matter to remove a tenured professor. Still, he had most likely committed a felony. She wanted to see Douglas prosecuted. At the very least, she felt, he should be dismissed and not simply allowed to resign. She wanted it placed on the record somewhere that the university found this sort of behavior wrong.

Manos held firm. As the university looked at it, the money had come from NEAVS and had since become the property of Tufts. Inasmuch as Tufts was the injured party, it was up to the university to either request or not request prosecution. Besides, Douglas was cooperating nicely. Hitchcock felt that Manos did not want her disturbing the delicate proceedings. He did not want her even talking to Douglas about it. This left her in a "hellishly awkward" position. Douglas, she knew, had already accepted another grant check from NEAVS. He was getting ready to hire more technicians. Still, for the greater good, she agreed to pretend it was business as usual.

SHORTLY before Thanksgiving, Hitchcock received a call from Nancy Douglas, who wanted to know if Bill was in some kind of trouble. Caught off guard by this overture, Hitchcock stammered that she had just learned of the possibility that funds had been misused.

Nancy announced, "I'll be right over."

"No," Hitchcock headed her off. "It's just that there are some problems. . . . He seems upset. He's not himself."

"If it's about the girl," Nancy said flatly. "I've taken care of that."

Hitchcock did not ask her what she meant. She could safely conclude from the drift of the ongoing internal investigations, however, that "the girl" to whom Nancy alluded must be Robin Benedict. For nearly a month now, Benedict's name had cropped up in invoices and vouchers bearing Hitchcock's name. The chairman had gone over these carefully with Thorngren, the auditor, and concluded that at least some of them had been signed in her absence by her secretary. Others had apparently been forged.

Douglas was presumed to be having an affair with Miss Benedict.

Whether she was a willing accomplice to embezzlement, no one yet knew. Shortly after Douglas had been called on the carpet by Steven Manos however, Benedict had submitted an invoice for $3,597. She had apparently been hired by the Human Nutrition Research Center as an independent contractor and was ostensibly developing a computer program to analyze human prostate tissues.

Douglas, Thorngren learned, had had a consulting arrangement with the HNRC. Up through the fall of 1982, he and Dr. Stanley Spilman had been volunteering their services on a pilot prostate project. When, in early October, it became clear that the funding for the program would continue, Douglas had made a proposal to the project head, one Dr. Frederick Merk, that he and Spilman would continue to serve without pay if the amount which would have been paid to them could be diverted to "a computer programmer, conversant in culture methods, located at MIT."

Thorngren froze the payment in the pipeline until he had a chance to grill Douglas on the particulars.

A little over a week after his first interview with Manos, Douglas showed up at the three-story frame house which housed the auditor's staff for his first day of questioning. He was, as Thorngren later recalled, "altogether docile" and not the least bit upset. Douglas asked if he could simply take notes on this first encounter. Thorngren agreed and proceeded to read off a list of sixty-six expenses which he had deemed questionable. When they met again two weeks later, Douglas had culled from that master list a set of twenty-six charges that he said were "problems." Among them were the Chicago hotel bills. Thorngren had frankly hoped for a direct admission of guilt. Douglas's statements so far had fallen short of a confession. His vagueness, in fact, was impenetrable. Rather than risk disrupting the precarious balance of negotiations, however, Thorngren continued to press Douglas gently but persistently over the space of the next five weeks. During this time, he presented for Douglas's perusal four airline refund checks. One of them had Nancy Douglas's signature on the back. Douglas identified Nancy as his wife and acknowledged having received all four checks. Still, he would not concede having done anything wrong. Thorngren then handed Douglas a receipt from the ABC Lock and Key Service for $127.90. Someone had altered the invoice to read $627.90. The address also appeared to have been altered to read "Lab 223 Brandon Hall."

Douglas did not deny tampering with the invoice. He simply termed it, too, a "problem."

Other charges, Douglas insisted were legitimate. The "biological fluid collection units," he claimed, were for a consulting project he was doing with Scott Labs, a private cancer research company in West Warwick, Rhode Island.

There was a questioned trip in early May to Saskatoon, where, Douglas claimed, he had visited Sergey Fedoroff. Beside this entry Douglas had written "OK." He also assured Thorngren that certain expenses incurred by his old friend Henry Holden were above board. These included a hotel bill from Howard Johnson for $74 and meals at Howard Johnson and Anthony's Pier 4 for $15.66 and $38.59, respectively, for a total of $128.-25. Holden, he said, had visited Tufts a week before the course started to make sure cells and supplies were ready.

For the present, at least, Thorngren accepted these explanations and directed Douglas's attention to a larger problem, the disbursement of some $13,580 in monthly fees to Robin Benedict. In reply, Douglas produced a handwritten work sheet on which he had broken down the various payments. He had indicated that four of these, totaling $7,000, were "problems." The rest, he insisted, were proper. Miss Benedict, he said, had been doing statistical analysis which required reviewing data and making sure it was significant. Between April 1 and September 27, he had paid her $1,980 for this work. Besides that, she had been doing image analysis which required taking a photograph of a cell under the microscope, outlining it on a graphics tablet connected to the computer, and then asking the computer to analyze the profile. For this, she had received, between April 1 and September 31, a total of $4,600.

The auditor asked him if he could substantiate those payments with work schedules or similar documents. Douglas said he could supply these if given a little time. He also promised to try to arrange for Thorngren to interview Miss Benedict. Once, just before Christmas, he managed to set up such an appointment, but Robin couldn't make it because of a snowstorm. Then she was away over the Christmas holidays. Since then, Douglas said, he had reached her by phone, but she was going out of town for New Year's. She promised to call him when she returned. After that, Miss Benedict was occupied with "moving." She had, in addition, "two personal problems" to deal with, but she would arrange a meeting with Thorngren after those things were taken care of.

In the meantime, rumors of an audit had reached Dr. Jeffrey Blumberg of the Human Nutrition Research Center. On January 4 he wrote a memo to his colleague Dr. Frederick Merk, asking him if he could lay his hands on a copy of either the program or the floppy disk prepared by Robin Benedict as well as a brief description of the "specifications/capability" of that program. Could he also locate a curriculum vitae or résumé for

Miss Benedict? Douglas received a copy of this memo and two days later penned this letter to Benedict:

Dear Robin,

Please forward to me at your earliest convenience a copy of your curriculum vitae. In addition, may I borrow the computer program you generated for the Nutrition Center. The Nutrition Center has requested a copy of the program for their review.

I look forward to receiving this information very soon.
Thanks.

Sincerely,
William H. J. Douglas
Director
Cell Culture Research Unit

That same day, Douglas dropped Dr. Merk a note explaining that Miss Benedict seemed to be taking a hard line. She hadn't yet been paid for the work she did on the project. No payment, no program. "She asked that I return [the program] to her until the time at which she receives compensation for the work," Douglas wrote. "I will prepare a brief description of the specifications/capability of the program. I have written Robin and requested a copy of her resume. . . . I will forward this information when I receive it. . . ."

Thorngren, meanwhile, had taken matters in hand and written Benedict himself, asking her to come in to discuss "certain monies" amounting to around $25,000. He mailed this entreaty to the last known address that he had for her, in Natick. He sent equally arch correspondence to Mr. Savitry Bisram in Randolph, Massachusetts. Mr. Bisram, Douglas had told him, was a gentleman who was working on the development of a computer program for yet another prostate project, this one for Dr. Peter Offner of the state labs at Shattuck. Mr. Bisram had supposedly worked 300 hours between August 2 and September 27, 1982, for a total of $4,500. He had received another $4,500 for programming work on a federal grant. Beyond that, he had also put in for and received a substantial travel advance of $2,400. Thorngren wrote,

Dear Mr. Bisram,

. . . A review of our records indicate[s] that the payments reflected on the statement that the University must issue to you might be as high at $11,400. In review of the substantial impact on your tax liability, it is essential that you contact me immediately. If I have not heard from you by January 31st, the statement will be finalized and mailed to you. . . .

Neither Miss Benedict·nor Mr. Bisram bothered to reply.

Karen Hitchcock, meanwhile, had been busy beating out brushfires. Around the first of December, Douglas had received another grant, a small one from Johns Hopkins, to study the toxic effects of red tide upon marine life. The chairman might not have known about this except that she had happened to see his letter of acceptance just as it was about to be typed. Douglas, Hitchcock knew, could not be allowed to involve the university in any more contractual obligations. She took the problem to Steven Manos, who, still unwilling to have her confront Douglas directly, instructed her to finesse it. "Just tell Bill, 'Don't send the letter now,' " he advised.

Hitchcock called Douglas into her office and told him he should delay accepting the new grant, "given the flux of the situation." It was the first time she had broached the subject even obliquely. A look of terror passed over his face.

"Are you all right?" she asked.

"I have no memory of it," Douglas blurted out. "I feel that I'm losing my mind. . . . I really can't talk about it now; I'm seeing a psychiatrist."

KAREN HITCHCOCK was not fully aware of how strange Douglas's behavior had become. He had taken, in recent weeks, to complaining that books and papers were being stolen from his office. In fact, he had asked a technician to research methods of marking his belongings so that they could be traced if stolen. She had looked into this and reported back to him that one could install an electronic system like the ones libraries used, but that could only stop someone at a checkpoint. Books couldn't be tracked down later. One could also put a strip of something in the bindings and use a metal detector, but that had very limited range.

Douglas finally settled upon a new and disturbing plan to irradiate all of his books with a radioisotope called Sodium 22. This, he imagined, would allow him to use a Geiger counter to scan the halls and offices of colleagues. Douglas set Stanley Spilman to work on the details. Spilman replied in an uneasy memo.

Bill,

The Geiger counter and the ^{22}Na arrived today. The ^{22}Na is on my desk in room 530 right now.

I don't know how to say this, but using ^{22}Na for a label is very tricky. It's as hazardous a radioisotope as you could find—worse than ^{32}P, which is very nasty stuff. . . .

If you unpack the ^{22}Na, realize that, as soon as you take it out of the lead container, each minute you're soaking up the equivalent of a lifetime's worth of X-rays. It's that bad—if you contact it, it is readily absorbed through the skin.

I'm not saying that it can't be used to label things in your office, but 1) an effort must be made to assure that the ^{22}Na is in a form which cannot be absorbed . . . and 2) if Health Physics finds out, they will go after us with an axe. . . .

When word of this spread around the lab, the technicians, two of whom were pregnant, went into a panic. To scope out the danger, Spilman, Ron Sanders, and a new postdoc named Tom Foxall hung around the lab until late one night when they were sure that Douglas had left. Then they entered his office with a Geiger counter and skimmed every inch of the desk, bookshelves, and file cabinets. They got no reading. Douglas, they later learned, had tested the isotope on the corner of a dollar bill, found it had a range of only two feet, and abandoned the plan.

Ron Sanders was becoming increasingly frustrated. Douglas was apparently being allowed to go about his business as usual. There seemed no guarantee that he would even be censured. Sanders was not privy to the deliberations of his superiors, but he was afraid that if they acted conservatively to avoid scandal, the whole story would never get out. On December 17 he met with Karen Hitchcock and handed her a letter which, since November, had been circulating anonymously throughout the department. The addressee had been obliterated, but it had clearly been intended for Pegeen Fitzgerald, president of the Millennium Guild. The letter read:

Since Dr. William Douglas has recently received a grant from your organization to do a pilot study in alternatives to the Draize test, you should know more about the man, his research and his ethics.

Dr. Douglas is currently under investigation by Tufts University for freud [*sic*], embezzlement and forgery. Monies involved are both federal and private, the latter coming from grants from the New England Anti-Vivisection Society. . . .

How is this man such a great animal rights activist, when the work in his laboratory relies very heavily on animal tissues in primary culture? Primary cultures mean repeatedly using cells directly isolated from fresh tissue for each experiment. The Mucin grant was originally written for *cat/kitten* trachea. A number of these animals were, in fact, sacrificed.

The writer went on to complain about various improprieties in the lab. A technician, Diane Romeo, had been denied certain credits due her. Worse yet, Stanley Spilman had been using the title "doctor" although he held no advanced degree.

> The University and the New England Anti-Vivisection Society have had proof of this thievery for well over a month. . . . Dr. Douglas is still on the faculty, still teaches and conducts business as usual. One can only conclude that some cover-up by both organizations is taking place, if this is not the case why then hasn't this man been charged in a criminal court?

While no one owned up to having written this letter, the author could have been any one of Douglas's disaffected colleagues or underlings. Sanders later speculated it was Romeo, because of the allusion to the photo caption. Romeo, in turn, surmised that the tone of the anonymous missive reflected more of the suppressed rage of Sanders. At any rate, the letter raised a problem which required Hitchcock's immediate attention. Had Spilman actually misrepresented his credentials? That same day the chairman called the University of California, where Stanley had supposedly gotten his Ph.D. It had no record of this degree. To make matters worse, the auditor Thorngren informed Hitchcock that among the dubious expenses were two travel advances—one for $2,000, another for $2,500—drawn by Spilman. Hitchcock was incredulous. Stanley was inclined to exaggerate a bit, but she did not believe that he could have gotten himself involved in anything criminal. Knowing the uncritical adoration he felt for Douglas, he had probably been an unwitting pawn. But if one or both of the charges were true, he would have to be let go. Hitchcock called Spilman into her office to discuss the allegations.

Confronted with the matter of his degree, Spilman explained that Douglas had overloaded him with work and that he hadn't gotten to finish his dissertation. It was his opinion that Douglas was "totally apprised" of his not having an advanced degree. If Douglas had given Spilman the title "Dr." for the purpose of the grants, he had done that strictly on his own initiative. As for the travel advances, Douglas had approached him in the fall with a predicament. He needed money to go on a business trip to Washington, D.C., he said, but he was having trouble with the accounting office. Spilman knew that the lab sometimes experienced cash shortfalls, so he agreed to tell the accounting office that he was the one who was going on the trip, and they gave him an advance. He could not remember this happening a second time. As reasonable as Stanley had made these occurrences sound, Hitchcock knew that, given the possibility of imminent scandal, he would have to leave.

As the New Year dawned, Thorngren was discovering that even those charges that Douglas insisted were proper were, indeed, false. Condoms were not required for Douglas's work at Scott Labs, which consisted chiefly of editing a products catalog. Karen Hitchcock ran into a pharmacist from Carl Martin's who fell cheerfully into a discussion of Douglas's standing order of condoms. Douglas had been ordering increasingly exotic Oriental brands, and there was a new line he ought to try out. Did Dr. Hitchcock know why Dr. Sanders had suddenly canceled the order? Beleaguered as she was, Hitchcock had found the "biological fluid collection units" perversely amusing. Who would have imagined Douglas had such a dry wit? To the pharmacist, however, she explained soberly that Dr. Douglas would not be requiring any more condoms.

Neither did the Holden paperwork hold up. Douglas's old friend had received a breakdown of expenses from the auditing department for his approval. He assumed there had been a clerical error. He had not been in Boston the week before Douglas's seminar. He scribbled "not correct" on the bottom of the letter, sent it back, and thought no more about it.

Dr. Sergey Fedoroff, however, was given pause. He received a call from a member of the Tufts auditor's staff saying that the university was checking its accounts and saw that Dr. William Douglas had spent a week in Saskatoon.

"Was he there?" the investigator asked.

"Oh, yes," Fedoroff replied. "He was here."

He went on to explain that Douglas had visited his class for the second year in a row to do some lecturing. For the last stint he had been paid an honorarium of $1,200 plus air fare of $700. The auditor did not suggest that these inquiries were anything more than routine. Still, Fedoroff was sufficiently alarmed to give Douglas a call.

"Bill," he said, "I'd better let you know that . . . I got this . . . phone call from somebody in the business office who was inquiring about your being here and asked about accountability and our payments."

"There's something funny going on," Douglas replied.

Someone was framing him, he claimed, by forging his name on invoices. He insisted that he was not involved and that everything was all right. Fedoroff, however, was not reassured. Something about Douglas's manner had not seemed right when he visited the preceding spring. Not that there was anything to which Fedoroff could point in his own interactions with the man. But others had witnessed strange behavior. Douglas had been lodged, as usual, in the student dormitories. Soon after he checked in, the resident manager came over to talk to Fedoroff. "This is the last time we will allow Douglas to stay at the University Residences," the fellow said emphatically. "Next time you better get him a hotel."

Fedoroff was shocked. It was a very serious matter if a senior visitor to the department was no longer welcome at the dormitories. In probing for details, Fedoroff found that the manager had not been able to find Douglas a suite with a private bath. He threw a tantrum and began shouting insults. The following morning, Fedoroff discreetly asked whether Douglas had found everything to his liking.

"Oh, yes," Douglas replied. "Everything is fine."

Fedoroff's lab personnel had also come to him with complaints. Douglas, they claimed, had been surreptitiously Xeroxing documents pertaining to research techniques in the Canadian lab. Presumably, he was planning to use this information in his own cell culture course coming up the following July. Fedoroff was perplexed by this. He would gladly have given Douglas anything he wanted, if he had only asked. That he felt compelled to obtain the material stealthily was peculiar. In the ten years that Fedoroff had known Douglas, he had never known him to do anything that might be considered dishonest. He was eager to get ahead, and that had led him to do some devious things. Fedoroff had always felt that Douglas's letter to the Jones family might have been an attempt to unseat his superior and take his place. Was this dishonesty or merely a clumsy attempt at advancement? Douglas had allowed himself to be apotheosized by the animal rights movement. Was that honest? He had no deep ethical commitment to the cause. To him, it was another vein of funding. Yet he had never professed to be a true believer. He had not deceived anyone into thinking that he had more than a purely scientific interest in the work. Was this not in itself a measure of integrity? For weeks after his brief conversation with the auditor, Fedoroff searched his memory for something in Douglas's career which might presage theft. There was self-interest, perhaps. An ambitious, politicking streak. But nothing that hinted at such a serious moral defect.

FEDOROFF was not the only one attempting to classify Douglas's apparent transgressions. The highest echelon of the Tufts administration had bent itself to this same task, with a much more practical intent. This was not a clear case of research fraud. If it had been, the trustees' course of action would have been laid out. The Association of American Medical Colleges had drawn up a set of guidelines for dealing with fabrication, falsification, or stealing of research data. It advised a discreet review by a committee of faculty peers. The accused must have a chance to confront his accusers and be given an opportunity to defend his actions.

The association said nothing about embezzlement—or its possible impact upon the quality of the investigator's science. It had, however, emphasized that those authors whose names appeared on scientific papers must have had a genuine role in the research so that they could be held accountable for it. One troublesome fact which had surfaced during the present inquiry was that Douglas had cowritten a surfactant paper with two other investigators for the prestigious British *Journal of Cell Science.* The last line of the credits read, "The authors wish to thank Robin N. Benedict for expert assistance in these studies."

One contingent of trustees was therefore calling for a peer review of Douglas's research. Among these was Vice-President Robert Levy, former head of the National Heart, Lung, and Blood Institute, the agency from which Douglas had received nearly $1.6 million. Levy wanted to be thorough. Given the apparent lack of integrity in dealing with research money, he reasoned, the science should be checked.

This raised the question of exactly what the university could or ought to tell those who inquired about Douglas. He had, it was learned, been sending out résumés since November. Assuming his science came out clean, could his superiors report that fact only, or were they obligated ethically to mention the funding irregularities? This issue was becoming a source of contention with Douglas, whose posture was becoming less conciliatory with each passing day. The pretense of goodwill began eroding when Manos asked him to sign a draft agreement wherein he promised not only to resign and repay the purloined funds but also to give the university permission to tell future employers that he had been asked to leave because of "misappropriated funds and falsified expense records."

During the first week in December, Douglas went to see an attorney, Harvey W. Freishtat, of the firm of McDermott, Will & Emery. The substance of that meeting was summed up in a letter sent the following week from Freishtat to Douglas.

December 14, 1982

Dear Dr. Douglas,

This is to confirm the results of our meeting of December 8 in connection with the difficulties you are now experiencing at the Tufts University School of Medicine.

During the course of our meeting, you described your background, experience, and current teaching, research, and administrative responsibilities as Director of the Cell Culture Research Unit and Tissue Culture Laboratory within the Department of Anatomy and Cellular Biology at the Medical School. You also described to me a series of personal events starting in the Spring of 1982, the net result of which was to cause you to expend thousands of dollars from a number of your research grants over a several month period for non-grant related purposes. You indicated that you have only a dim memory at this time of some of these events, and that you are currently under psychiatric treatment to address the issues giving rise to these events.

At the time of our meeting, the University was apparently requesting you to sign a statement which it had prepared with your assistance documenting the amount of misappropriated funds and seeking your agreement to provide restitution of those funds. In addition, the University is requesting you to resign your professorship and leave the University, with specific release for them to provide potential future employers with whatever information they deem appropriate regarding your situation.

At the conclusion of our discussion, I agreed to represent you in connection with these matters in order to seek a resolution which would be more equitable to you both personally and professionally. As I indicated, my agreement is conditioned upon some independent corroboration of your recitation of events, as well as an assurance that your difficulties relate solely to the financial aspects of your grant and not to the quality or integrity of your research. As to the former matter, I telephoned your psychiatrist with your permission subsequent to our meeting, and he has reinforced your description of the events. As to the latter matter, you indicated that an internal University Committee is being established to verify the quality of your professional work at the University. Pending the results of that investigation and on the basis of your assurance to me that your science has remained unimpaired throughout this period, I am pleased to represent you to attempt to restructure the resolution which the University has attempted to impose upon you thus far. . . .

Very truly yours,
Harvey W. Freishtat

Over the next few weeks, Freishtat won impressive concessions for his client. Douglas's own note-taking from the period indicates that Steven Manos was willing to give him an "assurance of non-prosecution." Freishtat then apparently contacted legal counsel for the New England Anti-Vivisection Society, who informed him there would be no NEAVS investigation. Judge Ford did not want to get involved in any meetings.

High on the list of Douglas's own priorities, however, remained the question of what Tufts could tell prospective employers. In his notes of conversations with Freishtat he wrote that whatever agreement was reached must provide that inquirers would be assured that he was "fully capable of science, that his science was not compromised." As for the university administrators, he insisted, they must realize that "he's having a personality problem he can't handle." He wanted to make sure that they realized the "bizarre cause" of his conduct.

The "bizarre cause" to which Douglas referred lay at the heart of the case he was preparing on his own behalf. According to this apologia, his peculiar behavior had been caused by dieting. Over the preceding year, he claimed, a breakdown of fat had released toxins called ketones into his blood, causing a chemical imbalance which, in turn, had affected his personality. To support this unorthodox theory, Attorney Freishtat had contacted his client's personal physician, Dr. James Patterson, of the New England Medical Center, who recounted the treatment Douglas had received over the past ten months.

Patterson had first seen Douglas on March 25, 1982, when he came into the center complaining of chest pain. Two days earlier, he said, he had been sitting at his desk and suffered a sudden, severe spasm in the "left lateral clavicle radiating to his sternum." It lasted for less than fifteen seconds. Patterson ordered an electrocardiogram, which turned out to be normal. He examined Douglas, who seemed to be in generally good health except that he was overweight at 317 pounds. The doctor put him on a low-protein diet, and when Douglas returned for a checkup on April 2, he had lost nineteen pounds. Patterson noted at that time that his patient was "very interested to lose weight." By April 29 he had lost a total of forty-three pounds. During May there was an increase of ketones in the urine. Patterson also detected a minor prostatic infection. The prostate was enlarged and the right lobe tender. But all in all, he reported, the patient "feels very well."

When Douglas visited Patterson again on June 11, his weight loss had leveled off to a steady one and a half pounds a week. Most significantly, he was showing no more signs of ketosis. His health had remained generally good after that except for a rather odd incident on June 15. On that occasion, Douglas reported, he had been pushed into a phone booth "by kids" who had then taken his wallet. During the attack, he had reportedly hit his head against the side of the booth. He was not knocked unconscious but did have a headache. The X rays were negative.

Patterson agreed to summarize this case history on New England Medical Center stationery for Freishtat's benefit. He concluded, "The overall picture here is of a massively obese man who successfully followed a protein sparing diet in March, April and May of 1982 which was liberalized by June. Urinary ketones were positive at examinations of April 2, April 22, April 29 and May 25 indicating that he had ketosis from the fasting."

Having lined up a credible witness who would attest that he had indeed suffered from ketosis, Douglas undertook to lay out its possible side effects. For this, he enlisted the help of an endocrinologist, Dr. Mark Molitch, of the New England Medical Center. Molitch contacted six experts in endocrinology and psychology, including one quite eminent Dr. Albert Stunkard. Questioned in the months thereafter, Stunkard could not recall having been contacted about Douglas. Yet Douglas's notes reflect that Stunkard had assessed his problems thus: "Quite possible all manic episode triggered by fast. $ and sexual issues triggered in certain predisposed . . . 2 phases. High and low, manic depression and mania, wide mood swings."

Douglas seemed to be suggesting that his profligacy had occurred during a manic episode. To support the theory that his mental aberration had been diet related, he also compiled a bibliography of a dozen or so scientific articles which described the effects of semistarvation diets upon overweight subjects. Several of these monographs had been written by a Dr. M. L. Glucksman, who described in painstaking detail the characteristic family background of the obese child. Such a child was often the youngest or only offspring, whose parents had used him as "compensations for their own frustrations or disappointments." His mother, usually possessing a stronger personality than the father, tended to regard the child as a "prized inanimate possession." In such a disturbed home, the child's feeding was not necessarily a nutritional consideration but a "bribe to keep [him] close, dependent and loyal."

Obese children, Glucksman observed, were usually highly intelligent. The knowledge of their own superior mental capability, coupled with their favored position in the family, often engendered in them a feeling of "specialness or potential greatness." This inflated sense of self-worth, however, disguised a deeper loathing for their own bodies and ineffectualness. As the child grew older and found himself the object of ridicule, he tended to become "shy, oversensitive and seclusive." He remained immature well into his adult life and was, more often than not, unable to tolerate frustration or delay gratification. Under stress, he resorted to overeating, which temporarily assuaged such discomforts as anxiety, depression, anger, boredom, and guilt.

Glucksman noted that certain obese patients who had been put on semistarvation diets had reported emotional difficulties, among these "increased anxiety, depression, hostility, [paranoia], sexual activity and near psychotic episodes."

Another of the authors cited in Douglas's bibliography, a psychiatrist named Hilde Bruch, observed further that some patients experienced "an exaggerated sense of well-being" during the early days of dieting. Losing weight, she concluded, became "the magical key opening the doors to the fulfillment of fantastic hopes and daydreams." As the fast wore on, however, the magic dissipated. The dieter, perceiving himself to be disintegrating physically, often became anxious, imagining himself helpless and susceptible to attack. Glucksman, in fact, had noticed the same phenomenon in the case of a twenty-six-year-old white man who lost one hundred pounds and subsequently dreamed he was attacked by a gang of men who slashed his arm. When he asked these dream bullies to take him to the hospital, they refused. The male dieter, Glucksman concluded, may develop a fear of injury at the hands of other men.

The experts also noticed that as the obese patient shed weight and became more attractive, his anxieties increased. His expanding opportunities for sexual encounters were often so threatening that he expressed his eroticism furtively—through fantasies, homosexuality, and promiscuity. Denied food, he often sought out other kinds of oral gratification, such as smoking, hoarding, thumb sucking, kissing, and breast fondling. Glucksman also noticed how, in the throes of fasting, a dieter might cling to maternal figures such as a mother or wife. Another expert cited in the bibliography agreed, observing that the dieter may cling desperately and dependently to another person as a source of security while dieting. If that relationship was cut off, he might lapse into a "dieting depression." In the face of this distress, he might very well try to establish control over his surroundings through obsessive-compulsive behavior and attempts to manipulate and dominate others.

If Douglas saw himself in the shy, plump child whose parents used him to fulfill their own dreams, or the magic boy who had the power to remake his own body, or the helpless victim preyed upon by phantom bullies, he did not come right out and say so. It was not his way to express himself so directly. Offering the arcane and impersonal observations of "experts" was apparently the closest he could come to offering an explanation for what he had done.

Douglas wanted to get a hearing before the university at which he could present this material. He was apparently nursing the hope that if he gave extenuating circumstances for his misdeeds and, more important, if he made restitution—Freishtat had suggested taking out staggered loans and liquidating his pension fund—the university might write the entire episode off as a lapse and let him stay.

For most of December, Freishtat worked to set up a hearing before a tribunal of high-ranking Tufts officials which included Steven Manos; Dean Henry Banks; Dr. Sol Gittleman, academic vice-president and provost; and Dr. Karen Hitchcock. It was finally scheduled for the afternoon of January 11 on the Boston campus.

That morning, Douglas called in to work instructing a secretary to tell Dr. Hitchcock that he would be arriving late. Hitchcock thought this was strange since for months now Douglas had not felt it necessary to account for his comings and goings. When he arrived later that morning, he telephoned the chairman from the lab and demanded that she come down and look at his office. Someone, he said, had broken into it. Hitchcock made her way warily to 530 M&V. Entering Douglas's warren, she saw it was in shocking disarray. Stacks of paper had been pushed onto the floor. His chair had been tipped over. Since the place was normally a shambles, however, it was difficult to tell what kind of mischief had been done.

Douglas seemed beside himself with anxiety. He explained how, for that past week, his home phone would ring. When someone picked it up, the caller would hang up or breathe heavily. Last night the calls began coming at half-hour intervals. When one of the children answered, the caller would say, "Did you know your father was a thief?" This was a deliberate attempt, he felt, to keep him from getting sleep on the eve of "the most important meeting of his life." Douglas said he couldn't bear to take stock of the damage and retired to the library to regain his composure.

All of this left Hitchcock feeling very uneasy. She recalled one thing in particular that Douglas had sputtered in his distress. The office, he felt, had been ransacked between 11:00 P.M. and 1:00 A.M., when there had been a two-hour break between calls. He thought that both the calls and the pillaging were the work of Lance Kisby and Diane Romeo. Hitchcock did not believe for one minute that those two young people would be persecuting Douglas. But there was obviously some sickness rampant in the lab. Either someone hated Douglas so much that he or she was harassing him or he was so disturbed that he was imagining it.

His accusation of Kisby stirred in Hitchcock the recollection of a conversation she had had just before Christmas with a faculty member who enjoyed a good relationship with Lance. Kisby had told his instructor some story about Douglas's wanting to douse the lab with a radioisotope. At the time when Hitchcock's colleague had passed the story along to her, there was no evidence that Douglas really intended to act on this scheme. Given recent developments, however, Hitchcock felt she ought to check again. The sodium 22, she discovered, was still in the lab!

Hitchcock quickly called Health Physics and asked it to remove the isotope. Then she hurried to the conference room, where the inquisition was scheduled to begin, in order to press her case before Douglas arrived. She told Manos and the others about the radioisotope and the supposed harassment calls. She described Douglas's ravaged office and the potentially dangerous hostilities running through 530 M&V. She wanted Douglas suspended regardless of the outcome of the day's meeting. The others were noncommittal. They were waiting to hear from Douglas.

Shortly after five Douglas arrived with his retinue, which included Harvey Freishtat, Dr. Molitch, and a psychiatrist, Dr. Peter Randolph.

Manos called the meeting to order. Then Douglas rose and in a high, plaintive monologue told of how much he had given to the university and how he had been overworked. He had been exhausted in the spring of 1982 when he had been placed on a strenuous diet. That resulted in ketosis, which, he claimed, had been known to cause "depression, paranoia, hysteria, a feeling of omnipotence and hypersexuality."

If Manos and the others were expecting him to elaborate upon the details of his financial indiscretions, they were to be disappointed. "The girl," as she was referred to discreetly, still lacked clearly definable form, and Douglas declined to give her any. He spoke of her in detached, almost scientific, terms as the catalyst for his "problems." Even when the proceeding was thrown open to questions, the tribunal shyly avoided inquiring about her. The questioning instead went to the heart of the ketosis claim.

"How long has your weight been stabilized?" someone asked.

Douglas replied, "October."

This was clearly at odds with his physician's report, which had specified June as the month when the weight stabilized and the ketones disappeared. Karen Hitchcock, having a passing familiarity with biochemistry, caught the discrepancy, pointing out that when the ketosis abates, behavior should return to normal. Many of the instances of alleged fraud, however, had occurred since October. The ketosis hypothesis did not meet with any warmer reception from other members of the panel. The whole argument smacked uncomfortably of the notorious "Twinkie" defense, which had been used without much success in certain criminal cases—its most celebrated failure being an attempt to exonerate Dan White, assassin of Councilman Harvey Milk, of San Francisco. White claimed that eating junk food had wrought a chemical imbalance which, in turn, had altered his behavior. The scientific community largely regarded the junk-food argument with contempt. The Tufts tribunal declined even to hear Dr. Molitch read excerpts from literature on the further effects of fasting.

Throughout the entire meeting, Douglas flirted with admissions of guilt, but he never came out and said, "I stole the money." Once again, Manos urged him to sign the "misappropriation" agreement. Douglas refused and departed with his retinue. The administrators agreed that the next morning, pending Manos's notification of Douglas's attorney, Hitchcock should declare him "suspended."

Flush with this mandate, Hitchcock arrived the morning of January 12, determined to expel Douglas. She made arrangements with Tufts security police to change the locks at 530 M&V. Sergeant Bruce Govostes, who had been briefed on the strange goings-on in the lab, warned her that she must not, under any circumstances, be alone with Douglas. She sat in her office and waited for the final okay from Manos.

By ten o'clock it became clear that this was not going to be a clean break. Freishtat was apparently instructing Douglas to hold fast in his cluttered office. Manos would not give Hitchcock the signal until he had concluded his conversations with the attorney. Hitchcock was afraid that Douglas might do something desperate. When the legal bickering extended into the afternoon, Hitchcock called Manos and proposed that she go down and sit with Douglas to make sure no harm came to anyone until the legal niceties were worked out. Manos agreed.

Hitchcock went down to Douglas's lab. She took a chair by his desk. The hour she passed there was most awkward. During that time, he gave her a two-page memo on which he had made an inventory of things he claimed had been stolen from his office. It included, two phone-answering machines, two tape recorders and microphone, and an Apple II Plus computer. She said she would inform security.

It was difficult to think of anything to say to a man whose career was on the verge of ruin.

"Do you need anything, Bill?" she asked.

He replied, "Do you think this is fair?"

Hitchcock didn't know how to answer.

The phone rang, and he announced he had to take a call from his attorney. Hitchcock stepped discreetly outside his office, and he closed the door. After several minutes, she heard him stirring inside. When the door opened, he had his coat on. "I'm ready now," he said. Hitchcock walked him to the elevator. There he hesitated for a second before leaving meekly by the stair.

DURING the months to follow, Hitchcock thought often and painfully of this leave-taking. It was not the sort of humiliation that a professional reputation could survive. Perhaps Douglas might teach high school or junior college in some rural community where rumors of his disgrace might not penetrate the isolation. But to the world of academic research, where reputation counted for so much, he was now a pariah. Once, while commiserating with one of her faculty friends, she was overwhelmed by pity for Douglas and started weeping.

Yet the query "Do you think this is fair?" plagued her. When she considered it, her sympathy became alloyed with irritation. Was it fair, indeed! When Hitchcock considered the enormity of Douglas's transgressions, she wondered how he had even summoned the nerve to ask that question. He had stolen, lied, and betrayed the trust of colleagues. He had imperiled, perhaps ruined, the careers of the young postdocs who admired him. Heaven only knew what he had done to his family. And yet he could ask if this was fair!

During months to follow—dreadful months when the compassion she felt for Douglas had finally given away to anger—Hitchcock would be reminded of one of the last things he had said to her as he was poised on the brink of expulsion, a comment which served to dispel her sympathy for good.

"If Robin Benedict calls," he had asked innocently, "have her call me at home."

ROBIN

IT WAS during the spring of 1982 that William Douglas—pushing up against the limits of his abilities as a scientist, confronting a mysterious coldness at home, passing without passion or the distinction which he desired into the uncertain reaches of middle age—went in search of something he would later describe as "a new hope for living." He found it—or so he imagined—in the Combat Zone at a bar called Good Time Charlie's.

Charlie's was not a place that called attention to itself. Tucked unobtrusively into one end of an alley known as Lagrange Street, its entrance was marked by a small Busch Bavarian sign. The recessed doorway beneath opened into a dim, high-ceilinged room dominated by a horseshoe bar. Down the center of it ran a runway where from 8:00 A.M. to 2:00 A.M., a succession of forlorn strippers gyrated in twenty-minute sets to the insistent, ever-present pulse of disco.

Even by the slipping standards of the Zone, Charlie's was considered déclassé. Other lounges had the odd pretension to refinement. At the Naked i, for instance, the management went out of its way to leave the impression that its dancers were just nice girls making a living. Its "All New College Girl Revue" conveyed to randy young men from Harvard and MIT the tacit assurances that their aesthetic enjoyment would not be marred by scars and tattoos. For the record, at least, the girls from the Naked i were not for sale. They were restricted to "clean mixing." That is, they could mingle with patrons in order to persuade them to buy drinks. The clean mixer's repertoire of tactics included nuzzling, flattery, any-

86

thing short of a hand job under the table. For grittier action, the patron had to move down the line to the Pussycat or Caribe, where the women were older and uglier. They did, however, engage in dirty mixing in the semiseclusion of dark booths. If a girl propositioned a guy at the bar, nobody complained as long as she wasn't obvious. At this echelon, sexual transactions took place behind a scrim of discretion. Not so at Charlie's, which was a flat-out hooker hangout.

When Charlie's opened, in 1971, on the site of an old antique shop, it professed to be a legitimate after-work lounge. It was no secret, however, that the main attraction was a covey of working girls who began showing up every afternoon around three. The prostitutes and the bar enjoyed a relationship which benefited both. Management let them cruise, and in the process they increased the house's profits by encouraging prospective johns to buy them watered-down drinks at $8 a pop.

If a patron was worried about getting mugged or contracting a disease, he might slip $50 to the bartender or doorman and ask, "Who's halfway decent?" More often, however, it was a working girl who took the initiative, circling the bar, sidling up to a prospect, and whispering, "You wanna go out?"

If she got a nibble, she would write an address on a slip of paper and meet her date twenty minutes later at a designated trick pad or hotel room. The going rate in those days was $30 for a trick called the "half and half" or, more evocatively, the "suck and fuck." Everything, of course, was negotiable. A girl working on the margin might agree to a hand job in the backseat of a car for $10. A specialist might contract for an evening of domination at $500. The fact was, an energetic hustler could make substantial money at Charlie's. If she could turn twenty standard tricks—a stiff but not impossible pace—she would come away with $600 a night. That came to over $4,000 a week.

Charlie's also provided some basic protection. On the street, a girl didn't always get a chance to screen for weirdos. In the bar, however, she could sit and talk to a guy for a while. If he was sweating and wouldn't look her in the eye, that was a bad sign and she could make a quick exit. On the street, furthermore, one had to conduct one's business in full view of the police. In Charlie's, dates could be made more discreetly. In theory, at least, officers from Boston's Vice Control Section made a turn through Charlie's seven or eight times a day. Their approach, however, was usually heralded by a doorman who kept surveillance on the street through a one-way mirror. When the shout of "Vice!" punctuated the din, the girls got clear of the bar, and the cops entered to find them lounging innocently against the wall.

These precautions notwithstanding, by 1974 over thirty girls had been convicted of using Charlie's as the site of "solicitation or immoral bargaining." In February, Charles Sicuso, brother of the club's owner, was found guilty in Boston Municipal Court of "knowingly allowing a cafe to be used for immoral solicitation." Charlie's had been feeling pressure from the police, not because it harbored prostitutes. In the pantheon of urban evils, prostitution was considered pretty harmless. The fact was, however, that a good number of those prostitutes were also thieves who would cruise Lagrange lifting wallets and then slip back into Charlie's to unload the goods. One prosecutor likened them to "whorelets coming out of the nest, stinging people, and returning to the nest." If Charlie's was to stay in business, it would have to crack down on thieves. So, in a gesture of reform, the Sicusos brought in Willie Moses.

Willie was a dapper black man in his late forties who hailed from South Carolina. He was a jack-of-all-trades. During his checkered career in Boston, he owned a pest control business, played jazz saxophone, and worked as an assistant manager of a lounge called the Teddy Bear, in Park Square. At the time the whip came down on Charlie's, he was an assistant manager of the parent corporation, Charlesbank Restaurants. Two months after Sicuso's conviction, Willie was made manager of the lounge on Lagrange.

Willie had big plans for the place. Upstairs he put in a jazz club, where prostitutes weren't allowed. Downstairs he laid down the law. First rule: Any girl who wanted to work Charlie's had to abide by a dress code. No blue jeans. Second rule: No pimps. They got in the way and sometimes made trouble. Willie instructed his bouncer, Juan, to keep troublemakers out. Third rule: No street whores. If a girl had been working the streets, she was probably also a pickpocket. Willie made it clear that he would turn over a girl without question if she was suspected of thievery. This accommodating attitude sat well with the authorities, who were launching their own offensive. In the fall of 1974, they bore down on the whorelets with a novel strategy.

The architect of this plan was a boyish riot trooper by the name of Billy Dwyer. Dwyer came from Dorchester, a hard-core Irish neighborhood on the southern outskirts of Boston. His parents were divorced when he was six, and he was raised by a strong-willed mother who schooled him in "American values." Dwyer could be moved to tears by the national anthem. During the sixties when free sex and radical sentiments were afoot in the land, he joined the Boston police force because it seemed the last stronghold of decency.

Although he lived at home until he was well into his thirties, he liked to project the image of a carefree womanizer, and for a time he dated a girl who worked at a clean club on the edge of the Combat Zone. She didn't get off until 2:00 A.M., and he would usually sit outside the club and wait for her. That gave him a chance to study the street. He watched the girls grabbing guys by the balls, robbing them, sometimes stabbing them. Where you had girls working the streets, you also had robbery, rape, murder, everything short of treason. And cruisers drove by doing nothing! They had just conceded the field to scum. That set Dwyer's imagination working. If this was war, why not send in commandos to take back the streets?

Since the spring of 1974, Dwyer had been a member of the Anti-Crime Unit of the Tactical Patrol Force, Boston's elite riot squad. The ACU specialized in decoy actions against muggers and purse snatchers in high-crime areas. Dwyer, who was endowed with a surfeit of manic energy and cunning, had become the brains of this operation, designing disguises and coordinating electronic surveillance of the decoys. In the fall of 1974, Dwyer prepared to lead his men into battle against the dark forces of Lagrange.

On November 23, 1974, at 10:30 P.M., six police decoys strolled out onto the alley, where for the next three and a half hours they submitted to solicitation and pickpocketing. Their comrades documented the encounters with hidden cameras. At 2:15 A.M., when the bars closed and the street action was at peak frenzy, the Tactical Patrol Force sealed off both ends of Lagrange Street and herded about one hundred prostitutes into the parking lot across the street from Charlie's. There, police made identifications and nearly fifty-six arrests before packing the shrieking, protesting girls onto a bus and off for booking. The genius of Dwyer's plan was that it had assured witnesses to the crimes. Ordinarily, the most difficult part of getting a conviction against a prostitute was persuading her john to testify against her. In this case, there was a willing "john" and supporting photos to support every arrest.

The specter of riot troopers lurking in the shadows kept Lagrange clean for about two months. Dwyer was gleeful to have shown the street element who was in control. He was busy preparing for other blitzes when the Tactical Patrol Force was ordered to South Boston to help enforce the busing order. The whorelets returned to Lagrange, where for the next three years they plied their trade in relative peace. In January 1977 Dwyer was reassigned to the Combat Zone, this time as part of a new cadre of detectives who replaced the ones fired in the wake of the Papuolo killing. The new regime was given a mandate to clean house.

Billy Dwyer became, by his own reckoning, a legend in the Zone. It was not a humble assessment, but then he was not a humble man. He enjoyed walking down Lagrange and observing the scum part like the Red Sea. He liked being able to arrest a girl for no particular reason, and he enjoyed her knowing that he could abuse his power if he chose. Billy Dwyer was the law in the Combat Zone, and as long as people realized that, everyone got along fine.

Willie Moses played the game. When Dwyer strolled into Charlie's on his daily rounds, Willie was all helpfulness and humility. Dwyer privately sneered at Willie's pretensions. A dress code for hookers, for God's sake! That's what happened when you gave a street nigger a little authority. Still, the two of them developed an understanding. Dwyer turned a blind eye to the goings on in the bar as long as the girls were discreet. In return for this courtesy, Willie turned over pickpockets.

What most endeared Willie to Billy, however, was his hard line on pimps. Above all else, Dwyer hated pimps. He regarded them as cockroaches that crawled all over something beautiful, nibbling at it, soiling it until it became garbage. Pimps actually believed they had the right to make money off of white girls. They knew how to spot the weakness in a sweet little blond from the suburbs. Maybe she was a little plain. LeRoy convinced her she was beautiful. Maybe she was lonely. Tyrone showered her with attention and clothes and jewelry and drugs.

Once he got a hook into her particular need, he loosened her up sexually. He'd persuade her to sleep with one of his friends for a favor. From there, it was a short step to persuading her to sleep with a guy for money. There was no shame, he'd tell her. That was the line they all used. Pretty soon she'd actually believe that turning tricks was a quick, easy, respectable way of earning money. Respect, like beauty, after all, is in the eye of the beholder.

Dwyer considered himself a worldly guy. He could understand the attraction that money might hold for a young girl. What kind of job is she going to get that pays $500 to $1,000 a day? If a girl decided to temporarily put aside everything that had been bred in her, worked for two years, and then invested the bucks, well then, fine. But to turn it over to a pimp! It defied logic. If a pimp had a stable of six girls doing $500 a day, he would be bringing in $3,000 a day, $15,000 a week. And this with almost no risk to himself. Because pimps knew how to make themselves scarce, they were rarely arrested and almost never convicted. To put a pimp away, you would need his whore to testify that she had been supporting him with her earnings. The girls were usually too well-trained to give up their pimps.

The best way, then, to get at a pimp, Dwyer discovered, was to cut into his earnings. If a girl was busted, she would lose a night's wages. And Dwyer knew whom to hit to hurt whom. He kept impeccable records.

Every time he saw a new girl in the Zone, he would jot down her identifying traits in a notebook. A scar, perhaps. A southern accent. A street name. Then he set about finding out who her pimp was. This he could usually do by trading on his goodwill at Charlie's. With this intelligence he could fit her into the complicated web of relationships in the Zone. He could tell if she was one of the "wives-in-law" of a particular stable. He could tell if she belonged to Comfort, or California Palm, or Finesse, or Sweet George.

In the spring of 1982, however, Billy Dwyer caught sight of a girl who seemed to belong to no one. He was patrolling Lagrange Street with his partner, Mark Molloy, when he spotted the newcomer. She was a young woman with dark hair and large brown eyes. Dwyer had noticed her off and on since about April. About four o'clock every afternoon, except weekends, she pulled her battered green Toyota into the Fitz-Inn parking lot on Lagrange. Then she made a beeline across the street to Charlie's. She was usually dressed in a blazer and skirt and walked with a brisk secretarial gait, which marked her instantly as an outsider. You could usually tell a prostitute from the way her pelvis was thrust forward and knees turned out in a funk strut. In the badlands of Lagrange, this tidy brunette looked so respectable she called attention to herself.

She was on her way from Charlie's to the parking lot when he intercepted her. He later recalled their conversation.

"Is something wrong, officer?" she asked sweetly.

"Well," Dwyer replied, "as a matter of fact there is. I just saw you comin' out of Good Time Charlie's."

"Is there something wrong with that?" she countered.

"Nope. But now we're on the subject, what are you doing in there?"

"I just went down to visit a friend. Oh, oh. You think I'm a work—I'm not a working girl."

"Oh, of course you're not," Dwyer replied. "And that means I'll probably never see you again. . . . It's been very nice talkin' to you."

A few days later, however, he saw her in the parking lot getting into her car.

"Hi, there," he said. "May I see your driver's license, please."

To his surprise, she carried a full set of identification. Most unusual for a working girl. Her name was Robin Nadine Benedict. Once again she appeared ingenuous.

"Something wrong, officer?"

"Yeah," he replied. "Now there's no doubt in my mind. You're a prostitute just like the rest of them."

"Oh, no," she responded enigmatically. "Not just like the rest of them."

ROBIN BENEDICT did not, in fact, seem "just like the rest of them." She did not project the weary resignation of a failed actress whose misguided dreams had led her to pose nude, then strip, then sell hand jobs in the alley. She was clearly no runaway playing the street action. She seemed far too fresh and prepossessing to be a junkie. From where, then, had Robin Benedict sprung?

It would be quite a few months before the details of Robin Benedict's past would come within Billy Dwyer's reach. By that time, her reputation would already have exceeded the narrow boundaries of the Combat Zone. By then, she would be emerging in the public imagination as a woman whose loyalties were mysteriously divided between a pimp and an adoring family. A woman who seemed to move with apparent ease between two worlds: that of "Nadine," the working girl who haunted the bars and hotel lobbies of downtown Boston; and that of Robin, sweet Robin, thoughtful girlish Robin, who felt conscience bound to spend weekends with her parents in a backwater milling town of northern Massachusetts.

JOHN BENEDICT had an incorruptible faith in beauty. On his first visit to the Merrimack Valley as a young man, he had been overwhelmed by its loveliness. All along the river's scalloped course from Lowell to Haverhill, the banks were on fire with autumn colors. The sunlight which fell on that blaze of yellow and vermilion captured it like the click of a shutter. Over the next thirty years, Benedict photographed the valley with as much devotion as a man scrutinizing the face of his beloved. He learned how the changing light of seasons transformed the landscape. On a winter morning he could catch the abandoned textile mills and tenements along the river in a mood of steely desolation. If he waited until four or five, the late afternoon light would soften their outlines. There was nothing that could not be made beautiful if it were cast in the right light.

Benedict's passion to document was a way of claiming the country as his own. He was not a New Englander, or even an American, by birth. His passport read "Native of Trinidad," a phrase which always caused him to wince, as it suggested—he thought—an aboriginal with spear and a loincloth. He was always careful to point out that his maternal ancestors were Spaniards—the Calendar family of Alcántara—who emigrated to Venezuela. The men became tailors. One uncle rose to the position of supervisor in a petroleum factory. Another became a headmaster of a commercial academy on Trinidad, off the northern coast of Venezuela. The family acquired property there, growing coffee and plantains and marrying into the local melting pot of Indian and African locals.

Juan Mathias de Trinidad Lopez, as he was christened, was raised by his mother, a tall, dark-skinned woman, who worked as a seamstress. While Juan was in his teens, she married an Italian American field engineer and moved with him to Baltimore. Juan stayed behind in Trinidad working for the Alcoa Steamship Company. Then, at the age of nineteen, he left to join his mother in America.

He was a handsome young man with full, sensual lips, wavy hair, and a wide smile that revealed a slightly chipped front tooth. Though dark, he was not as dark as his mother, and after he had been out of the equatorial sun for a while, he could even pass for Caucasian. Eager to be accepted by his "adopted country," the reverential terms in which he referred to America, he legally changed his name to the more English-sounding Benedict. When a clerk asked him for a middle name, he replied, "None." And that is how it went down on the form. John None Benedict became a citizen, joined the Navy, and was assigned to a tugboat in Norfolk, Virginia.

It was in Norfolk that he met Ellen Shirley Menzies, a short, fair-skinned girl from northern Massachusetts. Shirley was in Virginia visiting an aunt and showed up one night at the Servicemen's Club. The attraction was immediate and mutual. Years later, as they tried to define exactly what it was they saw in one another, John jokingly singled out Shirley's hair. She had been trying to grow it out and was wearing it in a stubby little ponytail. As for Shirley, she simply found John Benedict the handsomest man she had ever seen. Within the week he took her to visit his mother. Two weeks later he asked her to marry him.

When Shirley took him to her family home in Methuen, slightly to the north of Lawrence, her mother found him "rather dark." After they were married, however, Ma Menzies became his greatest supporter. She wouldn't hear a bad thing said about him. When John took his bride back to Norfolk to settle her into an apartment, the landlady, announcing that she didn't approve of mixed marriages, threw the keys at them. The newlyweds resolved to ignore spite and prejudice. They were eager to start a family. John wanted one boy and one girl. But when Shirley went for an examination, the doctor told her she probably couldn't carry a baby. There was considerable cause for celebration, then, when John Benedict, who had shipped out for the Mediterranean aboard the communications ship *Taconic*, received a cable from Ma Menzies that Shirley had given birth to a baby boy and that mother and child were doing well.

Over a period of four and a half years, John and Shirley Benedict had five children, a feat which caused Shirley to crow to amused friends, "We showed 'em, didn't we, Johnny." The boys were all born in Norfolk. First Rickie; fifteen months later, Ronnie. During Christmas 1959, when Shirley was about five months pregnant with Robbie, she was photographed kneeling beside a small fir tree. She was wearing a royal blue cheongsam, which John had brought her from Gibraltar. Her large, dark eyes were bright, and her face glowed with satisfaction.

Shortly after Robbie was born, John got out of the Navy. The Benedicts moved to Shirley's hometown of Methuen, where John, who had worked as a photographer aboard the *Taconic,* got a job at Raytheon photographing weaponry.

No sooner had they settled their infant and two toddlers into a rented house in Methuen than Shirley was pregnant again. On July 19, 1961, she gave birth to Robin Nadine. John Benedict was thrilled. From the roof of the house, he hung a sheet with big bold letters reading "IT'S A GIRL."

The birth of Robin was such a momentous event that the arrival of her sister, Rhonda, only ten months later was, by comparison, an afterthought. And it was with the birth of his daughters, John Benedict considered his family complete. Rickie, Ronnie, Robbie, Robin, and Rhonda.

The Rs had started as a joke that kept gathering momentum. John Benedict liked reeling off the names. They sounded like a jingle and, as such, had a curiously American quality. The life he had been putting together for his family was a pastiche of idealism and guesswork. He was not completely sure of what the good life included, but, like many immigrants, he felt the path to it lay in hard work and discipline. It also meant enduring deprivation with pleasant humor because in a land of opportunity, discomfort was surely temporary.

In pursuit of that hazy goal, the Benedicts bought a small five-room cottage on Lowell Street. All of the children slept in one bedroom. Rhonda, Robin, and Robbie had their own cribs. The older boys were stacked in bunk beds. Shirley went to work for a local jeweler doing repossessions. Every morning, John would take three of the children to one sitter. Shirley would call a cab and take the remaining two to another. No sooner did they get home in the evening than they would set to work feeding the babies and washing diapers. In the morning it started all over again.

By the time Rhonda was out of infancy, the Benedicts had saved enough to buy a modest tract house in a development northwest of town. They were fiercely proud of it and worked on it constantly, converting the basement to bedrooms and a recreation room. Onto the back they built a wide porch outfitted with green, all-weather carpet and a padded black leather bar. In the sloping backyard they installed an elevated swimming pool.

Every Sunday, John Benedict barbecued enough ribs or chicken to feed a small battalion of friends and relatives who had a standing invitation to drop by for a dip. Among the regulars at these pool parties were the Ramoses, Andre and Sallie and their five children, who were so close in age to the young Benedicts that they came to be known as the cousins.

The Ramos children belonged to Northstar, a drum and bugle corps which competed in tournaments throughout eastern Massachusetts. The corps were very popular in small towns like Methuen and Beverly, where they were believed to instill in adolescents such virtues as patriotism and discipline. This appealed to John Benedict, who was reminded of his own studies at the Halcyon Commercial Academy in Trinidad. His uncle, the headmaster, would play a game called battlin'. This required lining students up in a row and asking them questions. A wrong answer would send a combatant to the back of the line tingling with shame. Competition and peer pressure built what he perceived as character.

John Benedict thought the discipline of marching drills might do his children some good. Robbie was a bookworm and needed to be drawn out of his shell. Rhonda walked knock-kneed, like her mother. Ronnie had become infatuated with fast cars and motorcycles. What was worse, he was a little stooped, and that particularly bothered his father, who had always tried to teach his children that "bearing was everything." So thrilling did John Benedict find the sight of youngsters marching in step that, after his oldest son, Rickie, joined the Lawrence White Eagles, he became a codirector of the corps.

Unlike the Northstars, who were champions in their division, the White Eagles were a rag-tag crew. Once they climbed into the first echelon of competition, but they were beaten so badly they settled back forever into "Category B." They could not find sponsors among local businessmen. They had only two horns that, as Benedict used to say, "the Salvation Army would throw away." The equipment truck leaked oil from every gasket. Unable to afford dry-cleaning, they washed their flags and sweaty hats in the Benedict's pool and laid them to dry on the lawn. They had no practice hall, so the musicians convened at the Benedict house, where soprano brass took over the bathroom and the tympani took over in the kitchen. Benedict's appeal for a gymnasium brought no offers, so the corps had to drill under a bridge at the Lawrence Municipal Parking Lot.

When the White Eagles marched in perfect step, infrequent as that was, they validated John Benedict's theories of bearing. No matter that the truck wouldn't start and the instruments were falling apart, cutting an impressive figure was what counted.

Of all of Benedict's children, the one who cut the most impressive figure was Robin.

When she joined the White Eagles, at the age of eleven, Robin was assigned to a highly visible position as a member of the color guard. Years later her parents recalled in a eulogy, "We will always remember her tasseled boots and the shiny saber she held high with pride when she led the corps in competition throughout the state."

If Robin Benedict was memorable, however, it was not because she was beautiful. She had small breasts and short legs, which were a little plump in the thigh. She tended to bite her nails, and her left front tooth was chipped from years of opening bobby pins. She had an abundance of rich, dark hair, but, as she could never decide whether it should be long or short, it always seemed to be in a unruly growing stage. In profile, her nose was hooked at the tip. Her eyes, as hard and shiny as a pair of black marbles, were pretty and flirtatious but inscrutable. What transformed those rather ordinary Hispanic features into beauty was her smile. It was a smile that exploded like a sunburst streaming rays of pure energy. The aura it created suggested such vitality that it could not be ignored.

Just how aware Robin was of the effect of her own adolescent charm is unclear. In her parents' admittedly idealized recollections, she was utterly devoid of cynicism. Many years afterward, when her character was undergoing intimate scrutiny, she remained in their minds a loving, un-complicated little girl. On the rare occasions when she was irritated, she made a slight *psst* sound with her lips, a habit she picked up from her Trinidadian grandmother. On the even rarer ones when she was unhappy, she would sit cross-legged on her bed and play the flute. During these funks, she found solace in listening to Barry Manilow.

Robin, as her parents recalled her, was the one who picked out Holly Hobby cards for everyone's birthday. She was the soft touch who lent everyone money. She would bring her mother gifts, usually a red rose. As she handed it over, she would poke Shirley Benedict's belly and quip, "Doughboy."

If there was a hint of a taunt there, Shirley never let on that she cared. She knew that having five babies had made her "dowdy." She accepted this with pleasant humor, even as she tried to bolster her fading looks with jewelry and cosmetics. Each week, a beautician teased and lacquered her hair into an amazing sculpture of ringlets. Every now and again she would take out her wallet and display a photo of herself taken not long after she and John were married. Her eyes were dark and luminous. Did she not, she would ask, look a little like Robin?

When John Benedict looked at his oldest daughter, he saw less of her mother than of himself. She had his hair, cocoa skin, and high cheek-bones. She resembled him right down to the chipped tooth. John didn't feel as close to Rhonda, somehow. She was light-skinned like her mother and had a mind of her own. She tended to pick fights with him. Robin, on the other hand, was eager to please, always jumping on his lap and hugging him. Benedict was an affectionate man—his wife always said *too* affectionate—and in Robin he found someone who returned his affection in full. Once at a wedding, Benedict got a little drunk and summed his feelings up to a family friend, "I got a bunch of kids, but I only got one little girl."

John Benedict laid claim to her as he did to anything beautiful, with a camera. As she was growing up, he photographed her continually. One of the shots he liked best was taken when she was one year old. Bin Bin, as she was nicknamed, had been swaddled in terry cloth and perched on a high chair trimmed with a ruffle. The hair on the top of her dark head had been twisted into a curl. Her mouth was open, hinting at the dazzling smile to come. Only rarely over the years did he catch her pensive. Once, when she was fourteen, he noticed some interesting light coming in the picture window. He asked Rhonda to pose, but she cocked her head oddly, and he never bothered to develop the frame. Robin, however, seemed to know exactly what he wanted. She tilted her head back, allowing the twilight to pour over the contours of her face, filling the hollows with shadows. She seemed to be looking to him for approval, her eyes filled with a desire to please.

From the time she was in grade school, it was clear that Robin had inherited her father's artistic sensibility. She would sit on the living room floor sketching the faces of animals and fanciful creatures with large eyes. She signed her work "Robin," dotting the *i* with a tiny sketched bird. When she got older, her father gave her a Minolta, and soon she could hold her own discussing f-stops and light readings. Sometimes John Benedict picked up extra money photographing weddings. Robin usually went with him to help him set up the equipment. The effusive brunette girl and her tall, dark father—who looked much younger than his age, thanks to the good offices of a hairpiece and gold chains—made a very attractive pair.

Robin seemed destined for a career in commercial art, and it was decided that rather than go to Methuen High, she should attend the Greater Lawrence Vocational School. John Benedict did not think there was any stigma attached to that. It was honorable to learn a trade. (Personally, he always thought Shirley could have learned to do something more interesting than work in a jewelry store, but she enjoyed doing it, so he let her alone.) Robbie had gone to vocational school to study drafting. And so, in the fall of 1975, Robin Benedict enrolled as a freshman.

On paper, at least, Robin's career at the Voke was exemplary. She had a perfect attendance record and nearly straight A's. She was rarely without a zippered portfolio in which she was collecting pieces of artwork to show to prospective employers. Building that portfolio seemed to be foremost in her thoughts. She was unabashedly ambitious, but there was something in her full-speed-ahead enthusiasm that was endearing.

At least to Norman Salem.

Norm Salem was Robin's class sponsor. He had met her when she sat in the front row of his math class during her sophomore year. A shy man with a paralytic arm, Salem was a connoisseur of female beauty, and he found Robin "gorgeous, very very lovely." Robin, he later remarked, had a beauty that "flowed."

Salem was in charge of extracurricular fund-raisers, for which Robin was a regular volunteer. Among these was a sweets sale where students hawked caramel-almond crunch bars for fifty cents a shot. Robin turned out to be a super saleswoman. Salem was amused at how she used her "pretty ways" to sell candy.

He was so impressed by her willingness to work that in 1979, when the Voke decided to put out the first school yearbook in its history, Salem, as faculty sponsor, turned the project over to Robin, granting her almost total autonomy over the photo selection and layout. Given this much influence, Robin, it seems, could not resist inserting photos of herself all over the book. It opened with a full-page shot of her, Minolta hanging around her neck, her eyes fixed upon some distant point in a visionary gaze. It concluded with the baby photo of herself in the ruffled high chair. One could hardly turn a page in between without encountering her playing the flute at a talent show or receiving the Presidential Certificate of Merit. She had, unconsciously perhaps, documented her own metamorphosis through successive prom photos. In her junior year she had on little makeup and was wearing a simple white dress with spaghetti straps. The following year, she was decidedly more sophisticated in heavy eye makeup and a black, accordion-pleated gown. Robin's penchant for clothes was acknowledged in the class accolades, in which she was deemed "best-dressed." Her entry in the class will read, "Robin Benedict leaves behind her flashy wardrobe and goes stark naked into the world."

This display of vanity caused her classmates to mutter complaints. There was no doubt that Robin Benedict was Mr. Salem's pet. She had spent many hours with him working on the yearbook. He knew that Robin's classmates criticized her as a self-promoter, but he chalked this up to jealousy. The way he figured it, Robin had done most of the work, why shouldn't she do what she wanted with the book?

Salem would later say that he knew Robin was no angel. She ran with fast company, a Hispanic crowd, and Salem suspected that she was "far from a virgin." When Robin was about fourteen, she had begun dating an upperclassman named George Beltre, a Dominican from the automotive shop. Beltre was, in Salem's estimation, a "wild kid." In the cafeteria he had once grabbed a knife and held it to the stomach of the school cook. He was suspended for that, and afterward Robin came to Salem weeping, asking him if there was anything he could do. Salem couldn't resist a plea from Robin. He intervened to have Beltre reinstated.

Still, it infuriated Salem to see the way George treated Robin. The sponsor chaperoned dances every Friday night at the Voke, and he would see her standing around waiting for him. When he finally arrived, he would pat her behind. Robin didn't seem to mind. Beltre, however, seemed to realize that his fondling Robin drove Salem crazy. He would look over and grin as he did it. After a while, George would take Robin home, then come back to the dance to pick up somebody else. Salem never told Robin about that. He liked her so much; he didn't want to hurt her. He hoped she would eventually get rid of the troublemaker, but she was apparently in the throes of young love. He just tried not to think about her having sex with George.

John Benedict was no more enthusiastic about his daughter's choice in men. Like most fathers, he had trouble imagining any guy who might be good enough for his daughters. It made him uncomfortable when they brought dates home. He could not see why his Robin, who might have anyone, was wasting her time on George Beltre, whom he considered "unlucky," a fellow with no prospects. Beyond that, there was the ticklish issue of race.

Benedict prided himself on his own open-mindness. The crowd that gathered at his Sunday pool parties was largely Hispanic. Because he was sensitive about being thought a "native of Trinidad," Benedict made it a point never to question a visitor about his background. He extended that, in principle at least, to his daughter's boyfriends. But Robin's birth certificate listed her as "white." If she chose her companions well, she might move into privileged circles, among artists perhaps. Robin, however, seemed to prefer the company of auto mechanics. And she definitely preferred dark men. Throughout her high school years, she never dated a white boy.

IN JANUARY 1978, George took Robin to a basketball game at the Voke. It was an exhibition match which pitted the faculty against six professional football players from the New England Patriots. Norm Salem had sponsored this event as a fund-raiser, which included raffling off twenty tickets. The winners would go to dinner after the game with a handful of Patriots, including the tight end Don Hasselbeck and the linebackers Steve Nelson and Raymond Costict.

The Patriots routed the faculty handily. The crowd, however, was not disappointed, because it had come not for suspense but for the opportunity of seeing pro ballplayers in the flesh. The Pats' presence was made more wonderful by the fact that they had actually deigned to step off the big-time circuit and travel to a backwater town like Lawrence. The professionals clowned adorably. Ray Costict, in particular, was a real crowd pleaser, slamming, dunking, exaggerating long shots.

Among those delighted by Costict's antics was George Beltre's fourteen-year-old sister, Ida. George had let Ida tag along with him and Robin that night, an indulgence which proved fortunate when Ida turned up holding one of the winning tickets. This development apparently aroused George's opportunistic impulses. He got himself and Robin invited to the postgame party, which was to be held at a Lebanese restaurant called Bishop's. George sent his sister home to get dressed up, and she arrived at the restaurant wearing an orange pants suit. Her long, dark hair, which had been wound in a bun at the game, had been loosened, so it fell straight down her back. She joined her brother and Robin, who were sitting directly across from Ray Costict. Norm Salem, who was keeping an interested eye on all these interactions, noted that Costict was flirting with Ida. George noticed it, too, and capitalizing on the momentum, he persuaded Ida to invite Costict to come home with them after dinner.

The Beltres lived just across the street in the projects, and after the party at Bishop's broke up, George, Robin, Ida, and some friends ushered Costict over to the apartment to meet George's parents. Everybody was trying to be cool about it, but the electrifying fact was, *the Beltres had a real live ballplayer in their living room!*

By pro-ball standards, Costict was not an awesome figure. At two hundred pounds and a shade under six feet, he was one of the smaller linebackers in the National Football League. He had been hailed as a "ferocious tackler" at Mississippi State, but since signing on with the Patriots the preceding July, he had never been a starter. He was mostly a special-teams performer and a spot player. He certainly wasn't drawing a star's salary, like his friend and sometime roommate Ray Clayborn, who was the 1977 number one draft choice.

Costict found Boston a cold, racist city. Nothing in his background had prepared him for living in the Northeast. As one of an extended family of fifteen brothers and thirteen sisters, he was used to having people around. He missed Sunday afternoons when people brought their babies over and when his mother, who had worked as a cook in soul food restaurants up and down the Gulf Coast, would be tending a pot of greens. Costict's mother was a devout Jehovah's Witness who instructed her children to resist carnal defilement. From about the age of twelve, Ray had struggled to hold to the righteous path, but every once in a while he went into a "phase" doing drugs and "talkin' to women." Before he was twenty, he had gotten his childhood sweetheart pregnant, and she had borne him a son out of wedlock. When he was drafted by the Patriots, he left for the Northeast in a sort of self-imposed exile. He would not return to Mississippi until he could figure out what to do about his southern sweetheart and little Ray, Jr.

By January 1978, the end of Ray's first season, most of his teammates had broken camp and were heading for home. Costict found himself facing his first winter in Boston alone. He was pleased, therefore, to find himself the center of attention in Lawrence. When George Beltre invited him to come back and hang out, Costict agreed.

During the next two years, Costict got away whenever he could to visit "his people." He usually cruised into town in his roommate's black 280Z. George would service it for free. He'd hang out at George's second-floor studio apartment, or they'd go over to visit Beltre's friends Danny and Freddy Sanchez, who owned a Sunoco station on the Methuen-Lawrence line. The Sanchezes would make him Dominican drinks and then take him for a good Caribbean meal. George's mother cooked savory rice dishes, knowing Costict was partial to Spanish food. He also had a fondness for Spanish women, and the Beltre apartment was full of them. He courted Ida cautiously, but despite her brother's prodding, she did not seem receptive to his advances. Ida's parents were not keen on her becoming involved with a professional ballplayer. They thought she was too young. So every place Ray took Ida, they had to be chaperoned by George and his girlfriend, Robin.

It was clear that Robin liked Ray Costict. Whenever she saw Norm Salem, she would give him long, enthusiastic accounts about going to Patriots games at Schaefer Stadium, in Foxboro. She, George, and Ida usually ended up sitting with the players' wives, and Robin enjoyed the special treatment she got hanging around with that crowd. Most of all, she would go on about what a gentleman Costict was and how well he treated Ida.

Robin began inviting Costict to the Sunday barbecues at the Benedicts'. Costict found it "cozy" there. Most of the couples were racially mixed. There were John and Shirley Benedict and their friends the Ramoses. The next generation included Robin and George. There were also Richard Ramos and his fiancée, a "fine blond white chick" named Sharyn. Only Rhonda seemed to be dating a white guy, an older fellow whom she'd been seeing since she was twelve. The fact that the Benedicts seemed to have so many dark-skinned friends put Costict at ease.

DURING most of her senior year, Robin had been having trouble with George. He was pulling a macho routine, trying to keep her in line by acting tough. Robin knew she should get rid of him, but, as one friend later put it, he was like a "bad habit." About the time she graduated, in the spring of 1979, George had given her the key to his studio. One night she arrived unannounced and caught him in bed with another girl. It took some pretty quick talk, but George managed to smooth this over. The following evening, however, she made another surprise visit and caught him with the same girl.

Robin jumped in her car and drove twenty miles to see Ray Costict. It was the off-season, and he was living alone in an apartment in Quincy on the South Shore. When she arrived, her eyes were red and puffy. She told Costict what George had done. This put Costict in an awkward position. He knew the girl Robin was talking about. He had seen George with her two or three times. She was real fine with big breasts. She was young, and Costict could tell by the way she danced that she was kind of fast. He hadn't said anything to Robin, because George was his friend. He didn't want to rat on him. Ray told Robin he would talk to George and try to straighten him out. When he got hold of Beltre he said, "Man, you're a fool. Never take [a chick] to your place when you know your girlfriend has a key."

When Robin finally mustered the nerve to break it off with George, he was shocked and set about actively wooing her back. She intended to make it stick, however, and declined to invite him to the Benedict's Fourth of July barbecue. Ray Costict came and, as he later recalled, spent most of the day downstairs with the guys. At one point, Ray left the gathering to get another beer. He had entered a narrow hallway where the laundry room was when he ran into Robin coming through the door. They kind of bumped together. Costict grabbed her and kissed her playfully. Then things got out of hand. She put her hand around his neck and kissed him. Really *kissed* him. Costict broke it off, ran upstairs, and cracked himself a beer. He was a little scared.

In the weeks to come, Robin told him that she had first started having sexual feelings about him one night when they had run into each other at a local night spot called the Rendezvous. When Costict got there, he didn't know any of the girls but Robin, so he asked her to slow-dance. Robin later told him, "I felt myself in your arms, the way you held me. I've been thinking about this all the time."

That was the way Robin talked.

Costict was aloof at first. He didn't think you should let women know you liked them, or they'd walk all over you. He kept her humble with insults. "You're gonna get fat like your mother," he'd say. He had her dieting and exercising all the time. Sometimes he'd set up a date and then stand her up. Robin never complained until one time he really did forget to meet her at the Rendezvous. She drove all the way to Quincy, where she slammed some books down and cursed, "Shit. You're gonna straighten up and do right." He had never seen her mad, and it scared him into behaving better.

On the whole, he found Robin easygoing and "freehearted" with her love. She was so "gulliver," as he put it, that she'd believe anything anyone told her. He saw that her brothers and sister took advantage of her generosity by borrowing money. He scolded her for being so easy. But she seemed to be able to enjoy giving her family things. Since graduation, she had been working as a draftsman at an outfit in Wilmington called Screenprint. Danny Sanchez had gotten her the job there. He had also taken her to Queen City in Manchester, New Hampshire, to pick out a used car, a green 1978 Toyota. She was proud of having her own income and her own car, and although she lived at home she was a very independent girl.

She was also, Costict would insist in the months to come, a "nice, clean lady." Robin was no sleep-around, although some guys might have gotten that impression because she was so "freehearted with her friendship." Costict was usually careful not to let Robin spend too much time around the other players, particularly the white guys who would assume that she was trash for sleeping with a black. Neither did he want her partying too much with his buddies, who, he felt, might steal her away. He rarely took her out nightclubbing in Boston with anyone but his good friend Ray Clayborn.

Clayborn as a rule didn't trust women. He was riding high in the media just then and making big bucks. A lot of women hit on him, wanting him to buy things. He liked to take ladies out, but he didn't let any one of them get her claws in too deep. Robin was effusively affectionate to Clayborn. (Costict interpreted this as her cozying up to his friends to get closer to him.) Clayborn, in turn, urged Costict to bring Robin along whenever the two of them were going out. It was good for a black man to be seen with a fine white chick, he said. It attracted other fine white chicks.

"Costict, man," Clayborn would tell Ray, "if you don't want to take her out, let me take her to Boston. All I have to do is flirt around like she's with me, and I'd just get all the ladies I want."

Just to be safe, however, Costict deliberately avoided taking Robin into

Boston. He was just as happy to idle away their time together by the Benedicts' pool, where, just as in the Beltre household, there were also plenty of women.

On sunny summer afternoons, the girls would all be sunbathing. Rhonda, in particular, was always out there, slicked down with suntan oil. Unlike Robin, she couldn't tan for anything. Rhonda was not as pretty as her sister. Although her teeth were straighter, her full lips were usually pursed in a pout. She did, however, have lovely long legs and a toughness which Costict found sexy. Rhonda and Ronnie, he perceived, were the wild ones in the family. Sometimes when Rhonda ambled by in a bikini, Ray would tease her, "You need a good fuckin' and that'll settle you down. You wild." She'd snap back, "You're crazy," and walk on by.

Whenever these thoughts arose, Costict knew he was going into one of his phases, and he reached for the Bible, which he read and studied until the feelings passed. He knew his sins made him unfit for witnessing door-to-door but he tried to pass the Gospel on the sly to his teammates. This met with disappointing results. Clayborn tolerated his proselytizing, but it never made one bit of difference in how he lived. In Robin Benedict, however, Costict found a more ingenuous listener.

He would open up the Bible and let her read about how it wasn't God's purpose for mankind to die. God never told Adam he was going to die unless he sinned. God's purpose for mankind was for them to live forever on earth, which would be turned into a paradise. He instructed her to imagine Paradise.

"Do you see any hospitals or graveyards?" he asked.

"No," she replied dutifully. "Not in Paradise."

These drills were important to instill in a potential convert the conviction that there is no need to fear death. But death never seemed to bother Robin. She didn't seem afraid of growing old. She didn't in fact, seem to be afraid of anything.

When Robin started going to meetings at the Kingdom Hall in Methuen, Ray was real proud. He somehow never found time to go with her, but she gave him reports of the Bible study which she took one night a week under the tutelage of a stout, devout woman named Linda Fales. Normally, a spiritual counselor such as Fales would have gone to the house of the pupil, but Miss Fales sensed she wasn't precisely welcome at the Benedict home. Once Robin brought the elders over to meet her father, but John Benedict wasn't about to be preached to. He felt he knew as much Scripture as those supposed wise men and handed it back to them verse for verse.

Whatever expertise John Benedict had in the Gospel had come from indulging his secular curiosity. He and Shirley had never been particularly religious. Each Sunday morning they had sent their children off to the Mt. Carmel Catholic church alone. Robin had been confirmed there. Her brother Rick taught church school. But that was the extent of the Benedicts' spiritual involvement. It was Linda Fales's conviction that Catholics never learned how to use the Bible "correctly." Robin, she discovered, was virtually ignorant of the Gospel. Every Tuesday night, Robin would drop by the second-floor apartment which Fales shared with her elderly mother, and they would proceed methodically through *The Truth That Leads to Eternal Life.* At the end of each paragraph, Fales would stop reading and they would discuss the main thought, supplementing it with the appropriate scriptural passage.

Robin appeared to enjoy these sessions. The scheduled hour often went on for two. On weekdays, she would take her Bible to work and sit hunched in concentration over it during the lunch break. This perplexed coworkers, who had not exactly pegged Robin as the spiritual type. She had, after all, been George Beltre's old lady. She hung out with football players. She was a regular at the Rendezvous. From a local perspective, at least, she was considered a little fast. Could anyone be blamed for not taking this sudden piety seriously? Robin made a few timid attempts to proselytize, but if she encountered a coworker who actually knew something about the Scriptures, she became flustered. She tried to induce Richard Ramos's fiancée, Sharyn, to come to meetings at the Kingdom Hall, but Sharon demurred, saying she wasn't a religious person. She tried to enlist Danny Sanchez, whom she had often persuaded to go discoing with her. Sanchez's answer was an invariable and emphatic no.

Reports of these overtures got back to Linda Fales, who was elated. When novitiates start telling others about what they've learned, that's usually a sign that you are reaching the heart. Fales liked to think she was reaching Robin's heart, but it was difficult to tell. As far as she could tell, her spiritual charge was a sincerely sweet girl, pliant and eager to learn. She exhibited a Christian generosity. Once when the Fales' car broke down, Robin pressed $100 into her hand and said to pay her back whenever it was convenient. Still, she was not sure that Robin's motives were perfectly pure. She knew about Ray Costict and could tell from the way Robin talked that she was crazy about him. It was possible that Robin's apparent thirst for Scripture was an attempt to please a man.

Robin also had a reckless streak which worried Fales. Once she blurted out, "Last night I went swimming at twelve o'clock."

"You did?" Fales asked dubiously.

"Yeah, I just got out of bed and felt like going swimming, so I went."

Fales had no sure way of knowing what Robin did when she wasn't at meetings. If she would take off on a whim like that, that late at night, what else did she do? Fales knew that she had had a boyfriend since she was a young teen, and since kids nowadays were into sex, she assumed that Robin was too. Fales's suspicions had to be confirmed or denied. If there was some persistent moral defect, it had to be flushed out. As Robin drew near the end of her course of study, she would be preparing for door-to-door work. The church could not send her into the field if she was continuing to sin. She had to be admonished to cleanse herself of every defilement of the flesh and spirit, perfecting holiness in God's sphere. One Tuesday evening after Bible study was complete, Fales looked Robin in the eye and asked, "Do you smoke or do drugs? Do you commit the sin of fornication?"

"No," Robin replied simply. "I'm not doin' that."

On that assurance, Fales took Robin with her on the door-to-door rounds so that she could see how it was done. They went out twice, an hour each time. Robin had been admonished to say nothing. She hadn't earned the right to speak. Not until she had shown herself perfectly clean and sincere would she be allowed to witness for the faith.

NEARLY a year had passed since Robin had kissed Ray Costict in the downstairs hallway. That summer, 1980, Robin left for Providence to take a couple of summer courses at the Rhode Island School of Design. She wanted to learn airbrushing. Her father, clearly pleased that Robin had been accepted—even if only for summer study—by such a prestigious institution, bought her a compressor for her airbrushing class. Throughout August, Robin ostensibly immersed herself in the mysteries of three-dimensional forms such as cones, cubes, cylinders, and spheres. Her magnum opus was a scoop of orange ice cream melting over its cone in big, splashy drops. She did not manage to complete it before the end of the course. But study was not the main reason that Robin had gone to Rhode Island. Her most pressing need was to be near Costict, who was in training camp at Smithfield, only twenty miles away.

Costict, in fact, did not want Robin hanging around camp, where other guys could meet her, but it was no use trying to dissuade her once she had made her mind up. She would come if she wanted and stand outside the locker room all night if she had to. Sure enough, Robin showed up one afternoon for a game, and Costict had to admit she was the best-looking thing in the crowd. She was wearing a green top and hot yellow shorts that fit real nice. She had her Minolta around her neck and was dashing around taking pictures of him from every angle. Since they had started "talkin' " to one another, she had taken dozens of photos and even made a few sketches of him in his helmet and uniform.

It appealed to Costict that Robin considered him a superstar, and he was not inclined to disabuse her of her naïve notions. That year, in fact, he did have a shot at becoming a starter. Sam Hunt had been traded, and there was talk of Costict's replacing him as a middle linebacker. That dream, however, died during a preseason scrimmage when one of his teammates dived into the pile and landed on the back of his right knee. A surgeon had to remove smashed cartilage and tighten the ligaments, and for the rest of the season Costict was confined to the stands.

Clayborn insisted that Costict move in with him. He lived in a garden apartment in Quincy at a complex called Presidential Estates. It was a pleasant development set into outcroppings of rock like a miniature Alpine resort. It sat overlooking Quincy Bay, a pleasing enough vista if one's gaze breached a stretch of smokestacks and rusting containers on the waterfront.

Presidential Estates afforded Costict some comfort and diversion in his infirmity. There was a balcony for sunning and an exercise room, where he could work his leg. The apartment itself, however, had the perpetually disheveled appearance of a bachelor pad. Clayborn was a penny-pincher who didn't like to spend anything on furniture, so the living room was practically bare except for two pieces of an old sectional couch. Costict and Clayborn spent most evenings sprawled out on their respective lengths of sofa, studying game film or watching TV. Usually, they fell asleep right on the couch. There was a nice queen-sized bed in the bedroom, but it was always unmade and was used only if one of them had a girl over.

Throughout the fall of 1980 Robin was a regular visitor. Every day after she got off work at Screenprint, she drove forty-five minutes to Quincy. She would breeze in the door, give Ray a kiss, and set to work cleaning. She started with the dishes which Clayborn invariably left in the sink. Then she would work her way through the rest of the apartment.

Costict suspected that Robin was taking advantage of his injury to make herself indispensable, but he allowed her to lavish attention upon him. She was useful to have around. If he needed a paper or something, she could run out and get it. Whenever a player had a birthday or anniversary, she picked out the presents. She kept him stocked with provisions—collard greens, cabbage greens, red beans, butter beans, seafood, and the makings of spaghetti creole. If she saw he was running low on rice or onions, she'd bring some with her the next time she came and never asked to be reimbursed. If he tried, she'd leave the money on the bed. When he sent her out with cash for groceries, she'd shop for bargains and bring him back the change. Robin was not the kind of girl who expected a guy to pay and do.

Costict came to rely upon her more than he would have liked to admit. While she was waiting on him like a servant, she was also extending her influence over him. She even took charge of his rehabilitation, massaging his injured knee. When he got lazy about exercising, she would pick up the leg and flex it for him. Costict relied upon this prodding because the injury had thrown him into a funk. When self-pity got the best of him, he consoled himself with painkillers and cocaine. He knew that it was wrong and that there would be hell to pay if the elders found out about it. Costict would later insist that Robin disapproved. If she saw him smoking a joint, she'd cry. One Monday night, as the two of them sat watching a game, he felt one of his phases coming over him and slipped away to the bathroom to sniff. Robin walked in on him and, the story goes, cried, "Okay, I'm going to do it too."

Cocaine set Robin off on a rampage. He couldn't control her. She insisted he take her out dancing in Boston. On his bad leg, yet. In the early hours of the morning, she dragged him home to the queen-sized bed and made love to him. Robin was normally a sensual lover, but on this particular occasion, she carried on like a wild woman. She even insisted upon sleeping beside him the rest of the night—something he had never let her do. Usually, they would work in a little sex in the late afternoon, and then he would send her home to Methuen. Her family, he figured, knew perfectly well that they were lovers. Her brother Rob had taken him aside to assure him, "Look, man. What you do with my sister is your business." But Costict felt it was a good idea to keep up appearances, particularly as there was already an uncomfortable situation developing with John Benedict. Robin told Costict that her father had been scolding her for seeing a black man.

"My father ticks me off so bad," he later remembered her saying. "He tells me all of my sense is in my pinky finger. . . . All our life . . . they just let us go our own way. Now he wants to tell me what to do. And tell me what's right and what's wrong. I know what's right and I know what I want. He can't tell me what to do."

Costict couldn't make any sense of this. Robin's parents had a mixed marriage and openly prided themselves on racial tolerance. It seemed to him that if John Benedict had been as upset as Robin said, he would have slipped some inadvertent hint of his displeasure. On the weekends that the family invited him for barbecue, however, Benedict treated him as warmly as a son. It was only after Costict left, Robin told him, that her father would start "crawling down her throat."

Costict felt that maybe this was because Benedict hated to make a scene. He was, after all, a man who valued appearances. Perhaps, Ray suggested to Robin, he should approach her father and discuss it man to

about her rival and wangled tickets to sit with the players. Robin didn't speak. She just seemed to want to taunt him with her presence.

Costict didn't dare tell his girlfriend what happened, or she would have thought he had planned it. She had heard gossip about Robin and opined angrily that the white girl had probably used oral sex to snag him.

So it went, and Costict felt himself getting into the kind of bind that only a man who had been in love with two women could understand.

Late in December, Costict told Robin that he intended to spend the off-season in Mississippi. The news hit her very hard. Sharyn found her weeping. Robin didn't understand why he was doing this, she sniffled, but she really loved him enough to see him through this if he would just give her some hope to keep on trying. Costict was scheduled to drive back to Mississippi on New Year's Eve. That day Robin drove to Quincy, where she found him loading a U-Haul. Was there anything she could do, she asked, to get him to change his mind?

"No," he told her. "No way."

Costict later insisted that it took everything he could muster to turn her away. But he wanted to start fresh with his people back in Mississippi, and he didn't want some northern white girl messing up his mind.

ROBIN seemed to rebound admirably. By spring the weeping had stopped, and she moved into an apartment of her own on Howe Street. Rent was $225 a month, a little steep, given her earnings from Screenprint. She supplemented her income by selling vitamins and throwing Tupperware parties. These entrepreneurial ventures, however, took a backseat to one high-priority, top-secret project—a twenty-fifth-anniversary party for John and Shirley Benedict. Though all the children were in on the plan, Robin had taken charge of the logistics and had worked on it for almost a year, lining up guests and renting the VFW Hall. She used the facilities at Screenprint to design elegant silver-and-blue stickers that read "John and Shirley." Through the Jehovah's Witness network, she had found a local artist named John Petralia who painted commemorative portraits from snapshots. Robin brought him separate black-and-white photos of her parents, and over tea in Petralia's basement studio they plotted out the final product. Shirley should be wearing earrings. Robin had brought models along. Her father, Robin noted discreetly, was of mixed racial heritage. Petralia had once worked with John Benedict at Raytheon and knew to endow him with ruddy skin tones.

On the night it was to be unveiled, John and Shirley were lured to the hall on the pretext of a surprise party for another couple. Once they were inside, Robin ran in the door carrying a bouquet of roses, and the hall exploded with the laughter of over two hundred well-wishers. If the dazed Benedicts had any doubts as to whether they had lost Robin's affection, this extravagant display of daughterly devotion must have put their minds at ease.

The departure of Ray Costict had seemed to usher in a new period of intimacy between Robin and her father particularly. Although she had moved a little farther out of his reach on Howe Street, he had gotten her a CB so that she could stay in touch with him when she drove to work. Somewhere along the route to Wilmington of a morning, "Little Bird" would get a call from "Calypso." Once she got to work, she generally called her father to talk once more during the day.

Robin had, it seemed, gone out of her way to restore harmony. Or at least the appearance of harmony. These acts of kindness and solicitude were probably genuine. They managed at the same time, however, to obscure a project which Robin was pursuing with even more secrecy and industry than the anniversary party—getting Ray Costict back.

Throughout the spring, she called Costict in Mississippi, begging him to meet her someplace halfway. Her peripatetic Nana had alighted in Virginia, and Robin could go visit her without arousing suspicion. Then she could meet Costict in a nearby motel.

"No," he reportedly told her. "I know what it's gonna do."

Costict knew he was still weak for Robin, and he didn't want to walk right into temptation. To hold her at bay, he told her he was planning to be married. This was something he had not yet discussed with the prospective bride. But as he had come right out and said it, it didn't sound like such a bad idea. That same week, he proposed to his girl back home. They set the date for June 27.

Once more, Robin seemed to accept the inevitable, but now when she showed up for weekly Bible study, she was quieter than usual. On June 18, Robin left with Linda Fales for a four-day district convention in Providence. The gloom which had settled over her became even more noticeable. At night in the motel room, which she shared with three other young Witnesses, Robin would sit cross-legged on the bed and play her flute. Word got back to Fales that she would go out jogging near the Civic Center, a quarter inhabited by porn dealers and winos. She insisted upon going alone.

FALES felt that Robin was hiding something and that it was gnawing at her. Perhaps she didn't want to tell her spiritual adviser, for fear of hurting her. Fales felt it was best to wait and see if Robin would come out with it. Sure enough, a few days after they returned from Providence, Robin confided that she had been doing cocaine. Fales hastily summoned a pair of elders, who intoned to Robin the familiar admonishment: her body was a gift; she must not defile it. Robin said she understood.

Her conscience uncorked at last, Robin's confessions flowed freely. She had not only done drugs but done them with another Witness, Ray Charles Costict—with whom she had also committed the sin of fornication. These revelations found their way, as Robin doubtless knew they would, to the elders of Pascagoula, Mississippi, who were getting set to marry Costict and his fiancée that very week. Two days before the scheduled nuptials, the elders called him in and confronted him with the charges. It took some fancy footwork, but he managed to plead, with the most abject contrition, that he had been through a phase and that the affair with the white girl was over. The elders were apparently convinced, because the wedding went off as planned. And Costict breathed easier knowing that he was now a safely married man.

AFTER the wedding, Mr. and Mrs. Raymond Costict had one whole week of happiness. They left Ray, Jr., with the bride's mother in the projects in Pascagoula and took off for a honeymoon in Fort Walton, Florida. There they stayed at the Ramada Inn, which had a big beach right behind it and two giant swimmings pools, one of which had a bar in the middle. The warm glow which lingered through the drive home faded abruptly as they pulled into the projects. Ray saw smoke coming out of his mother-in-law's apartment. He stopped the car in the middle of the road and ran to the front lawn. His mother-in-law had gotten out, but the little boy was still inside. Ray crashed through a picture window into the black smoke but couldn't find his son. The child, it turned out had been removed through a back door and was lying on the ground. He died of smoke inhalation.

Little Ray's death was hard on his mother because she wasn't a devout Witness. Costict himself believed so strongly in the Resurrection that he knew he would see his boy again. The world would be coming to an end very soon, and loved ones lost in death would be brought back. Consoled by faith, he left for training camp.

His knee was in good working order, thanks largely to Robin's solicitude. Since high school he had been an inside linebacker, which had pitted him against players much larger than himself. He was willing now to learn a new position, in the hope of spelling a couple of veteran outside linebackers, Mike Hawkins and Rod Shoate.

But these hopes were crushed the second week in August when he found out he was to be traded to the New Orleans Saints.

This news, coming on the heels of his boy's death, laid Costict low. In his despair, oddly enough, he was plagued by thoughts of Robin Benedict. He was still mad at her for trying to sabotage his wedding, but he was irresistibly drawn to her for comfort. He called her from a pay phone in Smithfield. Robin seemed less excited than sad. She told him she had cried when she read about his son. That affected Costict so much that he was almost ready to forgive her for spilling the beans to the elders. He told her he wanted to see her again, to get the air clear between them before he left Boston for good.

Costict knew there was some risk in this. He kept telling himself he didn't want to start up with her again, but he also knew that his resolve crumbled whenever he got near her.

"I have to hold her and stuff," he told Clayborn, "and if I don't have nobody with me, I'm gonna get weak and I'm gonna be doing wrong 'cause I'm married now."

Taking Clayborn along as "insurance," Costict drove two hours from Smithfield to Methuen. Sure enough, Robin met him with the familiar plea to start over.

"We gotta stop," Ray told her. "I can't see you, because like I'm married now."

They talked about it so long and so late that Costict and Clayborn had to sleep over. Clayborn took the couch, but that created an awkward situation since there was only one bed in the apartment.

"Look," Costict said, "I'm not going to sleep in your bed. I'm going to sleep on the floor."

Robin then ordered Clayborn off the couch and into the bedroom and, tossing the sofa cushions onto the floor, lay there beside her Ray Charles all night talking and crying.

By the time the sun came up, Robin saw that it was useless.

"Okay, Ray Charles," she said. "If that's the way it's gotta be, I'm going on ahead . . ."

She got up, put on her sweat suit, and took off for a morning jog. She didn't even see him to his car.

SOON afterward Robin Benedict dropped religious instruction. She called up one day and said, "Linda, I'm just not gonna study anymore." Among the reasons she gave was money. The expenses on her apartment and car were driving her under financially, and she needed more time to free-lance. Then she quibbled over ecclesiastical points. It was the contention of the Witnesses that only a "little flock" of 144,000 would go to Heaven and reign as kings with Christ. All of the rest of the good people in the world would stay in a more modest version of Paradise wrought upon the earth. Robin now said she didn't believe that the little flock would be made up only of Jehovah's Witnesses. She couldn't help believing that there would be good folks from many different religions. Never before had Robin shown the slightest inclination to question the church's teachings. Linda Fales felt she was fabricating an issue to make the separation easier. That was, at any rate, the last the Witnesses heard of her.

When Robin's friends learned she had dropped Witnessing, they were relieved. Her reappearance on the disco circuit seemed to confirm that she had returned to her old self. Others were not so sure.

SOMETIME in the early fall of 1981, Robin's coworkers at Screenprint caught glimpses of a short, well-built black man in the parking lot. He dressed casually in blue jeans and sneakers. Nothing about him would have drawn particular attention except that he drove a late-model Mercedes. Robin finally introduced him around as Junior, sometimes known as J.R.

She wouldn't tell anyone what Junior did for a living, but her boss, a fellow named Eddy Ratyna, suspected he wasn't up to any good. It didn't square, somehow, a young guy with a car like that. He figured it had to be drugs or something. Robin, he knew, smoked dope once in a while, but that was no big deal. He could not imagine her into anything heavier. Robin dropped occasional comments about having gone to New York with Junior. Ratyna warned her to be wary of J.R., but Robin assured him she knew what she was doing. She liked Junior, and that was that.

Over the years, Robin had tended to confide her various tribulations with George Beltre and Ray Costict to Danny Sanchez. But on the subject of J.R. she was mysteriously silent. Sanchez would later insist that he knew almost nothing at all about Junior.

"Tell me what this guy does for a living," Sanchez recalled asking her.

"No," she replied. "I'm not going to tell you."

All that he could apparently elicit from her was that Rogers was a hairdresser and part owner in a couple of businesses. Robin added cryptically that he "moved money."

One morning Robin called him at the Sunoco station.

"Dan," she said, "I need to see you today." She sounded a little harried.

"I just can't make it," he replied. "If you gotta talk to me . . . meet me when you get outta work. . . . I get out at three."

"No," she insisted. "You gotta meet me for lunch."

Sanchez was all by himself at the station and couldn't get away. Next morning he called up to make amends and suggest they meet for a bite at noon.

"Today?" she said. "You blew it. Yesterday I was gonna tell you what he did for a living, but now I'm not gonna tell you."

"C'mon Robin," he urged. "You gotta tell me. We gotta discuss this."

"I just won't," she replied. "Don't even try."

JOHN AND SHIRLEY BENEDICT had also heard things about Robin's new boyfriend. This sparse intelligence came from Ronnie, who was temporarily down on his luck and had moved into Robin's apartment on Howe Street. They learned that the guy's name was J.R.—Robin called him Junie—but no one seemed to know his last name. Robin's new aloofness worried her father, but his fears were not made concrete until one weekday when he was doing business at the bank in Methuen and fell to chatting with one of the guards. This fellow, who was sort of sweet on Robin, said that she had told him recently she was moving to Natick, a western suburb of Boston.

It hurt John Benedict to think she would do this behind his back. The next time she visited, she bounded as usual into the house and tried to kiss him on the cheek, but he turned away. Later, when Robin dropped by unannounced with J.R., her father refused to meet him. Junior stayed in the car.

The impasse might have remained unbroken had Robin not scored a diplomatic coup. One afternoon she came over with an adorable three-year-old in tow. His name was Taj, she said, and he was J.R.'s son. Robin had apparently calculated that this precocious elf might soften the heart of her mother, who had a well-known weakness for babies. If she could win her over, she would have an ally to help woo her father.

Shirley Benedict predictably fell hard for little Taj, who referred to her daughter as Mama Robin. Just who his real mother was wasn't clear, but he apparently lived with her someplace out in the suburbs. The introduction of the child imparted a human quality to J.R. Could the father of such an adorable child be all bad? It was Shirley Benedict's nature to give the benefit of the doubt. This inclination was not born solely of naïveté. She had reasons to suspect that Junior might not be on the up-and-up. But she also had the sense to see that rigidity might not be what this delicate situation required. Robin was twenty and, under the law, an adult. Shirley Benedict was realistic enough to see how easily Robin could move beyond her influence. She had given notice at Screenprint telling the company, of all things, that she might be moving to California. Would it not be wiser, Shirley Benedict reasoned, to keep the lines of communication open?

Robin moved to Natick in early November and shortly thereafter invited her parents to dinner. Her father declined, persisting in his boycott of J.R. Her mother, however, accepted, and drove out to Natick one evening without him.

Robin and Junie, as Robin called him, lived in a tidy complex of garden apartments that lay alongside an industrial highway, Route 128. It was occupied mainly by young professionals who worked between Route 128 and Boston. The apartment had one bedroom with an adjoining bath. The living and dining areas were in one, long room. Robin had apparently tried to make the space look larger by hanging squares of mirrors with peel-off adhesive backs. The walls were rather drab brown. But Robin liked tans and had furnished the place in earth tones.

Junie didn't say much, just busied himself in the kitchen while the women talked. When he emerged, it was with Cornish game hens. Robin seemed happy to leave cooking up to J.R. He was a genius with a wok, she intimated. Then she proudly displayed her new haircut. Junie had done that too. They presented a comforting domestic tableau. With a lighter heart, Shirley Benedict said good-bye to her daughter in Natick and promised to keep in touch.

AS THE New Year dawned, Ray Costict felt the urge to see Robin again. He hadn't been getting along well with his new wife, who was still recovering from the death of Ray, Jr. To make matters worse, she had found out about the stunt Robin pulled, her telling the elders about her and Ray. She was *mad!* Good grief, she was mad. She told Ray that if she had known about it at the time, there wouldn't have been a wedding.

Costict was beginning to feel that maybe he had chosen the wrong woman. Putting the two side by side, he found Robin the more honest. His wife, furthermore, had a mind of her own, whereas Robin was submissive. She gave a man his proper "headship." Ray's curiosity got the best of him, and he called Clayborn to find out what she was doing. To his dismay, he learned that she had been seeing J.R. Rogers.

Costict had met Rogers at a get-together at Presidential Estates around Christmastime 1980. The two Rays had just gotten back from two weeks on the West Coast when they were invited to another apartment, belonging to a guy named Matt. A large, dark-skinned fellow in his early thirties, Matt had a big white girlfriend named Pam.

Matt had been over to their place several times before to visit Clayborn.

He clearly liked the idea of hobnobbing with professional athletes and was always begging them to come over to his place. This time they agreed. Shortly after they arrived, Matt gave his girl about $25 in bills and told her to go out and buy a bottle of Rémy Martin. She obeyed without a word.

All that afternoon they sat around Matt's kitchen table, drinking. They had just finished off the fifth when Junior Rogers showed up. Junior was dressed in a casual black shirt, blue jeans, and loafers. He looked like a regular guy except for a ring set with three diamonds, which flashed every time he moved his hand. The party went on at Matt's for another two hours or so; then the Rays went back to their own place. For some reason—Costict could never remember why—J.R. came with them. Shortly after they had gotten home, Robin arrived. She had on a nice white top and black pants and set to work as usual cleaning the kitchen. According to Costict's recollection, Robin seemed not to notice Rogers at all. J.R., however, made a point of asking who she was. Clayborn reportedly told him, "That's Costict's old lady."

Costict recalled seeing J.R. only two or three times after that and never had what he would call a conversation with him. He later claimed to have been a little wary of Rogers and so tried to avoid that crowd. He had a good suspicion that Matt was a pimp. Not that he looked the part. He wasn't one of those cute guys with a full-length mink. And he always acted as if he didn't have any money. The girl Pam apparently supported him. It was her behavior more than anything else that had Costict convinced. He knew that pimps have their women trained to be submissive around men. When the guys gathered, Pam never spoke, never even looked them in the eye. The night that he and Clayborn had gone to Matt's, Pam and J.R.'s girl—a skinny little thing who was not, in Costict's estimation, too fine—took themselves into the bedroom. He heard one of them say, "Aw, we ain't nuthin' but bitches anyway."

Matt had all but admitted to Costict that his girl Pam wasn't bringing top dollar. And he seemed, by the same token, taken with Robin.

"Man," he had told Costict once, "I need that girl right there in my stable, man. If I could just set her down, I wouldn't have to worry about money no more."

"Not her, man," Costict laughed. "She'd never go for it."

Now Clayborn was telling him that Robin was involved with Junior Rogers, who was apparently trying to put her out on the street! His campaign was subtle. He had stopped bringing other women around. He wooed her like a lover. He had probably told Robin that once they got enough money put away, he would marry her. Matt, who was an amused bystander to all this, had been giving Clayborn a play by play and was laying odds that Junior would succeed.

Clayborn told Costict he didn't think Robin would tumble. Every time he had seen her, he said, she seemed to be the same effusive girl she had always been. She had run up, held him by the neck, and kissed him.

"No bitch do that," he assured Costict. "If a bitch is a prostitute, if anybody comes in they don't even speak, they don't even look at him as if [he was] a guy. . . . No, Ray. She ain't out there yet."

But Clayborn's encouraging reports gave way to more disturbing ones. Robin had been seen in the Combat Zone. He couldn't believe it and asked Matt to take him down there to check it out. They had gone to a tumbledown strip joint on Lagrange Street, and there Clayborn saw Robin. He tried to speak with her, but she pretended not to know him.

"She'll come out of there if you come talk to her," Clayborn urged. "She'll be so scared if you walk in there. . . . Man. You know that ain't none of Robin."

Clayborn even offered to pay his air ticket. But Costict couldn't leave. His absence from home would be too conspicuous. Whenever he went anywhere during the off-season, his wife insisted upon getting his ticket and dropping him off at the airport. He couldn't go to Boston without her knowing, and if she found out about Robin, she'd hit the roof.

So he was stuck in Mississippi, tormenting himself, wondering how this could have happened. Had he misread Robin? Had she faked everything? The sweetness, the generosity, the interest in Scripture? She had seemed to have a good heart, but, as the Bible says, the heart is the most treacherous thing. In sorting through his memories of her, he couldn't recall anything but "a very innocent girl." Robin was never a sleep-around, and he couldn't understand how a girl who wasn't a sleep-around could go into a prostitute phase.

It could be, he considered with a smarting conscience, that he had hurt her so badly that she was trying to hurt him in return. At the very least, he had left her vulnerable on the rebound. He knew how easily Robin fell in love. When she was head over heels for a guy, she'd do anything he asked. He had seen her do it with George Beltre, and later she had done it with him. Costict frankly couldn't see why Robin would fall for a little, bitty shit like J.R. Rogers. The only thing he could figure was that maybe he reminded her of Beltre. They were about the same size and color. Costict had a hunch that Robin had gotten more deeply into cocaine. He knew from his personal experience that you could get chicks to do all sorts of things when they were on coke. Crazy sex and going swimming naked. Things you could never get past them if they were straight. He also remembered when Robin did coke with him and how out of control she was. Whether it was cocaine, or sweet lies, or a combination of the two, Robin had apparently tumbled for J.R., and whatever it took to please him, she'd probably do it.

Costict figured that Clayborn was right, that Robin would still listen to him. He tried to get her phone number, but this was not an easy matter. She had moved out of the Howe Street apartment and into a place with Junie, but no one in the Presidential Estates crowd seemed to know her new number. At least, no one was giving it to him. Costict figured if anyone would know how to reach her, it would be Shirley Benedict. Robin always stayed in touch with her mother. Costict called Shirley and confided his suspicions that J.R. was a pimp and Robin was into prostitution. To his surprise, Shirley said she thought so too.

"Mrs. B.," Costict said, "I need to talk to her. . . . I can get something out of her."

But Shirley refused to give him Robin's new number. Robin did not want it given out. So Costict offered another plan. The next time Robin visited, Shirley should go to the back room and call him to let him know. Then Costict would call right back, as if out of the blue, and ask for Robin. Shirley refused to budge.

This bewildered Costict because he had always thought Shirley liked him. Maybe, he thought, her husband had finally gotten to her. Maybe Robin's parents had decided that she was into this mess because she had gotten involved with black guys in the first place. Maybe they figured if they could get her away from J.R., she'd be free for good, so they didn't want Ray Costict edging back into the picture. It seemed peculiar to him that the Benedicts were keeping so aloof from the situation. He had gotten the impression from talking to Shirley that she was just keeping Robin talking, trying to persuade her to stop hooking. But why wasn't her father doing something? It was possible that he just didn't want to say or do anything that would hurt anyone's feelings. But if it had been *his* daughter, Costict opined, he would probably have his shotgun broke down waiting for J.R. to pull up.

He was pondering these strange occurrences when he received a call from none other than J.R. Rogers, who was furious, having just heard that Costict was calling him a pimp. How would he like it, he asked, if he got Ray's wife on the line and started telling lies to her?

Something in J.R.'s manner was unnerving. Not that Costict was worried about the threats. He didn't give a damn. If there hadn't been so much distance between them, he would have broken the little shit's neck. It was, rather, the tone of aggrieved righteousness with which J.R. denied he was a pimp. If you didn't know better, you might *believe* him.

Costict felt more urgency than ever to speak with Robin. A renewed appeal to his contacts at Presidential Estates turned up the number—655-0174. When he dialed it, Robin answered. He asked her what she was doing. She was silent for a moment. Ray knew from the quality of that silence that she was not alone. Finally she spoke in a trembling voice.

"I don't need any more men friends," she said, then hung up.

II

ON FRIDAY NIGHT, April 9, 1982, Detective Billy Dwyer and his sergeant, Eddie McNelley, had just gotten off duty and were heading out in search of cocktails when they heard a call for "any vice unit" to come to 478 Beacon Street. The detectives knew from the address that 478 Beacon was a first-floor back-alley apartment of the sort favored by prostitutes who lured their johns from the Combat Zone to the broad, tree-lined boulevards of the Back Bay. By the time the detectives pulled into the alley, uniformed police had already arrived and were questioning three men who stood around a mattress on the living room floor. In a bedroom off to the left were three women. Dwyer recognized one as a Sylvia Contalis, who worked under the street name Silver. The second was a West Indian girl named Savitry Bisram, also known as Savi or Indian Debbie. The third was Robin Benedict. Dwyer remembered having stopped her for questioning a few weeks earlier.

One of the men, named Perez, had been trysting with Savitry Bisram in the bedroom. He had apparently left his pants outside the door, and when he retrieved them, $110 was missing.

"Billy, Billy," Savi bawled. "I didn't take this asshole's wallet. Tell 'em I'm not a thief."

At that point Robin Benedict chimed in, "Detective Dwyer, nobody took this guy's money."

Dwyer was inclined to believe them. Although Sylvia was known to work the streets, he had never arrested her for pickpocketing. Savi was pretty straight. She was from Trinidad originally and lived in fear of being deported. Whenever she was busted, she used the name Debrah DiSola so that it wouldn't get back to immigration. It wasn't likely that she would take a chance on lifting wallets. As for Robin Benedict, she had never even been arrested for prostitution.

Dwyer told the uniforms that the girls were not known thieves, but he saw that the presumption of credibility was not running in their favor. It was, after all, highly unlikely that Perez would have gone to the trouble of contacting the police if he hadn't actually been robbed. So McNelley arrested Savi and charged her with both larceny and allowing the premises to be used for purposes of prostitution. Robin was charged with accepting $50 for "unlawful sexual intercourse" with a certain Italian john who had the misfortune to be caught in the Perez complaint.

The girls were taken to the station house on Commonwealth Avenue and booked. Savi, who was clearly not happy about this turn of events, sulked during her mug shot. Her full lips were pursed in a pout, and her eyes—large, wild eyes like a jungle cat's—smoldered with anger. Robin's face, by contrast, was as serene as if she had been posing for a license photo. In profile, she even seemed to be smiling a bit.

Sergeant McNelley later recalled taking her aside for some fatherly advice.

"You're gonna end up like the rest of them," he admonished.

"Oh, no. Not me. I got it all figured," she replied.

Robin refused to name her pimp, and Dwyer made a note to find out who it was. Through a stroke of good luck, however, the answer fell into his lap. It was just a little over a week after Robin's first bust. She had been arraigned and was out on bail awaiting trial when she was spotted by John Ridlon. A ruddy, garrulous fellow, Ridlon was a detective with the General Investigative Unit. He did not normally handle vice cases, but happened to be driving through the Combat Zone with his partner, Mike Ingemi, when he saw an unusually pretty girl coming out of Charlie's. Ridlon thought she looked out of place, so he called her over to the car. When he asked her what she was doing at Charlie's she admitted, inexplicably, that she was a prostitute. After that she became evasive. Ridlon therefore took her down to police headquarters on Berkeley Street for questioning.

Several things were peculiar about this girl. For one thing, she carried a full set of IDs that seemed to check out. And when they asked how to contact her parents, she gave him their names and number without hesitation. It was in the early hours of the morning when Ridlon called the Benedict household in Methuen. He got John Benedict and told him his daughter had been picked up by police. Would he please come to Boston to talk about it. Benedict, who had apparently just awakened from a deep sleep, sounded confused and mumbled to his wife to get on the extension and write down the directions. Two hours later they showed up at headquarters, where Robin was sitting in an office with Ridlon and Ingemi.

The Benedicts, Ridlon later recalled, seemed dazed. Shirley Benedict was crying, saying how things were going to be all right. Robin Benedict was cold and emotionless. John Benedict began to explain how Robin had been fooling around with the Patriots and gotten into a fast crowd. To which Robin reportedly replied, "Don't say those . . . things. That isn't true."

Ridlon finally agreed to release Robin to the custody of her parents, and she consented to go with them. Then he took John Benedict to Lagrange Street to retrieve Robin's green Toyota from the parking lot. She had left her keys at the bar in Charlie's, and Ridlon went in alone to get them. He had recalled Robin's father saying something about taking a baseball bat to the place—something John Benedict later denied. When the Benedict family pulled off down Berkeley Street that night in two cars, Ridlon assumed they were heading home to Methuen.

At some time during the discussion with Ridlon, John Benedict had mentioned that he was a photographer. The detective asked if he could get a picture of Robin's supposed boyfriend. Benedict promised to see what he could do, and shortly thereafter Ridlon received a five-by-five close-up of a black man who was apparently sitting in the driver's seat of an automobile. He wore a light fringe of beard, and his face was contorted in a playful grimace.

There was also a note from Shirley Benedict explaining that the photo had been taken outside the Benedict house in Methuen. The fellow's name was J.R., but she and John still couldn't find out what his last name was. He supposedly owned a barbershop, but they couldn't confirm it. Shirley had learned that J.R. traveled periodically to New York and Florida. During those absences, he called Robin but left her no way to get in touch with him. Ray Clayborn knew J.R., she said, and the Patriots' summer camp would be starting soon. If she could find anything out, she would give Ridlon a call.

As the pursuit of pimps was out of Ridlon's jurisdiction, he sent the photo along to Vice, where it ended up on the desk of Detective Billy Dwyer, who identified it in an instant. The face in the photograph belonged to Clarence "J.R." Rogers.

Throughout the vice squad Rogers enjoyed a reputation as a small-time hustler from Mattapan, a black neighborhood south of Roxbury. Junie, as he was known on the street, was a running partner of one Walter "Chink" Martin, a black man of about forty-four who had a stable of five or six girls. Junie and Chink were co-owners of an outfit named the World News Agency—doubtless the result of some inside joke. From the outside, the "news agency" looked like a barbershop. It was actually a gathering place for pimps. When a player brought his stable into town, he would stay at a friendly house up on Blue Hill Avenue and come down to World News to socialize. The shop gave the pimps a professional affiliation. They could say they were hairdressers.

Junie was seen only occasionally around the Combat Zone. For a while he used to hang out at a lounge called Togethers, a former jazz club that had been taken over by pimps. He sometimes put in an appearance wearing his glad rags—diamond jewelry and a full-length mink. Junie was not a classic pimp like Sweet George, who had seven or eight girls living in the same house with him. Nor was he a Pepsi Cola pimp, an amateur who might work one girl for a little spare change. Junie fell somewhere in between. He was a small-time player who would usually groom and send out one girl at a time.

Savitry Bisram had been the first. Not that she would ever admit it. Dwyer sometimes hung out around the bar with Savi. To hear her go on in her street talk cum Creole, you would not think she was quite all there. Even when she was sober, she tended to slur. When she was high, she was often incomprehensible. Yet Savi knew the street and was a good source of intelligence. No matter how drunk she got, however, she would never rat on Junie. Through other sources, Dwyer had learned that she had been "hired" by Rogers in 1974 and worked for him about two years until she became pregnant. Savi really wanted the baby and went ahead and had it. She named the little boy Taj. Once the baby arrived, J.R. was said to have been thrilled. The baby, everyone declared, looked just like him.

His delight notwithstanding, Junie replaced Savi soon thereafter with a perfectly exquisite little blond named Cynthia Plowden. Businessmen, Harvard boys—everybody was crazy for Cindi, whose appeal won her the appellation Queen of the Combat Zone. During the three years of her reign, she earned an estimated one to one and a half million dollars for Junie before she finally ran out on him.

During the seven years that he worked Savi and Cindi, J.R. had rung up a modest rap sheet. In 1978 Eddie McNelley had busted him and an accomplice for receiving stolen credit cards. He was convicted but given a six months' suspended sentence. McNelley nabbed him again in May of 1981, for unarmed robbery. Cindi Plowden was leaving Charlie's and heading toward the parking lot one night when she was ambushed by two muscular females who grabbed her gold chain, diamond ring, and about $400 cash. J.R. showed up about then and somehow retrieved Cindi's valuables. Then McNelley happened on the scene, saw J.R. scurrying away, and arrested him for the theft of Cindi's belongings. McNelley had a pretty good idea that he couldn't make this charge stick. The two Amazons—an eighteen-year-old black girl named Theresa and a nineteen-year-old named Myra—told him they had taken Cindi's things to get back at J.R. The day before, they had been walking on the Common when J.R. allegedly whizzed by on roller skates—much in fashion at that time—and ripped off their chains. When J.R.'s court date arrived, Cindi predictably couldn't be found, so the charges were dropped.

J.R. Rogers now had a new girl, it seemed. Though where Robin Benedict fit into Junie's extended family, Dwyer wasn't quite sure.

THE PERSON Dwyer knew could provide some answers was a working girl named Pam McGrath. Pam was a big, buxom brunette who had been around Charlie's for eight years, longer than just about anybody else. She was grande dame of that seedy salon. Every day from early afternoon to closing, one could find her at Charlie's perched on a stool, leaning heavily onto the bar, and swapping throaty obscenities with the clientele. Pam's seniority relieved her of the necessity to be kittenish.

Pam's father was a police officer, and there was no love lost between them. When she dropped out of high school three months before graduation, he yelled at her to get a job. She found something in accounts receivable which was an awful bore. When the opportunity for advancement presented itself, she went for it. Eight of her chums from Brookline High hung out regularly at Charlie's turning tricks. One of them offered to get her in.

There was a saying around the Zone that if you could get past the first trick, all the others were easy. Pam found it easy from the start. She loved everything about Charlie's. Hanging out, drinking, making money. Particularly the money part. You could blow $300 on a pants suit just because you knew you could go out and earn it right back. Pam wanted to puke when she heard bleeding hearts trying to figure out why girls became prostitutes. The fast life, that's why. No one could *make* a girl turn tricks. She does it because she *wants* to.

Dwyer knew that Pam worked for a pimp called Matt. He had had a run-in with the guy once. Matt and a friend named Moses had seen a free-lancer on the street and tried to bully her into working for them. The girl came running to Vice, and Dwyer locked Matt and Moses up. When it came time to file charges, of course, the girl was long gone. Matt, Dwyer knew, was also a friend of J.R. Rogers. Pam, he figured, must know something about Robin Benedict.

It was hard to find Pam around during the summer of 1982. The word was that she was pregnant with Matt's kid and spending most of her time at home at their apartment on the South Shore. Dwyer, however, managed to pick up enough bits and pieces from the girls at Charlie's to form a rudimentary profile of Robin Benedict. She was working under the street name of Nadine or sometimes Nadine Porter and had come into the bar under the wing of Savi Bisram. Savi was showing her the ropes. Where to buy rubbers. How to line up trick pads. That sort of thing. Dwyer gathered from talking to the girls that they were none too high on Nadine.

Her arrival had, in fact, exacerbated an already strained political situation at Charlie's. While Pam McGrath's dominance in the roost was largely undisputed, she was nudged every now and then by a girl who didn't know her place. Savi was one of those who sometimes got above herself. Pam thought Savi was a phony, always swaggering around trying to act like a tough black girl. She was a great one at pretending to be your friend and then talking about you behind you back.

Pam was not sorry to see Savi lose her hold on Junie. She just wasn't pleased to see him take up with Cindi Plowden. Cindi was Pam's younger cousin, and she felt sort of protective of her. They were "family." Little Cindi's parents were divorced when she was three. She was raised by her mother, who worked at the phone company. From the time she was ten, she had been hanging out and doing drugs in school. When she was about seventeen, she had started coming down to Charlie's to visit Pam. The doorman would toss her out, but she'd always be back.

As much as Pam loved "the life," she was not sure she wanted that for Cindi. Pam, after all, had some common sense, whereas Cindi was reckless. She was crazy on drugs and seemed not to care about anything, not even herself. Beyond that, Pam knew that the family would all blame her for corrupting Cindi, which of course was a big laugh. There was not much she could teach her cousin that she didn't already know. Still and all, she was not pleased when she came out of Charlie's one afternoon and saw Cindi in the parking lot talking with Junie. When Pam asked Cindi what he was up to, she couldn't get a straight reply. Cindi was always very secretive about things.

Pam didn't like J.R. much. He was always critical, making fun of other guys' cars, picking on girls for the way they wore their clothes and hair. But Cindi was dazzled. J.R. took her to the discos on Lansdowne Street and introduced her to his friends, who were all decked out in jewels and furs. She figured she could do a lot worse. She went to work for him early in 1977.

Like Savi before her, Cindi started out in a massage parlor. Junie felt it was the safest way to break a girl in since the club watches over her and calms her down if she gets a little nervous. Cindi never seemed nervous, but Junie insisted she serve an apprenticeship of about seven months at the Parisienne Sauna in Peabody, an industrial town on the North Shore. Junie, meanwhile, had moved out of an apartment he was sharing with Savi in Natick and into a new place with Cindi on the South Shore.

Although Savi despised Cindi for unseating her, she knew her salad days were over, and she was enough of a politician to feign goodwill toward Junie's new favorite, taking her under her wing and showing her the ropes.

CINDI was crazy for Junie. He had the ability to make a girl feel so beautiful, so good about herself. "You're so special," he would say. "You're a *star!*"

He told her how to do everything. How to dress and act. But in such a way that she didn't feel like she was being bossed around. Unlike some pimps, he didn't insist that a girl make a quota. If she made only $300, he'd say, "That's okay. But I know you can do better." That made Cindi push herself to please him. She'd call home during the evening for little pep talks. If she was at $300, he'd inspire her to go on to $500 or even $1,000. At the end of a working day, she'd never *hand* him the money. Instead, she left the bills, sorted by denomination, on the top of the bureau. Junie, in turn, always gave back as much as he got. Cindi would come home to find a new silk dress laid out on the bed. He'd think nothing of buying her $1,000 necklaces. During the four years they were together, Cindi never really thought of herself as Junie's whore. On Easter, he would take her home to an attractive middle-class neighborhood in Mattapan to visit his mother. Junie went out of his way to make you feel respectable. He was just a "classy guy."

Early in 1981, however, Cindi began growing despondent. Her own mother had been suffering from cancer for two years and was now in the final stages. Cindi was so wrought up she needed to get away from Junie and Charlie's for a while. She dropped out of sight to get her head straight. Not even Cindi remembered for sure what happened during that period. She was reputed to have gone to Canada. Her cousin Pam learned for a fact that she married a guy she had known for only two weeks. The marriage lasted only three weeks after that. When she returned from this disjointed odyssey to reclaim her domain, she found that it was too late. Junie had found another girl.

For the time being, at least, Cindi figured it was best not to rock the boat. Junie had not actually fired her, so she accepted her demotion to wife-in-law. After about two weeks of this nebulous status, however, she took Junie to lunch for a showdown. Junie assured her, Cindi later recalled, that he definitely did *not* love Nadine. But he had already gotten her into a massage parlor in Newton. When she heard this, Cindi knew that Robin Benedict was now so deeply entrenched that there would be no unseating her. Not long after that, Cindi left Junie to become the mistress of an elderly Italian grocer. She missed Junie awfully, but it gave her peace of mind knowing that he didn't love Nadine. It was only business. She harbored the hope that someday he would call her back as his number one. And if that happened, she knew she'd come running.

THE RECORDS of Robin Benedict's tenure at the Newton Health Club are sparse and only hint at the nature of her apprenticeship. What is known for sure is that the club, tucked into a small shopping center on Charlemont Street, had opened in August of 1981 under the auspices of one Robert McIntosh of Burlington, Massachusetts.

McIntosh was a short, rotund man in his late thirties, whose businesses included home renovation and the manufacture of light aircraft. He also claimed to be a rock promoter and sometime journalist. His father, he once announced with a perfectly straight face, was president of the Bank of England.

McIntosh had grand plans for the health club and ran newspaper ads promising massage by one of "New England's most talented masseuses" in an atmosphere of "elegance and dignity." In the weeks after it opened, the club attracted a brisk traffic of businessmen.

A patron seeking to avail himself of these services entered a small lobby and stepped up to a window staffed by a shift manager. There he paid a fee of $30, entitling him to the use of a whirlpool and sauna as well as to a forty-five-minute massage by a "licensed therapeutic masseuse." The shift manager handed him a towel, a robe, a set of locker keys, and a receipt. The patron then made his way through a pair of swinging doors that opened onto a locker room. There he stashed his clothes, donned the robe, and crossed the corridor for an optional dip into the whirlpool or sauna. After that, he followed the hallway to a recreation room rimmed on three sides with sofas. Strewn along those couches, like so many throw pillows, were between fifteen to thirty masseuses. When the patron entered, one of them rose automatically to offer him coffee or juice. Then he picked out a girl who appealed to him and handed her the receipt, and she led him into one of eight "therapy rooms."

McIntosh would always insist that what went on in those rooms was therapeutic, not sexual. His masseuses were, in fact, hired and licensed in strict accordance with city ordinances, and Robin Benedict seems to have been no exception. When she came to the club for an interview on October 25, she filled out an application giving her actual name and her Howe Street address in Methuen. The interviewer indicated "ok" on counts of "neatness," "personality," and "character." On "ability," someone had scribbled "no."

She was hired on the spot.

Three weeks later Robin visited the Newton Health Department to apply for a masseuse's license. The secretaries later recalled that she was "cute as a peanut." In order to qualify, she had to show evidence of training or previous experience. She wrote that she had been employed by the "Gentlemen's Club" of Hudson, New Hampshire, from September 1979 to July 1980. Such an establishment, it was later discovered, never existed. But Robin's performance on the written exam indicated that she had done her homework. Asked to name three lubricants used in massage, she dutifully cited "powder, vegetable oil or baby oil and lotion." Asked the definition of "effleurage," she wrote, "Stroking done with hands fingers or ball of thumbs, stroking in direction of the heart to increase circulation, calms the nerves." She scored a respectable 89 out of 100 points and was issued license No. 63, which was to be mounted on the wall of the Newton Health Club.

On paper at least, it was possible that Robin Benedict, as well as the other "independent contractors" who worked for the Newton Health Club, were actually capable of giving a therapeutic massage. McIntosh's assertions that these ministrations were strictly on the up-and-up lost credibility, however, after one disaffected shift manager went to the Newton Police Department in the spring of 1983 with his own account of how the club actually did business.

According to the informant, McIntosh held a staff meeting once a month for the purposes of briefing neophytes. At that time, he laid out a strict set of rules from which they were not to vary. No tardiness. Girls who arrived late were fined $5 a minute. They must wear skirts and blouses. No slacks. Nothing overtly sexual. For a while, he even talked of requiring nurses' uniforms.

Then, the informant claimed, McIntosh laid out a schedule of fees or "tips" for certain services above those included in the $30 cover charge. This tariff specified $25 for a hand job, $40 for a "clothed French" (the "French" being a blow job), $45 for a "nude French," and $50 for a "half and half," which included a blow job and intercourse.

The girls were not to charge more than the going rate. According to the informant, McIntosh was concerned that overcharging not only ticked off those operators who stuck by the rules but also alienated patrons. If a guy so much as complained about being overcharged, McIntosh would give him a credit slip entitling him to another trip to the club with cover charge waived. The girl would be summarily reprimanded and fined. Everyone, and he was emphatic, *everyone* was to use a condom when engaging in full intercourse. Girls who didn't were not only liable to disease but also enjoyed a competitive advantage over those who didn't.

An operator who let a guy off without a condom would be fired on the spot.

If the patron paid by credit card or check, McIntosh deducted allegedly 2 percent as a service charge, but otherwise a girl could keep all the money she made on tips. The average take was between $1,500 and $2,000 a week. As consideration for these opportunities, the masseuses were to make themselves available to the managers, who could obtain the services of any girl for any session for any sexual specialty as long as they paid the going rate.

McIntosh was said to be meticulous about security. Each customer, according to the informant, was required to indicate whether he was a regular or a "nonmember." The masseuse was to ease more carefully into her solicitation of a "nonmember" to make sure she wasn't moving a cop. If anyone suspicious walked through the door, the shift manager would stall him as long as possible while hitting a switch on the back of the office door. This dimmed the lights in all eight therapy rooms, alerting masseuses to keep their activities conventional. If the newcomer continued to arouse suspicion, he would be routed to Therapy Room No. 2. Hidden in a speaker was a microphone connected to earphones and a tape recorder in McIntosh's offices. The entire session would be taped with the intent of using it against the officer in the event of a bust. The informant estimated that McIntosh made about eight tapes a week and stored them in a refrigerator in his office.

McIntosh's wariness was not idle paranoia. The Newton city fathers, particularly Police Chief William Quinn, had been keeping an eye on the health club from the time it opened, in the summer of 1981. Chief Quinn had made a tour of the facility with the city health inspector and deemed the atmosphere "a little too sexual." That December, police raided the club and charged McIntosh with "knowingly suffering a female to be in or upon said premises for the purposes of unlawful sexual intercourse." In other words, "being the owner of a house of prostitution." (The following June a trial judge ordered a directed finding of not guilty, saying that the prosecution had not proved that McIntosh knew his establishment was being used for illicit purposes.)

There is no indication that Robin was on the premises the night the club was raided. Records show, however, that Robin continued working at the club until January of 1982. At that point, her apprenticeship was presumably complete, and she moved on to the main arena.

ROBIN BENEDICT came into Charlie's the easy way. If she had been some waif with a Pepsi-Cola pimp, then maybe Savi or Silver might have walked up and knocked her off her stool. Then she would have had to come back clawing to show how tough she was. Robin, however, was spared that hazing because she came with letters of introduction. The fact that everyone knew that she was Junie's girl put her under the protection of Savi and her friends. And the fact that Junie and Matt were friends gave her diplomatic relations with Pam McGrath's clique.

Nadine, it seemed, was heiress apparent to Cindi Plowden's crown. She dressed like a college girl in sweaters, skirts, and blazers. She kept her makeup looking fresh. She didn't drink. Early on, at least, she didn't do a lot of drugs. She insisted upon condoms—the mark of good training. Despite her youth—she was only twenty—she projected a willingness to take responsibility for a client's pleasure, a considerable asset since many a family man who wandered into the Zone was looking to be relieved momentarily of the pressure of putting his wife in the mood. By middle age a guy caught himself longing to once—at least once—turn himself over to the skill of a competent seductress.

Robin exploited her appeal with great success. Before long, she was doing an estimated $800 to $1,000 a night. Such industry was normally admired in the Zone. But ambition sometimes clouded her judgment. Perhaps it was a false sense of security she had gotten from Junie's connections or perhaps it was just natural arrogance, but Robin began breaking rules.

Willie Moses had laid out a strict protocol which prescribed that the first thing a girl must do after entering the bar was to salute the house by buying a drink. As soon as she connected with a date, she must see that he bought a drink for the both of them. Then she must see that the bartender got tipped. Whenever Robin arrived, however, she went straight to working the bar and grabbed a date without encouraging him to run up a tab. If Willie saw her without a drink, he'd throw her out, but she'd just turn around and do it again.

If Robin was contemptuous of the house, she was even less courteous to her colleagues. There were a couple of unwritten rules at Charlie's: you didn't move in on a guy if another girl was talking to him, and you sure didn't steal someone's steady date. Robin routinely flouted these warnings, hustling any sucker who looked ripe. Then sometimes she went low on her prices to undercut the competition. If the agreed-upon floor for a half and half was $50, she'd take $35, which created temporary anarchy in the market.

Privately, the girls at Charlie's found it irritating enough that Nadine was pretty and popular, but she was greedy as well. Greedy and reckless. In her eagerness to make her evening's quota, she'd take unnecessary chances, like hopping into a car with four or five guys. Any girl with half a brain knew this was stupid. One guy, you could control. Get five of them together, and they'll just take it from you without paying. If Robin didn't get smart, the cats whispered, she was going to get herself into trouble.

AS THE SPRING wore on, Robin diversified. Sometimes she would top off her night's quota by selling condoms to other working girls. Someone had put her in touch with a pharmaceuticals outfit that was supplying her with gross orders of Ramses. Unfortunately, these rubbers were about a year past their expiration date and tended to pop in the heat of battle. This fact did not improve Robin's standing at the bar.

She had also gotten into "girlie girlie" gigs. The girlie girlie was a simulated lesbian act which was in heavy demand at small bars, private parties, and VFW posts. If the host asked for a "salt and pepper" routine, Robin usually went with a slender black girl named Lorna Johnson. If a white-bread act was required, she teamed up with another working girl, named Julie.

Julie was a tall redhead with a scar that ran across one cheek. She had started working at Charlie's just a little before Robin did, although she had not enjoyed such favored entrée. She had just come up from the South with a black pimp. Unfortunately, he had no name recognition, and she had had to bully and scratch her way into a seat on the exchange.

Julie couldn't see where these Boston girls got off acting so superior. It seemed to her that there was a deplorable lack of standards in the Combat Zone. At least her pimp was from the old school. He saw that a girl observed all the proper "respects." She opened his doors, lighted his cigarettes, and poured his drinks. She wasn't allowed to swear. If she even talked to another pimp, she incurred a "charge" of $200 or more. In the Northeast, however, you had a lot of bubble gum pimps who wanted to live off women but didn't want to set any rules. You could walk down Lagrange and see them hitting on another pimp's girl. What disgusted Julie most was the lack of professionalism among the Boston whores. There were certain "dog bitches," as she liked to call them, who went out on a date—and then stayed with the guy all night because they liked the sex!

Liking sex or not liking sex, in Julie's informed estimation, was really not the issue. Liking money was. Julie loved money. She had left home at seventeen and for the next five years lived on and off the streets, from Miami to West Palm Beach. She ran into a couple of guys who paid her bills, but nobody who could really get her "the nice things in life." After spending a year or so in Jamaica, she came back to Fort Lauderdale totally broke. It must have been flashing like neon, because she was jogging on the beach and this black guy from Providence, Rhode Island, stopped her and told her he knew how she could make some money.

When she asked him if he was a pimp, he said no. "Oh, yeah," she laughed. "Then what do you call yourself?" He said that he had two girls who were "friends" of his who "helped him out." Every day after that, he was out on the beach to intercept her. He promised she would have a nice apartment and nice clothes, and after a month she was persuaded to join his stable. It wasn't because she was in love with him. A lot of girls believed they loved their pimps, but that wasn't it. Sex with him was no better than doing it with a trick. But he did make good on his promise to show her how to make money. For the next year she traveled with him and his two black whores through the Carolinas and Atlantic City. She got the nice things of life in bits and pieces. It was supposed to happen big when they got to Boston because the city was wide open. Bail was only $60 at the time, and you could get dozens of cases before being sent up to Framingham. Unfortunately, the general lawlessness took its toll on her pimp, and he ended up a junkie. He got violent, so she left him and just lived in hotels rooms for a while.

Julie had to admit that when she was down, some of the older girls at Charlie's went out of their way to help her. They steered her to Back Bay apartments with rooms she could rent for $10 a trick. Now and again one of the veterans would pass along a steady date who was looking for a kinky experience. Julie was happy to accept these referrals because she was looking to build up a specialty clientele. Since coming to Boston, she had apprenticed herself to an older girl who was an expert in domination. Under her tutor's guidance, Julie learned to trill the whole scale, from a light paddling on the buttocks right up to whips and chains. She didn't mind accommodating specialties. One guy liked pins stuck in his balls. Another liked to be ridden like a horse. There was one who enjoyed having his head stuck in a toilet. You had to figure that a guy who asked for these things wasn't all there, but it wasn't her place to pass judgment. Most guys only wanted verbal humiliation that they could jerk off to. If you were blessed with a gift for gab—as Julie was—you could earn $500 for a five-hour session. It meant less wear and tear on your own body than if you were fucking twenty tricks a night.

The girlie girlie, while not nearly as lucrative, was a similarly low-impact gig. Some girls were squeamish about lesbian acts, but Julie tackled them with the same professional detachment that she tossed off a hand job. Whether Robin felt any qualms about the girlie girlie, Julie really didn't know. Robin rarely talked about her business, and Julie respected her for that.

All she knew about Robin Benedict really had come through rumors circulating around Charlie's. Some of the girls were saying that Robin was a snob, a prima donna who didn't like to give blow jobs. Julie thought this was a little strange. Most of the guys who came to the Combat Zone were looking for things their wives wouldn't do. Blow jobs were right at the top of the list. How could a girl build a following if she went around behaving like a *wife?*

This diffidence seemed not to have affected Robin's popularity. She had worked out an arrangement whereby if a john insisted upon oral sex, she would pass him along to other girls who were glad for the business. One of those she sent out for special servicing was a guy named Bill.

BILL was sort of a sweet, shy fellow. He was overweight but not, Julie thought, as repulsive as some trick with polio or a kid with his face all zitted out. No one could remember for sure when he had started showing up at Charlie's, but he would come in while it was still daylight and just sit and drink. He was rumored to have hung out before that at a place called the Two O'Clock Lounge, where he had developed a series of worshipful crushes on the girls. He would fix all of his attention on one. Then, if she left his side, he would focus intently upon the next. He seemed most ardently attracted to a thin brunette, but she soon left the Zone to start a dog-grooming business in Vermont.

Bill had the markings of a classic sucker. He was docile, plain, and in serious awe of women. Cocky jocks might give you hassles and then stiff you, but not the sucker. He always paid up. He was always grateful. He could be counted on for special favors, like to bail you out when you got busted. While the sucker was the object of open ridicule, he was also something of a prize. When Robin took up with Bill, in April of 1982, she was credited with having hooked a safe, well-paying trick.

Bill was some kind of big shot over at the medical school. He seemed to have his hands on a lot of cash. Robin once mentioned, within earshot of Julie, that he would just casually hand over $200 or $300 to help her make her night's quota. For nothing! Once when Julie and Robin returned from a double date, Julie saw Bill parked along an alley near Charlie's. Robin apparently had some special arrangement with him, because she walked over and got into the car and they drove off. He insisted upon seeing her every night for at least two hours, at the rate of $100 an hour.

Robin didn't seem to go out of her way to accommodate him. She blew him only occasionally and then only with a rubber. If he wanted to be sucked off without one for a change, she'd pass him along to one of the older girls. Still, Bill followed Robin around like a little dog. He was even trying to lose weight to please her, and she was encouraging this by supplying him with drugs. She had given him speed for a while, but he didn't care for the effect. So she switched him to cocaine, which he liked much better. All in all, with the sessions every night and the coke, you had to figure he was dropping a wad.

Pam McGrath was a little contemptuous of this dog-and-pony show. Robin, she reasoned, had probably led Bill to believe she was in love with him, and his "heart went right through his dick." It was crazy for a guy to fall in love with a working girl. You had to keep emphasizing, "This is not love!" If he got to be dependent, he got to be a pest. If you tapped him out, he got desperate. A sucker in love was not so harmless as he might seem. In Pam's opinion, it was Savi's place to set Robin straight. But Savi seemed to encourage this thing with Bill. Robin would pass him along to Savi now, and then and she, too, was making money off of him.

Pam wasn't one to meddle. She was leaving the Zone anyway, for at least nine months. Matt had told her he wanted a baby, so she was going to give him one. Early in the summer she left for a sabbatical and sort of lost track of Robin and Bill. So, for that matter, did most everyone. Since Robin had such a good thing going with the professor, she didn't have to work the bar for a while. During the summer of 1982 Robin and the professor confined their meetings to the Back Bay.

After that, Robin showed up only rarely in the Zone. During the late fall she was spotted at Charlie's by a recruiter for a talent agency called DeeJay Productions. Robin had at least one documentable gig for DeeJay. Around the first November the agency sent Robin and a white partner to a bachelor party in Framingham. The girls brought their own disco tapes and did a fifteen-minute strip, for which they received $150 apiece. Then Robin and partner retired to a second-floor bedroom to service a group of stags who had formed a line in the hall.

Junie, for his part, stayed well clear of Charlie's. He and Robin could be seen together on weekends at a club called Jason's in the Back Bay. Jason's was a stylish place which was enjoying a vogue among sports celebrities. It also had the reputation of a pickup spot for young urban professionals. Among others who hung out at Jason's was a barrel-chested white dude named Arthur Rodman. Rodman worked as a shift manager at the Newton Health Club and had become friendly with Robin during her stint there. Although he later claimed never to have patronized her as a prostitute, he would explain they had dated from 1981 to 1983. She seemed generally to rely upon him for favors. Rodman, by his own reckoning, was a good-hearted schlemiel who lost a lot of money by lending it to girls. Once when Robin was having her old green Toyota painted, she borrowed a friend's car. It was rammed during a hit and run in Boston, and she hit Rodman up for the $2,000 in repairs. Naturally, he never got it back. Robin would meet Rodman after she got off work, and they would go out for a bite to eat. It pleased him that she trusted him to hold her money for her.

Robin liked to dance, and sometimes Rodman took her to Jason's, the same spot she frequented with J.R. Rodman later claimed never to have met J.R., although he did seem to know that she was living with a black man. This was perplexing since Robin had told him she didn't like black men. She would never go out with blacks at the health club. When he took her home to Natick at night, she would say, "Drop me at the corner," and go home alone.

Rodman had a friend who was a habitué of Jason's, a graphic artist named Paula. For a while she was dating a guy who took her there every Friday night. One night Paula was at the club with a girlfriend who used to date Rodman. While they were standing at the bar, Robin walked up and started talking. Rodman introduced her to Paula and her friend, explaining in an aside that they were "heavily involved" in a "serious relationship." Paula had difficulty believing that. Robin treated Rodman in a "very light" manner. Paula, however, found Robin "highly intelligent" and "versatile." They were both in graphic arts and thus had something in common. When Robin learned that Paula was single, she offered to introduce her to a "top executive" at an ad agency. Robin reportedly said she thought it might a good business contact, possibly a romantic liaison. With that, she gave Paula her number on Marlborough Street.

Soon after this congenial overture, Paula was at Jason's once again, when J.R. Rogers approached her. He had a business proposition for her. She could, he suggested, be making $250,000 a year. That was what Robin was making, he reportedly said, adding, "All of it goes to me." Robin, who was nearby, verified that this was true. He had bought a new Mercedes—Paula estimated that it must have cost between $38,000 and $40,000—with that money. In exchange Robin received "protection."

That was late October. Robin was the only girl he had working for him at the time, but they wanted another. Paula thought the idea of turning all that money over to a pimp was foolish, and she turned the offer down.

DETECTIVE BILLY DWYER, meanwhile, had been making persistent inquiries into the affairs of Robin Benedict. The charges against her and Savi stemming from the Perez incident had been dropped, since neither of the johns had shown up to testify. For a while Dwyer pursued rumors he had heard along the disco circuit that Robin was lugging cocaine for the Patriots. Nothing heavy, just bringing an ounce or so into parties. But he could never tie this down.

During the last week in November, Dwyer's partner, Mark Molloy, took a call from a male complaining about a girl working out of an apartment at 400 Marlborough Street. From the description, Dwyer suspected that the girl must be Robin Benedict. He took the photo of J.R. from his files and set out with Molloy for the Back Bay. As they were cruising down the alley that ran behind Marlborough, Dwyer spotted Robin wearing a green corduroy pants suit. She was walking with a heavy man in spectacles.

Dwyer pulled Robin aside without ceremony and showed her the photo of J.R. "You do recognize this?" he asked her. She denied knowing the man in the picture. Molloy, meanwhile, had gotten identification from the heavy man. He was Dr. William H. J. Douglas, a professor at Tufts University. The girl, he claimed, was his assistant.

"She is a hooker," Dwyer replied. "And she has a pimp. That girl works at Good Time Charlie's, and you're a trick."

"No. No," Douglas insisted. "She's a friend of the family. I've been to her house."

Dr. Douglas was very calm. He had apparently been coached. Since he wouldn't admit to giving Robin Benedict money, Dwyer couldn't arrest her. He sent her off with a warning to move out of 400 Marlborough.

About a week later, Sergeant Eddie McNelley got an anonymous phone tip about a girl working out of a pad at 280 Commonwealth Avenue. He turned the complaint over to Dwyer and Molloy. Again, the description matched Robin's. By the time they arrived, however, they saw the trick slip out the door. All Dwyer could do was order Robin out of this apartment too.

Dwyer later professed to have been mightily irritated by Robin Benedict. There was something slightly superior in her manner that he found offensive. A whore was a whore. Robin thought she was better than that: "not like them." In some perverse way, her contempt for the Zone was an affront to him as well. She didn't realize that on Lower Washington Street, nobody condescended to Billy Dwyer. He would have liked nothing better than to arrest her and send her to the women's correctional facility in Framingham.

The opportunity came three days later, on December 9, when Dwyer saw her coming out of Charlie's and heading toward her silver Toyota. He knew she'd be going to pick up a date somewhere. He followed her as she pulled around the corner to the intersection of Washington and Stuart streets. There she waved to a guy on the curb. He was an ordinary-looking kid in his early twenties. As the boy attempted to slide into the passenger's seat, Dwyer caught the door.

"Boston police," Dwyer told him. "Do you have some identification?"

"Did I do something wrong?" the kid replied. "She's just givin' me a ride."

"She's a just givin' you a ride? . . . Do you read the *Boston Globe?*"

"Huh?" By now, the kid was as terrified as Dwyer had hoped he would be.

"Your picture's gonna be in there tomorrow," he said soberly.

The boy began a frantic explanation about how he was a student at the Berklee School of Music and how this could ruin his career.

To that Dwyer reportedly replied, "I'm not gonna destroy your career as long as you cooperate with the Boston Police Department. . . . All I want to know is the truth. She's a hooker. I know you were with her at Good Time Charlie's. I want you to tell me what the financial arrangement was. If you don't tell me, we're gonna lock you up and you'll be held without bail."

This was nonsense, but the music student was sufficiently terrified to blurt out, "Okay, okay. It was fifty dollars."

Robin, who realized the game was up, chimed in, "What happens now?"

"You know what happens now," Dwyer told her. "You're going to jail."

ROBIN, of course, did not go to jail. Her case was postponed five times as, on each of these occasions, the music student failed to appear. Billy Dwyer noted with satisfaction, however, that Robin was feeling the heat of his arrests. She appeared to have moved out of the Marlborough and Commonwealth trick pads. And the word on the street was that she was persona non grata at Charlie's. Another working girl had seen her pick someone up in the parking lot and squealed to the bartender, who told Willie, who tossed Robin out for good. It appeared that bad breaks and Robin's own recklessness had conspired to end her career. By January 1983 she had, as far as Dwyer could tell, left the Zone for good.

JOHN AND SHIRLEY BENEDICT were similarly encouraged. It had been nine months since they first learned that Robin had been picked up on suspicion of prostitution, and during that time they had been pursuing a delicate strategy. The night she was released by Detective Ridlon, they had fully intended to take her back to Methuen, but she refused. They followed her to the apartment in Natick. Junie was not there. He had dropped out of sight. For the next two hours they pleaded with her to come home.

Later John Benedict would explain that he had thought about taking her home forcibly but had abandoned that idea. What would he do once he got her there? Tie her to the bed and stay home from work to see that she stayed put? She was an adult under the law, and he didn't have any right to take her anywhere she didn't want to go. The Benedicts finally gave up trying to persuade her and went home alone. When they got there, John Benedict broke down and cried like a baby. Neither could understand why Robin was doing this. Was she deliberately trying to hurt them for something? Since she was of age, it wouldn't have been necessary for her to have given the police her parents' names. It was almost as if she wanted them to know.

The Benedicts decided between themselves that, for the time being at least, they should keep quiet. The only thing they told Rhonda and the boys was that they weren't to try to borrow money from Robin anymore. Apart from that, they would go on pretending that nothing had happened. They would keep the lines open and encourage Robin to come home for visits. Perhaps the appearance of harmony would bring it to pass.

AS THE SUMMER wore on, this charade became increasingly easy to sustain. There were no more calls from the police in the middle of the night. Robin came home at least once a week, exuding the same bubbling enthusiasm she always had. The convivial atmosphere, which everyone seemed intent upon maintaining, lent credence to Robin's explanation that the police had picked her up by mistake. There was one anxious episode when it slipped out that Shirley had sent J.R.'s photo to the police. Robin was furious. Junie was *not* her pimp, she insisted. She and Junie were in love. They were going to be married and adopt little Taj. By August even John Benedict had accepted this as inevitable.

One afternoon she came home for a visit, wearing a soft yellow suede top that made her look particularly pretty. Her father later recalled a flush of sadness at the thought of losing her. He reached for his camera and caught her face turned slightly toward him. The bright summer light made each detail stand out with merciless clarity. The kohl on her lower lids had been applied too thickly. There were shadows under the eyes. Her chipped tooth appeared more prominent than usual. Her hair, now past shoulder length, was slightly tangled. Robin's imperfect features, however, were redeemed by an expression of such seductive mirth that she was undeniably beautiful. It had been John Benedict's implicit creed that what was beautiful must also be good. If those playful eyes concealed treachery, he really didn't want to know.

Whatever fears John and Shirley Benedict still harbored at the end of the summer of 1982 were gradually allayed by evidence that Robin seemed to be building a very respectable middle-class life for herself. Her credit rating seemed excellent. She had gotten a loan from the Baybank of Norfolk for a little over $4,000 and had bought herself a silver Toyota Starlet.

A car salesman named Ed Willis later recalled how J.R. Rogers had come into Wellesley Toyota one Saturday morning, wearing a blue jogging suit. Willis stepped up to help him, and Rogers said he was looking for something for his "fiancée."

"It will be her decision," he said. "I'll be doing the groundwork."

Rogers wanted a car that got good mileage, and Willis said he had just the thing, a lovely silver Toyota Starlet that was being used as a demonstration car. J.R. asked if they could drive it out to Natick so he could show it to the prospective owner. Willis was reluctant to leave the showroom on a big selling day, especially since he wasn't sure how serious Rogers was about buying the car. He agreed, nonetheless, and when the two men arrived at the apartment complex, J.R. went upstairs and brought Robin down to the parking lot. She was wearing a burgundy velour jogging suit and looking drowsy.

As Willis remembered the episode, Robin didn't say much. J.R. did all the negotiating. The asking price for the Toyota was $6,000. Rogers wanted to offer Robin's 1977 green Toyota Corolla as a trade in. It had 100,000 miles on it and needed a major overhaul. J.R. conceded it was "in real rough shape," adding, "She doesn't take care of it at all." In addition to the shabby Corolla, Robin agreed to put down $3,000 in cash, which kept her payments to a modest $100 per month.

A few days later, Robin came by herself to pick up the car. It was rush hour, about four or five in the afternoon. She was wearing a sheer dress, black- and white-striped with a black belt. Something, Willis thought, like what a secretary might wear. Whereas earlier she had looked drowsy, she now seemed hyped up and ready to go. The back of her green Toyota was filled with junk—books, papers, odds and ends. She just grabbed the mess in an armload and tossed it into the back of the new Toyota. Then she drove off into the rush-hour traffic.

THAT FALL, Robin and Junie started looking for their "dream house." They settled upon a ranch house in an expensive section of Ashland and hired an interior-design consultant to redo it with a "contemporary look."

The consultant had drawn up a complete layout of the rooms, right down to the wallpaper, when they called him with the news that the financing had fallen through. By the middle of October they had managed to secure a loan from the Medford Savings Bank and by early December had closed on a house in Malden, a working-class suburb five miles north of the city.

The house at 8 Cliff Street was nothing special, just a gray, two-story frame. But Robin, as far as her mother could see, was delighted with it. Everything was being done to her specifications, she said. She didn't want them to see it until it was done. Then she would invite them all over for dinner. Through the Christmas holidays she furnished reports about the workmen who were knocking down walls and hanging wallpaper. The color scheme apparently was her favorite, unremitting browns. The bedroom set was an alabaster finish from the Henredon line. Her carpets were deep-pile morocco tan.

Robin said that she and Junie were replacing the porch themselves and asked her father if she could borrow one of his hammers. He agreed. John Benedict was still not reconciled to J.R. Rogers, but Robin's portrait of her fiancé rolling up his sleeves to lay floorboards was something that a father could relate to. The Benedicts had spent most of Robin's teen years tinkering and toying with the house on Emsley Terrace. And if J.R. Rogers was a man who took pride in his home, then there must be something domestic and, therefore, dependable in him.

He certainly seemed good to Robin. He was always buying her nice gifts. In November he had gotten her two jackets from Lord & Taylor. One was black leather, the other a beige corduroy blazer. For Christmas he had bought her a flute. She had also turned up wearing a full-length mink, presumably Junie's largess.

The Benedicts did not apparently inquire too pointedly into where they were getting the money for all these things. J.R. seemed to be doing well in his mysteriously diversified enterprises. In addition to working as a hairdresser, he apparently helped locate exotic cars like Corvettes and Lamborghinis for a specialty dealer on the South Shore.

Robin told them that she was illustrating a medical text for a professor at Tufts University. He had vouched that she was making $19,000 a year, and on the strength of that she had gotten both a Visa card and a MasterCard. John and Shirley Benedict had no reason to doubt this. Robin, after all, had worked professionally as a graphic artist. To believe she had now been hired as a medical illustrator did not require an enormous leap of faith. Her account gained credibility when, as she and Junie were preparing to move from Natick to Malden, she had her mail forwarded temporarily to Emsley Terrace. Among the items addressed to her were copies of a technical journal called *In Vitro*. Obviously something to do with Robin's work for the professor. There was also correspondence from Tufts University. Shirley found that it contained a 1099 form indicating that the university had paid Robin $13,600 during the year 1982. If anybody asked, there it was in black and white. John and Shirley Benedict's daughter Robin was working as an artist.

BUT these felicitous omens were illusory. Unbeknownst to her parents, who were rejoicing over her 1099 form, beyond the purview of Willie Moses, who had tossed her out of Charlie's, out of eyeshot of Billy Dwyer, who was congratulating himself for squeezing her out of the Combat Zone, Robin Benedict was still in business. During the first week in January of 1983, as she and J.R. were putting the finishing touches on their supposed love nest, she had returned to work as a masseuse, this time in a town called Saugus.

Saugus was an old foundry town, site of the first ironworks in colonial America. Long after the ironworks shut down in the late seventeenth century, it evolved into a blue-collar suburb inhabited largely by elderly Italians from East Boston. It was a drowsy little community of very conservative character. The residents were intent upon keeping it that way, not an easy task in the face of the iniquities which lapped at the city limits. Saugus lay just off Route 1, a cacophonous commercial corridor that ran seven miles from Boston to the North Shore.

The Strip, the *Boston Phoenix* once noted with voluptuous precision, "is a neon state of mind. It's an attitude. It's lounge lizards and G-strings and 'gimme 'nother Budweiser.' It's combs, cologne and condoms spilling out of vending machines. It's lonesome souls with double-knit delirium in swizzle-stick heaven."

It was also a sort of sexual free port. Lovers hoping to elude the notice of spouses and associates escaped by afternoon to one of the many cheap motels that forested the Strip. Men seeking more anonymous encounters were attracted to three massage parlors positioned as innocuously as tobacco shops in the crazy quilt of commerce. The Roman and the Parisienne sat on the upper stretch of highway south of Peabody. The Danish Health Spa was tucked into the back of a tiny mall on the northbound lane near the Saugus exits.

It was the Danish that had the citizenry of Saugus up in arms. In February 1978 the club had been evicted from a West Peabody shopping center that was hoping to upgrade its image. The following October the spa's owners managed to get an operating license in Saugus.

As was standard in a club of this kind, the girls were allowed to keep their tips. These usually ran $40 to $50 for a clothed French, $50 to $60 for a nude French, and $60 to whatever else could be negotiated for intercourse. Most girls tried to avoid intercourse and thus cultivated specialties. A girlie girlie viewing was about $200. Special accommodation was made for one fat old fellow whose wife had slipped on a waxed floor, hit her head, and died. He would come in and buy up an evening's worth of sessions with one of the younger girls for $500.

The Saugus city fathers were not particularly worried about elderly widowers who sought comfort at the Danish. What had them concerned was the influx of businessmen from Boston and the attendant prospect that Saugus was getting a reputation as the Combat Zone North. So, a month after the Danish opened in 1978, the Board of Selectmen passed a resolution affirming, "The business community is desirous of maintaining the highest possible reputation in an environment that encourages family purchasing of goods and services within our town." Accordingly, they tried to rescind the Danish's license. That was not as simple as it seemed, since the license had been issued in accordance with the statutes, and the city had no proof that the masseuses were engaging in prostitution.

So, the Danish operated unmolested for four years, until the spring of 1982, when the Essex County District Attorney's Office sent state troopers undercover, hoping to get criminal indictments. During the first week in April, Trooper Bradley Hibbard went to the Danish posing as a client. His subsequent reports of that excursion told how he had entered from the parking lot into a foyer and there encountered a solid wooden door with a peephole. He rang a buzzer and was admitted by one of the managers, who asked him if he had ever been there before. When Hibbard said no, he was given a tour of the sauna, whirlpool, locker room, and steam room. Last stop was the lounge, which was furnished with an Advent TV and about eight to ten masseuses in "blue-green tight-fitting bathing suit-type garments."

Returning to the front desk, he paid $40 for a one-hour massage and received a towel, a red wrap, a lock, and a "receipt." After he had stashed his street clothes in a locker, he put on the red wrap and walked into the lounge, where he gave the receipt to the masseuse of his choice. His pick, "Lisa," led him through a pair of swinging louvered doors to a massage room. There he disrobed and lay face down on the table.

According to Trooper Hibbard, Lisa then began massaging his legs and moved easily to his genitals.

"I like to give all the muscles a good workout," she reportedly said, adding, "Don't worry about the time. I like to play."

Without breaking the rhythm of the massage, she climbed up and straddled his legs. Had he been there before? she inquired. When he said he hadn't, she placed her hand on his thigh and asked if he "wanted to have fun."

"What's included in the $40?" he asked.

"That goes to the management," she replied. "The girls make money on the tips."

When he asked her how much the tip was normally, she held up three fingers "for a little," and she put her other hand around his penis. Then she held up five fingers and said, "To make love with you."

Trooper Hibbard said he thought that $40 was a little steep. He was in town from New York for only a week, and he didn't want to run himself short.

"We take Mastercharge and Visa," she advised him.

When she apparently satisfied herself that he wasn't interested in sex, she told him to call her and make another appointment. She was usually booked up, she said, because she was very good at what she did.

The following week Trooper Hibbard returned and drew a masseuse named Dawn. She seemed aware that he had been with Lisa the first time and asked what she had done for him. Hibbard replied, "The usual."

"Nice young men usually like a French," Dawn affirmed.

She then asked what Lisa's tip was, and he told her $30. Dawn said that she personally would not do a French for less than $40, because she "couldn't get into it" and would have to cut it short. She offered to give him a "hand release" for $30.

Meanwhile, a few rooms down, one of Hibbard's undercover comrades, Trooper Patrick Keane, was in the thrall of an operator named Cleo. Keane, whose report reflects that he declined to remove his red wrap, had asked for a $20 oil massage, and Cleo was trying to talk him into a French for $40. He promptly placed her under arrest. With that he knocked on the door of Dawn's room, signaling Hibbard to take her into custody.

The city fathers of Saugus kept a close watch on the litigation, since a conviction would give them the standing they needed to yank the spa's license. During the ten months that the case dragged on, the Danish's owners, (realizing they were) standing in the shadow of the axe, appeared to go out of their way to comply with city health ordinances, increasing the amount of light in the massage rooms, installing windows in the doors so that city officials could cruise through at will and witness for themselves the therapeutic nature of the massage. During the first week of January, however, the owners suffered a lapse in prudence when they hired Robin Benedict.

Under the circumstances, it was extremely risky to be taking on a working girl from Boston. You couldn't tell what kind of trouble she might be bringing with her. Ever since the Newton Health Club had opened up down south, however, the Danish had had trouble keeping masseuses. Whatever reservations the owners might have had apparently dissolved in the face of the fact that Robin was very pretty.

The first week of January she was hired as a trainee, which meant she could observe but not give actual massages. According to accounts from other masseuses tendered many months later, however, Bobbie Benedict, as she was known, went to work right away. As it was commonly the practice to showcase a new acquisition, the owners set her up with their most valued clientele.

Bobbie made an impressive debut, showing a willingness not only to perform the standards but to submit to bondage as well. Within two weeks, however, this facade was faltering. Bobbie was getting a reputation for not delivering. If a position paid for a French, she'd try to get by with a hand release. She seemed not to realize there was a certain honor in giving a guy what he paid for. Bobbie also seemed to have a stubborn aversion to oral sex. On the sly, she would slip a condom into her mouth, hook the rim to her teeth and let it unroll over the submerging organ. One client, however, got wise to this maneuver and informed the owners, causing Bobbie's stock to dip.

Robin was regarded somewhat coldly by the other masseuses, who resented having their best clients diverted. They whispered that she was shooting coke through her veins. That she was a greedy little hustler who was going to bring trouble down on them all. Sure enough, around the second week in January, the spa got two calls from a guy claiming to be from a Saugus citizens' group complaining about Bobbie. At first the owners made a big show of protecting their own. But then, on January 21, the Danish received a visit from the city health inspector, who announced that a Mr. Schloss had called City Hall complaining that Bobbie Benedict had propositioned a friend of his and tried to sell him mescaline to boot. This time the owners didn't argue. The city probably couldn't get Bobbie on either the prostitution or the drug charge, but she was unlicensed in Saugus. If the health department could even establish that she had been doing something as innocent as giving a massage, it could put the spa out of business. The owners told Bobbie to clear out her things. She was gone in half an hour—done in by the mysterious Mr. Schloss.

ABOUT the same time, John and Shirley Benedict's earlier success in convincing themselves that Robin was out of difficulty was being undermined by new and troubling developments. Every other day or so they had been receiving collect calls from a stranger who used several different names, none of which they recognized or could even later remember. Sometimes the caller's voice was unquestionably male. At other times he seemed to be affecting a falsetto. He usually said something indistinct about trying to locate Robin. Sometimes there would be more calls in the early morning hours, between one and four o'clock. When either John or Shirley picked up the phone, there was no one on the other end.

One evening, late in January, the phone rang. John Benedict answered, and someone identifying himself as Detective Sheehan told him that his daughter was in a lot of trouble and was going to jail. The Benedicts, he said, had better be in court at nine the following morning. John and Shirley found their way to Boston Municipal Court, in Pemberton Square. When the elevator opened onto the second floor, the bewildered pair found themselves propelled into a milling mob of working girls, some strutting the corridor in bored defiance, others conferring with attorneys on a bank of hard wooden benches.

The events of this morning, as the Benedicts later described them to police, seemed to unfold not according to any coherent logic but rather with the menacing whimsy of a nightmare. Robin emerged from the crowd and tried to suggest that this was all a mistake.

Robin stood to be tried that day, after many lengthy delays, for soliciting the music student. She seemed less concerned about her own predicament, however, than about the fact that her parents had been summoned to court. When she saw Billy Dwyer step off the elevator, she approached him and said, "Can I talk to you? Why did Frank Sheehan tell my parents?"

Dwyer was reportedly surprised to hear this. Frank Sheehan was a detective from District Four, which covered the Back Bay, but as far as Dwyer knew he had nothing to do with this case. Out of curiosity more than anything else, Dwyer called Sheehan at home and asked him if he had had reason to call a family named Benedict. Sheehan seemed not to know what he was talking about. He had, in fact, arrested a girl named Robin Benedict around the middle of April the preceding year. A couple of officers from District Four had seen some traffic around 478 Beacon Street, so Sheehan had been keeping an eye on the place. One night he saw a Chinese fellow walking in the alley. Sheehan picked him up, and the guy admitted that Robin had solicited him for $50. He took her in, but charges were dismissed when the john didn't show.

Sometime later, however, Sheehan's sergeant handed him a complaint from someone from a Bay Bay tenants' group about an apartment at 400 Marlborough. Sheehan knew this trick pad also belonged to Benedict. As he turned into the alley, he saw a large man coming his way. When the man saw Sheehan, he ran in through the back door of the apartment.

Sheehan got out of his cruiser and banged on the door, shouting, "You son of a bitch." But the heavy man had already warned Robin's trick, who escaped through the front door. Sheehan didn't have a warrant to get in and couldn't get anyone to come out.

Detective Sheehan had, in fact, seen the heavy man before. On half a dozen occasions he had showed up at the courthouse when Robin Benedict was scheduled to appear. He might not have drawn attention to himself except that he was conspicuously large and wore a bright green satin jacket zippered up the front. The detective had heard he was some kind of professor, but he seemed to be just a typical, lovesick fool.

That was all Sheehan knew about the Benedict girl.

About the time that Billy Dwyer returned to the corridor to report to Robin Benedict that Detective Sheehan had not called her parents, Robin was introducing them to a large man in a heavy winter coat—Dr. William Douglas. He was writing a book, he told John and Shirley, and Robin was doing some artwork on the project. His familiarity apparently so disarmed Shirley that she began confiding in him about the annoyance calls. Douglas claimed that he was being bothered in exactly the same way.

Dr. Douglas then launched into an unsolicited explanation of how, if someone tried to harm Robin, he would take care of it. He kept some sort of liquid in his laboratory, he said, and if you put a drop of it on a person's lips, they would die. Not only that, but the body would disappear. Even the teeth. This struck Shirley as "a rather unusual" conversation. But when Dr. Douglas said he wanted to keep in contact with the Benedicts regarding the crank caller, Shirley did not discourage him.

One day shortly after that January court date—Robin's case was continued once again—Shirley got a call from Dr. Douglas. He had just found out that Robin was living with someone named J.R., he said. Did Shirley know that J.R. was black? Did she know what kind of person he was? How long had they been going together? Douglas speculated that it was this Rogers who was making the annoyance calls. On the day of her court appearance, Robin had taken her mother aside and told her not to say anything about Junie, because Douglas didn't know about him, so out of deference to this incomprehensible intrigue, Shirley Benedict played dumb. Douglas, however, was persistent. He called again toward the end of February claiming that several of Junior's buddies had beaten him up. When Shirley questioned him further, the assailants dwindled to one attacker. In the revised account, Douglas claimed that either Junior or one of his friends had punched him in the nose while he was walking down the street from Tufts.

The Benedicts frankly didn't know what to make of Douglas. On the one hand, he seemed to be genuinely concerned about Robin. One weekend in January, John Benedict had taken a U-Haul to Boston to help Robin move out of 280 Commonwealth Avenue. The Benedicts knew perfectly well that this apartment was a trick pad. The fact that she was dismantling it and putting the contents into storage seemed to signify Robin's intent to make a clean break. It was significant that when John arrived, he found Douglas there willing to lend a hand with the mattress and bureau and, in effect, get Robin out of the life. Given the awkward nature of this encounter, the two men did not exchange many words. What registered itself in John Benedict's memory was not Dr. Douglas, but the glimpse he caught of a woman who stood some distance away on Commonwealth Avenue. She appeared to be watching them load the truck. Benedict wondered after he got home if it might not be Douglas's wife.

The Benedicts weren't sure what Douglas's domestic situation actually was. He was clearly paying a lot of attention to Robin. He had a crush on her, at the very least. If Robin was reciprocating his affection, however, she didn't let on. Toward the end of February, in fact, she mentioned to her mother that Douglas was becoming a pest. He had started following her around, and when she confronted him with this, he denied it. Robin had finally taken matters in hand and called Douglas's wife, to complain about her husband's conduct. Mrs. Douglas, Robin reported, seemed blasé about the whole matter.

On Wednesday, March 2, Robin came back to Methuen for a visit. When her father arrived home from work, he heard her joking around in the bedroom with Rhonda. Robin had let her sister try on her new corduroy coat, but the sleeves were too short and the jacket too tight across the back. Rhonda also found fault with the collar, which was too high for her taste. Quipping that Robin could "keep the coat," she tossed it into the hall.

When Shirley Benedict got home, the family gathered in the kitchen, where Robin sampled a piece of cake that Ma Menzies had sent over. She began teasing her father. He had made a deal with her to give up smoking if she would quit biting her nails. She therefore drummed her fingertips on the table so that he could hear the click. Robin also gave her mother a little diamond ring that she wanted taken to the shop for more antiquing. Shirley noticed in passing that Robin was wearing what looked like gold shell earrings and a single diamond in one ear.

Overall, Robin seemed in excellent spirits. The unpleasant situation with Dr. Douglas seemed to be resolving itself. Things appeared to be going well with Junie. John Benedict had just about brought himself to the point where he was willing to sit down and talk with his daughter's fiancé. Robin had been trying to engineer a meeting. She wanted to have her parents over for dinner to talk things out. This would happen, she promised, after the rooms were wallpapered on the coming weekend.

That Saturday, March 5, was a chilly but sunny day. Robin had errands to run. At about ten in the morning, a neighbor whose kitchen window overlooked Robin's driveway saw her leave the house wearing a brown corduroy jacket and get in her silver Toyota. By two or three o'clock, she had returned. J.R. later told police that the last time he saw her that day, she was getting ready to go out shopping for a present for Savitry Bisram's little boy, Taj, whose birthday was Sunday. As J.R. left the house to visit a friend, he noticed that Robin had laid her brown pants and beige shirt out on the bed in their room. Her brown corduroy jacket was hanging on the door.

Robin dropped in at Charlie's at around a quarter of eight to tell Savi Bisram that she would pick up her and little Taj and take them to the Ground Round, where some of the girls and their kids were going to give him a party. She was on her way, she said, to meet a trick who lived in the West End. As nearly as her progress can be traced, Robin Benedict left Boston around ten o'clock and drove south on Route 95 toward Braintree. She stopped at a Howard Johnson to phone William Douglas; then she took the expressway toward Sharon. At about a quarter of eleven, she pulled into the cul-de-sac at Sandy Ridge Circle. She rang the door of the Douglas house, and someone let her in—whereupon she vanished.

II
THE INVESTIGATION

THE DISCOVERY

JOSEPH PLOTEGHER'S sweet, moon-faced wife, Cissy, had warned him to stay away from the highway, but he wouldn't listen. Every winter he got laid off road construction and had to find odd jobs to support her and their little son. Joe's father had gotten him a job at the car auction in Walpole, where he drove the clunkers around for prospective bidders to look over. It was there he had met Bob Jewell, a retired state worker, who invited him to go out scavenging. Even before the bottle bill went into effect, seven years earlier, Plotegher had discovered that you could bring in about $200 a week with cans. Combine that with unemployment, and it was pretty good money.

Plotegher liked scavenging. You could find incredible things up there on Route 95, rummaging through the trash at the rest stops. Cissy and his father had a bad feeling about the highway. No good, they felt, could come of poking around the stuff that strangers discarded in the night. He'd be better off sticking to the side roads and back streets. But Plotegher knew the stakes were higher around the blue barrels on Route 95. Sometimes people dropped their jewelry. Once he found a ten-dollar bill.

During the first week of March, Plotegher and Jewell had turned up more than seventy-five cases of bottles and cans between them. They set out on the morning of Sunday, the sixth, to salvage what they could before the barrels were emptied the next day. It was about 9:00 A.M. when they arrived at the Mansfield rest area, one of the better-appointed stops on the northbound lane between Boston and New York.

Jewell agreed to take the right side of the lot, and Plotegher took off to the left behind the tourist information pavilion. Just past a fleet of sleeping truckers lay several blue barrels. Plotegher peered into the first. Lying on top was a brown garbage bag secured by a neat, tight knot. As he lifted it, the weight excited him. That probably meant he had scored a cache of bottles. He tore into the side of the bag and examined the contents. There was a woman's corduroy jacket and a man's blue shirt. Both were spattered with what appeared to be blood. Lying loose among those garments was a hammer.

"Come over here quick," Plotegher called to Jewell. When the older man arrived, he showed him the bag. "Put it back," Jewell directed, "and let's get the hell out of here."

For the rest of the morning the bag and its contents tormented Plotegher. When he got home, he was so pale Cissy thought he might be ill. He finally decided he ought to let someone know what he'd found. It was nearly one o'clock when he phoned the state police barracks in Foxboro and told his story to the desk officer, Frank Mendes. There was nothing particularly alarming in the report. What appeared to be blood often was not. On a busier day Mendes might have disregarded the call. But on a Sunday afternoon there was rarely much to do at the Foxboro barracks, unless there was a Patriots game at nearby Schaefer Stadium, so Mendes turned to a fellow trooper.

"Got one for you, Paul," he said. "Guy from Foxboro just called saying that he found some clothing and a hammer in a trash barrel in the Mansfield rest area. Said they had blood on them. Can you check it out?"

Trooper Paul Landry took the report and read it with casual interest. He was not actually supposed to be doing any real work. Although he was relatively young, only thirty-two, his health was poor. A short man, about fifty pounds overweight, he suffered from hypertension. His head often ached, and sometimes he woke up in the middle of the night short of breath, his heart pounding. Police work had always excited him, but that was the problem. The excitement made him feel worse. Now and again he ran into a situation that sent his blood pressure soaring.

Early one morning the preceding spring, he had pulled into the Mansfield rest area to make a routine check and had become suspicious of two men sitting in a car. He called for backup, and as he and another trooper walked toward the car, the driver opened fire. The marksman escaped into the woods, but Landry managed to grab the passenger and disarm him. The two turned out to be members of a terrorist gang suspected of murdering a New Jersey state trooper. Landry emerged from the fracas a hero, cited by the governor for "swift and courageous" action. Unfortunately, he just didn't have the constitution for heroism. His condition continued to deteriorate, exacerbated by problems at home. He and his estranged wife were locked in a struggle over their young son. Landry decided it was best to take early retirement so that he could concentrate on winning custody of the boy.

On that Sunday afternoon in March, Landry had only twenty-five days left on the job. He had promised his station commander that he would just wind down, get his paperwork in order, and not get involved in anything complicated. When Mendes handed him the Plotegher report, it seemed routine enough. Landry drove out to Mansfield and into the truckers area, where he found the bag that Plotegher had described lying undisturbed on top of one of the barrels. Inside were the blue shirt and the hammer. The jacket which Plotegher had mentioned was apparently hidden. Landry figured it was probably innocuous refuse, but on the off chance it was significant, he called down to the Rhode Island border to Trooper Bud Petrucci, who always kept a camera in his cruiser. When Petrucci arrived, they spread the items on the ground. There was a light blue long-sleeved shirt. It appeared to have been ripped at the armpits and mended with darker blue thread. The woman's jacket was brown corduroy with a stand-up collar and high nap. It emitted a strong floral fragrance. The hammer looked like about a two-and-a-half-pound sledge. It had an iron head with blunted ends mounted on a lacquered wooden handle about ten inches long. It was large enough that a man would probably need two hands to hoist it. A mounting hook had been screwed into the end. Near the hook was a drop of reddish residue that was still wet and sticky.

Landry's curiosity was aroused. His first impression upon hearing about the items in the barrel was that they were probably the cast-off belongings of someone who had put a dog out of its misery. But seeing the shirt and jacket lying there beside a bloody hammer caused him to reconsider. Paul Landry had an odd tick that impelled him to pursue a routine assignment further than the evidence might seem to warrant. It was a habit that had started when he was fresh out of the State Police Academy. He was riding radar with his trooper coach when a car cruised by slightly over the speed limit. It was Landry's inclination to let it slide, but his coach said, "That could be the murderer, and you let him get away. Maybe he has a girl tied up in the backseat. Maybe there's a body in the trunk. Maybe it's the *big grab.*" The big grab came to mean the case that makes your reputation. Nabbing the terrorist at Mansfield had caused a pleasant flurry of attention, but twenty-five days away from retirement Paul Landry still felt something missing. His career, exemplary by most standards, still lacked the crowning distinction that makes a man feel his life has been worthwhile. Landry decided to follow this Mansfield thing a ways to see how far the trail would lead.

Landry took the barrel items back to the barracks, where he logged them into the contraband journal. Then he called Joseph Plotegher and asked him to come in for questioning. Plotegher was clearly sorry he had gotten himself into this predicament, particularly since he now seemed to be considered a suspect. Landry had him fingerprinted, read him his rights, then asked him to tell his story from the beginning. Plotegher explained how he had seen the corduroy jacket and, not realizing that it was a woman's, lifted it out thinking to try it on. When he saw the blood, he dropped the whole bag. Landry called Bob Jewell, who verified this account; then he put both of their names into the computer to see if there were warrants for their arrest. The search turned up nothing. Landry decided that Plotegher was just what he appeared to be—a scared kid grubbing for bottles to keep his family fed—and he sent him home.

But the items in the barrel continued to intrigue Trooper Landry. Later that day he sent a teletext message to the New England states, requesting receiving departments to check their files for missing persons, homicides, or assaults. The following morning he sent the coat, shirt, and hammer off to the State Police Laboratory at 1010 Commonwealth Avenue, in Boston. Common sense told him this was probably a lot of fuss about nothing. Every now and again, however, he would check the wire for replies.

THAT Monday morning in Boston, someone was, in fact, preparing to report a missing person. J.R. Rogers walked into the Central Secret Service Bureau, at 19 Temple Street, and announced he wanted to hire a private detective.

The Central Secret Service Bureau, its sonorous title notwithstanding, was a small operation founded during the 1950s as a detective and auto recovery agency. Its rates were reasonable enough, $20 an hour as opposed to $500 a day charged by a topflight investigator. Economy may have been what attracted J.R. Rogers. Just how Junie actually decided upon the CSSB, as it was known more succinctly, he never explained.

After a perfunctory screening by the receptionist, he was passed along to Detective Jack DaRosa, a stout, hulking fellow with a snaggled tooth. Before him sat a black man with gold chains and manicured nails wanting to locate a missing girlfriend.

Was the girl white or black? he asked.

Undaunted by DaRosa's apparent skepticism, Rogers confirmed that the person in question was a white girl named Robin Nadine Benedict. She had disappeared the night of March 5. One of her friends, a girl named Debbie, had told him that she had been on her way to see a Dr.

William H. J. Douglas. Robin had been working for Douglas at Tufts Medical School. Douglas was "crazy" about her, Rogers said, always calling and wanting to see her. Robin had apparently agreed to go out to Douglas's home in Sharon on Saturday night to pick up some income tax forms that he had filled out for her, and she hadn't come back.

DaRosa's first impression of J.R. Rogers was that he might be a pimp who, having disposed of one of his girls, was hoping to bolster the appearance of innocence by hiring his own private investigators to look for her. The detective overcame his qualms, however, when Rogers put down a deposit of $300 and promised to come in the next day with another $1,200. DaRosa advised his new client to report Robin missing to the Malden police.

That afternoon DaRosa and his partner, Jim Smith, visited the medical school in Boston. Douglas was not there. No one seemed to know very much about him. So the detectives set out for Norfolk County, hoping to catch the professor at home. When they arrived at 38 Sandy Ridge Circle, no one answered their knock. So DaRosa left a card on the door with a note asking Douglas to call him at the agency.

By the following morning he had received no reply. But sometime before noon J.R. came into the office with new information. Robin's friend Debbie had been calling around. She had managed to reach Douglas's wife, who said her husband was in Washington, D.C., attending a conference. He was staying at the Hotel Washington, on Pennsylvania Avenue. J.R. Rogers seemed convinced that Douglas, who had apparently been trying to persuade Robin to go on a vacation with him to St. Thomas, had coerced her into going along with him to Washington. Perhaps, J.R. speculated, he had even kidnapped her.

The shuttles were grounded because of bad weather, and DaRosa was not able to get a flight to Washington until late afternoon. At National Airport he picked up a rental car and drove to the Hotel Washington. Shortly after checking in, at 5:45 P.M., he spotted Douglas in the hotel dining room. J.R. had given him a description. A big man in his early forties, with gray hair and glasses. DaRosa followed Douglas back to his room and hung around in the hallway for the next four hours waiting for something to happen.

At about 10:30 P.M., Douglas received a phone call. DaRosa managed to eavesdrop on a conversation Douglas was having with a person he continued referring to as Debbie. Douglas was telling her that he had not seen Robin since midnight the preceding Saturday, when she left his house on the way to see someone named Joe. Douglas urged Debbie to call Robin's boyfriend and ask him to look in her black address book to see if there was a number for "Joe in Charlestown."

When the conversation ended, DaRosa knocked. Douglas appeared wearing a T-shirt and gray slacks, standing in his stocking feet. There was a bandage about three inches square over his left temple. When the detective asked, "Mr. Douglas, could I ask you a few questions with reference to a missing person, Robin Nadine Benedict?" Douglas ushered him in without protest.

He inquired how DaRosa had found him, but the detective ignored this question and began surveying the room. There was a briefcase on the floor and papers spread all over the bed. Keys and loose change had been dumped on the dresser. He wandered into the bathroom and looked into the shower stall. He peered into closets and under the bed. He poked audaciously through the contents of Douglas's suitcase. There was no trace of the missing girl.

DaRosa turned to Douglas and asked, "Do you know Robin Benedict?" Douglas replied, "Yes, I do."

Robin, he said, had done some work for him. The last time he had seen her was the preceding Saturday night at his home in Sharon. She had arrived at about 10:45 and they sat for a while, viewing slides of cell cultures.

"When she arrived at your home . . . were your wife and family there?" DaRosa asked.

"I was alone," Douglas replied. "The rest of the family were in New Hampshire."

Robin, Douglas said, had left around midnight on her way to Charlestown to see someone named Joe. Douglas claimed not to know who this was.

"Do you know Robin's boyfriend, Clarence Rogers?" DaRosa asked.

"No, I do not," Douglas replied. "But I have heard of him through Robin."

Douglas went on to explain that J.R. was a pimp who had several girls working for him. Robin, he knew for a fact, was a prostitute. She had a friend named Debbie, also known as Debbie the Indian, who had a little boy and lived somewhere in Randolph. Debbie's real name was Savitry Bisram. Nadine, which was Robin's working name, Debbie, and a couple of their friends, Pam and Lorna, all worked out of a place called Good Time Charlie's, in Boston. Once when Robin was charged with prostitution, he had gone to court with her mother and father. He was a "friend of the family," he said. He had met the Benedicts when Robin had been arrested by a Boston vice detective named Billy Dwyer. This Dwyer, Douglas claimed, was his "friend."

"Did you ever go out with Robin?" DaRosa asked.

"Only on a business basis," Douglas insisted.

A moment later, however, when the detective asked him if he had ever tried to get Robin to go to St. Thomas with him, he conceded that he had but that he had "changed his mind" about going with her.

"Bill," DaRosa asked more familiarly, "where did you get that injury on your forehead? The bandage looks new."

"I hit myself on a cabinet door before leaving for Washington yesterday," Douglas explained.

"Is it a bad bruise?" DaRosa queried.

"No," came the terse reply.

After questioning Douglas for about an hour and a half, DaRosa returned to his own room and called his client with a report. J.R. Rogers seemed alarmed by the bandage over Douglas's eye, and he instructed DaRosa to keep leaning on him to see if he could learn anything else. So around midnight, the detective returned to Douglas's room and knocked on the door, rousing the suspect from his sleep.

"Are you sure that you injured your head at home?" DaRosa persisted.

"What do you mean?" Douglas replied.

"You told me that you hit your head on the cabinet door at home in your kitchen, didn't you?"

"No, you must have misunderstood me," Douglas corrected. "I was almost robbed at the Amtrak Station in Washington. They tried to steal my briefcase, and in the struggle I was hit on the head by the briefcase."

"Did you notify the police?" DaRosa asked.

"Yes."

"Are you sure that you did not have an argument with Robin before she left your house?" DaRosa persisted.

"Yes, I'm sure. My wife was there when she left the house at midnight."

Simple drowsiness could not explain the inconsistencies in this new account. Douglas had previously insisted that his family was not at home when Robin arrived. Now he was saying that his wife had been around at midnight when Robin left the house. It was possible, of course, that Mrs. Douglas had come home during the hour when Robin had been there and that he had simply failed to mention it. There was no way, however, that his new account of the head wound could be reconciled with the first. If it was true that he been assaulted by thugs, he would certainly have recalled it when DaRosa first inquired about the bandage.

DaRosa wanted one more shot at questioning Douglas and extracted from him a promise to meet for coffee the next morning. So on Wednesday, March 9, a little before 8:00 A.M., the detective joined the professor in the dining room and renewed his inquiry on behalf of J.R. Rogers, who was still convinced that Douglas had somehow spirited Robin away. Once again DaRosa asked Douglas if he had invited Robin to go to St. Thomas with him. This time Douglas replied, "Yes, but she refused to go."

"Are you going to St. Thomas Island from here?" the detective asked.

"No, I'm going home from here," Douglas said, adding that he would be leaving by train.

"Is Robin anywhere in Washington—maybe in another hotel?" DaRosa pressed.

Douglas had become wary.

"Robin did not know that I was coming to Washington, and I came here alone," he replied. "Are you charging me with anything to do with the disappearance of Robin?"

DaRosa assured him that these questions were routine, then excused himself at the next graceful juncture, saying he had to get back to Boston. Instead, he continued trailing Douglas, who took the elevator up to a conference room on the mezzanine. When that meeting broke up, at a quarter of two, DaRosa followed his quarry—not to the train station, as he had indicated, but to the airport, where he caught a New York Air commuter flight to Boston. Agent Smith, who picked up the surveillance at the other end, observed Douglas being met by a woman—presumably his wife. Shortly after that, however, the Central Secret Service Bureau lost the trail.

THAT SAME EVENING at about eight, the Benedicts were clearing the dinner table when the telephone rang. John answered. A man identifying himself as Robin's "insurance agent" said he needed to talk to her. Did the family know where she could be reached? Benedict was suspicious. It had been a whole week since he had heard from Robin. She had visited the preceding Wednesday, the night she had let Rhonda try on her brown jacket. The following Friday and Saturday, her mother had left messages inviting her home to see Casper, the family's new poodle puppy. She did not get back to them. Finally Rhonda had called the Malden house and gotten the service. She left a message saying, "Cut the shit and answer the phone." But even that hadn't roused a reply. Since the weekend, John and Shirley Benedict had felt an uneasiness which was gradually turning to dread.

"Well, I haven't seen her since Wednesday," John Benedict replied. He declined to say more. The caller told him he should call a number in Malden. When Benedict dialed it, Clarence Rogers answered.

"Where's Robin?" John Benedict asked curtly. There was still considerable strain between him and J.R. Rogers.

"She's been missing for three days," J.R. replied. And he began to cry.

When Junie recovered his composure, he explained how he had hired the detectives to look for Robin. The supposed insurance agent was actually his private investigator. Rogers then called DaRosa and gave him permission to tell Benedict about his encounter with William Douglas in Washington, D.C.

Benedict was still absorbing this briefing when he received another call—this one from Douglas himself. Benedict had seen the professor on only two occasions—at the court appearance and the day they moved Robin out of 280 Commonwealth Avenue. Douglas, however, seemed to regard him as an old friend. He had heard Robin was missing, he said. She had been at his house the night of March 5 but had left at about a quarter of twelve. Then he added cryptically that Robin had told him that if anything happened to her, he should tell her father to take her jewels and furs from the house at 8 Cliff Street. She didn't want Clarence to get them.

While Douglas was explaining this, Benedict recalled something that DaRosa had told him.

"Do you have a mark on your head, a bruise or something?" he asked Douglas.

"No," Douglas replied. "I don't."

John Benedict didn't know what to make of these conversations. Junie seemed to be pointing the finger at Douglas, and Douglas, in turn, seemed to be implicating Junie. Benedict felt he should tell this to someone in authority. The first person who came to mind was Bill Dwyer. As far as the Benedicts could tell, Robin seemed to have enjoyed an amiable, even cozy, relationship with the detective. The day they all met at court, Shirley had seen her playing with Dwyer's collar. Dwyer had shown enough concern about Robin to tell the Benedicts that if they ever wanted to call him, they should feel free to do so.

That night John Benedict called Bill Dwyer. But the detective, who appeared to have forgotten his earlier offers of assistance, seemed distracted. When Benedict told him Robin was missing, he replied, "I hardly knew your daughter." He advised Benedict to report Robin missing in the appropriate jurisdiction, which seemed to be Malden.

No sooner had Benedict called police headquarters the following morning than he found himself lost in red tape. The officer on duty informed him that because the girl was twenty-one and not a dependent, she could not technically be considered a missing person for another forty-eight hours. Benedict called someone he knew in the Methuen police, who in turn called Malden and applied pressure through private channels. By Friday afternoon, an alert went out to the New England states.

Benedict was stung by this indifference. Would the police have been so casual had they not known she was living with a black man? They had apparently written her off as a lowlife. Robin needed an advocate, someone who could impress upon the powers that be what a sweet and beautiful girl she was. Benedict was not a shrewd man in many respects, but some visceral instinct told him that Robin's beauty was bound to attract notice. And if he could just make them see her face—really *see her face*—they would realize she was somebody's daughter.

He had extra prints of the photo he had taken in August, a shot he had snapped with eerie prescience at the thought of losing her. And that weekend he set out distributing copies to everyone he could think of. To Robbie's trucker friends and to paramedics, people who covered a lot of territory and could broadcast the photo as widely as possible. On Sunday morning he took the portrait to Channel 7 in Boston. The weekend staff agreed that this was a "neat-lookin' lady" and that night WNEV ran the picture with a forty-five-second voice-over asking anyone who had seen Robin Nadine Benedict to please contact the Malden police.

The following morning, Monday, March 14, Paul Landry got a call at the barracks from James O'Donnell, a trooper who happened to have been at the Wrentham District Court, west of Foxboro, when he overheard a conversation between two police officers about a girl who had been reported missing on the evening news. He knew of Landry's teletype query and thought this lead might be worth checking. Without a name there was not much to go on, but Landry called the six major Boston and Rhode Island stations as well as two UHF stations to see if they had broadcast anything about a missing girl. No one could place her.

Several hours later, however, Landry got a call back from the news director of Channel 7 to confirm that he had, in fact, run a report on the six o'clock broadcast about a missing girl from Malden. Landry took down the particulars, but he did not see any logical connection to the Mansfield rest area. Malden was twenty miles to the north. As it happened, however, he knew someone in the Malden PD, a vice detective named Charlie Borstel. The two had gone to high school together in North Cambridge. Landry called Borstel and asked if he knew anything about a girl named Benedict. Borstel, an amiable St. Bernard of a man, recalled obligingly that he had sent out an alert the preceding week. Landry was perplexed. He hadn't seen any reports about a missing girl. Borstel's message, he discovered, had gone out only as a stolen-car report on a 1982 Toyota.

A week ago Monday, Borstel went on to explain, a fellow named Clarence Rogers had come into headquarters to report his girlfriend missing. The Benedict girl, he later discovered, was possibly working for Rogers as a prostitute. She had disappeared March 5 after going to visit someone in Sharon.

Landry snapped alert. If Benedict had been in Sharon the night of March 5, then that placed her only five miles north of Mansfield, where the bloody clothing was found the following morning. Landry described the barrel items to Borstel, asking him if he had any idea what the Benedict girl had been wearing the night she disappeared. When Rogers had last seen her on Saturday afternoon, Borstel recalled, she had on a beige shirt and slacks, and a tan jacket.

The jacket was the galvanizing discovery. Word of it moved like a current through the growing society of interested parties. Borstel called the Central Secret Service Bureau, which called J.R. Rogers, who passed the news along to John Benedict. Late that afternoon, Paul Landry took a call from Jack DaRosa of the CSSB wanting information about certain bloody items found in a barrel along Route 95.

Landry, who could hardly suppress a chuckle when he heard the name Central Secret Service Bureau, told DaRosa that he would have to see his credentials. The detective agreed to come to the Foxboro barracks later that afternoon. Before he could arrive, however, a tall, dark man identifying himself as John Benedict asked to see Landry. Benedict, who was visibly upset, handed the trooper a photo of a dark-haired girl. He had heard, he said, that a brown blazer had been found. His missing daughter, Robin Nadine Benedict, had one matching that description. Landry found it odd that John Benedict had such specific knowledge of his daughter's clothing if she was no longer living at home. Benedict assured him that he remembered the brown jacket very well. Robin had let her sister Rhonda try it on during her last visit home, on Wednesday, March 2.

While they were talking, Jack DaRosa and Jim Smith arrived. Landry introduced Benedict to the detectives and ushered all three men into the guardroom for questioning. At Landry's request, DaRosa explained how his client, J.R. Rogers, had strong suspicions that one Professor William Douglas of Sharon was responsible for the disappearance of Robin Benedict. DaRosa had followed Douglas to Washington, D.C., where he had found the professor with a head wound. He claimed to have been mugged at the train station in Washington, D.C., an attack which he supposedly reported to the police, but DaRosa had since checked with the Washington PD, and it had no record of it.

Although Central Secret Service Bureau was technically pursuing Professor William Douglas, the detectives seemed to have reservations about their own client and were openly speculating that he was a pimp. Landry cast an uneasy glance toward John Benedict. But Benedict just sat and listened. How, Landry wondered, could a guy who looked so completely normal have a daughter who was a hooker?

Landry had offered to take Benedict and the detectives to state police headquarters in Boston to look at the jacket. Before leaving the barracks, he called J.R. Rogers and asked him to meet them at 1010 Commonwealth Avenue. Remembering the strong scent on the corduroy jacket, Landry asked him to bring along all of Robin's perfumes sealed in separate sandwich bags.

When Rogers met the company on the sidewalk outside headquarters, he seemed nervous in the presence of John Benedict. But as far as Landry could tell, Benedict displayed no particular hostility toward J.R. Attempting to prepare Benedict for what might be coming, Landry explained, as they made their way to the third floor, that the state chemist had found a dark brown human hair lodged between the head and the shaft of the hammer. This probably meant nothing, he hastened to reassure Benedict. But, in fact, there was nothing at all comforting about this new revelation that the hammer could now be linked to a human with brunette hair. The only thing which could dispel the mounting suspicion that Robin Benedict had come to harm was for her father to look at the jacket and say that he had never seen it.

When the chemist came into the lab carrying the jacket, Benedict began to cry. J.R. Rogers lost his composure, shouting, "No! No! That's hers. No!" And while a handful of curious technicians looked on, he tried to flee the room. Landry caught him and steered him back inside the lab.

"Take it easy," he said. "How do you know it is her jacket?"

"I'm positive it's her jacket," Rogers replied. He had bought it for her at Lord & Taylor the preceding November.

Landry asked him if he could identify the perfume which even now rose in a cloying cloud from the corduroy. It was Molinard de Molinard, Rogers replied, the only fragrance Robin ever wore. He had bought it for her at Filene's sometime between October and December of 1982.

Landry frankly didn't trust Rogers and decided it was time to put Rogers's grieving-boyfriend number to the test. He took J.R. downstairs to a room off the Communications Section to interrogate him. He did not invite John Benedict to come along, because he figured the revelations might be too painful. DaRosa and Smith, however, were allowed to stay. Landry knew this wasn't proper. They weren't state police, and, even worse, they were in Rogers's own hire. But they seemed to be as skeptical of J.R. as he was.

Landry read Rogers his rights and then asked point-blank what he had done with Robin Benedict's body.

J.R. did not seem rattled. He replied softly that he hadn't killed her. They had never even fought.

Why, Landry asked, had he hired private detectives?

"Because I love her," Rogers explained in the same even, low voice. "We were planning to be married."

At Landry's urging, he described how he had met Robin around two years ago through a friend, Raymond Clayborn. They dated for a while, then lived together in Natick before moving to Malden. Robin worked in a bar called Good Time Charlie's. She also did illustrations for a Dr. William Douglas, of Sharon, with whom, J.R. observed obliquely, "there may have been some sex involved."

When pressed on this point, J.R. apparently realized that it was in his best interest to level about Robin's professional life, if for no other reason than to shift the focus of inquiry from himself to where he felt it more properly belonged. He conceded that during the spring of 1982 Robin had been working as a prostitute, using the street name Nadine. In April or May she had been working a bar named Good Time Charlie's, where she picked up William Douglas. For about a month after that, they saw each other every night. Douglas would meet Robin around 2:30 to 3:30 A.M. He wanted to be the last one to see her. The amount of time he demanded kept increasing. He began taking her to plays and concerts. For every moment of these outings he was "on the clock" at the rate of $50 an hour.

Douglas had become "obsessed" with Robin, Rogers continued. There were times when she came out of her apartments with other dates and would see Douglas parked nearby. He had apparently decided that if he couldn't be with her, neither could anyone else, and he began, J.R. suspected, calling the vice squad with tips. It got so that whenever Robin showed up at one of her apartments, the Boston PD would arrive. The pressure had become so intense that she had to move out of her two trick pads.

Almost daily, Douglas sent Robin some card or love letter. For her birthday, in July, he had given her a Panasonic answering machine so that she would always be able to receive his messages. The machine had come with a beeper to allow her to pick up her messages by phoning home. Several times when Robin was at home, she had heard the machine click on without warning. This led Rogers to suspect that Douglas had kept a duplicate beeper and was phoning in for Robin's messages. Robin finally gave up on machines and got an answering service. She did not give William Douglas that number.

By the beginning of 1983 Robin had gotten fed up with the letters and phone calls and was trying to break the relationship off. Around the first of March she had gone to the Ellis Nursing Home in Norwood with the intent of talking to Douglas's wife. Learning that Mrs. Douglas was not at work, Robin called her later in Sharon and told her that Bill kept wanting to see her but that she did not want to see him. Mrs. Douglas said okay. Nothing more.

Although Rogers had originally told Jack DaRosa that Robin had gone out to the Douglas home on March 5 to pick up tax forms, he now amended his explanation to suggest that she had made the trip to Sharon to tell Douglas she did not want to see him again.

Robin seemed "quite happy" the afternoon when she disappeared, J.R. recalled. He left while she was still dressing and went to visit a friend, a car salesman, who lived near the Fenway. He had stayed there until about 8:30 P.M., then came home and watched television for the rest of the evening. Shortly after midnight, the answering service called and gave him two messages. The first, which had come in around 10:00 P.M., was for Robin from a "Joe in Charlestown." It said that Robin had been invited to a party from 10:00 P.M. Saturday to 6:00 P.M. Sunday. The second, time-stamped 11:45 P.M., was for "J.R. from Robin." It indicated that she had left Sharon and was on her way to "Joe's in Charlestown." J.R. professed not to know who "Joe" was.

For the rest of the night, Robin didn't get in touch with him—which, he said, was not her practice. She called him and left messages whenever she was going to see or was leaving a client. The next day, the answering service took a call at 3:13 P.M. It was from "Robin to J.R." and said, "Will be at John's at Longfellow." He became increasingly upset, he said, when he did not hear from her for the rest of the day. The following morning he hired the detectives to find her.

J.R.'s account neatly begged the question of whether he was or was not Robin's pimp. Landry had checked his criminal record and found he had never been charged with pimping. His rap sheet showed only an arrest for unarmed robbery and the conviction for receiving stolen credit cards. There was also a warrant outstanding for a traffic violation. Landry, however, told J.R. he wouldn't arrest him. By cutting Rogers a break, he calculated, he could build some rapport and keep him talking. He was also curious to see if J.R. was reliable. As the interview drew to a close, Landry sent J.R. off to the courthouse in Weston with instructions to turn himself in and pay his traffic fine.

THREE INVESTIGATIONS were now under way. Despite the growing number of interested parties, Landry was under the impression that the Benedict matter was still a secret, a situation he wanted to preserve. The girl might have been reported missing in Malden, but her bloody jacket had been found in his jurisdiction. Landry sensed that he might be onto something big, and he needed a little time to make sense of it all. No sooner had he returned to the barracks, however, than he received a phone call from the *Boston Herald.*

The *Herald* was cheerfully and unabashedly the city's premier scandal rag. The tabloid was a sampler of sensation trading in oddities, lotteries, and lunacies. Its reportage had become more strident than usual during the spring of 1983 as the paper was fighting for its life. This struggle was the culmination of a curious evolution. The earliest incarnation of the *Herald* had been a rock-ribbed Republican paper catering mainly to the interests of State Street financiers. Its political nemesis was the *Boston Globe,* a progressive Democratic paper which championed the interests of the Irish Catholic working class. During the mid-1950s, the two papers were fairly evenly paired rivals, matching each other ad for ad, edition for edition. The *Globe* was the more congenial of the two, its owner and patriarch, Charles H. Taylor, proclaiming, "My aim has been to make the *Globe* a cheerful, attractive, and useful newspaper that would enter the home as a kindly, helpful friend of the family."

By the early sixties, however, this banality had given away to bite. The *Globe* won its first Pulitzer and earned a following for its hard investigative reporting. Over the next five years it gradually surpassed the *Herald* in suburban circulation and by the early 1970s had emerged preeminent, not only in Boston but throughout New England. The enfeebled *Herald* was bought by the Hearst Corporation, which hoped to revive the paper by switching its format, from a tabloid to a broadside. Still, circulation continued to drop.

In the summer of 1981 Hearst took radical steps to fatten the *Herald* for sale. The paper was restored to a tabloid format and staffed with energetic, if underpaid, recruits who were exhorted by their embattled editors to wage guerrilla warfare with the *Globe.* The one area in which they could hope to best the competition was crime reporting. Not that the *Globe* didn't have the resources to cover these stories; it just seemed to consider them beneath its dignity. *Herald* reporters, unfettered by such pretensions, got down and dirty with cops who frequented a working-class bar called J. J. Foley's, located just around the corner from the newsroom. They were dispatched to cover national criminal trials, which were reported and showcased on the grand scale of morality plays. The characters were invariably very good or very bad, and those exaggerated attributes were trumpeted daily in bold, alliterative headlines like "Hinck's Shrink Stinks" and "Claus Is a Louse."

The front page took a nastier turn in December of 1982 when the *Herald* was purchased by the Australian press lord Rupert Murdoch. Recast in the image of Murdoch's sensational *New York Post,* it abandoned its clever banners for slasher heads like "Coed Held in Kinky Sex Slaying." Murdoch cut his news staff to the bone, insisting that the beleaguered few who remained in the newsroom accelerate their campaign against the *Globe.* Outmanned and outgunned, the survivors scrambled for tales of woe. The medical exploits of "Cancer Baby" and "Little Liver Girl" washed across the pages in waves of bathos.

And so when John Benedict walked into the newsroom a little before noon on March 14, bearing photos of his missing daughter, it quickened the pulse of the assistant managing editor, Charlie O'Brien.

Missing girls were one of the *Herald*'s staples. There was a formula for dealing with these creatures. They were invariably idealized. There was a joke around the newsroom that a girl who had more than one eye was a "beauty." If she could spell her name, she was a "coed." O'Brien was shrewd enough to know that he had before him a classic of the genre, a distraught father in search of a pretty daughter. A missing beauty.

There happened to be no crime reporters in the newsroom, so O'Brien led John Benedict over to the cubicle of Shelly Murphy, a blond, blue-eyed imp in her early twenties who had been one of the few new staffers hired that spring. Murphy was a consumer affairs writer who usually had her hands full with a column that ran seven days a week. But whenever the city desk was short a body, as it often was, she would be assigned to news.

"We don't have anyone here to interview this guy," O'Brien told her. "Do you mind taking the story?"

Murphy could see that O'Brien had taken a special interest in this one. When Benedict handed her the photo, she could see why. The missing girl's face, with its playful, haunting expression, was almost certain to occupy most of the next day's front page. She laid her column aside and asked Benedict to take a seat.

The portrait Benedict painted of his daughter was a glowing one. She was a commercial artist who, he claimed, had graduated from the Rhode Island School of Design. She was also a good, dutiful daughter, who kept in touch with her family. She had last been seen at the home of a professor from Tufts University.

"What was she doing there?" Murphy asked.

"She dropped papers off," Benedict replied. "She was supposed to get there earlier but didn't make it till late at night."

This late-night errand struck Murphy a little odd. Before she could pursue it, however, Benedict received a telephone call. When he got off the line, he seemed worried. The police, he told Murphy, had found clothes matching the description of those Robin was wearing the night she disappeared. Benedict asked directions to the state police barracks in Foxboro, then hurried out.

Before leaving, Benedict had given Murphy the number of Robin's boyfriend, one J.R. Rogers. Murphy dialed his number and found him eager to talk. Rogers gave her essentially the same story with one exception. Whereas John Benedict seemed reluctant to point the finger of suspicion at anyone, Rogers clearly suspected she had come to harm at the hands of a certain Dr. William Douglas.

Murphy was convinced she was not getting the straight story on Robin Benedict from either of these two men. The late-night visit still bothered her. Robin must be into drugs or something equally shady. J.R. Rogers had given her the telephone number of his private detective, so she gave DaRosa a call. DaRosa also seemed happy to talk and gave Murphy the highlights of his interview with Douglas in Washington, D.C. When she asked if Robin was a prostitute, he replied thoughtfully, "All of her girlfriends are prostitutes. I would say she was a prostitute."

Murphy was not sure how Charlie O'Brien was going to take this. He was obviously counting on this story and had been running over to her desk all afternoon asking her how it was coming. Now she had to tell him that his missing beauty was probably a missing prostitute. To her surprise, however, O'Brien seemed delighted. The weirder the tale got, in fact, the more he seemed to love it. First a solicitous father and his lovely lost daughter—now a possible pimp and a midnight rendezvous with a scientist in the suburbs. He told her to keep working leads.

At about four o'clock Murphy made her way out of Boston with a throng of rush-hour commuters returning home to Norfolk County. Arriving in Sharon, she wound her way through the pine hills to Sandy Ridge Circle. Pulling into the cul-de-sac, she parked in front of No. 38, walked up the drive, and knocked on the door. A woman in a white uniform answered. Murphy introduced herself as a *Herald* reporter and explained that she was doing a story on a young woman named Robin Benedict. The woman, who she assumed was Mrs. Douglas, remained silent.

"Well, do you know Robin Benedict?" Murphy pressed.

"No, I don't know her," the woman said. She began to shut the door when Murphy interjected, "Well, her boyfriend says that Robin called you and told you to have your husband stop callin' her. Isn't that true?"

"No," the woman insisted. "I don't know anything about it."

With that, she shut the door.

MURPHY returned to the newsroom and was preparing to tell Charlie O'Brien she had struck out when she received a call from William Douglas.

"Oh, I'm so glad you called me back," she bubbled gratefully.

When she inquired how he knew Robin Benedict, he told her that he had advertised for the services of a free-lance artist and that she had answered the ad.

"Did she always drop off her artwork that late?" Murphy asked.

"Not so much at that hour," Douglas replied. On the day in question, he added, she had called several times and was very disturbed and said she'd like to just get away for a couple of weeks.

Murphy said she had heard that he had been harassing Robin with phone calls.

"That's just absolutely not true," Douglas replied indignantly.

"Look," she said at last. "She wasn't at your house deliverin' artwork, was she? There's more to this, isn't there?"

Douglas hesitated.

"Well, I can't really tell you . . . I'm kinda afraid of her boyfriend. He's kind of tough . . . I wouldn't want it to get back to him that I told you what's goin' on here . . ."

"What is it?" Murphy probed. "Prostitution?"

"Yes," came the reply.

"Is that why she was at your house?" Murphy pressed. "Because she's a prostitute?"

"No."

"You mean you never had anything to do with her being a prostitute?"

"Oh, I was telling the truth," Douglas hastened to assure her. "She [did] artwork for me."

Murphy started to laugh.

"No, really," he insisted. "I tried to help her. I think she's a very nice girl."

The reason she had showed up so late the night of March 5, Douglas went on to explain, was that she had been having trouble with her boyfriend. It wouldn't be surprising, he intimated, if J.R. was now trying to blame him for Robin's disappearance.

"So what are you saying?" she asked. "That this is a setup?"

"Well, I don't know," he replied. "What do you think?"

"Well . . . ," Murphy said matter-of-factly, ". . . it doesn't look too

good, does it? Her boyfriend says you're obsessed by her. . . . You gotta
bump on your head. . . . Doesn't look too good to me, you know."

"Well, keep in touch," Douglas concluded pleasantly. "And let me
know if you find out anything."

It was going on 7:00 P.M., and Murphy was running up against the
deadline for edition. Charlie O'Brien was pressing her to get a third
confirmation on the prostitution business. She called a source in Boston
Vice, who replied, "I know exactly who you're talking about. Her father
was here with pictures lookin' for [her]."

"Oh!" Murphy exclaimed. "So her father knows she's a prostitute?"

"Yeah," the source replied. "He's been in court with her before."

There was now no doubt in Murphy's mind that Robin Benedict was
a hooker. But the third confirmation did not set her mind at ease. John
Benedict had struck her as a decent fellow. The fact that he had apparently misrepresented his daughter to her seemed less deceitful than desperate. The poor man was wandering around Boston wearing the em-
peror's new clothes. If the media had the power to create illusions, it
certainly had the power to unmask the illusions of others. John Benedict
probably never guessed that a reporter, in the course of ordinary business,
was in the position to find out all of his secrets. And now he was about
to be stripped naked before the world.

When O'Brien came around for that third confirmation, she appealed
to him, "She's still a missing kid. And she's his kid. Do we have to say
she's a prostitute?"

"Shelly," he explained, "you feel bad about a lot of things. But it's true.
. . . If it was totally irrelevant to the story, that would be one thing, but
it doesn't appear to be."

Murphy knew he was right. Even as she was framing her fragments into
a missing-prostitute story, however, she heard O'Brien—out of sight,
beyond the partition of her cubicle—arguing with his own superiors. The
executive editor had been led to expect a missing beauty whose face could
run on the cover accompanied by the story of a father's anguish. He now
seemed reluctant to let the ideal be sullied by a reporter's sordid discoveries. O'Brien argued that, like it or not, it had become a "prostitute
disappeared—last seen at doctor's house" story. As the debate wore on,
Robin Benedict slipped irretrievably from the cover to page seven.

With only minutes to deadline, Murphy was working frantically, cutting, rewriting, and recasting the lead to suit the prevailing whim of the
editors. The story which finally reached the copydesk was a compromise
hammered out to placate both camps. Running under the head "Distraught Father Hunts Daughter," it read:

A distraught Methuen father yesterday launched a search for his 21-year-old daughter, who disappeared without a trace ten days ago.

"Her disappearance is shrouded in mystery," the account continued, on a darker tack.

Police sources working on the case said the missing girl is a prostitute, and was at the home of Dr. William Douglas of 28 Sandy Road, Sharon the night before she was reported missing.
[A] blood-stained corduroy jacket found on Rte 95 in Mansfield, next to Sharon, was identified as Benedict's yesterday by her live-in boyfriend of 1 1/2 years, Clarence "J.R." Rogers—described by police sources working on the case as a pimp.

At about seven the following morning, John Benedict went out to the Quick Stop in Methuen to pick up the *Herald.* When he returned home, Shirley could tell from his face that he was angry. He placed a call to Trooper Landry asking who these "police sources" were. Landry assured him that he hadn't said anything to the media. But he, in turn, was dismayed that the *Herald* had gotten so quickly into the heart of the matter. He called Shelly Murphy.

"You are so irresponsible," he berated her. "How could you write that story, saying that about that poor father? Do you know what you've done to that family? They're devastated."

"I'm sorry," Murphy replied. "But can you tell me that it's not true?"

No sooner had she deflected this harangue than she received another call from John Benedict.

"How could you use that!" he charged angrily. "I thought you were a nice person. What kind of person are you?"

"Look, I am sorry," Murphy returned. "I really feel bad. I didn't want to use it. But I got that from three sources."

"So if three sources say you're a prostitute, does that make you one?" Benedict retorted.

By now Murphy was losing patience with the hypocrisy which seemed to pervade this affair.

"Well, I haven't been to court, Mr. Benedict. [From] what I've been told, this is no surprise to you. You didn't just learn this from reading it in the paper."

Benedict hung up.

Murphy was recovering from this new assault when she got a third call, from William Douglas.

"Good story," he commended her. "You were fair and very accurate.

I just want to let you know that I heard the Benedict family is going to sue you. And I just wanted to let you know that I'll stand by you and say, 'That's the truth. She was a prostitute.' "

He had, he said, another story he wanted to discuss with her. Murphy asked if it had anything to do with the Benedict case.

"No," he replied. "I'm having some problems at Tufts with my job."

"Well, what is it?" she asked.

"I can't say," he replied. "I'll just have to think this over. I'm not sure I'm ready to talk, but if I am, I'll talk to you. . . . Could we meet on your day off or after work?"

Shelly said she would check with her editor and get back to him. She took this up with the desk, but by now Robin Benedict had been submerged in the flux of fresh sob stories.

"No," the editor on duty told her. "The guy sounds like a nut. Why don't you just stay away from him."

THE DISTRICT ATTORNEY

WHEN William Delahunt, the Norfolk County district attorney, arrived at his office in Dedham on Tuesday morning, March 15, he found on his desk a clipping from the *Boston Herald* regarding a girl—a very pretty girl judging from her photograph—who had disappeared in Sharon. Although she had apparently dropped out of sight ten days earlier, he'd heard nothing about it. He inquired of his assistants; none of them knew anything either. The *Herald* mentioned "police sources." If there was a case of this apparent stature being investigated in his own county, he should know about it. It was embarrassing to learn about this sort of thing through the media.

Delahunt was very sensitive to media. He was first and foremost a politician. However, unlike the pugnacious Irish pols who had historically dominated the district attorney's offices in the four counties encompassing Boston, Delahunt was of a new, more refined generation of suburban prosecutor. He was a handsome man, tall, perennially youthful, with casually cropped silver hair that framed a set of centurion features. Elected to the state senate in the early seventies, he had been hailed as a rising star. Upon meeting him, people were flattered to be admitted to his charmed presence. He had the inestimable political gift, according to one intimate, of being whatever his listeners wanted him to be. A foe of abortion, he was nonetheless a favorite of pro-choice advocates, who found him "reasonable." A law-and-order man, he was on drinking terms with the ACLU. The media gravitated to him for a witty quote or an attractive headshot on the evening news.

Nothing in his style or appearance suggested the hack. Yet he was completely attuned to the political protocol of Boston, which was in essence an overheated hamlet occupied by old friends who stayed in business by doing each other favors. Among the tribe of Boston Irish, Bill Delahunt cut a flamboyant figure. Once, it was said, when he and a couple of drinking cronies were being baited by a carload of thugs, he fired a pistol into the street. Though Delahunt sturdily denied that episode, it became part of his legend.

Delahunt took over the post of district attorney in 1976, when his predecessor resigned in midterm, under a hint of scandal. The new DA proved a conscientious reformer. Until that time the Norfolk office, like others throughout Massachusetts, had been staffed by part-time prosecutors. Insisting that this system created potential conflicts of interest, Delahunt assembled a staff of full-time assistants of a disciplined, tenacious character curiously unlike his own. Delahunt never tried cases himself. Instead, he parceled them out to this carefully picked staff. That cadre included a contingent of "pit bulls"—indefatigable old warriors who, while lacking finesse, rammed through convictions on stamina. More significantly, it included a handful of technicians trained to wrestle with the abstractions of white-collar crime and circumstantial cases. One of these was John Payton Kivlan.

Kivlan was a thin, taciturn man with an emotionless gaze. He did not socialize much with other members of the DA's staff but lived a quiet, semireclusive life with his wife and two daughters on a rural Norfolk County estate. During the early part of the century, Kivlan's grandfather had made a sizable fortune manufacturing glass preserving jars but lost it all with the arrival of tin cans. As a charm against the fickleness of fortune, John Kivlan displayed an ostentatious austerity.

He had a dark blue suit, his "lucky suit," which he wore on important trial days, but most of the time he preferred shark gray attire with few adornments. Each day, without fail, he walked into the office carrying a brown lunch sack which contained a small sandwich—either tuna fish or egg salad on dark bread. It was cut into neat halves, both wrapped meticulously in cellophane. On Fridays he brought a can of sardines.

So unyielding was John Kivlan's personal code of honor that he was known, with good-natured derision, as Johnny America. It was said that he was reluctant to borrow a quarter, because it placed him in a lender's debt. He made it a habit to be in debt to no one, a trait which set him apart from the fraternity of favors which governed Boston politics.

Many of these odd ways he had learned from his first boss, the former Middlesex County district attorney John Droney. Although Droney had been an intimate of John Kennedy, he stayed aloof from machine politics.

If you were his friend, it was said, he was less inclined to do you a favor than if you were a stranger. Droney kept those who tried to lean on him in check by threatening to call them before a grand jury. He was beholden to no one.

When Droney took ill in the late seventies, his office fell into a state of confusion. Kivlan showed up, without the endorsement of any political patron, on the doorstep of Norfolk County, looking for a job. Delahunt had reservations. Kivlan's reputation was not that of a dazzling trial attorney. Far from exciting, his style was flat and sometimes monotonous. Yet he had an impressive record of public corruption convictions in Middlesex. The DA hired him to fill out his new white-collar crime unit, and three years later, when Kivlan managed to get a conviction in a notoriously convoluted and celebrated insurance fraud case, Delahunt crowed that his young ADA might be "the best prosecutor in the Commonwealth."

Kivlan was particularly good at putting together circumstantial cases. His tolerance for minutiae seemed limitless. He attacked each new prosecution with Jesuitical zeal. What drove him was not clear. It did not appear to be personal ambition. Certainly not political ambition. He actively shunned the press. His conviction, rather, was that of one who revered the law as though it were some earthly edition of the universal order. Defendants, by the very fact that they found themselves in the compromising position of being charged with crimes, were a threat to this order. An arrest aroused in Kivlan an almost involuntary instinct to pursue. It was natural, then, that Delahunt, confronted with the *Herald*'s perplexing account of the disappearance of Robin Benedict, would assign the matter to someone with a proclivity for sorting out chaotic details. He handed the clipping to Kivlan, who had dropped by to confer on another matter, and said, "Why don't you look into this?"

Kivlan returned to his own office, a room he shared with two other assistants on the attic floor of an old frame house two blocks away. The Gray House, as it was known, caught the spillover from the central office. It was more shabbily appointed than the main facility, its chief drawbacks being poor ventilation and a gloom that even the spring sunshine could not dispel. Kivlan pulled out the clip and read it in the dim light.

It occurred to him, as he digested this perplexing account, that Benedict's disappearance might be linked to those of five other girls, all of whom had been found murdered along or near Route 95 over the past four years. There had been a couple of hitchhikers from Lincoln, Rhode Island. Another girl who had been found in northern Worcester, and still another in southern Bristol County. In November of 1981 Kivlan had been called out to a sandpit near Sharon to check out the body of a fourteen-year-old who had been killed with three shots from a handgun. She was later identified as Patricia Harvey of Providence. The Harvey girl, like the others found along the highway, had been a prostitute. Her history and associations were so murky he could never turn up any leads. Patricia Harvey always bothered him: first, because he couldn't understand how a girl so young could find herself in a position that she'd be shot to death; and second, because her killer remained at large.

As for Benedict, it wasn't clear into whose jurisdiction she fell. She had residences in Methuen, Malden, and Boston, but she had apparently disappeared in Norfolk County. Police in one of these areas had already begun an investigation, and he needed to find out who was on the case. By afternoon he had confirmed through the captain of detectives at State Police Headquarters in Boston that it was being handled by Paul Landry, a trooper assigned to A-Troop in Foxboro.

It was highly unusual for an investigation into a criminal matter to be handled by a road trooper. This was more or less the exclusive province of a cadre of the plainclothes troopers assigned to the district attorney by the State Bureau of Investigative Services. When Delahunt first took office, he had twelve such trooper detectives at his disposal. Each of these men customarily ran his own investigations, but when the DA brought in his full-time prosecutors, he transferred control to them, setting off a long-running struggle for autonomy over cases. Delahunt finally cleaned house, ridding himself of the dissidents and reducing the trooper contingent to a core of six, most of whom had offices in the Gray House. They were under the command of Detective Lieutenant James Sharkey, a garrulous old Irishman who had kept his office in the main building next to the district attorney.

Kivlan called Sharkey that afternoon and asked him if he had ever heard of Paul Landry. Sharkey didn't recognize the name. He'd never heard him spoken of as a cowboy or a troublemaker, he said, but he would check him out with Tim O'Leary, the sergeant at Foxboro. Sharkey got back to Kivlan with a report that Landry was a "top quality guy." It bothered Sharkey that he had apparently taken off on what would later be termed "an unsupervised frolic." But Kivlan was inclined to give him the benefit of the doubt. True, it was unusual for a road trooper to keep a homicide investigation for ten days. But you could argue that, for all Landry knew, the bloody clothing had come from an accidental injury. There was, after all, no body. That afternoon, Landry was summoned to the Gray House to brief Kivlan.

, When the trooper showed up, shortly after four, he had shed his uniform and was wearing plainclothes. He appeared knowledgeable about the case and outlined the developments energetically. Kivlan liked Landry. After he left, the prosecutor called Sharkey and asked that Landry be assigned to the case. With the trooper contingent at low ebb, they were shorthanded. He could use Landry's knowledge and enthusiasm. Sharkey was not so sure this was a good idea. He was dubious of road troopers who fancied themselves detectives. They might be able to gather evidence, but they didn't know what to do with it. Landry had no investigative background. Besides, Sharkey argued, Sergeant O'Leary had told him that Landry was set to retire at the end of March, just a little over two weeks away. Kivlan offered to intervene with the state police to get Landry's retirement postponed if he could just have him for a while longer. Sharkey finally agreed to allow Landry to remain on the case, with the stipulation that he be closely supervised.

LANDRY had brought with him that afternoon Detective Charlie Borstel of the Malden PD. Borstel had taken the original report from J.R. Rogers. In light of recent developments, he had set up an appointment with Professor William Douglas for questioning. Kivlan told Borstel to keep the appointment, which was scheduled for the following morning.

On Wednesday, March 16, Douglas arrived in Malden at 8:00 A.M. He was going to work, he said, and that's why he had to come in so early. He was a little condescending, and this made Borstel ill at ease. The detective wasn't used to interviewing someone who he imagined to be so much his intellectual superior. He asked Douglas if it was all right if he took notes, and the professor said yes.

What was his relationship to Robin Benedict? Borstel asked.

Robin was a prostitute, Douglas replied matter-of-factly. She had been banned from a bar called Good Time Charlie's for soliciting on the street. Douglas admitted that he himself had been an "occasional client" of Robin's. He admitted having bought her an answering machine in the spring of 1982. "If Robin was bound and determined to continue working," Douglas explained, "at least she would not have to work the streets."

Borstel noted a Band-Aid on Douglas's left temple. How, the detective asked, had he gotten his head wound?

It was on the evening of Sunday, March 6, Douglas explained. His wife had dropped him off in Foxboro, where he had taken a bus to Logan Airport. From there he had caught a subway to South Station. He was hungry, he said, and wandered over to Kim Toy's Restaurant in nearby Chinatown for a bite to eat. There he was jumped by two men, one white and one black, who stole his briefcase and hit him over the head with a metal pipe. The injury was not so severe, however, that it prevented him from making the 10:15 P.M. train to Washington, D.C.

This account varied from earlier ones in three important respects. For the first time Douglas had admitted being one of Robin's johns. While he had told DaRosa he had left Boston from Route 128 on Monday, he was now saying he had left from South Station on Sunday night. And the Kim Toy episode was the third explanation of how he had gotten his head wound.

Borstel observed the incongruities and made a mental note to pass them along to Kivlan. Still, Professor William Douglas seemed to him a far less likely suspect than J.R. Rogers. Paul Landry shared these suspicions. Neither could shake the conviction that J.R. was a pimp who had knocked off an unruly prostitute. If Rogers had murdered her at the house in Malden, they reasoned, there might still be bloodstains or other telling clues. They had no warrant to search but devised a plan whereby one of them would keep J.R. occupied while the other wandered around the house a bit. Later that morning, the two investigators paid a visit to 8 Cliff Street.

J.R. seemed unperturbed by this surprise call. He asked Landry and Borstel if they wanted coffee, which they declined. Then, unprompted, he led them through the cellar, which was being outfitted as a small gymnasium; through the dining room, where a new hutch was being built; through the kitchen, where marble tile had just been laid; to the bedroom, where a large curving mirror had been installed over the bed. Landry searched the walk-in closets. There was no trace of Robin Benedict and no sign of foul play.

After taking leave of J.R., Borstel had another lead he wanted to check out. A friend of his, a policeman in neighboring Everett, knew a young woman named LuAnn Lussier. LuAnn lived with her brother and elderly mother, whose kitchen overlooked Benedict's driveway. During the past few weeks, LuAnn had seen workmen coming in and out of the house. She couldn't help noticing Clarence Rogers and his friends, however, because the neighborhood was not integrated, and black men stood out. Sometimes she would see Robin Benedict leave with an overnight bag and return the following morning. LuAnn had supposedly seen Robin the night she was reported missing.

LuAnn worked at a place called Pete's Donut Shop on the Everett-Malden town line. After leaving Cliff Street, Landry and Borstel dropped into Pete's see her. LuAnn was nervous and indicated she did not care to discuss the matter. The two policemen finally coaxed out a rudimentary account of how, on Friday, March 4, at a little past noon, she had seen J.R. and another black man move a brass bed, two twin mattresses, and a brown couch from the house and load them onto a Hertz truck. Rogers pulled off about dinnertime and didn't come back until around ten Saturday morning. Sometime earlier than that—LuAnn thought it was about eight-thirty—Robin had left the house wearing a tan corduroy blazer and carrying a "tote type" bag. Then she got in her car and left.

Had she seen Robin return in the evening?

No, LuAnn replied. She never saw Benedict again.

LuAnn's account seemed to confirm Rogers's claim that Robin had not returned to Cliff Street that night. Though not yet convinced of his innocence, Landry and Borstel had to concede that J.R.'s story seemed to be checking out pretty well.

SHELLY MURPHY'S missing-girl opus, meanwhile, was sending ripples into increasingly obscure inlets of Boston society. On Newbury Street, in the Back Bay, an English realtor named John Conroy read the *Herald* account the Tuesday morning it appeared and had a pang of recognition. Conroy worked for the A. F. Doyle Company, which served as agent for a landlord at 397 Beacon Street. Only two weeks earlier he had rented Robin Benedict a one-bedroom apartment in that building.

Benedict had come to him as a referral from a firm called Boston Common Realty. He had had only one, brief encounter with her when she came into the office to pick up her key. That was either March 2 or 3. She had paid the first and last month's rent—$950, mostly in $100 bills. At the time Conroy thought the thing smelled a bit. Not that she looked like a working girl. He would later describe her as "very fresh and clean and well-scrubbed" with a lovely smile. But you could never really tell. There were perfectly respectable little girls who worked for insurance companies by day and came to the Back Bay at night to do a little hooking.

Benedict had given her occupation as "research assistant" for a Dr. William Douglas of Tufts University. Her salary was listed as $18,500 a year. When Conroy phoned Tufts personnel, however, they had no record of her. He then called the Department of Anatomy and got a secretary who explained that Robin Benedict had worked for Dr. Douglas in the past on special projects but that she had never been and would never be an employee of the department. Later that day Conroy received a call from a man identifying himself as Dr. Douglas.

"You've been inquiring about Robin Benedict, who works for me," he said. "You've spoken to a new girl in my office, and she's not aware of the fact [Robin] does work for me."

Conroy's suspicions were aroused partly by the testiness of the secretary's reply, partly because Douglas confirmed the exact figure of Robin's income. In the realtor's experience, legitimate tenants usually inflated their own income, and the employer confirmed a figure that is lower. The apartment in question was also a first-floor rear apartment, which is what the hookers always asked for. Conroy passed along his reservations to his superior, who—noting that Benedict and the A. F. Doyle Company shared the same answering service—called the service to get a discreet reading on her. He was told that Robin Benedict was "a nice girl."

Whether she was a prostitute or not, Conroy thought, it was sad to see a father so desperate to find his daughter. The realtor tried to locate a number for a John Benedict at 8 Cliff Street in Malden. There was no such listing. He phoned the Malden police but was told he would have to call back on another shift. Annoyed by the indifference, he decided it would be best to take this matter to the press. Reporters seemed to be able to get the attention of the police when ordinary citizens couldn't. The following morning, he called the *Herald* and asked for Shelly Murphy.

At the time Conroy's call came in, Murphy was up against a deadline, but she was intrigued by the prospect of having another go at Professor William Douglas. To her disappointment, however, the city desk was unwilling to give her the assignment. Her first story had raised so many hackles, her editors doubted that she could continue to report the story effectively. Conroy was therefore passed along to Beth Holland, a southern reporter who specialized in sick-kid cases. Holland was currently up to her neck in the Jamie Fisk liver transplant, but she had found the Benedict case "incredibly odd" and agreed to take the call. She jotted down the particulars and, with photographer in tow, set off for the Back Bay.

At 397 Beacon she found a shabby brownstone with an arched entryway recessed between two sets of bay windows. The door to the inner foyer was locked. Holland and the photographer waited until a young man came up the walk carrying a bag of groceries. Edward Vaughn was a resident of 397 Beacon. Beth showed him the photo of Robin Benedict and asked if he recognized it. Yes, Vaughn replied. He had seen the girl. She was a graphic artist who lived on the first floor. He invited the reporter upstairs to talk to his girlfriend, Monique Cuartero, who, he said, might know more.

Cuartero also recognized the girl in the photo. She had moved in on March 5 or 6, she thought. That Saturday, Vaughn and Cuartero had been home when Benedict came running up the stairs to ask the time. The following Tuesday, they thought, they had heard someone downstairs playing flute and singing in a high voice. Holland and her photographer then went downstairs to the foyer and settled into a pair of decrepit chairs, where they sat waiting, staring across the hall at Benedict's locked door.

Sometime after 1:00 P.M. Detectives DaRosa and Smith arrived on the scene. The investigators had actually been tipped off to the existence of this new trick pad by Holland herself, who, before leaving for the Back Bay, had left a message at the Central Secret Service Bureau. Holland now introduced herself, hoping that the investigators had some means of getting into the apartment. But, as luck would have it, neither had a key. DaRosa contacted J.R., who seemed strangely indifferent to the news. He had known about the new Beacon Street apartment, he said. In fact, he had helped Robin move into it. He hadn't mentioned it, because he didn't think it was important to the investigation.

Landry was summoned, and, equipped this time with a key provided by J.R. Rogers, the little party made another assault on 397 Beacon.

By this time night had fallen. The locked door, lit dimly by an incandescent hall light, stirred as much anticipation in the searchers as the entrance to a tomb whose artifacts, however grim, might shed light on the recent past. Members of that little party knew that behind that door they might find Robin Benedict's corpse. It was also possible they would find her in flagrante delicto with some john. Someone turned the key in the lock. It opened into a small, sparely furnished apartment. In the center of the living room, which had apparently been used as a bedroom, was a box spring mattress on a Harvard frame. There were no sheets on the bed, and extra mattresses were piled against the wall. Except for a couple of paintings on velvet, the apartment was devoid of decoration. There were three cane-back chairs, a pair of night tables, and a dresser which was empty except for business cards bearing the inscription "Nadine." A couple of robes hung in a closet. The kitchen cabinets were empty. Next to the bathroom was a sort of utility room full of women's shoes, pocketbooks, and trash bags filled with debris.

Next to the bed Landry found a brown paper bag containing used condoms, tissues, and the discarded wrappings of a hobby knife and blades. There was a sales receipt from the Pill, Inc., hardware store on Massachusetts Avenue, indicating that the items had been purchased on Saturday, March 5. Except for that knife, which could conceivably have been used as a weapon, there was nothing to suggest foul play.

Paul Landry was not prepared to acknowledge that either the discovery of the apartment or the statements he took from Vaughn and Cuartero indicating that they had heard flute music as late as Tuesday really meant that Robin Benedict was still alive. He had concluded that Benedict was dead and seemed to resent any evidence to the contrary. He had awakened that morning moving surely toward "the big grab," which hovered at a stationary point just beyond his reach. Now it appeared to be moving away as quickly as he moved toward it. His worst fears seemed to be confirmed when he turned on the TV later that evening to see District Attorney William Delahunt speaking to News 7.

CHANNEL 7, which had run the original photo of Robin the preceding Sunday, had picked up the thread of the story on Tuesday during the 3:30 P.M. story conference with the Eleven o'Clock news team. A young reporter named Mike Lawrence called attention to the Shelly Murphy clip, remarking, "This looks interesting."

Lawrence was frankly dubious about the prostitution angle. With the *Herald* you often couldn't be sure where fact ended and speculation began, but he found the business about the professor intriguing. That afternoon he worked some of his sources at Tufts and learned that there was more to Douglas than a liaison with a beautiful girl. There were apparently financial problems with the research. It wasn't clear whether or not these related to Robin Benedict, but she had apparently been listed as an "image analyst" on a grant from the New England Anti-Vivisection Society. She and Douglas had apparently taken trips together to Chicago and Washington, D.C.

The following day, Lawrence made a trip to Norfolk County to see what he could get from the district attorney. Lawrence liked Delahunt, whom he considered not only an excellent DA but also a good politician who probably knew that he had a hell of a case about to break. He found Delahunt uncharacteristically coy. The DA was apparently unable to tell exactly what he had, a missing person or something more. Lawrence was nonetheless able to worm enough from Delahunt and the state police to go on at eleven o'clock with the report of a "police stakeout" at Robin Benedict's Boston apartment.

He was also able to persuade the district attorney to go on camera to announce, "The individual might very well be alive at this point in time, and we're trying to track that down to determine what, in fact, the situation is."

This was a fairly cautious statement. It nonetheless infuriated Paul Landry, who interpreted it as a sign that the DA was intending to drop the case. His anxiety undoubtedly increased the following morning when Beth Holland's story appeared under a headline proclaiming, " 'Missing' woman traced to her Boston apartment." Landry set about salvaging his teetering grab. Edward Vaughn had mentioned another tenant, named Dale DeJoy, who formerly occupied Robin's apartment at 397 Beacon. Vaughn didn't know DeJoy's new address but thought he had moved to Brookline. Landry called directory assistance and got listings for every DeJoy in that area. Shortly before noon on Thursday, he found his man.

Landry asked DeJoy if he had met the woman who had moved into his apartment.

"Sure," DeJoy replied. "I introduced myself to her."

He had run into her while he was checking for mail at his old address.

She had told him she didn't use the mailbox, because she had a private post office box on Charles Street.

"When was that?" Landry asked. "Do you remember—what date?"

"Sure," DeJoy replied. "It was the Friday after she moved in—the eleventh of March."

This was disappointing.

"Are you sure?" Landry pressed.

"Positive," DeJoy replied. On that same date he had been to the post office to fill out a form to have his address changed.

Landry asked DeJoy if he would do him a favor and check the date with the post office. DeJoy agreed.

Late in the afternoon of the following day, DeJoy called Trooper Landry at the Foxboro barracks to inform him that he had been mistaken. He had seen Robin Benedict at the mailbox on Friday, March 4, not the eleventh. If DeJoy had been mistaken about dates, wasn't it also possible that Vaughn and Cuartero were similarly confused? Landry gathered these arguments for rebuttal in the event that the district attorney's office was starting to lose interest in the case.

In fact, quite the opposite was true.

During the March 15 briefing, Paul Landry had handed over to Assistant District Attorney Kivlan certain documents he had received from J.R. Rogers. Among them were a packet of love letters from William Douglas to Robin Benedict. Over the following week, Kivlan had read and reread this correspondence with growing excitement.

Spanning the period from April 1982 to January 1983, they plotted the progress of a peculiar obsession.

April 19, 1982

Dear Nadine,

This gift is given to a very special person! If the curator at the Gallery was correct, you should be able to sell this when your first child is ready for college and pay for their entire college tuition. I hope this is true and it turns out to be a super investment.

Please, never lose your wonderful smile!

Your friend,
Bill

There was no allusion to what the expensive gift was. To this letter, however, were attached a set of handmade gift certificates for the following:

ONE COMPLETE SET OF SUPER EXPENSIVE COSMETICS OF YOUR CHOICE!

ONE BIKE OF YOUR CHOICE!

A VIDEO RECORDER AND PLAYER FOR YOUR TELEVISION!

A HAIR PERMANENT AT A SALON OF YOUR CHOICE AS OFTEN AS YOU WISH!

NAILS BY DOROTHY AS OFTEN AS YOU WANT THEM!

By May he had adopted a more personal, confessional tone.

Wednesday, May 12, 1982

Dear Robin,

I hope everything is well with you, Dear. I miss your warm wonderful smile. May I wish you a wonderful day, Dear, you are a beautiful person and deserve only the very best in life!

On Sunday, May 2, 1982 my lab group at Tufts had a cook-out for one of my postdoctoral fellows that is working for me and is going to have her second baby soon. I wanted to ask you if you could go with me to this party (normal rates, of course) but Nancy would not tell me until the last minute if she was going or not (she did not) and I did not want to ask you at the last minute. Next lab party I am just going to ask you and not tell her about the party.

At that May 2nd party, one of my graduate students showed up in a sweat shirt. On the front of the shirt was the skyline of Boston with many of the sky scrapers. Across the buildings was written in large capital letters— WHJD—. He suggested that all lab members in William Henry James Douglas' lab get one. I thought the sweatshirt was a novel idea.

Dear, I am ready to return to Boston now! Saskatoon is very nice, however I miss my children and you! Brief chats daily on the phone with all of you are super! However, I would rather see the four of you in person.

Take care fantastic lady,
Bill

By the end of May, Douglas had apparently formalized his business arrangements with Benedict. To that end, he addressed her once more by her street name.

Sunday May 23, 1982

Nadine,

Attached is a copy of the information we discussed 3:30 AM–5:00 AM this morning. I also enclosed another copy of the list of appointments we made.

As you know, I truly enjoyed our meeting this morning!
Thank you for being there!

> Your Friend,
> Bill

[Schedule attached:]

Tuesday June 1st—	2–4 PM
Friday June 4th—	You work 4 PM until 2:30 AM we meet 2:30 AM–5:00 AM
Wednesday June 9th—	You work 4 PM until 2:30 AM We meet 2:30 AM–4:30 AM
Sunday July 18th—	2–4 PM Pier 4 to celebrate your Birthday
Wednesday July 21st—	You work 4 PM until 2:30 AM We meet 2:30 AM–5:30 AM at my house in Sharon. We drive down in your car together

There were no letters documenting the events of the summer and only a couple of saccharine friendship cards sent during the early fall. By October there were indications of trouble. Douglas composed some crude blank verse which he entitled "Some Thoughts Passing Thru My Mind."

I am very glad I met you
I love seeing you
I appreciate all the kindness you show me
I appreciate the special things we do and talk about
QH's are GREAT so are hand and arm squeezes

Kivlan mused over the "QH's." "Quick hugs"? "Quick hands"? "Quaalude highs"?

Your smile is marvelous
Phone calls from you are special events
We have interesting times together

I wish I never caused you any problems. Believe it or not I am working hard at this . . . but not hard enough. I will try even harder. Today Oct. 9, 1982 will be day 01 of hopefully a long streak of good days.
I am VERY VERY SORRY, EMBARRASSED AND ASHAMED FOR THE WAY I ACTED LAST NIGHT. I WISH I NEVER SAID THOSE THINGS. PLEASE FORGIVE ME DEAR!!!!!!!!!!!!

> Your friend,
> Bill

There was an undated letter sent around this time.

Hi Dear

I am truly sorry I said that phrase about the house and furniture. I was hurt and striking out defensively.

My Dad taught me that DEEDS speak much stronger than words. Therefore, I hope you can forgive me and forget those words and let my deeds, love and friendship speak for me

Your good friend
Bill

By the beginning of the new year, Douglas had apparently fallen from favor and could scarcely control his anguish. On Monday, January 3, Douglas wrote Robin a long letter. It was sent under a cover sheet dated January 6, 1983. The note read:

Hi Treasure

I read most of this to you Wednesday night, but I am mailing it because I want you to have a copy

I am truly sorry for
the way I acted
Bill

Monday, Jan. 3, 1983

Dearest Robin:

I hope that it is OK to write you. If you prefer that I do not write you just call the office and leave the following message. . . . "This is Robin calling, I want to leave the following message for Dr. Douglas. . . . The cells are not doing well and therefore will not be ready for the experiment as planned."

As you know, the truly wonderful times in my life this last year were those times I spent with you. You shared so much with me . . . our thoughts, our lives and we had so many special meaningful times together that can only happen between friends. I cherish those memories and look forward to the time when we are together again. Robin, *I treasure you* and for you to know fully what that phrase means to me, you have to know what the word treasure means to me. When I say the word treasure, I think of something that is precious, a one-of-a-kind possession, something that is priceless and must be protected at all costs. For the present time I have lost the privilege of seeing you, which is another way of saying I have lost a precious treasure.

You know I am sad that it happened but I have only myself to blame. I will change my ways! I will work hard on trying to act like an adult when I interact with you and not some love-struck teenager. I must learn to think through a situation clearly before acting and not to be a pest or a NAG. During the time we are apart I will work hard on these problem areas to correct the defects. Actually when I look back over the mistakes I have made in our relationship I realize how foolish I have been. Robin I am very thankful to you that you did not say the following "Bill, I will never see you again." Believe me, I will change! I have to change! I never want to be in a position to hear that phrase from you! I thank you dear for not saying that yet. . . . Though I certainly have made enough mistakes.

Dear, when I was a teenager growing up I used to dream about designing a machine that would reverse time and let you relive times and places that you have already had. I guess all kids have thoughts like that. Today I wish I was clever enough to make one of those instruments for 2 reasons. For one reason to go back in time and change the stupid things I did and to do it right. These are some of the things I would change!

NOT   calling you back time after time
NOT   crying and pleading with you
NOT   arguing with you in your home and then leaving and calling you
       many times
NOT   making a fool of myself
NOT   being a pest
NOT   being a nag
NOT   repeating myself over and over again
NOT   making an appointment at the club and then canceling it
NOT   following you
NOT   being a problem for you at a time when you need a truly
       supportive friend

>   The second reason for wanting the machine is to act the
>   appropriate way when I am with you, so that I could be someone
>   you are proud of, someone that you respect, someone that you
>   care to be with! I guess if I had one wish, no two wishes They
>   would be the following

#1   To see you again
#2   To be someone you are proud of, someone that you respect and
      someone that you care to be with

>   I just received your 8:35 AM phone call, telling me NOT to mail
>   this letter and that you are leaving town. I hope you will be proud
>   of me that I did not try to call you back.
>   I pray to God that you do not leave town and that I do see you
>   again. Unfortunately that decision is yours because of the stupid
>   mistakes I have made I have lost the privilege of talking with you
>   except when you call me.

Dear, I look forward to the time when my phone rings and you are on the line, at least when that happens, I will hear your voice again and I can pray that you will say . . . "What's up Doc, would you like to get together"

My dearest precious Robin may things in our lives straighten out soon, we have had enough hell.

Douglas went on to reminisce about the last memory he had of her, watching her leave with her father from Commonwealth Avenue the day he and John Benedict had helped her move from her trick pad. If she did decide to leave town, he suggested in a desperate attempt at humor, they should spend a "GRAND" day together. The grand, he said, would come in handy, and he would love to see her.

I will never forgive myself that I have upset you and angered you. Robin you have been wonderful to me. You gave me a new hope for living, you were my guiding light for and motivation for losing weight and the finest friend I have known and for these things from you, I will be forever thankful. Robin, I thank you for sharing your life with me during the last few months. I will cherish these memories forever:
Your playing AMAZING GRACE on
your flute
QH's
hand squeezes
our special talks when we shared
our thoughts and lives
walks in the park
feeding the ducts [sic]
velamint transfers
pizza in the park
early morning walks
feeding the ducts [sic]
your smile while watching the plays we
saw together
you being YOU YOU YOU YOU YOU
I am sorry for causing such a wonderful person problems at a time when you needed my support. I hope you can forgive me, I have been in living Hell wishing that I had acted differently. . . .

Your supportive friend,
Bill

Sometime over the next couple of days, Douglas and Robin enjoyed some sort of apparent reconciliation. On Thursday, January 6, Douglas wrote euphorically:

Dearest Robin:

. . . It was a pleasant surprise to hear your voice last night around 6:30 PM and a tremendous joy for the opportunity to see you. During the two hours we were together, I tried to act in an appropriate manner and I hope that I succeeded. As you know, Dear, I treasure those two hours with you.

I hope and pray that our troubles are now over. . . .

I also hope and pray, my treasure, That your anger toward me is decreasing. I am so sad, knowing that I have upset you terribly. Not being able to talk with you frequently and to share parts of our lives leave me with a large void in my life. Unfortunately, I have no one to blame but myself. I look forward with enthusiasm to the time when things return to the way they were.

If indeed our troubles are over perhaps you will feel safe leaving the answering machine at the joint. That way you could receive calls AND if you permitted, I could leave you messages. . . . I am sure that decision will be made sometime in the future.

Dear, I hope things work out so you do not leave town. You have one friend here, who will do *ANYTHING* for you that you require in order to stay in town.

As the weekend approaches, I hope we can spend time together. Its been a while since Rocky Horror. . . . I think we are about due.

Have you heard any comments about Airplane II? I wonder if it is as funny as Airplane I?

Are you beginning to get an attack of the hungries for crab legs from Pier 4?

Naturally I am presuming alot by mentioning these things. I will wait patiently until I hear from you regarding when, where and for how long we can meet.

My treasure, I love seeing you!

> Take good care, my love
> Your friend,
> Bill

By the following day, his spirits had taken another plunge.

Friday Jan. 7, 1983

Dearest Robin:

It was wonderful to hear your voice last night, I am sorry you had difficulty reaching me. You would have been impressed if you could have seen the elaborate "call-forwarding" and "search and locate" plans I had for my people to locate me yesterday when you called.

I hope everything is OK for you. I hope and pray that the bull crap has stopped and that you can now settle down to a more normal existence. I worry about you precious lady, especially now that we are apart and I no longer am able to share a part of your life.

Naturally I was very sad and sorry to hear you say that you would not see me Thursday night and that you did not think you would see me Friday— Because you did NOT want to see me. I am so sorry I angered you. It tears me apart and brings tears to my eyes to hear you say that. Unfortunately I have only myself to blame. I understand why you feel the way you do. Believe me, Dear Robin, if I ever am lucky enough to see you again. I will never upset you!

Robin, give me another chance, I will not prove to be a disappointment to you again! More than ever NOW I need that machine to reverse time . . . if only I could redo Those problems I caused for you.

I am a foolish person, Dear, to have angered you so and to have lost a treasured friendship. I know now how stupid I have been.

God bless you, Robin! May only good things happen to you! I look forward to hearing from you at the appropriate time.

To handsqueezes and QH's in the future!

I love seeing you
your friend always
Bill

Two days after his suspension from Tufts, Douglas wrote Robin as follows:

Fri Jan 14, 1983
Morning

Dearest Robin,

Dear I hope you don't mind if I asked the lady to put this in your mail box. . . . I wanted you to receive this note as soon as possible.

Robin, I need your help! I am so depressed and sad. Everything in my life is going wrong lately. I truly need a friend that I can talk with and share things with.

Yesterday I tried to be near my home phone as much as possible hoping to hear from you. Last night I could not reach Debbie to get a message to you.

Dear since I have known you, I have always tried to be by your side in time of need. Now I desperately need some help from you. . . . I know you don't want to see me while you're working days—but Dear I desperately need to be with you. Please reconsider letting me visit you while you work—Dear I am so sad—

As I told you Wed night I will pay to have you call me or if you give me your number I will pay each time I call you.

Dear, I can't believe I am writing and begging you this way but I need to see you very much right now.

Please don't turn yourself away from me NOW!

I need you

Dear

Bill

PLEASE BE THERE
I NEED YOU, LOVE

PS Is there any chance you could call me in the morning between 7–9 AM. I will be by my home phone these hours for the next few days—also 5:30–7:30 P.M. in the evenings?

Remember when I used to see you every day. Dearest can we do that again this coming week, I need your support during this difficult time for me!

And another postsuspension note.

Dearest Robin:

I decided to get a telephone message service for one month. Now that I will not be in the office it will come in handy.

I asked the Lady at 104 Charles if I could drop off the note for box 115 That way you can have my message number sooner than if I mailed it.

The phone number is 367-0810

Please call me! If you don't reach me at home please leave a message for me at the answering service

Right now in my life—its important for me to see you WHENEVER you agree to see me. The message service may help in this regard.

He signed this "I love you" but then altered it to read, "I love seeing you, Bill."

The unrequited yearning reflected in these letters left no doubt in Kivlan's mind that William Douglas had something to do with the disappearance of Robin Benedict. The intensity of the January 3 letter, in particular, suggested to him that Douglas would know where this girl was at every minute. Now that she was missing, he seemed implausibly casual.

Early on Thursday, March 17, Kivlan called Landry and told him to bring Douglas in for questioning as soon as possible. But Douglas, Landry told him, was temporarily unreachable. Landry had received word from Shirley Benedict that Douglas had called her Wednesday night for no apparent reason other than to say he was going to be out of town until the weekend.

Kivlan instructed Landry to keep an eye out for Douglas's return. In the meantime, he said, the trooper should again contact J.R. Rogers to grill him about the days and hours before Robin's disappearance.

Once again J.R. seemed eager to cooperate, explaining that on the preceding Friday morning he and a friend had met Robin at a U-Haul storage warehouse so that she could sign papers authorizing them to move her furniture out of storage. He took some of these items over to the Beacon Street apartment. After that he returned to the house in Malden and loaded the brass bed onto the truck. When he arrived back at the warehouse at about 2:00 P.M., Robin was there waiting for him because he had the key to 397 Beacon. She took it and set off to clean the new apartment.

Later that evening, around 9:30 P.M., Robin called her answering service and was told that a Mr. Rogers had just phoned and picked up their messages. Robin knew that J.R. always identified himself as J.R. or Clarence Rogers, so she found this strange. She called J.R., who said he hadn't made any such call.

On Saturday, between 3:30 and 9:00 P.M., there were three calls for Nadine from someone named John who lived at 1 Longfellow Place, asking her to call 742-2929. After that, there were two more messages. Rogers showed them to Landry.

| 03/05 | 10:07PM | *To* Nadine *from* Joe-Charlestown | YK # Party from 10:30 Sat. nite to 6PM-Sunday PM Your invited |
| 03/05 | 11:42PM | *To* J.R. *from* Robin | Left Bill's on way to Joe's in Charlestown has materials |

J.R. still claimed not to know who this mysterious "Joe" was.

There were no further calls until Sunday afternoon, when Nadine got two messages—one at 12:48 P.M. from a Sgt. Nichols leaving the number 367-8850, and another at 1:02 P.M. from the persistent John asking her to call 1 Longfellow. According to J.R., he had received a message reporting a call from Robin at a little after 3:00 P.M. that Sunday saying she would be with "John at Longfellow." Such a call, if it existed, raised the possibility that Robin was alive as late as Sunday afternoon, and it was critical to confirm it. That afternoon Paul Landry went to Brookline to visit the Americall Answering Service.

There he learned that six operators had been working the weekend of March 5. Landry showed J.R.'s messages to them. They all agreed that the slips looked accurate. Maura Armstrong had taken the one reading, "Left Sharon, going to Joe's in Charlestown." She was new at Americall and couldn't distinguish many of the clients' voices yet. She would, she believed, have been able to recognize Clarence Rogers. She couldn't say anything specific about the "Joe from Charlestown" call except that it had not been left by Mr. Rogers.

Elizabeth Valeri recollected that on Sunday, March 6, at around 11:00 A.M., she had received a call from someone who said, "This is Nadine. Any messages?" Judging from the slips in Landry's possession, there were none to be relayed. Winnie Farley vaguely remembered a call in which someone seemed to be imitating a woman. It was possible that this was the midafternoon message to J.R. from "Robin." But nobody seemed to be able to find the slip. Landry urged the operators to keep looking.

In the meantime, Landry conferred with the state chemist Ronald Kaufman on the progress of forensic tests. Kaufman had made a study of the stain patterns on the two garments found in Mansfield. The jacket showed a thin smear across the left front. There had not been sufficient blood to soak through the nap. Neither was there much on the shirt. Just a reddish brown oval near the right shoulder. Kaufman's guess was that both articles had been stained from rubbing up against the head of the hammer.

Kaufman tested the blood from the hammer and found that it contained human protein. It had not been used to kill an animal. Further tests showed all of the blood on the Mansfield items to be type A. The next logical step was to compare it to Robin Benedict's blood, but there seemed to be no record of it. Her parents didn't know it, and it apparently hadn't been noted on any of her medical records. Landry called J.R. Rogers to see if he had any ideas where to look. J.R. produced Robin's Brigham and Women's Hospital card indicating that she had been treated on March 19 and 26, 1982. Landry served a subpoena on Brigham and Women's and got records showing that Robin had been examined for venereal disease. The tests came back positive, but the hospital had not, in the process, typed her blood. The DA's office also checked with Northgate Medical Care in Revere, where Robin had been examined by a Dr. E. A. Golia. Unfortunately, Dr. Golia had done no serological tests. For the time being, at least, the blood inquiry had reached a dead end.

Returning to the events of Saturday afternoon, Landry hoped to find out more about John of 1 Longfellow. J.R. was vague on this subject but gave Landry the number of Savitry Bisram in Randolph. Savi told Landry that she was Robin's "closest friend" and that when she didn't show up for a birthday party on Sunday, March 6, Savi made some calls to try to find her. One of these was to a guy named Sargent Nichols, who lived at 1 Longfellow Place, a high-rise apartment in the West End. The doorman there was a fellow named John Baldwin.

Shortly past seven the next evening, Landry dropped in unannounced at 1 Longfellow Place. Baldwin was sitting at a glassed-in security booth. When he learned what Landry had come for, he was wary but helpful. He had met Nadine, he said, around the end of February in a bar at the Park Plaza Hotel. He had bought her a drink, and they talked for a while. Then she gave him her card with the answering-service number. At the time, Baldwin said, he had not been sure that she was a prostitute, but after that he tried to get in touch with her to find out more about her line of work.

He had made a series of calls on March 4 and 5 trying to arrange a date for her with one of the tenants, a real estate entrepreneur named Sargent Nichols. Nadine finally returned his call on Saturday afternoon, and he secured her services for that evening. She arrived at Longfellow Place at about 7:30 P.M., he recalled. They chatted briefly before she took the elevator to Nichols's apartment, on the thirty-second floor. She was upstairs for about forty-five minutes; then she came back down and handed him another card before leaving the building.

Several minutes after she had gone, Nichols came downstairs to tell Baldwin how impressed he had been with Nadine's intelligence and charm. He would like to date her again, he said. Landry asked to speak to Nichols. Baldwin said he wasn't home but took a message to have him call the Foxboro barracks. Later that evening, Landry received a call from a man who introduced himself in a low, brusque voice as Sargent Nichols.

Nichols, by his own account, was a well-heeled bachelor who, on the weekend of March 5, had found himself without female companionship. All of his girlfriends were out of town. On the informal advice of his attorney, he had decided to seek the services of a prostitute. His doorman offered to put him in touch with Nadine, a working girl whom he had met over a drink.

Nichols estimated Nadine's arrival time at considerably later than Baldwin. She had appeared at 8:40 P.M.—he was sure of this because his business required him to be precise about time. If he slipped up on a detail like that, he said, he could lose a million dollars. After he let her in the door, he got her a drink. This Nadine was "very attractive," Nichols recalled. Very articulate and well dressed in blouse and pants. He would have felt comfortable taking her anywhere on a date, he said, even the "Harvard-Yale game." Nadine told him she had attended the Rhode Island School of Design and was "doing this" for a couple of years so that she could invest her money and go back into commercial art work.

After they had chatted for about half an hour, Nadine said, "We ought to make some sort of financial arrangement." Nichols tried to persuade her to spend the night, but she was interested only in "something quick." They did not have sex, he insisted, but he paid her $30 for her time.

Before she left, she asked to use the phone. This was about 9:30 to 9:40 P.M. Nichols overheard her telling the party on the other end, "I'll be leaving shortly. I'll be there in about a half hour." After hanging up, she observed lightly that she had to "run in and out between the wife and the children."

Nadine's tone did not suggest there was any tension in the conversation. Was it possible then that Robin was simply running out to the Douglas residence that night to turn another trick? There had been a suggestion in the love letters that Robin was not a stranger to the Douglas household. In the missive of May 23, Douglas had scheduled a session with Robin at his home in Sharon. They were to meet at 2:30 A.M., when Robin got off work, then drive in her car to Sharon, where she was to stay until 5:30 A.M. This tryst would have occurred on Wednesday, July 21, while Nancy and the kids were camping in Narragansett.

Whether Robin had actually made that rendezvous, Landry had no way of knowing. But an obscure incident report which he had secured from the Sharon PD revealed that Robin had made a visit to the Douglas house a little over a week before her disappearance. On the morning of February 23, Douglas had called the department, insisting that someone was trying to extort him. Detective James Testa answered the complaint. Testa knew the Douglas family. He had coached young Billy Douglas in Pop Warner football. He had seen Nancy Douglas at the basketball banquets held every year and found her "solemn, not a joyful person."

When Testa arrived at 38 Sandy Ridge Circle, a little after nine, Nancy Douglas was nowhere to be seen. The children were getting ready for school. Professor William Douglas was agitated. He told Testa that he had been up in Lynn, on the North Shore, the night before with an assistant named Robin Benedict. He had begun having chest pains and had to be taken to the Lynn Union Hospital for treatment. During that time Miss Benedict had stolen important slides and papers from his briefcase. The reason he had called was that now she was on her way to his house in an attempt to exchange these things for something. Douglas didn't specify what.

Benedict arrived soon thereafter, and when Douglas went to the driveway to meet her, they began arguing energetically. Testa couldn't make out what they were saying, but fearing they might make an unpleasant scene in front of the children, the officer invited Douglas and Benedict to the Sharon PD for a chat. There Benedict volunteered that she and Douglas had been "involved" for about a year and a half and that she had come to Sharon to bring things to a head with Mrs. Douglas. Testa, who interpreted this situation as a lover's triangle, advised them to get a lawyer or marriage counselor to straighten things out. As for the missing papers,

Testa told Douglas he should go to the Lynn police if he wanted to pursue it. The crime, if it was a crime at all, had occurred there, not in Sharon.

Landry relayed these developments to John Kivlan, who had been charting the pattern of hostility that seemed to have begun sometime in the early fall. In his letter of October 9, Douglas had first alluded to difficulties, lamenting, "I am very very sorry, embarrassed and ashamed for the way I acted last night. I wish I never said those things. Please forgive me dear!!!!!!" In January the drift of his letters suggested she had cut him off completely. Now, according to Testa's account, the two had been cozy in Lynn the night of February 22, an encounter which brought Robin to Sharon the following day in search of something and ended in a quarrel on the Douglas lawn.

The dispute appeared to have carried over to the beginning of the following week, when Robin called Nancy Douglas to tell her she didn't want to see Bill. And it apparently came to a head on Saturday night when, according to J.R. Rogers's revised story, Robin went out to Sharon to tell Douglas to leave her alone. Kivlan hadn't a clue about what had occurred between them during the intervening four or five days until J.R. anxiously phoned Paul Landry to report that a $200 check that Douglas had written to Robin had been returned stamped "Payment stopped." The unnumbered check, drawn on the account of Dr. William H. J. Douglas and Nancy Douglas at the Sharon Co-Operative Bank, had been written on Wednesday, March 2. Robin had apparently deposited the check in her own account on March 4. Sometime before that or shortly thereafter, either William or Nancy Douglas had canceled the endorsement.

Kivlan felt a sense of renewed urgency to get to William Douglas. The professor had been remarkably loquacious to date, giving detailed statements to DaRosa and Borstel. Reviewing the reports of these conversations, Kivlan was gratified to see the mounting inconsistencies. Three separate stories of the head wound; two different dates and locations for his departure from Boston. In one place he claimed to be a friend of Robin's family; in another, one of her johns. His apparent eagerness to talk made him seem almost naïve. Kivlan, however, suspected this was disingenuous. He had pegged Douglas as a man who held a very high opinion of himself. A man who was confident that if he created the appearance of innocence by cooperating with the police, they would handle him respectfully. Douglas, the prosecutor reasoned, felt protected by his own prestige, and such people often miscalculated the dogged intrusiveness of the law.

On Saturday morning, March 19, John Kivlan sent Paul Landry out to Sharon to see if he could raise anyone at 38 Sandy Ridge Circle.

THE SEARCH

UPON arriving at the cul-de-sac, Landry spotted the Douglas house, a light green split-level on the left side of the street. There was certainly nothing in its external appearance to suggest it had been the scene of a death struggle. It stood serene and shadowless in the morning sunlight alongside six similar houses, whose uniformity seemed somehow to attest to the respectability of the neighborhood. Landry knocked on several doors and asked the occupants if they had noticed anything strange at No. 38. No one had. As far as the neighbors were concerned, the Douglases were just a "normal" family with "well-behaved" kids who went on camping trips and to sporting events together.

When Landry finally rang the doorbell at No. 38, Pammy Douglas answered. Her parents were not there, she said. They had gone to New York. Landry asked if she would have her father contact him when he returned. That afternoon at around three, Douglas called Landry in Foxboro. He would be happy to discuss the missing girl, he said, but he would rather not do it at his home. His wife could drop him off at the barracks. He arrived ten minutes later. Landry noticed he had a scar on the left side of his forehead. The rosy incision ran from the right of the part into the hairline. It was a wavy line, thin in the middle, broadening out at both ends like the extended wings of a sea gull.

Douglas seemed relaxed, almost nonchalant. The impression he seemed to want to leave was that he was doing the police a favor. Landry had been instructed not to discourage this illusion. He settled Douglas comfortably in the sergeant's office, then brought him coffee from the kitchen.

"More sugar, Bill?" he asked.

"No, no thanks. I'm fine."

Waiving his rights without any apparent qualms, Douglas began to tell the story of his dealings with Robin Benedict.

He had met her a year earlier when he had been looking for someone to design tables and charts for a project he was working on. He had placed an ad in one of the dailies, and she had come into his office with a portfolio of her work. He had told her that the job paid $5 an hour on a contingency basis and hired her without checking references. They swapped phone numbers. She gave him one for her residence in Natick and another for an apartment in Boston.

About three to four weeks after he hired her, Robin approached him for a "date." At first he thought she was kidding, but then he took her up on the offer, paying her not $5 an hour but $50 an hour for these newly negotiated services. He would visit her two to three times a week, he said. Sometimes they had sex, sometimes they didn't. He had continued to see her more frequently up to the present.

In about December or January, Robin had been barred from a place called Good Time Charlie's for working on the street. Landry asked what he meant by that, and Douglas explained that the prostitutes who worked out of Charlie's were supposed to stay in the bar and generate business for the establishment. A working girl named Genna had seen Robin soliciting in a parking lot and turned her in to the owners, who put out the word to the bartenders that Robin was not to be allowed in the lounge.

Douglas spoke with authority, indeed a peculiar familiarity, about these matters. He seemed to enjoy throwing around terms like "working girl," as though this argot admitted him to some secret fraternity.

Landry asked what he knew about Robin's house in Malden.

Robin, Douglas replied, had been excited about finally having a place of her own. She had been renovating it all through January and had moved in the following month. Shortly after that, however, she had started sleeping at various motels along Route 99, which ran northeast through Malden. That, she told him, was because her boyfriend was bringing other girls home. Robin never stayed over at her trick pads, Douglas insisted, because, as he put it primly, "Robin would never sleep where she worked."

The events of March 5, as Douglas now recalled them to Landry, were much the same as those he had rendered to DaRosa. Robin called him all day long, postponing her arrival, finally arriving at a quarter of eleven. She was wearing slacks. He couldn't remember what else she had on.

When he asked why she was late, she told him that she had had a "disagreement" with her boyfriend. Robin then gave him two slides, which he projected on a wall to study. They discussed his impending trip to an ophthalmological conference in Newport, Rhode Island. He outlined some of the new drawings he needed for the Draize project, then paid her $35 to $45 for her work on the finished slides.

Landry asked if Robin had anything to drink that evening, and Douglas replied that Robin didn't smoke or drink, except for an occasional glass of wine.

As Robin got ready to leave, Douglas continued, she put on her jacket—he suddenly remembered she had been wearing a jacket—and said she was going to "Joe's in Charlestown." This Joe, Robin had told him, was a "good date," meaning he paid well. She then got into her car and drove away. After she left, Douglas said, he went into the kitchen and fixed himself some cookies and milk before going to bed. His wife, he believed, got back from New Hampshire at around 12:30 A.M.

The following morning, Sunday, he awoke between nine-thirty and ten-thirty. He showered and shaved and began getting "organized" for his trip to Washington, D.C. At about eleven-thirty he went down to the Cumberland Farms on South Main Street in Sharon to buy a newspaper.

At this point Douglas's narrative took an unexpected turn. For some inexplicable reason, he began describing an event which had occurred the Tuesday prior to Robin's visit. He had gone alone to see the early evening showing of *Tootsie* at the Saxon Theatre across from the Prudential Center, in Boston. He had parked his Toyota on Marlborough Street; when he returned, he found that it had been stolen. He took the train back to Sharon and reported the car missing to the Boston PD.

The following day, Douglas said, he called Good Time Charlie's and left a message with Debbie that he was looking for Robin. That evening he took a train back into Boston and met her at ten-thirty at the White Hen Pantry, a convenience store near her Marlborough Street pad. They went to a Susse Chalet in Boston, where, Douglas said, they had had sex several times before. They registered under Douglas's name and spent about an hour. Then, Douglas said, as he was approaching the cashier's window to pay the bill, he was kidnapped by three black men. They forced him into a white van, blindfolded him, and pushed him onto the floor. For the next six and a half hours, they drove him around telling him to "stay away from Nadine." At about 6:00 A.M. the van stopped. His abductors ordered him to get out and lie face down on the pavement, where he was to stay for thirty seconds before moving. Douglas counted to thirty, removed the blindfold, and found he was on a small side street near Kenmore Square. Next to him was the car which had been stolen the day before. The keys were in the ignition.

Landry asked him if he had reported the kidnapping, and he replied he had not, because he didn't want his family to find out that he had been with Nadine.

Douglas's story was extremely strange. Landry excused himself and called John Kivlan. All that Saturday afternoon the prosecutor had been working with another assistant district attorney, Matthew Connolly, coauthoring an affidavit in Landry's name. Even if Landry could not elicit a confession from Douglas in Foxboro, an extended interview might still lay the groundwork for a warrant to search the house at 38 Sandy Ridge Circle. Landry summarized Douglas's statement to date. Kivlan was pleased to hear that Douglas seemed so unwary.

"Just keep him talking," he told Landry. "Whatever happens, keep him talking."

Landry got Douglas more coffee, then steered him back onto the subject of his trip to Washington, D.C., asking him how he had gotten the scar on his forehead. Douglas replied that he had been wounded the evening he left for Washington. When he arrived at South Station, he said, he had had time to kill, so he checked his suitcase and shoulder bag into a locker and, briefcase in hand, walked over to Chinatown. He never let that case out of his sight, he explained, because it contained eight very important grant applications that he had reviewed for the Veterans Administration. He dropped into Kim Toy's Restaurant and ordered some takeout. On his way back to the station, he was attacked by "two black boys" who hit him on the head with "something metal" and stole his briefcase.

Landry interrupted him to point out that he had already told Detective DaRosa that he had hit his head on a kitchen cabinet and later that he had been mugged in Union Station.

Douglas thought a moment, then said he didn't even recall DaRosa asking him about the injury.

The trooper then moved back in time to late February, asking Douglas to explain what had happened between himself and Robin Benedict to cause them to be taken to the Sharon police station. Douglas obliged, explaining that on Tuesday, February 22, the night before Robin visited him in Sharon, he had arranged to meet her at a place called the Ship Restaurant, in Saugus. When she arrived, she got into his car and they drove around the North Shore for a while. Douglas couldn't remember whether they stopped somewhere to have sex. During their ride, however, he began having severe chest pains and thought he might be having a heart attack. Robin drove him to the emergency room of the Lynn Union Hospital, where he was given an electrocardiogram. The results were negative, but the doctor advised him not to drive.

Douglas then said he called his wife at home in Sharon and asked her to pick him up. When Nancy arrived at the hospital with their neighbor, a Mrs. Greeley, Robin came over and introduced herself as Chris. Douglas then recalled Nancy saying to him, "That's the girl, isn't it?"

At some point Robin left surreptitiously in Douglas's Toyota, driving it back to the Ship Restaurant to pick up her own car. While pretending not to know where the car might have been taken, Douglas described how he subtly steered Nancy and Mrs. Greeley to the Ship's parking lot, where they found the missing Toyota with the keys in it. Nancy drove him home. Only later did he realize that his briefcase containing grant papers and slides was missing.

The following day Nancy left for work at about 6:30 A.M. At around 8:45 Robin called the house saying she had his briefcase and wanted to exchange it for money. Douglas then called the Sharon police to report that he was being extorted. Officer Testa arrived at the scene. Shortly after that, Robin pulled up and Douglas ran out to meet her in the driveway and asked her what was going on. Robin, he recalled, was "very upset" and wanted to go into the house. He tried to stop her, but she insisted. When she saw Testa, the "conversation got very loud." Testa suggested they all go down to the station, where he urged them to get some kind of counseling. After the officer dismissed them, Douglas began walking home. Robin, who had driven off in her Toyota, did a U-turn, picked him up, and took him back to his house. Douglas said they talked for a while in her car during which time, he said, she relented in her demands for money and gave him the papers.

Landry drew Douglas's attention to a $200 check he had apparently written to Robin on that same evening. Douglas explained that the check was for sex. He had actually given it to Robin on Friday, March 4. Then, when he saw her on March 5, he gave her $200 cash, so he canceled the check. Landry stopped him here. Why, when they had been going so methodically over the events of Saturday, March 5, hadn't he mentioned that he had given Robin that much cash. Douglas claimed simply to have "forgotten."

"Did you love Robin Benedict?" Landry asked him finally.

"Not now or at any time," Douglas replied.

LANDRY knew Douglas was lying. Still, he felt sort of sorry for him. Just looking at him, you could tell he had been really hurt. Here was this big, fat, plain-looking fellow with glasses who had gotten crushed by a girl. Landry knew what it felt like to be used and hurt. This guy had given a girl everything there was to give. He had even risked losing his wife and kids and job, and she had just said "tough shit." Landry saw where he might have worked up the rage to kill her.

Landry became blunt. Why, he suggested, didn't Douglas tell him what really happened? Had she done something to make him mad? Had she hit him first? Had he maybe just defended himself?

Douglas was silent.

Landry couldn't help him unless Douglas let him, the trooper prodded. Still, Douglas said nothing.

The trooper realized there was no use pushing him any further.

Later that evening—over Douglas's objections—Landry called a reluctant Nancy to the barracks, asking her to reconstruct to the best of her ability the events of Saturday, March 5.

She recalled leaving the house some time before 1:00 P.M. to go shopping at the Manchester Mall in New Hampshire. That evening she arrived home around supper time to find a note from Bill on the kitchen table. It said that he had gone for a walk and that "Nadine" was going to drop off some materials at around 7:30 P.M. As it was already 7:00 and Nancy "didn't want to be around," she took her son Bill to McDonald's and afterward to a mall to shop. At 11:30 P.M., Nancy said, she and her son returned to the house. But when she saw Robin's car in the driveway, she turned around and left. On her way out of the cul-de-sac, she met Pammy, who was returning from baby-sitting at a neighbor's. The three of them drove around for a while.

Nancy repeated that she didn't want to be around while Nadine was in her home. So, she drove aimlessly for forty-five minutes, and when she returned, at 12:15 A.M., the car was gone. She went into the house, looked into the master bedroom, and saw her husband asleep in the bed.

Landry asked if she had seen a cut or bandage on his head, and she replied no. Nancy then said she went to sleep on the living room sofa.

Why there? Landry asked.

Nancy said it was because she was upset over her husband's relationship with Robin Benedict.

The next time Nancy saw Bill, she said, was at 9:00 A.M. on Sunday. They did not do much talking that day. She noticed no wound on Bill's head. Neither did she see any sign of a conflict. At around 3:00 P.M. she took her older son to a basketball banquet. That evening she drove her husband to the bus station at Foxfield Plaza. She didn't wait around to see him off, she said, because the two of them hadn't been talking much of late.

Landry told Nancy frankly that her husband was a suspect in the disappearance of Robin Benedict. He also related to her what he knew about their relationship. Nancy appeared distraught but said she refused to believe it. At length, Landry drove her back to Sandy Ridge Circle, where she asked him to drop her off at the top of the street so that she could walk the rest of the way home.

IT WAS PAST ten o'clock when Landry finally arrived at the district attorney's office to put finishing touches on an affidavit which laid out the details of the investigation to date, concluding as follows:

> . . . There is probable cause to believe that the location of the hammer, blood or blood residue as well as items used to clean blood as well as clothing or materials similar to the blood stained man's shirt . . . may be found at the home of William Douglas. . . .

The clerk of the court in nearby Stoughton, having been alerted to the possibility of a search, remained at the courthouse until nearly eleven, when Kivlan brought the warrant in for his signature. Then the prosecutor ferried the document to the Sharon police station, where a search party was assembling. Besides Landry there was the chemist Kaufman and Corporal William Anderson, a photographer and fingerprint technician from the state crime lab at 1010 Commonwealth Avenue. There were two road troopers who had been recruited to secure the area in case there was a leak to the press. There was Assistant District Attorney Matthew Connolly, who had helped write the affadavit. Finally, there was Lieutenant James Sharkey. Kivlan had asked Sharkey to head this expedition. House searches, he knew, could be very chaotic, and he wanted this done in an orderly fashion. Sharkey was fussy about detail. He was also a good-natured schmoozer who, Kivlan felt, might be able to catch Douglas off his guard.

In the best of all worlds, Douglas would open the door, discover the cadre of troopers about to storm his foyer, and be jolted into confessing on the spot. Landry seemed to think he was teetering on the edge of an admission. Sharkey had been instructed, in the event this did not work, to isolate Nancy Douglas and encourage her to break ranks with her husband. Landry was to get to the children if possible.

The troopers and forensics team were to look for anything which might link the items found at Mansfield to the Douglas house. It had been over two weeks since Benedict had disappeared, so Kivlan was not optimistic about finding much in the way of blood. One of the family, however, might identify the hammer or shirt. Perhaps Douglas had a work area with tools mounted with eyehooks similar to the one on the sledgehammer. Finally Kivlan hoped, although he knew this was a long shot, they might find something that Benedict had taken with her the night she disappeared. Something that Douglas had no right to have in his possession.

Around 12:40 A.M. a silent convoy of cruisers and unmarked cars pulled into Sandy Ridge Circle. All the lights were out at No. 38. The family was apparently asleep. Kivlan and Connolly waited outside in a Malibu sedan while Sharkey and Landry led the party to the door. Landry knocked. Getting no answer, he rang the doorbell. When William Douglas finally appeared in a white shirt and pants, Landry handed him the warrant. They could search the house, Landry told him, or he could simply step outside and tell the truth about Robin Benedict.

"I have told you all I know, and that's all I can do," he replied simply. "Why don't you come in."

Douglas let the search party onto the landing, which faced two flights of steps—one going up, the other down. He led them up the stairs, then left down a hallway to the kitchen at the back of the house. When he flicked on the light, the troopers were shocked by what they saw. What appeared to have once been a pleasant suburban kitchen, papered with cheerful yellow poppies, had been overrun with clutter and filth. Dirty dishes lay stacked in the sink. A brown formica table, enclosed on three sides by a leatherette banquette, was littered with dirty socks and old newspapers. The floor around it was strewn with grocery bags, discarded towels, and hockey sticks.

The living room across the hall was a similar jumble. At one end of the room stood a grand piano. Near it, an exercise bike. The surrounding space was full of sports equipment and discarded clothing. Philodendrons and cacti were growing in plastic pots in front of the bay window, but they were dying from lack of care. A stick of butter lay open on the bare wooden floor. In the midst of it all, little Johnny Douglas was sleeping on a large red futon.

Nancy emerged from a rear bedroom, and Sharkey quickly took her in tow. Apologizing for the intrusion, he beckoned for the evidence bags, and Landry produced the blue shirt. Nancy allowed that it looked "like a shirt that Bill might have owned." When Sharkey showed her the stitching in the armpits, she conceded that it looked like her sewing. She brought him two rolls of thread, one light and one dark, which could possibly have been used to mend the shirt.

Sharkey was delighted to get this admission because it linked the shirt to the Douglas household. Nancy Douglas was being so cooperative, he did not think it was possible that she could be involved with Benedict's disappearance. If he could isolate her from her husband, he felt, he could win her over. By now, however, she was trembling. She asked if she could wake her children and take them away someplace, to her father's perhaps. Sharkey took her hand soothingly and told her she could, by all means. Nancy went to the living room to awaken Johnny, then to a bedroom at the opposite end of the hall to rouse Pamela. Billy was sleeping over at the house of a friend.

As the Douglas children were dressing, Landry showed them the stained shirt. Neither could remember seeing it before. He brought out the sledgehammer. They couldn't identify that either. Landry showed it to Nancy Douglas, who looked it over carefully and said that it was unfamiliar to her. As far as she knew, she said, the family did not own any hammers of that kind. The trooper then took the mallet to the kitchen, where Sharkey was preparing for some conversation with Douglas. Sharkey asked Douglas if he recognized it. He replied, "It is not mine, and I have never seen it before."

Sharkey invited Douglas to take a seat across from him at the cluttered table. Then, pulling out a notepad and a ballpoint pen, he asked Douglas to please answer slowly so that he could get everything down. Douglas produced a pad on which to take his own notes.

Trooper Landry, meanwhile, began searching the kitchen cabinets. In the storage area at the base of the sink, he found a box of Hefty trash bags that were brown on the outside and black on the inside. At first glance, they appeared identical to the bag found in Mansfield. Landry went outside, where Nancy was packing her children into the Toyota, and he gave the car a quick once-over. Under the front seat, he found a clear plastic bag from Shaw's Supermarket. It contained several brown-and-black bags similar to the ones he had just found in the kitchen. He asked Nancy and the children if they could explain how they had gotten into the Toyota. No one professed to know anything about them. Landry took the new bags inside and showed them to Douglas, who also pleaded ignorance.

The troopers began working their way down the hall toward the bedrooms. The first door on the left opened onto a bathroom. On the green tiled floor were piles of towels, discarded socks, and sneakers. A television set had been positioned on a low table in front of the bath. Someone who had apparently been watching TV and eating popcorn there had left a greasy bowl in the tub. Landry waded through the debris to the medicine cabinet to check for bandages matching those Douglas had been wearing in Washington. He found nothing.

Across from the bath was a child's room papered with bold red gingham poppies. It was apparently Pamela's. Here, too, the floor was cluttered with textbooks and teen magazines. At the end of the hall was what appeared to be a boys' room done in blue and red poppies. The mattress was bare and the floor covered with stuffed toys and greeting cards. To the left was the master bedroom.

This chamber was small, dominated by a double bed, which was positioned with its head flush against the far wall. The bed, in turn, faced a bureau that was as cluttered as nearly every other surface in the household. On it sat a large lamp with a columnar base festooned with the same wide-petaled poppies found on the kitchen walls. There was a loose passport and a large German beer stein. Behind that was an earthen pot of artificial flowers. Even these looked neglected.

Running parallel to the bed along the left wall was a closet with a sliding wooden door. The interior was filled with old wire hangers and men's shirts. On the floor beneath them was a large Seagram's box atop which sat a Kodak carousel projector. Landry removed the projector, revealing a stack of hard-core pornographic materials. The troopers, who had been numbed somewhat by the incessant disorder of the preceding rooms, now had to stop to take this in. There appeared to be fifty or more publications with titles like *Tower of Deviant Lust* and *Gang Up on Gail.*

The collector had scissored out advertisements for live S&M shows at the Belle de Jour and Bizarre Theater in New York City. There were also clippings advertising the services of young women with New York phone numbers. One featured a photo of a supremely poised girl dressed in a cowl-neck sweater and jacket. Her long brunette hair was piled on top of her head. The ad read:

STOP
wasting your money on girls who don't care.
For satisfaction, friendliness, courtesy, discretion and much more. . . .
    My real name is Jennifer, I really care if you return.

There was another for "Rena a True Submissive." Rena, who was got up in black stockings and suspended by ligatures, urged the reader,

Spank me, whip me, tie me up—I am your slave. Use me for your pleasure and fantasies. I am yours to command. That is really my picture and as you can see I have a young lush body awaiting your masterful demands. My lovely, rounded ass beckons and yearns for the penetration of your male hardness.

Lying among the pornography was a manila envelope which appeared to have contained business correspondence addressed to Douglas. Landry opened it and discovered a pair of sheer pink panties. Inside the panties he found a piece of chewed gum in a Trident wrapper.

Landry could not believe what he was finding. There was a remote controller—a beeper—for a Panasonic answering machine. There was also a black book about four and a half by seven inches. It contained names and phone numbers in code. Alongside it lay a slightly larger red book which contained headings for "addresses," "birthdays," and "card list." Stuck into the back of the red book was a phone bill and other personal papers, belonging to Robin Benedict. Among them were her Visa card and MasterCard.

"Look at this!" Landry shouted. He hurried down the hall to the kitchen door and signaled for Sharkey to come with him. Sharkey excused himself and followed Landry to the bedroom to check out the panties, notebook, beeper, and two other items which the troopers had found in a yellow plastic bag at the top of the closet—an Armstrong flute and a dark rectangular pocketbook in which Landry thought he detected the scent of Molinard de Molinard.

What could have possessed Douglas to keep these things in his closet? Sharkey wondered. How would he now account for them? In light of the closet discoveries, Sharkey returned to the kitchen and took up a new line of questioning.

"Did Robin have any credit cards or charge cards that you were aware of?" he asked Douglas.

"Yes," Douglas replied, ". . . either a Mastercharge or a Visa. I'm not sure which one. It may have been both."

Had he seen either of these cards?

"Not that I remember," Douglas replied.

Had he ever had any of Robin's charge cards in his possession?

"No," Douglas replied. "Like her car, she would never give those to anyone. I couldn't imagine a circumstance where she would either lend her car or let someone use her credit cards."

Landry entered the kitchen carrying the Panasonic beeper. Sharkey asked Douglas if he had ever seen it before. For the first time, Douglas lost his composure.

"Shit," he said. "I have no idea of how that beeper got into my closet. . . . When that reporter Sheila Murphy called, she said, 'Boy, Dr. Douglas, someone is trying to do a number on you,' and is she right. . . .'"

In the doorway behind Douglas, Sharkey could see Landry holding up the purse. It was was deep blue leather, almost black. Picking up the cue, Sharkey asked Douglas if he could recall how Robin was carrying the slides she had brought with her the night of March 5.

"I think she had them in a bag," Douglas replied. "But she always had her pocketbook with her, and she always had money."

Sharkey asked Douglas if he could describe the pocketbook that Robin had been carrying.

"I think she has a black one," he gestured holding his hands apart at a distance of about twelve to fourteen inches. "And it's about seven inches long. . . . I would recognize it if I saw it."

Despite the discrepancy between the two descriptions, Sharkey saw that Douglas's gesture matched the length of the bag Landry was holding. Landry handed the pocketbook to Sharkey, who opened it to look at the contents: cherry-flavored lip balm, Visine, a bottle of nail hardener. There were ticket stubs from an Olivia Newton-John concert, and eight Ramses condoms. Sharkey then handed the purse to Douglas. It had been found, he said, in the bedroom closet.

"Unbelievable," Douglas replied. "I have no idea of how this got in my house or my closet. This is Robin's pocketbook." He picked up the condoms and examined them. "It certainly looks like it, with the contraceptives inside."

"Doctor," said Sharkey. "Don't you think it is fair to say or at least surmise that [this] is a bit incriminating?"

"I know it," Douglas replied. "It's unbelievable, and things don't look good. I don't know how that got in my house, and I don't know how my shirt got in that trash barrel."

Sharkey held up the black book, asking him if he had ever seen it.

"Could I look at it?" Douglas asked. After examining it, he replied, "This is Robin's date book. I know it's Robin's. She showed it to me many times before."

"Doctor," Sharkey asked pointedly, "how do you explain this being in your bedroom closet . . . ?"

"I don't know how that got in my house," came the reply.

Landry then brought out the pink underpants. He had found them in an envelope addressed to Douglas. Could he explain to whom the panties belonged and what they were doing in the bedroom closet?

"Those are Robin's," Douglas replied. "I don't know how they got in my house. You mean there are more."

Before he could recover himself, Landry handed him the red address book, opening it to the back pocket to reveal the credit cards. If he had never seen or had access to Robin's charge plates, Sharkey prodded, how could he account for their being found in his bedroom closet?

"This is hers," Douglas said, apparently bewildered. "These are her cards. I don't know how any of these things got in my house."

The only thing Douglas claimed not to recognize was the phone bill.

"I've never seen that before, as opposed to the other things you have shown me," he insisted.

"How did all this stuff get here, Bill?" Landry asked him.

"I don't know," Douglas replied. "Maybe J.R. put them there." Perceiving that this was not going over well, he pressed on. "Well, I work and my wife works and we're not here and the kids are off to school, so it very easily could have been planted there by J.R."

THE CHEMIST Kaufman, meanwhile, had been poking around for signs of blood. It made him feel a little strange to be wandering through the Douglas home like this. When the professor had opened the door, Kaufman recognized him instantly as one of the commuters who, like himself, took one of the last trains from Boston to Norfolk of an evening. He seemed harmless enough. A neighbor. Through some improbable circumstances he had become an outlaw whose belongings had been transformed into pieces of evidence to be bagged, tagged, taped, scraped, soaked, and examined in microscopic detail.

A quick scan of the rooms hadn't turned up any visible stains, but even if someone scrubbed a spot until it was invisible to the naked eye, it left a residue which could be detected for many years. Kaufman went to the living room, opened his tool kit, and took out a piece of laboratory filter paper. He chose a section of floorboard and rubbed it with the tissue. Then he took out two bottles filled with reagents. He applied two drops of the first to the paper, waited a moment, and applied the second. If blood was present, the paper would turn a deep aquamarine. There was nothing. Kaufman tried a few more places in the living room, then moved along to the master bedroom, where he tested a throw rug and the bare floorboards. He got a couple of "slow reactions," but these were common in a dirty house where decaying vegetables like potatoes could give a response similar to that of blood.

Kaufman opened a hallway closet near the master bedroom. Hanging there were two or three nylon jackets and some sport coats. There was no blood that the chemist could see. He tested the first couple of garments, with negative results. Then, spying a windbreaker, he rubbed the outside of the pocket with filter paper and, applying the reagents, got a strong reaction. He showed the results to Sharkey, who took the jacket into the kitchen and asked Douglas if it was his.

"Well, it looks like mine and I would say it was mine, but I don't know," Douglas replied. "Could I try it on?"

Douglas pulled on the coat and zipped it up the front. It appeared to fit him perfectly.

"It looks like mine, but I'm not going to say it was mine. I couldn't really say it was mine," he insisted, adding that he hadn't worn it for two years.

Sharkey searched the pockets and found a couple of scraps of paper. On them, someone—apparently Nancy—had written notations about her patients. There was clearly a possibility that the windbreaker belonged to, or at least was used by, Nancy Douglas.

Sharkey felt it was time to confer with Kivlan. The prosecutor couldn't risk setting foot inside the house, for fear of being called as a witness. He had confined himself to the Malibu, smoking unfiltered Luckies and waiting for reports from Landry about the amazing discoveries inside. As he listened to Sharkey's account of blood on the nylon jacket, something occurred to him. Sharkey should go back in and try to get Douglas on record saying that he had never been near Robin's car. That way if the car were found and his fingerprints turned up on the vehicle, they would have him trapped.

Douglas, however, seemed to be anticipating this. He hadn't been in Robin's car that night, he said, but he had ridden in it "one of three days" before her disappearance.

Sharkey touched on another point Kivlan wanted clarified. When exactly had Robin left his house that night? To this he now replied, "A few minutes before midnight." He had widened the cushion of time before Nancy Douglas arrived home.

There was still a third matter that Kivlan wanted to get cleared up. Exactly how did Douglas perceive his relationship to Robin Benedict? He had first represented himself as her employer, then as a friend of the family. He had told Borstel, then Landry, that he used her services as a prostitute.

How long, Sharkey asked Douglas, had he and Robin been in love?

Douglas bridled at this suggestion, insisting that Robin was "a friend." During the year he had known her, they had had sex, though he couldn't say how many times. When Sharkey asked abruptly how much he had paid her, he replied, "I don't have a dollar figure on hand." He couldn't even come up with an estimate.

Was it possible, Sharkey tendered, that she was shaking him down?

"No. No," he protested, apparently revolted by this suggestion. "That never happened, and she wouldn't do that."

But, Sharkey reminded him, he had reported to the Sharon police that Robin filched his slides in exchange for money. Wasn't that extortion?

Douglas conceded that it was. "But," he emphasized once again, "she wasn't really like that."

SHARKEY wasn't sure what to make of William Douglas. There were times when he had looked at the professor and tended, like Paul Landry, to see a poor soul who had allowed himself to be tortured and provoked until he finally returned a blow. That was understandable. Douglas had just closed a case where a sweet old codger had knifed his nagging wife to death and was acquitted. But the professor was clearly more complicated than that. Although he had slipped up inexplicably on the head wound, he seemed wary in other respects, parrying the attempt to link him to the car, distancing Nancy further and further from the crime. He was sometimes clever, evasive, and, Sharkey thought, a little arrogant. The more he talked, the more Sharkey tended to agree with Kivlan's assessment. Douglas was convinced that he was too smart to be caught, too important to be prosecuted. Sharkey decided it was time to drop the pretense of respect.

"Doctor," he announced gravely, "I must tell you that I find your handling of the truth careless and believe you have something to do with Robin Benedict's disappearance or murder."

"I'm awfully sorry you feel that way," Douglas replied quietly.

"If you killed Robin," Sharkey pressed, "would you please be gentlemanly enough to tell us where the body is so that she could have a decent Christian burial? If you have any principles, morals, or scruples—or any concern whatsoever for your wife and children—you will do the right thing and lead us to her remains."

"I didn't kill her, and everything I told you is the truth," Douglas insisted. "I only wish I could help you more."

Sharkey leveled his final salvo.

"You are the worst liar I have ever encountered in my thirty years as a police officer."

Douglas gave a start.

"I don't know why I am talking to you," he said. "I want a phone, and I want to call a lawyer. In fact, you told me when you read that little card that you would get me a lawyer. Now I want you to get me one right away."

Sharkey left Douglas fussing with a phone book, and he went back outside to break the news to Kivlan. Douglas had not confessed and now probably would not confess. He was looking for an attorney. Kivlan knew that whatever else he hoped to get from 38 Sandy Ridge Circle would have to be gotten before a defense attorney rang down the curtain. He sent Sharkey back into the house to try to persuade Douglas to give fingerprints and a blood sample. Douglas refused.

With that, he wandered down the hall to the master bedroom, curled up on the bed, and appeared to go to sleep.

Sharkey was taken aback by this development. Not knowing what else to do, he went back out to the Malibu and told Kivlan, "Can you believe it? This guy's taking a nap!" Kivlan didn't know what to make of it either. He turned to Matt Connolly and asked if he would like to take the last shot at Douglas.

Connolly went into the house, roused the sleeping professor, and led him to a couch in the boy's bedroom. He asked him for a blood sample. Douglas refused.

"A girl was seen at your place last," Connolly said. "Are you sure you don't want to tell us where the body is?"

He looked at Douglas's face. It was empty, an insipid mask whose inscrutability was betrayed only by his eyes, which darted now and then from Connolly to Sharkey and back. The assistant DA could not read that expression, only imagine what he would be feeling in Douglas's position. Desperation and terror, no doubt. If he were Douglas right now, he thought, he would either confess or commit suicide.

It was not to be a confession. For the last time, Douglas insisted he had told all he knew.

By then it was 2:40 A.M. The search party had been at work for two and a half hours. Connolly, who saw no more to be done, signaled the troopers it was time to leave. As they hauled their booty to the cruisers, Kivlan kept an eye on the house, hoping to get some clue as to what Douglas might do in the wake of this intrusion. He caught a glimpse of a figure through a glass panel that ran down one side of the front door. Douglas was locking up. Then the lights went out at 38 Sandy Ridge Circle.

CLUES

BY NOW John Kivlan was convinced that Douglas was not going to confess. The next move, he felt, was to go after his wife and children. Paul Landry disagreed, and this contention lay at the heart of the strain that was building between them. Although Kivlan had originally stepped in to champion Landry when Sharkey was expressing doubts about his ability to handle the case, he was now beginning to feel that he had made a mistake. He had figured Landry for a good soldier who would take direction. But now Landry, in his view, was becoming possessive of evidence and authority. He seemed to consider the Benedict case *his* case. Kivlan, who had a rigorously impersonal view of public service, considered this unhealthy. To the prosecutor's way of thinking, an investigation belonged not to one individual but to the Commonwealth. And now, when Kivlan felt it was critical to isolate the wife and children, Landry was advancing his own ideas about how to proceed. The trooper frankly felt sorry for the children, and he hated the thought of having to say to them, "Look, your father is a murderer." He wanted to continue working on Douglas himself. He was gaining the suspect's confidence, he felt, and if he could just keep the pressure on for a day or two more, he assured Kivlan, he was sure he could get him to crack.

Kivlan prevailed upon Landry, however, to ride out on Monday morning to the Ellis Nursing Home to confront Nancy Douglas with some of the more unpleasant details of the search. Arranging a meeting with her in the parking lot, he showed her a pair of women's shoes that had been found on the floor of the master bedroom closet. They were brown, size

9B, and inscribed with the brand name Pretties. She identified the shoes as her own. Landry then showed her the Armstrong flute. Nancy said she thought that belonged to her daughter Pam. The dark leather pocketbook, however, she could not place. Nor did she know how the address books with credit cards belonging to Robin Benedict got into her closet. Her husband had told her that nothing of evidenciary value had been taken during the search.

"It's gonna be in the papers," Landry told her. "He's hurt you. He's hurt the kids. I understand you're married to the guy. I understand your loyalties and everything else. But how much can you live with? Can you sleep with that?"

Nancy, Landry later recorded in his notes, appeared "visibly shaken and emotionally upset." And she said she wanted to talk to an attorney. When Landry relayed this back to Kivlan, the prosecutor pushed him to go right over to the house and try to get to the kids. Landry, however, was still reluctant to do this and argued that Douglas was surely on the verge of confessing.

That night Landry called Douglas and implored, "If there is anything that you can tell me now, so I don't have to talk with the kids, tell me. . . ." Douglas thanked him but said he would like to have until morning to think about it. Landry agreed. But the morning and, indeed, the entire day passed with no word from Douglas.

Kivlan's patience was at an end. Landry, he insisted, must contact the children without delay. The question was whom to approach first. In recounting the events of March 5, Nancy Douglas had been a little vague about which of the boys had been with her as she drove around waiting for Robin to leave. Landry thought he had heard her say Billy. By contrast, Nancy had been specific about picking up thirteen-year-old Pammy on her way down the road. Landry had checked with the couple for whom Pam had been baby-sitting. Marsha and Elliot Eisenberg, who lived a couple of houses up on Sandy Ridge Circle, explained that Pammy had a standing Saturday-night engagement with their children. On the night of March 5, Pam baby-sat while they went to the Home Show in Boston. They had left about six to six-thirty and returned to Sharon around eleven-thirty to midnight. Pam left about then to go home. This was independent confirmation that the girl was in the neighborhood at the time Robin Benedict was at the Douglas house.

Landry drove out to the Sharon Middle School and asked to see Pamela. But the principal refused, explaining that the parents' attorney— one Daniel J. O'Connell—had requested that the girl not be allowed to speak to anyone.

Kivlan, as it happened, knew Dan O'Connell very well. His father had

been an important figure in the Boston Irish legal establishment. He had
been executive secretary to Governor Foster Furculo and after that a
superior-court judge. Danny O'Connell was connected to the hilt. Kivlan
and O'Connell had studied law together at Boston College and later
shared an office as young assistant district attorneys in Middlesex County.
Though Kivlan's reserve usually precluded socializing with coworkers, he
and Dan had gone out for dinner occasionally with their wives. They
considered themselves close friends. O'Connell, Kivlan knew, was a dogged, pugnacious advocate. If the Douglases succeeded in hiring him, the
state might lose all future access to them. He urged Landry to take
another shot at Pam.

It was midafternoon when Landry arrived at Sandy Ridge Circle.
Douglas invited him into the house, then proceeded to explain that, on
his attorney's advice, he could not allow Pamela to be interviewed. Just
then Pam emerged from the hallway and yelled in a high-pitched voice,
"Why is everyone trying to get something on my father?" Then she ran
back to her room, weeping.

Landry turned to Douglas and said, "Why don't you tell your kids
exactly what is going on here?"

EVEN as he was making forays into Sandy Ridge Circle, Paul Landry was
trying to make sense of the evidence taken during the search. On Monday
morning he called J.R. Rogers and asked him to come down to the
barracks. Rogers swung by on his way back from karate practice. He was
wearing a T-shirt, blue jeans, and baseball cap, looking almost self-con-
sciously ordinary. As far as the DA's office was concerned, Rogers was now
in the clear. The search had settled suspicion squarely upon the Douglas
household. What's more, J.R. had settled his score with the traffic court
in Weston, something which increased Landry's confidence in him.

Landry led Rogers into the evidence room where, after briefly recap-
ping the search, he showed J.R. Robin's Visa card and MasterCard. It was
Landry's opinion that Robin was dead. J.R. began to pace back and forth.
Then he sat, looked at the ceiling, and started to cry.

The trooper withdrew certain other items taken from the Douglas
house in hopes that J.R. could provide some additional explanations.
Among these were the black and red address books. J.R. did not acknowledge ever having seen the books but declared that the writing in them
closely resembled Robin's hand. He went on to explain that when Robin's
Marlborough Street apartment had been burgled in December, the intruder had not only ransacked the place but also taken a TV set, telephone, and other odds and ends. Among these, Robin had told him, was

one of her "black books" as well as the Panasonic answering machine which Douglas had bought for her.

During the second break, a week later, the intruder had used a key. This time he took $300 in cash and a cheap Record-A-Call answering machine with which Robin had replaced the Panasonic. In the aftermath of these thefts, Douglas bought Robin another Panasonic, identical to the first.

After the black book was taken, Robin's clients began receiving harassing phone calls. Their wives would be told about "the prostitute" Robin Benedict. Robin also began getting strange calls, mostly hang-ups. She told Douglas about this, and he said he had a friend who worked for the phone company and could catch the culprit. It was J.R.'s impression that this supposed friend had Robin's phone bugged while they were living in Natick.

Landry then played for J.R. a tape which had been found on the bedroom bureau. This one had been made by someone, presumably Douglas, affecting a falsetto. "Hello, hello," it began:

Is your whore from the Combat Zone working tonight? . . . The one who calls herself Bobbie. Robin Benedict. You know we're going to close that fucking place of yours for bringing whores from the Combat Zone back here to *our town* of Saugus.

There was an interlude of coughing. Then the speaker made another attempt. This time in a more authoritative voice.

This has got to stop. We don't want this type of person coming up to Saugus. Call the Danish Health Club—the number is 231-0068—and complain. If [they don't] fire her, we will picket. We will demonstrate, and we will get it so that no man will go inside that place.

(The speaker made yet a third try.)

This is Tom McAllison. [His voice dropped suddenly.] Tom McAllison. I'll speak very quietly because I don't want to be overheard. . . . I'm at the Danish Health Club. Route 1. Saugus. One of their masseuses propositioned me for sex for money. Tried to sell me some dope. I will testify to both of these because we as the good citizens of Saugus are going to rid ourselves of the stench of this place.

J.R. was able to shed some light on this. Robin, he said, used to work at a place called the Danish Health Club in Saugus. She used the names Nadine Porter and, sometimes, Bobbie. Douglas would go to the club frequently when she was working. He used the name Hank. Then the owners of the club began receiving anonymous phone calls saying that Bobbie was a whore from the Combat Zone. The Saugus Board of Health also got calls about Bobbie because one of their investigators went to the club and told the owners to fire her.

THAT SAME DAY, Landry contacted the fraud department of BayBank Middlesex, which had issued Robin's MasterCard, to see if her plate had been reported missing. It had not. Among those charges which Robin had made during the three weeks prior to her disappearance, however, was one for an air ticket on Bar Harbor Airways. It had been issued for travel on February 17 or 18 from Boston to Albany, connecting to a flight into Plattsburgh, New York. Landry called J.R. for more details on the Plattsburgh trip and learned that Robin had flown up to join William Douglas, who was attending a seminar. Douglas had made some sort of "attractive proposition" to get her there. She had flown up on Thursday, February 17, and driven back with Douglas on Saturday, February 19. J.R. didn't seem to know any more than that.

Three days later Landry got a call from Shirley Benedict, who had found a two-minute toll call which Robin had charged to her parents' phone. She thought it might be "significant." Landry checked into it and found it had been made on Friday, February 18, at about half past noon from a phone booth in Elizabethtown, New York, some fifty miles south of Plattsburgh. The number she had dialed was a Charlestown exchange listed to one Joseph Murray.

CHARLESTOWN which lies north of Boston, is a gritty precinct bordered on three sides by waterfront. In the early 1820s the Irish moved there to work in the navy yards. During the potato famine twenty years later, Charlestown was overrun by immigrants who supplanted indigenous Yankees on Breed's and Bunker hills, latticing the slopes with rows of cramped three-decker houses. After that Charlestown remained a clannish Celtic enclave—tough, chauvinistic, and suspicious of outsiders. It was not the sort of place in which Robin Benedict might be going to a fashionable party.

From the point they had first been queried by investigators, J.R. Rogers and Savi Bisram insisted they did not know this "Joe from Charlestown." That was not surprising, since the townies on Bunker Hill had no use for dark skin. It was possible, of course, that J.R. knew more than he was telling. Three days after he had hired the Central Secret Service Bureau, he had passed on a "tip" to them that they should check with someone named Bucky, who owned a place called Angie's Deli on Broad Street, near Government Center. Bucky was supposed to know who Joe was. DaRosa and Smith visited Angie's but were not able to locate Bucky.

The house search had turned up one new bit of information about this Joe. There was a notation in Robin's black book that was different from the rest of the entries. Penciled in a hand that did not appear to be Robin's, it read, "Joe with house."

Landry called the Charlestown number and got Joe Murray, who agreed to meet him later that evening in the parking lot of the Howard Johnson on the Southeast Expressway in Quincy. At around seven-thirty Murray showed up. He was a thickset man in his late thirties. He had a large head and short gray hair, the quintessential Charlestown tough. At first he didn't seem inclined to talk. Even when Landry threatened to have him brought before a grand jury, he wouldn't be rattled.

"I've been before the grand jury before," he replied.

When Landry stepped back into a more conciliatory pose, Murray relented, saying he had read the *Boston Herald* story about Robin's supposedly going to visit a "Joe in Charlestown" and that he knew the police would be looking for him. He promised to cooperate any way he could.

He said he was a businessman. He owned a company called Harbor Oil, which leased all kinds of vehicles, cars, motorcycles, motorboats, and aircraft. He had met Robin Benedict a couple of years earlier at a Boston bar called the Saint and had seen her on "many occasions" since, sometimes as a "client," sometimes as a "friend." She would come to him for advice when she was in a scrape.

Murray insisted that he had given no party the night of March 5 and had not called Robin's telephone service. He had been at home all night with his wife, Suzanne. The last time he had seen Benedict, he said, was around February 18, when she and a male companion drove into the neighborhood at about 9:00 to 9:30 P.M. They were in a light blue, late-model Datsun or Toyota. Robin's companion, he recalled, wore glasses. Robin, who had gotten out of the car to talk for a while, indicated that they were on their way back from New York.

During that same conversation, she happened to mention that around Christmastime a client—a "young guy" whom she had taken to her apartment on Beacon Street—had tried to strangle her. She had run out of the place leaving all of her belongings—including her black book—and the assailant apparently took it. Since then she had been getting strange phone calls. Murray then told Landry that during the week before Robin disappeared, his wife had also been bothered by a nuisance caller.

Landry phoned Suzanne Murray from a booth in the parking lot to get her account of this. She told him about a man who had called her to say that Joe was going out with "a whore from Boston named Nadine." The next call seemed to be made by a man using a high-pitched voice. He identified himself as Nadine, someone who was having a relationship with Joe. Suzanne Murray said she had heard Robin's voice before and knew this was a phony. She told the caller, "So what," and hung up. Then, two or three days ago, there had been another call. Nobody said anything, but she heard a typewriter clicking in the background.

Before he left Murray in the parking lot, Landry asked him if he would be willing to take a lie detector test. Murray replied that he would be happy to, "any time or any place," because he had "nothing to hide."

MEANWHILE, in the perennial dusk of the Gray House attic, John Kivlan had been sorting through the jumble of clippings and memorabilia in the Seagram's box. The panties, the wadded-up gum, the notebooks, the credit cards. Why had Douglas kept these things? For sentimental reasons? Were these mementos of Robin through which he continued to pursue his obsession?

One of the most curious items he found lying among the pornographic matter was a set of clippings about prostitutes. The oldest dated back to 1979 when the Boston vice squad had picked up a number of women ranging "from a peasant grandmother in a babushka" to a "sweet-faced 15-year-old who could easily have been her granddaughter." The hookers in this sweep seemed to specialize in oral sex. Another clip from the *Providence Journal* of the preceding October told how prostitutes had infiltrated an old West End neighborhood, making it difficult for decent women to walk the streets.

At the very least, this told Kivlan that the professor had a fascination with working girls going back four years, to a period when he had recently moved to Sharon. This was also around the time when the bodies of teenage prostitutes had started to appear along Route 95. The prosecutor had not dismissed the possibility that Douglas might be a serial killer. On the other hand, it was possible that the clippings had some more private significance. Perhaps they were like specimens whose provocative details had been fixed in newsprint, to which Douglas could return and study whenever he liked. It was, perhaps, the only way that an academic, lacking knowledge in how certain human contacts are made, could hope to penetrate a world of women who were as available as they were forbidden.

One thing that Kivlan found odd was that nowhere among these mementos was there a photo of Robin. If Douglas had been into fetishes such as panties and gum, would he not at least have kept her picture around, even if only her license photo? Landry had learned from J.R. that Robin kept her license on her whenever she drove. He had searched the Cliff Street house and was unable to find it. As Kivlan reviewed the events of the preceding Saturday night, he realized that neither Landry nor Sharkey had searched Douglas's pockets. It was possible that he might still have Robin's license in his wallet.

On Saturday, March 26, Kivlan got a second warrant, this one for Landry to search Douglas's house and person. Landry and another trooper arrived midmorning at the Douglas house. At Landry's request Douglas handed over his billfold; as Nancy and the children looked on, Landry went through it. There was a white business card imprinted with the name Nadine. There was also a card from "William C. Dwyer, Detective, Boston Police Dept." But there was no license.

Landry took the opportunity to check out a couple of other areas he had given short shrift during the first search. On the dining room table he had noticed an Apple II Plus computer. When Landry had asked Douglas if it belonged to him, Douglas assured him it did. The computer had an identification tag on its underside. Landry now wrote down the serial number.

Returning to the master bedroom closet, he went looking for something specific, a brown tote bag. It was a foot long and five or six inches deep, flanked by two carrying handles. It bore a leather tag engraved "LEICA." It appeared to have been used for camera equipment. The interior was divided into several compartments, and there was a back pocket into which Douglas had slipped a number of papers. Landry had done a quick search of the bag the preceding Saturday and had removed a handful of odds and ends.

Now he wanted to go through the satchel again to see if there was anything he had overlooked. Sure enough, in the back pocket were some twenty pages of notes in Douglas's hand, which appeared to reconstruct the events leading up to March 5. At the bottom of the bag was a small red plastic case imprinted with the logo of the Bank of Boston. When Landry opened the flap, he found two razor blades and some white powder wrapped in paper.

Douglas, who was lounging across the bed, exhibited casual curiosity. "What's that?" he asked.

"It looks to me like it might be cocaine," Landry told him.

"Well," Douglas asked innocently, "how did it get in my bag?"

It occurred to Landry that Douglas might have lured Robin down to Sharon on the pretext of needing coke for the weekend. A "Can you supply me?" sort of line. He put in a call to Kivlan and asked him if he should arrest Douglas for possession. The prosecutor thought for a moment. The amount, from what he could tell from the description, was less than the statutory minimum for a jail sentence. That would mean that Douglas would be taken down to Stoughton District Court and released on his own recognizance. Worse, from the prosecution's point of view, was that it would open another criminal case. From a practical standpoint, any defense attorney could then use the discovery process to require the state to turn over reports on the house search. Kivlan did not want to risk having the homicide investigation derailed by a peripheral issue, so he told Landry to hold off making an arrest.

Landry had in the meantime turned up another item, which seemed to demand more immediate attention. Under a stack of textbooks to the right of the bureau, he had found a pad of tan stationery with writing, which seemed to belong to Nancy Douglas. She had penned a lament to no one in particular. It read:

> I wish I knew what was going on—those horrible feelings of loneliness, distance and despair are back again and I don't think I can deal with it again. I need someone to talk to, someone just to hold me. All I can do is cry. Why is this happening? Why don't he just come home? Why does he hate me? . . . I think he's on drugs too. Oh, God. Please help me. Please, please help me. I can't take any more.

Nancy wrote that she wished Bill would go to see a certain "Dr. Randolph." For the most part, however, she blamed herself for the family's troubles, faulting herself for neglecting the children. Suicide, she mused, would be so "nice" if she didn't have responsibility for the kids. She ticked off an eerie litany of methods. Slitting her wrists, running the car into a wall, carbon monoxide.

Landry was alarmed. He had caught glimpses of Nancy's face during the last search. She appeared dazed and unresponsive to what was happening around her. Now he felt that she might actually be on the brink of taking her own life. Only the day before, Landry had gotten an unsolicited phone call from a Stephen Boulton, who identified himself as an attorney and police officer in West Warwick, Rhode Island. Boulton was also Nancy Douglas's brother. He had been talking to his sister, he said, about the disappearance of Robin Benedict and would like to find out more about the case. After turning up Nancy's letter, Landry called Boulton back to say he was concerned that his sister might do harm to herself. There was also a possibility that William Douglas, threatened with exposure, might go off the deep end and do something to Nancy and the children.

Boulton came immediately to the Foxboro barracks, where he identified the writing on the tan pad as Nancy's. He confided to Landry that it was his opinion, based on several conversations with his sister, that she might be hiding something for Bill's sake. Boulton did not seem particularly fond of his brother-in-law and told Landry he would try to get Nancy away from the house to talk with her privately.

Two days later Boulton called Landry with unexpected news. The sledgehammer found in the Mansfield barrel probably belonged to his father, who had lent it to Nancy when she and the children came down to West Warwick for Thanksgiving. (Douglas didn't come with the family that day, claiming he had to remain at Tufts with his experiments.) Nancy had said she needed the hammer to repair her porch. She never returned it.

Kivlan was elated to hear this news. The hammer, which by now was widely assumed to be the murder weapon, had so far eluded identification. The troopers had found nothing in the search which indicated that it might have come from the Douglas house. Each of the Douglases had been shown the instrument, and each had claimed not to recognize it. Now Nancy's own father was saying that he had lent his daughter just such a hammer a little over three months earlier.

The following day Landry and a trooper named Brian Howe drove down to West Warwick to meet Stephen Boulton and his father, John, at the police station. Landry showed the sledgehammer to the elder man, who examined it carefully. John Boulton seemed hesitant to express an opinion but finally conceded that, while slightly more worn, it was "fairly identical to the hammer [he] had." In fact, he was "99 percent" sure that it was the one he had lent Nancy. John Boulton then took the troopers home to his cellar workshop. There on a wall each of his tools, except for the missing sledgehammer, hung meticulously in place, suspended by eye screws. A package of these hooks was hanging from a pegboard on the wall. With Boulton's permission Trooper Howe removed them, put them into an evidence bag, and took them back to Dedham.

EARLY the following week, Kivlan received word of yet another macabre discovery—one that promised to link Robin even more closely to Sandy Ridge Circle. In going through William Douglas's blue windbreaker, the chemist Kaufman had found a mass of grayish material, compressed and flattened to about the size of a quarter and stuck to the inside of the right pocket. Taking a pair of tweezers, the chemist managed to peel it off intact, leaving a slight ring on the fabric. He tested a portion of it to see if it contained blood or protein which would identify it as human, but got negative results. He then set the specimen in formalin and sent it off to

Dr. George Katsas, a widely respected forensic pathologist who had once served as medical examiner for Suffolk County. Katsas, Kaufman hoped, could determine microscopically what kind of tissue it was.

Dr. Katsas was not optimistic. Over three weeks had passed since the Benedict girl had disappeared, he observed. If the tissue was hers, it might be so deteriorated as to defy analysis. When he saw the specimen, however, he marveled at how well preserved it was. Its pristine condition was apparently the result of its having been pressed and dried in a fairly sterile environment.

The formalin had caused the fragment to solidify slightly. Katsas cut a thin slice and placed it under the microscope. It had the distinctive architecture of brain cells and even appeared to contain a fragment of skull tissue. He could not say on the basis of this histological examination, however, that it was from a *human* brain. Observed microscopically, the brain tissue of a monkey is indistinguishable from that of a man. Katsas could only infer from Kaufman's tests, which found human blood and protein on the surrounding pocket fabric, that the brain tissue had come from a human being.

That the tissue could not be unequivocally deemed human vexed John Kivlan. He was interested to learn, however, that the specimen was composed of white cells normally found beneath an exterior layer of gray matter. The sample would have to have come from a depth of at least one-fifth of an inch. This meant that it could not have escaped easily from a superficial wound. The brain, Katsas explained, was completely enclosed, with no natural openings, so the victim would have had to have suffered a severe injury to the head for brain tissue to escape from the wound or be forced through the nose or mouth. The wound from which the matter came, Katsas continued, would have had to have been inflicted by a gunshot, which characteristically scattered tissue, or from a blunt injury with massive, extensive laceration of the skin and fracture of the bone so that brain spilled out. Either way, he concluded, it must have been a very open injury.

The other possibility, Kivlan knew, was that the tissue had come from some experiment that Douglas was conducting at Tufts. Perhaps a lab specimen that spilled into his pocket. Kaufman did not think this was likely. The tissue did not appear to have been artificially fixed prior to being set in the formalin. At Kivlan's request, Landry had called Karen Hitchcock at Tufts to ask if Douglas had done any work with human brain tissue. The chairman checked around and reported back that several months earlier some of Bill's colleagues had been working on a brain project where they had used only animal tissue.

Douglas, at any rate, was not a collaborator on that project.

JOHN KIVLAN, meanwhile, had discovered yet another investigation in progress. From a box next to the bureau in the Douglases' master bedroom, troopers had taken an interim audit report dated January 26, 1983. Therein, the auditor Richard Thorngren had enumerated Douglas's suspected financial misdeeds and placed the university's mounting losses at $46,127.96.

In the same box where they had found the audit, the troopers also recovered a set of handwritten notes wherein Douglas had sketched out his troubles with Tufts. These random thoughts, which he had scribbled on strips of paper and then stapled to a larger sheet, had apparently been composed for the benefit of a psychiatrist or an attorney. Kivlan could not tell which:

> Used all of our savings to see girl, then started to use Tufts money by turning in false trips. By Mid-August, Nancy was getting suspicious and started questioning the continued long hours, credit card charges and my activities . . . so there were more pressures at home. . . . In Oct. Nancy was accusing me of seeing someone. She confronted me with evidence. The VP called— meet with auditor & on my birthday (Nov. 1) met with you.

Douglas had then composed what appeared to be a little script of what he intended to tell the auditor.

> I'm very troubled by this . . . I want to cooperate.
> It's important that I answer your questions accurately & right now the anxiety level is very high.
> I am having difficulty remembering what are real charges and what are not.

Douglas had refined these ruminations further in one of the cassettes taken from the bedroom bureau. In this tape he seemed to be rehearsing a story to tell the auditor. He chose his words slowly, stopping the tape at intervals to form new thoughts. Most peculiar, he seemed to be addressing himself to an unidentified companion, who occasionally offered suggestions in a low, androgynous voice. Douglas began,

> Always worked hard and have had twelve-, fourteen-, fifteen-hour days. But I always felt in control because I could pace the workload. At night, I still had enough time for myself and for my family and for some life outside of work. But since January [or] February of '82 . . . things changed for the worse . . . duties were added constantly. . . . I've always had trouble saying no to things, but it got to the point where I had to sleep at work because I couldn't afford the half hour commute each day. . . .
> And during all this added pressure, something snapped. Something just

. . . in talking about it now with my wife, I realize that I was a different person. . . . Something must have happened to me personality-wise because I've always been a very hardworking individual, a very honest individual and I'd never think of cheating or taking anything that wasn't mine. And, in fact, you know, if I'm employed by someone I always give them 150 percent instead of 80 percent or 100 percent. . . . And it just does not seem in character for me to have faked travel . . . uh . . . ummm travel vouchers and so on and so forth, and I think that's symptomatic that that was a problem. And it's unfortunate and heartbreaking to realize that no one at work, where I spent all of my time, noticed anything or said anything to me about it. And the first I knew that there was a problem was when I got a call from the vice-president of the university.

So, the question is, why did I do the things with the travel advances? And the one possible answer is "I don't know." I don't remember doing it. All of that activity is blocked from my mind and although down deep I feel that I did do it . . . I don't remember any part of those activities and I guess that really scares me. And that's why I went to see Dr. Randolph because I felt that something was seriously wrong. The question is "What did you do with the money?" versus "Why did you do it?"

At this point, Douglas's mystery companion interjected in a muffled, sexless voice, "Scheming . . . sounds like you were deliberately scheming to take money from your grants at the university. We don't have any of the money."
Douglas continued,

But the question is what did I do with the money? Here's one possible explanation for what we did with the money. It was 3:00 A.M. one morning and I had my car parked . . . in the parking lot across the street and I was just very tired and decided to go out and get a cup of coffee to stay awake because I'm not a coffee drinker. And so I went up to . . . was going to drive up to one of the all-night . . . restaurants in Kenmore Square and get a nice big coffee to go. And . . . okay, so I was walking across the parking lot to my car and a girl in the parking lot who looked like Joanne Sateriale, who used to work for me, said, "What's up, Doc?" And that's a phrase Joanne Sateriale always used to use. And I said, "Joanne, what are you doing here?" She said, "I was down at the hospital bringing some tissues from the Retna Foundation." I said, "At three o'clock in the morning?" . . . trying to say . . . that was not Joanne Sateriale, that was another girl. That was the hooker, but she looked a lot like Joanne Sateriale, and when I called her Joanne, she just played right along with it. And I told her I was going out for a cup of coffee, and she said, "Well, why don't you come over to my place and have a cup of coffee?" And then, so I went over and had coffee with her, but first she gave me some apple juice before . . . while she was making coffee, since I was thirsty. And that . . . I passed out, and then when I woke up . . . then when I woke up, she and her boyfriend had taken pictures of me with her in bed and said that they were going to show my kids and my wife. And then that's what started the blackmail.

Douglas paused to address his companion. "My idea stinks," he said blankly. "What's yours?"

There was silence for a moment; then Douglas resumed his litany of mounting stresses. The department chairman, he claimed, had been pirating his ideas. He was spending so little time at home that when he was there he couldn't relax and relate "normally" to the family. Something as minor as repairing the dishwasher became intolerable.

My wife actually saw the problem, and she said I was taking on too much and I was working too many hours and that the strain was beginning to take its toll. And my response to her [was] that she just wasn't supportive anymore. All of a sudden, I started seeing someone else because that was one place I could go and relax and there wouldn't be any problems. . . . So this girl actually became a crutch to help me through this difficult time. In looking back on it now, she obviously was a very bright person because she could see the problems that I had at work and was having when I went home and she decided to capitalize on it. It first started by the using the $15,000 that we had at home . . . then when that was gone, we started using money from work.

In August, the pressures at work were not relieved and the home situation became worse because my wife, poor dear, finally decided . . . [Here, the mystery companion gave a deep chuckle.] . . . finally caught on to what was going on and became . . . very suspicious, so she was questioning every move I made. . . . Through all of this, obviously, I was leading two lives, but I was so busy that I didn't have a chance to really reflect on it and realize what was wrong and put a stop to it, which is what I would have done on any normal circumstance of having time to breathe and to reflect and to think about things. And then when my wife met me at the airport when I came back from a trip to Washington, and [said] the vice-president called, these two things just hit me that there obviously is something wrong and then everything has begun to fall into place. The money was given to the girl so she would continue to see me.

Am I crazy? My wife thinks I had a nervous breakdown. . . .

By his own account, Douglas had clearly been going through some kind of crisis. He was under pressure at work. Things were apparently not going well at home. So he had sought an antidote to his discomfort in the company of a pretty hooker.

Kivlan was not convinced that this added up to "crazy" in a clinical sense. But as he listened to the remarkable recitation in what would come to be called the "What's up, Doc?" tape, he became convinced that the suspect was a pathological liar. In one breath he was all tears and contrition; in the next he was framing a deliberate lie.

Who was the mystery companion? Who would have been close enough to him to listen and critique his deceptions? The respondent had used the pronoun "we."

"We don't have any of the money."

It was obviously someone familiar with Douglas's situation at the university. Robin? A coworker, perhaps? Kivlan asked Landry to check out Tufts to see who knew what about Douglas's affair with Benedict.

The auditor Thorngren's interim report seemed to suggest that the security department at the Bank of Boston had a considerable amount of information about both Miss Benedict and her financial arrangements with William Douglas. So Landry called the bank, where he located Joseph Gibbons, an officer referred to in the auditor's memo. Gibbons acknowledged familiarity with the case. Tufts University, which kept its own accounts at the Bank of Boston, had asked him to look into the financial activities of William Douglas, Savitry Bisram, and Robin Benedict. Bank cameras at the 710 Washington Street branch had caught all three negotiating Tufts vendors checks totaling $70,000 to $80,000. The bank had been trying to get in touch with Benedict and Bisram to question them, but without success.

Landry asked Gibbons about a pair of keys found during a search of Douglas's house. He had checked with the company which manufactured them, and confirmed that they belonged to a safety deposit box at the Bank of Boston. They were both tagged No. 920.

Gibbons confirmed that lock box 920 had been rented by William Douglas on July 1, 1982. His application specified that the account was to be held jointly with his "wife," Robin N. Benedict. The last time anyone had entered the box was on February 23, 1983, when Robin Benedict signed in at 8:51 A.M. Landry recognized that as the morning when Douglas and Robin had had their tiff on the lawn in Sharon. A check of his notes revealed that Robin had entered the vault only seven minutes after Douglas called police to complain that someone was "extorting" him.

Late Monday morning, March 28, Landry visited the Bank of Boston at 710 Washington carrying a warrant. The vault attendant brought Douglas's lock box to a private room where, as Landry watched, the bank manager took one of the keys and opened the box. It was completely empty.

Shortly after noon Landry called the Tufts University police, asking if anyone had observed a girl matching Robin Benedict's description coming in and out of the building. One security officer, a Michelle Benkovic, thought she might have seen Douglas with a short, dark-haired woman after hours. But all visitors who entered M&V after six o'clock were, in theory at least, required to sign a log book, and there was no record of a Robin Benedict.

John Kivlan secured a warrant to search Douglas's office, and on Wednesday morning Landry set out for Tufts with Trooper Brian Howe.

Trooper Howe was a lanky, sober man. A former Marine pilot, he also had an M.B.A. and was noted for writing scrupulously detailed reports. For the preceding five months he had been working out of the fire marshal's office in Boston. Only recently had he been assigned to Norfolk, to investigate a spate of suspicious fires. Howe had found the arson detail dreary work and was eager to get back into regular investigations. So when Sharkey called him in to assist Paul Landry, he was glad to do it.

Howe knew Landry casually. The two been classmates at the State Police Academy in Framingham. They had even roomed together for three or four weeks. Howe liked Landry well enough. He had been to his home once and was surprised to find it a small museum of state police artifacts: mugs, insignia, and other memorabilia. All in all, Landry's zeal for police work struck him as a little excessive.

Operating, as he did, on the periphery of the Norfolk County office, Howe was not really aware of the politics surrounding the Benedict case until he and Landry rode down to West Warwick together to check out the hammer. Landry grumbled about how he thought the DA's office was going to screw him. He had done a lot of work on this case, he said, and he wasn't going to just step aside and let all of it go to someone else. Howe shrugged, saying that he didn't know anything about that. On the trip to Tufts that Wednesday morning, Howe took pains to avoid any discussion of office politics.

The troopers arrived at the Boston campus slightly before noon. Passing the guard's station on the ground floor, they took the elevator to the fifth and made a quick right into the office of the department chairman. Karen Hitchcock was friendly and eager to help. She would assist them, she said, in any way she could. When Landry presented her with the warrant, she explained that they could expect to find Douglas's office in some disarray.

Hitchcock then led the troopers down the maze of pastel corridors to 530 M&V. She unlocked the outer door to the lab, then the door to Douglas's private office, revealing a disorder to which her earlier description had not done justice. Howe began sorting through newspapers and documents that lay in boxes on a table to the right of the door. Landry applied himself to the desk. On the right-hand surface he came across a manila envelope. He opened it and found condoms—twenty-two Ramses, one Trojan, one Sanitary Laboratories Inc., and one exotic number wrapped in gold foil with Oriental characters. In the top desk drawer he found a mirror, which he guessed had been used in cutting cocaine. In the right desk drawer he found paperwork relating to travel and other expenses for William Douglas, Robin Benedict, and Savitry Bisram. Among these was a receipt for 500 business cards imprinted "Nadine." It was for $23 and had been paid by William Douglas on October 4, 1982. There was also a contemporary card which featured an anxious little oculist pointing to a screen which read,

HAPPY BIRTHDAY
Did you know that
Too Much Sex
can impair
your vision?

The punch line was delivered in blurred letters.

But
what the heck

you only
live once!

Have a
happy day!

It was addressed "To my favorite Prof" from "Me."

In the desk drawer Landry also found a small brown "Name Saver" address book. There were forty or fifty entries in what seemed to be Robin's trick code. She had apparently started a new black book, but this one, too, had been stolen almost as soon as it had been started. On the wall next to the desk, Landry found a list of thirteen priority callers. The first six were

Nancy Douglas
Billy Douglas
Pammy Douglas
Johnny Douglas
Robin Benedict
Nadine Porter

Trooper Howe, meanwhile, finding only research materials in the box on the table, had moved to the bookshelves, where he discovered more Benedictiana. On the inside cover of a volume entitled *Lung Development: Biological and Clinical Perspectives,* there was written:

> May our friendship grow more wonderful as time goes on. Let's keep it strong as we help each other to achieve all that we've talked about. . . .
>
> Friends always,
> Robin

In another text, *Research Animals and Concepts of Applicability to Clinical Medicine,* she had penned:

> To my favorite Prof
>
> In recent months, the amount of work you've accomplished is an abundance of wonderful works.
> It makes me very happy to know that such a wonderful person is finally getting what he deserves. And I'm glad and grateful that you're letting me be a part of it all.
>
> Your friend always . . .

Running beneath these endearments, however, was a more ominous current of memoranda. Among these was a note to William Douglas from one Stanley Spilman, warning of the dangers of a radioisotope called Sodium 22. There was another, dated 1/11/83, which read:

> Bill,
>
> I would have sworn that once I was kicked out everything would quiet down. I'm shocked, and I'm not the shock-prone sort. More than ever, I'm willing to deal with whoever is responsible for this on a very personal and violent level.
> I've moved nearly all my papers out of M&V 530; there is too much to lose at stake.
> Talk to you tomorrow.
>
> Stan

Brian Howe inquired about Spilman, and Karen Hitchcock told him he was someone who had enjoyed a close relationship with Douglas. He had written the isotope memo during a period when Douglas was behaving very strangely, claiming that items were being stolen from his office. Around that same time Spilman was found to have been using an academic title to which he was not entitled, and Tufts had to let him go.

Howe mentioned that an internal audit memo taken from Douglas's house indicated that Spilman had incurred $4,500 in questionable travel advances. Hitchcock said the auditor had asked him about this and had satisfied himself that Spilman had simply taken out the advances as a favor to Douglas.

Howe got a better idea of the relationship between Douglas and Spilman from Dr. Ronald Sanders, who seemed relieved that someone in authority was trying to get to the bottom of this matter. Douglas, as Sanders represented him, was a petty man who terrorized secretaries and quavered in the face of superiors. He was cunning, devious, and a manipulator of people, among these Stanley Spilman. Spilman was naïve and tended to believe whatever Douglas told him. If Douglas asked him to get money for him, he would probably do it blindly without questioning the propriety.

That evening, when Howe returned to the troopers' office in the Gray House, he reported to John Kivlan what he and Landry had found in the office as well as what he had learned about Dr. Stanley Spilman. Was Spilman the mystery companion for whom Douglas had spun his "What's up, Doc?" story? Perhaps they had conspired to embezzle funds, and the $4,500 in travel advances was part of that. Spilman had written, "I would have sworn that once I was kicked out everything would quiet down." Was he referring to a money scheme, or had he egocentrically misinterpreted the fracas over his credentials as the cause for Douglas's ouster?

Kivlan knew it was important to get in touch with Spilman, if for no other reason than to make sure he would be a friendly, or at least neutral, witness. He did not want him turning up on behalf of the defense to say, "Douglas was with me that night, so he couldn't have killed her." Kivlan asked Howe to call Spilman to check out his story.

By now Spilman had returned to the West Coast to continue work on his disputed doctorate at the University of California at Davis. The last number anyone had for him was his parents'. Howe dialed it, got Spilman's mother, and told her it was urgent that he get hold of her son. Several days passed and he heard nothing. Once again he called the mother and this time told her that if he did not hear from Stanley an officer from the Norfolk County District Attorney's Office would be dispatched to the coast to escort Stanley back east. Within fifteen minutes, Spilman returned the call.

Spilman seemed unpleasantly surprised, but not inordinately nervous, to hear of Douglas's predicament. He had not, he said, been with Douglas the night Robin Benedict disappeared. When Howe summarized the content of the "What's up, Doc?" tape, Spilman denied any knowledge of it, insisting he had had no discussions with Douglas concerning Robin.

Spilman sounded sincere enough. It was possible, Howe thought, that he was lying, but he had no way—short of matching voice prints—of proving it. Even then, the fragments of the mystery voice on the tape were so muffled and fleeting that it might be impossible to make a comparison.

For the time being Howe and Kivlan decided to let the matter slide.

WHEN Kivlan needed things done, in what was now the third week of the investigation, he found himself relying increasingly upon Brian Howe. Lieutenant Sharkey, in fact, had made up his mind to phase Paul Landry out altogether. The lieutenant had never been comfortable delegating such authority to a road trooper, and now he felt his suspicions were justified. Landry, in Sharkey's opinion, was swollen with the importance of his unorthodox promotion and suffering from "delusions of grandeur." More serious, however, Landry was not doing his paperwork. Sharkey was a stickler for reports. "If a guy can't write," he was fond of saying, "he's only half a cop." And with all that had happened, Landry had not filed a single report.

He was also running up against a deadline for filing returns, listing for the benefit of the magistrate who had issued the warrant everything that had been taken in the first two house searches. If these were not filed promptly and properly, Douglas's attorney could get a motion to suppress the evidence. With so much riding on Landry's performance then, it made Kivlan uneasy to learn from state police higher-ups in Boston that the trooper was having personal problems arising from his divorce. The prosecutor was further surprised to hear that after he had gone to the trouble of interceding to postpone Landry's retirement date, Landry had been pulling strings behind the scenes so that his retirement would go through on schedule.

Kivlan called a meeting with Landry to find out what exactly was going on. The trooper, it turned out, was indeed intent upon retiring as scheduled, on March 30. He was not, however, planning to give up the Benedict case. He wanted the district attorney to hire him as a private investigator. That way he would be getting his retirement plus a fee. Kivlan found this unacceptable.

During the awkward days that followed, Sharkey turned over the case to Brian Howe. Landry seemed reluctant to relinquish control of the evidence. He hinted further that this was a state police case and that if he chose he could file his reports through headquarters in Boston rather than through the district attorney's office. If Landry went that route it might open up a jurisdictional dispute and throw the maintenance of evidence into question. And if Douglas's defense attorney could suggest that the evidence had not made its way through an orderly chain of custody from the Douglas house to the courthouse, this too would be grounds to suppress. Kivlan felt he had to move decisively to quell this mutiny.

On April 1, the day after Landry officially retired, Kivlan called him at the Foxboro barracks and told him that if he did not deliver that report soon, he would be called before the grand jury. When John Kivlan said he would call you before the grand jury, it was not an idle threat. There was a dark joke which circulated around Norfolk that if Kivlan got in a bar fight, he wouldn't land punches, he'd serve subpoenas. Like his old mentor John Droney, Kivlan saw the grand jury as the natural ally of the prosecutor, and he was not above using it to bully a wayward trooper into line.

Landry was stunned. He had liked Kivlan. During the early, intense weeks of the investigation, he had even come to think of him as a friend. The prosecutor's threat now struck him like a blow to the stomach.

"I don't work for you," Landry shot back. "I don't work for anybody anymore." And he hung up.

Presently Kivlan called back to smooth things over. Landry, his feelings still tender, nonetheless agreed to start his report the following Monday morning. Working from a pile of notes, filling in with memory, he began to hunt and peck a voluminous account of the case. Every day, Kivlan sent a trooper down to Foxboro barracks to pick up the latest installment. Page by page, article by article, the report and accompanying evidence were transported back to Dedham until each piece of the expanding puzzle was securely lodged at the Gray House—under the exclusive jurisdiction of the Norfolk County district attorney.

THE GRAY HOUSE

SINCE the night of the first search, when Robin Benedict's credit cards and trick book had turned up unexpectedly among the belongings of the William Douglases, the missing girl had seemed tantalizingly accessible. So accessible, in fact, that John Kivlan was convinced that it was only a matter of days before she would be found. The prosecutor knew from experience that a human body was a far more difficult thing to dispose of than most people imagined. If dumped in a harbor, it tended to bob up and wash ashore. If abandoned in the woods, it stood to be discovered by hiking Girl Scouts. If buried, it was likely to be unearthed by a curious dog. Corporeal bulk was so buoyant, and at the same time so solid, that it was nearly impossible to make it disappear without some telltale trace. If one gave Douglas the benefit of the doubt and assumed he was not possessed of any particular criminal instinct or expertise, then it was reasonable to assume that he had disposed of it in a panic, hence carelessly. The law of averages would cause it to surface.

Early on, the Norfolk troopers had searched the marshes behind Sandy Ridge Circle, but there seemed no logical place to dispose of either a body or a car. The water was shallow and had, at any rate, been frozen solid during the first week in March. Kivlan and a handful of investigators had driven along Route 95 between Sharon and Mansfield, thinking Benedict might have been discarded in the open, as were the bodies of the other prostitute runaways they had found since 1979. One trooper, perched on the back of a flatbed truck, traversed the four-lane interstate from Mansfield to Providence and back, but he found no sign of her along the wide shoulder between the pavement and a high chain link fence that paralleled the highway.

During the time which Matt Connolly had spent in the Douglas house on the night of the first search, he had nosed around quietly to see if there was anyplace where Douglas might have stowed a body. Descending the stair that led from the main landing, he had found a rumpus room strewn with toys and wine bottles. Off to the left was an unfinished utility area, and against the far wall was an upright freezer. Connolly had considered it with trepidation. It seemed too small to accommodate a body intact. But what if Robin had been dismembered? Douglas, after all, was an anatomist and might have the means and skill to perform a hasty vivisection. The ADA had opened the door to discover, with some relief, that the vault was nearly empty.

The idea of a corpse on the premises was a ghoulish one, but Professor William Douglas had demonstrated rather unusual proclivities. Given his habit of hoarding intimate and illicit tokens of passion, was it so strange to imagine his concealing the very object of that passion? Connolly was among a growing contingent who felt that it was possible that Douglas had hidden Robin somewhere where he could return to visit her, to venerate her. If Douglas had the means to dismember Robin, might he not also have the means to preserve her in some fashion? One sentence from his letters seemed to ring prophetic.

I used to dream about designing a machine that would reverse time and let you relive times and places that you have already had.

The notion that Douglas might visit the site where he had disposed of the body seemed plausible enough to Kivlan that he placed the professor and his family under surveillance for most of the late afternoon and nighttime hours. From a wooded rise, some seventy-five or eighty yards from the point where the main road turned off into Sandy Ridge Circle, one could park an unmarked car and watch the Douglas's comings and goings unobserved.

Beginning the last week in March, Brian Howe and two other troopers took turns on lookout, and from what they could see, life in the Douglas household seemed to go on with amazing normalcy. Nancy left for and returned from work as usual. She continued ferrying the children to and from athletic events. Neither did William Douglas seem fazed by recent developments, including two searches of his home. One Sunday afternoon, he even took young Billy to Lechmere's to shop for video equipment. All in all, the Douglases presented to the world a placid, unworried exterior.

The only thing slightly out of the ordinary was Douglas's habit of taking midnight drives. The trooper on duty would follow him into the heart of town, then out onto the highway for a while, then back to Sandy Ridge Circle. He rarely stopped anywhere, just drove and returned home. By and by, Kivlan concluded that Douglas had gotten wise to the surveillance and that these nocturnal meanderings were a deliberate attempt to frustrate the trooper on his tail. The suggestion of evasion stirred in the prosecutor the same impulse to pursuit that the sight of a darting mouse arouses in a cat. He expanded the surveillance to include the morning hours.

While the troopers dogged Douglas's steps, Kivlan turned to Paul Landry's report in order to determine more precisely what terrain Douglas had covered during the days immediately following Robin's disappearance.

Landry had noted that Douglas made at least two trips to West Warwick, Rhode Island. The first was on Thursday, March 10, the day after he returned from Washington, D.C. The second was on the following Thursday, March 17. On the evening preceding each of these excursions, Douglas had placed a call to the Benedicts telling them that he was going to West Warwick on business and giving a number where he could be reached. Why would he drop a dime on his own movements? Kivlan wondered aloud to Matt Connolly. Matt speculated that the calls might be Douglas's twisted way of consoling the Benedicts, assuring them, in effect, "The situation is under control. I'm going to visit Robin."

The number he had given the Benedicts was listed to Scott Laboratories, which, Kivlan discovered, was a research supply company headquartered in an old textile mill sitting astride the Pawtuxet River near the heart of West Warwick. What was Douglas's business at the laboratory? Kivlan wondered. Was it possible that he had access to chemicals which might, as he had suggested to Shirley Benedict, dissolve a body without a trace? Perhaps he had used Scott as a staging area, a place to prepare Robin for burial in the thick woods surrounding West Warwick. At Kivlan's request, Rhode Island state police investigators visited Scott Laboratories to question the personnel. They learned that Douglas, on both of his recent visits, had spent his time editing a products catalog. He had enjoyed no actual access to the labs or to any chemicals.

Douglas, Kivlan knew, had more than professional ties to West Warwick. Nancy's family lived there, and the Douglases, he had learned, had also purchased property down the coast. During his interview with Landry on the afternoon of March 19, Douglas had let slip that he and Nancy owned a lot in Narragansett. Kivlan inquired of local police about the parcel—Lot No. 32, Plat S-1 on Hope Lane—and he got the impression that it was a densely wooded lot. "Bet that's where he hid it," the prosecutor said to himself, when he heard the description.

Late Sunday evening, after the first house search, John Kivlan and Paul Landry drove to Rhode Island for a look. Following the coastline past Providence and West Warwick, they continued south to the peninsula, at the tip of which lay the resort town of Narragansett. Kivlan had notified local authorities that he would be coming, and they promised to put whatever resources they possessed at his disposal. It was well after dark when he finally pulled into Hope Lane, and he was surprised to find a sizable detail of West Warwick and Narragansett police outfitted with searchlights and digging equipment. The area upon which this contingent was set to concentrate its formidable resources, however, was scarcely a quarter of an acre. Though overgrown with marsh wheat and scrub brush, it was hardly the "densely wooded" grove that Kivlan had been led to expect. There was no freshly turned earth. The lot, furthermore, was flanked on either side by homes, making it unlikely that anyone, particularly a man as large and ungainly as Douglas, could have succeeded in burying a body there unobserved. The search was over in three minutes.

ABANDONING the Rhode Island tack temporarily, Kivlan stepped back to review the broader scope of Douglas's movements during the three weeks after March 5. It was apparent that sometime within two days after Robin disappeared, he had traveled—by train, he said—to Washington, D.C. When Jack DaRosa had seen him there on the night of the eighth, he was alone. The detective had kept him under surveillance until the ninth, when he caught a plane back to Boston. There had been no sign of Robin Benedict.

There followed the two trips to West Warwick. On the second of those excursions, on March 17, Nancy had accompanied Bill to Rhode Island; then the two of them had continued on to Chazy, New York, about twelve miles north of Plattsburgh. Chazy was the site of Miner Institute, a student-training facility operated by the State University of New York.

Brian Howe called the institute and spoke to the director, Dr. William Graziadei, who informed him that Douglas had been to Chazy several times during the past year. Douglas's relationship to the university went back a long way, he explained. Douglas had received his B.A. in biology there, and later, as a senior scientist at W. Alton Jones, he had been made an adjunct professor.

When, in the fall of 1982, Douglas approached Plattsburgh looking for a job, the university was eager to entertain his application. Hiring Douglas, administrators felt, would not only give them one of the leading experts in cell culture but also entrée into the TCA. Douglas was offered a full professorship with tenure.

During the second week in December, he visited Chazy for two days to discuss the terms of his employment. Then, during the week of February 13 to 18, he returned to lecture on cell culture. During that visit he stayed in a room above the library at the Faculty Duplex, about fifteen yards from the labs on the Chazy campus.

At that point news of Douglas's financial difficulties had not reached Plattsburgh. The first indication of anything out of the ordinary occurred during the February visit. On the first morning of classes, Valentine's Day, Douglas had begun receiving calls from a young woman introducing herself as Robin. The secretaries assumed it was his daughter. Douglas, however, seemed extraordinarily anxious, popping periodically into the office to see if he had gotten any calls. He was apparently expecting them at a certain hour, and he instructed the staff to interrupt him no matter what he was doing. When the calls came, he insisted upon taking them behind closed doors.

On Thursday evening he appeared at a social gathering with a young woman wearing light beige linen pants and a blazer of the same color. She had a nicely tailored appearance, except that she was wearing sandals which, the center secretaries agreed, spoiled the ensemble. Douglas introduced her as Chris Costello. She was a graduate student, he said. She would be coming with him to Plattsburgh to pursue her own studies and wanted to look over the facilities. Although such a situation was not unusual in the world of academe and would not in itself have raised eyebrows, the office staff recognized Chris's voice as that of the Robin who had called so many times the preceding week. The girl said she had flown in from Montreal the night before. This caused even more snickering among the secretaries, who knew perfectly well that there were no direct flights from Montreal to Plattsburgh.

The Costello girl had attended Douglas's lecture on Friday morning, and a little before noon the two of them left, presumably for Boston. Two weeks later, unknown to the Miner faculty, of course, Robin Benedict disappeared. Graziadei did not see Douglas again until March 17, when he and his wife, Nancy, showed up to check out the community. They had been looking for property and assessing the school system. During their stay the Douglases were guests at the Faculty Duplex. They left for home early on the morning of March 19.

A little over a week after that visit, a former student sent the department a news clipping from the *Boston Globe* which told of Douglas's being linked to a missing girl. There had also been rumors of financial indiscretions. This news was greeted with disbelief. Graziadei put in a wary call to Douglas, chatting at first about general things, hoping Bill would bring the subject up. He did not. Douglas simply sounded depressed and indicated that he was encountering some "difficulties." Hoping to get to the bottom of the situation, Graziadei's superior, Dr. H. Z. Liu, spoke with Karen Hitchcock and Vice-President Steven Manos, who verified that Douglas was under investigation. Upon learning this, Graziadei told Howe, Plattsburgh formally withdrew its offer of a teaching position.

AFTER returning from Plattsburgh with Nancy on March 20, Douglas took a train trip on March 24 to Cherry Hill, New Jersey. He arrived home on Saturday, March 26, just in time to greet Trooper Landry, who was there to search his house a second time. Landry learned that Douglas had returned from a meeting of the executive board of the Tissue Culture Association.

A check with the TCA revealed that prior to the meeting in Cherry Hill, members of the executive board had gotten wind of Douglas's difficulties at Tufts. In November, one of the board members had received an anonymous letter. The sender had attached Xerox copies of an application nominating Robin Benedict for membership in the Tissue Culture Association. It had been submitted to Tufts for reimbursement. The $400 claim far exceeded the usual $50 fee.

Before making the trip to Cherry Hill, Douglas had called a friend on the board to see if his presence would be an embarrassment. On the contrary, he was encouraged to come and offer an explanation. On Friday night after dinner the board gathered in the chairman's suite at the Hyatt, and Douglas explained that a disgruntled student whom he had given a bad mark was trying to do him in.

None of the board members—indeed, none of the eyewitnesses to Douglas's activities after March 5—could recall his being in a state of unusual anxiety. There was nothing to suggest that he had just killed a woman and was in the process of disposing of her corpse. On each of these trips, he had taken commercial transportation or driven his own car. Both of the Douglas vehicles had been impounded and checked for evidence of blood, but the tests had come back negative.

Norfolk had alerted police departments in the New England states, New York, New Jersey, and Washington, D.C., to keep an eye out for a 1982 silver Toyota, license 665HXG, with a black racing stripe. The rim of its right front wheel was bent. There was a small dent in the body near the door on the driver's side and a key scratch on the hood. At Trooper Howe's request, Amtrak police checked all the lots at stations between Boston and New York, but with no results. Kivlan had a hunch that Douglas had driven Robin's car on one of his excursions to Rhode Island or Washington, D.C. The critical trip, he suspected, was the one from Boston to Washington. How, he wondered, had Douglas really traveled to the Veterans Administration meeting during the two days following Robin's disappearance?

Brian Howe called New York Air, the carrier Douglas had used on his return, to see if Douglas had been holding reservations for March 6 or 7, but the airline did not keep those records in its computer. After that he checked with the BayBank Credit Card Fraud Division to see if there had been any travel charges on Douglas's Visa card around the critical weekend, but as of the last week in March he was still awaiting a reply.

IT WAS getting on toward April, and if the body did not turn up soon, John Kivlan realized, he would have to sit down with the district attorney to decide whether it was necessary to build a circumstantial case. To prosecute a homicide without a body, however, was a forbidding task. The difficulties had been demonstrated three years earlier in Suffolk County, where a twenty-one-year-old Charlestown woman named Anita Doiron disappeared one night after getting off work from a veterans hospital in Jamaica Plain. She had supposedly accepted a ride from a fellow named George Walker, a boiler attendant at Fort Devens, in Ayer. Walker was indicted and brought to trial, where the prosecutor produced blond hair "similar" to Doiron's. It had been discovered in Walker's car as well as in a boiler at Fort Devens. Walker even admitted going to the fort that night. Still, he was acquitted because the jury could not be satisfied that Doiron was dead.

No-body cases, as they were called, required the state to leap a double hurdle. Before it could hope to prove that an individual defendant had committed murder, it had to establish, through purely circumstantial means, that a murder had actually been committed. The odds against conviction were enormous. Yet there was a narrow window of opportunity which had been opened during the middle of the preceding century by the Massachusetts Supreme Judicial Court in the celebrated case of the *Commonwealth v. Webster.*

The plaintiff, Dr. John Webster, was a Harvard chemistry professor accused of murdering a colleague, Dr. George Parkman, scion of one of Boston's first families. One Friday afternoon Parkman went to the medical school to collect from Webster a debt of about $2,400, and he never returned home. The following day the police set out to hunt for him. The search led to the medical college, where a janitor found a human pelvis in a vault beneath Dr. Webster's privy. This spurred investigators to a more exacting exploration of Webster's laboratory, where in one drawer of a tea chest they discovered a human thorax and chest. From the furnace where Harvard anatomists disposed of animal remains, they recovered, embedded in cinder, the fragments of human bones and pieces of false teeth. Webster was arrested and charged with stabbing Parkman, striking him on the head with a hammer, and "kicking, beating and throwing" him to the ground.

News of these grisly findings caused public hysteria. A throng of hoodlums and curiosity seekers surrounded Webster's house, shouting insults to the doctor's wife and three daughters inside. A crowd of antivivisectionists descended upon the medical college with the intent of burning it. Irish immigrants from the nearby "Black Hole" tenements threatened to join rioting which had already broken out in other areas of the city. Perhaps it was the recognition that evil dwelt everywhere, even in the midst of eminence. Maybe it was some innate human revulsion from vivisection that roused these passions. Whatever the cause, Boston society had been knocked out of kilter, releasing in the citizenry terrible impulses of destruction. The entire city police force, fortified by the militia, was required to suppress it.

The tension that remained could be discharged only by some final dispensation of justice. The trial of John Webster in the summer of 1850 became the most highly publicized criminal proceeding in national memory. Until that time no one had successfully prosecuted a case without a body. There had been a burden upon the prosecutor to prove to the point of "absolute certainty" the corpus delicti—that is, the fact that the murder had actually occurred. The Webster case, however, eased the burden upon the state by introducing a new standard of evidence. In his instructions to the Webster jurors, Chief Justice Lemuel Shaw pronounced that they needed only conclude beyond a "reasonable doubt" that the crime had occurred. This meant that for the first time a jury could consider circumstantial evidence, such as that introduced by the prosecution to suggest that the dismembered corpse in the laboratory belonged to George Parkman. Although no one could identify it with certainty, the corpse's trunk was extraordinarily hairy, as Parkman's had indeed been in life. What is more, the artificial teeth found among the ash were identified by Parkman's dentist, who had made them to order only two weeks earlier.

The Webster jurors were persuaded beyond a reasonable doubt that Parkman had been murdered. And they were convinced, in accordance with the further instruction of Lemuel Shaw, that the chain of evidence led to John Webster and no one else. They found the defendant guilty of murder, and in late August of 1850 Webster was hanged in the presence of an angry mob.

In the years to follow, legal scholars would argue whether the chain of

*Robin Benedict—the "Missing Beauty" photo (Wide World
Photos/John Benedict)*

TOP LEFT.
Robin, age one
(John Benedict)

TOP RIGHT. Robin and her
sister, Rhonda

ABOVE RIGHT. Senior class
photo

MIDDLE
LEFT. Robin
during summer
vacation in
California

LEFT. Robin and her yearbook
staff

TOP LEFT. Robin and George (R.) at the junior prom

MIDDLE LEFT. Robin and George at the senior prom

BELOW LEFT. Robin playing her flute at a talent show

MIDDLE RIGHT. Raymond Costict (New England Patriots)

BELOW RIGHT. Robin accepting a prize for exceptional scholarship

Lagrange Street, Good Time Charlie's on the left
(Village Voice/James Hamilton)

One of Robin's trick pads in the Back Bay
(Village Voice/James Hamilton)

Mug shots taken during Robin's arrest in April 1982

Robin Benedict and William Douglas photographed cashing a check illegally at the Bank of Boston

The sledgehammer photographed shortly after it was discovered in the trash barrel at Mansfield (Massachusetts State Police)

TOP. The William Douglas home at 38 Sandy Ridge Circle (Village Voice/James Hamilton)

LEFT. Nancy Douglas getting into her car (Boston Herald/Kevin Twombly)

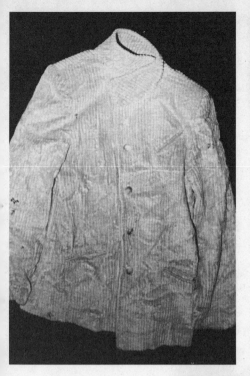

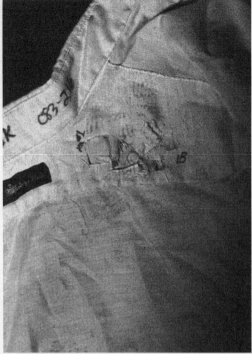

ABOVE LEFT. The corduroy jacket (Tom Neff)

ABOVE RIGHT. Bloodstained blue shirt (Tom Neff)

RIGHT. William Douglas showing head wound to state troopers the night of the first house search (Massachusetts State Police/William Anderson)

LEFT. Billy Douglas answering door (Boston Herald, staff photo)

BELOW. Robin's silver Toyota after being discovered in New York City (Massachusetts State Police)

RIGHT. Pamela, John, and Billy Douglas leaving the Norfolk Superior Courthouse after refusing to testify before the grand jury (Boston Globe/Joe Runci)

BELOW. Douglas after his arrest in the custody of Lieutenant Sharkey and Trooper Howe (Boston Herald/John Landers)

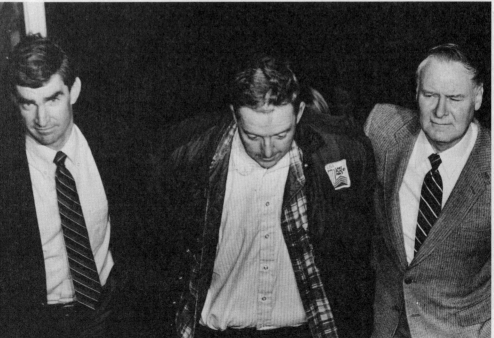

*John and Shirley Benedict (*Village
Voice*/James Hamilton)*

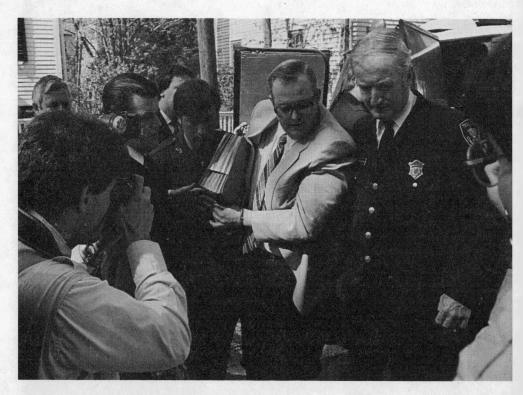

William Douglas in handcuffs on the courthouse steps
(Village Voice/James Hamilton)

*J.R. Rogers shouting an obscenity as William Douglas changes
his plea, as Shirley Benedict looks on (Quincy
Patriot-Ledger/Bill Green)*

LEFT. Prosecutor John Kivlan (Quincy Patriot-Ledger/Bill Green)

BELOW. William Douglas awaiting his sentence with Attorney Tom Troy (Wide World Photos/Bill Green)

evidence did, indeed, lead to Webster and to no one else. There were inconsistencies in the janitor's testimony that made him suspect. He testified that he had seen Webster, late in the afternoon of the alleged murder, leaving the medical college by the back stair. But Webster's daughters were willing to affirm that their father was at home with them at that time, taking tea. The janitor, it was also discovered, engaged in an illegal trade of acquiring human bodies for medical vivisection. Was it not possible, then, that he had planted the remains of a pauper in Webster's laboratory in order to collect the reward money offered by the Parkman family? Even Attorney General John Clifford, the principal prosecutor, indicated in his confidential notes that he, too, was suspicious of the janitor. But, under pressure to find a culprit, he concluded emphatically, "Somebody must answer!"

Long after Webster was hanged, doubts lingered as to whether he had been the victim of a too radically liberalized use of circumstantial evidence. In the 1920s the "reasonable doubt" standard was tightened by the Supreme Court, which held that "the circumstances surrounding the disappearance of the victim must be such as to convince the mind to a moral certainty of death, and to the exclusion of every other reasonable hypothesis."

That, then, would be the hurdle that lay before John Kivlan in the event that Robin Benedict's body could not be found: to convince a jury to a moral certainty that Robin had been murdered at 38 Sandy Ridge Circle the night of March 5, 1983. Unfortunately, he had nothing as tangible as a hirsute torso or charred dentures to affirm her demise. There was only the brain tissue, a few fragile cells which one of the most distinguished medical examiners in the country had conceded might have come from a monkey. Kivlan noted ruefully that in the history of the Commonwealth, there was no instance of a conviction without an identifiable body part.

EVEN AS Kivlan ruminated upon the weakness which lay at the center of his case, he remained convinced that Douglas would make one misstep that would lead the Gray House to the body. In pursuit of this anticipated clue, the prosecutor pored over the documents and handwritten notes recovered from Douglas's bedroom, focusing his attention upon one particular set taken from the Leica bag during the second house search. These notes, in Douglas's handwriting, seemed part of a strange, interior monologue chronicling the events of March 5. As in the "What's up, Doc?" tape, Douglas seemed to be constructing a tale for the benefit of some unknown person. This éminence grise was someone who had apparently told him to sit down and get his story straight. He had penned three progressively more polished drafts. Inasmuch as Landry had not found these writings during the first search, it appeared that Douglas had written them during the period between March 20 and March 26. Kivlan went over the accounts line by line, looking for Douglas to make a slip.

To his chagrin the accounts were remarkably consistent with what Douglas had previously told police. Kivlan, however, spotted three significant variations. Douglas had written, "She was wearing brown slacks, a light tan blouse, a tan waist length corduroy jacket and a brown pocketbook."

When Douglas had been queried on previous occasions about Robin's arrival, he claimed he could not recall what she had been wearing. His own notations now revealed that he remembered her attired in a "tan" jacket. This was also the first time he had mentioned a "brown pocketbook." During his interview with Sharkey the night of the first search, Douglas had described the purse as black.

When Douglas got around to recounting his own activities the following day, he recalled having been mugged on the way back from the Chinese restaurant by "two black men." In the version he had given Charlie Borstel, only one of the men had been black.

Douglas seemed aware of the risk of inconsistency. At one point he made a weak attempt to reconcile the accounts of the head wound. "I told DaRosa he never asked me about the bruise," he wrote for the benefit of his éminence grise. "I never told him I walked into a door."

What seemed to nettle him most was the suggestion, made by Landry and others, that Robin's call to Nancy meant that she had lost affection for him. In a passage carefully indented for emphasis, he wrote:

> If Robin wanted to break relationship with Bill, he would never see her again—She had done that with several dates. She saw Bill because she wanted to—in fact in the Sharon Police Report she stated that she was in love with Bill.

Douglas then launched into an angry refutation of certain things that Landry had told Nancy. Among them was the allegation that he had been stealing Robin's phone messages.

"NOT TRUE," he wrote in a bold hand.

Who, Kivlan wondered, was Douglas trying so hard to convince? Nancy, perhaps? It made sense that Douglas would want to persuade his wife that he was not so obsessed with Robin Benedict that he was stealing her messages—although it was now apparent to Kivlan that he had been doing precisely that.

From a box sitting to the right of the bedroom bureau, Landry had removed five sheets of paper on which Douglas had composed a careful handwritten record of Robin's phone calls. He had apparently stolen from Robin's apartment or mailbox a set of phone bills covering a period from mid-August to mid-November. These billings, which he had stuck into the back of her red address book, were for 247-1197, a number listed to one of Robin's trick pads. Most of the calls Robin had placed were to her apartment in Natick. Douglas had made an effort to find out to whom she had made the remaining calls. His notations read:

Boston—617-338-5979—   She was not working this Saturday night but she called home from this number at 8:48 P.M. Not in service for incoming calls—They can call out but we cannot call in. . . .

Framingham 617-872-8772   She called this number of 11/8 at 5:17 P.M. EJ Productions. . . .

(This was actually *DeeJay* Productions, the outfit which hired Robin and her partner for the bachelor party in November of 1982.)

A couple of other notes suggested that his intelligence had been gleaned through more direct observation:

On Thursday Dec. 2nd at 3:10 A.M. there was a call from apt. to another phone. I had to leave room during call. Was this to home phone.

Douglas appeared not to have picked this up off of a bill, since he would have known if she had called home. It seemed to indicate that he was with Robin at one of her trick pads when she made the call. Kivlan surmised that she had probably asked him to step out of the room, whereupon he made a mental note to enter the call into his records.

From about mid-November on, however, Douglas had begun keeping another list composed exclusively of messages which appeared to have been beeped off of Robin's answering machine. He seemed to be struggling to identify her living companion.

Nov. 24   Met 4–8P.M. & 11:30 P.M.–3:30 A.M. She called [someone] I believe [Douglas appeared to be trying to make out a name like "Jerry or Jay"] at her home # Told him she and I had a conflict . . . , said she wanted to hear his voice. . . .

Nov. 29   10:00 _____ she left another message on her home phone kiss, kiss, kiss, kiss—sweetheart its me are you there?

Douglas jotted down this succession of endearments with dispassionate precision. It was almost as though he had taken samples of Robin's life which he had then fixed and magnified for study in greater detail. His entries betrayed no emotion until he got to a call on November 30 which seemed to give him pause. Between ten-thirty and eleven-thirty that evening, Robin called in with the message "Sweetheart. This is your woman talking. I'll talk to you later." Douglas bracketed these words in bold doodling. Hearing Robin refer to herself as "your woman" had apparently fascinated him.

Reading these notations left no doubt in Kivlan's mind that, throughout the fall of 1982, Douglas had cold-bloodedly stalked Robin Benedict. But had he meant simply to find out whom she was seeing, or had he been forming an intent to kill her? The prosecutor read and reread Douglas's handwritten account of the days surrounding the disappearance of Robin. Sometimes he took drafts home with him to Milton, where late at night he spread them on the living room table and pored over them until the early hours of the morning. Sometimes he cracked himself a beer hoping that a light buzz might put things in a clearer light. But Douglas would not give himself away.

WITH each passing day, the missing body loomed a little larger as a stumbling block in the investigation—and as a reproach to the prowess of the prosecutors and troopers lodged in the Gray House. As ungainly and inept as William Douglas appeared, he was emerging in the collective imagination of those investigators as an infuriatingly stubborn and even cunning adversary. As such, he aroused in them a certain competitiveness, an eagerness to match wits. That he could have disposed of the body without a trace was unthinkable. Finding it, then, was becoming an obsession.

Late of an afternoon when the formal business of the day was complete, the Gray House investigators would gather in John Kivlan's attic office to spin hypotheses. Among them were Peter Casey and Gerry Pudolsky, assistant prosecutors whose desks were wedged into the same cramped room with Kivlan's. They had no actual responsibilities on the case but were nonetheless fascinated by it and eager to enter into the intrigue of conjecture. Joining them were Troopers Bobby Murphy and Rick Zebrasky, who were conducting much of the surveillance work at Sandy Ridge Circle along with Brian Howe, who now had primary responsibility for fieldwork. Through most of these sessions, Howe would sit tilted back slightly in a hard plastic chair, eyes half closed, simply listening. Thinking. Howe harbored a scarcely veiled contempt for Douglas, whom he considered an unprincipled weakling. Yet he referred to him with scrupulous formality as William. Lieutenant Sharkey, who had supervisory duties at the main office and dropped into the Gray House sessions only occasionally, had adopted a more charitable attitude toward the suspect, customarily alluding to him as Billy, while Matthew Connolly, who saw rather more humor in Douglas than did most of the others, fell into the habit of calling him Dr. Bill.

Like Kivlan, the other Gray House investigators held to the belief that Douglas would do something—or perhaps already had done something—to give himself away. Flush with this conviction, they reviewed what they knew, assembling a set of coordinates from which emerged a rough picture of what had happened the night of March 5.

J.R. Rogers had seen Robin around three o'clock in the afternoon. Indian Debbie then saw her about 7:45 P.M. when she dropped into Charlie's. According to Sargent Nichols, Robin had arrived at his apartment around 8:40 P.M. and placed a call to someone, presumably Douglas, at 9:40 P.M. Shortly thereafter she left Longfellow Place. At 10:07 P.M. Americall received the call for "Nadine" from "Joe" inviting her to the party in Charlestown. Then, at 11:42 P.M., Robin supposedly left a message for J.R. saying that she was on her way to Joe's. The following day, at 3:13 P.M., the service supposedly got a third call from Robin saying, "Will be at John's Longfellow."

The Gray House investigators suspected that Douglas had made those last three calls himself to shift suspicion to Joe in Charlestown. Just how familiar he was with the actual Joe Murray, the investigators could not tell. It seemed likely that he had gotten Joe's number from Robin's black book, into which he had scribbled, "Joe with house." There was a growing consensus among the investigators that at the moment the 10:07 P.M. call was placed, Robin was still alive. Why, then, had Douglas made this call? Matt Connolly opined that it was part of a conditional murder plan. Late in March he framed a memo for the benefit of his Gray House colleagues crystallizing this theory. In it he wrote:

Assuming Douglas made this call, we can see that he was thinking of a couple of things at that time: First, he wanted anyone who was interested in Robin's whereabouts to think she may be at Joe's party . . . ; second, and more significantly, this demonstrates that Douglas, at this point, has decided to kill her.

He has clearly waited until he has heard from her and she is on the road before making this call since he does not want her to call her answering service and receive this message since it may somehow prevent her arrival at his house. However, the message is clever, because it leaves open the possibility that he may not kill her. He may yet hope to resolve their difficulties. . . . So, if they got back together, when Robin later calls her answering service, she would just think it was Joe calling who was just hoping she would show at his party.

. If he has decided to kill her, he may have already made plans for the disposal of her body. His wife said that when she came home from New Hampshire in the afternoon or early evening . . . he left a note saying Robin was coming over and he was out for a walk. Could this have been a walk in the woods to dig a grave?

Brian Howe was dubious about the grave-digging scenario. It was true that the woods around the pumping station were close by the Douglas house. They were also sufficiently dense that one could dig a grave unobserved. Still, Howe could not believe that Douglas had actually gone out for a stroll that afternoon. His surveillance of Sandy Ridge Circle had led him to conclude that Douglas was not a man given to walking any farther than from his car to the counter of a Burger King. He found it extremely unlikely that Douglas, doubtless aware of his own limitations, would consider lugging the body any distance at all. Besides, the ground had been frozen so solid in early March that it would have been difficult or impossible to dig a grave.

"Why does Douglas decide to do her in at his house?" Connolly continued.

Is it he can better commit the [murder] if he does it this way?
    Could Douglas' wife be in on the initial murder plans? (No—would have involved kids).

The idea of premeditation continued to perplex Connolly. If Douglas was so much in love with Robin, he reasoned, he would have wanted to make one last pitch. Accordingly, the assistant district attorney laid out the following reasoning:

There can be no question that after her arrival she took off her coat and put her pocketbook down. I cannot see Douglas whacking her with the hammer as soon as she walked in. He is still madly in love with Robin. He would want to enjoy her company for at least a while, see her smile again, hear her talk, while hoping that he can have her back again. Douglas, the donkey, had to believe at some time that Robin also loved him. He would not have played his hammer trick without one last attempt at reconciliation. . . .
    She commences doing business with Douglas. (Note: What was this business that evening? Obviously, it was not as Douglas maintains, for her to bring two slides to him, since he had lost his job and had no need for these. In this regard, we have to remember Robin called Douglas's wife a couple of days before this time. She told her she was tired of being bothered by Douglas. If

this is the case, what would motivate her to go to his house? . . . We have Robin going . . . to Sharon to see Douglas, a person who now offends her, her tormentor, she turns down a night's pay from Nichols, commits at least two . . . of her productive hours to visit Douglas. . . .)

Did she make one final big demand? "Look, Bill sweetheart! Thanks for the memories. It's all over! Oh! By the way—unless you give me $5,000 ($10,000?) for all my efforts (or past moneys owed or promised)—I take these pictures [tapes or letters] and show them to your wife (kids—*Globe*—employers.)" [Douglas] wanted only one thing—Robin. So he must have lured her out with the big pay day.

. . . Douglas professes his love, goes through his sad sack . . . rejected lover routine, and makes no headway. Robin is adamant, "give me the money and get out of my life." . . . Douglas sees his love is no more than a hardened whore who he would still love but she won't have him. If that's the case, she won't have anyone. Douglas tells her he'll get the money. He gets the hammer and raps her on the head. She falls down either dead or unconscious.

Connolly speculated that Douglas, now pressed for time, had to get rid of the body before 11:30 P.M., when his daughter was scheduled to arrive home from baby-sitting. He carried Robin out of the house, head resting on his shoulder. This had caused the bloodstain on the shoulder of his shirt. (If she was bleeding, Connolly noted, it was possible that she was still alive.) Then he loaded her into a car. Since neither of the Douglas cars showed bloodstains, Connolly concluded, he must have used the silver Toyota.

If one assumed that Douglas left the house with the body at around 11:00 P.M., it meant that he could have gone only fifteen to twenty minutes in one direction—spending five to fifteen minutes hiding the body—in order to get back to the house to make the call at 11:42 to Robin's answering service. In light of this, it seemed unlikely that he had buried her. Instead, Connolly proposed, he had left her body by the highway, making it appear that she had been on her way to Boston or Charlestown. (Perhaps, Douglas might suggest, Robin had been victimized by a hitchhiker.) He then drove south to Mansfield, with the intention of discarding the bloody items as far away from the body as time allowed.

On Sunday, Connolly theorized, Nancy had driven Douglas to where he had hidden the car the night before. Then Douglas either drove the car to the garage at Longfellow Place and caught a train to Washington or he drove the car to New York and took the train from there.

"We will better be able to tell this," he concluded, "after we know from which point Douglas went to Washington, D.C."

THAT CRITICAL piece of the puzzle hovered out of reach until April 1, when a security officer of BayBank's Credit Card Fraud Division finally got back to the DA's office with the charges on William Douglas's Visa card. Among them was an Amtrak ticket purchased in New York City on March 6.

Brian Howe called Amtrak Police at Penn Station in New York and found that a ticket had indeed been charged to William Douglas's Visa card for travel between New York and Washington, D.C. Further checking revealed that the ticket had been sold at 7:58 P.M. on March 6 at Penn Station. It was then collected and punched on train No. 67, departing Penn Station for Washington at 3:33 the following morning. When the train arrived in Washington, D.C., at around 7:59 A.M. the ticket was removed from the used-ticket pouch and stored with Amtrak records officials in Washington.

These revelations opened a new vista of speculation. How had Douglas gotten to New York? It was possible he had left Boston by train the morning of Sunday, March 6, but if so, he had paid cash, because Amtrak could not locate a charge from that point of origin. One also had to assume that he had spent seven and a half hours in New York after buying the ticket. Why such a long layover? He could have caught one of several other evening trains to Washington before the one that left at 3:33 A.M. On an Amtrak timetable which had been taken from Douglas's camera bag during the first search, he, or someone else, had jotted down two times on the back, "12:30 and 3:30." He had apparently entertained the possibility of leaving on the earlier train.

Howe did some rudimentary computation and concluded that during the layover, Douglas could not have strayed beyond a fifty-mile radius of New York City, and that presupposed his having a car. The most convincing scenario was that Douglas had driven Benedict's Toyota to New York that Sunday morning, parked it, bought a ticket to Washington, and spent the rest of the day disposing of the car. Maybe even of the body.

John Kivlan, though delighted to have linked Douglas to a specific location in New York City, was dissatisfied with Amtrak's computer record of the sale. Douglas, he feared, might try to suggest that Robin or one of her associates had stolen his card and forged the charge in an attempt to frame him.

At the prosecutor's request, Amtrak recovered from its Washington warehouse the ticket stub bearing the scrawled, childlike signature of "William H. J. Douglas." Kivlan made a note to have this analyzed by a handwriting expert. He then dispatched Brian Howe to New York in hopes of finding someone who had seen Douglas during the weekend in question.

Howe showed Douglas's photo to the ticket agent Norma Diggs, an attractive black woman in her midthirties who, Amtrak records indicated, had sold Douglas the ticket on Sunday, March 6. Diggs could not identify him and could remember nothing of the exchange. Howe had also asked to speak to the conductor who had punched Douglas's ticket, but Amtrak authorities were having trouble finding out exactly who that was. Under normal circumstances such a thing was simple to trace. Management assigned each conductor his or her own distinctive punch. Any spent ticket could then be checked against the registry to determine who sold it. Douglas's ticket had a punch mark the shape of a crescent with a nob at the lower end of the arc. For some reason, however, Amtrak did not have a record of this particular punch. It was possible, Amtrak detectives explained, that the punch had become worn with use and that the mark was therefore difficult to identify. Sometimes a conductor lost his punch and was afraid to report it for fear of being disciplined. Rather than run that risk, he perhaps went to a novelty store and purchased a renegade punch. Amtrak promised to continue trying to locate the missing conductor.

A little over a week after Amtrak found the ticket, the Gray House received an even bigger windfall.

Trooper Bobby Murphy—a good-natured, foul-mouthed country boy—had been conducting surveillance on the Douglas house in the early hours of a Saturday morning. It was trash night on Sandy Ridge Circle, and on the sidewalk in front of No. 38 Murphy spied five plastic bags—three green and two black.

The trooper cruised quietly into the cul-de-sac and scooped up the bags. Repairing hastily to a convenience store, he bought fresh trash bags. He had filled them with coffee cups from a nearby dumpster when he realized to his dismay that all five were green. Returning to the store, he bought black bags, filled two of them with refuse, and set the five dummy sacks back on the curb in front of the Douglas house, where, he hoped, no one would be the wiser.

Trooper Murphy's midnight raid turned up a treasure. Lying among the debris was a piece of lined paper containing addresses and phone numbers of Douglas's family and friends. The list was made in a steadier hand than the one John Kivlan had come to associate with Douglas. After studying this document, the prosecutor concluded that Nancy must have been canvassing these supporters for contributions. At the bottom of the list, the writer had added the note "When you call dial o–area code–phone number. When operator answer[s] say charge to area code 617-956-6680." The number was a Tufts exchange.

On Monday morning Murphy went to the medical school on the

Boston campus to check this out. Douglas, he found, had three phone lines, two for his office and one for his lab. The lab and one of the office numbers had credit cards issued to them. Douglas's personal credit card number was 956-6680. Happily, Tufts had received records of the charges which had come in from the first week in March. Among them were six credit card calls made during the late evening of March 5 and the early morning of March 6. There was one at 11:43 P.M., then two which came very close together at 11:54 P.M. and 11:56 P.M. After midnight there had been calls at 2:12 A.M., 5:29 A.M., and 6:51 A.M.

Douglas, or someone using his card, had been making calls all night long.

Matt Connolly prevailed upon contacts at New England Bell to pinpoint the phone booths from which the calls had been made. The results came as a stunning climax to nearly two days of suspense. The tolls laid out an itinerary which showed the caller traveling an erratic course between Boston and Providence.

The call at 11:43 P.M. had been made to Robin Benedict's answering service from a pay phone at the Bradlee's Shopping Plaza in Foxboro, a drive of only five or ten minutes from Sandy Ridge Circle. The calls at 11:54 P.M. and 11:56 P.M. had been made to the Douglas house from a pay phone at the North Attleboro rest stop on Route 95 South.

North Attleboro, the investigators noted incredulously, lay diagonally across the highway from the Mansfield rest stop. Now Douglas, or the person using his card, could be linked in time to a location only a few yards from where the bloody clothing was found!

At 2:12 A.M., after a more than two-hour hiatus, the caller again phoned the Douglas residence, this time from a pay phone near South Station in Boston. After a long gap of over three and a half hours, at 5:29 A.M., there was a call from a Leo's Shell Station in Pawtucket, Rhode Island, then another, at 6:51 A.M., from the Bonanza Bus Terminal in Providence. These, too, had been made to the Douglas home.

The following day at 1:02 P.M., the user of the credit card had called Robin Benedict's answering service from a pay phone at Cobb's Corner in Canton. (Had the caller hoped to conduct business out of the earshot of children?) This call corresponded in time with the message for "Nadine" from "John" asking her to call him at Longfellow Place. The last call billed to the credit card was one made at 9:17 P.M. on Sunday to the Douglas home from Fairfield, Connecticut. This was during the seven-and-a-half-hour gap between the time when Douglas bought the Amtrak ticket at Penn Station and the time when he caught the 3:33 A.M. train to Washington, D.C.

Could investigators reasonably assume that the caller was Douglas?

Perhaps not. If the sheet of listings which Murphy had liberated from the trash was any indication, the Douglases had apparently handed that number around freely to friends and relatives. Even Robin, it turned out, had been making calls on the card. Among these were the one she had made to Douglas from Sargent Nichols's apartment at 9:40 P.M. and another, at about 10:06 P.M., from the pay phone of a Howard Johnson on the Southeast Expressway. If Douglas was not the nocturnal caller, then someone might have been working a deliberate deception through the answering service to frame him.

In the ensuing days, Brian Howe followed the route laid out by the tolls and found that Douglas could have negotiated these distances easily, even traveling five miles under the speed limit.

Trooper Murphy checked out the southern half of the route, ending up at the Bonanza Bus Terminal in Providence. Murphy learned that the first departure Douglas could have made from Providence after the 6:51 A.M. call was bus 152 at 7:30 A.M., heading for Logan Airport in East Boston. This bus also made a stop at Foxfield Plaza near Sharon. Bonanza officials told Murphy they did not keep actual tickets, but their records indicated that of six passengers who got on in Providence, only one got off in Foxfield. Murphy looked up the driver who had taken bus 152 to Logan that night. Samuel Rao, who had driven for Bonanza for twenty years, explained that on the Providence–Logan run hardly anyone ever got off at Foxboro. On the morning of March 6, he had called out that stop and, glancing in the rearview mirror, happened to notice a man crouching to peer out the window. The passenger had a round face and thick glasses and, Rao observed, "looked like a professor." The fellow would not have stood out except that he was glancing from left side to right as though he was confused. When Murphy showed Rao the photo of Douglas taken the night of the house search, however, the driver was unable to identify it as being of the man on the bus.

MATT CONNOLLY had started keeping a running computer log of events which preceded and followed Benedict's disappearance. He now updated it to include the credit card calls as well as tolls charged to the Douglas residence. From that chronology emerged an enlarging scenario.

On Friday morning someone at the Douglas house placed a series of calls to the Ellis Nursing Home. Since Nancy would have been at work and the children at school, the caller was most likely William Douglas, who had an apparently urgent need to speak to his wife. John Kivlan speculated that they might have been discussing the $200 check to Robin Benedict. The district attorney's office had finally gotten a copy of the stopped-payment order and discovered that it had been initiated on that Friday, March 4, by Nancy Douglas herself!

This discovery lent substance to a growing belief that Nancy Douglas knew more about the events of March 5 than had originally been imagined. When Landry interviewed her on the afternoon before the first search, she had conceded knowing that Robin Benedict was coming to her house Saturday afternoon, but she had represented herself as a passive, shrinking woman who had temporarily abandoned her turf to the enemy to avoid a confrontation. When Sharkey had questioned her during the search, she was so cooperative in identifying the blue shirt and digging up spools of thread that the lieutenant was convinced she was not involved in Benedict's disappearance. During the warm spring afternoons that the Gray House investigators spent spinning hypotheses, they had tended to shy away from assuming a role for Nancy Douglas. Part of this diffidence was simple deference to the woman's suffering. More realistically, as Matt Connolly had observed, it was hard to imagine Nancy involving herself in something as radical as a plot to murder a young rival. That would almost certainly place her children at risk.

Although the Gray House had been inclined at each turn to give Nancy the benefit of the doubt, they were now faced with a document indicating she had involved herself directly in the money squabbles preceding Robin's disappearance. While stopping Robin's check did not, by itself, indicate that Nancy was helping to formulate a conditional murder plan, it did suggest that she was helping to engineer some sort of showdown. Perhaps she had stopped the check in anticipation of Bill's giving Robin a large cash payment. Maybe she had instructed Bill to invite Robin to Sandy Ridge Circle Saturday afternoon with the intent of buying her off—then stayed clear of the house so that he could close the deal. But why, the question kept arising, would she have chosen the house as the negotiating site? If a pretty young woman walked up to the door in the middle of the day, might that not cause gossip, particularly since Robin's last visit had resulted in a scene on the lawn? Perhaps Nancy had reasoned that if Bill met Robin in the more provocative atmosphere of Boston, they might end up in bed, giving Robin the bargaining advantage and Bill the disincentive to make a clean break. If, on the other hand, this summit was held at the very seat of Bill's domestic life—amid the clutter of toys and homework and mending—then Bill might be chastened to keep his mind on the business at hand.

Whatever plans were or were not being hatched on Friday, March 4, William and Nancy Douglas were apparently on the phone to one another for most of the morning.

Toward noon Douglas began placing calls alternately to Robin's answering service and to her residence in Malden. The investigators knew from talking to J.R. that he suspected Douglas had been calling into Americall that afternoon and picking up Robin's messages under the guise of Mr. Rogers. At a little past eleven in the evening, Douglas got hold of Robin, or someone else at her home, and talked for fifteen minutes. Kivlan speculated that Douglas had made this call to plead with her to come to Sharon.

The following morning someone at the Douglas house spoke for five minutes to someone at the Malden residence, then, throughout the late morning and early afternoon, made calls to the Norwood Taxi Service. Perhaps, Kivlan mused, Douglas had taken a taxi somewhere to arrange the later disposal of her body. Perhaps he had actually gone into Boston to meet her, as his private notes suggested.

Norwood Taxi, unfortunately, kept no records of any kind.

About a quarter of noon on March 5, someone, probably Robin, had called Douglas using the Tufts card number from a pay phone at Despina's Pizza on Massachusetts Avenue. They had spoken for about twenty minutes. That afternoon around three-thirty John Baldwin called the answering service asking Robin to call him at work. Forty-five minutes later there was a call from Sharon to the answering service—apparently Douglas picking up Robin's message from Baldwin—and he placed a call one minute later to Longfellow Place. Douglas was evidently trying to locate this person he knew only as John to find out what arrangement he had with Robin. The investigators checked with Baldwin, who had no recollection of speaking with anyone identifying himself as Douglas.

Baldwin then left two more messages, which Robin apparently received because she showed up at Longfellow Place that evening, staying until around 9:40 P.M., when she called Douglas on the credit card. At ten o'clock Douglas called the answering service, apparently checking for messages. At 10:06 P.M. Robin called Douglas from the Howard Johnson on the expressway.

Matt Connolly speculated that Douglas had asked her to call when she was truly on her way. Maybe she was picking up some coffee or pastry to soften him up. A minute later, at 10:07 P.M., someone at the Douglas house in Sharon placed a call to Robin's answering service. That was exactly the moment when Americall had received the message from "Joe" inviting Robin to the party in Charlestown. This, according to the Connolly theory, was the call which laid the groundwork for the conditional murder plan. An hour and a half later, at 11:42 P.M., Robin was dead and Douglas needed to cover his tracks with the call from Bradlee's to the answering service announcing that Robin was on her way to Joe's.

Now that the investigators knew that Douglas had not hurried back to the house to make the 11:42 P.M. call, it significantly expanded the time and geographic range in which he could dispose of the body. After driving south as far as North Attleboro, where he made the calls at 11:54 P.M. and 11:56 P.M., he apparently swung north, dumping the bloody items at the Mansfield rest area en route. Two hours later, at 2:12 A.M., he was at South Station. That was perplexing since, in the wee hours of the morning, it usually took no more than forty minutes to drive from Mansfield to Boston. What had he done in the two intervening hours?

Assuming that the caller was William Douglas and that he had arrived in Boston around a quarter of one, the investigators asked themselves, where would he logically have gone? Given that Douglas was the compulsive type, a creature of habit, he would most likely have gravitated to the area in which he felt at home. Probably to the five-block district encompassing Tufts, the Combat Zone, and South Station. A subpoena of Douglas's charge slips had turned up an $8.54 charge made at a Mobil oil station on Berkeley Street, near the medical school. Brian Howe had paid a visit to the station and talked to one Symeon Papadopoulos, the attendant who worked the early-morning shift. Papadopoulos acknowledged that he must have made the sale because his initials, "SSP," had been written on the slip. The transaction had obviously occurred while he was on duty, between 1:00 A.M. and 8:00 A.M. He could not pinpoint the time any more precisely. Neither could he identify the photo of William Douglas. During that shift, he explained, there would have been approximately three hundred customers.

The pumps were self-service, so before a customer could get gas he had to come up to visit Papadopoulos, who was shut up in a control booth, and present his license and credit card. Papadopoulos required a driver's license to ensure that the photo matched the customer's face and that the name on the license was the same as that on the credit card. Apparently, he had been satisfied that the person signing the charge slip was William Douglas.

The Mobil slip established a couple of important things. First, that it was probably William and not Nancy Douglas who was in Boston at this hour. It was possible that Nancy was a passenger, but who would have been receiving the calls in Sharon? The children, perhaps? Was Robin also in the car at this time?

Gerry Pudolsky reminded the others that there was a lot of construction going on along Washington Street, part of the urban renewal program which was whittling away at the Combat Zone. Douglas might have been intending to dump her in one of the massive open pits and throw sand over her, in which case she might now be immured in the foundation of a high-rise. The Gray House group couldn't reasonably accept that hypothesis, because it led to a dead end.

The proximity of South Station to Tufts, only about four blocks away, led Peter Casey to suspect that Douglas might have disposed of the body somewhere on the Boston campus. Douglas was intimately familiar with those buildings. Since Tufts was in the business of training young anatomists, it undoubtedly had an incinerator for disposing of remains. (That method had worked well enough for John Webster some hundred and thirty years earlier.) Since Douglas had spent so much time there at night, his presence in the early hours of the morning would not necessarily have drawn attention.

The problem with this scenario, Kivlan pointed out, was that since mid-January, Douglas had been officially locked out of his lab and was therefore persona non grata with the security force. The sight of him lugging something heavy through the lobby would therefore have been a likely cause for alarm. Even if Douglas had found an entrance through which he could sneak unobserved, the prosecutor continued, he would probably not have been strong enough to carry 120 pounds of dead weight. He could have dismembered her, but Kivlan felt that would have taken more time than was available to him, even in the first long gap. Even assuming he had been able to vivisect her and sneak her parts past security, he would have had to stoke up the incinerator on a quiet Sunday morning, which would almost certainly have drawn notice from someone. While Kivlan did not dismiss the incinerator theory out of hand, he found it highly dubious.

Matt Connolly then introduced an alternative scenario. What if Douglas hadn't actually turned north after placing the calls from North Attleboro? What if, instead, he had continued south on 95 to Rhode Island and there stashed the body in one of his old haunts on the Brown campus or in the wooded vicinity of West Warwick? Among credit card tolls, investigators had found one on March 10 to the College of Mount Saint Vincent in the Bronx (to a colleague, it turned out) and another on March 17 to the Ellis Nursing Home. Both had been made from the Midland Shopping Mall in Warwick, Rhode Island. Perhaps this, Connolly reasoned, was where Douglas had disposed of the body, and he was returning periodically to the location to check it.

Brian Howe drove down to Warwick to survey the mall and found that the toll phone from which both calls had been made was located in a corridor leading to the upper-level parking lot. The booth was opposite an Eastern Airlines ticket vendor and a branch of the Hospital Trust National Bank, where the Douglases, it had been learned, had an account.

Howe interviewed owners and salespersons in nearby boutiques, including one salesgirl employed by Frederick's of Hollywood. The salesgirl looked at Douglas's photo and said she thought she had seen him in the store on several occasions, but she wasn't sure he had ever purchased anything.

Significantly, however, Howe had discovered during this outing that the traveling time between North Attleboro and the Midland Mall was only an hour round-trip. Because the drive to South Station took another forty-five minutes, that meant that Douglas could have squeezed in a trip to Warwick in the first two-hour time gap.

Matt Connolly resumed his scenario making at this point, speculating that after disposing of the body, Douglas had made the trip into Boston to park the car in such a location as to incriminate either Joe Murray or John Baldwin. Working against that supposition, however, was the fact that both Charlestown and the area around Longfellow Place had been searched thoroughly and nothing been turned up. If the car had been parked in Boston, it would most likely have been reported by now. In light of this, Connolly revised his theory to suggest that Douglas had had second thoughts about disposing of the Toyota in such a visible location. Perhaps he reasoned that one of Robin's associates might see him. Or that the Boston police might find the car immediately, notice the blood, and send out an alarm. Maybe he wanted to buy himself more time. The call home at 2:12 A.M. could have been to confer with Nancy on this point. Perhaps they had decided, for whatever reason, that it would be best for him to take the car back to Rhode Island and dispose of it more securely. What seemed certain was that, after the call from South Station, Douglas had started south to Providence and gotten rid of the car during the second time gap, between the 2:12 A.M. and 6:51 A.M. calls to Sharon. Then he had taken the 7:30 A.M. bus from Providence to Foxboro, where Nancy probably picked him up at the station.

On Sunday afternoon, the investigators concluded, Nancy had dropped her husband off at Foxboro, where he caught a bus, not to Boston as he had claimed, but to Providence. There he retrieved the car and drove it to New York City. After buying the ticket in Penn Station at 7:58 P.M., they speculated, he drove, for some inexplicable reason, to Fairfield, Connecticut, where at 9:17 P.M. he placed a call home to Sharon.

The Fairfield call had the Gray House stumped. Technically, there was plenty of time for Douglas to have bought the ticket, driven north on Route 95 for eighty-five miles to Fairfield, and gotten back to Penn Station in time for the 3:33 A.M. departure. But why hadn't he conducted whatever business he had in Fairfield on the trip down? Perhaps he still had the body in the car, intending to leave both near Penn Station, then got cold feet and thought the body should be placed away from the car outside the city. Perhaps he had driven north as far as Fairfield and, losing his nerve, turned at the overpass, ducked into the Howard Johnson on the southbound lane, and made a call home for instructions or moral support.

It was more likely that he had only the car to dispose of at this point and that he drove to Fairfield, which seemed a discreet distance, intending to leave the Toyota in or near the parking lot of the commuter rail depot. Trooper Murphy had checked and found that there had been three departures from Fairfield to Grand Central Station that Douglas could have taken in order to make the 3:33 train to Washington. Unfortunately, the commuter rail was on strike—something Douglas may have learned only after making the trip up to Connecticut.

The round-trip to Fairfield, including phone call, probably took only about three hours. What had he done during the rest of his layover in New York? In perusing the refuse taken from Douglas's front walk, the Gray House had found a narrow box of matches imprinted with the name Ginsberg and Wong, a Jewish Chinese restaurant in Cherry Hill. Trooper Murphy checked with the owners and found that they had started giving out these matches shortly before March 6. Douglas could have made it to Cherry Hill and back to New York within four hours. It was possible he had dropped the body somewhere along the Delaware River Valley and then stopped in for sweet-and-sour corned beef before returning to Penn Station. It was equally likely that he had picked up the matches when he was in Cherry Hill for the Tissue Culture Association meeting later in the month.

Neither owners nor service personnel could identify his photo.

The tolls were at once intriguing and maddening. Each new time and location that Matt Connolly fed into his computerized chronology seemed to hold the promise of a breakthrough. After the discovery of the credit card number, John Kivlan had been certain that Robin Benedict's body would be found within twenty-four hours.

Three week passed. Still nothing. The Gray House continued mulling over the bits, turning and reassembling them in hopes of finding the scenario which would accommodate them all. But the tolls were like crystals in a kaleidoscope. A slight twisting of the lens caused them to fall into a new pattern as distinct and coherent as the last. The Gray House investigators began to feel themselves at the mercy of their own imaginations. Elaborate theories had emanated from the Fairfield call, among others, but what if it was simply a clerical error? What if the phone company had made a mistake and Douglas had really made the call on his way to New York? Or perhaps Amtrak had been wrong about the time the ticket was purchased.

The Gray House investigators were nettled by the possibility that this game of matching wits with Douglas was, after all, misguided pride. Perhaps they had endowed the suspect with gifts of logic and enterprise that he did not actually possess. Perhaps he had done nothing more complicated than drive aimlessly up and down Route 95.

There was a chance that all of this elaborate conjecture was nothing more than an attempt to impose rational motives upon a confused and wholly irrational man.

STRANGE BEDFELLOWS

IT WAS ordinarily the district attorney's policy to keep a victim's family informed of developments. But by the first week in April, John and Shirley Benedict had been edged quietly to the periphery of the investigation. John Kivlan was afraid that news of the tolls and Amtrak tickets might leak out to the press. Even though the media seemed to have lost track of the story (a development which the prosecutor observed with profound gratitude), he felt he could not take chances. The Benedicts, while well meaning, were not discreet and could not, Kivlan felt, be entrusted with confidential details. And so, as the investigation took twists they were not privileged to follow, the Benedicts found themselves on the outside, not sure whom to trust.

IN THE VERY BEGINNING, at least, they had been willing to give Professor William Douglas the benefit of the doubt. He had first presented himself to them in the guise of a delivering angel, the man who could verify that Robin was indeed engaged in the pursuit of a conventional career. In the midst of their bewildering pilgrimage to Boston Municipal Court, Douglas had emerged to assure them that Robin was in his employ. The Benedicts were understandably reluctant to let go of Professor Douglas as a touchstone of respectability.

On both occasions when he had called the house following Robin's disappearance, he had assumed the peculiar intimacy of a friend of the family, passing along the confidence that Robin did not want J.R. Rogers near her valuables. At that point the Benedicts were still not yet sure what to think about J.R. They did not doubt that he had gotten Robin into prostitution. "A girl doesn't just get there by herself," Shirley would later confide in friends. It was possible, after all, that he might even be responsible for her disappearance. Yet the Benedicts had recent, vivid recollections of Robin's apparent affection for her Junie. The "dream house." The engagement. All the trappings of domesticity and respectability. The Benedicts were loath to dismiss these as deceptions. There was also Junie's apparent solicitude for Robin. His grief at her disappearance. His diligence in hiring the private eyes. As weeks wore on, the Benedicts found themselves turning increasingly toward J.R. Rogers for information and theories.

It was Douglas, J.R. continued to assert, who was responsible for Robin's disappearance. His allegations gained credence when, on the morning of Monday, March 21, Trooper Paul Landry called the Benedicts to say that over the weekend Robin's personal belongings had been found in Douglas's bedroom closet. Until then, they had been nursing the hope—which J.R. professed to share—that if Douglas had been involved with Robin's disappearance, it was only to spirit her away and keep her against her will. Not even Junior could believe that the professor was capable of murder. But with the discovery of brain tissue in Douglas's windbreaker, there seemed no choice but to acknowledge that she might be dead.

Shirley Benedict had spent most of the day after Landry's announcement trying to rouse herself from a paralysis of dread, when she received yet another call from Dr. William Douglas.

Douglas greeted her nervously. She suppressed a surge of anger. Her desire to get information was stronger than grief or rage. She was curious to see if he would mention the search.

He did not. He was apparently waiting to see if she would bring it up, but she would not oblige him.

Douglas then began telling her how on the Saturday night when Robin had visited him in Sharon, she had shown up with a black eye. J.R. had given it to her, he intimated. They had had a fight over a girl he had brought to the house.

Shirley Benedict did not believe him. Nonetheless, she listened quietly. She had learned, over the months since Robin's activities in the Zone had come to light, that it was often necessary to make a display of civility toward those whom one distrusted if there was a possibility of getting information from them. She wanted to leave the door open for Douglas to call and talk. The more he talked, the more he might incriminate himself. Perhaps he would even confess.

Douglas did not confess that night, and he never called again.

IN THE WEEKS to follow, the Benedicts began to see more of J.R. Rogers. On occasion he brought little Taj up to Methuen, where Shirley received him as affectionately as a grandchild. Eventually his picture took its place alongside the baby photos of Robin and her siblings in the Benedicts' curio-filled living room. Once Taj asked innocently if "Mama Robin" didn't like him anymore and if that was why she didn't come to visit. Hearing this, Junie was reputedly overcome by emotion and went into another room to cry.

The Benedicts' sympathies were further aroused when Junie confided that he was the target of an anonymous caller who told him that if he went out to the toolshed, he would find Robin's body wrapped in a rug. This proved false, but thereafter Junie professed to be too frightened to live in the Cliff Street house alone, and he made arrangements to move back to Mattapan with his mother.

As he dispersed the household, he passed along certain things he thought the Benedicts would like to have. He collected her personal effects—an assortment of lingerie, nylons, hairbrushes, curlers, and makeup. There were many blouses, slacks, suits, dresses, and shoes, including a new pair of brown leather boots. There was the black leather jacket he had given her the preceding November and, finally, the valuables—a full-length mink coat and several pieces of jewelry, among them a sapphire ring and three gold chains, one set with twenty-one diamonds.

While cleaning out the closet, Junie had also found a piece of artwork, a block print featuring an ominous, disjointed figure against a green background. When one first looked at it, the eye went to the top of the image and fixed upon what appeared to be interlocking spikes. After a moment's reflection, one realized that these were fingers. These fingers were attached to arms, and as the eye followed these arms to the bottom of the canvas, it found the grimacing face of a black man.

J.R. said that William Douglas had given it to Robin, telling her it would appreciate in value. She didn't like it, however, and had turned the grimacing face toward the wall.

DURING the first week in April, Junie confided to John and Shirley that Robin had been to see a psychic. He didn't know many of the particulars, such as why or when she had gone, but he did have the name of the medium, a certain Gloria James, who lived in the South Shore town of Hingham.

John Benedict, who considered himself a man of reason, was dubious of such hocus pocus. But over a month had passed since Robin's disappearance, and the state police, from what he could see, had turned up nothing. He was now amenable to considering extraordinary measures. It seemed worth making a visit to James, who, having met and consulted with Robin, might shed some factual, if not supernatural, light on her whereabouts.

On Wednesday, April 6, Shirley called Miss James's appointments secretary, who told her to come down that same day.

The psychic lived in an unassuming white frame house guarded by a pair of stone lions. She held audiences in a back room filled to overflowing with religious statuary and gifts from supplicants who had credited her with setting their careers or love lives on a more stable footing.

James's assistant ushered the Benedicts and J.R. Rogers into the audience room, the far corner of which was occupied by James herself, enthroned on a green Naugahyde lounger. She was a wizened woman, whose tough talk and unrestrained delivery of baleful tidings had earned her the title Prophet of Doom. The Benedicts acknowledged this dour presence. Shirley took a seat in an armchair opposite her. John and J.R. sat on a daybed.

The psychic had not been told why they had come. The Benedicts had been careful not to relate any particulars of the case. But as Gloria James later recalled the reading, she addressed her first comments to Shirley, asking, "Who's missing?"

Shirley explained that it was her daughter Robin, a former client of James.

"That goddamn kid," James said. "Is she the kid I told, 'Don't go into stripping. Don't go to Florida,' 'cause I saw her posing naked? I said, 'What the hell you posing naked for?' "

Robin had apparently not given her a direct answer.

After that burst of recognition, the psychic slipped into another persona.

"I'm always on the go," she intoned. "I'm back and forth . . . what am I doing in New York? . . . There's blood around me. There's bloodstains and it's in a car, but I'm in New York. But I'm not sure if it's New York City or upper state New Jersey. . . . I'm involved with several people. . . . I guess two people are in a professional field."

"What about a professor?" Shirley Benedict asked.

"Yes, I've seen the professor. I go out with this . . . schoolteacher, whoever he is . . . but I'm also in sports. . . . I don't know what sports mean to me. . . . Something about sports around me, and I'm frightened."

James's staccato pronouncements then became a series of alternating voices:

"I can't keep my word to you. You owe it to me. You owe me. . . . And I'm running upstairs. I am frightened, but a woman's with me. I have female characteristics around me. I'm a female also. There's a female, and I'm in a uniform. But why should I have a uniform? What am I doing in a uniform as a female?

"But I walked in unexpectedly. . . . I'm looking around and I'm crying for somebody. . . . There's a child around me and I'm frightened, but I don't know why I'm frightened. But there is a child somewhere. A child is looking in or a child walked in."

Gloria James began receiving impressions of a metal instrument, a sword perhaps. She gripped the imaginary object in her right hand. Her arm began to rise and fall.

"I kept her alive for a while. . . . She was shifted back and forth. It's like . . . I'm putting you here and there and nowhere."

THE PSYCHIC'S SCENARIO was chilling; her knowledge of particulars, extraordinary. It was possible, of course, that she had chanced to read the *Herald* account about the finding of a hammer, but James maintained in the months thereafter that she had read or heard nothing about the case. She could not, at any rate, have known that Douglas's wife was a nurse who customarily wore a uniform, because that had not been reported anywhere.

The Benedicts found James credible on several other counts. She had said that Robin had a wound on the inside of her thigh. As it happened, Robin had been injured there some weeks before her disappearance by a box which fell from the top of her closet. The psychic also mentioned a weak ankle. That apparently referred to an injury which Robin had incurred while hanging wallpaper in the bathroom. She had slipped and fallen into the tub.

In at least one respect, Gloria James seemed to know more about Robin than even the Benedicts themselves did. At one point the psychic asked if Robin had ever had an abortion. John and Shirley hastened to assure her that this was impossible.

Junie winced and said yes. She had had one when she was sixteen.

The Benedicts were stunned. The ethical considerations of abortion aside, they were grieved that Robin could have gone through such a thing without telling them. When had she managed to do it? She had never missed a day of school and had even gotten an award on Class Nite for perfect attendance.

Robin, the psychic continued, had wanted the child, but she was forbidden to have it by "a doctor and someone else."

"There was something wrong with her insides," James said, "and a gynecologist was treating her for it. But he didn't cure her."

These provocative revelations notwithstanding, James could not seem to provide the one thing that the Benedicts had come for, the location of Robin's body. The impressions she was receiving were too diffuse, she claimed. She was left only with a sense of Robin's being "here and there and nowhere."

The next week they followed up on a lead provided by John's mother. Nana had made the acquaintance of mediums who made the round of psychics' fairs in northern Massachusetts, and one of these had told her about a woman from out west named Marie Stephenson. Stephenson was well known for her powers of second sight and spiritual healing. Police departments around the country frequently used her to help locate missing persons. When an Iowa toddler disappeared from his parents' farmhouse, she had pinpointed the cornfield in which he was later found, dazed but unharmed. This exploit had been chronicled earlier that spring on "That's Incredible."

Shirley Benedict put in a call to Stephenson, who lived in a trailer park in Tucson, Arizona, and offered to pay her way back east if she would agree to assist them in locating Robin. Stephenson declined to accept money. She was planning to travel to Massachusetts the following week with one of her clients, who was suffering from cancer. They were scheduled to visit a faith healer in Worcester. She would be happy, she said, to consult with the Benedicts at that time.

Several days later, when John and Shirley set out for the appointed meeting place, a Howard Johnson in Weston, they swung south into Norfolk County to pick up Paul Landry. The family had gotten to know Landry during the three weeks he been on the case. He had been willing to share information, and now, even though he was no longer assigned to the case—he had retired, as scheduled, at the end of March—they still perceived him as a possible lifeline to the investigation.

Landry, for his part, was eager to keep on good terms with the Benedicts. While there was no chance that he would be formally reattached to the investigation, there was another avenue for achieving the big grab he desperately desired. He would write a book about it. So when the family invited him to come along to the meeting with Marie Stephenson, Landry—though as skeptical of psychics as John Benedict was—saw an opportunity he should not refuse.

When the three of them entered the lobby of the Howard Johnson, they found Stephenson, an attractive middle-aged woman with a dimpled chin and frosted hair rolled up in a bun. She was in the company of her spiritual charge, a pale, sullen woman named Fern. Together the five of them took a booth in the restaurant. Stephenson put her hand on Shirley Benedict's arm to comfort her and pulled out a legal pad to make some notes.

She wanted, she said, only the barest circumstances of the case to provide grist for her meditations. Shirley took the lead, explaining how Robin had been doing artwork for a professor. She had gone out to his home in Sharon, where she disappeared.

The psychic had a feeling—a "knowingness," she later called it—that the girl might be into prostitution.

"She's a call girl," she said bluntly.

The Benedicts appeared surprised but acknowledged that this was true. Shirley seemed eager to impress upon Stephenson that her daughter had indeed been a "call girl" and not a common prostitute.

Stephenson then asked that the Benedicts go home and get together some of Robin's personal belongings. These should be things that Robin had worn close to her body. Things that she liked. The following day, while Stephenson took Fern to the faith healer, the Benedicts returned to the motel and dropped off several items: a chain necklace, a tortoise-shell headband, a hairbrush, and a bathrobe. In addition, Paul Landry agreed to send photos of the barrel and hammer, as well as a map of the area around Mansfield.

Stephenson took these articles back with her to Tucson. When she arrived home at her New Moon trailer, she laid them out on her kitchen table and waited until dark. She preferred nighttime for metaphysical work. Strong light interfered with her mental images. There were a lot of electrical disturbances out there to begin with. But when one was dealing with a violent crime, the transmission could get hopelessly garbled.

She adjusted a light fixture which hung above the table. There were five bulbs, each of a different color. Yellow gold, orange, green, sky blue, and a purplish blue. She unscrewed all but the two blue ones, which she considered particularly useful in neutralizing the turbulence of a murder.

With this, she pulled out her legal pad and put on the necklace and headband. Sitting quiet and still in the pool of blue light, Marie began receiving images of a man with a narrow nose and thin face. She figured it must be Douglas. She saw him in a hat. A soft hat that was not in style. The hat had a dark band, and the man appeared to be wearing either glasses or sunglasses.

"Turmoil surrounded their last meeting," she wrote. "Complacency followed. But not total peace, catching Robin off guard."

Stephenson thought she saw Robin making a telephone call from a mall or a plaza, where she was met by someone who then took her away.

Then she saw a trunk bound with a leather strap. It seemed to be sunk in a bloody mire.

She turned to photos of the hammer. These, for some reason, triggered a stream of intimations concerning Robin's relationship with Douglas.

"A man who was yearning to be flamboyant, but couldn't hold onto that image of himself," she wrote. "He was very disappointed to not be able to do that."

In Robin she perceived something of the "con artist." She exercised total control over Douglas and enjoyed the power. "When people get that kind of control," the psychic observed, "their ego goes out of whack."

"Robin bullied Douglas," Stephenson wrote, "demeaning him and this led to turmoil."

"False call took her somewhere else," the notations continued. The terms "admonished and threatened" came to mind, but she couldn't tell which way the threats were running. She didn't think that Robin was threatening Douglas, and she felt certain that Robin wasn't threatened by him.

Stephenson wrapped herself in Robin's bathrobe and sat for a while in contemplation. She heard the words "Stonebridge," "Sturbridge," or possibly "Stony Brook." She consulted the map which Landry had sent her and found a "Granite Reservoir" near Sturbridge, west of Boston, in Worcester County. She wrote, "Just possible we are looking for reservoir." Stephenson also admitted the possibility that it could be "Sandy Ridge" and scribbled a note which advised looking around the area where Douglas lived.

Running her hands over the hairband, brush, and necklace, she finally received the impression of "a place where intermittent blasting goes on—could be a furnace."

JOHN KIVLAN, meanwhile, was dismayed to hear that the Benedicts were running around the countryside in the company of psychics. Such undignified conduct, in the prosecutor's opinion, could only work against them if the case came to trial. Since the victim was a prostitute, it would be very easy for a jury, particularly one selected from the predominantly white, well-educated, well-to-do population of Norfolk County, to decline to take a charge of murder seriously. Particularly when the charge was leveled at a purportedly respectable professional like William Douglas. The tables might be turned, however, if Robin Benedict could be shown to have been a normal, loving little girl from a normal, loving, middle-class family. The more unorthodox the Benedicts' behavior became, the more they stood to weaken this gambit.

One of the most troubling things about the Benedicts from a public relations standpoint, of course, was that they appeared to embrace their daughter's pimp. The Gray House investigators found this very queer. The line the Benedicts were now taking was that Junie was actually Robin's "fiancé." Brian Howe had learned from contacts in the Boston police that Robin's father had not been happy with her relationship to J.R. and that when he found she had been nabbed for suspected prostitution, he turned over a photo of Rogers to Vice. Robin was subsequently able to persuade her father that what the police had told him was not the truth. Howe's impression of John Benedict was that he was not the type to confront his daughter directly and say, "Are you a prostitute?"

Like Landry before him, Howe could locate no actual convictions establishing that Robin was a working girl. The records of her court appearances had been sealed. He managed, however, to obtain copies of Boston police reports with accounts of her arrests, and these were fairly incriminating. Likewise, there was nothing on record to establish that Rogers was a pimp. He had never been arrested, and there were no surveillance reports which would involve him in prostitution. The intelligence coming out of the Boston vice squad about Rogers could—if it became necessary to rehabilitate J.R. in the eyes of a jury—be discredited as street talk. On the other hand, Rogers had been living with Robin, which left him open to charges of deriving income from a prostitute.

Both Kivlan and Howe knew J.R. stood to take a severe bruising at the hands of opposing counsel. They also realized that he wasn't telling everything he knew. While they didn't want to play into the hands of Douglas's defense by unearthing any more unsavory details than necessary, neither did they want any surprises. J.R. was summoned to the district attorney's office for further questioning.

Kivlan preferred to hold J.R. at arm's length, leaving the interviewing to Howe. The atmosphere surrounding that meeting, which took place in the Gray House attic, was scrupulously formal. Just as Howe insisted upon the rather elevated form William when referring to Douglas, the trooper addressed Rogers as Clarence.

Howe went back over Rogers's history with Robin from the time they began to "date," in the fall of 1981, asking Clarence if he wouldn't elaborate a bit upon his relationship with Robin.

She had been into prostitution when he met her, Clarence said. The calls she made back to the answering service were of a precautionary nature. His position was that Robin's business was her business, and she didn't bring it home with her. That was all he would say.

While Howe found the relationship between Robin and J.R. "unusual," he did not get the feeling that it was a classic pimp-prostitute arrangement, in which she came home and handed him the cash. Judging from Robin's real estate transaction, which left the house clearly in her name, J.R. did not seem to take a very active role in her temporal affairs. If he was indeed her pimp, Howe reasoned, his role must have been more protective than supervisory.

J.R. claimed never to have met William Douglas, but Robin had told him that Douglas had confided to her that he and his wife had not had sex for two to three years. She had had some kind of operation and blamed Douglas, who called her the Android. Robin said that Douglas was "depressed at work" and could relax only when he was around her. Robin told J.R. that she thought Douglas was a "big baby."

Of the bitterness between Douglas and Robin, J.R. insisted he knew little. In February, Douglas had been arguing with Robin, threatening to expose her for her supposed role in the embezzlement. She, in turn, threatened to expose him by going to the *Globe.*

On the afternoon she disappeared, Robin had laid her clothes out on the bed while she showered. Besides the beige ensemble, she had worn panties, but not the pink ones found in the professor's closet. As near as J.R. could remember, Robin had also been wearing a knotted gold ring and gold shell earrings. Most significant, however, he now seemed to recall her having taken, not the bluish black purse found in Douglas's closet, but a smaller brown clutch bag.

This seemed to support the existence of the "brown pocketbook" to which Douglas had referred in his handwritten notes. It didn't make any sense. If Douglas had kept one of Robin's purses, why hadn't he kept the one she had brought with her to the house the night of March 5? Howe made a note to follow up on the brown clutch.

ONE SUGGESTION which Clarence Rogers passed along to Brian Howe, was that when he talked to Savi Bisram, he shouldn't call her Debbie. She didn't like that name. Accordingly, when Howe telephoned her requesting an interview, he was careful to address her as Savi. He asked her if she could come into Dedham for an interview and, finding she didn't have a car, agreed to drive the five miles east to Randolph to pick her up.

As Howe pulled into Presidential Acres, he was surprised at how nice it was. Clean, well-cared-for children played on the grounds. Professionals outfitted with Walkmans and Reeboks jogged along the paved sidewalks that connected the units. Presidential Acres was a sprawling complex of garden apartments laid out on a flat meadow. Each building was named for an American president. Savi lived near the back of the complex in "Franklin Pierce."

Howe buzzed Savi and waited. After a moment she appeared, a tall dark-skinned woman of about twenty-five, wearing tight jeans and high heels. She got into the trooper's cruiser, and the two of them set off for Dedham. Howe was interested to see that Savi did not try to hide the fact that she was a prostitute. Her only concern, apparently, was how her involvement in this matter would affect her little boy, who, she said, was being cared for by her sister.

"I don't care what they say about me," Savi told him. "but I don't want my kid to have to put up with anything."

She was originally from the West Indies, she said. She wanted to go back for a visit but was afraid that if she left the country, she might have trouble getting back in.

This called to mind a pair of notations Howe had seen among the piles of notes taken from 38 Sandy Ridge Circle. Douglas had written, "Debbie—2 yr old son problem with immigration."

Among the tapes found on Douglas's bureau, there had been one with a scarcely audible conversation between Douglas and Savi that seemed to have been made as he was driving her home one night from Boston. Above the growl of the car motor, one could hear Savi explaining in a crazy, lilting Creole how her brother was getting a new Volvo. She really didn't want a car and would rather live in Boston. Douglas agreed sympathetically that if she lived in Boston, she'd "get more sleep." He, too, would like to live in Boston, he said. As he let her off, he apologized for "the trouble."

Howe assumed that this "trouble" referred to the difficulties with Tufts. He surmised that Douglas might have been subtly suggesting to Savi that he was in a position to blow the whistle on her.

Had Savi ever gone out with Douglas? the trooper asked.

"Oh no," Savi replied. She wouldn't have minded having a good date like Douglas. After Robin had taken up with him, she didn't have to work weekends. Savi lamented that she herself had to work just about every day because she liked nice clothes and had the rent to pay. But Douglas, unfortunately, didn't like "dark-skinned girls."

After they arrived at the Gray House, Howe managed to extract from Savi a sketchy account of her own role in Douglas's financial misconduct.

Around the middle of October 1982, Savi said, Robin had asked her if she would cash a couple of checks for Douglas. Savi agreed.

A few weeks later Savi began getting correspondence from Tufts asking her to clarify some payments made to her. Savi asked Robin about it, and Robin said she would talk to Douglas. When Robin didn't get back to her, Savi called Douglas at his home to ask him about it. Douglas said he wanted to meet with Savi to straighten things out. The prospect of Douglas's knowing where she lived made Savi uneasy, so she had him pick her up at a Friendly's on Route 28 in Randolph. On the way into Boston, Douglas explained that the university had a new computer system that had been fouling things up. She would receive four inquiries about the checks she had cashed, but these were routine, and she was not to worry about them.

Douglas dropped Savi off in the Combat Zone at about 3:00 P.M. and said he would drive her home later. Savi told him she wouldn't be done until very late, but Douglas said he didn't mind and returned to pick her up at 1:00 A.M. She got in the car with him and, against her better judgment, allowed him to drive her back to Presidential Acres. It was during that trip to Randolph, apparently, that Douglas had taped Savi without her knowing it.

Howe relayed this episode to Kivlan, who found it rather bizarre. Why tape a prostitute? Had Savi or Robin been threatening to cooperate with Tufts? Were they extorting him? Was he taping them to establish proof of blackmail? Perhaps he was preparing to threaten Savi with immigration troubles if she appeared inclined to rat on him?

If that was the subtext of the ride to Natick, Savi professed to be unaware of it. Douglas had assured her that everything was all right. The only unpleasantness she could recall was an uneasiness bordering on fear.

THE GRAY HOUSE troopers, meanwhile, kept a close eye on the comings and goings at 38 Sandy Ridge Circle, but they made no move to arrest William Douglas. It was Kivlan's intent that he should remain free for as long as possible.

Even though the first search had turned up more than enough evidence to bring him in, the prosecutor was not convinced that—without a body— it was sufficient to obtain an indictment, or, more unlikely still, a conviction. What is more, he knew that Douglas was aware of the odds against a successful prosecution. During the second search, troopers had recovered a page of notes on which Douglas, after a consultation with Dan O'Connell, had scrawled confidently, "Kivlan may not indict (without) car or body."

That notation gave Kivlan a valuable clue to O'Connell's strategy. He would have the luxury of taking several positions. The first was "You cannot prove that she is dead, let alone that my client killed her." If Robin turned up, he could fall back on "She might be dead, but my client didn't do it." Given Robin's lifestyle, he could point to one of several suspects— J.R. and Joe Murray among them—who might have had motives to kill her. O'Connell clearly intended to concede nothing.

The hand that Kivlan chose to play, therefore, was to leave Douglas at large for the time being, but to turn the matter over to the Norfolk County grand jury.

The grand jury was an august body whose deliberations were normally shrouded in extraordinary secrecy. Every Monday morning nineteen citizens, selected from the voting rolls of Norfolk County for a six-month tour of duty, convened in the oak-paneled grand-jury room of the Superior Courthouse to hear evidence against accused felons and decide whether the state had sufficient evidence to take those cases to trial. The matters presented to the grand jury were, for the most part, fairly straightforward. Petty larcenies and barroom assaults. The jurors might hear five to ten of these in succession, handing down as many indictments in the course of an afternoon. Occasionally, however, the jury was called upon not only to hear evidence but also to assist in an investigation of an unindicted suspect. In this capacity the grand jury enjoyed such impressive authority that it could often summon witnesses and command evidence that were beyond the reach even of the district attorney. While this body was theoretically independent of the state, a clever prosecutor could nonetheless manage to win over the jurors and exploit their considerable power to his own advantage.

John Kivlan was uncommonly adroit at persuading a grand jury to see his point of view. What he now wanted, in regard to the William Douglases, was to persuade the jurors to call Nancy and the children to testify. When he brought this matter before them late in March, they obliged, promptly petitioning the superior court for three summonses requiring Nancy, Billy, Pamela, and John to appear before them on Monday, April 4.

Kivlan knew that even if Nancy showed up, as she was obligated to do under pain of a contempt citation, she would probably say nothing. As William Douglas's wife, she enjoyed a "spousal privilege," which meant she could not be required to say anything that might incriminate her husband. This protection—long honored in common and statutory law— had grown out of the theory that requiring one spouse to testify against another would disrupt family unity.

Strangely—and happily from the prosecutorial standpoint—no such privilege apparently existed for the children. Kivlan thought he had a good shot at getting the young Douglases to talk. He had explained to the grand jury that it wasn't simply a matter of wanting their testimony to bolster someone else's account of the night of March 5. Rather, he felt that Billy, Pamela, and John possessed potentially *unique* testimony. Although the prosecutor didn't believe that the children had actually witnessed Robin Benedict's supposed murder, he felt with some certainty that they had been privy to the comings and goings of their parents that weekend. At the very least, they could say whether their mother drove away from the house, as she claimed, or whether she went inside.

To date the children themselves had not actually refused to testify. Pamela's tearful complaint to Landry that everyone was trying to "get something" on her father suggested that she and her brothers had come to see the police as enemies. Other than that, the only indication of what the youngsters might be thinking came from a set of notes seized during the second search.

"My kids are terrified . . . cry to sleep at night," read one of the jottings. "My Wife doesn't want him [Landry] to talk to the kids PERIOD. . . ."

Kivlan could only guess at how the Douglases might react to the summonses, but he thought he detected the first reverberations in a seemingly unrelated occurrence up north in Methuen.

On the Saturday afternoon that Nancy was served, John Benedict received a Western Union telegram which read, "Happy Easter. I'm working in Las Vegas and things are well. Please don't tell J.R. where I am. Love to everyone. Love Robin."

That message, which should have inspired joy, struck John Benedict as suspicious. First of all, it was unaccountably formal, addressed to "Mr. and Mrs. Benedict." The sender had, furthermore, gotten the address wrong. It had been given as "41 Emsley Terrace," but the Benedicts lived at No. 44. Finally, Benedict noticed that it had been signed Robin, whereas his daughter would probably have used the nickname Bin Bin.

John Benedict reported this to the state police, who called John Kivlan at home. Kivlan, too, thought the telegram sounded specious. He contacted Western Union and tried to find out if the message had indeed originated in Las Vegas. Company officials could not identify the point of origin. All they could tell him was that shortly before one that Saturday afternoon the message in question had been taken by operator 122. Kivlan was put through to the operator, who said she remembered the message "vaguely." The phrase that stood out in her memory was "Don't tell J.R. where I am." The voice, she thought, was that of a female. It struck her as that of a "young woman." By that, she explained, she meant someone who was not elderly. She was not completely sure that it was, after all, the voice of a woman.

The operator was certain that the caller had said "41 Emsley Terrace." She would, as a matter of procedure, have read it back for confirmation. The caller had said that he (or she) did not want his (or her) telephone number to appear on the telegram.

The timing of the telegram led Kivlan to the conclusion that the Douglases, alarmed by the grand-jury summonses, had engaged in desperate subterfuge to deflect attention from themselves. It was possible that Nancy might try to ignore the summons, placing herself in contempt of the grand jury, in the hope that a furor over the telegram would overshadow her absence.

The following Monday, however, Nancy and the children showed up at the somber granite Superior Courthouse in Dedham, as though nothing had happened. As expected, Nancy invoked her privilege not to testify. Attorney O'Connell, recognizing that the interests of parents and children might not necessarily be the same, had arranged for a friend of his, an attorney named Brian McMenimen, to represent the three youngest Douglases. McMenimen quickly moved to quash the subpoena issued to his clients on grounds that it was a "violation of their rights under the Constitution." A superior-court judge denied that motion but agreed to hold off enforcing the subpoena for ten days to allow McMenimen a chance to appeal it.

Often, when there is such urgency that a matter cannot be held for hearing before the full Supreme Judicial Court, a single justice will agree to hear the case. That is what happened in the matter of the Douglas children—discreetly labeled "Three Juveniles," in an attempt to preserve their anonymity and avoid attracting the notice of the press. On April 13 McMenimen argued before Supreme Judicial Court Justice Neil Lynch that his motion to quash the Commonwealth's subpoena was wrongly denied, since it robbed the Juveniles of privacy protection accorded to families under the Constitution. He pointed in particular to the Fourteenth Amendment, which established "the right to marry, establish a home and bring up children." It was possible, he said, that the Juveniles might be jailed for refusing to testify, something, McMenimen claimed, which would cause "enormous and irreparable emotional harm."

A week later the Three Juveniles' parents, acting under the pseudonyms John and Jane Doe, filed a motion to intervene as an interested party to the proceedings. The Does reported that they had informed their own attorney, who had informed the attorney for the Juveniles that it was their wish that the children not testify.

While Justice Lynch appeared sympathetic to the concept of a parent-child privilege, he nonetheless decided that the matter was sufficiently grave and the legal questions sufficiently novel to warrant a hearing before the full bench when it convened the first week in May.

In the meantime the Norfolk County grand jury postponed further official attempts to contact the Douglas children until the Supreme Judicial Court had had its say.

JOHN KIVLAN —foreseeing that some or all of the Douglases might soon be declared off limits—decided to hazard one, last assault upon 38 Sandy Ridge Circle.

He did not have to look far for a pretext. During the second house search, on March 26, Trooper Landry had jotted down the serial numbers of the Apple II Plus computer in the Douglas dining room. Tufts security had verified that the computer was the one Douglas had reported "stolen" from his office on January 12. The knowledge that stolen equipment was sitting in the Douglas house provided ample grounds for another search warrant. The new initiative was set for Friday, April 22. That was the day William Douglas was scheduled to be away in Newport, attending his ophthalmological conference.

That afternoon Sharkey and Howe arrived at Sandy Ridge Circle, intercepting Nancy just as she was loading her children into the car. She did not seem alarmed. After glancing at the warrant, she told the troopers that she would be taking the children to the dentist but that they were welcome to search in her absence. Howe replied that he was uncomfortable with that arrangement, so Nancy led them into the house and canceled the doctor's appointment.

As Howe set about confiscating the Tufts equipment, Sharkey turned his attention to Mrs. Douglas.

The lieutenant was, in fact, a little embarrassed that Nancy had made a fool of him. The sight of her shivering in terror during the first search had aroused his sympathy. She had struck him—her corpulence notwithstanding—as frail. If she had done anything wrong, Sharkey then believed, it was only to have turned her back on what was going on. He felt she had probably come home the night of March 5, sensed something had gone awry, and gotten the hell out of there. Women, he knew, had uncommon intuition in these matters.

But if she was innocent, why did she continue to stick by her husband? If J.R.'s "android" reports had any validity, the Douglas marriage had been in trouble even before Robin Benedict entered the picture. Why did she now appear to feel such loyalty to him?

Sharkey was at this point ready to concur with the growing conviction at the Gray House that Nancy was more involved than he had originally imagined. But if that was so, he asked himself, why had she cooperated so readily the night of the first search? The only thing he could figure was that, taken by surprise, Nancy made a pretense of cooperation in order to take her children and get clear of the scene. He did not intend to let her slide out from under him again. As Howe and Zebrasky made a last turn about the house, Sharkey informed Nancy Douglas that she was, without question, a suspect in the murder of Robin Benedict.

That was technically true. If Nancy's role in Robin's disappearance was limited to knowing about the murder and saying nothing, that would make her only an accessory after the fact. Under Massachusetts law, wives or blood relatives who harbor felons are immune from prosecution. But, by her own account, Nancy knew that Robin was coming to her house the afternoon of March 5. If it could be proven that she also knew about a plan to kill the girl and had taken an active role in furthering that plan, it wouldn't matter if she had not done the actual killing. She would be considered an accessory before the fact and tried on an equal footing with the killer.

Sharkey removed from his wallet a Miranda card and read the individual warnings to Nancy Douglas, who replied that she understood. At the conclusion of that formality, she asked why she was being considered a suspect.

"Well, Mrs. Douglas," Sharkey replied, "we are aware that [William Douglas] called you early Sunday morning from Attleboro, later from Boston, and after that from Providence, Rhode Island. . . . We feel that he was having conversation with you and that he was [not] in this house and asleep like you led us to believe. You deliberately lied to us. . . ."

"How do you know that?" Nancy parried. "I don't sleep in that room. I told you that."

Sharkey then reminded her that when shown the hammer on the night of the first search, she had denied ever seeing it before.

"You lied outright to me . . . about the hammer. We have . . . established that the hammer belongs to your father and that he lent it to you. How in God's name do you explain that?"

"The hammer wasn't for me," she insisted. "Why don't you ask my father? He'll tell you."

"I think you know where Robin's body and vehicle are," the lieutenant pressed. "Why won't you tell us, and let the young lady have at least a decent burial?"

"Don't use the word 'you,' " Nancy protested. "I don't know where the body is. I don't know anything."

"Is there any question in your mind that your husband killed Robin?"

"I know that's what you think," Nancy replied. "But I don't even know there's a body."

"I'll tell you, Mrs. Douglas," Sharkey replied, "there is a body. . . . And so we don't misunderstand each other, we took a section of that body out of this house the night we searched. . . . Doesn't that make you suspicious?"

"I'm not saying anything to that," she insisted.

"Mrs. Douglas," Sharkey finally pleaded, "you know your husband was out early Sunday morning when you told us he was in bed asleep. . . . Why don't you tell us where he was and what he told you so we could recover the automobile and the body?"

"No, I can't, I'm sorry," Nancy replied plaintively. "You would have to be married to a man twenty years to understand."

Sharkey continued working at Nancy Douglas for half an hour, but at length he saw it was no use to continue. She could not be moved. With a gesture of resignation, he rose to join the troopers, who were carting the purloined electronics to the cruiser. Before taking his leave, however, he turned to Nancy and fixed her in his gaze. "The crime of murder does not have a statute of limitations," he reminded her. "As time goes on, the pieces will just fall into place like a large puzzle."

ODD JOBS

DANIEL J. O'CONNELL III was a stout, round-faced man whose bearing and expression suggested the disposition of a bulldog. He was quick to anger under the best of circumstances. But when he received the news that John Kivlan had scored another search of 38 Sandy Ridge Circle, O'Connell exploded, firing off a letter of protest to Norfolk County.

It had come to his attention, he said, that state police had conducted another search of the William Douglas home, during which time Lieutenant James Sharkey had taken it upon himself to interrogate Mrs. Douglas about "the body" and to inform her that he felt she was "involved" in an alleged homicide.

"Any questions or inquiry by police officials is an obvious attempt to circumvent the attorney-client relationship and intentionally interfere with the right to counsel," he complained. "I regard this matter as a serious Constitutional infringement aside from the ethical questions involved."

One week later, on May 3, Kivlan sent his old friend an arch reply.

"Dear Mr. O'Connell," he wrote. "It is neither necessary nor appropriate for me to respond to either your factual representations or legal conclusions other than to state that I possess no information that would indicate any 'Constitutional infringements' have occurred or any 'ethical questions' have arisen. . . . I am certain that, in the future, as in the past, any contact with [the Douglases] by police investigators will be conducted appropriately."

EXACTLY what constituted "appropriate" contact with the Douglas children was now a question for the Supreme Judicial Court to decide. During the two weeks since Justice Lynch had referred the matter of the Three Juveniles to the full court—an interval which allowed little time for preparation—both sides had engaged in a frantic bout of legal research. McMenimen and O'Connell had scoured the constitutions of country and Commonwealth for specific mention of a child-parent privilege but turned up nothing. Looking to common law, they found a number of cases in which a child who had been raped by a parent or seen one parent assault another had been required to testify. But those rulings did not apply to the present situation, where the parent stood accused of a crime against someone outside the family.

O'Connell found one decision which encouraged him. It had come down only recently, in Nevada, where the son of a reputed mobster named Agosto had gotten a protective order to prevent a federal grand jury from questioning him about his father. The court held that forcing a child to testify against a parent places him in "a psychological double bind in which he is scorned and branded as disloyal if he does testify and jailed if he does not."

But even the *Agosto* ruling was slightly off the mark. The "child" in question was an adult. The Douglas children were minors living at home. As such, they might not be capable of an informed opinion or even have a legal right to assert a privilege.

On the morning of May 5, O'Connell, McMenimen, and the Commonwealth's attorney, a Norfolk ADA named Charles Hely, repaired to the Supreme Judicial Court, in Pemberton Square, to present arguments before the seven-member bench. The hearing was closed to the public. Neither John and Jane Doe nor their children were present. Affidavits, briefs, and tapes of the proceeding were later impounded in an attempt to ensure the privacy of the Three Juveniles.

During the ten minutes allotted to him to summarize his arguments, McMenimen appealed to the court to fashion a rule similar to the spousal privilege. O'Connell then rose to argue that even if the court did not see fit to create a privilege, one was already implied in the U.S. Constitution, which had created a "zone of privacy" surrounding family affairs. Except in those cases of crime against another family member, no one in a family should be made to do anything that would pit one against the other.

The Commonwealth's Charles Hely, however, warned that creating a parent-child privilege might damage the state's ability to prosecute child- and spouse-abuse cases. "It should not," Hely insisted, "be a device by which an adult can use the child as a shield for his or her criminal acts."

"A total or partial parent-child privilege," he went on to urge, "might well destroy the court's only remaining means for establishing who the killer is." He pointed to an even more serious threat: "If a parent is in a position to have eliminated an inconvenient girlfriend, what is to prevent him from eliminating someone else, perhaps even a family member, at a future time if the community is unable to intervene and question the only available witnesses at home."

Hely asked the justices if they would announce their finding as soon as possible, saving the full opinion for later. The Commonwealth's ability to investigate this murder, he observed, was diminishing with the passing of time. The court agreed. But even with the SJC moving on this accelerated schedule, the Norfolk County District Attorney's Office resigned itself to the fact that a decision might not come until late summer.

BEHIND the scenes of this Olympian contest, William Douglas was engaged in a grittier struggle. He had squared off against the board of trustees of Tufts University and was making a last-ditch attempt to keep his job.

Shortly after being locked out of his lab the preceding January, Douglas had written a letter to the president of Tufts, Jean Mayer. Without alluding to any particular wrongdoing—at that point the only charge against him was embezzlement—he appealed to Mayer, the nutritionist, to consider the role that diet might have played in this affair. He had been in contact with six experts around the country, all of whom "were of the opinion that [his] difficulties could well have stemmed from the circumstances of a severe diet." Yet, he complained, the Tufts tribunal had declined to entertain these opinions or even read excerpts from the literature of obesity which he had provided.

In light of the revelations which had emerged in recent months, the "literature" had taken on new and ominous significance. Douglas's experts had described their hypothetical dieter as immature and unable to tolerate frustration or delay gratification. Douglas's apparently irascible behavior with Robin Benedict had caused her to describe him as "a big baby." The hypothetical dieter was afraid he would be attacked by other males. Douglas now seemed obsessed with being mugged and kidnapped by black men. The hypothetical dieter clung to a maternal figure as a source of security while dieting, even going to pathological extremes to keep that person under control. Douglas's dependence upon Robin Benedict had caused him to monitor her activities through the most insidious means.

The letter to Mayer continued, "It is particularly disturbing to me that there seems to be such insensitivity or lack of understanding of a nutrition-ally-originated problem by a University so highly regarded in the area of nutrition. . . ."

Douglas closed with a plea for Mayer to assemble a panel of experts to consider his condition from the "psycho-nutritional viewpoint." Mayer, who chose to maintain an imperial distance from this sordid affair, did not respond.

Vice-President Steven Manos, meanwhile, was still trying to induce Douglas to resign of his own free will. On the table was the agreement in which he had been asked to attest that he was leaving because of "misappropriated funds and falsified expense records." Douglas refused to sign it. The university began withholding his salary, hoping to weaken his resolve. That tactic, however, elicited not a signature but a series of angry, plaintive phone calls from Douglas to Karen Hitchcock describing the hardship his family was being forced to endure. He had not even been able, he said, to buy his children Easter baskets.

His pleading filled Hitchcock with disgust because, only a few days before Easter, Trooper Landry had called her with the news that Douglas was under suspicion of murder. That word had been passed up to the highest levels of the Tufts administration, no doubt increasing the sense of urgency to get Douglas off personnel rolls before all hell broke loose.

Still, Douglas would not sign.

It is possible that he grasped his own situation so imperfectly that he actually believed his legal troubles would blow over—that this episode would be forgiven as the temporary aberration of an overtaxed genius—and that he would be restored to his former eminence. To resign would destroy the delusion that he could be redeemed, leaving him face to face with his own ruin. But there was at least one other consideration that kept him from putting his name to that document. Dan O'Connell had apparently advised against it. In one of the sheaves of notes taken from Sandy Ridge Circle, Douglas had written, "Dan's instinct—resignation now will add fuel to fire that State is trying to create in respect to motive." O'Connell apparently felt that to acknowledge "misappropriated funds and falsified expense records" was to acknowledge that stolen money was at the heart of Douglas's relationship with Robin Benedict. From that, the prosecutor could construct any number of scenarios of greed and betrayal leading to murder. It was better to concede nothing.

In the face of Douglas's implacable refusals, Manos at last turned the matter over to the board of trustees, which had the power to dismiss him. A meeting was called for May 27 to dispose of the matter. Firing Douglas would, of course, increase the potential for scandal, and the trustees knew they would have to proceed very delicately. He had not been convicted of—or, indeed, charged with—any crimes. His science had not been impugned. The peer review authorized by Vice-President Robert Levy had turned up no irregularities in Douglas's research. As a practical matter the panel had realized that there was no way of assessing Douglas's science accurately without opening his books and going line by line through the data. That was likely to take one or two years. Instead, they consulted with collaborators who had relied upon Douglas's in vitro work to see if they had reported any problems with their cells. When it turned out they hadn't, the panel accepted this as an "internal check" and reported to Levy that there were no grounds for a more extensive audit.

That Douglas had stolen research money, there seemed no doubt. But Richard Thorngren had never in his eight or so conversations with Douglas been able to elicit an outright admission of guilt. Neither, for that matter, had Manos or the Tufts tribunal. Yet Douglas had conceded that there were "problems," and this admission, combined with the mounting heap of documentation that the auditor had assembled, seemed suitably damning grounds for dismissal. Up to the very eve of the trustees' meeting, Thorngren scurried about town, tying up loose ends. On the morning of Thursday, May 26, he went over to MIT to get a notarized letter attesting that the institute had never employed a Robin Benedict or Savitry Bisram. Letter in hand, he returned to his office to discover the good news. Douglas had agreed to resign!

The trustees had offered him a revised agreement containing softer language. The new document made no mention of "misappropriation or falsification." Neither did it specify what the university could or would tell those who requested references. It made no mention of restitution. It simply stated, "The University has requested that Dr. Douglas resign his position as Associate Professor on the faculty of the University." Douglas signed the agreement on May 27 and that same day sent a letter of resignation to the dean of the medical school.

JOHN KIVLAN, meanwhile, had been following this drama intently. As O'Connell had suspected, the prosecutor hoped to use Douglas's financial difficulties to "create a fire" with respect to motive.

Motive would become increasingly important if Robin's body were not found. Should he be forced to proceed with a circumstantial case, Kivlan would have to be able to establish three things: that Douglas had not only motive but also the means and opportunity to murder Robin Benedict. The bloody hammer would suffice as means. And Douglas, by his own admission, was alone with Robin for almost an hour before midnight on March 5, leaving him ample opportunity to kill her. But the motive was as yet obscure.

Late one evening, after the troopers and prosecutors had abandoned their theorizing, Kivlan stayed to review the evidence. Pulling out the documents from the file, he traveled inch by inch over the arch of Douglas's and Benedict's tortured relationship to see if he could pinpoint what had led up to their final conflict.

Shortly after their meeting in April, Douglas's mood was euphoric. (She had given him—how had he put it?—"a new hope for living.") He praised her smile. He sent her little gifts. He was expansive. His letters tried to create the impression of a man of the world who took pleasure in spending money carelessly.

Among the the items that J.R. Rogers had handed over to the DA's office was a black binder which Douglas had given Robin, apparently hoping to impress her. It was filled with copies of his articles and correspondence containing flattering allusions to work. This collection contained two papers he had written on the Navy submarine project. They had apparently been sent to Robin under an undated covering letter in which he wrote, "I look forward to discussing additional aspects [of] the present study with you and hope we can realize full potential of their benefits."

There followed a letter dated May 21, 1982, which read:

Dear Robin,

   This letter is written to clarify our collaboration on the U.S. Naval Submarine project. In my view this will be a 50:50 collaboration; that is, we will share equally in the design of experimental protocols, conduct of experiments, authorship on publications, patent rights and other benefits which may develop from the above mentioned study.

   I look forward to discussing with you the design of our preliminary experiments and the beginning of the experimental investigations.

   With warm regards,

                                                  Sincerely,
                                                  William H. J. Douglas, Ph.D.
                                                  Director
                                                  Cell Culture Research Unit

The Navy grant, Kivlan had learned from Ron Sanders, was practically used up. The talk of "patent rights and other benefits" had clearly been bravado to dazzle Robin. Doing favors and dispensing largess left him feeling confident. Every time he was able to bestow a favor, he apparently felt he had increased his control over her.

By the first week in October, however, something had happened to cause Douglas to drop the pose of the carefree man about town. "I am "VERY VERY SORRY, EMBARRASSED AND ASHAMED FOR THE WAY I ACTED LAST NIGHT," he agonized in his letter of October 9. Robin had probably sensed that his money was drying up, and her new indifference was causing him to panic. Shortly after that, Savi Bisram had cashed the two checks amounting to over $12,000. Was this an attempt on Douglas's part to assure Robin that his credit was still good? If so, it apparently did not have the desired effect, since after that Douglas embarked upon his campaign of harassment and surveillance. If one could assume that it was he who had broken into Robin's trick pad, one could also assume that he was the one who had stolen her black book and was calling her customers. He was without doubt stealing her phone messages. Douglas appeared to be trying to isolate Robin from her source of income so that she would be dependent upon him alone.

By early 1983 his funds had dried up. Still, he had managed to lure her to Plattsburgh with the inducement of what J.R. had described as an "expensive gift." And it was in Plattsburgh, Kivlan was sure, that they had become embroiled in a dispute which two weeks later led to Robin's disappearance.

THERE was no doubt in Kivlan's mind that Douglas had intended to run away with Robin to Plattsburgh. Douglas, Kivlan figured, had probably concocted some fantasy that Robin would settle down as the wife of a professor on a small-town campus. She would decorate their house in browns and tans, colors for which they both seemed to have an inexplicable fondness. She would play the flute charmingly for visitors, and night after winter night she would sit across from him in an overstuffed armchair and listen to him spin out yarns about the effects of high carbon dioxide levels on the human lung. And everyone in that small academic world would marvel at Bill Douglas, remarking how they had all misjudged him. Never mind that he had always struck them as a compulsive drudge. Still waters run deep. Beneath that drab exterior, he must be far more amusing and passionate than anyone imagined, in order to have captured such a beauty.

What Kivlan found most ironic was that Plattsburgh had in fact offered Douglas his "new hope for living." Not a fantasy hope that would purportedly lift him above his personal disappointments and professional failures, but a real and honest hope of rescuing his family from the pain his excesses had caused them. If he had played his cards right at Chazy during the week of February 14, he might have gained the chance to live down whatever rumors might eventually have filtered up from Tufts and go on with his life and work. But Douglas had apparently been too firmly in the grip of his obsession to recognize what a precious opportunity lay before him. He made a choice. And on the heels of that choice he plunged into a still steeper decline. Now, slightly over three months after the pivotal days in Plattsburgh, he was being investigated for larceny and murder. He had been drummed out of academe in disgrace. And he was nearly destitute.

The seriousness of the Douglases' financial difficulties had been revealed to the prosecutor in a set of documents found in the Leica bag during the first search. Around the first of the year, the family had consulted with a credit-counseling firm and had filled out work sheets which were to form the basis for a debt management plan. Douglas listed his monthly income as $3,975 and his wife's as $372. Their overhead was $2,937, leaving them only $1,410 a month to pay off what then amounted to almost $36,000 in debts. They were apparently considering filing for limited bankruptcy but for some reason decided against it.

By the middle of March, Douglas had lost his salary. He owed Attorney Freishtat a couple of thousand dollars in legal fees. The family borrowed about $16,000 from HFC and took out a second mortgage of $24,000 on their home. Burdened with debt, Douglas began to look for odd jobs.

Amid the clutter of his bedroom, searchers had found several help-wanted ads clipped from the *Globe*. He had circled one for "chemist." A Quincy consulting firm was seeking "a mature person for entry level position." There is no indication that Douglas ever applied for this position. By late May, however, he was working part-time as a polltaker for the Becker Research Corporation. He wrote on his application that he was a "free lance writer" available for "sporadic weekday work." He agreed to a wage of $3.50 an hour.

The Gray House troopers who had kept him under surveillance now found themselves following him two or three times a week to the station at Route 128, where he caught the commuter train into Boston. In the evening Nancy picked him up and took him home. Then he sometimes took the Toyota and headed out again to the interstate, stopping at rest areas en route to Providence. This curious behavior aroused the troopers' suspicions. Was he still parceling out Robin Benedict's belongings? As they got closer, however, they could see as he bent over the barrel that he was not putting things in. He was taking things out. As they strained to see what it was, they realized with disbelief he was picking through the

trash for bottles and cans. Dr. William Douglas, whose exaggerated sense
of protocol had once kept him from associating too intimately with academic inferiors, had now sunk to the society of the scavengers whose
discoveries at Mansfield had been his undoing. Dr. William Douglas, the
man whom the New England Anti-Vivisection Society had once hailed
in the same breath with Albert Schweitzer as scientist and humanitarian,
now found himself rummaging for returnables.

ON THURSDAY, May 4, Douglas answered an ad for the position of "night
clerk" at the YWCA. When he called for information, he was told he
must come not to the main building on Clarendon Street, in the Back
Bay, but rather to the hotel for women in the South End.

Much of the South End was ghetto. The Berkeley Residence, however,
was located on its gentrified northern border. The austere gray bunker
abutted a bank of neat brick row houses. Visitors entering through a pair
of large glass doors were carefully scrutinized by the desk clerk on duty.
Men were asked their business. If they had none, they were sternly
requested to leave. The residence prided itself upon being a place to which
fine families could entrust the welfare and safety of their daughters.
Around the corner on Columbus Avenue, hookers were strutting their
wares. Only four long blocks to the east, pimps and junkies played the
street life in the Combat Zone. But vice did not penetrate the prim
sanctuary of the Berkeley Residence. In a city fraught with perils for
young women, it was a haven of decency.

The person in charge of maintaining these high standards was the
resident manager, a gentle young woman named Cynthia Cajka. Miss
Cajka suffered from a palsy that affected her speech. But she was philo-
sophical about her debility, arguing that it had made her a keen judge of
human nature. Deceitful people made her nervous. And when she got
nervous, her speech impediment became worse. But she wasn't menaced
in the least by Bill Douglas. She would later recall that when he came in
for an interview on May 4, she found him comfortably "old shoe."

Douglas told her that from June 1978 to the present he had been a
"self-employed biomedical writer" and that he was looking for something
to supplement his income. The night shift on Saturdays and Sundays
would suit him fine. Miss Cajka was eager to have him start right away.
The summer season was coming, and she needed a night clerk who could
help pick up the slack when regular staff members took their vacations.
The following day she wrote him a warm letter verifying that he had been
hired to work the front desk. His contract ran from May 4 until the end
of the calendar year. His work schedule would be determined by the "need

of the residence," and he would be paid $4 an hour. There were, unfortunately, no fringe benefits, such as holiday or sick pay, for temporary positions.

Douglas was responsible for checking guests in and out and for operating the switchboard. It was not a difficult job, and Douglas mastered it quickly. He seemed eager to do more than was required of him. If he found that Miss Cajka was short on clean towels, he would offer to do a load. He would even bring them up to the front desk to fold them. If someone got sick, he would offer to work on the spur of the moment. If the ice chests were running low, he would take it upon himself to haul a bucket up from the kitchen to refill them. Miss Cajka came to think of Douglas as a "kind man."

Besides those daughters of good families and professional women on their way up, the residence housed those less graced by fortune: widows whose pensions couldn't buy them any more affordable security; "special cases" such as the woman who slept with her arms folded like a corpse and got up at night to howl at the moon. There was also a group of amiable, rather excitable, ladies who took their meals together in the residence dining room. The members of this society included Miss Cindy Segal, a good, simple soul who worked as a messenger at Boston City Hospital, and her friend Mrs. Pamela Anderson, who was legally blind but made her way around quite sprightly with the assistance of a white cane. There were two innocents named Annie and Ann Marie. There was also Miss Deborah Woodman, who sometimes taped the casual conversations of friends and played them back as a prank. The informal leader of this assembly was Miss Mary Thawley, a slender, red-headed woman who was reputed to be "a very holy character." Miss Thawley was a member of the Third Order of St. Francis, which was committed to humility and good works. It was said that all she had to do was to think something spiritual, and the woman who howled at the moon would get up and leave the dining room. Such were her powers.

Miss Thawley also suffered from heart trouble and in the spring of 1983 sued the phone company, where she worked selling space in the Yellow Pages, for refusing to let her take off during the week and see a doctor. She had written a letter to the *Globe* detailing this injustice. To her amazement and delight, it was published on the editorial page. Miss Thawley was so pleased that she showed the clipping to everyone who might possess the critical faculties to appreciate it. That included William Douglas.

Bill, as he was known to the ladies of the residence, had a reputation for being a man of letters. He brought books to read during the slow periods and was forever scribbling notes on a legal pad. Miss Thawley didn't yet know Douglas, but she had heard that he was a free-lance writer, so she went up to the desk one day, introduced herself, and showed him the editorial. He was so enthusiastic that she was taken aback. It was wonderful, he said. She was so talented! He bustled off to the Xerox machine and made ten copies. Miss Thawley was flattered by the fuss. Whenever she found him on duty, she would stop to chat. He was invariably polite and solicitous. Yet, pleasant as he was, Miss Thawley would later say she found something odd about about him.

She couldn't quite put her finger on it. But for one thing, he had seemed a little too gushy over her *Globe* article. She imagined that a free-lance writer would be a little more blasé about seeing things published. Whenever she asked him about his own writing, he seemed not to want to talk about it. And he had the peculiar habit of taking his brown valise with him wherever he went, even to the rest room. Miss Thawley wondered what he had in it that was so valuable that he couldn't leave it at the desk for a couple of minutes. One of the other desk clerks, a girl named Millie, got so curious she just came right out and asked him what he carried in there. He told her, "Pepsi cans."

Miss Thawley's friend Elizabeth Sanborn said that Douglas gave her the creeps.

Betty Sanborn was a petite, talkative blond in her early forties. For most of the year she lived and taught school near Nottingham, New Hampshire, but she had spent her past four summers at the Berkeley Residence. Sanborn had fallen in love with the city as a child, when her mother brought her down on the train to go to the circus or the ballet. She lived on time-worn memories of the hard French rolls at Schrafft's and the swans in the Public Garden. It had been her dream to move to Boston for good. In the spring of 1983 she decided to take the plunge. Teaching had not left her with much of a nest egg, and her only asset was a 1974 Gran Torino which had 160,000 miles on it. She would have to sell the car—which she had come to know fondly as Bette Lou—as soon as she arrived in Massachusetts.

Sanborn pulled into town, as she always did, on Sunday of Memorial Day weekend. She liked to celebrate the end of a long New England winter with an afternoon sunbathing, and so took off alone for Castle Island Beach. When she returned to the residence that evening around six, she noticed a new night clerk, a heavy man with glasses. When he saw her, he jumped to his feet and cried, "Betty, I hear you have a car to sell."

Sanborn was startled and not a little self-conscious. She was, after all, standing in the lobby in her swimsuit and the center of a strange man's attentions.

Offering a hasty introduction, Douglas explained that he and his wife were having to share a car and that he needed one so that she wouldn't have to bring him in to work. He wanted to test-drive the Torino right then and there. Sanborn figured she knew what was proper and what wasn't. And she thought it decidedly improper to go out alone with a man she had just met. She spied Annie, who was lounging in the lobby, eating yogurt from a carton, and recruited her as chaperone.

Bette Lou was parked on a side street. Annie climbed into the back, Betty got into the front passenger's seat, and Bill took the wheel. He had a terrible time getting the hang of the gears, and Bette Lou jerked all the way up Commonwealth Avenue to Kenmore Square. After that fitful ride, Bill announced cheerfully that he would like to buy the car. They haggled over price a bit and struck upon a figure of $200. Betty knew she should be thankful for her own good fortune, finding a buyer so soon. But she was a little depressed to see Bette Lou go. She had to return to New Hampshire for a couple of weeks to tie up odds and ends, she told Bill. She would hand over the car when she returned.

In those days, Sanborn didn't exactly dislike Douglas. But neither did she trust him. He had "laughing eyes," and sometimes during the days following their first meeting, she thought she caught him winking at her. She had no way of knowing, of course, about the serious trouble he was in. Neither she nor any of her friends had read the *Herald* account of Robin Benedict's disappearance. Even if they had, they would never have made the connection between Professor William Douglas, who entertained prostitutes in the suburbs, and Bill Douglas, the free-lance writer who folded towels at the front desk.

Even as Douglas was haggling with Sanborn over a used car, he was under fresh assault from the Norfolk County District Attorney's Office. This time John Kivlan was literally out for blood.

THE CHEMIST KAUFMAN'S TESTS had shown that the blood on the hammer, shirt, jacket, and windbreaker was all type A. This seemed consistent with its coming from one person, possibly a victim. But Kivlan still could not locate Robin's blood type. Her parents had no record of it, and an ongoing search of her medical history hadn't turned up the critical information.

It complicated matters that A was a very common type. Nearly 60 percent of the population had it. There was a high statistical probability that William Douglas and Nancy were also type A. If so, they might claim that the blood on the items had come from one of them. But if Kivlan could establish that the Douglases were B or O, the blood on the evidence would have had to come from a third person. A jury could reasonably infer that it was Robin Benedict.

Getting blood from the Douglases was not going to be a simple matter. The courts were usually discinclined to allow the state to go after "evidence" if it required invading a person's body. Complicating things was the fact that neither William nor Nancy had been charged with a crime, and Kivlan could find virtually no precedent in which police had managed to get blood samples from someone who was not in custody.

If Kivlan went to court to request blood in the name of the Commonwealth, he would have to establish that there was probable cause to believe that a crime had been committed. If, however, he could manage to persuade the grand jury to request it, the jurors would need only to establish that there was a reasonable basis for believing that the samples would assist them in determining *whether* a crime had been committed.

On Friday, May 29, Kivlan took this petition to the grand jury, which voted to require the Douglases to appear the following Tuesday to give blood.

This maneuver infuriated O'Connell, who wrote Kivlan and charged that he was "continuing to use subpoena power under the guise of valid Grand Jury process to harass and inconvenience" his clients. O'Connell took his suit to the Norfolk Superior Court, where he complained to Judge Thomas Dwyer that Kivlan had pulled a fast one by finessing the Commonwealth's own request through the grand jury.

Judge Dwyer was not anxious to interfere with the prerogatives of the grand jury and so addressed himself exclusively to the question of whether it violated constitutional protections against unreasonable search and seizure to take blood from a pair of suspects who were not in custody. At length, he denied the Commonwealth's request.

John Kivlan promptly appealed the decision to the Supreme Judicial Court.

WHILE waiting for that hearing, which was yet a month away, Kivlan altered his blood strategy.

Back in April he had learned of a "no-body" case in which the state of Oklahoma had gotten a conviction based on some very sophisticated blood testing. A twenty-seven-year-old Oklahoma City man named Gary Lee Rawlings and his former wife, Sally Jean, had during the early months of 1982 been engaged in a custody battle over their little daughter, Kimberly. In May of that year Sally Jean suddenly disppeared. Gary Lee claimed she had given him custody of Kimberly and left town. But police investigators found blood in his car and in a plane he had rented shortly after his wife disappeared. They had reason to suspect he had killed Sally Jean and dropped her body from the aircraft into the Gulf of Mexico. He was charged with murder.

The prosecution took the samples of the blood to a private laboratory, which analyzed it for "genetic markers," a set of proteins and enzymes which are determined by heredity. Up to that point, the state hadn't any way of knowing if the blood belonged to the supposed victim, since it had no corresponding sample of her whole blood with which to compare it. It did, however, have the next-best thing—a twin sister, whose genetic composition was identical to Sally Jean's. The markers matched, enzyme for enzyme. Even this test could not establish with absolute certainty that the blood in the plane was that of the missing woman. Nevertheless, the state of Oklahoma was able to infer it with such a high statistical probability that a jury convicted Gary Lee Rawlings.

This technique, called electrophoresis, intrigued Kivlan. He did not have a whole blood sample from Robin Benedict. He did not even have a twin sister. But he did have her parents and four siblings. If a serologist could map their blood genetically, he might be able to establish to the satisfaction of a jury that the person whose blood was on the evidence was a child of John and Shirley Benedict.

The state lab did not have the capability to do such sophisticated blood work. The prosecutor in the Rawlings case had used a private lab, but Kivlan was reluctant to approach the same firm, fearing that its chemists might be discredited as witnesses for hire. He favored instead the Federal Bureau of Investigation, whose methods and interpretation of results were notoriously conservative and whose integrity, Kivlan felt, was above reproach.

During the middle of April, Kivlan had instructed the chemist Kaufman to send blood samples to the FBI crime lab in Washington, D.C., to see if it could establish "a more definite link" between the items found at Mansfield and the windbreaker in Douglas's closet. The Norfolk samples went to Agent James Kearney, a serious, methodical man who was considered cautious even by FBI standards. While the private labs tested for markers within twenty or so systems, as they were called, Kearney had faith in only eleven.

Any sample of whole blood would contain one marker from each of these eleven systems. The question was, How many of these markers could be raised from blood that was dried and beginning to decay?

Kaufman had already run the ABO system and found that all of the samples contained type A. Kearney accepted those findings and turned his attention to a system called adenylate kinase. AK, as it was more familiarly known, was a very stable enzyme, which stayed intact even in dried blood for long periods of time. The serologist prepared a bit of bloody extract from the hammer and placed it in a slot at one end of a glass plate covered with gel. The plate had a negative and a positive pole. Each enzyme and protein had its own electrical charge, so when the current was turned on, the marker was drawn out of the extract and carried across the surface of the plate, leaving a distinctive banding pattern in its path.

When the current stopped, Kearney discerned one very dark bar surmounted by two lighter ones—the banding pattern for a marker called AK 1-1. This was encouraging, but during the course of the afternoon he was able to pull up only two more. The hammer showed another enzyme, AD 1-1, and a protein, HP 2-1, turned up on a bloodstained section of the blue shirt. Unfortunately, Kearney could find no blood or human protein on the blue windbreaker and thus was unable to establish the "link" Kivlan was looking for.

There were, however, other uses for those markers. Kearney could compare them with the markers of William and Nancy Douglas and perhaps eliminate the possibility that it was their blood on the evidence. But with the Douglases out of reach pending the appeal, Kivlan laid that plan aside for the time being and went after what was available to him. On the afternoon of June 22, John and Shirley Benedict came to the district attorney's office in Dedham to give blood. The vials were labeled K1 and K2—indicating that they were the first "known" samples to be compared with the "questioned" blood on the evidence—and were sent off to Washington for analysis.

KAUFMAN, meanwhile, had a handful of other tests in progress. He had dusted the hammer, shirt, and jacket for fingerprints but had not been able to find a single one. He had then compared the thread used to sew the underarms of the blue shirt with that from the two spools Nancy had given Sharkey. The smaller of the two spools was plainly too dark to have been used to stitch the shirt. The other, a larger spool of spun polyester fiber, was a closer match. Kaufman compared this to the mending thread under the microscope. They appeared similar, but he thought they warranted a more detailed examination by a fiber expert. He sent all three samples along to the FBI.

Kaufman then turned to a lead he felt held considerable promise. Two sets of trash bags had been taken from the Douglas house the night of the first search. Eleven had been recovered from a Hefty box under the sink; three others had been found in the Shaw's Supermarket sack shoved under the seat of the Douglas Toyota. All were brown on the outside and black on the inside and appeared identical to the one which Plotegher and

Jewell had discovered in the Mansfield barrel. Kaufman had done very simple tests on the bags from all three locations and found that they were all made of polyethelene. He delivered these findings to Kivlan and encouraged him to look for a lab that could analyze the chemical composition further. He had heard of instances, he said, where bags had been identified as having coming from the same dye lot.

This inspired in the prosecutor the prospect of linking the bags in the Douglas car to the one in which the bloody hammer and clothing had been disposed of. He instructed Brian Howe to contact the Mobil Chemical Company, which had manufactured the bags, and see what he could find. Howe was able to determine that the bags from the sink area had been manufactured on the preceding January 27 at the company's plant in Washington, New Jersey. They had been part of a run of many thousands. Each bag in that run would have the same chemical composition and, even more important, similar coloring defects.

Frequently during the manufacturing process not all of the pigment was satisfactorily mixed and clumps of it streaked the plastic. This left a "characteristic flaw" in every bag in the run. A Mobil chemist examined the Mansfield bag and found a small orange lump visible to the naked eye. Nothing similar was detected in the bags found under the car seat. The same ruddy defect, however, had turned up in the bags under the sink. Further testing showed that the Mansfield and the sink bags were identical in chemical composition, whereas the car bags were distinctly different.

These results caused Kivlan to readjust his thinking. When Landry had presented the bags from the Toyota to Douglas on the night of the first search, he denied ever having seen them. This suggested to the prosecutor that Douglas had used those bags to dispose of the bloody evidence. Perhaps he had simply taken a few from the box, stuck them in a bag, and carried them to the Toyota. But Mobil's findings indicated that the two sets of bags were from entirely different batches. Where, then, had the bags under the seat come from? It was not possible that he had bought them at Shaw's after he was on the road. The supermarket closed at 10:00 P.M., forty-five minutes before Robin reportedly arrived at his house. Could Robin have arrived much earlier than anyone had previously suspected? That was not likely, since she had been at Sargent Nichols's as late as 9:45 P.M., and it would have taken her at least three quarters of an hour to get to Sharon. One could argue that he had bought the bags in anticipation of killing Robin, but this again presupposed a conditional murder plan.

Of course, it was possible that the bags under the seat had nothing to do with Douglas's activities on the night of March 5, but Kivlan doubted that. He tended to believe that Douglas had used bags from two sources to discard Robin's belongings. Although he could not link the bags in the Douglas car to Mansfield, he could now argue that the ripped bag found there had probably come from the Hefty box in the Douglas kitchen.

BY NOW it was late June. Despite the internal activity it had generated, the investigation into the disappearance of Robin Benedict had been conducted in amazing secrecy. It had been over three months since a word about Douglas or Benedict had appeared in the Boston media. Beth Holland's *Herald* story of March 17 announcing " 'Missing' Girl Found" seemed to lay the matter to rest.

Nevertheless, Mike Lawrence, the young Channel 7 reporter who first made the connection between the missing girl and the missing funds, suspected something was up.

Lawrence swung by Dedham every now and then to chat up Bill Delahunt, who was always happy to make time for TV reporters. During the third week of June, Lawrence dropped into the DA's office to find out what had happened to the professor from Sharon. He could tell immediately that the case was not only alive but occupying the best efforts of the district attorney's office.

Delahunt wouldn't give details but observed slyly, "I'm surprised no one is picking this up."

Lawrence started calling his sources in the state police. Someone slipped him the word "Everything you're trying to get from us is in a public document in Stoughton."

It was true. Landry's affidavit as well as all the warrants and a list of the items taken from the searches of the Douglas house had been filed with the clerk of the district court in Stoughton. John Kivlan, fearing that details of those documents would leak out to the press, had requested that they be impounded.

When Lawrence went over to Stoughton and casually asked for the affidavits, however, there was a flurry of indecision among the clerks as to whether they should be given out. But as they couldn't find anyone to render a decision, they handed them over.

Lawrence skimmed the documents and, as he reached the details of the findings in the Douglas closet, whispered, "Holy shit."

Dashing for a pay phone, he dialed the Douglas home and got a young boy, to whom he explained that he absolutely must speak with Professor Douglas. Channel 7 was going to be running a story which raised the possibility that Dr. Douglas had killed Robin Benedict.

The boy began crying and hung up.

Douglas did not get back to Channel 7 with a reply. At six o'clock, Lawrence went on the air to report that the attractive young artist who had been hired to do graphic design work for Dr. William Douglas of Sharon apparently had a personal relationship with him as well. A relationship she had been trying to end. Lawrence got District Attorney Delahunt to go on camera to say that he thought Robin Benedict was dead and that the grand jury which had been used as "an active tool" in this investigation would surely return an indictment.

The following morning the *Globe* ran a brief, unbylined story announcing that "a Tufts University associate professor resigned under pressure last month after an investigation indicated he apparently misused thousands of dollars in research grants." William Douglas, the item concluded, was also being investigated by a grand jury in the disappearance of a young graphic artist who had been working on his research projects.

This squib, which the *Globe* had buried on an inside page, nonetheless tripped a lever of recognition at the *Boston Herald*.

Charlie O'Brien didn't see it; by then he had left the newspaper business. Beth Holland didn't see it; she had returned to Mississippi to get married. Shelly Murphy didn't see it; she was wrapped up in her column. But it did attract the notice of a court reporter named John Birtwell.

Birtwell was an affable fellow who had joined the staff of the *Herald* as it was making the passage from Hearst to Murdoch. During that tumultuous period he managed to navigate the treacheries of office politics with the assistance of an impious wit. He had a sense of humor about the melodrama which issued forth day after day from his own keyboard. Out of earshot of his editors, he lampooned the *Herald*'s menagerie of sick kids and missing coeds. Birtwell had a law degree from a reputable midwestern university and doubtless could have pursued a more respectable, certainly a more lucrative, profession. But the fact of the matter was, he loved writing for tabloids and could not imagine doing anything else.

On Friday, June 24, Birtwell came across the *Globe* item on the resignation of Professor William Douglas. It gave him a start of recognition. Douglas had been the target of the Murphy-Holland one-two punch back in March. He scissored out the item and tucked it away for safekeeping.

That weekend Birtwell agreed to fill in as editor on the assignment desk. Sunday's news budget was hard to fill under the best of circumstances. There were no meetings and no government news. The weekends preceding the Fourth of July were particularly slow. Birtwell, finding himself hard up for an assignment to give a reporter named Andrea Estes, handed her the *Globe* clip.

Estes couldn't remember having heard anything about Douglas. But she set out to see what she could find about this grand-jury investigation. On a Sunday afternoon the pick of sources was slim, but she managed to reach Peter Agnes at the Norfolk DA's office. He told her that the grand jury, which would normally adjourn at the end of June, had been extended at least through July.

The following morning the *Herald* reported, "The District Attorney's office wants a special witness to appear before the grand jury, but that witness has reportedly declined to testify. The DA is waiting for the US Supreme Court ruling on whether the witness can be forced to testify."

This cryptic report, which ran the following morning under the front-page banner "Mystery of Prof & Missing Beauty," did not go unnoticed at the *Globe*. Ordinarily a *Herald* headline would not have been enough to send the *Globe* clamoring in pursuit of a story. Particularly not a crime story, since the larger daily considered the salacious cases that were the *Herald*'s glory rather beneath its dignity. But on this morning an anonymous caller phoned the *Globe* with a tip about the "missing girl case." A co-op student who took the call transferred it to a general-assignment reporter named Mike Frisby. Frisby picked up the phone, and the voice on the other end said, "Hey. Why don't you check some documents down in Stoughton District Court."

Like Birtwell and Estes, Frisby had not seen the Channel 7 report which had capsulized the contents of the Stoughton documents. He thought he ought to drive down to the court to take a look. When he got there, the papers were still available to the public. What they contained was "a dream come true." He took the affidavits back to the newsroom on Morrissey Boulevard to show his editors, who pondered them with concern. Under normal circumstances, the *Globe* would not consider running allegations of homicide until a man had been charged. They were not convinced, despite the incriminating evidence that the Norfolk District Attorney's Office had managed to accumulate, that it could really get an indictment without a body. On the other hand, there was no sourcing problem. The entire story was laid out in a public document. Frisby was finally given leave to summarize its contents for the next day's paper.

When John Birtwell saw the *Globe* headline "Grand Jury to Hear Missing Woman Case," he blanched. The *Herald* had been caught napping. Birtwell sped down to Stoughton District Court and, handing the clerk a copy of the *Globe* story, said, "I want these."

The clerk delivered the awful news that they had been impounded.

Birtwell cleared his throat, lowered his voice, and trying to sound as official as possible observed, "They were in the *Globe* this morning."

The clerk, who could see as well as anyone that the Douglas affidavits were by now the worst-kept secret in town, relented. But, she said, it would be half an hour before they could be copied. Birtwell hung around fidgeting and fretting until he finally had the documents in hand. Then he fled, afraid of encountering anyone who might reverse the decision.

Like Lawrence and Frisby before him, Birtwell saw that the documents were a gold mine. He and Andrea Estes set to work mining nuggets. To their relief they found much that had not appeared in Frisby's story. While mentioning the pocketbook and credit cards, the *Globe* had apparently been reluctant to disclose some of the more titillating items found in the Douglas home. The *Herald* enumerated these with relish. There were not only "love letters" but also "newspaper clippings about prostitutes, a quantity of birth control devices, 55 pornographic books and a pair of pink panties."

The morning when the story appeared, Estes called Shirley Benedict to ask for an interview. The Benedicts were still stung by what they considered Shelly Murphy's betrayal. But they also knew that press coverage was likely to keep pressure on the investigation. It now appeared that the *Herald* was recanting its earlier heresy and intended to focus upon what a lovely young woman Robin was. Shirley Benedict agreed to an interview, demurring on the question of her daughter's prostitution.

"I prefer not to talk about it," she said. "They'll have to prove it to me."

She also sent Estes home with a wealth of photos showing Robin at various stages of her life. There was one of her as a ten-month-old toddler, sporting a big strawhat. There was a Christmas portrait of the children in which three-year-old Bin Bin and her defiant baby sister were standing beside dolls as tall as themselves. There was the one her father had taken of her bathed in twilight from the picture window. And, of course, the photo with laughing eyes—an image so evocative that the *Herald* had elevated it to the status of a logo with a legend reading "Missing Beauty."

But the story which Shirley Benedict expected to play as "Robin's Family Album" ran the following morning under the headline "The Two Lives of a Missing Beauty." To the Benedict family's horror, Estes had been able to uncover more details of Robin's forays into vice, including the fact that Robin had worked for several months at a Newton massage parlor, receiving $2,000 for four six-hour sessions.

Thereafter, reporters from the *Boston Herald* found themselves to be personae non gratae at 44 Emsley Terrace.

BY EARLY JUNE, there was still no sign of Robin Benedict. Frustrated by the lack of progress on official fronts, John and Shirley Benedict decided to embark upon a search of their own. They contacted an underwater salvage outfit called Inner Space Services. The company was owned by a Methuen man named John Mason, who ran the company out of his home. Mason had two daughters of his own and felt sufficiently sorry for the Benedicts to offer his services free of charge.

Mason operated on the theory that Robin's body could not have been effectively submerged without the car. A corpse invariably floats. As the weather gets warmer, the temperature of the water rises. That would hasten the body's deterioration, causing it to inflate with gases and rise. Even if Douglas had weighted her ankle with a brick, the ankle would rot and release her to the surface. No, Mason was certain that if Robin were to be found at all, it would be locked inside her silver Toyota.

John Benedict came over to Mason's house, where the two of them sat around the kitchen table studying maps, trying to pick the most promising prospects out of the hundreds of lakes, reservoirs, excavation pits, and harbors which indent southern Massachusetts.

Every weekend thereafter, John Benedict would accompany Mason and his crew to diving sites. They took as a starting point a small pond south of Douglas's house. Mason waded out to the middle of it and found it was only waist deep, too shallow to cover a car.

Then, guided by Marie Stephenson's divinations, they dove in the ponds around "Sturbridge" Mason grumbled a bit about being led around by psychics. John Benedict replied, "Well, I don't have a lot of faith in them either, but listen, what are we gonna lose?"

These forays turned up nothing of value.

By early July they had started making plans to dive in Boston and Providence harbors. The Benedicts approached the Central Secret Service Bureau for help.

The politics of this alliance was increasingly confused. John and Shirley were still on good terms with J.R. Rogers, but, by the end of May, J.R. had finally dropped the CSSB (leaving a bill outstanding). After that the owner of the agency, a tall, sad-eyed gentleman named Andrew Palermo, tried to persuade the Benedicts to pick up J.R.'s contract, but John Benedict said he couldn't afford it. The bureau nonetheless remained in the game because, as Palermo later told a reporter, "sometimes these cases just swallow you up. You can't stop looking."

On Thursday, July 7, the day before the dive, John Mason stopped by the Central Secret Service Bureau's office on Temple Street to confer with Palermo on strategy. The two men went down to the waterfront to locate the spots where a car could have been driven into deep water.

The following morning at eight o'clock, Palermo and DaRosa left Temple Street for Charlestown, where Mason's red-and-white tug, the

Uncle Tat was moored. John Benedict did not come. He was by now finding these excursions too wrenching. Every time Mason descended into some muddy pond, Benedict was simultaneously buoyed by hope that the divers would find something and racked by the fear that it would be Robin. He stayed in Methuen to wait for reports of what seemed to be the most promising dive to date.

On the night Douglas had presumably been dashing around the countryside disposing of things, he had made a call shortly past 2:00 A.M. from a phone booth near South Station and the waterfront. Mason and Palermo had found a spot nearby at the intersection of Atlantic and Northern avenues where Douglas could have pushed the car into the Fort Point Channel, a long inlet which divided downtown from South Boston.

The search party made a short voyage south along the Boston waterfront to a parking lot at Atlantic and Northern on the east bank of the channel. About thirty feet from shore, Mason and another diver strapped on thirty-five-pound weights and dove to a depth of fifteen feet. They went down another fifteen feet and followed the shore north. They spotted a Subaru, a Volkswagen, and a Chrysler, but no Toyota.

They crossed the channel again to South Boston, this time following a granite wall beneath the Northern Avenue Bridge. They found several more cars resting on the bottom of the channel, but these were so badly deteriorated that the divers assumed they had lain there for years. The search was called off before noon.

The following week John Mason took three divers to Providence Harbor. The channel, however, was so deep and murky that it resisted exploration. And this failure seemed to bring to an end all reasonable hopes of finding the silver Toyota.

BETTY SANBORN, meanwhile, was becoming increasingly irritated with Bill Douglas. It had been her understanding after their Memorial Day spin that he had definitely decided to buy the car. But nearly two months had passed, and still she couldn't pin him down on when he intended to take possession.

In the early round of negotiations, he had told her that he wanted the Gran Torino for himself. But over the intervening weeks he had come up with a couple of other not too convincing stories. First, he said he was obtaining the car for an auto body shop which wanted to use it as a "learning tool." Then he claimed to be procuring it for the son of a wealthy friend.

On July 3 he had slipped into Sanborn's mailbox the following note:

Betty,

   I am going to have the boy and his father come into Boston to see you and
THE CAR.

Bill Douglas

But neither the boy nor his father materialized. So, a week later, Sanborn sold the car to the boyfriend of a woman who lived at the residence. Bette Lou promptly died on him, however, and the buyer asked for his money back. Worse yet, the Torino had stalled on a back street where it stood to be ticketed or towed. Late one night as Sanborn was fretting over this problem, she was buzzed from the front desk. When she got downstairs, the girl on duty told her that she must call Bill. It was "urgent."

Douglas was upset to learn that she had sold the car and promised to come right into Boston and take it off her hands. He showed up at around 1:00 A.M. and, managing somehow to stir life in Bette Lou, drove her off, jolting and sputtering into the summer night. No money exchanged hands. Douglas had simply promised to get the best offer he could from the "boy and his father."

The following day Douglas left another note in Sanborn's box enclosing $28, which he described as the "best offer" he could get. He asked her if she would also supply him with the registration and plates.

Sanborn had expected a good deal more than $28 dollars, and she got Douglas on the phone to say she wasn't about to hand over the registration or plates until she got at least $200. The following evening, she was sitting in the lobby, chatting with Miss Thawley, when Douglas barreled through the front door in a huff. He came over to where she was sitting and banged his fist down on a table, shouting, "I want the plates!"

Sanborn could see that his eyes were bulging and his face turning colors. She was alarmed by this unprecedented display of fury.

"I want my money back," he yelled.

"That was $28," she replied. "You were supposed to give me $200 . . ."

"I couldn't sell the car," he sputtered. "Nobody wanted the car."

By and by, when Douglas cooled down, he said that if Sanborn wanted her car back, she should come out to Sharon by train the next day to get it. He would meet her at the station. She agreed. In light of his recent outburst, however, she thought it best not to go alone. So she enlisted the company of Ann Marie, who was delighted by the prospect of an excursion into the countryside.

It was 2:30 P.M. when they got off the commuter train at the Route 128 station. Looking around her, Sanborn saw tracks and trees and a huge expanse of parking lot filled with commuter vehicles. But Douglas was nowhere to be found.

She got the strangest feeling that her Bette Lou had been kidnapped, and now she was stranded with Ann Marie out in the wilderness. She began to cry. The phone at the station didn't work, so she went across to the street to an auto body shop and asked a man working there if he knew Douglas.

"We know him," the fellow replied cryptically. "His name has been in the papers."

Sanborn then phoned the Douglas house and, getting no answer, said, "That's it. I'm calling the police." Within a few minutes, an elderly officer responded to the call, and she poured out the story of Douglas and Bette Lou. The officer wrote out a report, but he didn't promise to check it out. Sanborn was totally frustrated by the time she got back into Boston that evening. To make it worse, she found yet another note in her box. It was dated that same day, Thursday, July 14, and read:

Dear Betty,

As so often happens in the free-lance writing business, when I returned home last night, there was a phone message for me. It was from a client who wishes to review a manuscript I drafted for him. He wants to meet me today from 9:30 AM until 3 PM.

Therefore, I will *not* be able to meet you at the Sharon train station at 2:30 P.M. . . .

I got the impression last night from you that you think I am driving your car all over. Let me assure you, I am not! All I wanted to do was to try and help you sell your car.

In light of the way you feel, I suggest you drive home with me tonight at midnight, pick up your car, return the $28 to me, and drive your car back to Boston. . . .

Bill Douglas

Sanborn called Douglas and told him he'd better get into Boston right away. When he arrived, she pushed him to a private office out of earshot of the ladies idling in the lobby, and called him a "liar and a cheat."

Then she told him about the police report.

"This is terrible," he said emotionally. Sanborn noticed that the rims of his eyes were red. He suggested that she go immediately with him to

Sharon and drive the car back. But she had no intention of doing anything of the sort. It was already late in the evening, and the hours at which Douglas insisted upon doing business made her feel like a hooker.

Once again Sanborn enlisted Ann Marie to wait out on the sidewalk in front of the residence for Douglas to return. At one-thirty in the morning he showed up driving Bette Lou. Behind him was a large woman in a blue Toyota. She looked straight ahead. Her expression seemed chiseled in stone.

By this time Douglas was quite irritable and called Bette Lou a piece of "junk." He nonetheless told Sanborn to look the car over to satisfy herself that it had not been damaged. In fact, she noted to herself, the license plates were bent and so was the shift lever. But she didn't want to make a fuss. Douglas finally got into the passenger side of the blue Toyota next to the woman, and the pair drove off.

Sanborn was just relieved that Douglas had not asked her for the $28, which by now was all spent.

FOR the next three days the clerks at the desk made Sanborn feel just terrible for persecuting poor Bill Douglas. Filing a police report on him. Imagine!

That Sunday, July 17, was a glorious, hot summer day, and Sanborn decided to celebrate the return of Bette Lou with an excursion to the North Shore for a picnic at Revere Beach. She had invited a handful of the ladies, including the trusty Ann Marie. For some reason—no one could ever remember why—an argument broke out, and Ann Marie was asked to remain at the residence while the others set off for their summer frolic.

What happened thereafter was to enter into the popular mythology of the Berkeley Residence as "Ann Marie's epiphany." The poor woman, left behind by her comrades, retired to her room and cried herself to sleep. As it happened, she had left the television on, and when she awoke a little after 6:00 P.M., the evening news was on. And whose face should she see on the screen but that of Bill Douglas! A man's voice was explaining something about bloody clothes in a barrel.

Uncomprehending, Ann Marie threw on a red terry cloth bathrobe and ran downstairs to where Douglas was folding towels at the desk.

"Bill, Bill," she cried, "you're on TV."

Douglas did not blink.

"Oh, no, Ann Marie," he said calmly. "That's another Bill Douglas."

"Welllll, it looks like you," she persisted. "I believe it is you."

Ann Marie was very upset that Douglas did not believe her. She was so distraught, in fact, that she wandered out of the residence and roamed the streets for most of the night. In the morning, as Betty Sanborn, Miss Thawley, and the others were coming down to the dining room for breakfast, they greeted Ann Marie as she stumbled through the door in her terry cloth robe.

After listening to her nearly incoherent account, Sanborn rushed up to the Guild drugstore and picked up a *Boston Herald.* There on the second page was a photo of Douglas. The caption beneath it read, "William Douglas—ex-Tufts anatomy professor suspected in beauty's disappearance." Sanborn brought the paper back to the residence and excitedly showed it to the ladies. Miss Thawley, whose heart was none too good, had to rest her head on the dining room table.

The headline read:

COPS FIND LOST BEAUTY'S CAR
BLOODY AUTO IN PROF CASE ABANDONED IN NEW YORK

THE SILVER TOYOTA

IT WAS Saturday evening, July 16, when New York City police found the silver Toyota. Officer Christine Miller and her partner, Cornelius Dever, were on routine patrol through Sector F. This five-block area encompassed Manhattan's Garment District—notably the fur district—and was plagued by thefts, so Miller and Dever made it a point to drive slowly, examining the cars parked along the curb for anything out of the ordinary.

At a little past 9:00 P.M., Dever had turned into West Twenty-ninth Street, when Miller caught sight of a 1982 Toyota Starlet parked in a tow-away zone. It had no plates. Dever pulled over and walked to the Toyota's passenger side. It was unlocked. The vehicle's inspection sticker was missing from the dashboard. Someone had also scraped the dealer's decal off the rear of the hatchback. When Dever checked under the hood, he saw the battery was missing. On the engine block, he found a vehicle indentification number—the one easily traceable number that the person who had obliterated the other identification had apparently overlooked. Officer Miller then read the VIN over the car radio to central dispatch.

The Toyota was not in the system as a missing car. Miller figured there must have been an error in transmission. She copied the number off the engine block and returned with Dever to the station house to run it again. This time it came back with an alarm. The car had been reported stolen in Massachusetts and its "owner possibly involuntarily missing."

Detective Kenneth Bowen was dispatched to the scene to examine the Toyota. When he opened the door, he was enveloped by a foul odor. Bowen, who had been a supervisor in the midtown homicide squad for

317

six years, recognized the smell as that of decomposing human tissue. Pulling the driver's seat forward, he examined the hatchback with a flashlight. There were two large reddish stains on the black vinyl matting and what looked like dried blood around the wheel well.

Bowen notified the agency which had originally sent out the alert—the Malden, Massachusetts, police. Malden, in turn, called the state police in Foxboro. By coincidence, Trooper Bobby Murphy was at the barracks gassing up his cruiser when he overheard the news. Murphy roused John Kivlan at home in Milton to tell him that Robin's Toyota had been found in New York City. Only two blocks from Penn Station.

"Go get that car," was the prosecutor's terse reply.

Murphy borrowed a flatbed truck and set off at midnight down Route 95. At a little past five on Sunday morning he arrived at the Midtown South Precinct, where he was met by Detective Bowen and Joseph Pirrello, commander of the detective unit.

Bowen recounted in more detail the events of the preceding evening, then showed Murphy the car, which had been hauled into the impound garage at headquarters. Its peculiarities were identical to those listed in the description of those on Robin's Toyota. It had the black racing stripe. The right front wheel rim was bent. There was a small dent in the body near the door on the driver's side, and there was a key scratch on the hood.

Pirrello took Murphy to the spot on West Twenty-ninth where the Toyota had been found. The trooper had hoped to ask around to see if anyone in the neighborhood had seen the car being parked or who parked it, but it was Sunday and businesses were closed. That afternoon Murphy interviewed Officer Miller, who told him there was no way the Toyota could have been there during her last patrol, which was between 4:00 P.M. and midnight the preceding Wednesday, July 13. She had checked the street thoroughly and would have seen it. On Thursday she had done an overtime tour out of the precinct. Friday was her birthday, so she had it off. So, Murphy concluded, the car must have been parked on West Twenty-ninth sometime between Wednesday and Saturday.

The trooper loaded the Starlet onto his truck, covered it with a tarp, and drove it back to the Foxboro barracks. It was after midnight when he called Kivlan to tell him the Toyota had been tucked into bay No. 3.

Later that morning Kivlan and Matt Connolly went down to the barracks to check out the car. As Detective Bowen had reported, the battery was missing. So was the radio. The feature which attracted the prosecutors' keenest interest, however, was the driver's seat. It had been pushed far back from the pedals. Robin, at five feet four, would not have required that much legroom. It had apparently been adjusted to accommodate someone over six feet tall. William Douglas was easily six feet, and Nancy Douglas was much taller than five four.

The following day a forensics team from the state lab dusted the Toyota for fingerprints but could find none. (The state crime lab did not have a particularly good record of turning up prints. In fact, John Kivlan, in his eagerness to peer inside the car, thoughtlessly braced himself against a window with his fingertips. Even these did not show up.) When the chemist Kaufman tried to open the hatchback, he found it jammed so tightly that it resisted prying. Going through the front, he pulled the seat forward so that he could survey the deck mat.

The mat was hard black rubber, around four feet wide and three feet long, contoured around two bulging wheel wells. There appeared to be a light stain covering most of it. Kaufman lifted the mat, revealing the steel underplating of the Toyota. Blood had seeped onto this surface. Some of it had even dripped onto the fabric at the bottom of the driver's seat. The only other place the chemist could find stains was on the vinyl near the handle on the passenger's door. He clipped samples from the door and seat as well as a section chosen at random from the deck mat and took these back to the lab.

When the chemist examined the section of deck mat with his naked eye, he could see only a film of dried fluid. But when he placed it under the microscope he discovered, to his mounting excitement, that there was another piece of tissue—gray, like the fragment found in Douglas's windbreaker, only much smaller, less than a centimeter in diameter. Unlike the first specimen, this one contained blood. It was type A.

Kaufman hastily dispatched this specimen to Dr. Katsas, who confirmed that it, too, was brain tissue. Inasmuch as it contained human blood, he could say with certainty that it was *human* brain tissue. The medical examiner could not, however, confirm that it was from the same organism as the tissue found in the windbreaker.

LIEUTENANT SHARKEY, meanwhile, had been on the phone with the Midtown South Precinct, trying to determine more precisely when the Toyota had been parked on West Twenty-ninth Street. Early in the week of July 18, he had spoken to a Lieutenant Bernard Gillespie, who claimed to have seen the car while on a surveillance detail at about 4:00 P.M. on Friday, July 15. The Starlet caught his eye, he said, because it was covered with a thick coating of dust. That night there had been a heavy rainstorm. When Miller and Dever found the car the following day, it was clean.

The dust cover suggested to John Kivlan that the car had been garaged somewhere for quite a long while. The prosecutor was now operating on the assumption that Douglas had driven the Toyota to New York on March 6 and left it in a parking garage in the vicinity of Penn Station before catching his train to Washington. It had stayed there for over four months. Then, for some reason, someone had moved it to the street. If Officer Miller had not seen it on her July 13 rounds and Lieutenant Gillespie had seen it on his July 15 surveillance, it must have been parked between Wednesday and Friday.

Kivlan hoped to trace the movements of the car back to the lot where it was first parked, on the off chance of finding an eyewitness who had seen Douglas drive it in the night of March 6. When Brian Howe visited New York to locate the Amtrak ticket, he had done a quick survey of fifty-five parking garages but had turned up nothing. Now, Kivlan felt, these warranted a closer look. On Tuesday, July 19, he sent Trooper Rick Zebrasky to New York to canvass the lots around Penn Station.

On Wednesday morning Zebrasky and a pair of detectives assigned to him by Midtown South Precinct hit the pavement. During the course of the afternoon, they visited ten garages. None of these had any record of a 1982 Toyota with or without plates. One of the lots, Meyers Parking System on West Thirty-first Street, kept its books not on the premises but in its main office, on West Forty-second. Zebrasky would have to call back the following day to get at them.

The New York detectives felt that Meyers merited further checking. About the same time that the Toyota had been discovered, another patrol had discovered a black Volkswagen parked on West Thirtieth. It, too, had no plates, but inside it police had found a Meyers ticket stub. It was possible that the garage had dumped these two delinquent vehicles on the street at the same time, in the same manner.

When Zebrasky finally got a look at Booker's records, he discovered that the Toyota Starlet first showed up on March 6—the same day that Douglas had purchased his train ticket to Washington at Penn Station two blocks away. The trooper went back down to West Thirty-first Street to speak with one John Isaacs, the attendant who had been on duty that Sunday night. From 2:00 A.M. to 3:00 A.M. of March 7, Isaacs had gone on his customary rounds, logging in every vehicle in the lot at that hour. On the second level he found the Toyota. It had been backed up against the wall. When Isaacs went around to the rear to check the plate, he found it missing.

Every night after that for about three weeks, Isaac noted the Toyota on a separate inventory sheet. He never saw anyone around or near the car. And he did not recognize the photo of William Douglas.

The Boston media, having just digested the remarkable revelations in the Stoughton affidavits, now greeted the discovery of the silver Toyota with renewed and ravenous appetite. This time Channel 5 found itself at the head of the pack.

WCVB was located in Needham, only two miles north of Dedham. By virtue of its proximity to the county seat, the station usually enjoyed an inside track at the Norfolk County District Attorney's Office. One of Channel 5's reporters, a serious fellow named Ron Gollobin, had spent quite a bit of time on the crime beat and was trusted and well liked by troopers both at Foxboro and in the DA's office. He was, moreover, a close personal friend of William Delahunt.

Gollobin had been aware of the Douglas investigation in early March when one of his trooper friends had confided to him that state police were looking for the body of a hooker. At the time he was absorbed with the investigation of an organized-crime figure in New Bedford and didn't follow up on the lead. A month or so later, however, he heard once again from the trooper, who was calling on behalf of Paul Landry, wanting to know if Gollobin knew of anyone who might help Landry write a book.

"I do a little writing myself," Gollobin told the trooper, who agreed that he'd be perfect.

Landry and Gollobin met a few afternoons later at the Red Coach Inn in Norwood, where Landry gave a sketchy account of the case. Even these few details evoked for Gollobin the story's intriguing possibilities: A geek who would have given up all his academic honors for one moment of macho glory. A beautiful, middle-class girl who heeded the call of the streets. A retiring cop hungering for the big grab. Gollobin told Landry he was very interested in writing this book and invited the trooper out to his home in Brookline. There Landry sat under a tree in the front yard and told his story for the next twelve hours. Gollobin's wife, Helen, took notes. She ended up with forty pages.

Gollobin had to admit that Landry was not one of those guys with lightning-fast insights. But he had a good grasp of detail, and he built and built until finally he had something. In this case it was not quite clear what he had. One of the cornerstones of the story was how the big grab had been within his grasp until it had been snatched away by the district attorney. This was a very dramatic aspect of the story and could not, of course, be ignored. Yet that placed Gollobin in a bind.

Bill Delahunt was his good friend, but here he had Landry freely confiding his bitterness toward Norfolk, completely unaware of Gollobin's friendship with the DA. Signing a book deal with Landry would mean walking a thin ethical line, but Gollobin decided it was worth a try. He decided not to tell either man about his relationship with the other.

Gollobin was not quite sure how these deals were consummated, but he hoped to keep the arrangement with Landry informal. A straight fifty-fifty split. Gollobin saw no need to tell his news director what he was up to. As a practical matter it could only benefit the station to have a reporter on staff who knew so much about what was becoming one of the most titillating stories of the year.

Gollobin soon had the opportunity to reap the benefits of this new association when, on Saturday, July 16, he got a call from a "police source" telling him that Robin Benedict's Toyota had been found and was on its way back to Massachusetts.

On Sunday morning Gollobin, proceeding with the utmost delicacy, approached John and Shirley Benedict. Although Gollobin's ally, Landry, was still on good terms with Robin's family, it was now no longer possible to simply place a call to Emsley Terrace and get them on the line. The Benedicts had hired an attorney.

Anthony J. DiFruscia, a compact, dapper man in his early forties, was the son of a Lawrence ditchdigger. He had made his fortune handling personal-injury cases for workers in the factories that dotted the Merrimack Valley. During the late sixties, DiFruscia was elected to the Massachusetts House of Representatives, where he served three terms, gaining a reputation as a liberal reformer and an advocate of child abuse legislation. That brief but promising political career came to an end in 1970 when he failed in a bid to become the Democratic nominee for lieutenant governor. After that, DiFruscia settled back into his law practice, headquartered in a large Victorian house which he christened, with engaging egotism, the DiFruscia Building.

The Benedicts had first met DiFruscia back in the late 1970s when they had retained him to handle the affairs of the troubled White Eagles drum and bugle corps. In the spring of 1983 they turned to him again because they were dissatisfied with the investigation into the disappearance of their daughter. They were extremely unhappy about having spent so much time searching the swamps and ponds of southern Massachusetts when all the while Robin's car was sitting in some parking garage in New York City. DiFruscia had a local reputation as a "gunslinger," and the Benedicts apparently liked the idea of having an hombre of their own who could shoot his way into the Norfolk District Attorney's Office and demand answers. The disgruntled pair was also feeling a little overwhelmed by the forces of law and media which Robin's disappearance had set in motion, and welcomed a buffer against the storm. And so when Ron Gollobin called John and Shirley Benedict seeking an interview, he was obliged to petition their new champion.

Gollobin did not like DiFruscia much. Tony, he sensed, smelled big publicity, hence big money, in this case and was intending from here on out to dictate what the media said about Robin Benedict. Gollobin decided not to complicate matters by telling him he was thinking of doing a book of his own. Before giving Channel 5 a green light on the interview, DiFruscia insisted upon bringing John Benedict to meet Gollobin and his camerawoman at a Howard Johnson near Emsley Terrace. He wanted to set a few ground rules.

At the top of the list of prohibited topics was prostitution. "That," DiFruscia announced emphatically, "cannot be mentioned."

It struck Gollobin as a little foolish to try and rewrite history at this point. Details of Robin's "double life" were being reported freely in the *Herald* and elsewhere.

"It . . . *has* been mentioned," he observed. "If I didn't ask it, I'd be fired. If we can't get around that, I'll do the story without Mr. Benedict."

Naturally, he was bluffing.

Finally Gollobin and DiFruscia arrived at an understanding. The attorney would sit in on the interview and raise objections if he disapproved of a question. As a sweetener to the bargain, Gollobin promised to try to commandeer the station's helicopter so that John Benedict could survey the terrain around Sharon. With that he was given permission to come along to the Benedict house. Gollobin did not know what to expect of the childhood home of a prostitute. He found it eerily "ordinary." Shirley Benedict was in the kitchen looking as if she might cry.

Gollobin addressed his queries to her husband.

"When you think about Robin, what are the memories that come to mind?" he asked.

"All good memories. Always good memories," John Benedict replied. Then he began to cry.

After a decent interval Gollobin probed, "Were you close to her?"

"Yes, very close. Always close with Robin," Benedict responded. "I guess . . . somebody called her . . . Daddy's little girl. It's more than just that we were close, [a] father-daughter relationship. The line of work she was in, commercial arts. I'm in photography. We used to sit here many times and we'd talk about that type of thing. She'd do airbrush work or she'd be doing some drawings. And we'd sit down and talk about perspective, or whatever. Whereas, my other daughter is in a different line of work. She didn't know what we were talkin' about. It was over her head. She and Robin were very very close. But I think Robin and I were . . . close is the best word I guess you'd call it. We were very close. She is very affectionate. I'm very affectionate. In fact, my wife says a little too affectionate. We'd sit here and we'd hug up or she'd sit on my lap and we'd talk about different things. Yeah, we're very close. . . ."

Did he know his daughter was a prostitute? Gollobin queried gently.

"I don't believe it," John Benedict replied. "It'll have to be proven to me. And even if she is, I don't think it has any bearing. She is my daughter. She's a human being and she's missing. And I think that is the most important thing of all."

At six o'clock Newscenter 5 broke the news that Robin Benedict's Toyota had been found and that the girl's parents felt a "very great sadness."

ONLY about three hours before WCVB ran its story, the *Boston Herald* got a tip of its own that the car had been found. There was no way that the *Herald* could scoop the stations. The earliest the paper could get anything into print was Monday morning. Nevertheless, John Birtwell sprang into action, hoping to come up with a next-day's story that would transcend a rehash. He called the *Herald*'s sister paper, the *New York Post*, attempting to locate a photo of the car on the spot where it was found, but the *Post* didn't have one. Then he placed several ingratiating calls to the NYPD, where he finally reached one Sergeant Graham who seemed eager to be of help. On the basis of Graham's intelligence, Birtwell managed to put together a story which gave more details on the car's actual discovery.

The following morning Birtwell, Estes, and a photographer drove out to Sandy Ridge Circle, where Birtwell marched boldly up to No. 38 and knocked on the door. Billy Douglas answered. Seeing the reporters, the boy announced, "My Dad's not here."

"That's all right," Birtwell said. "We'll wait for him."

An hour passed and Douglas did not show up. The photographer managed to bag a couple of shots of the children before the reporters abandoned their stakeout and moved along to the state police barracks in Foxboro, where District Attorney Delahunt was scheduled to hold a press conference. Unfortunately, they had gotten the time wrong and arrived in Foxboro to find the conference over. There was nothing to do but photograph the silver Toyota, sitting dirty and forlorn in bay No. 3.

Having lost out in this round, Birtwell nonetheless rebounded shortly with a discovery which had escaped the vigilant Boston press.

Birtwell had been scanning a South Shore paper called the Quincy *Patriot-Ledger*, where he found a brief article telling how the Norfolk district attorney was trying to compel testimony of the Douglas children and that Dan O'Connell was willing to take this issue to the U.S. Supreme Court. Birtwell snapped alert. This must mean that the case was currently under consideration by the Supreme Judicial Court.

He hurried up to Pemberton Square and found that during the court's last sitting, in May, it had heard arguments in a case that was listed simply as *Three Juveniles v. Commonwealth.* No names were given, but the facts were identical to those of the Douglas case. Birtwell could see that the Three Juveniles had gone first to a single justice, by whom it had been referred to the full bench. He found that the papers and exhibits filed with the single justice had been sealed. His disappointment was quickly assuaged, however, when he learned that the papers filed with the full court had somehow escaped impoundment.

Birtwell walked out of the clerk's office with 140 pages of briefs as well as a cassette tape of the arguments presented to the full bench on May 5. He took these back to his cubicle in the newsroom, where he and Estes sorted through the impassioned pleas. They found a passage where Assistant District Attorney Hely explained how Nancy Douglas had invoked her spousal privilege. At that point, one of the justices interjected, "[This] may also indicate she wants to protect herself." To which Hely replied, "Sure. There's evidence that she is . . . doing that."

More damning still was an affidavit from John Kivlan explaining how William and Nancy Douglas had denied ever having seen the blood-stained hammer, and yet Mrs. Douglas's father had identified the instrument as the one he had lent the pair three months earlier. Nancy had been caught in an apparent lie.

Birtwell called the Douglas house and asked for Nancy.

"Mrs. Douglas," he began formally, "we have learned that the hammer belonged to your father."

There was a moment or so of silence before Nancy replied, "Please don't print that." Her voice was shaking. Birtwell thought there was a pleading quality to it.

"We're very willing to tell another side of the story in whatever form you'd be willing to do it," he offered.

"I'm sorry," Nancy replied. Her attorneys had forbidden her to talk about the case.

The following morning the *Herald* announced unequivocally that Nancy Douglas was under investigation in the disappearance of Robin Benedict.

WHEN Michael Frisby picked up the *Herald,* he saw he'd been trumped. *Globe* writers were normally encouraged to keep a gentlemanly distance from their stories. To report them dispassionately. The paper never indulged in the logos or the long-running obsessions which gripped the *Herald.* But the Benedict case had aroused a proprietary streak even on

Morrissey Boulevard. One morning, early in the game, there had been some new development on "the missing beauty." Frisby's editor had called him and complained that he had seen a *Globe* truck driver parked somewhere reading a *Herald*. "Let's get on the story and stay on it," he said. Since then Frisby had begun to think of the Benedict case as *his* story.

Frisby knew he had to come back from this day's defeat with a forceful salvo. Fortunately, he found a source who was willing to fire the necessary rounds. Attorney Anthony DiFruscia was itching to take on two of his clients' peeves—the Boston *Herald* and the Norfolk County district attorney. When Frisby got him on the line that afternoon, DiFruscia assailed the *Herald* for naming Nancy Douglas as a suspect. "On the basis of information that I have received, there appears to be only one reasonable suspect in the case," DiFruscia huffed. Then he lambasted the Norfolk investigators for "playing to the media" for political reasons.

Frisby knew that Delahunt had a weakness for publicity. It was highly unusual for a district attorney to be making statements in the middle of an investigation. The DA's press conference on the silver Toyota had been broadcast on the heels of Gollobin's interview with the Benedicts. In light of this, Frisby surmised that DiFruscia might also be a little irritated that Delahunt was cutting in on his press. It would not hurt to play one off against the other.

That afternoon Frisby called the DA for comment.

"In any case that attracts media attention," Delahunt replied coolly, "the dissemination of information is always a problem."

Privately, the district attorney was not amused. He directed Lieutenant Sharkey to call Attorney DiFruscia and tell him that any more such incendiary comments would get him prosecuted.

DiFruscia replied, on a more conciliatory tack, saying the Benedicts wanted to help the investigation along by offering a pair of rewards; one, in the amount of $5,000, for information leading to Robin's body, another, in the same amount, for information leading to the conviction of her killer. Sharkey relayed this proposition to John Kivlan and the district attorney for their consideration. An incentive as generous as this couldn't hurt, they decided. The danger in this plan was that it might lead to critical information being channeled through the Benedicts or DiFruscia, and God knew in what form it might eventually reach the DA's office. Delahunt, however, finally agreed to the rewards, with the proviso that all information should be given directly to the Norfolk investigators.

DiFruscia agreed. On July 24 he issued a press release announcing the rewards. The money would be paid after the probating of Robin Benedict's estate. Out of respect for the "privacy" of the Benedict family, DiFruscia asked that all information be given to the state police.

THE TROOPERS stepped up their surveillance, not confining themselves to the promontory but taking periodic swings into the cul-de-sac with various vehicles. Sometimes it was a black van. Sometimes a truck borrowed from the phone company. Sometimes even a cruiser. By now the troopers were not even bothering to hide their presence. In revealing themselves more brazenly, they hoped to apply enough pressure on Douglas to elicit the long-hoped-for confession. The only effect it seemed to have, however, was to force the Douglases into diversionary tactics like parking their blue Toyota behind the house so that no one could see if they were home.

Kivlan decided that the troopers needed a lookout which would give them a better vantage point for watching the back door. Brian Howe had spotted an orchard at the top of the slope behind the Douglas house and got permission from the owner, an elderly Italian gentleman, to use it for surveillance. Every night after that, whoever was on duty would drive down a dirt path, which ran through the orchard, and park on the edge of the woods which overlooked the Douglases' backyard.

One night Trooper Bobby Murphy spotted a red compact parked at the back of the house. Taking down the license number, he ran it and found that it belonged to the Crimson Car Rental Company, headquartered in Cambridge. Murphy, as it happened, knew Crimson's East Boston manager, a short, sandy-haired fellow named Sal. East Boston was a stronghold for organized crime. Rental cars were routinely used for robbery, murders, and drug deals, and Sal had been cooperative with the Norfolk District Attorney's Office on a couple of previous investigations. Murphy called Sal and learned, to his surprise, that Douglas was currently working for Crimson.

When Murphy pressed him for details, Sal explained that around June or July Douglas had answered an ad for a shuttler, a driver to ferry cars among the company's four Boston locations. He had been hired at the rate of $4 an hour, and nobody had any complaints about him. It was amusing to see him hustling his bulk across the lot, squeezing in and out of compacts, but he was a good worker, surprisingly dedicated to the job, always asking if he could do a little more. The red compact that Murphy described was supposedly at the shop having its transmission overhauled. Douglas had apparently taken it home, which was against company policy. Murphy asked Sal not to make an issue of it, just to monitor Douglas's movements so that the DA's office could locate him quickly if it had to. Sal agreed to keep an eye on his new employee—a promise that would prove very useful in the days to come.

MEANWHILE , a delegation from the Norfolk County District Attorney's Office went calling on Robin Benedict's last known appointment, Sargent Nichols.

John Kivlan had never seriously considered Nichols a suspect. His doorman, John Baldwin, had seen Robin walk out of the building after her date with Nichols and was willing to testify that she looked perfectly healthy at that point. Nevertheless, the prosecutor knew that any defense counsel worth his salt would try to divert suspicion to Robin's johns. (Kivlan had deliberately avoided trying to decode Robin's black book, for fear of unearthing more suspects who would create "red herrings" for the defense.) But Nichols's encounters with Robin had been recorded in some detail in Trooper Landry's report. He apparently was, moreover, the last person, other than Douglas, to see Robin alive.

There were still certain discrepancies between the accounts given by Baldwin and Nichols as to the times when Robin arrived and left. On the last Monday in July, Kivlan and Howe went to Longfellow Place, to set the record straight.

They passed the doorman's booth (John Baldwin was not there, for he had been relieved of duty when the Benedict incident came to light) and took the elevator to Nichols's apartment. Nichols answered the door. He was a beefy man who appeared to be in his mid to late forties. He seemed a little nervous but eager to be of help. His apartment commanded a stunning view of Boston Harbor. The furniture was tasteful and contemporary. On the left wall of the living room hung a portrait of Thomas Dawes, son of the Patriot William Dawes who ran one leg of Paul Revere's ride. He was one of Nichols's own forebears. Nichols, in fact, could trace his line back through the passenger list of the *Mayflower* to one lord mayor of London.

Nichols confirmed, for Kivlan's benefit, his earlier estimate of Robin's arrival time. "Nadine" had gotten there at around 8:40 P.M. He was disappointed to notice that she was wearing slacks. He had wanted to be able to see her legs. But on the whole, he was delighted to see how attractive she was. He considered himself something of a sociologist and had her pegged at "lower-middle SEC (social economic class)."

She took a seat on a section of couch which left her face to face with old Thomas Dawes. Robin and Nichols had engaged in "general conversation" for about fifteen minutes. She told him that she was a graduate of the Rhode Island School of Design, and he was impressed.

They engaged in "light conversation" for about ten more minutes, after which Nichols recalled giving Robin $40—one twenty and two ten-dollar bills. Although he insisted that they had not had sex, he felt he should pay her something for her time. After she left, Nichols went to the lobby to thank Baldwin for sending up someone who was not "unpleasant or difficult." Then he went back to his phones for an evening of work.

This scenario checked out. If Robin made the call at 9:40 P.M. and stayed ten more minutes, that would have taken her out of Longfellow Place shortly before ten. If she had moved fast, she could have made it to the phone booth on the expressway at 10:06 P.M. and on to Sharon by 10:45 P.M.

Kivlan asked Nichols whether he would come forward and testify when the case came to trial. Nichols seemed willing but was nervous about possible publicity. Did Kivlan think there would be any press at the trial? Kivlan shot a furtive glance at Howe, then replied, "Oh, no. I shouldn't think so."

THROUGHOUT most of July, the Gray House investigators occupied themselves with odd jobs, waiting to hear from the Supreme Judicial Court on the two critical questions. Could they get the children? Could they get the Douglases' blood? On July 12 a single justice, Herbert P. Wilkins, had heard arguments on the blood issue, then set about his deliberations.

On the last Monday in July, the Justice came back with a precedent-setting decision. Reversing the trial court's ruling, he declared that drawing blood samples from an unindicted suspect did *not* constitute an invasion of privacy. While granting that the Commonwealth could take samples from William Douglas, he did not, however, extend this mandate to Nancy Douglas. Rather, he sent that request back to the trial judge, to whom the district attorney's office would have to show more proof of need.

The court had left the door open for Kivlan to continue pursuing Nancy, but he hesitated. Nancy's involvement was far more difficult to pin down than was her husband's. Trying to build a case against her at this stage might divert attention and energy from the main focus of the investigation, which was, without question, William Douglas. The prosecutor decided to put his request for her blood on hold for the time being. He could push for it later, if it was needed.

Two weeks after Justice Wilkins's decision, William Douglas came to the district attorney's office, where the Dedham medical examiner drew his blood. Gates then passed the sample along to the chemist Kaufman who labeled it "K3"—indicating that it was the third "known sample"— and sent this along to the FBI.

By this time Agent Kearney had completed a serological workup on John and Shirley Benedict, and he concluded that the blood on the Mansfield items was "consistent" with having come from one of their offspring. Working with extracts sent from the Massachusetts lab, however, he had been able to locate only four out of the six standard markers. Kearney felt it was still possible to raise the remaining two if he could test the whole items. Accordingly, Kivlan sent him the Toyota deck mat, Douglas's nylon jacket, the hammer, and the corduroy jacket. The FBI lab was carrying a heavy load—and it was obligated to handle its own cases first—but Kearney promised to get back as soon as possible with test results from the whole articles as well as with an analysis of William Douglas's blood.

BRIAN HOWE, meanwhile, had stumbled onto yet another account of how William Douglas had gotten his head injury.

The trooper had contacted the Veterans Administration, hoping to flesh out the details of Douglas's trip to Washington, D.C. The VA, in turn, referred him to Dr. James Bodley, chairman of the Merit Board, which had convened in Washington the week following Robin's disappearance. When Howe reached Bodley at the University of Minnesota, the chairman told him about a conversation he had had with Douglas the morning of March 8. Bodley had inquired about Douglas's head wound, and Douglas told him that he had been mugged at La Guardia Airport on Sunday. Bodley thought Douglas had said why he was in New York, but now he couldn't recall. At any rate, Douglas had told him that he had been in the area between the security check-in booth and the loading gate, when he was assaulted by "two black males," who hit him with a pipe, knocking him to the floor. Then they took his briefcase and ran. He had bled "profusely" on the carpet. When he went to the security booth to report the assault, a policeman told him that "this sort of thing happened all the time." Douglas informed Bodley that he had been clutching the briefcase to his chest, which had probably given the thieves the impression that he was carrying something valuable. He vowed never to do this again.

This newly discovered account stood to benefit the prosecution. For the first time Douglas had admitted being in New York City during the hours after Robin Benedict disappeared. True, La Guardia was located in

Queens and was a $20 cab ride from Penn Station. But it was not impossible that Douglas had parked the car at Meyers, gone over to Penn Station to buy the Amtrak ticket, and then, for some reason, taken a taxi to La Guardia, where he caught a flight to Washington. Douglas himself had told Landry that he had originally intended to fly to Boston. Brian Howe had checked New York Air—the airline on which he flew on the return trip—but the carrier's computers no longer had any records of cancellations on that flight.

The hypothesis that he flew from New York, however, was a little too cumbersome to be credible. There was growing evidence that Douglas had taken the train. As of the middle of August, Douglas had still not disputed the Amtrak charge on his Visa billing (there was no corresponding charge for air travel on March 6 or 7). And if Douglas had not taken the train, why had Amtrak turned up a punched ticket stub bearing his signature?

Kivlan suspected that Douglas would come up with a story to the effect that J.R. Rogers had stolen his credit card, forged his signature, and perhaps even fabricated a conductor's punch. But then Douglas would also have to suggest that J.R. gone so far as to ride to Washington, D.C., so that the incriminating stub would be planted in Amtrak's warehouse. All this strained credulity, but Kivlan did not intend to give Douglas the latitude to spin such a tale. Amtrak had still been unable to locate the conductor on Train 67 to Washington. If he could identify Douglas, the problem would be solved. In the interim, Kivlan set about to establish to the probable satisfaction of a jury that the signature on the Amtrak ticket belonged to William Douglas.

Again the prosecutor turned to the FBI, this time to the handwriting expert Charles Perrotta. Agent Perrotta was finicky about the kinds of identification that he would attempt. He took one look at the Mobil slip Kivlan had sent him—hoping he could tie Douglas to the gas station on Berkeley Street in the early hours of March 6—and informed the prosecutor that a positive identification would be impossible. Because Douglas himself had the kept the original, only the carbon was available. Perrotta routinely declined to try and identify carbon signatures, whose wavy lines and blunt ending strokes gave them the same characteristics as a forgery. He held out more hope, however, for the Amtrak signature, which was an original inscribed into a hard, almost cardboard-like paper. It would be useful, Perrotta told Kivlan, if he could get Douglas to give fresh handwriting samples on the same kind of paper, managing, if possible, to approximate the conditions at Penn Station.

Accordingly, Kivlan ordered a number of regulation ballpoints as well as original ticket stock from Amtrak. When those arrived, all that remained was to summon Douglas.

That proved a relatively simple matter. Inasmuch as the Supreme Judicial Court had already agreed to allow the grand jury such intimate evidence as Douglas's blood, there was no practical impediment to its getting relatively public "nontestimonial" evidence like handwriting samples. And so, at the grand jury's request, Douglas appeared with Attorney O'Connell at the district attorney's office on Tuesday, August 23, to give exemplars.

Lieutenant Sharkey invited Douglas and O'Connell into his office, where Brian Howe was waiting. There he bade his visitors take a seat. Then he instructed Douglas to write his name over and over again in a "natural, unaltered manner." Douglas complied, filling several sheets of lined paper and using three separate pens.

Then, without warning, Howe asked Douglas to stand. Before him on the desk sat a lectern, which provided a writing level at about the same height as the teller's window at Penn Station. The trooper placed before Douglas a set of twenty-five voided Amtrak tickets. To this point, neither Douglas nor O'Connell knew that Norfolk had turned up the punched ticket stub. Brian Howe would later testify to the grand jury that Douglas's facial expression changed into an apparent look of "surprise and concern." Nevertheless, he signed all twenty-five tickets, after which Sharkey quipped, "Okay, Dan. . . . Just have him write where the body is and that'll finish it out." O'Connell bristled and shouted no.

Kivlan forwarded the exemplars to Perrotta, who examined the series of signatures. They were highly erratic. Some were printed. Others cursive. One did not have to be a handwriting expert to see the distortion. Sometimes the D was rounded liked the ones on the Mobile and Amtrak signatures. At other times he had made it angular like a triangle. What interested Perrotta most was the way he signed his initials $H.J.$ The letter H showed extremely wide variations. One time he would execute it without lifting his pen. The next time he would make it in three separate strokes.

On the basis of this examination, Perrotta wrote back to Kivlan that it could not be definitely determined whether William H. J. Douglas, the writer of the exemplars, had written the signatures on the Amtrak ticket and Mobil charge because of "distortion and possible disguise in much of the known writing." Perrotta did note, however, that there were certain similarities between the exemplars and the two charge slips which "prevent the elimination of Douglas as the possible writer of these questioned signatures."

Perrotta held out hope that if Kivlan could gather samples of Douglas's known writing from the past two years, he might be able to make a more positive identification. These, he instructed, should be things written during the "normal course of business"—memos, contracts, and applications.

Kivlan went through the evidence files and pulled out Douglas's handwritten notes and the correspondence with Robin Benedict. He showed these things to Karen Hitchcock, who said they appeared to be in Bill Douglas's writing. She could definitely identify the memo that he had written to her regarding the items "stolen" from his office as being in his hand. Next, the prosecutor subpoenaed contracts, time sheets, and cashed checks from Douglas's recent employers, the marketing research firms and the YWCA. He also secured the guest registration forms from the Susse Chalet motor lodges and inns where Douglas had spent time with Robin. The prosecutor could be fairly sure that these signatures were in Douglas's hand because the Susse Chalet required a guest to show a driver's license if he wanted to charge a room. William Douglas's ID must have checked out because he had been allowed to use his Visa card.

Kivlan sent these things to Perrotta and waited for a reply.

WHILE the Norfolk investigation found itself in a holding pattern— waiting for results of blood tests, waiting for handwriting analysis, waiting for permission to speak to the children—William Douglas found himself in trouble on yet another front.

Sometime in the early spring Tufts had completed its own investigation into the missing money and found that $8,687 of it was federal. This raised the specter of prosecution by the U.S. attorney. On April 6, representatives from the university had met with those of the National Institutes of Health and inspectors from the U.S. Department of Health and Human Services to discuss the alleged misappropriations. The feds decided to conduct their own on-site review to verify just how much of the missing funds had come from the government. Three months later the Office of Audit published a report confirming that it had found some $11,962 in questionable direct expenses.

The government decided not to make an issue of it. By this time the university had already reimbursed the National Institutes of Health and the Department of the Navy for their full losses. It had also settled accounts with the New England Anti-Vivisection Society to the tune of about $41,600. In turn, Tufts was reimbursed by Hartford Accident & Indemnity, the company which had issued its "blanket crime policy," which covered among other things, "employee dishonesty loss."

With the feds placated, NEAVS satisfied, and its own losses restored,

Tufts would have liked to forget about the whole affair. That became impossible when it learned that the Suffolk County district attorney was investigating Dr. William Douglas.

Up to May 27, the day Douglas resigned from Tufts, no one had bothered to report his suspected larceny to the Suffolk DA's office, whose jurisdiction covered Greater Boston, including Tufts University. Kivlan had not been eager to alert Suffolk. The relationship between the two counties was civil but not warm. Kivlan feared that if Suffolk got on the case, its investigators might get in the way of his own. By late May, however, much of the groundwork had been laid for Norfolk's prosecution. Kivlan reasoned that a larceny investigation might not only increase the pressure on Douglas to confess but also ferret out details of his financial relationship with Robin Benedict. Almost immediately after Manos called him with news of Douglas's resignation, Kivlan put in a call to the Suffolk County District Attorney's Office, where he alerted an assistant named Gerry Muldoon to the possibility of embezzlement and intrigue at Tufts University.

Muldoon, a slow-talking, easygoing fellow, promised to look into it. In the days thereafter he was to pursue a more limited, less exhaustive investigation than the one in progress down in Norfolk County. With the help of one "financial investigator"—a young civilian employee who had an M.B.A.—he did nonetheless manage to pick his way slowly but deftly through the maze of questioned expenses.

The investigator, Arthur Shabo, canvassed the various banks at which Robin had either cashed checks or made deposits. In the process of reviewing her activities at the Washington Street Branch of the Bank of Boston, he interviewed Michael Durant, the vault attendant who had been on duty that morning in February when "Mrs. Robin Benedict" had come in to check the safety deposit box which she shared with her "husband," William Douglas.

Since Douglas rented the box the preceding July, Durant recalled, he had visited it about once a week. Whenever he carried the box to the private viewing room, it felt empty. He had never seen Mrs. Benedict until the morning of February 23. Then she visited it three times. The first was around 9:00 A.M., just as the bank opened. She came back two times shortly after that. At some point she had telephoned William Douglas in "Philadelphia," reversing the charges. Durant overheard this conversation and recalled hearing Mrs. Benedict calling Douglas "sweetheart" in "endearing tones." She had laid it on so thick that he suspected that the two were not really married. Douglas had apparently told her there was "money" missing from the box. Durant had then shown her the vault's access records, which revealed that no one but William Douglas had ever signed into the vault.

The Bank of Boston's security department also gave the Suffolk investigators photos of Robin cashing eight checks drawn on Tufts University. Douglas was present in two of these. These shots were taken long before the pair was actively being investigated by anyone, but the bank kept film of every transaction, no matter how routine. There were also two shots of Savi Bisram, though Muldoon was disappointed to see that Douglas was not in them.

Muldoon had requested a detective assigned to the Suffolk DA's office to contact certain street detectives who pulled Savi in for questioning. Muldoon found Savi amazingly nonchalant. By this time she had been questioned repeatedly by Landry, Howe, and others and was something of a veteran at handling inquisitors. As she lounged at the end of the conference table in his office, Muldoon showed her a photo taken on October 19, 1982. Savi identified herself standing at the teller's station at the Bank of Boston. She was cashing a $9,000 check, she said, as a "favor for a friend."

What Muldoon had here was a woman cashing a check to which she clearly was not entitled. She readily acknowledged that she did not work at Tufts. But she also claimed that she did not keep any of the money, receiving only a small courtesy tip for her troubles. Under cross-examination Savi would be savaged by a good defense attorney. Still, she was an eyewitness to Douglas's fraudulent dealings with Tufts and the Bank of Boston. Muldoon was intent upon preserving as much of her integrity as he could.

When the Suffolk grand jury began hearing evidence in the middle of August, Muldoon called Savi to testify. Under Muldoon's discreet probing, she acknowledged that it was her "custom" to spend evenings in the area of Good Time Charlie's where, about two and a half years earlier, she had been introduced to Robin Benedict, who became a "friend."

The prosecutor produced a check for $2,400 drawn on the account of the Trustees of Tufts College and made out to Savitry Bisram. Savi acknowledged that she had cashed that check on October 14 at the Bank of Boston near Tufts. Robin had picked her up in Randolph; then they drove into town, where they met Bill Douglas at the bank. He handed her the $2,400 check and said, "Cash it," but the bank wouldn't accept her signature. Douglas then went with her to the service desk and showed his own ID. A girl wrote down the information, Savi signed the check, and they finally succeeded in cashing it. When she got to the car, she handed the money to Robin, who handed it to Douglas.

Muldoon showed her a request for a travel advance for which the $2,400 check had been cut. Her "signature" was in the lower right-hand corner. Savi said she had never signed a request form. She insisted, furthermore, that she knew nothing about computer programming and had never taken any business trips at the university's expense.

Regarding the $9,000 check, which she acknowledged having cashed a week later, on October 19, she explained how she and Robin again met Douglas outside the Bank of Boston. Douglas handed her the check, and the two of them went directly to the service desk. This time the girl called her supervisor, who okayed the check. When they got back to the car, she once again gave money to Robin, who handed it to Douglas.

Muldoon then called a series of financial officers, who testified to the flow of funds in and out of Robin Benedict's own accounts. On October 14, the day Savi had cashed the $2,400 check, Robin deposited $7,290 to her savings account at the Natick Trust Company. Then, on October 20, the day after Savi cashed the $9,000 check, Robin opened a savings account at the Framingham Trust Company and deposited that exact amount.

A little over two weeks later, on December 3, Robin withdrew the balances in both accounts, amounting to some $14,500 in treasurer's checks. That same day she went to the Medford Savings Bank and took out a mortgage in the amount of $25,000 for the house on Cliff Street. This testimony strongly suggested that Douglas had made his last-ditch raid on Tufts to help Robin make a down payment on her new house. All in all, Muldoon felt he could make a case for Douglas's having stolen about $50,000 of the $67,000. (The balance could not be substantiated with photos and canceled checks.) For the purposes of indictment, he managed to reduce Douglas's freewheeling moral turpitude into ten separate schemes of larceny, which included falsifying expenses, authorizing checks and phony travel advances, altering vouchers, stealing equipment, and, not least, ordering "biological collection units" under false pretenses.

The Suffolk grand jury would consider these charges for well over two months before coming to a vote.

DURING the week following its Toyota scoop, station WCVB decided to do an in-depth report on the Douglas case for its evening magazine, "Chronicle." An editor named Jerry Kirschenbaum approached Ron Gollobin and asked if he would do the honors. Gollobin, observing the media frenzy the Toyota had provoked, was becoming a little worried that his best material would leak into the public domain. He told Kirschenbaum, "I'll give you the information. You write it."

Gollobin asked his wife to messenger the whole Landry file over to the station. He had intended for her to send it directly to him so that he could sort through it and pass along only the material he could afford to part with. She misunderstood and sent everything, including all forty pages of notes from their twelve-hour interview with Landry, directly to Kirschenbaum. Assisted by this unexpected windfall, Kirschenbaum took the myriad details of the case and fashioned them into a remarkably rich and coherent account. So skillfully did he juxtapose the Douglases' own accounts of their movements on the fateful weekend with the credit card tolls that there could be little doubt in a viewer's mind that William and Nancy had spent the early morning hours of Sunday, March 6, on the phone to one another in apparently urgent conversation.

When John Kivlan saw the "Chronicle" account, he did a slow burn. Since the discovery of the Toyota, the investigation had been plagued by press leaks, but this was by far the worst. WCVB had revealed the details of the Douglases' confidential statements. Worse still were excerpts from a long interview with Paul Landry sitting in his yard spilling details about the search of the Douglas house. Someone tuning in cold would think that Landry was still assigned to the investigation and that the district attorney's office had given him permission to speak.

Perhaps most damaging from a public relations standpoint, however, was that the broadcast questioned the propriety of calling the children to testify. Gollobin had sought out one of Boston's most flamboyant and controversial defense attorneys, Thomas C. Troy, who railed grandiloquently against those who would reach into the hallowed sanctum of the family and pluck out infants for persecution. "This is not Russia," he fumed. "Ya cannot expect 'em to go in and testify against their parents!"

By now it was late July. There was still no word from the Supreme Judicial Court on the fate of the Three Juveniles. John and Shirley Benedict were bitter at the delay. The Douglas children, they were convinced, knew something and were not being allowed to tell it. They found the situation intolerable. "It is incredible," Anthony DiFruscia mused to the *Globe*, "that the chief suspect in a murder (investigation) is able to control what may be the key witness. . . ."

On August 1 John and Shirley Benedict filed a motion calling for the Douglas children to be taken from their parents and placed in the care of a guardian ad litem,—an attorney or counselor who looks after the interests of those who are too old, too young, or too infirm to look after themselves.

DiFruscia had consulted with several psychiatrists, who told him that if a child witnessed a parent committing murder in the home, the resulting trauma would qualify as "psychological abuse," ample grounds for the state to intervene. While expressing sympathy for the young Douglases, the Benedicts' motion raised the possibility that they might also want to "unburden" themselves of certain terrible knowledge. It was critical to the children's mental health that they be given a truly independent attorney with whom they could discuss such things. If, in fact, these children were exposed to such a heinous crime, the Benedicts concluded pointedly, "their parents may not be able to provide them with the necessary care and protection to insure their rights to normal mental, spiritual and moral development."

The SJC denied the Benedicts' motion, but three days after it was filed, the court came back with its own, long-awaited decision. The justices ruled four to three that while a child might not be forced to reveal the contents of a confidential conversation with a parent, he had "no privilege to refuse to testify as to what he may have seen or heard." A parent, furthermore, enjoyed no right to assert such a privilege on his child's behalf.

It was an unequivocal victory for the Commonwealth. John Kivlan wasted no time in calling the children's attorney, Brian McMenimen, to inform him that he would be summoning the young Douglases to appear before the grand jury. McMenimen should also see that the children were at the Norfolk County Courthouse for a hearing where a guardian ad litem would be appointed to replace him.

This appointment was to be made by a superior-court justice named Roger Donahue, who happened to be assigned to Dedham during the second week of August. Judge Donahue had a reputation for delicacy in domestic matters. He boasted a background that was markedly profamily. His father, Judge Frank J. Donahue—known to his contemporaries as Daisy—had served on the superior-court bench for forty years, longer than any jurist in the Commonwealth's history. During his tenure he became known for three things—his harsh sentences (by the time one expired, the felon would be pushing up daisies), his wit ("I have always loved the law," he was reputed to have said. "Some may think it is monotonous hearing the same things every day, but there is always something new—usually perjury"), and, not least, his concern for children. Fathers who deserted their children were anathema to old Daisy, and he went after them with a vengeance, sending nonsupporters up the river for stiff terms. This fraternity of convicts was known informally as the Daddy-Owe Club.

Judge Roger Donahue—who though well into his fifties was referred to as the Kid—was now in the position of unseating the children's present attorney, a man whom they had apparently come to trust. It was an act in which he took little pleasure. He had known young McMenimen's father, who was also a judge. He was acquainted with the son only slightly, but well enough to know that he was a friend of O'Connell's and that there might be, if not an actual conflict, then a "perceptual" one. Donahue decided to appoint in McMenimen's stead an attorney who had served as guardian in several child custody matters. Stephen Keefe was a retired major general in the Air Force, and the judge, an old Air Force man himself, considered Keefe's background and integrity to be above reproach. Best of all, Keefe was a member of the civil bar and so had no apparent ties to O'Connell.

On the day Donahue announced Keefe's appointment, the Douglas children were not in the courtroom. They had chosen to remain outside on the courthouse steps, where Keefe later joined them to tell them the outcome. The extent of their displeasure was revealed one week later, when O'Connell and McMenimen managed to get an emergency hearing before a single justice of the Supreme Judicial Court. McMenimen reported to Justice Ruth Abrams that the children emphatically did not want a guardian ad litem.

O'Connell now complained to the court that no one had consulted William or Nancy Douglas before Keefe was named, and they wanted his appointment revoked. Justice Abrams demurred, however, saying she did not have the power to do that. The matter was referred quickly to the full bench, which declined to halt the children's next appearance before the grand jury, which was scheduled for the following day.

That morning Nancy Douglas and her children arrived at the courthouse in a borrowed 1980 Oldsmobile sedan. When Nancy pulled around to the back entrance, the children, who had been crouched out of sight on the floor, sprinted "whooping and hollering" past reporters and TV cameras to the door of the courthouse. For the next six hours the children, who were dressed shabbily in T-shirts and blue jeans, were sequestered in an upstairs conference room where, the *Herald* later reported, they spent the next six hours "munching on sandwiches and pizza and huddling with their lawyers."

Just before 3:00 P.M. Billy was called to the grand jury. He stayed, by the *Herald*'s accounting, only four minutes and thirty-nine seconds before returning "grim-faced" to the waiting room. John spent two minutes and thirty-nine seconds and Pammy only two minutes in the grand-jury room before emerging, "her eyes brimming with tears."

It was clear to reporters, who hovered in the corridors jotting down the most mundane details hoping that one might shed some light on the comportment of the Douglas children, that they had not been persuaded to say very much, if anything at all.

After Pamela's brief appearance, the grand-jury foreman, a middle-aged secretary named Dorothy Brennan, reported confidentially to Judge Donahue that the children would give only their names and addresses. Donahue then summoned the children into his office. The details of his conversation with them were never made public. The judge would later say only that he explained to them the importance of the supreme court's order and that they had a duty to testify. He suggested that they confer with Mr. Keefe before their next grand-jury appearance, which was scheduled for three days later, on Friday, August 19.

Stephen Keefe did manage to speak to his charges, but his urgings were in vain. When they returned to Dedham on Friday, they were even less talkative than before.

The grand jury was now running out of patience with the young Douglases. It had asked the district attorney's office to take any steps necessary to persuade them to testify. That extended to their being confined in a "suitable facility." Hoping to head off this drastic measure, Donahue called the children in for another chat. This time he reportedly took a sterner line, explaining to the three what it meant to be held in contempt. They could be fined or possibly even imprisoned. The Douglas children maintained their stubborn silence.

Over the next two weeks Kivlan called the Douglas children twice more without success. During that same period—unbeknownst to the prosecutor or the grand jury—Billy, Pammy, and Johnny were undergoing an interrogation of quite a different sort.

During the three weeks since his appointment as guardian ad litem, Keefe had managed to arrive at an uneasy détente with Nancy Douglas. He had persuaded her to let the children speak to a psychiatrist, Dr. Sheldon Zigelbaum, whose evaluations might be useful in case of an appeal. Dr. Zigelbaum had two one-hour sessions with the children. On the latter occasion he also spoke with Nancy for about fifteen minutes. The psychiatrist then summarized his findings in an affidavit:

My clinical evaluation of these children demonstrates that they are all now showing signs of a severe anxiety disorder including disorders of sleep, frightening intrusive thoughts, inability to focus and concentrate on their day to day lives in a manner appropriate for their age groups, a growing lack of concern about their personal surroundings and personal appearance stemming from their level of anxiety, a firm unremitting sense that the actions of the state are frightening them, dividing their family structure and asking that they go against their natural instincts as part of an intact, caring family unit.

The publicity surrounding these three children has caused them to withdraw from normal peer and social relationships. They now feel insecure when separated and feel they are most safe when within their own family unit. An anonymous threatening phone call made to the children, announcing that if the children did not testify that one of them would be killed, is a consequence of their identities being available to the public in general.

(The incident to which Zigelbaum referred had occurred the evening of August 30. The phone rang and when Pammy answered, a woman caller asked for "the professor." Pammy reportedly told the caller that her father was not at home. The woman then said, "Well, you tell him this. Unless one of you comes up and admits to the murder, one of you is going to die." Pammy started screaming and hung up.)

These children have already discovered that their experience of a police investigation is frightening and "unfair." They have heard their father called a "murderer" by police while in their home. They have heard the police distort "factual testimony" so that their trust in authority figures is now corroded. . . .

Without . . . relief of stress, my prognosis is that the children's condition will worsen, their anxiety disorder will exacerbate, further, they will all require long-term psychotherapeutic intervention rather than crisis intervention which may be successful at this point in time and the family's integrity as a family may be injured beyond repair.

In early September, Keefe took the psychiatrist's affidavit and appended it to an appeal of the SJC's decision, which he then filed with the U.S. Supreme Court. As a precautionary measure he also asked the high state court for a stay of any further appearances pending the Supreme Court's decision. That motion was denied, and Keefe appealed that ruling, too, to the Supreme Court.

The plight of the Douglas children, meanwhile, was arousing increasing public sympathy. Despite its allegiance to "the missing beauty," the *Boston Herald* could not resist exploiting the compassion value of the three denim-clad urchins who ran in and out of the grand-jury room, "eyes brimming with tears."

Since Attorney Troy's "This is not Russia" tirade on the "Chronicle" broadcast, others had joined in the protest. This included the head of the Massachusetts Civil Liberties Union, who gave a TV interview protesting the "heavy-handedness" of the Norfolk district attorney.

The CLU's attack gave District Attorney Delahunt pause. He prided himself on his good standing among liberals, and the fact that both civil liberties and profamily contingents were up in arms demonstrated the possibility that public sentiment would be aroused in a backlash against the state. The DA's next move against the children would have to be undertaken with extreme caution. Delahunt met privately with Roger Donahue to review the options. Although the judge had what he later termed a "personal reluctance" to cite the children for contempt, he was nonetheless prepared to carry out his duty if they remained in violation of the court order. He could find them guilty of criminal contempt and either fine them or sentence them to serve a specified period of time as punishment. Or he could deem their recalcitrance civil contempt, in which case he could order them detained until they complied.

If they were to be jailed, the two men agreed, it should be under the most humane conditions, in a juvenile facility perhaps. Delahunt had conferred with his office's Family Services Unit, which said that the children could be held in custody for as long as the court ordered in a detention center in Boston. There they would not be forced to mingle with other juvenile detainees, or they might be kept in a foster home, where—removed from the influence of their parents—they might develop a more trusting relationship with their guardian ad litem. *Then,* perhaps, the DA's office could work discreetly through Keefe to elicit written statements from the children, obviating the need for them to make any more tearful visits to the grand-jury room.

Delahunt mulled over these options and decided for the time being to do nothing. He had asked a caseworker from his Family Services Unit to try to visit the Douglas home to see what condition this "intact caring family unit" was actually in. Perhaps relations were so strained that William and Nancy were ready to separate. Perhaps Nancy would turn on Bill, or Bill on Nancy. Perhaps whatever hold the Douglases had on their children would also loosen, and someone would break silence.

District Attorney Delahunt felt that the Commonwealth's best hope lay in the passage of time.

THE ARREST

WORDS could hardly describe the mortification which poor Miss Cynthia Cajka felt when, on the Monday after the silver Toyota was found, a desk clerk showed her Bill Douglas's photo in the *Boston Herald*. It was the Berkeley Residence's God-given mission to shelter women, particularly young women who hadn't the cunning to protect themselves against the evils of the city. But now Douglas, who had been hired as night clerk charged with keeping a lookout for danger, stood accused of murdering a twenty-one-year-old girl.

Miss Cajka knew that Douglas must never be allowed back into the building. He was not due to return to work until the weekend, so she had some time to maneuver. The following morning she requested an urgent meeting at the main building on Clarendon Street, where she confided the problem to the personnel director, Jean Webbert. Douglas had a contract. Could they legally fire him? Webbert relayed this ticklish problem to the personnel committee, which, after hasty deliberation, decided that Douglas, who had not been convicted of any crime, could not be fired. He could, however, be suspended.

That very day Miss Cajka called Douglas to tell him he was being temporarily relieved of duty. He seemed to be expecting this call. The only thing he said was "Fine." To make the break official, the director sent him a letter confirming that he was suspended immediately because of "adverse publicity" surrounding his pending investigation. When those inquiries had been concluded, she assured him, the residence would review his employment status.

343

Miss Cajka had handled this matter as discreetly as she knew how, and now she earnestly hoped that it had been laid to rest. Her hopes were dashed when she received a call from Lieutenant James Sharkey, who wanted to make an appointment to speak with Elizabeth Sanborn. A detective at the Sharon Police Department had turned up a complaint which Sanborn had filed on July 14 saying that Douglas had taken her car.

The following morning Sharkey and Trooper Brian Howe visited the Berkeley Residence. Miss Cajka made them comfortable in her office, then summoned Sanborn, who gave a complete and enthusiastic account of her misadventures with Douglas and the Gran Torino. Where was the car now? Sharkey asked. Sanborn replied that she had given it to her friend Ann Marie's boyfriend, a fellow named John Vargas. Sharkey took down Vargas's address in East Boston, then dispatched a police chemist to give the Gran Torino the once-over.

Douglas's intense, if erratic, interest in Sanborn's car caused the detectives to suspect that he might have wanted it to transport the body. When he had first approached Sanborn about buying it, Robin had already been missing for three months. It was possible, however, that he wanted to move her from one hiding place to another and needed a vehicle that would not attract attention. Sanborn reported that Bette Lou had been returned with a bent gear shift. She had also detected a certain "fishy smell."

Sharkey's chemist could find no evidence of blood or tissue and, in checking the odometer, discovered that the car had not been driven any great distance. When the tests proved negative, Sharkey abandoned this tack and put the Gran Torino incident out of his mind.

Not so the ladies of the Berkeley Residence.

The news of Douglas's alleged atrocities—followed so soon by the visit of detectives—had lent a tinge of danger to life at the Y, which, for all its gentility, was rather drab. Betty Sanborn, Miss Thawley, and their friends were at once horrified and thrilled by the thought of having had a madman in their midst. The prospect of having been witnesses, however peripherally, to a crime imbued them with a sense of extraordinary importance.

Every night after dinner, which they customarily took together in the residence dining hall, they met to discuss the matter at length. On these occasions they usually managed to work one another up into a frenzy of delicious fright. One of the ladies had seen Douglas just recently on the Green Line. He had looked the other way and gotten off the train at the first possible moment. Another had spotted him—or so she imagined—on Park Street. It was incredible to Miss Thawley and her chums that this man, who stood accused of so many heinous crimes, was still apparently allowed to roam at large. That the majority of residents had once considered him kind, considerate, and generally innocuous was now forgotten in nightly orgies of denunciation. Sanborn recalled how she had always gotten "wicked bad vibes" from him. Miss Thawley, who had once read an article about serial killers, proclaimed that they were generally over forty, successful at their careers, and unhappy at home. Douglas seemed to fit the profile. The fact that he had lost his temper with Sanborn seemed to confirm his homicidal bent. That he had tried to stiff her on the car provided further testimony to his innate depravity. It was like a bit of Scripture Miss Thawley was fond of quoting, "If you sin in the small things, you'll sin in the large."

Since the detectives' visit, the ladies were convinced that Douglas's dealings with Sanborn lay at the very heart of this case. It was entirely possible, they felt, that he might now try to get at her and "stop her testimony." So they made a pact to travel, whenever possible, in groups of two or three. This informal arrangement led them to form a "protective society," which rapidly evolved into a "secret society" known as the Agatha Christie Crimestoppers Club.

This was the idea of Miss Thawley, who besides being a very devout woman was an amateur detective. She was an avid reader of Sir Arthur Conan Doyle and Agatha Christie, having inherited a complete set of Christie's mysteries from her mother's cousin. Missing persons held a particular fascination for Miss Thawley, who had researched the career of Amelia Earhart and concluded that the aviatrix's disappearance was due to heart failure during her final landing approach. She had postulated this theory in a scholarly—albeit unpublished—paper entitled "The Heart of Earhart."

Now that an honest-to-goodness mystery had washed up on her own doorstep, Miss Thawley could hardly resist the impulse to do some sleuthing. She and her fellow Crimestoppers were doubly inspired by the $10,-000 reward offered by the missing girl's parents. They would solve the crime and divide the money equally.

As a secret society must have the proper accoutrements, Miss Thawley designed official T-shirts, white with the insignia ACC in red lettering. She held a rite of initiation wherein she inducted each of the seven members into the Crimestoppers by tapping them on the shoulder with a penknife. Miss Thawley, naturally, was "president." Betty Sanborn was "prime minister." Miss Deborah Woodman was "secretary," and Miss Pamela Anderson was designated "superspy." Since Pamela was blind, most people thought she was deaf too, and she could sit stone still in the lobby, hands resting on her white cane, and overhear the conversations around her. In these perilous times the Agatha Christie Crimestoppers felt that no one was above suspicion.

The ACC held its meeting in the downstairs lobby until the baleful glances of resident personnel drove them up to the mezzanine. They finally took to convening in Miss Thawley's room to review the "evidence." On the day before the detectives were scheduled to arrive, Miss Thawley had prowled through the premises looking for clues. In a linen closet on the sixth floor, she found a deep porcelain sink with a dark red stain in the bottom of it. It turned out to be rust. In another closet she found a dirty novel, but didn't pay much attention to it. One of the maintenance men was rumored to hole up in the rest room with those things. Near another one of the sinks, however, she found a razor and a piece of bloody tissue with dark hair on it. Careful not to get her fingerprints on anything, Miss Thawley sealed the items in sandwich bags and filed them in a bookcase in her room.

The Crimestoppers had no doubt that the bloody tissue and razor related somehow to Bill Douglas. In fact, every inexplicable occurrence at the Berkeley Residence was elevated to the status of a clue. Miss Thawley recalled how one day she had gone across the street to a convenience store to buy plastic trash bags. Her mother was visiting, and she wanted to clean up a bit. When she got back to her room, however, she discovered there were only five bags in a purported box of ten. Had Douglas stolen the rest? Around the same time there had been a dog barking at some trash sitting on the sidewalk behind the residence. When a resident got near one of the bags, she discerned a "terrible smell." Another resident had picked a long, tan trench coat out of the trash. The inside was heavily bloodstained. On still another occasion, a young music student who was late for class bustled out of the back of the residence to see Douglas trying to open the hatchback of his blue Toyota. In one hand he had a filled trash bag and, although he was struggling with a key in the lock, he would not put the bag down. The meaning of these isolated occurrences was not clear, but the Crimestoppers were sure that if they persisted, the pieces would eventually come together like those of a great puzzle.

Miss Thawley, who had started keeping a scrapbook of newsclippings, had found an account in the *New York Post* which suggested that Douglas had "hacked [Benedict] to bits and buried the pieces along a trail from Boston and New York to Washington." A spokesman of the Norfolk County District Attorney's Office had been quoted as saying, "With an expert knowledge of anatomy, a person could easily dissect [a body] and hide the pieces." This seemed to support a theory, already evolving in the minds of the Crimestoppers, that Douglas had applied for the job as night clerk with the express intent of disposing of Robin Benedict's body within the Berkeley Residence. It would be simple enough, they reasoned, for him to have brought her in piece by piece in that bulging briefcase. (Pepsi cans, indeed!) Or perhaps one night he had smuggled her in in her entirety and hidden her in one of the empty rooms. As front-desk clerk, he had only to look at the guest register to see which rooms were vacant. He had enjoyed access to all the keys. The Crimestoppers recalled his odd habit of hauling ice up and down the elevators on a dolly. Perhaps he had preserved Miss Benedict and was shuffling her from room to room as new tenants arrived. The point of all this activity was to hide her until such time as he could get possession of Betty Sanborn's car and dispose of the body for good.

Inasmuch as he did not get the car, the Crimestoppers reasoned, the body must still be on the premises. For the next few weeks, they poked surreptitiously around the residence, searching empty rooms, linen closets, and ice chests for a concealed corpse. All to no avail. Miss Thawley, however, thought it might be a public service to inform Lieutenant Sharkey of the "evidence" she and her cohorts had been uncovering. She wrote several letters. All of which he received and promptly discarded. Sharkey, who had been besieged by flakes and fortune hunters spurred on by the reward, felt that the ladies at the Y were hitting on only four out of six cylinders, and he did not want to encourage their fantasies.

LATE IN AUGUST, Anthony DiFruscia announced mysteriously to the Herald that "an agent" of the Benedicts would be conducting a search for Robin Benedict's body within a ten- to fifteen-mile radius of the Douglas home in Sharon. This agent was, in fact, a psychic named Edith Locke—a dark, voluptuous woman with wide, bright lips who billed herself as a "criminal astrologer."

Locke had drawn up Robin's "birth chart," which showed, among other things, that it was her "time to die." The psychic was also getting readings that the body was in the "Sharon dump" and that it was "hidden but not buried."

Their hopes once again raised, the Benedicts assembled a search party of friends and relatives who would agree to accompany the psychic to Sharon on Sunday, August 28. Once again they called upon Paul Landry, asking him if he would come along to clear things with the Sharon Police Department.

Landry later claimed that he didn't want anything to do with this expedition but that he did it to "keep [the Benedicts] happy." His deal with Gollobin had fallen through shortly after the "Chronicle" broadcast, and he was casting around for a new writer. It would not hurt to do a favor that would keep the Benedicts in his debt.

That Sunday a search party of twenty-five people left in a caravan from Methuen to Sharon, where they were met by a news team from Channel 4. Edith Locke, who cut a flamboyant figure in an enormous pink peasant blouse, was photographed circumnavigating the cul-de-sac at Sandy Ridge Circle. After inspecting the terrain, the psychic announced, "She was dead by 11:00. That was all hogwash about 11:30. She was dead in her car right here. There's Mercury through this whole thing. With Uranus. And it was very sudden. It wasn't planned. . . ."

The search party and camera crew milled around the cul-de-sac for about twenty minutes. (If the Douglases were inside the house observing these goings-on, they did not reveal themselves.) Finally, the Benedict party moved on to the Sharon Police Station, where Landry assured the personnel on duty that his companions were not troublemakers or trespassers but a bereaved family hoping to explore the town dump. By now, however, the psychic was getting intimations that the body wasn't in the dump, as she had originally thought, but in a place "where cannon balls are made." This seemed to suggest the Old Forge historic site on the shores of Lake Massapoag. The search party wandered through the maze of hiking trails for much of the afternoon without results. Locke could not seem to pinpoint a location. (The psychic complained that Trooper Landry's cynicism had spoiled the atmosphere.)

Over the weeks that followed this outing, Locke would come up with another intimation, that Robin had been "frozen" and stored somewhere at Tufts University. Locke was not the first to propose the theory that Douglas had somehow preserved Robin. In June a tipster had called the Benedicts informing them that several fish companies kept frozen food lockers on Atlantic Avenue. Inasmuch as Douglas had made a call from nearby South Station, the informant thought it was possible he had stored the body there. The Benedicts had relayed this to the Central Secret Service Bureau, which promised to check it out. Like so many other leads, it led to nothing.

Shirley Benedict harbored hopes, born perhaps of grief and frustration, that Robin would be found in some whole and recognizable form and that she could look once again into her daughter's face. She was haunted by Douglas's comments the day they all met at Boston Municipal Court. If he had the power to make someone disappear by putting a chemical on the lips, would he not also have the means to preserve a corpse perfectly intact? There were a couple of reasons why Shirley and John believed Douglas might have been disinclined to bury Robin. They, like the Gray

House investigators, felt that he might have been so obsessed with her that he had transformed her into an effigy of her former self to visit and venerate. But he might also have been aware of Robin's horror of being interred. Several years earlier, when her paternal grandfather died, the members of the family all went down to the funeral home to pay their respects. She had touched her papa's cheek and said, "Look. He's still got his wrinkles." John Benedict recalled being proud that she had seemed unafraid of death. But then she remarked that *she* never wanted to be put in the ground. She didn't like the idea of worms' eating her. John and Shirley thought she had perhaps told this to Douglas, who, out of deference to her wishes, might have kept her, as Locke put it, "frozen at Tufts."

Attorney DiFruscia, meanwhile, was nursing a pet theory of his own. He believed that after killing Robin, Douglas had brought her body to Tufts, not to freeze it, but to incinerate it. The second psychic, Marie Stephenson, had made reference to a "furnace," which could be loosely construed as an incinerator. Throughout July and August, DiFruscia had tried to interest the media in this scenario. He called Ron Gollobin and postulated that Douglas had carried the body in through the back door and stashed it in the morgue. Then perhaps he carried her up to the incinerator. But Gollobin, who was wearying of intrigue, didn't rise to the bait. DiFruscia also called Mike Frisby, who had given him his home number, and ran the same theory past him. But Frisby had begun backing off from DiFruscia, knowing that the *Globe* was not likely to publish such bizarre speculation.

The incinerator theory, however, found an enthusiastic advocate in the person of John P. Foley, a reporter for radio station WCCM, in Lawrence. Foley was young, aggressive, and eager to make a name for himself. The Benedict story therefore held obvious attractions for him. Here was a local girl who was getting big-time Boston coverage. Foley had managed to win the confidence of Shirley Benedict by feeding her tidbits of information he had managed to turn up. She, in turn, told him things that she trusted him not to publish—and she leaked him a few things that he could go with, like the contract Robin had signed with the Human Nutrition Research Center the preceding October. At a time when Tufts was claiming it had never employed Robin Benedict, a signed authorized agreement was a nice little scoop.

Shirley had told Foley that when she disappeared, Robin had been wearing a diamond in one ear. It was also possible that she had been wearing gold shell earrings. These things had never been found, but if she had indeed been incinerated, Foley reasoned, her jewelry would have survived the flames. The reporter did a little checking around and found that there were three incinerators at the medical and veterinary schools. He went over to the medical school one day and mingled for a while in the hallways with the crowd of students starting the new term. He discovered in the process of this reconnoitering mission that the incinerator closest to Douglas's lab was on the fourth floor of Stearns, one building over and one floor down. From M&V one could reach Stearns easily through a connecting hallway, but the fourth floor, which had been dubbed the "animal farm," was under continual quarantine. One could not reach it by stair, and the elevator did not stop on that floor without the turn of a special key. Other than that, security seemed remarkably lax. Once, at two in the morning, Foley managed to slip past the security guard, who was drowsing over a newspaper, and get on the elevator. Then he managed to slip out again without being seen.

The ease with which Foley, a total stranger, managed to navigate the labyrinth of the medical school suggested to DiFruscia that Douglas, a man who knew the terrain, could have made it in and out without being seen. He might be aware of passageways that only a habitué of the campus could know.

(Douglas's position and duties had never entitled him to have a key to the "animal farm." Most insiders at the medical school, however, knew how to jimmy the elevator lock at the fourth floor. As one descended from the fifth floor, one simply turned the elevator off and then back on. It stopped automatically on the next level.)

It seemed to DiFruscia that the Norfolk investigators were giving short shrift to the Tufts angle. So in mid-September he sent a letter to the district attorney, demanding to know what investigation had been made into the movement of William Douglas in and out of the medical school between the hours of 11:00 P.M. and 1:30 A.M. on March 5 and 6. What areas other than Douglas's laboratory had actually been searched? Had the investigators looked into Tufts's procedures for embalming and burying cadavers?

"I would like very much to meet with you," DiFruscia concluded, "because I would prefer to work with you rather than to point out these inconsistencies publicly. With your assistance, I believe I will be able to have Miss Benedict declared legally dead through the probate court system."

In fact, the Norfolk investigators had not yet checked the Tufts incinerators. When Peter Casey had brought up the cremation prospect at a couple of the early Gray House sessions, it had been shot down so thoroughly that it did not resurface in subsequent discussions. Kivlan seemed to get testy when the subject arose. A good part of his aversion to the theory was that embracing it meant accepting once and for all that there would be no body. He liked the idea of Douglas's knowing that the dragnet continued unabated. Beyond these tactical considerations, however, he felt that no matter how bad Tufts security was, it would have been impossible for Douglas to drag 120 pounds of dead weight into the building and up to the fourth floor unobserved. The fact that security officers had orders to evict Douglas on sight made it doubly unlikely that he would risk a shot at the incinerator. It was possible that he had carried dismembered portions one or two pieces at a time, but that would increase his exposure dramatically.

The district attorney was leery of being drawn into the incinerator scheme for another reason. DiFruscia, he suspected, was hoping to establish that Tufts had been negligent in allowing Douglas access to the facilities where he could dispose of Robin. Tony DiFruscia clearly had his eye on a large judgment from the university, and Delahunt had no intention of being enlisted in that enterprise. Although DiFruscia seemed to be suggesting that it would be in the state's interest to help him get Robin declared dead, the district attorney scoffed at the notion. Even if Robin were declared dead under civil law, a criminal court would not recognize the ruling. Delahunt did not respond to DiFruscia's letter.

JOHN FOLEY, meanwhile, was continuing to learn what he could about the process of incineration. He had talked to a pathologist from the state Department of Environmental Quality Engineering, who told him that if one took scrapings off the walls of the oven and analyzed them, it was possible to tell if someone had incinerated human tissue there. In order to burn human waste, Tufts needed a license, but Foley hadn't been able to locate one among the folds of bureaucracy. If he could get to that incinerator and take samples which turned up human tissue, he could establish, at least, that a person had been cremated there illegally. And if, perchance, he could find the diamond . . .

Foley decided he would try to breach the battlements of the "animal farm."

Foley was careful never to suggest that he undertook this mission at the request of his station or Tony DiFruscia, who was in fact the station's attorney. As he later explained it, he received "tacit approval" from his news director to take a vacation day and see what he could find out. When Foley told DiFruscia what he intended to do, DiFruscia reportedly thought it was "great." But, Foley would hasten to add—and DiFruscia would later verify—"It certainly wasn't his idea."

On the morning of Thursday, September 22, Foley put his plan into action. He got himself up to look like a college student in dungarees and cotton shirt. He carried his notebook on top of a couple of college texts which he had borrowed from his brother—a business major—and stuck a tape recorder in his hip pocket.

At about 9:30 A.M. he entered the Medical and Veterinary Building. Crossing over to Stearns, he boarded the elevator, hoping to find some congenial passenger who could secure him access to the fourth floor.

Foley rode the elevators for two hours, without success until at last a maintenance man stepped on board. He was carrying a ring full of keys.

"Tell me," Foley asked, "how do I get up to the fourth floor to see Professor Hamilton?"

"Fourth floor?" the maintenance man said. "I can get you there." With that he inserted a key, and the door opened onto four. For twenty minutes Foley wandered aimlessly through the corridors. Past a sign that read "quarantine." Past rooms with cages of rats. Some were being used for hideous experiments. One, Foley noticed, was pinned spread-eagled on his back. Above him was a jar of liquid that was falling in steady, rhythmic drops to the creature's liver. But nowhere in this chamber of horrors could Foley find the incinerator.

At length he ran into another maintenance man, to whom he explained that a Professor Hamilton had sent him up to get ashes for a carbon study. The second maintenance man was as helpful as the first, directing him to the incinerator room, which, Foley discovered, was kept unlocked. The incinerator itself was a tall metal vault with two doors, one above the other. The top one was apparently for stowing the carcass to be burned. Foley measured it with his hands. It was about two feet square, large enough to accommodate a human body. The lower door was for shoveling out the ashes. Climbing down on his hands and knees, he opened it. There were flames above, and it was "hotter than hell." Foley took a teaspoon he had brought with him and began scraping ashes off the bottom of the vault. He put these into an insulated, two-ply ice cream bag.

As Foley was absorbed in this anxious labor, someone kicked his feet! He turned in terror to see a very stern man in a Tufts security uniform staring down at him. Sergeant Bruce Govostes took Foley downstairs for questioning. Foley's story did not hold up long. There was, in fact, no Professor Hamilton. After receiving a stern warning, he was released.

Although Foley came back to Lawrence empty-handed, the very fact that he had been able to get into the incinerator excited DiFruscia's imagination. Once again he began pressing his suit to the DA's office, charging that its apparent disregard of the crematorium was indicative of a "slipshod" investigation. Almost seven months had passed, and the body still had not been found. Douglas had not been indicted. The Benedicts were unhappy with this apparent lack of progress. DiFruscia was now demanding a meeting with the district attorney to be "briefed" on the status of the case.

Kivlan himself did not relish the idea of such a meeting. He was still convinced that anything his investigators told the Benedicts was likely to end up as tomorrow's headline. But the advantages of confidentiality had to be weighed against those of community relations. The Benedicts were eager to be a part of the case, and the more isolated they felt, the more they relied upon psychics, private eyes, Paul Landry, and now Attorney DiFruscia, who Kivlan felt was actively fanning the flames of their frustration. He agreed to a meeting on Tuesday, September 27, at the offices of the district attorney.

That morning DiFruscia brought his clients down to Dedham in a chauffeured Cadillac limousine. As the Benedicts and their entourage were ushered into the district attorney's library, both sides did their best to establish a civil tone for the ensuing encounter. This fragile goodwill deteriorated quickly, however, when DiFruscia began presenting a set of demands. Why hadn't investigators checked the incinerator? Why hadn't the DA's office arrested Douglas? he asked. Kivlan, whose irascible nature was ill-suited to these missions of diplomacy, interrupted DiFruscia to inform him that it was not his position to be making demands, then went even further, accusing him of "pandering to the media . . . misleading these people and showboating." At this tense juncture William Delahunt walked into the library and managed to smooth ruffled feathers. The district attorney gave the Benedicts a quick update on the case. Then he explained that while he was sensitive to their grief, the investigation had to be guided by principles that transcended personal feelings. As much as they might want to see William Douglas behind bars, it was not their prerogative to demand his arrest. It was up to the Commonwealth, and only the Commonwealth, to decide who was going to be arrested and when.

AT THE MOMENT Delahunt delivered his lecture to the Benedicts, the prospect of arresting William Douglas still seemed far away. After seven months of intensive investigation, Norfolk still had no body. It could not get to key witnesses, and the FBI's forensic tests had yet to turn up a smoking gun. This impasse, however, was broken by a series of rapid-fire developments.

During the second week in October, Agent Perrotta got back to John Kivlan with exciting news. After comparing the new batch of known writing with the questioned signatures, he was now confident that the signature on the Amtrak ticket did indeed belong to William Douglas. He had, furthermore, detected enough similarity between the known samples and the Mobil charge to say that Douglas had "probably prepared this signature also."

On the heels of these welcome tidings, the FBI fiber expert who had been studying the thread used to sew the armpit of Douglas's blue shirt, determined that it had the same diameter and chemical composition as that from the large spool which Nancy had turned over to Lieutenant Sharkey the night of the first search. This served to link the bloody shirt even more closely to the Douglas house.

Most exciting, however, were the results of Agent Kearney's latest blood tests. In going over the Toyota's deck mat, he had managed to raise one more marker, an enzyme called phosphoglucomutase, or PGM. The marker in question was PGM 2-1. This could not possibly have come from William Douglas, whose blood was PGM 1-1. For the first time, Kearney had been able to find a marker which eliminated the possibility that *all* of the blood had come from William Douglas.

The grand jury, which had been occupied through most of the late summer with getting the children to testify, had entered a state of suspended animation awaiting a decision from the U.S. Supreme Court. But now John Kivlan felt that, even without the body or the Douglas children, he was in a position go back to the jury and get an indictment on the basis of this powerful new circumstantial evidence. Accordingly, he sent out a barrage of subpoenas summoning over thirty witnesses to appear before the grand jury during the week of October 24.

Dan O'Connell had an inkling that Kivlan was moving in for the kill. The defense attorney was not, of course, privy to the FBI reports which had imbued the Commonwealth with its new optimism, but he could not fail to see something stirring in Dedham. For one thing, both William and Nancy Douglas had been subpoenaed to appear once again before the grand jury. For another, the Suffolk County grand jury had already ceased its deliberations and on October 11 voted to indict William Douglas on sixty-one counts of larceny and filing false expenses.

The Suffolk indictments were predictable, and O'Connell had apparently hoped to manage the damage by arranging for a gentlemanly surrender. It was in his client's best interest to leave the impression of a civilized man who, though hounded unconscionably by the state, could be counted upon to deliver himself into custody. And so, after learning that a warrant had been issued for his arrest, Douglas came into Boston and turned himself in at a precinct station four blocks west of the Combat Zone. He gave his occupation as "driver."

As Douglas was escorted up to Pemberton Square for arraignment, the media had its first opportunity to get a good look at him. Before this time they had only caught glimpses of him bustling in and out of the courthouse in Dedham, his face shielded by briefcase or windbreaker. The one good photo of him, head bowed displaying his wound, had been published repeatedly because it was the only one available. In that shot his face appeared fairly slender as a result of the weight he had lost for Robin's benefit. His large horn-rimmed glasses made him look a bit like Woody Allen. But now Douglas had gained some weight. His face was again round, soft, and childlike. Clad in a blue windbreaker and running shoes, he carried a tiny broken umbrella. The *Herald* observed that he looked "meek and disheveled." In a "feeble, high-pitched voice" he pled innocent to all sixty-one counts. After being released pending a hearing scheduled for three weeks hence, Douglas accompanied by O'Connell made a mad dash down the back steps and across Courthouse Square, pursued by a pack of reporters and news cameras. It was not the altogether dignified conclusion O'Connell might have wished for a gentlemanly surrender, but, all things considered, the day had not gone too badly. William Douglas, who was facing charges which carried a total of 450 years in prison, was free on his own recognizance.

O'Connell, hoping for an equally civilized arrangement with Norfolk, had written to Kivlan, saying that if an indictment were returned, Douglas would surrender. O'Connell was hoping that bail might be set at $25,000, or $2,500 in cash. (One of Douglas's elderly aunts from Lake Placid had sent Nancy Douglas a check in that amount the preceding week.)

Kivlan was so contemptuous of this suggestion that he did not even bother to reply. O'Connell, he felt, was trying to create the impression that his client was somehow too special to be treated like a common suspect. Kivlan intended to emphasize that this was not so. Douglas was accused of the most serious crime in the Commonwealth. When the time came—if it came—he would be led away in cuffs just like any other criminal defendant.

AS THE WEEK of the grand-jury hearings drew nearer, John Kivlan was plagued by a number of worries. Chief among them was the impression that his star witnesses—a suspected pimp and a handful of prostitutes—were likely to make on the all-white, middle-class grand jury. To the average resident of Norfolk County, the Combat Zone was distant and unreal. The characters who inhabited it were fearful creatures of the night. That they had been enlisted as allies by the Commonwealth would not confer upon them automatic credibility. When John Kivlan thought of J.R. and the girls roaming the sedate corridors of the Norfolk County Courthouse, he winced. At best they would appear exotic; at worst they would appear criminal.

To date Kivlan had done his best to keep J.R. Rogers at arm's length. But as the hearings approached, the prosecutor called his prospective witness up to the Gray House for a last-minute briefing. There Kivlan told Rogers point-blank that he thought he knew more than he was telling about certain things, like Joe Murray and the Tufts money. He was convinced that J.R. also knew a good deal more about the hostility that had been building between Robin and Douglas during the final days of their relationship. While it might be embarrassing for him to admit to the Benedicts and the world that he knew about these things, the important thing was the truth.

J.R. Rogers continued to insist that he had told all he knew.

ON THE first morning of hearings, Tuesday, October 25, J.R. showed up at the courthouse alone, clad in a very expensive and conspicuously conservative business suit. Kivlan knew that the defense would try to discredit J.R. right off the bat by bringing up his criminal record. The prosecutor intended to diffuse this assault with a preemptive strike. No sooner had J.R. taken the witness stand than Kivlan bore down on him, asking if he did not have a prior record of arrests. J.R. answered with an unflinching yes. Only one of these, however, resulted in conviction, for which he had received a year's probation.

Kivlan directed his attention to the weeks preceding Robin Benedict's disappearance.

"Did she tell you that Mr. Douglas was making threats about revealing her participation in taking money from Tufts . . . ?"

"Yeah," J.R. replied. ". . . but also that he could get her into trouble because she was a prostitute."

On the night Robin disappeared, J.R. continued, she had gone out to Douglas's house to exchange some of his "papers" for some of her tax forms.

That evening, J.R. said, he arrived home around eight-thirty and was in bed by midnight, at which time the answering service called with two messages. One was from "Joe" about the party in Charlestown. The other was from Robin saying that she was on her way to Joe's. The next day, he called the service and was told that Robin was on the other line saying that she was "going to Longfellow Place." J.R. said that when he questioned the operator a few days later, she had told him that the caller sounded like a man "disguising his voice as a woman."

One of the jurors interrupted J.R. at this point to ask why Robin would have called the answering service rather than dialing home directly. J.R. explained that Robin would normally try the Malden number first; if she got no answer, she'd call the service. If J.R. was correct about Robin's habits, then she would have called home, not the service, sometime before 11:42 P.M. to tell him she was on her way to Charlestown. He had not heard a ring at that hour, suggesting that it was someone other than Robin who made the "Joe from Charlestown" call.

ALL IN ALL, J.R. had acquitted himself admirably. John Kivlan had no faith, however, that Savi Bisram would do nearly so well. After weighing the possible consequences of putting her in the witness stand, he decided against it. "Savi," Kivlan would later remark, "had a head of mush." Her memory for dates was poor and her testimony inconsistent. What she would say to a grand jury might differ substantially from what she would say to a criminal court, giving the defense the opportunity to pick her testimony to pieces. It would be better, Kivlan felt, to save her for the trial. He felt it was absolutely necessary, however, to call Lorna Johnson.

Douglas had reportedly given Lorna his credit card number. If O'Connell picked up on that fact, he would undoubtedly use it to suggest that many of Robin's dubious associates had access to that number and that one couldn't necessarily assume that it was William or Nancy Douglas making the calls along Route 95. Again, Kivlan decided to make a preemptive strike by calling Lorna himself.

Norfolk's first efforts to reach Lorna were unavailing. Brian Howe had called Detective Billy Dwyer, self-styled legend of the Combat Zone, to see if he could use his contacts to get Lorna to come in. In a few days Dwyer reported back to Howe that he had talked to Lorna, who denied ever having had such a conversation with Douglas.

Howe did not believe that he was getting the whole story. Dwyer apparently hated J.R. (at least, J.R. thought so). Dwyer and Douglas were apparently on friendly terms (at least, Douglas had claimed this to Landry). J.R. had been convinced from the start that Douglas was calling Dwyer with tips on Robin and her johns. J.R. also insinuated that there might be some kind of hanky-panky between Dwyer and Robin.

In the months to come Dwyer would deny vehemently that he ever had any sort of romantic dalliance with Robin Benedict. Neither was he a "good friend" of Bill Douglas. Yes, he conceded, he had given Douglas his business card, but that was perfectly appropriate under the circumstances. Douglas seemed to want to get a young girl out of the life—if only to keep her to himself—so why not develop some rapport? You had to develop contacts. You had to work people. The "staties" out in Norfolk, he would grouse, had no idea of what it took to get along in the streets.

Dwyer had, in fact, been furious on learning that Paul Landry had come right into Boston and conducted a search of Robin's trick pad without bothering to inform Vice. That was, at the very least, a breach of professional courtesy. Dwyer had called Landry repeatedly, trying to find out what was happening with the investigation, but the trooper never returned his calls. Dwyer reflected frequently and ruefully upon the night that John Benedict contacted him to say his daughter was missing. Dwyer had casually advised him to report her missing in Malden. He could just as easily have told him to file in Boston, where she kept her trick pads. If Benedict had done that, he—William Dwyer—would now be principal investigator on the Douglas case!

After days of delays Howe finally went down to Charlie's to ask the bouncer if he knew Lorna Johnson. Under ordinary circumstances the bar might not have been so willing to turn one of its girls over, but since Robin Benedict's disappearance there had been a string of troopers, private eyes, reporters, and vice cops poking around for information. The bouncer's job was apparently to get them out of there as quickly as possible. So he pointed to Lorna, a short black girl with a pug nose. Howe walked up to the bar and handed her a subpoena to appear in Dedham on Tuesday, October 25.

On the morning of her appearance, Lorna gave Howe a scrap of paper on which she had written Douglas's credit card number as well as the room number of his Washington Hotel. When Kivlan called her to the witness stand to query her about these notations, he began discreetly, "I don't mean to embarrass you, but were you involved in . . . prostitution activities?"

Lorna, who seemed not embarrassed in the least, replied yes.

The prosecutor directed her attention to the last time she had seen Robin, the evening of March 5.

"Do you have any recollection of talking to her that day?" he asked.

"Like 'hi,' you know," Lorna replied.

"Do you have any memory of what she was wearing that day?"

"A corduroy jacket, like a couple of days that week."

"Now," Kivlan continued, "recalling the night of March 7, which would have been two nights after she disappeared, did you receive a call from William Douglas?"

"Yes," Lorna replied. "He wanted, I think, Indian Debbie. He was leaving calls for Indian Debbie or Nadine all the time, and he told me—he said, 'Sorry to bother you,' real pleasant-like. And then he gave me his credit card number."

By getting Lorna on the record with this account, Kivlan had succeeded in establishing that she could not possibly have been making the calls on Douglas's credit card during the hours after Robin disappeared, because she had not received the number until the following Monday evening.

OF ALL the working girls Kivlan sought to call before the grand jury, the long-legged, red-haired working girl Julie was the most accessible. On the Friday night before the hearings were scheduled to begin, Trooper Rick Zebrasky went warily into Charlie's, where Julie greeted him with a simple "I was expecting you."

The following Tuesday morning when Julie showed up at the court-house with Lorna Johnson, Brian Howe took her into a conference room to question her privately about her association with William Douglas. Julie told him that she had gone out with Douglas twice. The first time was in January or February after Robin had been barred from the Zone. The second was about a week after Robin's disappearance. Most of the other girls had heard that Douglas might have done something bad to Robin and were steering clear of him, but Julie hadn't gotten the word. Both times they had gone to a motel in the Back Bay, where one of Julie's girlfriends had a room. Both times he wanted oral sex. No touching. Each time she worked only fifteen minutes and received $100. Julie recalled that everything she did was okay with him. He was very gentle-manly. Very, very polite. Most guys, she observed, are not that polite.

Then, about a month after the second date, Julie recollected, Douglas called her from the parking lot across from Charlie's, asking her to go out with him. By this time Julie had heard the news about Robin and refused to meet him outside the club. She tried to persuade him to come inside, but he wouldn't agree. After getting off the phone, Julie called Billy Dwyer, who came as quickly as he could, but Douglas was already gone. After that, Julie got the feeling that he was watching her as she left the bar. Once she thought Douglas followed her home, but she wasn't sure about that.

When Howe conveyed the essence of Julie's story to Kivlan, the prose-cutor decided not to call her before the grand jury. While the business about Douglas's going back into the Zone after Robin's disappearance provided a fascinating detail, it did nothing to further the case. At best it would make Douglas look bad. If he claimed his affair with Robin had been an isolated incident, Julie's account would commit him to a lie. But

Kivlan was frankly doubtful that a judge would allow that testimony into evidence. It could probably be employed to better advantage at the time of sentencing to establishing that Douglas was not some poor sap who had strayed temporarily from the straight and narrow but a lustful, unrepentant recidivist who did not deserve leniency.

Relieved of the obligation to testify, Julie nonetheless hung around for most of the morning in the lower lobby of the courthouse waiting for Lorna Johnson to finish. She found herself pacing the same narrow stretch of corridor with Robin's man, Junie. Of course, the same rules that held in the Zone held here; she didn't dare go up to him and say hello. She didn't even dare look him in the eye. Junie was chatting familiarly with the Benedicts, who seemed not to bear him the slightest ill will. Julie, who was normally not given to sentimentality, felt a flush of pity for the Benedicts. She had not known Robin well but considered her a nice girl. As Julie had always been something of an outsider, she had not shared the general dislike of Robin that permeated the inner circle at Charlie's. Screwing up her nerve, she walked up to John Benedict and told him how sorry she was about Robin. He seemed to appreciate the thought and was just as nice to her as he was to Junie. Julie thought about saying something to Mrs. Benedict as well, but, somehow, it just didn't seem proper.

Shirley Benedict stayed a little aloof from the gathering. She was learning that her role as bereaved parent required something special from her—a display of dignity. Beneath this veneer of grief, however, Shirley's curiosity was as active as ever, and as Julie studied her, she studied Julie and her chum Lorna. In the process she caught Junie giving Lorna a wink. Junie was clearly reveling in the irony of the situation. Here he was a black man—a black man whom the Boston vice squad was eager to nail as a pimp—and through some strange quirk of fortune he had found himself under the wing of two powerful protectors: the Benedict family, which needed, for appearance' sake, to preserve the illusion that he was Robin's "boyfriend"; and the Commonwealth of Massachusetts, which needed his testimony. It was little wonder J.R. Rogers could scarcely conceal his mirth.

If Shirley Benedict was offended by his impious gesture, she never let on. She and her husband tended to regard J.R.'s foibles with limitless tolerance. And this was something that worried John Kivlan. On the one hand, the Benedicts' apparent goodwill toward Junie stood to help the prosecution. Jurors might tend to be reassured by the Benedicts' apparent faith in their daughter's fiancé and give Junie the benefit of the doubt. On the other hand, a jury might be so put off by the sight of a middle-class couple cozying up to their daughter's pimp that they would dismiss not only J.R.'s testimony but the Benedicts' as well. For that reason Kivlan knew that he had to preempt any possible backlash against the Benedicts by emphasizing their most sympathetic trait—their close family ties.

On Tuesday, October 25, Kivlan called Shirley Benedict to the witness stand and asked her to tell the grand jury how, even though Robin was out on her own, she had "frequent contact" with the family. Shirley testified to Robin's daughterly solicitude, explaining that she had come home as recently as the Wednesday night before she disappeared.

Kivlan also called Rhonda to ask her about that same visit. Did she recollect whether Robin was wearing a tan corduroy blazer?

"Yeah," Rhonda replied. "She was."

"How do you remember that?" Kivlan probed.

"Because I tried it on that day, 'cuz every time she came over, I tried on all her coats."

Rhonda verified that the next time she saw that brown jacket was at the state police crime lab at 1010 Commonwealth Avenue.

Kivlan then called John Benedict, whom he asked to give his own account of the atmosphere that surrounded that Wednesday-night encounter.

"We had just come off a little father-daughter argument type of thing because she had done something I didn't like," Benedict began. "We were just starting to get back and 'gel' again to the way things were supposed to be. So I didn't have her Malden address, because she told me that she was working on the house and she's fixing it up but in another couple of weeks the house would be all done and then we're going to go over and see what the house looked like and have dinner there and everything else. I said okay; at that time too I wanted [her] to come over that week and bring Junior and have dinner with us so I could patch up my misunderstanding. . . . She said, 'Fine. Everything's starting to get together.' But since then, we couldn't get a hold of her. I got a phone call from Dr. Douglas. He had just gotten back from Washington, I guess it was, and he said to me, 'Do you know where Robin is?' I said, 'No. We've been trying to get ahold of her.' "

Douglas, John Benedict recalled, had told him that Robin had been at his house on Saturday night. She was supposed to have come earlier in the day but had been delayed hour after hour. It sounded to Benedict as if Douglas were reading from a prepared script. Finally, Douglas said, Robin had told him that if anything should happen to her, he was to tell her father to take her valuables because she didn't want Clarence to have them. John Benedict thought this was "kind of silly," since it was Clarence who had bought her all these things to begin with.

THUS FAR, the first day of hearings had gone off without incident. But Kivlan was alert to the possibility of trouble from Joseph Murray. A few days before the hearings, he had received a call from Murray's attorney, a former Norfolk prosecutor named Judd Carhart, who announced that his client intended to take the Fifth.

Since the middle of March, when he had spoken so freely to Paul Landry, Murray's legal problems had gotten considerably more complex. Almost a month to the day after Robin Benedict disappeared, federal agents had raided a South Boston warehouse owned by Murray's Harbor Oil, finding over eleven tons of marijuana. The FBI had been investigating Murray since the preceding August and had reason to believe he headed a gang of Boston Irish hoodlums who smuggled drugs through the waterfront. Murray's operation was so big, the snitch claimed, that he was the largest single importer of marijuana in Massachusetts.

As the result of an ensuing raid on Murray's warehouse, both Joe and his brother, Michael, were indicted. So were a pair of small-time operators named Jake Rooney and Arthur "Bucky" Barrett, who were part of what the FBI identified as the Joe Murray crew. (Only Michael Murray and Jake Rooney were ultimately convicted.)

Bucky was a stocky Irishman who liked to party and was seen quite a lot in the Combat Zone. He was an expert at disarming sophisticated burglar alarms, and his skills as a safecracker were reputed to be in much demand by the New England mob. Bucky owned a restaurant called Angie's Deli, near Government Center. His wife, Elaine, ran a waterfront bar with Jake Rooney. The FBI suspected that this establishment, called Little Rascals Deli, was the scene of much of Joe Murray's drug action.

Robin Benedict appeared to have been tied up with these people somehow. Less than a week after Robin disappeared, J.R. Rogers, who professed not to know anything about Joe Murray, had directed his private detectives to look up Bucky Barrett. DaRosa and Smith went over to Angie's Deli, but Bucky was not in. Their inquiry ended there. That Robin had introduced Douglas to Jake and Bucky was revealed in a letter among Robin's belongings. Douglas had apparently written it to Jake Rooney during the early summer of 1982. It read:

Dear Jake:

I met you and Bucky on Thursday afternoon . . . through a mutual friend, Nadine. We indicated at that time we are interested in having Little Rascal's Deli supply food for two lunches for 42 people on each of two days. . . . It is my understanding that the platters will include corn beef, roast beef, turkey, ham, potato salad, cole slaw, pickles and rolls. . . . Will condiments be included or should we plan on supplying those. . . .

There was a good chance that when Douglas wrote his letter to Little Rascals trilling inanely on the subject of cold cuts and condiments, he had no idea what heavy company he was running in. It was possible that he was simply hoping to impress Robin by throwing business to her friends. The catering bill, as it turned out, was not insubstantial. (The auditor Thorngren turned up invoices amounting to $1,030 from Little Rascals which he deemed "invalid.")

On the other hand, there may have been a more cunning subtext to Douglas's correspondence with Jake Rooney. As in the letter in which he authorized Robin's work on the Navy submarine project, Douglas may here have wanted to establish a history of correspondence with Jake and Bucky so that their names would not be questioned if they later turned up on fraudulent invoices.

John Kivlan, however, chose not to explore these questions too deeply. He was chary of exposing a drug connection that might detract from the homicide investigation. He was, moreover, disinclined to flesh out the outlines of Robin's shadowy associates for fear of raising more potential suspects. Bucky and Jake he did not need. Joe Murray he did. It wasn't until the day of his grand-jury appearance, however, that Murray named the price for his testimony.

On the morning of the twenty-fifth, Murray and his wife, Suzanne, a tall, weary-looking woman with long blond hair, showed up at the courthouse in the company of Attorney Carhart. Brian Howe spotted them and alerted Kivlan, who took the Murrays aside for a chat. During that palaver, he learned that Murray wanted a quid pro quo. He would testify if Kivlan would intervene in—or, as he put it, "take care of"—his federal drug charge. The prosecutor reportedly told him that he was in no position to intervene in the U.S. attorney's case even if he were so inclined. Consequently, Murray appeared before the grand jury but refused to confirm his earlier statements to Paul Landry. The jury agreed to give him time to reconsider before taking any drastic measures.

THE FOLLOWING MORNING, October 26, did not commence on a more encouraging note for the Commonwealth. William Douglas arrived at the courthouse with Attorney O'Connell and asked to confer with Kivlan outside the grand-jury room. When the prosecutor arrived, he informed Douglas that although he had the right to remain silent, he could use the opportunity to testify and bring any information he wished to the attention of the jury. In reply, Douglas pulled out a sheet of paper and read a statement declaring that because of the "unfair and illegal manner" in which he had been treated by law enforcement officials, he did not feel that anything he might say to the grand jury would be "received and evaluated in an unbiased manner."

With that, he left the courthouse.

Following Douglas's refusal, Kivlan called Landry and asked him to re-count before the grand jury a phone conversation he had had with the suspect on the Monday evening following the first search. As Landry stepped up to testify that morning, he did not seem angry or bitter, only slightly reserved. At Kivlan's urging, he told how he had called William Douglas at about 8:30 P.M. on Monday, March 22, and offered to get him an attorney or even psychiatric care if he would agree to tell everything he knew.

"I said to him," Landry recalled, "possibly something had happened in that house; possibly you were being extorted; possibly Robin Benedict might have struck you first in which case . . . it's a self-defense type of thing. I said if there's anything you can tell me . . . then talk to me. And he paused . . . and he thought for a while. And again he thanked me, and he said, 'Well, I just want to have time to think about it and talk to a lawyer. . . .'"

"Did you, in effect, feel he was going to confess to you about it?" Kivlan probed.

"It was my feeling," Landry affirmed, "that he was on the edge of confessing to me at that time."

For the balance of the day, the grand jurors heard testimony from several witnesses, including Jack DaRosa, who read verbatim from his interview with William Douglas in Washington, D.C. He arrived at the point when he had gone back to Douglas's room, at J.R.'s request, to grill him on the circumstances under which he and Robin had parted on the night of March 5.

DAROSA.   Are you sure that you did not have an argument with Robin before she left your house?
DOUGLAS.   Yes, I'm sure. My wife was there when she left the house at midnight.

A juror seized upon this, asking DaRosa, "Did I understand you right? Did you say that he told you that his wife was there, that they didn't have a fight? That his wife was there when she left at midnight?"

"When Robin left at midnight, right," DaRosa replied.

Brian Howe had been to Good Time Charlie's trying to find Pam

McGrath. She always seemed to elude him. Finally, just before the third day of hearings, he managed to intercept her at her apartment at Presidential Estates. Pam disavowed any intimate knowledge of Robin's relationship with Douglas. Most of it had occurred during the summer that she was out pregnant with little Matt. Four or five months after the baby was born, she had been invited to a birthday party that Savi Bisram was having for her little boy, Taj. On the afternoon of March 6, about ten girls and their children got together at the Ground Round, a steak house in Prudential Center. The kids all had hamburgers and birthday cake. Through most of it, little Matt slept on her shoulder. A couple of the girls asked why Robin wasn't there, but Savi didn't say anything. Nobody thought much about it.

When Howe told Pam that Douglas was claiming that she had borrowed Robin's car, she became angry. Douglas, she suspected, had tried to set her up so that when the bloody car was found, she would be a suspect. She accepted her subpoena and on Thursday, October 27, appeared before the grand jury, where she gave a brief, emphatic statement to the effect that she had not seen Robin on March 5, much less borrowed her car. She had, furthermore, *never* asked to borrow Robin's car.

Kivlan thanked her and excused her from further testimony.

THE NEXT WITNESS was a man whose name was virtually unknown to the grand jury. He had not even come to the attention of the Norfolk investigators until one Thursday in late July when Lieutenant Sharkey got a message to call Lieutenant Joseph Pirrello of the Midtown South Precinct in Manhattan. When Sharkey reached Pirrello at home, the commander told him that after his officers had found the silver Toyota, he had received a call from one John McManus, who identified himself as a private detective working for the defense in the Douglas case. McManus had been rooting about for information and apparently tried to appeal to Pirrello's sense of camaraderie by telling him that he was a former homicide detective with the Boston Police Department. Pirrello was reportedly unimpressed, making it clear to McManus that he considered him not a police officer but an *ex-*police officer—and one now working for "the other side."

According to Pirrello, McManus had tried to convince him that Douglas was innocent and that Robin Benedict had been killed by her pimp. McManus wanted to speak further with Pirrello, he said, either in New York or on Cape Cod. As Pirrello recalled it, McManus then promised that such a chat would be worth his while, as there were "a few bucks" in it. The commander interpreted this as a bribery attempt and let McManus know "in no uncertain terms" that the New York City Police Department was not for sale.

After hearing from Pirrello, Sharkey had done some checking around and reported to Kivlan that McManus was indeed a former cop and was, in fact, Daniel O'Connell's private investigator. If what Pirrello said was true, and Kivlan had no reason to doubt the word of a high-ranking officer, then McManus had left the defense team's flank open to attack. First, he had flat out called J.R. a murderer, something for which he would have to be called to account. Second, he had tried to bribe a police officer, something for which he stood to be indicted. By calling McManus before the grand jury and confronting him with these charges, Kivlan hoped to accomplish the twin goal of shooting down another rumor about J.R. and discrediting the defense with charges of impropriety.

When McManus showed up at the courthouse on the morning of Thursday, October 27, he had no idea why he had been summoned. He clearly suspected that the inquiry might turn treacherous, however, because he brought Daniel O'Connell along to advise him. Once McManus had taken the witness stand, Kivlan explained to him that he was being given the opportunity to provide whatever information he had pertaining to the disappearance of Robin Benedict. McManus replied that he would not be answering questions, because he was protected by O'Connell's attorney/client privilege with William Douglas.

Kivlan was undaunted. "Now, directing your attention to on or about July 28 of this year, 1983," he continued, "did you make a telephone call to Lieutenant Joseph Pirrello of the New York Police Department?"

McManus and O'Connell, who were apparently caught unprepared by this line of questioning, ducked into the hallway for a conference. When they returned, McManus again invoked his "attorney/client privilege" and refused to answer.

"Now, this isn't meant to be verbatim," Kivlan persisted, "but I am asking you if in substance you told Lieutenant Pirrello that Dr. Douglas was innocent and that the pimp had killed Robin Benedict. Did you tell him that?"

Once again, McManus and O'Connell left the jury room, after which McManus declined to answer "on advice of counsel and based upon the attorney/client privilege and the attorney work product doctrine."

"I'm not sure I caught all of that," Kivlan returned. "Are you also asserting a Fifth Amendment privilege?" It was a sly query intended to underscore the fact that McManus was in a position to incriminate himself.

"I think the witness's answer speaks for itself, Mr. Kivlan," O'Connell interjected. Kivlan shot back, "Mr. O'Connell, you know . . . that you are not permitted to address me or the jurors in the grand-jury room."

The antagonism which had been simmering for nearly eight months erupted in a shouting match before the grand jury. A serious breach of etiquette. One juror moved to cite O'Connell for contempt, claiming that he took his outburst as "a personal insult."

O'Connell was humbled. "I do not mean it as such," he replied.

HAVING neutralized that potential offensive against J.R. Rogers, Kivlan moved to preempt another threat to the credibility of his star witness. He, like Howe, suspected that Detective Billy Dwyer had deliberately misrepresented his conversation with Lorna Johnson to obstruct the Norfolk investigation. After the grand jury summoned her, however, Dwyer had become considerably more conciliatory, saying that he must have "misunderstood" her. Kivlan was willing to let bygones be bygones, but he was afraid that Dwyer was in a position to do still more harm to the Commonwealth's case. The vice cop doubtless knew a great deal about J.R. that could be damaging if it were allowed into evidence. Kivlan intended to smoke out this testimony and see what he could reasonably hope to discredit.

When Billy Dwyer appeared before the grand jury on Thursday afternoon, he described the various occasions on which he had stopped Robin Benedict. "Do you recollect any conversation with Douglas during those times?" Kivlan asked him.

DWYER.   Yes, I spoke with him on a couple of occasions relative to her activity and her employer, so to speak.
KIVLAN.   Her activities and her employer? What do you mean?
DWYER.   I informed Douglas that she was working for a pimp and he would be much better off disassociating himself from this type of activity. He insisted that I was in error and that [he] was just a friend of the family accompanying her to court; that sort of thing.
KIVLAN.   . . . Did you tell him who you thought the pimp was?
DWYER.   Yes. I even showed him a picture at one time.
KIVLAN.   Who was that?
DWYER.   Clarence Rogers.

Kivlan framed his next question narrowly. "Did you at that time or do you now possess any evidence or do you have any witnesses with any evidence or testimony that would show that Mr. Rogers is a pimp, other than street talk?"

Dwyer, who knew in his heart that Rogers was a pimp, was nonetheless obliged to answer no.

IN THE PROCESS of troubleshooting, Kivlan also hoped to tie down a couple of facts he had not been able to verify to his satisfaction. The first was the identity of the person who made the call inviting Robin to the party in Charlestown. Kivlan was sure that it had not been made by Joe Murray, but now that Joe was taking the Fifth, the Commonwealth would not be able to rely upon his emphatic denial to shift the suspicion to William or Nancy Douglas. During both the second and the third days of testimony, Kivlan called Maura Armstrong, the Americall operator who had supposedly taken the "Joe from Charlestown" call, hoping that she could remember something specific that would help identify the caller as Douglas. To his dismay, however, her memory was worse than when she had spoken to Trooper Landry in the spring. Now she professed not even to remember taking the call.

The second bit of equivocal testimony concerned John Boulton's identification of the hammer. Although both Landry and Howe thought they had heard Mr. Boulton say that he was "99 percent sure" that it was the hammer he had lent Nancy on Thanksgiving, he had quibbled, saying that the Mansfield hammer seemed much more worn than this own.

Kivlan now called Boulton to the witness stand in the hope that he would make a positive identification for the record. To his dismay the elderly gentleman backed off even further from his earlier testimony. When asked if he had identified the hammer he had been shown as the one he had lent his daughter, he replied, "No. I told them I couldn't positively identify it. . . . The hammer that I lent had been in fairly new-looking condition and this hammer looked like it had been probably weathered out in the weather or something like that."

"Well, let me ask you specifically," Kivlan pressed, "did you tell Trooper Landry and Trooper Howe that you were 99 percent sure that that was the hammer that you had lent to them?"

"No," Boulton replied. ". . . I told them that I couldn't positively identify it, because of the condition it was in when it was shown to me."

Privately, Kivlan felt sorry for Mr. Boulton. The moment was clearly difficult for him. Kivlan also suspected that during the months since he had first identified the hammer, the old man had been fed a seriously distorted view of events by Nancy and had come—as the children apparently had—to believe that the state was persecuting William and Nancy Douglas for no good reason.

"I know this is difficult for you, Mr. Boulton," the prosecutor continued, "and I don't want to make it any more difficult than it is, but I have to ask you these questions." Kivlan read him Landry and Howe's reports of the encounter in the West Warwick Police Station. Both contained the words "99 percent sure." Boulton conceded that he "might" have said it and just didn't remember.

Kivlan asked Boulton if he had discussed the hammer with Nancy. The old man said he couldn't recall that either.

"Let me bring something to your attention that might possibly refresh your memory," Kivlan persisted. He produced a copy of Lieutenant Sharkey's interview with Nancy Douglas during the house search of April 22. He read aloud the exchange where Sharkey reminded Nancy that although she had originally denied ever seeing the hammer, her father had admitted lending it to her. "How do you explain that?" he had asked her. "The hammer wasn't for me," she had replied. "Why don't you ask my father. He'll tell you."

"Now that seems to indicate," Kivlan continued, "that apparently Nancy might have talked to you about this and in fact might have explained to you who did have the hammer. Did she?"

John Boulton said he couldn't recollect any such conversation with his daughter.

KIVLAN knew he could expect more congenial testimony from Nancy's brother. Stephen Boulton had shown himself consistently more sympathetic to the Massachusetts state police than to his brother-in-law. Moreover, he did not he seem to be on particularly friendly terms with his sister. He was apparently worried about his father's health and angry that Bill and Nancy had drawn the old man into their problems. Stephen had found it extremely unusual that Nancy would have gone shopping in New Hampshire. He had never heard of her doing that before, and he had confided in the Norfolk investigators that he was not totally convinced by her alibi.

Taking the witness stand after his father, Stephen described for the grand jurors how he had first learned of his sister's troubles. Back in March, Nancy had called him out of the blue asking questions about a Boston lawyer that she and Bill were going to see. The attorney was demanding a fee of $8,000, and she wanted to know if that was excessive. Boulton said he thought so, unless, of course, it was a very serious criminal matter. She replied, "It very well might be that there is." Later on in that same conversation, Nancy told him that Bill had become the target of an investigation pertaining to a "missing girl."

Boulton decided to do a little checking of his own and called Trooper

Landry, who invited him to come in to talk about the case. A day later Landry called him with the news that a second search of the Douglas house had turned up what the trooper described as a "suicide type note," apparently written by Nancy. The following evening at around eight-thirty, Boulton and his father visited Nancy in Sharon while Bill was not at home. Stephen asked her what she knew about certain items that the state police had taken from her house, notably a sledgehammer which was believed to be the murder weapon. At first Nancy denied any knowledge of it. Then, as Stephen began describing it to her, trying to "shock her recollection," old Mr. Boulton piped up saying, "Don't you remember borrowing a hammer from me last Thanksgiving?"

Kivlan asked if he recalled what his sister had said.

"She did acknowledge it at that time," Boulton replied. "She said that she had forgotten all about the incident, that it had happened several months previous to this conversation that we were having with her. She did acknowledge, however, that they did borrow a hammer from him that was to be used for repairs to a wooden deck at the rear of the house, I believe."

"Now, did she . . . indicate in any way who was actually going to use the hammer or whether it was going to be Mr. Douglas?" Kivlan probed.

"She did not," Boulton replied, "and to the best of my recollection she indicated that after she had returned [with] the hammer to Sharon, Massachusetts, she had not seen the hammer since. . . ."

Kivlan asked him if his sister had ever told him that she had told Lieutenant Sharkey that the bloody shirt looked like her husband's.

"She never said that she admitted to the police that that was his shirt," Boulton testified. "She told me that she could not identify it."

A juror asked Stephen Boulton, "When you first spoke to Nancy regarding her coming home and seeing Robin's car in the driveway, she left then?"

"She said she had two children with her," Boulton replied. "One was baby-sitting, and two were with her and saw Miss Benedict's car in the driveway and she turned around. . . . She knew the automobile, and I don't know if she knew Miss Benedict personally but she knew of her. . . . I think she told me she went to McDonald's for, like, forty-five minutes and she returned to the house. At that point the vehicle, Robin Benedict's car, was no longer there; so she went into the house with at least the two children, and she might have told me that she stopped to pick up the third one, who was baby-sitting, and all three children might have been with her when she returned, according to her story."

When Nancy went into the house, she looked into the master bedroom and thought she saw someone in the bed. Boulton thought she had described the figure as a "lump" under the blankets. Then she went off to sleep elsewhere in the house.

"She was evasive in general pertaining to whether or not Bill was actually there or she had actually seen him in the bedroom," Boulton recalled. The next time Nancy saw Bill, she said, was the following morning when she found him roaming around the house with a hat on. (Boulton said this was not unusual, as Bill Douglas was in the habit of wearing a hat with a "little brim" on it.)

While Stephen was still questioning his sister, his brother-in-law called. Stephen got on the line and told him he would like to talk with him, and Douglas replied, "Fine. Come on and drive into Boston. I'm at. . . ." Boulton couldn't remember the name of the bar. Douglas was apparently using the phone in the manager's office. Boulton stayed on the line, talking to his brother-in-law at some length. During that time Douglas mentioned committing suicide.

"He said that that would seem the easiest way in light of some of the accusations that were being made regarding the missing money at Tufts and other such things," Boulton recalled. "He said he was going to do himself in."

A juror asked Boulton if he had gone into Boston to meet his brother-in-law at the bar that night, and the witness replied, "I did not because . . . he [was] threatening to do harm to himself. I didn't know what his mental state was. I wasn't about to drive into a strange place in Boston."

(Douglas was apparently absent that night at Nancy's request. "A lot of problems were fresh," Boulton explained, "and I think . . . she thought it was bad to have him there. So he . . . was spending most of the nights out of the house and he would come back during the day.")

Two days after Stephen and his father had had this heart-to-heart with Nancy, the troopers came to West Warwick to show old Mr. Boulton the hammer. Stephen had not heard his father say he was "99 percent sure." His father, he said, was "so overabundantly cautious" that he would never use an expression like that. Kivlan asked if it was possible that the troopers had said, "Are you 99 percent sure?" and he assented to it. Stephen affirmed, "In substance he stated that it appeared to be the same hammer with certain qualifications." Stephen went on to observe that the borrowed hammer was very likely the only one around the Douglas household since, as he put it, "Bill was not very handy, and I don't believe he had any variety or assortment of tools with which he could repair anything."

Sometime in April, continued Boulton, he himself had asked Douglas to come to John Boulton's house in West Warwick. There he had told his brother-in-law that he thought the police had amassed some very incriminating evidence against him. And to this Douglas replied that it would all come out that some "black gentleman friend of the missing lady" had planted the evidence in his house. "He also told me in the alternative," Boulton said, "that the state police had manufactured certain evidence . . . brought it into the house and . . . put it on the search warrant inventory."

When Boulton asked him about the cocaine that had been found in the Leica bag, Douglas was vague. He said that he had seen it but that it was "no problem." It was only five dollars worth of coke that he had taken with him on his trip to Washington, D.C.

Boulton told the grand jury how he had advised his brother-in-law to sign all the property over to Nancy and go away—far away—to upstate New York, perhaps, and start another life. If he remained at home, he would only continue to attract the police and the media, all of which was upsetting to the children.

"I was of the impression," Boulton explained, "that he should just relent a bit and call it quits as far as the marriage was concerned."

"Is it fair to say . . . that you were indicating to him that from what you knew," Kivlan pressed, "that it appeared that he was responsible for the disappearance and murder of Robin Benedict?"

"Well," Boulton replied, "being a policeman at heart and it looking that that was probably the case—and if it looks it, a lot of the time it is—I thought that that might very well be the case."

The prosecutor then called Stephen Boulton's attention to a statement he had made to Paul Landry, indicating that he thought his sister knew more than she was saying and that she appeared to be covering up for her husband. Did he remember saying anything like that?

"I do," Boulton assented, "and still, unfortunately, I find her story outrageous and unbelievable, some of it."

Stephen Boulton said he had urged his sister on several occasions to be more cooperative with the police. He had warned her that she might be accused of obstructing justice, but she swore that she had told him all she knew.

Boulton had asked his sister about the suicide note, and she acknowledged having written it. At the time she had put those thoughts to paper, she was "very depressed," but since then a psychiatrist or clinical psychologist had given her medicine which made her feel better.

Kivlan asked the grand jurors if they had any other questions. One asked Boulton if his sister wasn't also concerned about what might be happening to the children if Douglas remained with the family.

"She had considered that," he replied, "and in her deliberate consideration of it, she said that the children are better off having the father there than not having the father there. That the broken home with the father not present is not preferable . . . even though these problems . . . may continue. Her answer is that it's [in] the best interest of the children to have the father present regardless of what might have happened and that it would strengthen the family bind [*sic*] by people being supportive of each other rather than bailing out on each other."

THE FOLLOWING DAY, Friday, October 28, was the Feast of Saint Jude, patron saint of police and, more significantly, of impossible cases. It would also be the last day of hearings.

That morning Nancy Douglas herself was called to the witness stand. The woman on whom so much mystery turned sat stern and mute. When Kivlan tried to question her, she fixed him with a baleful stare. It was difficult to reconcile this cold, unrelenting figure with the writer of the suicide note. All of her wild anguish had now apparently been harnessed to a single resolve—stonewalling the prosecution. Nancy may have been no tactical genius, but she recognized that her strong suit was silence. The grand jury might be able to call her to the witness stand, but it not could force her to incriminate herself—and it could never force her to testify against her husband. And so Nancy sat there—cloaked in her privileges, keeping an impenetrable silence—until the grand jury finally gave up and dismissed her.

It was by design that Kivlan saved the forensic testimony for the last day. If there was any doubt lingering in the minds of the grand jurors that Robin Benedict was dead, he wanted to dispel it with an impressive display of test results. After calling the chemist Kaufman to summarize the blood work to date, Kivlan called Dr. George Katsas to address the likelihood that a human being could have survived a blow that sent brain tissue flying from the skull. Kivlan asked Katsas if, on the basis of his examination of both pieces of brain tissue, he could tell the jury from what part of the brain it had come.

KATSAS. Well, the brain tissue that I found in both specimens was of the nature or structure which usually we see at least a few millimeters under the surface of the brain . . . roughly about one-eighth of an inch below the surface of the brain. Now . . . if one considers the distance from the skin itself, that might be half an inch, depending on the size of the person [and] the thickness of the bone. . . .

KIVLAN. So is it fair to state that this brain tissue that you examined is from a deeper part of the brain?

KATSAS.   Well, it is deep enough. It is not from the surface of the brain, and
the basic thing is that it is brain tissue and one [that was] proven
to [come from a] human brain.

KIVLAN.   . . . Do you have an opinion as to whether or not the person from
whose brain this tissue came from is dead?

KATSAS.   Yes, sir. It is my opinion that the person is dead.

Around noon the grand jury retired to consider the testimony it had
heard during the preceding four days. What factors weighed most heavily
in its deliberation was never revealed. Of that clandestine session, only
two things can be known for sure: that it did not charge Nancy Douglas
and that it did indict William Douglas for murder in the first degree.

Judge Dwyer issued a warrant, which was typed hurriedly in the superior-court clerk's office and handed to Lieutenant Sharkey and Brian
Howe, who were poised to make the arrest.

For the past three months Bobby Murphy's pal Sal at Crimson Car
Rental had kept the Norfolk troopers apprised of Douglas's movements.
This was easy since Douglas had been placed in charge of a shuttle crew
and had to report back to the main office periodically over a radio unit
in his van. After Sharkey got the warrant, Murphy called Sal, who told
him that Douglas had just radioed in from East Boston saying he would
be going to the company lot in Cambridge.

Brian Howe called Trooper Zebrasky, who was standing by in the
Cambridge area, and instructed him to go to the Crimson lot to wait for
Douglas. Zebrasky found the lot on a dead-end street. He pulled into a
Burger King on the corner, from where he could see everyone entering
and leaving the street. A couple of rental cars drove into the lot, but he
did not recognize Douglas among the drivers. Sharkey and Howe arrived
shortly, and while the three troopers were talking, Howe pointed to the
street and shouted, "There he is!" Douglas, who was wearing a baseball
cap, had apparently slipped past Zebrasky unnoticed, and now he was
ferrying a car out into the late Friday afternoon traffic.

Douglas was being followed by a rental car driven by a young woman
coworker. Sharkey and Howe slipped in behind her. Zebrasky eased in
behind Sharkey and Howe. As this convoy approached a congested rotary,
Howe, afraid they would lose Douglas in the impending confusion, cut
in front of him and motioned him to pull over. Howe got out of his car,
went up to Douglas, and handed him the warrant. Douglas flashed a grin
and replied, "I surrender." The only complaint he made as Howe pushed
him up against the car and placed him in handcuffs was that his employer
was counting on him to ferry these cars to Park Square. By the time he

arrived at the Sharon Police Station to be printed and mugged, Douglas was still fretting about letting his employer down.

The Sharon police took Douglas's valuables—a brown wallet, a pair of sunglasses, and one subway token. By the time he reached the forbidding stone portals of the Norfolk County House of Corrections, he had only the clothes on his back. During admitting procedures, the clothing officer tried to find a pair of regulation dungarees large enough for him, but that proved impossible. For the time being, Douglas was allowed to wear his own pants with a general-issue blue T-shirt.

Sharkey took some pity on him and introduced him to an old friend of his, a good-hearted deputy named Peter Gagliardi.

"This is Billy Douglas," he told the deputy. "He's a good guy. He probably hasn't eaten tonight. He might not be able to sleep well. Get him some warm milk and a nice sandwich. . . ."

William Douglas passed his first night in jail in a separate wing for those in "administrative protective custody." There he was placed on suicide watch. (This precaution was reportedly undertaken when Nancy Douglas, having learned of the arrest, called the jail and expressed concern for her husband's mental health.) But William Douglas never uttered a complaint. Perhaps he sensed that the safest course was to play the good, dutiful boy. Or perhaps he had risen above shame to a plateau where he could appreciate the irony of his own predicament. It was exactly a year ago to the day that the Tufts vice-president Steven Manos had called him up to his office to confront him with his sins against Tufts. How relatively innocent those offenses seemed now. Back in those halcyon days he stood accused only of lying, cheating, philandering, and thievery. A year ago this very moment, Robin Benedict was still alive and William Douglas still had the chance to save himself. But he had thrown that chance away. He had pressed on, gaining altitude so recklessly that he went into a stall. And now he found himself lying on a hard cot in the wreckage of his own life— wearing a foolish grin.

ADVERSARIES

O'CONNELL was even more annoyed than usual at Kivlan for snubbing his offer of a surrender. The prosecutor had an ulterior motive, O'Connell suspected, and that was to humiliate Douglas by making a media spectacle of his arrest. He had succeeded. By late Friday afternoon the press had caught wind of the indictment and reporters gathered on the macadam outside the jail. The evening news had carried footage of a disheveled William Douglas arriving in handcuffs, head bowed, in the custody of Sharkey and Howe.

O'Connell was confident, nonetheless, that Douglas's impressive achievements would all but guarantee his release on bail. The long-term prognosis was also still good. It was one thing for a prosecutor to ram an indictment through a grand jury, quite another to get a conviction where there was no body. And there was still no body.

On Monday morning, October 31, Douglas was escorted by bailiffs from the jail to the Norfolk County Courthouse for arraignment. The defendant, attired in his customary brown sport coat and horn-rimmed glasses, sat, shoulders rounded, peering meekly at the floor. All in all, Douglas cut such an innocuous figure that the indictment, which was read over his head by the clerk of the court, seemed hardly intended for him.

". . . Jurors for the Commonwealth of Massachusetts on their oath, present that William H. J. Douglas, of Sharon, in the County of Norfolk, on or about March Fifth of 1983 . . . did assault and beat Robin Nadine Benedict with intent to murder her, and by such assault and beating did kill and murder said Robin Nadine Benedict."

"As to that indictment, sir, how do you wish to plead?" asked Judge Dwyer. "Guilty or not guilty?"

"Not guilty, sir," Douglas replied faintly.

John Kivlan stepped in quickly to allay any impression of harmlessness by summarizing the case against the defendant. "The evidence will show," he concluded, "that at the time [Robin Benedict] left to go to Mr. Douglas's house, Mr. Douglas had decided, at that time, if not before, to murder her."

Douglas must not be allowed bail, Kivlan argued, for several reasons. First and foremost was that the crime of which he was accused was the most serious offense known to the Commonwealth. Not only was he a potential threat to others, but he was a threat to himself as well. By his own admission to certain colleagues at Tufts University, he had suffered mental problems which he claimed had something to do with his diet and fluctuation of weight. This disturbance could well have been complicated by drugs, since cocaine was found among his belongings. On the heels of this instability, Douglas had confided to his brother-in-law that he was contemplating suicide.

The defendant, Kivlan claimed, also had every incentive to flee. While at first blush he seemed to have roots in the community, these were more tenuous than they appeared. A representative of the district attorney's Family Services Unit who had visited the Douglas home to investigate the background of the children had learned from Mrs. Douglas that the family situation was "volatile and explosive." Mrs. Douglas had even indicated that she and her husband might separate. As for employment, Douglas had been fired from Tufts and had since moved about from one job to another. Prior to his indictment, Kivlan argued, Douglas had apparently been under the impression that he could not be prosecuted without a body. Now that he had been made aware of the extent of the evidence, he had an even more compelling reason to jump bail.

O'Connell objected angrily to Kivlan's characterization of Douglas as unstable. His client, he said, had no history of mental illness or drug dependency. As for the rumor that he was suicidal, it was no secret that Stephen Boulton was "highly antagonistic toward Mr. Douglas." While conceding that Douglas's tenure at Tufts had ended in May, he had since worked continuously, sometimes as much as eighty hours a week. "He's gone from job to job because newspapers published articles," O'Connell charged. "Certain things get said that are not appropriate to be said and, indeed, may well be untrue . . . and have caused employers to terminate this man. . . ."

Finally, O'Connell took heated exception to the terms "explosive and volatile," which Kivlan had used to describe the Douglases' family life.

Naturally the family was a little tense since it had been under virtual siege by the press and the grand jury. But, O'Connell contended, "throughout all of these pressures these people have stayed together, pulled together, with all the dignity they can muster."

O'Connell's plea was poignant. Judge Dwyer nevertheless denied bail.

Decrying this ruling as "outrageous," O'Connell appealed it two days later to a single justice of the Supreme Judicial Court. Justice Francis O'Connor was also apparently less impressed by the defense's characterization of Douglas as a beleaguered man of honor than by John Kivlan's representation of him as a cunning, deceitful manipulator. The justice decreed that Douglas should be held in custody until he came to trial, a date that promised to be many months away. In the meantime, he would remain where he was, in the Norfolk County House of Corrections.

THE COUNTY JAIL resembled a cathderal whose architect decided midway through construction that his edifice should be consecrated not to God's glory but to man's misery. What had been intended to soar skyward was drawn back to earth by the weight of massive granite blocks. The walls were inpenetrable save for a few small gothic windows. The jail had been built, during the preceding century, in the shape of a cross, which allowed deputies patrolling the guardroom floor to stand at the intersection and have a clear view of the north, east, and west wings.

The east wing had a special tier reserved for defendants accused of particularly heinous crimes. It was here, in Row Seven, or "Murderers' Row," that the anarchists Sacco and Vanzetti spent the weeks prior to their execution. It was here also that William Douglas would spend six months awaiting trial. After his first weekend in jail, Douglas was moved from the holding tank to cell No. 10 in the maximum-security tier. It was furnished sparely with a nightstand, toilet, and two cots. The second of these was occupied by a twenty-two-year-old boy who had allegedly brutalized a Dorchester girl, throwing her out of his car and running over her, back and forth, until she was dead. Douglas's new cell mate had a penchant for unsavory pranks like urinating in the communal coffee pot that was passed each morning from cell to cell. These playful outbursts were not greeted with humor by others on the tier, and he engaged in one wrestling match where he came up holding a clump of his adversary's hair in his fist. Yet the boy's relationship to Douglas seemed comparatively tranquil. Despite a weakness for mischief, he had a sporadically generous nature. He was something of an artist and ingratiated himself with the professor by carving him pieces of soap sculpture.

The professor's presence in the jail aroused a great deal of curiosity among other inmates who took his young cell mate aside when they had the chance to ask him if Douglas had confided any details of his affair with Robin Benedict. The boy had to confess that he had not. (O'Connell had warned Douglas never to discuss his case.) For most of the day, he reported, Douglas sat on his cot wearing earphones that were connected to a TV against the wall. He would watch himself on the news and take a lot of notes. He kept those in an accordion file which he carried with him everywhere he went. Even to the shower.

Douglas had his breakfast, lunch, and dinner served through an opening in the bars. (The inmates in Row Seven were considered sufficiently dangerous that they were not allowed to eat in the mess hall with the general population.) He was, however, permitted to leave his cell when he had visitors. Only two people ever came to call, Dan O'Connell and Nancy Douglas. At least twice a week, for the twenty-six weeks that Douglas remained at the House of Corrections, Nancy would arrive wearing her white nurse's uniform. She and the other wives would wait on hard, wooden benches against one wall of the guardroom floor. The room had a long table in the center, and running the length of it was a long mesh screen. When the prisoners were brought in, Bill Douglas took his place on one side of the screen and Nancy on the other, and they conversed in low voices. If the Douglases were on the verge of separating, it was not apparent from their behavior. Nancy visited faithfully, and Bill called her whenever he could get to the inmates' phone on his tier. On these occasions, perhaps for the benefit of the deputies who were within earshot, he talked to his wife in the most extravagantly endearing terms, always ending a conversation with "I love you."

From nine to eleven in the morning and again from one to three in the afternoon, the doors of the cells of Row Seven were opened and prisoners were allowed to mingle and socialize. During these free periods the former professor William H. J. Douglas, whose sense of protocol was once offended by the notion of socializing with graduate students, made the acquaintance of his fellow inmates. These were mostly older men, whom he found "very supportive" and much quieter than the young punks who did a lot of yelling at night.

There was Mike Shea, a sickly man of about forty who was awaiting trial for allegedly disemboweling his former girlfriend. There was Joseph Barber, a short, weasely fellow who was accused of raping a mentally retarded girl. Leader of that little clique was a heavy, sagging man named Lawrence Goldman, who was being held awaiting trial for conspiracy to commit murder. Goldman was by far the most intelligent of the lot, and Douglas found he had the most in common with him. The two spent most of their free hours in Goldman's cell playing chess.

But if Douglas had managed to ingratiate himself with his peers on Row Seven, he was the object of ridicule in rougher quarters. Sometimes he would be taken to see a counselor, and on those occasions he would be led through the north wing, which was occupied by a particularly depraved lot of child molesters and rapists. The inmates would scream, "Fatty, fatty. I'm gonna kill you, fatty."

Douglas walked on as if he didn't hear. Stripped of his academic titles and research funds, he was not in a position to impress anyone. He was just a plain, fat man who was vulnerable to the taunts of common street punks.

THE ANNOUNCEMENT of William Douglas's incarceration was greeted joyfully by the Agatha Christie Crimestoppers, who agreed they would all sleep much better now that the mad-dog killer had been put behind bars. After that the ladies abandoned their habit of going out in pairs. The meetings which they had held almost every night in Miss Thawley's room now slacked off to once or twice a week. The ritualistic fervor with which they had once pondered the "evidence" had also abated. The clues still refused to form a coherent whole. And although the $10,000 reward still sat out there waiting to be claimed, the Crimestoppers were at a loss as to how they should proceed.

They were shaken from their torpor by Miss Debby Woodman, who bade her fellow sleuths recall a certain young woman who had lived at the residence for about two weeks during the summer of 1982. The girl had been in her early twenties, pretty, with short dark hair. It was difficult to tell how long her hair was because she wore a lot of wigs. Regina—the only name they knew her by—had caused a stir when it was learned that she worked as a dancer in the Combat Zone. She would wear what the ladies considered "floozy kinda stuff" and come flopping in at one or two in the morning with her skimpy little costumes on a hanger. But there was a brightness about her that was winning. She seemed a happy young woman and not the least bit haughty, always stopping to make conversation in a soft, bubbling voice.

Regina hadn't told very much about herself. Her parents, she said, weren't happy about her working as a dancer. She also claimed to be an artist. Miss Woodman asked to see some of her drawings, but she seemed a little shy about showing them. On several occasions she had said with a "smirky smile" that she was looking for a "sugar daddy."

One Thursday evening that summer the ladies had been sitting in the lobby when Regina came home wearing black satin shorts and carrying one of her outfits—a gold lamé top with round circles on it and gold briefs with black tassels. She saw them and wandered over to ask if they knew anything about an express bus to Providence. She had to go see her boyfriend in Rhode Island. They had had a fight, and she wanted to make him "understand something."

Now, Miss Woodman pointed out to her friends that what they knew of Regina's life bore a conspicuous similarity to that of Miss Robin Benedict. Miss Thawley retrieved one of the *Herald* photos of Robin and blocked out the girl's long hair with her cupped hands. All the ladies agreed that the resemblance to Regina was astonishing. Was it possible that William Douglas had come to work at the residence because his mistress had once lived here?

The evening of the "sugar daddy" conversation with Regina, Miss Woodman had been playing a little joke on her friends. She had gotten a new AM/FM cassette player and had placed it under her seat in the lobby, where she was surreptitiously recording conversations. As a consequence she had Regina's voice on tape.

Miss Thawley appropriated the cassette for "evidence." She thought about sending it along to Lieutenant Sharkey, but she hadn't seen any results from the series of letters she had sent him to date. While Miss Thawley was pondering what to do with the tape, she had an experience which frightened her thoroughly. She had been walking through the Haymarket when a black man with a camera came right up to her, snapped her photo, and ran off through the stalls. Someone, Miss Thawley speculated, had figured out that she knew too much and was setting her up for a contract hit.

There was no choice, Miss Thawley concluded, but to take her case to the media. That way if she disappeared suddenly, someone would know the full story. With this mission in mind Miss Thawley and Betty Sanborn took the Regina tape and walked unannounced into the Boston headquarters of Channel 7.

They were quickly handed over to Mike Lawrence, the young reporter who had broken the affidavits story the preceding June. Lawrence listened agreeably while the ladies recounted their labyrinthine tale of William Douglas at the YWCA. Lawrence found them oddly believable. As they told the story, he could see it being replayed in their eyes. But he wasn't sure what it all added up to, if anything. He thanked them for their help and, out of courtesy more than anything else, asked to keep the tape for future reference.

In fact, he knew perfectly well that the ladies from the Y had no credibility and that the tape would never make it to the air.

Miss Thawley, however, returned to the residence considerably reassured. The mysterious Mr. L., as she chose to refer to Lawrence for the benefit of the other Crimestoppers, had things well in hand. You couldn't be too careful when you were dealing with a clever creature such as William Douglas, who might well slip his bonds the moment that society dropped its guard.

UP TO THE POINT of the indictment, O'Connell had not been aware of the full scope of circumstantial evidence accumulating in the locker on the top floor of the Gray House. As counsel for an unindicted suspect, he had enjoyed no right to those reports. But now, as the attorney of a defendant, he was entitled to see every item that the Commonwealth intended to introduce into evidence. John Kivlan, however, had no intention of turning these over without a fight. When the defense formally requested the court to grant discovery, Kivlan refused on the grounds that O'Connell had a "conflict of interest" and should be disqualified from the case.

The prosecutor had gotten wind of this supposed conflict during the grand-jury hearings when Joe Murray had asked him to "take care of" his federal drug charge. Out of curiosity, Kivlan had sent for the documents on that case and discovered, to his amazement, that Murray was being represented by Dan O'Connell.

Kivlan could see why O'Connell would be loath to give up either Douglas or Murray. The first had enormous capacity to generate publicity; the second, presumably, was a big money-maker. But it was a principle well established in Massachusetts case law that an attorney in a criminal case could not represent both a defendant and a prospective witness. And O'Connell's potential conflicts did not stop there. As far as Kivlan knew, he still represented Nancy Douglas, who stood to be indicted herself. That would put O'Connell in the position of representing two criminal defendants whose interests might well be at odds.

Kivlan promptly filed a pretrial motion to disqualify O'Connell, arguing that the state should not be required to provide discovery until there was some determination as to whether O'Connell would be allowed to continue on the case. Judge Donahue, who was now handling all the matters pertaining to William Douglas, agreed to entertain the motion to disqualify. In the interim, however, he ordered Kivlan to turn over to O'Connell the discovery he was seeking.

A LITTLE over a week after Douglas's indictment, the FBI's Agent Kearney got back to Kivlan with his best news to date. He had examined every inch of the hammer and in the process had taken the head off the handle.

In the bore where the two were joined, he found more encrusted blood. Dampening a piece of cotton thread, he had run it across the blood with a pair of tweezers, then submitted it to electrophoresis. To his delight he found PGM 2-1, the same marker that he had pulled up from the Toyota deck mat and upholstery. Since Douglas had PGM 1-1, that meant it could not possibly have been his blood on the hammer. This placed John Kivlan in the advantageous position of arguing to a jury that it was the victim's blood on the supposed murder weapon.

Whether the crusted blood came from Robin Benedict, Kearney still could not say with certainty. But he had now managed to raise six markers from the bloody evidence, and he calculated that only 2 percent of the Caucasian population would have had this same combination. That was only about one in fifty people. In the Benedict family alone, two of Robin's siblings, Ronnie and Richard, showed the same set of six, suggesting that they had a close genetic tie with the person whose blood was on the evidence.

Even as he was digesting this new intelligence, Kivlan was busy pursuing another tack through which he hoped to persuade a jury that Robin Benedict was indeed dead. Consulting again the Sally Rawlings case, he noticed that the Oklahoma prosecutor had tried to establish that the victim was such a devoted mother that she would never have walked off leaving her baby daughter to the care of her ex-husband. She had fought for custody of the little girl. All of her future plans revolved around the child. Her absence, therefore, was a striking departure from her normal pattern.

Even as far back as the Webster case, the Commonwealth of Massachusetts had argued that Dr. Parkman, a God-fearing man with roots deep in the community, would never have abandoned his family voluntarily. "Life pattern" also proved crucial to one of the first of the modern no-body cases when in 1955 a Los Angeles prosecutor argued that a missing socialite named Evelyn Scott would not have voluntarily abandoned her Beverly Hills home—leaving her dentures and eyeglasses behind. Her husband was eventually convicted of her murder.

Establishing a pattern for Robin Benedict, however, presented a delicate problem. Most of her working hours—from about four in the afternoon to three in the morning—were spent in the Combat Zone, a revelation which was bound to raise questions as to how predictable a pattern she could have developed. Moreover, it raised once again the specter of her "associates", any of whom might have had a motive to kill her or abduct her or induce her to run away from her pimp.

Kivlan could, however, call Savi Bisram to tell how Robin loved little

Taj and would never voluntarily have missed his party on Sunday. He would call J.R. to have him tell how he and Robin had planned to get married, how happy they were, and how she would never have left him of her own volition. He could call Shirley Benedict, who would tell of her daughter's enthusiasm over her "dream house"—a home, humble as it was, that Robin would not have quit anymore readily than Evelyn Scott would have left her Beverly Hills mansion.

While Kivlan fine-tuned these scenarios, the Benedict family undertook its own methods to establish that Robin had not left town of her own accord. In late October, Attorney DiFruscia had put in motion his plan, outlined in his letter to the district attorney, to have Robin declared legally dead by a probate court, thus giving her parents access to her estate. This included her house, valued at $50,000, her car, at $5,275, and her personal property—including mink coat, diamonds, and gold jewelry assessed at a rather conservative $1,000. For three successive weeks DiFrusica ran advertisements in the *Malden Evening News* announcing that John and Shirley Benedict were petitioning to become receivers, special guardians appointed by the court to watch over their daughter's estate. The ad invited Robin Benedict, or any other person claiming an interest in her property, to come forward and object. It brought no response from Robin. It did, however, draw challenge from a new and hostile quarter. The trustees of Tufts entered an objection to the appointment of the Benedicts as receivers. The university had already filed suit against the estate, claiming that of the $67,400 that Douglas had stolen, at least $21,324 had gone directly to Robin Benedict for services never rendered. Now the trustees requested—and received—a $30,000 attachment on the "dream house."

DiFruscia, who delighted in a good fight, saw the chance to prove his mettle against the big boys at Tufts. He picked up the gauntlet, replying that the trustees' claim was absurd. In the first place, the university had already been reimbursed by Hartford for its losses. (The insurer, in turn, had gotten a lien on Douglas's house.) Furthermore, Robin Benedict had been working under a legitimate contract authorized by the officials of Tufts themselves. DiFruscia doubtless knew that Robin's employment was a sham. No one had ever produced one scrap of artwork that she had done for Douglas. There was no evidence that she had ever acquired the expertise to do "image analysis" or "statistical analysis." DiFruscia nevertheless felt that there was a case to be made on paper. Among the documents he was prepared to produce was the federal 1099 form for $13,600 in "nonemployee compensation." Another was the paper which Douglas had coauthored for the British *Journal of Cell Science*, in which he acknowledged Robin N. Benedict's "expert assistance." There was also the correspondence with her concerning their fifty-fifty "partnership" on the Navy submarine project.

Beyond this, DiFruscia had in his possession an intriguing memo which Douglas had written to Robin in what appeared to be May of 1982. While cleaning out the Cliff Street house, J.R. had reputedly found it stuck into the couch and had passed it along to John and Shirley Benedict. It read:

1   Hire RNB for image analysis project. RNB is a graduate student working on image analysis project. This, in addition to my letter to you of May 21, 1982, documents for the future your involvement in the U.S. Naval Submarine Project—including 50:50 division of patent rights!
2   RNB receives check of $200 per week for part-time work on project.
3   This $200 check will be used to cover WHJD's first two hour visits each week.
4   Only inconvenience to RNB. A) instead of receiving two $100 bills, you have to cash check. B) Social Security number required. BENEFIT— Employment Record and Tax Return.
5   Starts April 1982.
6   If you do graphic arts work for us, you will be paid extra for that work above $200 per week.
7   April 82 to September 82 is initial or starting period to see how it works. April 82—I would like you to have some form of documentable income/ employment. When you retire from "business" your resume will not have a five-year gap.
   Also IRS will have a record that you were employed by a Medical School and—there will not be a gap in your employment income.
   This will help in April 1983 when I do your tax return. . . .

This document, penned with such avuncular solicitude, was ambiguous. At least one clause left open the possibility that Robin actually had done—or at least had the opportunity to do—some artwork. DiFruscia thought that this might even be interpreted to suggest that Robin was actually involved in a top-flight government project.

As the Norfolk district attorney had suspected, DiFruscia was hatching his own plans to sue Tufts. Looking at the case from a personal-injuries perspective, DiFruscia reasoned that the university, through its negligence, had caused the "absence"—he could not legally use the word "death"—of Robin Benedict. The Tufts suit against Robin's estate gave him the impetus he needed to launch his own offensive. He filed a counterclaim for $1,000,000 in damages.

Tufts's purported negligence, DiFruscia was prepared to argue, took the form of sloppy accounting procedures which had permitted Robin to remain in Douglas's employ. This was a rather tortured argument, which Tufts's attorneys rebutted in correspondingly arcane civil terminology. The gist of their reply was that Robin had no business being there in the first place. She had known what she was getting herself into and failed, nonetheless, "to exercise due care for her own safety, and that . . . lack of due care was the . . . cause of whatever injury [she] suffered."

Tufts had filed its original complaint in Malden District Court, which did not allow a trial by jury, nor did it give adversaries the right to elicit information through discovery. DiFruscia reasoned that if he could get the case moved to superior court, he would have a chance to grill Tufts about its accounting and security procedures. Even better, he might be able to interrogate William Douglas. While Douglas could take the Fifth in a criminal proceeding, he might not be able to refuse a subpoena to supply testimony in a civil case against Robin's estate. This, then, would give the Benedicts their first opportunity to confront and question their daughter's accused killer directly.

The attorneys for Hartford Insurance had a similar idea to lure Douglas into civil depositions, but Dan O'Connell cut in quickly to argue that questioning Douglas on civil matters could contribute to the adverse publicity now surrounding the upcoming criminal trials. Douglas, however, refused to show up for depositions, arguing that to answer questions, even in a civil proceeding, would infringe upon his Fifth Amendment protection against self-incrimination.

One reason that O'Connell was so eager to keep his client out of the hands of civil plaintiffs was that he knew any revelations elicited during their questioning would surely fall into the hands of John Kivlan. The prosecutor, meanwhile, had stepped up his campaign to have O'Connell disqualified. Late in November and early December the combatants— Kivlan, O'Connell, and Joe Murray's attorney of record, Judd Carhart— gathered in the chambers of Judge Donahue to try and resolve the question of whether O'Connell could be allowed to proceed. The meetings were secret, but word leaked out that insults were flying fast and furious.

O'Connell finally withdrew from the case of his own volition, hoping "to avoid even the possibility" of a conflict.

The departure of Dan O'Connell left the Douglas in temporary disarray. Within hours, however, the defendant found himself courted by a number of young attorneys eager to take up the cudgel for such a celebrated client.

One of these was Damon Scarano, a nervous, talkative fellow whom Douglas had apparently found to replace Harvey Freishtat in his negotiations with Tufts.

As Scarano himself had no criminal experience to speak of, he invited a friend of his, a defense attorney named Stephen Hrones, to become attorney of record. Scarano would "assist" in the defense. Douglas apparently accepted this arrangement because a little over a week after O'Connell's withdrawal, Hrones entered his first appearance.

These developments, however, did not please Dan O'Connell. Even before he formally withdrew from the case, he had decided to bequeath it to his own, hand-picked successor, a close pal of his named Richard Clayman. O'Connell felt that Clayman was a good detail man, and this case clearly required the ability to marshal minutiae. O'Connell also knew that the money, of which Douglas had little, would matter less to "Richie" than the publicity. Clayman, like O'Connell, was trying to build up his criminal practice.

And so when it appeared that Scarano and Hrones were threatening to move in on their turf, O'Connell and Clayman made a hasty trip to the Norfolk County House of Corrections to try to convince Douglas he had made a terrible mistake. They succeeded without too much effort. Nancy Douglas, apparently not too fond of the team of Scarano and Hrones, was willing to defer to O'Connell's judgment. William Douglas sent a letter to Hrones informing him that his services would not be required.

Eager to show his stuff, Richie Clayman moved aggressively to lay to rest any suspicion that the defense was foundering. At a preliminary hearing on January 18, he presented the findings of a psychiatrist, Dr. John P. Hennessy, who had reportedly seen the defendant six times between his arraignment and the middle of November. Hennessy reported that Douglas was "oriented to all spheres." While showing "mild depression and mild anxiety," he displayed "no demonstrable signs or evidence of any suicidal or homicidal ideation." Clayman argued that this view of Douglas's emotional state belied the Comonwealth's contention that Douglas was a threat to himself and others and that he should, therefore, be granted bail. Once again Kivlan reminded the court of Douglas's own claims of a "mental aberration" arising from dieting and the use of cocaine.

Once again, bail was denied.

Clayman then dropped a surprise on the court. He had been contacted, he said, by a "well-respected" attorney who had reportedly seen Robin Benedict in the days since her disappearance. Clayman declined to give the witness's name, saying that he had to check out the lead to satisfy himself that it was reliable. Even if Clayman returned to report that his "well-respected" attorney did not exist—as was entirely likely—he had suceeded in casting doubt on the Commonwealth's assertions that Robin Benedict was dead. If he could arouse in jurors a *reasonable* doubt, then they would have to acquit.

Kivlan appeared unfazed and said he would investigate.

O'CONNELL, meanwhile, had passed his discovery materials along to Clayman. Confronted by the overwhelming bulk of evidence, Clayman thought it might be wise to bring in another attorney to help sort through it. He called on his own good friend Charles Balliro. The scion of a prominent Sicilian family from the Italian North End, Balliro was also well connected in the criminal-defense community. He was the cousin of one Joseph Balliro, reputed to be the leading criminal defense attorney in Boston. Charlie had spent several years in Los Angeles working as an immigration attorney and, having returned to Boston, was interested in establishing a reputation in criminal work like his cousin Joe's. As Balliros went, Charlie was strictly junior varsity, but he was a hard worker and enjoyed certain entrée that Clayman, a straitlaced Jewish boy from Chelsea, lacked. The Balliro family once owned a Combat Zone night spot called the Intermission Lounge. Charlie had worked there for ten years as a bartender while putting himself through law school. The street people knew him as Charlie Boy and were likely to tell him things they wouldn't tell some nosy private eye.

Charlie did a little checking among his contacts on Lower Washington Street and learned a thing or two about Robin and Douglas. For one thing, Douglas was reputed to have been fascinated by Robin's face. It was said that she rarely or never performed oral sex on him. He preferred that she straddle him so that he could see her features. Balliro himself later claimed he had once seen Robin eating dinner at a Chinese restaurant in the Zone and was struck by what he took to be her imperious look. Charlie, who had gone to college on an athletic scholarship, had nonetheless read a bit of Homer. In the months after Robin's disappearance, he would liken her, with flamboyant romanticism, to Circe the sorceress. He imagined her haughty stare to be saying, "I am beauty. I am heartless. Beware of me."

After reading over the case file, however, Balliro developed a somewhat softer opinion of the reputed vixen.

If the Benedicts could be believed, Robin had been a very dutiful girl, almost reverential toward her parents. She had, Balliro thought, a peculiarly Hispanic attitude toward family. Her main reason for cultivating William Douglas was doubtless pecuniary, but she may also, Balliro thought, have enjoyed the legitimacy he lent her. That she could claim to be doing artwork for a distinguished professor not only kept her family from prying too deeply into her affairs; it must have even made them a little proud.

Douglas, Balliro reasoned, also derived advantages from bestowing legitimacy upon Robin. By styling her an MIT graduate student, he was free to mention her name, both at work and at home. It gave a man a secret pleasure to speak his lover's name. And Douglas, Balliro concluded, was seriously in love with this woman. If a guy goes to the Zone to get blown, that's sex. But if he daydreams about sharing an evening over crab legs at Pier 4—well, that's love.

Charlie Balliro drew up a detailed chronology of verifiable events and toll calls and in the process came to a controversial conclusion. Robin Benedict, he felt, was just as likely to have been killed by Nancy as by William Douglas. If it was Nancy who had borrowed the hammer from her father, Balliro reasoned, might she not have had the hammer in the car intending to return it to him? When she came home that night and saw Robin's car in the drive, might she not have taken the hammer into the house? What, then, if she came into the bedroom and saw Robin atop her husband? Driven by the rage of a woman scorned, might she not have hit Robin from behind, giving Bill a glancing blow in the process?

Balliro chose to proceed on the theory that it was the wife who, as he put it, "slew" Robin Benedict. That would get Bill Douglas off the hook, and it would probably have only limited repercussions for Nancy. Balliro was convinced that the Norfolk district attorney would never dare to bring Nancy to trial. A good defense counsel could whip up so much sympathy for that poor, beleaguered woman that no jury would ever convict her. When Balliro ran this scenario past his client, however, Douglas was horrified. Nancy was apparently none too pleased herself. By the end of January she was already soliciting another attorney to take her husband's case.

"IN BOSTON", a native son named Lawrence O'Donnell, Jr., once wrote, "criminal defense is the specialty of the gritty Irish, Italian and Jewish lawyers who graduate without academic distinction from plebeian colleges and law schools. They could never win employment in the city's high-powered corporate law firms founded a century ago . . . by patrician Harvard Law School graduates. . . ."

O'Donnell might have added that they have a taste for the blood sport of criminal defense work that Brahmins find unbecoming to a gentleman.

There was certainly nothing gentlemanly about one of the leading exemplars of this scrappy fraternity, Thomas C. Troy, Esquire.

Troy was a florid old club fighter from the former Irish stronghold of Dorchester. His loyalties were governed almost exclusively by tribal affiliations. He had a parochial suspicion of females, blacks, and outsiders in general, but he could establish instant intimacy with a man who was a "fellow Marine" or a "brother attorney" or a "cousin cop." He hailed from a line of Boston policemen. When Tom was young, his father was killed trying to make an arrest in the South End and was subsequently immortalized by the premier crime writer of the day, a reporter named Johnny Sullivan. The deification was so extravagant that Sullivan's paper, what was then the *Daily Record,* managed to raise $33,000 for the fallen officer's fatherless children. It was through the good offices of the media then that young Tom Troy was raised to manhood, a fact which served to remind him continually of its power.

Throughout his seventeen-year career Troy had been fascinated by the press, mesmerized by its ability to elevate a man on a swell of adulation and then, without warning, turn and throw him into disgrace. Troy was careful to educate himself in the ways of the media. He learned that what reporters wanted was not complexity but pithy one-liners that would provide a lead for the next day's story. He became a favorite of old-time newsmen—particularly the indolent or gullible variety—who fed on his flash and bombast. They enshrined him in a legend spun from countless tales of Troy. He had wanted to be a priest but was rejected because he had a tattoo on his forearm. He had been a boxer, then a cop. The legend had it that he studied law by the glow of his cruiser domelight until he got a degree from one of those "plebeian colleges," the Portia School of Law.

Only six months after being admitted to the bar, Troy lucked into a notorious client. Albert DaSalvo, the so-called Boston Strangler, had quarreled with his attorney, F. Lee Bailey, over handling of the book and the soon-to-be-released movie based upon his supposed exploits. DaSalvo, who had never actually been convicted of the killings, only of multiple rapes, objected to being called the Boston Strangler and wanted Bailey to quit referring to him as such on talk shows. He also asked Tom Troy, who represented another client at the prison, to take his case. Troy seized the initiative with a flourish, claiming that *The Boston Strangler* was "one of the most perfect hoaxes this country has seen in years." He tried to get a restraining order against the release of the movie in Boston. He knew he had little chance of succeeding—and ultimately didn't—but he got out of it what he wanted, an enormous amount of publicity.

Over the years Troy built his practice on junk cases, cast-off cases, cases which were supposedly unwinnable. By the spring of 1984 he had tried around forty-six murder cases alone. Of these he counted forty-three as wins. His record, it must be said, was enhanced by creative plea bargaining. There was a joke around Foley's that if a client didn't go to the chair, Troy counted it as a victory. But he was undeniably effective for the defense. Having been a cop, it was said, he could think like a prosecutor. While weak on the fine points of law, Troy was expert at playing the spoiler, dropping the seeds of suspicion that would sprout into reasonable doubt. He knew how to exploit sentimentality to obscure a logical argument and—most important, perhaps—had the capacity to sway and beguile juries with his considerable charm. "A fat unattractive woman . . . that's Tommy's cup of meat," one Boston newsman observed, "He'll make her feel young again. Hell, he owns her."

Troy was undeniably one of the five best defense attorneys in Boston. Unlike that of F. Lee Bailey and certain others, however, his reputation had never moved outside the bounds of New England. At the age of fifty-four, he suffered from heart trouble and diabetes and, he had told the *Globe* a little over a year earlier, he was "tired."

"I'd like to get a Von Bulow type case," he had reflected wistfully, "and go out in a blaze of glory."

And then William Douglas, one of the most celebrated criminal suspects in the history of the Commonwealth, came begging for his services.

Tom Troy would later say that Nancy Douglas called him "almost daily" during the early weeks of 1984 asking him to undertake her husband's defense. At first he declined. Not because he wasn't intrigued. A professor accused of killing a hooker who had a black pimp! No witnesses! No body! This was definitely Tom Troy's type of case. The sticking point was that Douglas apparently had no money, and Troy usually required a $25,000 retainer to start. Nevertheless, when Mrs. Douglas persisted in her importuning, Troy's office manager, a shrewd and practical man named Pat McCann, urged his boss to reconsider, arguing that this was the kind of high-publicity case that would generate business.

One Friday afternoon in January, McCann paid a visit to the Norfolk County House of Corrections, hoping to talk with William Douglas. On the guardroom floor he happened to bump into Richard Clayman and Charlie Balliro. The latter, realizing what was afoot, offered to let Troy "assist" in the case. When McCann carried this account back to his chief, Troy was infuriated by what he considered the effrontery of these two young punks and determined to let them know with whom they were dealing. The following Monday morning he called Douglas and told him he would take up his cause.

Although Douglas had told Pat McCann that there were "available funds" in the form of a retirement account, Troy soon discovered that this was not true. That fund had already been attached by a previous attorney. In mid-February, therefore, Troy informed Judge Roger Donahue that his client—the eminent Dr. William H. J. Douglas—was "marginally indigent" and persuaded the judge to grant him a court appointment.

Troy then offered to let both Clayman and Balliro stay on if they agreed to "take instruction," but they declined and were shortly given the bum's rush.

TOM TROY got along well with the Norfolk DA, whom he regarded not only as a "brother attorney" but as a dear old friend. Troy was with Delahunt the fabled night that the district attorney, harassed by thugs, allegedly fired his gun into the street. While Troy was fond of Delahunt, however, he had no use for the DA's young assistant, John Kivlan. There were "quiet rules" which members of the clan of Boston Irish attorneys observed in dealing with one another. And Kivlan, in Troy's estimation, had broken those rules by turning on his old friend Dan O'Connell. Troy knew young O'Connell's father, a silver-tongued orator who would nearly climb right in the jury box to woo jurors. The son was no spellbinder, but Troy considered him a decent, capable fellow. Troy had been affronted on behalf of the O'Connell family when he heard how Kivlan had tried to humiliate Dan before the grand jury. He was further enraged to hear of Kivlan's treatment of McManus. Troy had known McManus when he was a Boston cop and was aware that he had a reputation for integrity and bravery. Troy suspected that this business about a bribe was one of the excesses of an overzealous prosecutor. He resolved to cut young Kivlan down to size.

One of the first things Troy set out to do was seize the media momentum from the state, which—to his way of thinking—had benefited from undeserved favorable publicity. After nearly a year of "missing beauty" coverage, the public now envisioned a sweet, innocent Robin persecuted by the diabolical professor. It was time, Troy felt, to create what he referred to delicately as the "proper atmosphere" for trying his case. He prevailed upon Judge Roger Donahue to impose a gag order on all attorneys to keep them from making further comments to the press. Troy knew perfectly well that, as a practical matter, a gag order is binding only upon the prosecutor. A defense attorney can tell the press anything he likes, as long as he is discreet. No one is going to be disciplined for selling his client to the press. So while the district attorney's office was forced to crack down on leaks, Troy mingled as freely as usual among his media buddies at Foley's.

"You're forgettin' the fact that she's a blackmailin' whore with a black pimp," he admonished them slyly. "You haven't got the balls to print the whole story. She's a *hooker!*"

From the moment he took the case, Troy never used the past tense in referring to Robin Benedict. All of his public statements, rather, were calculated to leave the impression that she had simply dropped out of sight for some perverse reasons of her own. Throughout the first few public hearings in February, Troy bellowed challenges calculated to infuriate the prosecutor.

"I fully expect Robin Benedict to walk into this room," he would say. "She's on my witness list."

Kivlan refused to be ruffled. Instead, he used Troy's motions to his own purposes. Calling the court's attention to the fact that the defense had asked for reports pertaining to "any post-mortem examination of the purported victim," the prosecutor noted that this was "interesting," adding, "He is asking for an autopsy report in a case where we don't have the body. Maybe he knows where it is."

In another motion Troy asked for the "medical records of witnesses," apparently hoping to get copies of Robin Benedict's hospital records. Kivlan corrected him, pointing out that the request specified only "witnesses."

"Robin Benedict," he reminded the court, "is dead!"

"Judge," Troy boomed, "he just said, 'She is dead. . . .' He has a glib tongue, Judge, and I'm going to start dancing on it in a minute."

"Go right ahead, Mr. Troy," Kivlan retorted.

Troy turned his back to the bench and muttered, "You're a piece of cake, kid."

As Troy bellowed at the prosecution and press for harassing his client, Douglas would sometimes grin, as pleased as a child whose mother has undertaken to dress down a gang of bullies in his defense. Every now and again he would cast a curious glance up to the bench to see what effect Troy's histrionics seemed to be having on the judge.

Roger Donahue had a reputation for running a tight court and would not normally have tolerated such high jinks. But he was inclined to give these spirited attorneys more rope than usual. Donahue knew both men fairly well. Kivlan he perceived as a rigorously moral fellow who saw human behavior as black or white. To Troy, however, there was no black or white—only infinite shades of gray. In a case which turned upon a man's fall from virtue, Kivlan and Troy were the perfect pair of adversaries, one arguing punishment and the other forbearance. It was natural, then, that they should strike a few sparks off each other's armor. It was Donahue's intent to give them maximum leeway during the hearings, reining them in sharply before the trial, which had now been set to begin on Monday, April 23.

As the hearings continued into February, Troy became even more provocative, attempting to lure the district attorney's office out into the open and onto what remained a potential minefield of public controversy. Around the first of the year the U.S. Supreme Court had quietly denied Attorney Stephen Keefe's "emergency request" to keep the young Douglases from appearing before the grand jury. The following month, it denied without comment the actual appeal of the Massachusetts high court's decision requiring the children to testify. The Douglases had run out of remedies. The children, if called, would have to testify or be found in contempt.

Troy knew that there was a powerful current of sentiment to be exploited here. It would not be difficult to invoke the specter of babes being torn from their parents' arms and forced to betray them. As he had told Channel 5's "Chronicle" over six months earlier, "This is not Russia!" Now when the question of the children arose, he would draw himself up self-righteously and intone, "Deliver unto me the children of the world. . . . I stand with the family."

He christened this principle "Troy's law."

The day after the U.S. Supreme Court's final rejection of the Douglases' appeal, there was a hearing in Dedham at which Troy demanded that Kivlan say what he intended to do with the children. In a conspicuous aside to the press gallery, Troy sneered, "He just wants to lock up the kids because they won't testify about Mommy and Daddy." Kivlan responded coolly that no decision had been made yet. But in reality both Kivlan and District Attorney Delahunt were extremely worried that Troy might be able to whip the public into such a frenzy of sympathy for the children that it would obscure the fact that their father was on trial for murder.

Kivlan made one more attempt to call the young Douglases. On March 7, a little over a week after the Supreme Court's decision, he called Keefe and asked him to make arrangements for the children to appear at the grand jury the following Monday, March 12, at 8:00 A.M. Keefe assured him that, Supreme Court decision notwithstanding, the children would not testify. Monday came, and they did not appear. By this time Kivlan had been pursuing the Douglas children for a full nine months. "Deliver unto me the children of the world" had threatened to become a battle cry. Rather than risk creating martyrs, Kivlan reluctantly dropped pursuit.

TROY, meanwhile, had been to interview his celebrated client at the county jail. While Douglas would later recall this meeting as "very, very enjoyable," Troy himself had a somewhat different take. He would never say that he came away from that first encounter convinced of Douglas's guilt. He was, however, convinced that his client was lying. When Douglas tried to suggest that the state police had planted Robin's belongings in his house, Troy reputedly turned off his tape recorder and said, "That's bullshit."

After that, Troy shrewdly allowed himself "minimal involvement" with Douglas. Instead, he arranged for the interviewing to be done by a young associate who had joined the firm just that February. William Doyle, a clean-cut, boyish fellow, was also the scion of a Boston Irish law family. His father had been an assistant to the Suffolk County district attorney in the early sixties, and before that his grandfather had served Suffolk as first assistant for nearly thirty years. Young Doyle had just come from the Massachusetts Defenders Committee, a state agency which represented indigent criminal defendants, and already had over fifty jury trials to his credit.

At least once a week Doyle drove to Dedham, where he met with Douglas in a little office that lay up a spiral staircase and down the second-floor corridor. The accommodations were austere, one institutional metal desk with two institutional metal chairs. One window with the blinds always drawn. At times the clanging of tier gates and the hiss of steam heat would nearly drown out Douglas's high voice.

During the first few meetings Doyle reputedly skirted the issue of guilt or innocence and tried to get some sense of what Douglas's relationship with Benedict had actually been. Very quickly, he found that the client's story varied from telling to telling. Sometimes Douglas would render the highly impressionistic account that he had spun for the edification of his mystery companion in the "What's up, Doc?" tape. (Douglas would not reveal the identity of his companion.) In this version, of course, he was waylaid by a hooker in the parking lot. She took him home, knocked him out with apple juice, posed him in bed nude, and took photos, intending to blackmail him. At other times he would claim that Robin had picked him up while trolling at Charlie's.

After hours of chasing after these fanciful filaments, Doyle concluded that Douglas truly was having a hard time distinguishing between reality and fantasy. The events of those months between April 1982 and March 1983 had the quality of a nightmare. His perceptions, Doyle felt, had been distorted by the trauma and fear surrounding Robin's disappearance—whatever those circumstances might be. Doyle was convinced that Douglas's faulty recall was compounded by the fact that during the period in question he had been using drugs.

After he and Robin had been going together for about a month, Douglas told Doyle, Robin had decided that she could "trust" him and so introduced him to cocaine and marijuana. The strongest substance that he had ever used before that was alcohol. Although Douglas wouldn't be specific about how much coke was involved, Doyle got the impression that he was doing only a couple of lines an evening. He hadn't apparently gotten into the more sophisticated applications, such as injecting or freebasing. His dependency, if it was a dependency, seemed to be less physical than emotional. Cocaine had apparently released him from his structured life, lifted him above the system of habits which had governed his actions to date, relieved him of the necessity of reading from his slavish, compulsive little scripts, and allowed him to be the person he had always wanted to be. A spontaneous, fun-loving thin man.

Over the ensuing weeks Doyle and Troy were able to piece together from their individual conversations with Douglas the extent of his erotic involvement with Robin Benedict. Although Douglas would later try to minimize the role that sex had played in that relationship with Robin, his attorneys estimated that it consumed a good 50 to 80 percent of his hours with her. Douglas was not getting any physical satisfaction at home and had gone to the Zone looking for oral sex. This would relieve his tension for a few days. Robin, however, expanded his expectations, providing the variety that, as Troy later put it, "made him sexual."

By the early spring of 1984, Douglas seemed willing to concede that Robin Benedict had been using him. If asked whether he had loved her, he would deny it. He took vehement exception to the notion that he had been "obsessed." A man obsessed is a man pursuing a baser sort of instinct. Douglas wanted to present himself as an intelligent, rational being.

When Troy offered him the face-saving observation that he had perhaps been "infatuated" by Robin Benedict, Douglas seized upon it gratefully. From then on out, he spoke of a passion which had once gripped him with the fury of a grand mal seizure as an indulgence which had simply turned his head. He had indulged in Robin Benedict much as he had indulged in cocaine. She relieved his tension. She had raised a mirror that allowed him to see himself the way he had always wanted to be. She had given him an exhilarating, if illusory, "hope for living." He had allowed himself to be carried away, to become dependent upon the rush that her presence and radiant smile and calculated adulation gave him. But obsessed? No. Dr. William Douglas could not recall having ever been obsessed.

DOYLE did not like Douglas much. Troy would later explain that his young associate's aversion was due to a puritanical streak found in a certain kind of Irish attorney, the type who says, "I know you're guilty but I'll defend you, you lousy bastard." But even Troy, who had little of the puritan in him, found Douglas "an awful whiner."

The attorneys' discomfort increased when, several weeks into the case, they received the discovery material which arrived in a huge box from Richard Clayman. Doyle scanned it quickly, then strode into Troy's office to announce, "We're in trouble."

The chain of evidence led straight to the Douglas household. There was material seeming to implicate both Douglases. Kivlan, however, had clearly focused his attention on William Douglas in constructing what appeared to be a nearly airtight circumstantial case.

As defense counsel, Troy did not have to build an equally airtight case establishing Douglas's innocence. All he had to do was to poke enough holes in the Commonwealth's case to raise a reasonable doubt. Troy hastily convened an ad hoc committee composed of Doyle, McCann, two young associates, and a law student and bade them go through the box of discovery. For a solid week this crew met around the clock in an upstairs library named the "Plot and Scheme" room, where they examined John Kivlan's chain of evidence for weak links.

THE SLEDGEHAMMER stood to be very incriminating—but only if Kivlan could convince a jury that it was the same one Nancy had borrowed from her father. He had done his best to establish that at the grand-jury hearings, but, in fact, his persistence had backfired. The Plot and Scheme group zeroed in on the statements of John Boulton, who testified that the Mansfield hammer looked much more worn than the one he had lent his daughter. He had also denied the "99 percent" comment. Kivlan's own witness could be turned against him.

The man's shirt was tougher to wish away. Troy would, of course, argue that blue shirts—even in large sizes—were extremely prevalent among professional men. This one, however, had stitching which Nancy Douglas had identified as her own. Since her admissions had been made in front of Douglas himself, they would probably be allowed into evidence. It was even more incriminating that the shirt had been found in close proximity to a coat which the Benedicts and J.R. Rogers had identified as Robin's. Plot and Scheme decided that its best line of defense was to argue that since Robin wasn't living at home, her parents couldn't really claim they were that familiar with her wardrobe. The bottom line would be that brown jackets, like blue shirts, exist in abundance.

Doyle was assigned to check the reliability of the tests which linked the Mansfield trash bag to the Hefty bags under the Douglases' sink. He had been a chemistry major in college and called an old classmate who assured him that such tests could be performed with amazing accuracy. The "characteristic flaw" was as distinctive as a fingerprint. The good news was that no chemist alive could identify a single bag as coming from a particular package. The Mansfield bag could have come from any number of boxes in the New England area. There were probably several boxes of bag with that orange fleck at Shaw's Supermarket alone.

Likewise, Plot and Scheme felt the Mobil slip could be dismissed with little difficulty. After analyzing the signature on the carbon, the best the FBI could do was say that Douglas "probably" wrote it. The pump operator couldn't identify Douglas and couldn't tie his supposed purchase down to any particular time. Only a shift. And even if Kivlan could somehow establish that it was Douglas at the station—so what? It didn't mean he killed Robin. Why is he there? someone might ask. Well, Troy would reply, he's a man who works strange hours.

The Amtrak ticket was tougher. The FBI had positively identified the signature on that ticket as Douglas's. Plot and Scheme hoped to rebut that with its own witness. This plan was dashed when a handwriting expert hired by Troy came to the office one afternoon and within a matter of minutes confirmed the signature as Douglas's. The best the defense could hope to do was muddy the waters a bit. Troy and his brain trust could tell from the police reports that the prosecutor had had difficulty locating the conductor who owned the punch used on Douglas's ticket. Doyle checked with an old friend of his at Amtrak who confided that the conductor had not actually been scheduled to work that evening and had just jumped aboard the train to help out. By raising the possibility of an off-duty conductor using his punch in an unauthorized fashion, Troy could suggest that Douglas's ticket could have been punched anywhere, not necessarily on a train pulling out of New York City.

The tolls were going to be brutal. Doyle for one could not imagine why on earth Douglas, if it was indeed Douglas who had used that card, had not used coins. Didn't he know that charging left a sharp set of hen tracks in the encoded bowels of AT & T? Was it because he had no money or because he simply wasn't thinking? Douglas was a very smart man, Doyle concluded, but that intelligence did not extend to common sense.

John Kivlan would attempt to show how the calls charged to Douglas's credit card or home phone matched the calls received by Robin's answering service. Americall's procedures, however, were demonstrably sloppy. One message slip had three different stamps on it, each suggesting a different time and date. Maura Armstrong, the Americall operator who testified before the grand jury, couldn't remember having taken either of the Charlestown messages which came in before midnight on March 5. Plot and Scheme proposed to draw up a large chart listing the tolls and to circle all the discrepancies in red. A juror might lose track of the intricate logic behind the calls, but when he went into deliberation he would remember those big red circles.

Plot and Scheme next turned its collective attention to the forensic evidence. As impressive as the FBI's blood analysis looked on paper, Troy knew that such subjective results were always open to challenge. Troy had wanted to send samples of blood and brain to Wraxall and Abbott on the West Coast. Judge Donahue, however, wouldn't allow the evidence to travel as far as California, which, he observed dryly, was a state "which the rest of the country seems to have some reservations about." As it happened, one of the lab's founders, John Cope Abbott, was opening up a new branch in Burlington, Massachusetts, and the prospect of testing there met with Donahue's approval. Doyle dropped into the state police lab at 1010 Commonwealth Avenue to pick up the samples, which he then drove out to Abbott's lab.

Abbott, who was not as conservative as the FBI, routinely tested for five more obscure markers, and in John Benedict's blood he reportedly found one which occurred most commonly among those of negroid ancestry. That marker had not shown up in the blood samples from the silver Toyota; this left Troy room to suggest that it did not belong to Robin. The problem with that argument was that Robin would also have been a product of her mother's genetic makeup and might not have possessed the negroid marker. On the more common markers Abbott's findings were perfectly consistent with the FBI's, leaving no latitude for faulting Agent Kearney on a technical basis. Troy's tack, therefore, would be to argue that while all of the blood samples on the evidence were consistent with having come from a Benedict offspring, that meant nothing. An estimated ten thousand people in the Boston area alone had that same blood profile. Not all of them were the children of John and Shirley Benedict.

Most potentially damaging of all the evidence, however, were the statements which Douglas had given before getting himself an attorney. Any contradiction at all was bound to hurt a defendant's credibility, but John Kivlan would no doubt make high drama of the fact that Douglas had given at least two accounts of how he had hired Robin, two different points of departure from Boston to Washington, D.C., and four accounts of how he had gotten his head wound. Troy would naturally try to get these statements excluded from evidence. He would argue that Jack DaRosa had been acting as an agent of the Norfolk County district attorney and that, inasmuch as he had neglected to read Douglas his rights, the Washington interview should not be allowed. He could argue that the other reports should be disallowed because Douglas thought he was in custody. He would present Douglas as a "baby" at the mercy of manipulative police officers who had coerced him into talking. Even if the statements were allowed in—and the consensus in Plot and Scheme was that Kivlan would pretty much have his way—Troy could argue that his client had contradicted himself because he was weary and confused. Landry had taken the longest and most damning statement just after Douglas had completed a tiring six-and-a-half-hour drive back from up-state New York. No wonder his wits were addled.

There was one encouraging thing about those statements. Each of them allowed Douglas the defense "She was alive when she left my house." This, in turn, offered Troy the possibility of shifting suspicion to other suspects. Because most of the prime candidates were scheduled to testify for the Commonwealth, Troy would have the added tactical advantage of turning John Kivlan's witnesses into defendants.

As Robin's last appointment before Sharon, Sargent Nichols was high on the list. But the men of Plot and Scheme found they really couldn't get far with this scenario. Nichols had no identifiable means or motive to kill Robin, save perhaps her refusal to stay for the night. Inasmuch as she had spent time at his place, he arguably had the opportunity, but Douglas himself admitted having seen her alive later in the evening. There were the calls from "Robin" on Sunday afternoon, saying she was on her way to Longfellow Place, but there was no evidence that she and Nichols ever had that second meeting. No. Nichols was too respectable to make a credible suspect.

The next likely prospect was Joe from Charlestown. If the Americall messages were to be believed, it was Murray, not Douglas, who was the last to see Robin alive. Troy asked Judge Donahue for permission to depose Murray, but Murray was still maintaining his silence, claiming that to discuss the Benedict incident might hurt him in his federal drug case. In early February, John Kivlan challenged this contention, pointing out that Murray had been acquitted of the drug charges in January and was no longer likely to endanger his Fifth Amendment rights. After much negotiation between Kivlan and Attorney Carhart, Murray had finally agreed to give the prosecution a brief written statement affirming that he had not seen Robin Benedict the night of March 5 and had not invited her to a party in Charlestown. He refused to make himself available for lengthier depositions but did agree to testify for the prosecution when the case came to trial.

Troy was mindful that the "Joe from Charlestown" scenario had serious flaws. "Robin" had left a message with her answering service saying that she had left Murray's and was on her way to Longfellow Place. Troy could try and discredit this call, but that would also cast doubt on the preceding night's message that she had been on her way to Joe's. While Murray arguably had the opportunity to kill Robin, he could not be linked to the hammer and had no discernible motive. Perhaps the best thing about having Murray to kick around was that it would allow Troy to invoke Robin's milieu, a shadowy world reputedly rife with drugs and sexual perversion. During the summer preceding Murray's trial, his codefendant and Robin's "associate," Bucky Barrett, had also disappeared without a trace. The judge presiding over the Murray case speculated publicly that one of the other defendants might have "sunk Mr. . . . Barrett in the soft mud of the South Bay." Such dark doings so close to the Murray camp stood to underscore what potentially lethal company Robin had gotten herself into. Robin could easily have been done in by one of those "associates."

This raised the question of J.R. Rogers. Tom Troy regarded Rogers with all the loathing and contempt that an old Irish cop could muster for a black pimp. To Troy, J.R. was nothing but a "slick-talking sewer rat." That the DA persisted in the charade that he was a sweet, cultured antique-car dealer was infuriating. Troy was itching to call J.R. to the stand and there bully him into showing his true colors.

On paper, at least, J.R. seemed the ideal candidate. He had the means to kill Robin. (If she had borrowed the hammer to do work on the house, J.R. would have had access to it.) And one could speculate on a number of motives. Perhaps Robin really was fond of Douglas. That was not so hard to imagine. Before meeting Douglas, she had hung out with jocks and street punks. Perhaps she actually enjoyed the company of someone older, more refined. Pimps were notoriously insecure, Troy reasoned. Perhaps J.R. was getting worried about all the time that Douglas and Robin were spending together. Jealousy, then, was one motive.

Douglas also claimed that Robin and J.R. had been arguing in recent weeks because he had been bringing other girls back to her dream house. Troy had heard through his own sources that J.R. was cultivating "upwards of eight" girls. Was it not possible that Robin was on her way out? Perhaps she and J.R. were having problems in the drug business. Maybe she had become inconvenient. "If she's dead," J.R. might have reasoned, "Tufts won't be coming after her. . . ."

But if so, why wouldn't J.R. have found a more inconspicuous way to get rid of her? It strained credulity to imagine a guy as streetwise as Rogers concocting a scheme that required planting evidence in the Douglas house. When, after all, would he have found the opportunity?

There was only one logical point at which J.R. could have broken into 38 Sandy Ridge Circle, and that was Saturday afternoon when Douglas went for his supposed walk. Still, a black man entering a home on Sandy Ridge Circle in broad daylight was likely to attract some notice. A more plausible scenario was that J.R. had accompanied Robin to Sharon that night and that when she returned to the car without whatever it was that she was supposed to get from Douglas, they began to argue. He hits her, panics, heads to Rhode Island, making toll calls to Douglas and hoping to frame him.

If by some happy chance, the Plot and Scheme group could establish that it was J.R. who had signed Douglas's name to the Mobil slip, it might have a shot at selling this convoluted story to a jury. But that hope was short-lived. Even though the FBI had been unable to say for certain whether the Mobil signature belonged to Douglas, the expert whom Troy called to examine the writing samples declared unequivocally, "It's his." In the pursuit of J.R. Rogers, the defense could not even count on the help of its own witnesses.

Among this handful of suspects was one whose name was so sensitive that it had to be whispered—so important, however, that it could not be ignored. This was Nancy Douglas. Technically speaking, Troy represented only William Douglas. Nancy, as one of the Plot and Scheme group later described her, "was just out there hanging." That left the defense free, if it wished, to try and shift the blame onto her, a plan which Bill Doyle felt was a strong gambit. Nancy certainly had access to Douglas's credit card—she had apparently been passing it around to relatives. You could argue that it was Nancy who ran around making phone calls and trying to get rid of the body.

Nancy Douglas had the critical triad of means, opportunity, and motive to commit murder. The hammer had been lent directly to her, not to her husband. She had admitted coming home and finding Robin's Toyota in the driveway. This placed both women in the same location at about 11:30 P.M. As for motive, who had a stronger motive than Nancy Douglas?

The beauty of "the wife" scenario was that it would explain away Douglas's contradictory statements. One could argue that he had been lying to cover up for her. The downside of this strategy was that it meant sacrificing Nancy. There was a chance that if Douglas agreed to shift blame to his wife and was still convicted, the Norfolk DA's office would not move to indict Nancy. If he was acquited, however, it might. Naturally, there was no possibility of proceeding on this tack without first sounding out Douglas on the plan. Accordingly, Doyle brought it up on one of his visits to the prison. Douglas, however, was no more receptive to the idea now than he was when Balliro had suggested it and so turned it down flat. He likewise rebuffed another alternative which Troy, after reading the discovery, thought might be prudent—a plea of insanity.

The groundwork for such a plea had already been laid in Douglas's negotiations with Tufts when he had claimed that whatever irregularities had occurred in the management of his research grants were due to his dieting. Troy was prepared to argue that he was suffering from this same condition when he killed Robin Benedict. He would argue, furthermore, that the combination of ketosis and cocaine had rendered the defendant incapable of forming intent.

Troy knew the risks of raising the junk-food argument. You might be able to sail it in California, where you had a bunch of lunatics on wheat germ, but an eastern jury was likely to view it more cynically. It would also require Douglas to confess. And that meant losing the advantage of having no body. That would be a very high price to pay for so speculative a defense.

Douglas, Doyle later recalled, "sort of liked" the idea of a junk-food defense but wasn't yet ready to admit to having committed murder. This more or less settled matters, leaving the defense team no choice but to fall back on its bottom line, "Robin Benedict is not dead."

IT HAD BEEN a year since Robin's disappearance. Kivlan still could not produce a body, and the burden still rested on the state to prove that a murder had occurred. All the prosecutor could offer was circumstantial evidence, but even Troy had to admit that it was pretty devastating. The brain tissue in Douglas's jacket would come as a ghastly revelation to jurors who might be shocked into an irremediable bias against the defendant. Troy would have to offer some innocent and rational explanation of how it found its way into Douglas's garments.

Doyle had been able to establish that Douglas had come into contact with human tissue. During the course of his surfactant work, he had collected aborted fetuses so that he could study their lungs. Perhaps the tissue had come from those specimens. If Troy could get his own expert to confirm that the brain cells belonged to an unborn infant, then they could not possibly be the remains of Robin Benedict.

The expert Troy solicited for this task was Dr. William Q. Sturner, medical examiner for the state of Rhode Island. Sturner, a stout, cheerful, man widely respected for his integrity, had learned about the Benedict case the preceding spring when one of his old friends, Dr. George Katsas, had alerted him to the possibility that the Benedict girl's body might have been dumped somewhere near Providence. When Sturner received the call from Troy, he asked Katsas, who was coming to Providence on other business, to bring a slide of the windbreaker specimen with him.

When Sturner placed the slide under his microscope, what he later described as "a juicy, large circumscribed homogenous neuron" jumped right out at him. This Betz cell, as it was called, was found only in an adult brain. The fetal tissue theory had collapsed.

Sturner did, however, express the opinion that the cells in question need not have come from the deepest structures of the brain and could therefore be the result of an injury less severe than the one suggested by his esteemed colleague Dr. Katsas. This observation left Troy the latitude to argue that Robin might have suffered a survivable wound. The case of the former presidential press secretary James Brady showed that it was possible for a person with even serious brain injury to pull through if he got medical attention. Kivlan would come to court armed with a list of hospitals he had checked to see if they had treated Robin or anyone matching her description. Troy would counter with an even longer list of hospitals that Kivlan had overlooked.

Troy had the prescience to guess that the prosecutor was going to trot out the girl's loving family and describe the progress of her "dream house" to convince the jury that she had not left town of her own accord. He figured he could knock holes in that fairy tale. Robin had been feeling heat from Tufts and arguing with J.R. about money, he would contend. She was beset by troubles, and cutting out seemed an easy solution. So what if she had to leave her new house? She had sufficient earning power that she could afford to buy another.

As for the loving family, Troy thought there was something fishy about the Benedicts' recollection that things had been swell between them and Robin. The grand-jury testimony would show that Robin and her father had been fighting two to three weeks before her death. If she had left town, she wouldn't necessarily have written them.

One theory the defense team found promising was that Robin had gone to the Caribbean. For three weeks or so before she disappeared, Douglas had been trying to persuade her to vacation with him in St. Thomas. It was also possible that since John Benedict had ties in Trinidad, she had gone to stay with relatives. Her passport had not been used, but that didn't mean she was necessarily traveling under her own name. If she had gone to the Bahamas, all she would have needed was a driver's license. And her license had never been found.

Furthermore, had not the Benedicts' received a telegram from her in Las Vegas? John Kivlan would try to suggest that it had been sent by Nancy or William Douglas. State police reports, however, indicated that the operator who took the call had told Kivlan that the caller had the voice of a "young woman." Bill Doyle, who did a little checking into the Western Union system, learned that there was no way to confirm where the telegram had originated, so it couldn't be traced to the Douglases. This ambiguity left Troy free to argue that Robin was now plying her trade along the Las Vegas Strip.

Perhaps she had wanted to shake off J.R. (Hadn't the Las Vegas telegram warned her parents, "Don't tell J.R. where I am"?) Maybe she figured the best way to break clean was to fake her own death, pinning the suspicion on Douglas. Robin had, after all, spent time in the Douglas house the night of March 5, so she would have had the opportunity to plant her belongings in his closet. As one of his nominal employees, she might have had access to some of the tissue from his research which she slipped into his pocket. She knew the number of Douglas's credit card, so she could have placed the toll calls to frame him. This scenario was scarcely credible, but it did not have to be airtight, just provocative enough to raise doubt.

In pursuit of doubt the Plot and Scheme team even came up with a plan to hire a model with long, dark hair to show up at the trial wearing a veil. Troy knew he would probably be held in contempt, but this would illustrate dramatically that Robin Benedict could walk in at any moment. Fortunately for the defendant, this caper never got beyond the drawing board. Probably because Troy had something even better: two witnesses who would testify that they had seen Robin during the weeks after she disappeared.

Shortly after taking the case, Troy received a call from one Florenzo DiDonato, who during the late summer of 1983 had taken his camera to a boat tournament in Mystic, where he photographed a dark-haired girl. Now he thought she might have been Robin Benedict. The defense team figured that DiDonato was most likely an attention seeker, but Troy nonetheless dispatched a private eye to the photographer's home in Arlington to check him out. The detective returned with a discouraging report. The face of the woman in the photograph was so indistinct as to defy identification. Moreover, the envelope in which DiDonato had stored the slide was marked "9/8/82." One could argue that the file had been mislabled, but one of Troy's assistant's caught something else, a van in the background with a political placard reading "Sam Rotundi for Governor." Rotundi had made his bid in 1982.

On the off chance that Kivlan wouldn't notice these inconsistencies, the defense decided to keep the photographer in reserve.

Far more promising was the "respected attorney" whom Richard Clayman had dangled so tantalizingly before the court during Douglas's last bail hearing. This mystery witness, Troy discovered upon receiving Clayman's notes, was a Miami civil attorney by the name of Malcolm Weldon.

Troy sent Morgan to Florida to interview Weldon, and the private eye came back with an encouraging account. "Mac" and his wife, Nardis, had made a combination business and pleasure trip to New York City in the summer of 1983. During the part of the trip allotted to business, they had stayed at the posh Helmsley Palace. When business was completed, they checked into the more modest Howard Johnson in midtown Manhattan. The following morning they brought their bags to the lobby and, having time to kill before their flight, repaired to the cocktail lounge for refreshment. They did not see many women in the crowd, and their attention was drawn to one, an extremely attractive girl with long, dark hair who was sitting at the bar. She was dressed in dark slacks with a lighter blouse or sweater. The girl left the bar a couple of times but returned on both occasions. The Weldons thought no more of it until they returned home and were leafing through accumulated newspapers. On an inside page, Mrs. Weldon spotted the photo of a missing girl and remarked to her husband, "Boy, doesn't she look familiar?" Scrutinizing the photo closely, the Weldons came to the conclusion that this was the girl they had seen in the bar the day before. Mac thought he ought to call Daniel O'Connell, whom the account named as the defense attorney, and tell him what he had seen. O'Connell had in turn relayed this tip to Clayman, who passed it along to Troy.

Morgan found the Weldons credible.

Late in March, when John Kivlan finally learned Weldon's identity through the process of reciprocal discovery, he promptly dispatched Sharkey to Miami to pay the attorney a call. Sharkey returned the following day with the reassuring report that the Weldons' account was full of holes. Nardis, who was much younger than her husband, tended to run on about the girl's big boobs. As a point of fact, Robin did not have large breasts. When Sharkey showed them photos of Robin at various ages, they became less positive that she was the girl they had seen in New York. Robin, for instance, had a chipped tooth. The girl at the bar had straight teeth.

Sharkey called Bill Doyle and announced with satisfaction that the Weldons would make "horrible" witnesses.

Like Weldon, DiDonato had to be neutralized. That proved simple enough. When the Gray House finally got Plot and Scheme to send over a copy of the Mystic slide, Kivlan seized immediately on the Rotundi placard, which rendered DiDonato's testimony worthless.

FOR THE FIRST TIME since the investigation began, however, the defense had the Commonwealth on the run. Kivlan found himself developing a grudging admiration for Tom Troy. While Troy often came off as a blowhard, he was actually very shrewd and apparently relentless. And so for a month preceding Douglas's scheduled trial date, Kivlan and his troopers ran around frantically plugging leaks.

Anticipating Troy's claim that the brown corduroy jacket was too nondescript to be positively identified as Robin's, Kivlan instructed Brian Howe to check with the records department at Lord & Taylor at South Shore Plaza, where the trooper turned up a sales slip identifying the jacket which J.R. purchased in November as that from a line called Aqua Mates. The Mansfield jacket bore the same label. This made it possible to counter Troy's argument that there were many brown jackets with the observation that this was a very particular brown jacket, identical to the one J.R. purchased for Robin.

Realizing that John Boulton's equivocation made the hammer argument vulnerable to Troy's assaults, Kivlan looked for means to link it once and for all to Boulton's tool bench. The prosecutor asked a state police ballistician to compare the eye screw found in the handle of the Mansfield hammer to the package which Brian Howe had taken from John Boulton's work area. The ballistician checked with the screws' manufacturer, Parker Metals of Worcester, and learned that the machines which twist, strike, and cut the lengths of metals for the hooks were reset at the beginning of every run. All of the hooks from that run would therefore, have the same distinctive strike mark on the head of the hook. The ballistician then compared the dent on the screw from the handle of the Mansfield hammer to those on the hooks from work area and found them to be identical.

Of all the points on which the state was vulnerable to Tom Troy's machinations, the most obvious was J.R. Rogers. Kivlan knew that Troy, with his solid connections in the Boston Police Department, was likely to come "prepared to the nines" on Robin's boyfriend. The "pimp problem" was aggravated further by an article entitled "Fallen Angel," which had appeared in *Boston* magazine that February. The piece had been written by a local reporter who had contacted Dwyer, proposing to write a book about the Douglas case. He had managed to interview the Benedicts, who, for the first time, let slip Robin's relationship with the New England

Patriots. Newman contacted Costict, who gave him an account of the party at Presidential Estates at which Robin supposedly met J.R. Rogers. Costict recalled J.R.'s remarking on that occasion, "That's the kind of child that you put out on the street."

Brian Howe placed a quick call to Costict, who, after reconsidering, revised his recollection, reporting that Rogers had actually said, "That's the kind of girl you *marry.*" This assertion was not altogether credible, but it would at least put Costict on record as denying the first.

EVEN as Kivlan was overseeing these urgent, last-minute chores, Troy and his minions were plotting a more visceral assault upon the heart of the Commonwealth's circumstantial case—the motive for the alleged murder.

Plot and Scheme had gone over the love letters with much care and had, predictably, arrived at an interpretation which differed radically from that of the Gray House. Whereas the Commonwealth would argue that this correspondence showed a passion which careened toward violence, the defense would introduce into evidence the parts of those letters which emphasized Douglas's essential sweetness, his puppylike adoration of women. To this end Troy intended to pull out the missive of January 3, 1982—which Plot and Scheme had dubbed "the young fool" letter—and read from Douglas's eager, effusive prose. He would make the jury see how this man yearned for something beyond himself, how he strained to articulate a passion he hadn't the emotional range or words to express. "Dear Treasure," Troy would read in his Dorchester lilt. "When I say the word 'treasure,' I think of something that is precious, a one-of-a-kind possession, something that is priceless and must be protected at all costs."

Did these sound like the words of a man who intended harm?

As for the stolen tapes and messages, they suggested not the insidious tracking of a killer but a man longing to hear the voice of his beloved. Troy was counting on the fact that every man sitting in the jury box could hark back to his first love. Maybe it was in grade school, when girls seemed like magical creatures and there was one little girl who bobbed beyond reach. And just looking at her or brushing her shoulder or hearing her voice made you dizzy. Day after day you would chase her, and when she allowed herself to be captured, you would suddenly realize that you were the one who had actually been caught. "Women," Troy would observe to those kindred males on the jury. "You chase them until they catch you!"

Kivlan, for his part, had no intention of allowing Troy to distract the jury with meandering ruminations on the nature of infatuation. Should this happen, he fully intended to bring the proceedings back to earth with a reminder that William Douglas and Robin Benedict were on a rather harsh business footing. They appeared, furthermore, to have been arguing about something very specific in the days before Robin's disappearance. What it was, Kivlan still didn't know. He had spent a good deal of time trying to find out. In the five months since Douglas was indicted, Kivlan had been developing and refining a scenario which he called "the dispute."

For purposes of "the dispute," Kivlan narrowed the time period under consideration to the month before Robin's disappearance. The final disagreement began, according to the prosecutor's reckoning, around Valentine's Day when Robin began placing calls to the Miner Institute. According to J.R., Douglas had lured Robin to Plattsburgh with the promise of an "expensive gift." (Slightly disconcerting, from the prosecutor's point of view, was the fact that Robin charged the airline tickets to her own credit card. If Douglas was in such a fever to have her come, would he not have bought the tickets himself? Perhaps not.)

For the two days she was at Plattsburgh, none of Douglas's colleagues noticed any strain between the pair. On Friday, February 18, they left by car for Boston. Robin did not show up again in the documents until Monday, February 21, when she was admitted to Massachusetts General Hospital for a "raw tongue." She had swollen tonsils and had been suffering from laryngitis since the preceding Saturday.

The following morning at about nine-thirty, Douglas made a call from the North Shore Motel on Route 1 in Peabody to an outfit called Garber Travel in Cambridge. Kivlan surmised that Benedict was with Douglas at the motel and that, during their tryst, he had called the travel agency to arrange their proposed trip to St. Thomas. When the prosecutor checked with Garber, however, the agents could locate no reservations for a William Douglas or a Robin Benedict.

Kivlan had secured medical reports from the Lynn Union Hospital which indicated that, late that same Tuesday evening, Douglas was admitted to the emergency ward with chest pains.

During the confusion at the Lynn Union Hospital, Robin had apparently taken not only his car and house keys but also his briefcase containing the key to their joint lock box at the Bank of Boston. Kivlan suspected that before chancing upon those keys, Robin never realized that the lock box existed. Agent Perrotta had checked the signature on her application card and found it was not hers. It had, most likely, been forged by Douglas. The bank had no records of her entering that lock box before the morning of Tuesday, February 23.

Robin had called Douglas several times that morning, and something she said must have alarmed him. At a little before nine he called the Sharon police to report that a briefcase with important papers had been stolen out of his car and that the thief was coming to his house. There was some confusion about what the thief wanted.

When Paul Landry had talked to Detective Joseph Testa back in March, the officer couldn't recall exactly what the thief was threatening to do to Douglas. As the prosecutor put finishing touches on "the dispute," he contacted Testa again and asked him to go over his notes to see if he could refine his earlier account. This time Testa recalled much more particularly that the thief wanted money and would be arriving at the Douglas residence within half an hour to "make the swap." Yet when Robin arrived, Testa heard her, in his words, "hollering at Mr. Douglas [something] to the effect of giving back her clothing and personal belongings and she'd give him back his briefcase, and if he didn't she'd tell everything to his wife." At the police station Robin explained that she and Douglas had been having an "affair" for the past year and a half and that she had come to Sharon to bring the whole thing to a head. Testa, anxious to be rid of the matter, told Douglas that if he wanted to pursue it, he would have to file a complaint with the Lynn police.

There was no need for that, according to Douglas, because the disagreement with Robin had supposedly been settled on the spot. After leaving the police station, she had had a change of heart, made a U-turn in her silver Toyota, picked him up, and taken him home. Before parting, he had said to Landry, she had given him back the stolen slides. This supposed reconciliation occurred well before noon. Kivlan, however, had received from the Lynn Police Department a copy of a complaint which Douglas filed at a little past 4:30 P.M. that same day. He reported his briefcase missing and named as the "suspect" one Robin Benedict. Kivlan felt it safe to conclude that by late afternoon of February 23 "the dispute" had still not been resolved.

What was it that Robin had hoped to find in the lock box. Money? Cocaine? No matter how Kivlan refined "the dispute," its precise cause remained elusive. What mattered, the prosecutor decided—the point he would hammer home to the jury—was that they had been arguing over *something.* And the antagonism had reached such a pitch during the week preceding March 5 that even before Robin reached Sharon for their final summit, William Douglas had formulated a conditional plan to kill her.

BY NOW it was late March. Douglas had passed five months in the county jail. In this tumultuous period he had gone through a total of five attorneys. Yet, for all the apparent stress and turmoil caused by his predicament, Douglas maintained an imperturbable calm.

He never made any trouble, and the deputies liked him for that. Every day when the chief administrator, Deputy Sheriff Bob Campbell, strolled by to ask how he was doing, everything—food, accommodations, everything—was simply wonderful. Whenever a menial work detail cropped up, he volunteered for it. Every week or so the tier had to be disinfected with a power hose, and it was Douglas who asked for that duty. As time passed, the deputies started coming to him for advice on their taxes or insurance problems. He was very keen at sorting out the intricacies of contracts. He had also picked up a bit of prison lingo. He talked about so-and-so doing his "bit"—a sentence—or gossiped that so-and-so was a "skid," a wimp who hadn't any serious crimes to his credit. Whenever anyone asked about his own case, he declined to give particulars, remarking only that he intended "to beat the rap."

His good behavior did not endear him to the young toughs who continued to scream insults at him when he passed on the catwalk. Still, he refused to acknowledge them, hoping apparently that if he was quiet enough they would forget about him. His passivity, however, only served to embolden his tormentors. Particularly Elmo Johnson. Elmo was a mean black dude, tall, heavily muscled, and possessed of a wild, demonic grin. While awaiting trial for an alleged robbery attempt accomplished with gratuitous cruelty, he was being held with a number of other hard cases in "One Row," a lower level of the guardroom floor. Periodically, he and his companions would be herded up to the guardroom level to make calls on the pay phone. On those occasions Elmo could see Douglas through the grill, and he took delight in screaming taunts.

Three times a week Douglas and his comrades from Murderers' Row were led, ten at a time, to the shower room. This brought him into occasional, and unfortunate, contact with Elmo. One evening Douglas had already showered and was toweling off when Elmo got out of the shower. On seeing Douglas dried, Elmo flipped him a shower of water from his Afro. For one startled moment Douglas remained motionless. Then with a swiftness neither Elmo nor anyone else could have foreseen, he jumped up, clenched his fist, and fixed his adversary in a murderous glare.

Elmo backed off. News of this remarkable showdown circulated throughout the jail. Bill scared off bad Elmo. As incredible as it seemed, the inmates understood why. Elmo Johnson, mean-spirited as he was, had never actually murdered anybody. Bill Douglas, it was charged, had. There was an unspoken understanding among the prison population: if a guy had the stones to kill once, he could do it again. Douglas was accused of murder. It was possible that all of his good manners and womanish ways concealed a violent disposition. After that the taunts ceased, and Elmo and his friends gave William Douglas a wide berth.

DOUGLAS'S public reputation had also grown impressively during the past five months. This was due largely to his attorney's efforts to set the "proper atmosphere" for trial. During the process of filing motions—the defense was burying the court under an avalanche of paper—Troy had succeeded in generating an enormous amount of publicity, much of it more favorable than any Douglas had enjoyed since the days when he was the darling of the animal rights movement. Troy, who knew that the hearings on the suppression of Douglas's statements were bound to release revelations that would make Douglas look bad, tried to get reporters excluded from the hearings. Failing in this, he took the initiative, releasing the first sixteen pages of Trooper Landry's report to a grateful press. This way, at least, the revelations were courtesy of the defense, not of the prosecution. Through the alchemy of Troy's image making, Douglas was now occasionally portrayed in the daily accounts of the *Herald* as a good citizen who had cooperated with the police. And there lay the tragedy. He was an innocent, framed by a pimp, manipulated by a cynical prosecutor, a "babe in the arms" of police.

Well into April, Troy continued inundating the court with motions. Judge Donahue saw this very clearly for what it was—an attempt to delay the trial past its scheduled date of April 23. Delay usually works to the advantage of the defense. Witnesses might die or simply forget what it was they had to say. The defense truly needed more time to prepare. As Troy would later point out, the Commonwealth had three hundred days to put its case together; he had only seventy-five. Judge Donahue, however, had run out of patience. When the tally of motions reached seventy-five, he declared "enough," announcing that the trial would start on time come hell or high water.

On the morning of Monday, April 23, both sets of attorneys convened in Dedham to begin the process of jury selection. Donahue, fearing that Kivlan and Troy might have difficulty in agreeing on a jury, had arranged for an unusually large pool of five hundred potential jurors who awaited their turn at voir dire in the pleasantly cool sanctum of the Allin Congregational Church, across the street from the courthouse. The *Herald* speculated that it might take over a week for both sides to agree upon the sixteen jurors, including four alternates, who would sit on this case. But the selection moved much more swiftly than anyone imagined.

Troy and Kivlan, as it turned out, seemed to have very similar notions of what constituted an acceptable juror. Kivlan, for his part, was looking for maturity. A young person, he felt, might not feel confident sending a defendant to prison. He also speculated that a man who held a respected position in the community might find himself offended when confronted with the full extent of Douglas's alleged depravity, which ran from embezzlement to murder. Troy, too, was partial to the middle-aged, middle-class male, for quite different reasons. He was looking for that juror who had fallen for that little girl in grade school and who could be counted upon to understand the disturbing nature of infatuation.

When selection was completed, early Thursday afternoon, the jury included twelve white males thirty years old or older.

ON THE warm, sunny Friday that was to have marked the opening rounds of *The Commonwealth v. William H. J. Douglas,* a seat in the courtroom was a highly desirable commodity. At 9:00 A.M., half an hour before the trial was set to begin, the press gallery was already packed with reporters who had abandoned their usual routine of cruising the hallways in favor of guarding their privileged vantage point on the impending drama. After a year of catching crumbs and foraging for documents trying to fit together the pieces of this puzzling tale, they stood, at last, to see it unfold before them with reasonable continuity. John Kivlan's witness list contained the names of over 150 people, many of whom were known only by the fleeting, mysterious references made to them in police reports. Plotegher and Jewell, Joe Murray, Dr. Ronald Sanders, Officer Christine Miller, and Pam McGrath and Lorna Johnson. Kivlan had included the names of Billy, Johnny, and Pammy Douglas, whom he had added to the list in order to keep pressure on their recalcitrant parents.

The press searched the spectators gallery for the Douglas family. Nancy and the three children, who had been frequent visitors to the halls of justice in months past, were nowhere to be seen.

At about a quarter past the hour, the Benedicts and their four children filed past the press gallery and took the only seats left, at the back of the courtroom. There was no danger of their being inconspicuous.

Their party included the impeccably tailored J.R. Rogers. John and Shirley had taken pains to seat him between them, in an apparent show of solidarity. This naturally caused a good deal of whispering. But the Benedicts appeared not to notice. As John Benedict had always told his children, "Bearing is everything."

John, who had forgone his customary gold chains and floral shirts for a gray suit, stared grimly ahead, his jaw elevated in defiance. Shirley was dressed in mourning, and her chin trembled. They were actors in a drama intended to sway the jurors toward sympathy for the victim. But by now they had also begun to feel that they had been cast in the starring roles of their own lives. Most of Boston and much of the country now wanted to know how they lived and what they were feeling. A stroke of tragedy had raised them from the status of an obscure middle-class family from the Merrimack Valley to "the Benedicts." A young reporter from the *Lawrence Eagle Tribune* was already urging them to sell him their rights so that he could do a book about their experiences. Writers from *US* magazine, *New York* magazine, and the *Village Voice* had contacted DiFruscia in the hope of securing the family's cooperation for their own accounts. Trooper Landry had found himself a collaborator, a former editor of *Boston* magazine, and he was apparently hoping to cash in on the goodwill he had secured over the months to solicit the Benedicts' assistance. John and Shirley Benedict had not yet entered into any agreements—nor had they even decided if they would—but they were clearly flattered by all this attention. And they were, to all appearances, bent upon playing to the hilt the role that fate had handed them.

Nine-thirty passed. Then ten o'clock. The lawyers had not appeared. There was no sign of judge or defendant.

At a quarter of the hour, the attorneys appeared and took their seats at counsels' tables. Kivlan looked grim and utterly implacable. Troy seemed weary. The clerk announced, "All rise," as Judge Donahue took the bench and the bailiffs brought in William Douglas, looking a little more somber than usual. As the court officer released his wrists from the cuffs, he lumbered over to take his seat between Tom Troy and Bill Doyle.

Kivlan rose and addressed the bench.

"Good morning, Your Honor," he began. ". . . I wish to advise you that Mr. Troy has advised me this morning that the defendant Douglas wishes to change his plea from 'not guilty' to 'guilty' to so much of the indictment . . . as alleges manslaughter."

Murmurs of surprise rippled through the courtroom. A deal had been cut. On the back bench Shirley Benedict rested her head on the shoulder of J.R. Rogers and wept.

The prosecutor explained briefly how Troy had approached him the preceding afternoon with the news that William Douglas was prepared to admit that he had killed Robin Benedict and wanted to plead to the lesser charge of manslaughter. Kivlan told how he had then discussed this prospect with the members of the Benedict family, who agreed that it was "something they wished to do."

Kivlan announced that the DA's office would demand "a full and complete account from Mr. Douglas as to how he killed Robin Benedict and where and how he disposed of her body." The prosecutor asked that Douglas not be sentenced until state troopers had had the opportunity to investigate Douglas's account of the killing and to attempt to recover, if possible, the remains of Miss Benedict's body.

Kivlan then turned to ask John Benedict, seated at the back of the courtroom, if this account of the family's participation in the plea was accurate. Benedict rose to reply, "Yes, it is."

"Mr. Douglas," the court clerk then addressed the defense table, "would you kindly stand."

Douglas stood.

"Mr. Douglas," Donahue took over. ". . . You have indicated, have you not, that you wish to change your plea from not guilty to guilty of manslaughter, is that correct?"

"Yes, sir," Douglas replied.

". . . Do you further understand that by agreeing to go ahead with your plea of guilty, you will not be allowed to withdraw your plea . . . at a later time?"

"Yes," Douglas persisted, "I understand that."

Donahue proceeded to define the concept of manslaughter. It was, he explained, "an intentional killing which would otherwise be murder and is only reduced to voluntary manslaughter if there is proof that there was adequate provocation for the killing and that the killing was done in the heat of passion."

" 'Heat of passion' is not confined to anger," Donahue stipulated carefully. "It may be fear, fright, or nervous excitement. The killing . . . must have followed the provocation before there had been a reasonable opportunity for the passion to cool, and there must be a causal connection between the provocation, the passion, and the fatal act.

"Now, keeping in mind the definition of manslaughter . . . are you willing in this case to admit to sufficient facts to constitute guilt as far as manslaughter is concerned?"

"Yes, sir," Douglas replied.

John Kivlan was called to the witness stand, where he stood for nearly one hour reciting without notes the intricate particulars of the Commonwealth's case against William Douglas.

"The evidence would show," he concluded, that "body or no body, the Commonwealth could prove . . . that Robin Benedict was killed on the night of March 5, 1983, and that the defendant Douglas killed her."

At the end of this recitation, Donahue asked Douglas, "Do you admit to your involvement as described by Mr. Kivlan of the events leading up to March 5 of 1983 . . . ?"

"Respectfully," Douglas replied, "I don't agree with every detail of what Assistant District Attorney Kivlan stated, but I do in fact agree with it substantially."

"Did Robin Benedict come to your house on the night of March 5, 1983?"

"Yes, sir," Douglas replied.

"While she was at your house, did an altercation between you and Robin Benedict occur?"

"Yes, sir."

"And during that altercation, did you take up a hammer or was there a hammer in your possession with which you struck Robin Benedict?"

"Yes, sir."

"Did you dispose of her body thereafter?"

"Yes, sir."

"Are you willing to cooperate with the law enforcement authorities and take them to where you placed Robin Benedict's body?

"Yes, sir."

Donahue was content to accept the plea.

Douglas then made an unexpected request to take the stand. "If I may, I would like to apologize to you," he implored the judge. "I know you are a very, very busy person and I have misused a lot of your time and I do apologize for that and to the court."

Douglas strove for new pinnacles of penitence.

"I would like to, with your permission, although I don't really have the right, to address the Benedict family."

From the back of the courtroom, someone yelled a harsh, bloodcurdling "Fuck you!"

Spectators, startled by the outburst, craned their necks to see the heckler. It was J.R. Rogers. His body was tensed and trembling, his face contorted into a mask of hate. Douglas recoiled a bit, clearly fearful that J.R. might try to leap the barricades and strike a blow. But then, seeing that there were at least four rows of bodies and five court officers between himself and the bully, he regained his composure.

"Shall I continue, Your Honor?" he asked meekly. Donahue nodded.

"What I wanted to do was to apologize to the Benedict family. I know Mr. and Mrs. Benedict, and they are fine people. They have raised a wonderful family unit," Douglas continued, "and, unfortunately . . ."

Once again J.R. shouted from the back of the court, "Shut up, you . . ."

This time Donahue threatened to have him removed from the court.

"Your Honor," Douglas resumed, "I am sorry, again, for this commotion. I did want to say I am sorry to the Benedict family because I have caused that family a great deal of pain and anguish and grief and sorrow and wondering about Robin Benedict, and for that I do apologize. And I would like to apologize to my family, my wife and three children, because I have caused them a great deal of suffering also."

From the back of the room Shirley and Rhonda Benedict sobbed audibly.

Donahue asked the clerk to take the defendant's new plea.

"What say you, Mr. Douglas," asked the clerk, "are you guilty or not guilty of so much of this indictment which charges you with manslaughter?"

"Guilty," came the reply.

THE CONFESSION

"GUILTY!"

The word, whispered so faintly that it was scarcely audible even in the breathless stillness, sent a shot of electricity through the courtroom.

Guilty! William Douglas is guilty!

Onlookers whispered fervently among themselves. Reporters raced for phones, and soon news sped along the wires that the killer had confessed.

In the midst of this pandemonium, one reporter thought to ask Tom Troy just why—at the eleventh hour—his client had chosen to come clean.

"It would have been folly to go to trial," Troy answered magnanimously. "I've realized for perhaps a few weeks, the evidence was insurmountable."

Troy, of course, had from their first interview suspected that Douglas was lying. For the purposes of the highly creative scenario making of the sort Plot and Scheme had engaged in for the past three months, it was not necessary to have the truth, only a credible hypothesis. But two weeks before the trial was set to begin, Troy had finally acknowledged the likely futility of going to trial and had begun toying in earnest with the idea of a plea bargain. On Easter Sunday, a day of redemption and new beginnings, Troy and Doyle had driven to Dedham in a rainstorm for an urgent conference with their client. Troy laid out Kivlan's entire case, concluding, "He's going to blow you away."

In one version of events which Troy delivered later, Douglas broke down and wept. In another, he was dry-eyed and calm. Whatever the truth of that encounter, Douglas did not confess on the spot. Troy would say that Douglas had suppressed so many painful memories that these had to be eased out of him over the course of several days.

Neither Troy nor Doyle would ever disclose precisely what Douglas told them during those meetings. But the essence of his fateful revelation was that Robin Benedict had come to Sandy Ridge Circle with a hammer in hand and threatened him with it. They fought, and he grabbed the hammer and struck her a fatal blow.

William Doyle personally found the hammer secenario ridiculous. The story would be entirely more credible, he felt, if the hammer could be placed somewhere in the house. But Douglas would not be dissuaded. Robin Benedict, he insisted, had brought that hammer with an intent to harm him.

While the scenario lacked credibility, it did have the advantage of establishing Robin as the aggressor. If she had indeed come to the house that night spoiling for a fight, then it could be argued that Douglas had used "excessive force during self-defense." And that entitled him to a plea of manslaughter.

Troy decided to approach the district attorney's office with an invitation to deal. By rights, he should have taken his suit to his counterpart, John Kivlan. But Troy suspected that he would find a more congenial listener in his old friend Bill Delahunt. A week before the trial was scheduled to begin, Troy called the district attorney to sound him out. Delahunt, well aware of Troy's propensity to bargain at the last minute, was attuned to the possibility of such an overture. He suggested a drink at the Bostonian Hotel. The place was crowded with out-of-towners, but very few locals went there—a fact which assured some anonymity.

For Troy, plea bargaining was just one more form of combat. He did not allow his fondness for Delahunt to obscure that fact. The Commonwealth was clearly under pressure from the media and the victim's family to find Robin Benedict. The body, therefore, was Troy's ace in the hole. He went into the meeting at the Bostonian dangling it before the district attorney. Over the course of forty-five minutes and two beers, Troy was deliberately vague, confiding to Delahunt only that Douglas had "left the body out of state" and that he could now lead investigators to the site where he had "last seen" it.

Delahunt went for the bait. He urged Troy not to tell anyone that they had had this little talk, but to contact Kivlan directly with an offer.

Troy delayed in approaching Kivlan—perhaps waiting to see if it was even going to be possible to get a jury. As the selection process was going into its third day, and the tenth juror had already been chosen, Troy finally sidled up to Kivlan—who still knew nothing about the meeting at the Bostonian—and intimated that he might be able to get Douglas to confess.

Kivlan was not eager to consider a plea. He believed in the case he had built against Douglas. He felt that the pattern of phone calls made the night of March 5 indicated that the killing was premeditated, a condition which warranted the charge of murder in the first degree. He felt confident that he could get a conviction.

But Kivlan was also a good soldier who did not question the judgment of a superior. And his superior in this case seemed inclined to strike a bargain. From the district attorney's standpoint, a deal was desirable for a number of reasons. It would save the trouble and expense of a lengthy trial and obviate the need to make any more controversial demands on the children. And it promised to produce the body, which in the public mind seemed to hold the key to this mystery.

There were other considerations which favored bargaining. A jury might decide to reduce the charge on its own initiative after hearing the evidence. If Troy could show that Douglas had been drinking or using drugs just before Robin's death, then that automatically knocked it down to murder in the second degree. It was likely to drop a notch further, to manslaughter, if a jury could be convinced that Douglas had committed the crime in the "heat of passion." Ironically, Kivlan's own "dispute" scenario could be turned against him to suggest that Douglas had been provoked to violence.

Even if he won a conviction, Kivlan reasoned, it could be appealed and reversed. A full quarter of all felony convictions in Massachusetts were reversed by the conspicuously liberal Supreme Judicial Court.

Kivlan was persuaded of the wisdom of the district attorney's position.

Troy had given Kivlan what the prosecutor later called a "rough idea" of what Douglas had done with the body. He had apparently stashed it in a dumpster near the Rhode Island border. Troy assured him that Douglas was now willing to do everything in his power to help locate the body. In exchange he would plead to manslaughter. Kivlan said he could not agree to anything without first talking to the missing girl's family.

The following day Kivlan summoned the Benedicts and J.R. Rogers down to Dedham and explained the offer on the table. If the Benedicts chose to refuse it, Kivlan explained, the Commonwealth was prepared to prosecute Douglas to the fullest extent of its abilities. The family, however, should be aware of the risks.

"There is no body," Kivlan reminded them, "and when there is no body, there is a chance that he may not be convicted. And [even] if he is, he does not have to say what he did with the body."

Armed with a go-ahead from the family, Kivlan went back to Troy for another round of negotiating. The DA's office was willing to reduce the charge, but only to second-degree murder. Troy wouldn't budge. It would be manslaughter or nothing. This was a calculated gamble on Troy's part. Opening arguments were set to begin the following day. The district attorney's office could plunge ahead with a trial that would probably drag on for three months—possibly ending with no conviction and no body. Or they could give in and get both. This gave the district attorney pause. As a practical matter, the sentencing difference between second-degree murder and manslaughter was very slight. Douglas would almost certainly be paroled after he had served a minimum sentence. For second-degree murder this was usually thirteen or fourteen years. For manslaughter it was twelve. The DA finally decided that the extra two years weren't worth the fight.

And so it was that both sides walked out of the courtroom that Friday morning with a face-saving trophy. Tom Troy had preserved his winning record. William Delahunt could announce to members of the press assembled on the sidewalk in front of his office, "I don't know of any other case anywhere in this country in the history of criminal jurisprudence where an individual has pleaded guilty where a body has never been discovered."

EVEN AS Delahunt and Troy were publicly applauding each other for a job well done, the DA's office was holding over Douglas's head the prospect of folding the deal if he did not cooperate. As a practical matter, however, Douglas did not have to say one more word. He had publicly admitted his guilt, and the court had accepted his plea. The Commonwealth could not back out even if it wanted to.

But neither did Douglas dare welch on his end of the bargain. Tom Troy knew that Bill Delahunt had placed his prestige on the line to make this deal. Above all else, Douglas dared not embarrass the DA. Delahunt had the power to make his life a living hell. If, for example, Douglas ended up doing time at the state maximum-security prison at Walpole, which lay in Delahunt's county, the district attorney could block his transfer to a more congenial medium- or minimum-security facility elsewhere in the state. The DA could also send his emissaries to parole hearings to say, "This lying, cheating son of a bitch does not deserve to be out on the street." With the public and press on his back, Delahunt would be in no mood for games.

The district attorney would now be asking for the maximum sentence, eighteen to twenty years. Troy was convinced, nonetheless, that there was a good possibility he could persuade Roger Donahue to grant a lesser term of only six to ten, which would mean that Douglas would be eligible for parole in about four years. Between now and May 7, however, Douglas would have to convince the judge that he warranted leniency. That meant he must confess himself sincerely and thoroughly.

DOUGLAS was led back to the jail, where he changed from his brown business suit back to prison blues. He was then escorted to the district attorney's office for interrogation. Troy, exhausted by the events of the preceding two weeks, went home leaving Douglas in the hands of William Doyle.

Douglas, Doyle, Lieutenant Sharkey, and Trooper Howe all took their seats around a desk in the district attorney's private office. A court reporter placed a small microphone in front of Douglas. Sharkey began the questioning.

"Now what I would like to ask you, Doctor—I will refer to you as 'Doctor.' You've earned the title—is if you would start in chronological order . . . from maybe three months before the murder. . . ."

Douglas had been advised by Doyle to try and keep the confession limited to the three weeks or so prior to the killing. The larceny case was still pending in Suffolk, and his discussing events of 1982 stood to implicate him in other crimes.

"If it's agreeable with you," Douglas demurred politely, "I'd like to start the week before February 18, and then if you want me to go back beyond that, I'll be glad to . . ."

Sharkey agreed to Douglas's preferred starting point—the same place at which John Kivlan had started tracing "the dispute."

"I was going back to my alma mater," Douglas began reverently. "I was going to be teaching in a course that I thought very highly of, the tissue culture course. And also, this involved a job offer because I was going to start on a full-time basis as a professor in the Department of Biology at Plattsburgh in September 1983. . . .

"So when Robin asked me about . . . accompanying me, I said no for two reasons; one, I couldn't afford it, and secondly, it just would not be proper . . . in a professional setting to have anyone accompany me up there except my wife and children."

Robin had begged to join him, he said, pleading, "Please, I'm having trouble with my boyfriend. I need the money. I want to go up with you.

I've always helped you. . . . Will you help me, because I really need the money now?" When he refused, she persisted, calling him in Plattsburgh to tell him she already had her tickets. He reportedly told her, "No. You can't come. I'm not going to pick you up at the airport." To this she replied, "Well, if you don't, I'll take a taxicab over and raise hell."

"I was just shocked and dismayed," Douglas told Sharkey. "And I told her no again, but she did come up, and I met her at the Plattsburgh Airport. It's about twenty miles away. She was up there with me that Thursday night. I taught Friday morning and then left about noontime Friday and returned to Boston. . . ."

On their way out of Plattsburgh, Douglas recalled, Robin wanted to stop somewhere to buy a nightgown. She said she might not go home that night because her "boyfriend" had been bringing other working girls to the house. Douglas pulled into the Grandway Shopping Center—the mall, he took pains to point out, where he used to bag groceries as a boy—and Robin bought a pink baby doll nightgown.

It was the panties from that set that had been found in his closet the night of the first search.

Then they took turns driving back to Boston. Robin was at the wheel as they approached the northern perimeter of the city. She drove into Charlestown, parked the car on a residential street, and went into a house, where she stayed for twenty or thirty minutes. The house belonged to Joe Murray. When Robin came out, she was carrying a sandwich bag about half full of cocaine. She told him it was worth about six or seven hundred dollars.

"Did she give you any?" Sharkey asked.

"A little to try it," Douglas replied. Robin, he explained, had introduced him to cocaine.

After leaving the house in Charlestown, Robin seemed "nervous and upset."

"As we drove back . . . toward Boston," Douglas continued, "she became convinced that someone was following her. . . . At one point, she thought she had lost the people who were following her. She asked me if I would check her into the Red Roof Inn. . . . I believe it was Natick."

"Who did she think was following her?" Sharkey asked.

"She said that she thought it might be one of J.R.'s associates," Douglas replied, "or someone else who she didn't tell me. . . . That's the first time that I've really ever seen her frightened. She usually is very calm and cool and collected. . . ."

Douglas went on with his tale: After checking Robin into the inn, she thought she saw her pursuer go by in a van. Seized by another spasm of fear, she insisted they leave. With Robin at the wheel, they traversed a maze of back roads between Natick and Framingham. At one point Robin thought she saw a yellow Volkswagen driven by someone she knew. She became even more frightened.

They checked into a "white motel" near a Fun and Games Arcade on Route 9. Robin had started to unpack when she heard a noise in the adjacent room. She called the desk to complain about it, but the manager insisted that no one was in there. When Robin persisted, the manager—a young lady with an attack dog on a leash—came down and opened the room to demonstrate that it was empty. Robin, however, was becoming increasingly anxious. She thought she had seen the suspicious van in the parking lot. Douglas looked out and saw a van, but he hadn't been aware that it had been following them.

"Up to this point . . . ," Sharkey asked, "did you know for a fact that she had taken any of this cocaine?"

"Yes," Douglas replied. "She sampled some."

"So she was on the cocaine at the time all this was occurring?"

"Right."

"How about you?" Doyle interjected.

"I had some too," Douglas replied.

"How much?" his attorney pressed.

"Oh, at that point, I wouldn't say very much; probably twenty dollars' worth or so. Just a small amount."

Robin, Douglas continued, was growing increasingly worried at the prospect of being found with the cocaine. She drove them through downtown Natick, turning onto a residential street near the library. There she instructed him to take the bag of coke and stick it into a snowbank.

Toward sunrise, Douglas said, he checked her into a third motel, a brick complex near Route 9. They took a room at the back. Now manic, Robin sent him out to retrieve the cocaine. He found the right street but couldn't remember in which yard he had buried the bag. After an hour and a half of futile searching, he returned to the motel and woke Robin. They went out together to look for it but had no better luck. At first Robin accused Douglas of stealing it. Then she concluded that someone must have seen them hide the cocaine and snatched it from the snowdrift.

Giving up the search, they returned to the motel, picked up Robin's luggage, and drove to the Revere Showcase Cinema, north of Boston, a site where Douglas had dropped her off on a couple of previous occasions. She said she was going to take a taxi home.

IT WAS two days later, Douglas said, when he and Robin met in Saugus at the parking lot of the Ship Restaurant. He couldn't remember whether he had contacted her or she him. Robin got out of her car and into his; then they drove up Route 1 and "talked." If they had gone to a motel, as Kivlan had suggested to the court, Douglas didn't remember. Their disagreement, he recalled, centered on money.

When he dropped her off in Revere two days earlier, she had told him that she wanted not only the $1,000 for her services in Plattsburgh but also $2,000 to cover the time they had spent on their whirl through the back roads of Natick. She felt she was entitled to $3,000 and wanted $5,000. The additional $2,000 was "interest."

During the course of the bargaining, Douglas began having chest pains. Robin drove him to the Lynn Union Hospital, where he was given an EKG. Doctors could find no damage but gave him a muscle relaxer to ease the pain.

Even as he lay on the examining table, Douglas claimed, Robin continued to persecute him, driving her fingers into his ears. When Nancy arrived with their neighbor Mrs. Greeley, Robin introduced herself as Chris. As a parting gesture, Robin removed her new pink panties from her luggage and slipped them into the pocket of his brown flannel jacket.

(Bill Doyle had counseled Douglas to emphasize this point, to offer some plausible explanation of how Robin's underwear had found their way into his closet.)

The following morning Douglas got a call from Robin telling him that she wanted to exchange the slides and grant applications for money.

"I told her then that I had the thousand dollars . . . but I didn't have the other two plus the other two."

"Where did you get [the thousand dollars]?" asked Brian Howe.

"The thousand dollars was borrowed from my father-in-law," Douglas answered. "In fact, I borrowed two thousand dollars from him through my wife."

"What did you tell your wife why you needed the money?" Doyle prodded.

"I don't remember specifically," Douglas replied, "but I probably told her that I needed the thousand to give to Robin. I honestly don't—and I'm not being evasive."

I did tell her that I had a problem. And she borrowed two thousand dollars from her father. And I remember specifically her father asking her on the phone what it was for, and she said, 'Don't ask.' . . ."

"But at this time," Sharkey persisted, "your wife was well aware of the situation existing between you and Robin?"

"Oh, yes."

"Is that the way you normally conversed with your wife?" Howe asked caustically. "You'd tell her that you needed money for a problem, and that was it? She'd just get it for you? Don't you find that somewhat unusual?"

"This had never happened before," Douglas replied. "Before I met Robin Benedict, things like this never happened."

Douglas resumed his narrative with the events of the morning of February 23.

"Robin called me that morning," he said. "I got the impression, and I guess it was wrong, but I got the impression from the phone call that she was coming down with some of her associates and if I didn't give her the money, there was going to be bodily harm. . . . That fear was probably prompted by the fact that she told me on several occasions, and I know for a fact, that if people bother her, people do pay for bothering her."

Douglas told about one night when Robin had gotten off work at Charlie's and they had gone to an all-night delicatessen in Kenmore Square. A cab driver from the Combat Zone came into the restaurant and began to make fun of her for being a prostitute. Robin supposedly said to Douglas, "Come on. Let's get up. We're leaving." Several days later, Robin asked, "Remember that taxicab driver? . . . He's in the hospital."

That was why Douglas called the Sharon police.

"She was very upset with me for having called the police," Douglas recalled. "There was some shouting in the house. That's for certain. Then the three of us left."

Douglas still insisted that Robin had given his slides to him on the way back from the police station. He also claimed that she had done it in a spirit of tenderness and reconciliation, without her usual insistence upon money.

"Did she know that there was a safety deposit box to which she had access?" Howe asked.

"Yes," Douglas replied. "I thought she was there at the signing."

(Howe knew this was untrue, since the FBI had established that Robin's signature was not genuine.)

"Okay," said Howe. ". . . What was she looking for in the box?"

"I think," Douglas replied, "she knew I kept money in there that I misappropriated from Tufts for her and on occasion she asked me to keep cocaine in there for her, which I did. . . . At that time, there was no money in the box. If there had been money . . . I would have certainly given her the five thousand dollars to get her off my back."

Douglas claimed that he offered to give Robin $1,000 on the spot, but she declined it, saying she wanted all or nothing. He met with her again on March 2 at the White Hen Pantry in Boston to try, he said, to persuade her to accept $2,000 rather than $5,000. Robin, upset that he still wasn't meeting the mark, charged him $200 for that half hour.

By Friday evening, March 4, he said, he and Robin were still arguing over money. The fifteen-minute call he made to her home from Sharon was, to the best of his recollection, to "reason with her." To get her to settle for the $1,000.

For most of Saturday, she kept calling him, as he had told police earlier, to say that she was being delayed. At first Douglas tried to suggest that he had made all of the calls to her answering service that afternoon to find out when she was coming. But when Brian Howe pointed out that the answering service hadn't taken any messages from him that afternoon, Douglas retreated, conceding that he might have been spying on her.

"I have done that in the past and I may have been doing that at that time," he allowed.

When she hadn't arrived by 10:00 P.M., he said, he came to the conclusion that she was stringing him along, and he decided to "tease" her by sending her on a "wild-goose chase" to Charlestown.

Douglas insisted that the call upon which John Kivlan had based his conditional murder plan had been nothing more than a joke.

"Now, Doctor," Sharkey interrupted, ". . . had you made arrangements with your wife and family this day to have them not be there . . . ?"

Douglas replied that his wife had been in New Hampshire during the day. In the evening she had taken Billy and Johnny "to get away, to not be around the house."

"In other words," Sharkey probed, "she was aware that she was coming?"

"Yes."

"And she didn't want to be there to make a scene?"

"Absolutely."

"What did you tell your wife was Robin's purpose of coming out that evening?" Howe interjected.

"May I think about that for a minute?" Douglas asked. By now he was smoking nervously.

Howe allowed a short recess, after which Douglas replied simply, "I don't know what I would have told her . . . I don't think I told [her] to leave. I don't tell my wife things to do. I probably discussed it with her, and she decided that she didn't want to be there."

When Robin arrived at 38 Sandy Ridge Circle that night, Douglas continued, she parked in front of the house going the wrong way, her nose pointed toward the cul-de-sac. He recalled that she was wearing brown slacks and a beige blouse. She was carrying a brown pocketbook and had a tan jacket over her arm.

"She came in, and I told her that I would get the money and I had the money in the bedroom," Douglas continued. "I walked into the bedroom . . . and she followed me in there."

"There was a reason for not doing it in the living room," Douglas explained primly. "As you know, we have bay windows and almost wall-to-wall windows in the living room and neighbors can see in, and I did not want neighbors to see her in my house."

For safekeeping, Douglas explained, he had put the $2,000 in the drawer of a microscope case at the bottom of his closet.

"I went into the closet and reached down to get into the microscope case, and pulled out the drawer, got the money, and told her that there was two thousand dollars and I don't have any more money, and that's when she hit me on the head with the hammer."

"Where did she get the hammer?" Sharkey asked.

"The hammer was brought to the house by her," Douglas explained awkwardly. "The hammer was loaned to my wife Thanksgiving—the Thanksgiving before."

"We know that," said Howe. "How did she get the hammer?"

"She asked—the reason that hammer was borrowed was because she asked me for that sledgehammer to use around her house. [Douglas later explained that Robin liked to garden and that he thought she was pounding some posts to mount covers for the winter.] That hammer was in Robin's possession from about two days after Thanksgiving until March 5."

"And she just happened to bring it that night with her?" Sharkey goaded.

"No, I don't think she just happened to bring it," Douglas replied archly. "She brought it with her."

"For what purpose?"

"I imagine to use it on me if I didn't give her the five thousand dollars." Sharkey was scornful.

"Someone as big as you, and she was going to come out there with a hammer and take money away from you? Doesn't that sound a little crazy to you?"

"I was very surprised when she hit me."

"You didn't see her walk in with a hammer in her hand?"

"No," Douglas replied. "The coat was over her arm like a waiter carries a towel."

Sharkey could scarcely contain his disdain.

"I think, Doctor, really you're having a little problem again with the truth."

"I'll be frank with you," Howe seconded. "That sounds ridiculous to me. . . . I mean you don't think that she could have found a more useful weapon with all of her alleged contacts than a damned two-and-a-half-pound sledgehammer . . . ? It would have taken both hands for her to pick the thing up . . . ."

"No," Douglas insisted. "Robin was a very strong person."

"All right," Howe relented. "We'll go back to that. Go on."

"Okay . . . . She hit me on the head with the hammer, and I fell down on the bed. She hit me several times on the body with the hammer, and I then grabbed her wrist or twisted it with one hand and took the hammer away from her and she continued to hit me, kick me and she bit me also on the leg."

He added almost anticlimactically, "And I hit her three times—two or three times—on the head with the hammer."

Robin went down on the bed and didn't move. He checked her pulse in two places, on the neck at the carotid artery and on the wrist.

"There was no pulse, and I panicked," he said. "I was scared to death."

"At this point," Sharkey asked, "how much damage was [done] to the skull and where did you hit her?"

"I hit her on the head," Douglas replied. "On the side of the head."

"What side?"

"Let's see—uh, it was on the—toward the front of the skull as opposed to the middle or back, and I believe it was on the right side, if I'm recalling correctly."

"How much damage did you see?" Sharkey asked.

"There was damage. The skull was cracked and I could see the internal part of the brain."

"So it was a vicious smash, not just a tap?"

"Oh, no," Douglas replied. "It was not a tap."

Brian Howe was skeptical about this scenario.

"When she struck you, was she facing you?" he asked.

"Yes."

"Didn't you see the blow coming?"

"I saw it as the hammer was in midair. Yes. And I couldn't stop it. I guess I don't have very good reflexes."

Sharkey asked how many times he struck her.

"Mr. Doyle asked me that," Douglas reflected. "And it was either two or three times that I hit her in rapid succession."

"She was laying on your bed at the time she was struck?" Howe asked.

"Either laying on the bed or trying to get up from the bed. . . ."

"Did she say anything after you hit her?" Sharkey asked.

"No," Douglas replied. "I remember when I hit her the first time, there was a surprised look on her face, and I just hit her once or twice again."

Robin lay motionless on the quilted blue liner of a sleeping bag.

"I guess the first thought that crossed my mind, if I can remember correctly, was that I had to get her out of there. I could not have my children coming home and finding her in the house. I just could not do that. There's just no way that could happen."

Douglas then told how, galvanized by thoughts of his children returning, he set quickly to work. From the hall closet he grabbed a brown shopping bag, into which he stuffed the hammer, his shirt, and Robin's jacket. Blood began seeping through the bag, so he ran into the kitchen and transferred the contents to a plastic garbage bag.

Returning to the master bedroom, he got some towels from the adjoining bath and wiped up the blood. There was a little on the floor—not much—and more on the radiator that ran behind the bed. Blood had spattered a few papers nearby, so he tore off the stained parts. There was blood on his brown trousers, which he washed off. He put the towels in the paper bag.

He was bleeding profusely, he said, from the blow Robin had dealt him. So he grabbed a few towels and applied pressure. In a closet cupboard where Nancy kept towels, mittens, and scarves, he found a knitted stocking cap and pulled it over his head to stop the bleeding. During the fracas Robin had bitten him through the leg of his pants, leaving teeth marks which, he claimed, stayed inflamed for the next ten days.

Douglas was a little confused about how the brain tissue could have gotten into his jacket pocket. At first he claimed that he put the hammer straight into the paper bag along with the bloody clothing. After more reflection, however, he concluded that he had grabbed the windbreaker from his closet during the time he was looking for the paper bag and had tried to jam the hammer into the pocket without realizing that the space was too small. He then changed to another coat with very large pockets. He slipped the hammer into one of those. Into the other he put the blood-soaked paper bag, which now contained not only the jacket and shirt but also the bloody towels. In this new version he went to the kitchen, withdrew the hammer from his pocket, wiped it clean of blood, and transferred it to the plastic garbage bag with the bloody clothing. The discarded windbreaker with its telltale tissue remained in the closet.

Most of the blood from Robin's wound had soaked through the comforter and the blankets beneath it. These bedclothes, in which Douglas's children had once burrowed and played, were now to become his mistress's shroud. Douglas described how he positioned the body in the center of the blankets so that "she would not be overhanging either edge." Then he dragged her into the kitchen, which had become a central repository for all the bloody refuse: The plastic trash bag with the shirt, jacket, and hammer; the paper bag with the towels; and now the corpse in the comforter.

Douglas explained how he went through Robin's clothing looking for her car keys and found them in her jacket pocket. He backed her Toyota into the drive, opening the hatchback. Then he pulled the body through the kitchen and out the back door onto the redwood deck.

The state chemist had found pine needles in the back of Robin's Toyota, a fact which had led the Gray House to speculate that Douglas might have tried to bury the body in the woods.

Douglas now explained, "Our deck had pine needles on it because after Christmas we leave our Christmas tree out there, and in fact it might still have been there in March. And that's where the pine needles came from. . . . I'm sure that's where the needles came from because I dragged the blue comforter out through the kitchen door onto the deck and down the stairs."

He had difficulty lifting the body into the car but finally succeeded in propping one end on the bumper. Grabbing the other end, he held it for a moment on his knees before heaving the "entire unit," as he called it, into the hatchback. It lay lengthwise, "parallel to the back bumper."

"At that point," Douglas explained, "the body was lying on the blue comforter, and under that was one or two blankets from the bed."

"And all her clothing except the jacket?" asked Sharkey.

"Oh, yes," he replied. "When you find her body, you'll find [it] completely clothed. There was no sex that evening, and there was no monkey business with the body."

Douglas then recalled carrying the trash bag out to the car, where he placed it in the front passenger's seat. (This possibly accounted for the blood stains on the vinyl near the door handle.) He also brought out the pocketbook which Robin had carried with her that night. It was a brown one, not the bluish black one that troopers had found in the Douglas house.

Douglas believed that he left the house not later than 11:30 P.M.

"I drove," Douglas continued his narrative, "and as we got to the top of our street, there's a little side road that leads you out to the main road. I did not drive out to the main road. I turned right onto one of the back streets down there [where] it's usually very dark at night. And I remember just pulling over and sort of catching my breath and wondering what the hell to do now with this body in the car."

Douglas had used the pronoun "we." "*We* got to the top of our street." Was it inadvertent? Was he referring to himself and the body? Or was there someone else with him in the car? Unfortunately, neither of his interrogators seemed to catch this slip. No one followed up on it.

In a later statement Douglas claimed that he sat at the top of the street, "literally shaking and screaming and, you know, just out of control. Just clearly out of control."

He sat there for a few minutes hoping that Robin would come back to life, because this was "just horrible, a horrible situation."

He did have the presence of mind to remember the call he had made to Robin's answering service just past 10:00 P.M. That, he claimed, had been to "tease" her. But now he thought he might be able to buy himself some time by leaving a follow-up message. He pulled out onto the main road and took a right turn into the Bradlee's in Foxboro, where he left the message for J.R. that Robin was on her way to Charlestown.

Traveling south on Route 95, he was approaching Mansfield when he spotted an all-night rest area furnished with both barrels and dumpsters. He considered disposing of the body there and then but was made nervous by a number of cars and tractor trailers parked with their lights on. Instead, he pulled up to a bank of phones in the area to call his wife.

"I asked her when she got home," he recalled, "and she said they just walked in the door. And I said, 'Is there anyone there or had there been any calls?' And she said, 'No. Where are you?' And I said, 'I just have a problem, and I'll tell you about it later.' "

As soon as he hung up, he said, he realized that he hadn't told her to lock the doors. "In our house we often don't lock the doors at night," he explained. He was worried that Robin's absence might bring some of her associates out to the house. That's why he made the second call.

He then purportedly made a U-turn and headed north into Boston and, pulling off into a rest area, dropped the plastic bag in a barrel.

"I remember when I dropped that, I let it go and I heard a thud at the bottom as it hit the metal," Douglas recalled, seeming to fixate on this point. "I remember that thud when the sledgehammer hit the bottom. . . . That's an eerie sound."

After that Douglas claimed that he drove northwest on a circuitous route to Boston. In a later statement to one of Troy's interviewers, Douglas would claim that he had a very special purpose in mind. "I had one officer on the vice squad—his name is Bill—Billy Dwyer. And I felt that maybe what I could do is just go up [to] him with the body and tell him what happened and, you know, get it over with." Douglas apparently lost his nerve. And he did not mention the Dwyer gambit in his first statement to Sharkey and Howe.

Instead, he claimed to have "no plan. None at all." He wended his way without direction toward South Station, stopping at the Mobil station for gas. He filled up, he explained confidentially, because "how can you run out of gas with a body in the car." He had given his own registration number on the charge slip, he said, so that it could not be established that he was driving Robin's Toyota.

He called Nancy again from South Station to ask if there had been any calls. Again she supposedly asked, "What's going on?" Again, he purportedly replied that he had "a problem."

Howe found this exchange a little tough to swallow and inquired acidly, "She must have gotten awful tired all the time hearing [about] you and your problems, huh? Now was that your standard answer to her—'I have a problem'?"

"I did have a problem," Douglas replied innocently.

AT THAT POINT, Douglas said, he considered the prospect of dumping the body in one of the large dumpsters near South Station, but he changed his mind and began driving west on Commonwealth Avenue. He later said that he had fallen into a sort of "trance." He did, however, recall entering a residential neighborhood in Brookline and stopping the car in front of a dumpster. He opened the hatchback, but as he started to pull on the body he heard something.

"It must have been moving the lungs or something," he explained, "because I heard a—not a breath—but a sort of eerie sound which I can't begin to duplicate for you. And I guess that was just residual air in the lungs being expelled."

"Could she have been alive at this time?" Asked Sharkey.

"No," Douglas replied with conviction. "There was no pulse. No. If she would been alive at my house on my bed, she would have been in a hospital, guarantee you."

As Douglas was preparing to hoist the corpse into the dumpster, however, a light came on in a nearby home. He panicked and fled. After wandering aimlessly through the Back Bay and downtown Boston for an undetermined amount of time, he headed south again down Route 95. It was nearing dawn when he reached Pawtucket—a trip which should ordinarily have taken only an little over an hour from Boston at that time in the morning. He couldn't remember what had taken him so long. At Pawtucket he stopped at a Howard Johnson to get a cup of coffee and call his wife.

As he was preparing to get out of the car, he noticed two uniformed policemen coming toward him, carrying ice cream cones. He froze, he said, sure that they had spotted him and could see the guilt on his face. Instead, they walked straight past him, got in their cruiser, and drove off.

After getting his coffee, Douglas drove to a service station a block away and made yet another call to his wife. He claimed to have awakened Nancy from a sound sleep. She was drowsy, he said, but not angry with him. Again, he asked her whether there had been any calls. She told him there were none.

From Pawtucket, he drove to Providence, taking an exit that led to University Heights Shopping Center. The center was an L-shaped complex which one entered through an access road on the left. One could turn right into the parking lot or continue straight into an alley that wound back behind the stores.

On a bluff above the alley were the tidy brown town houses of the University Heights housing complex. (Douglas made no mention of the fact that he and his family had once lived here. Or that the spot he had in mind as Robin's final resting place used to be his own backyard.)

Douglas drove the Toyota into the alley past a series of dumpsters. Doing a U-turn in that cramped space, he backed the Toyota up against one of the dumpsters. He recalled removing a couple of trash bags and then, with a great deal of difficulty, lifting "the material" into it.

" 'Material' being the body?" Sharkey queried cautiously.

"The body with the blue comforter, right," Douglas replied.

Douglas said he laid the body in the dumpster. Then he covered it with garbage bags, closed the dumpster lid, and was preparing to go when he looked up into the apartment complex above him and noticed a light in one window. There was a man standing there silhouetted against the light. Douglas seemed to recall some kind of red painting on the wall behind him. He could not say for sure whether that spectral figure noticed him but, he suggested helpfully, the man might be found to verify his story.

After that, Douglas claimed he got back on Route 95 and drove south. He stopped at the Garden City Shopping Center and found a spot around a Child World where there were many dumpsters. In one of them he discarded his coat, which by this time was covered with blood. (The brown bag with the towels was in his pocket at the time.) In another he dumped the bloody blankets which had lain under the comforter.

From there on, his memory was dim, but he thought he had driven north again to the Rhode Island Hospital in Providence and there disposed of Robin's purse in another dumpster. He kept the contents—her credit cards and red address book—and put them in his pocket along with $40 that he had taken from her corduroy jacket.

After that, he drove into the center of Providence, where he parked the Toyota in a concrete parking garage adjacent to the Bonanza Bus Terminal. There was no attendant on duty. He simply took a ticket and parked the car on the second level. Then he walked across the street to the terminal.

From inside the terminal, he again called Nancy, who by this time was "really panicky." He asked her to meet him at the bus station in Foxboro and promised to tell her what had happened. When he arrived, Nancy reportedly asked him, "What in the hell is going on?" Douglas said he tried putting her off, saying he was having "problems" and didn't really want to talk about it. But she wasn't buying that line any longer.

"This is where I have a problem," Douglas told his inquisitors. "And I am being honest with you. I promised my wife that I would never tell anyone that she knew, because that's the only time I told her and she got very upset with me that that happened."

Douglas, in his circuitous way, was admitting that he had told Nancy about the killing.

"I've only probably seen my wife really mad at me twice in my life," he continued. "I mean really mad—yelling and screaming." (In a later statement, Douglas had Nancy yelling, "Don't touch me! Don't touch me!") Douglas went on, "She's just not that type of person. She's a very calm person. She doesn't talk a lot, and she was just livid that I could do something like that."

When Nancy brought him home, Douglas said, he put Robin's credit cards and red address book in his closet.

"Why?" Howe asked him. "You went to great lengths to dispose of all the other stuff, and you kept that. Why?"

Douglas thought about this, then replied, "I guess I kept the red address book out of curiosity and fascination. I have no idea why I kept the credit cards. I would certainly never use them."

He recalled cutting Robin's driver's license into small pieces and throwing it away. He thought he had done this later, in Washington, D.C.

Douglas seemed to remember staying in his bedroom for the rest of the morning, with the door shut. He went into the bathroom and tried to remove the stocking cap which, he said, was stuck to his head with matted blood. He left the bedroom only to go out and make the call to J.R. to the effect that Robin had left Charlestown and was on her way to Longfellow Place.

That afternoon Nancy dropped him off at the bus station in Foxboro. He went into the knitting shop to buy a ticket to Providence, where he picked up the car at the parking garage. He drove straight south on 95—only fifty miles an hour, he said, because he didn't want to get pulled over. He stopped only once, in Connecticut, to call home and ask his wife how the basketball banquet had gone.

(This tale did not jibe with the New England Telephone toll, which showed him making the call from Connecticut later in the day.)

It had been Douglas's plan to leave the car at a parking garage in New York City and catch a bus to Washington, D.C., from Grand Central Station. But when he got there, he was told he would have to go to Penn Station, at Madison Square Garden. On his way across town, he stopped to get a Coca-Cola from a vending machine and accidentally locked his keys in the car with the motor running. His panic worsened.

Looking for help at a nearby gas station, he found a Yellow Pages, where he located the name of a locksmith.

At last, he found Madison Square Garden, where he pulled into a parking lot. But when he found that the management kept the keys, he reconsidered his choice. He wanted to be able to lock the doors. He left that garage and found one where he could drive in and take a ticket. This was the Meyers lot on West Thirty-first. He went up two levels, backed the car against the wall, removed the license plates, and scratched off all the other identification he could find with a ballpoint pen.

The license plates, Douglas claimed, then went into his suitcase. "I guess that's the other thing that . . . surprised [me]," he mused to Sharkey and Howe. "When DaRosa was in Washington, the plates were in my suitcase. And I'm almost certain that he searched [it]. . . . And he did not see the plates. . . . I disposed of the plates at the airport when I left Washington. . . ."

At about eight o'clock, he said, he went to Penn Station and bought a ticket to Washington, D.C., then waited around for the 3:00 A.M. departure.

"Why did you want to catch that one train?" Howe asked him. "There were other trains leaving between the time you purchased the ticket and that."

He was referring to the inexplicable seven-hour gap between the time when Douglas had bought his ticket and when he boarded the train for Washington. The Gray House investigators still suspected he had been busy trying to dispose of the body or the car. Douglas insisted, however, that he had passed those hours strolling around Penn Station.

The next morning, upon arriving in Washington, he took a subway to the Hotel Washington, checked in, and called one Howard Berman, his contact at the VA.

"Why did you tell him you lost your papers?" Howe asked. "What was the purpose behind that?"

"My purpose behind that," Douglas replied, "was because I had not written the grant reviews."

So Douglas had been lying all along. Robin had not stolen his grant reviews the night of the Lynn hospital incident.

BY NOW it was approaching 5:00 P.M., and Bill Doyle had to leave soon for another appointment. Spurred by that impending deadline, Sharkey began ticking off unresolved questions which only Douglas could answer.

"What were your intentions [in] trying to get a hold of Elizabeth Sanborn's car?" he asked.

"To buy . . . a second car, until I realized that it was really a rat trap."

"You weren't going to go to New York in it or anything and try to recover Robin's car?

"Not at all," Douglas replied. He claimed he never saw the Toyota again after leaving it at Meyers parking garage.

As for the story about being kidnapped by black men with a van, Douglas admitted that he had fabricated the whole thing.

"I think I made that up to make Robin feel sorry for me," he explained.

"Robin did not take your car?" Howe inquired, referring to Kivlan's theory that Robin was holding the blue Toyota hostage.

Douglas insisted she had not. The stolen-car report which he had filed on March 1 was completely false.

"One thing that bothered me," Sharkey interjected, "is . . . after you've murdered her, you still went back to the Combat Zone. You still engaged in sexual activity. How many times did you do this in the interim after you killed her? . . . This is something we know. Now give us an honest answer."

"As best I can estimate," Douglas replied, "between five and ten [times], but not with a hooker out of Good Time Charlie's."

"Out of where?"

"On the streets."

"And you went with them . . . ?"

"Wherever they would suggest. Around the corner. In a car."

"So you go down to the Zone a minimum of ten times, let's say," Doyle prodded. "You don't always hop in the back seat of a car or around down in the alley."

"It's not in the back seat of a car. It would be in the front seat . . . ," Douglas corrected primly. "And it's not sex."

"Personally," Howe cautioned Douglas, "I would like you to think about all the things you've told us to make sure when we talk again that your memory [has] improved. . . . Because at the conclusion, when we go to Mr. Kivlan, we are going to say, 'Listen, we think he is . . . telling us the truth,' . . . or 'We think he's lying to us . . .' And if that's the conclusion we reach, you've got some serious problems."

"I know," Douglas replied. "I'm not a fool."

BEFORE RETURNING to the county jail that afternoon, Douglas drew a diagram indicating to the best of his recollection the location of the dumpster where he had disposed of Robin's body. The shopping center, as he sketched it, was laid out as a backward L. The upright stroke paralleled the back alley. As one entered the alleyway from the top of the L, one passed the rear entrance of a Star Supermarket on the right. There was a huge trash receptacle attached to the rear of the building. Beyond that there were two large rectangular loading bays. The first was empty. The second had several receptacles in it. Douglas seemed sure that the dumpster in question was in the second recess, behind a Radio Shack store.

The dumpster, as near as he could recall, had been dark blue, about four yards across, with large metals pins protruding horizontally from each side. The front sloped backward to the base. There was a cover on the rear half of it. He could remember this because when he had removed the trash bags from the inside of the dumpster, he had set them on that surface.

The next morning, Brian Howe drove down to University Heights to look around. He found the second loading bay and the back of the Radio Shack. But the space was empty. Returning to Dedham, he called Bill Doyle to ask if he would mind rousing his client at the jail for a field trip. That afternoon, Douglas, in the company of Doyle, Sharkey, and Howe, set off for University Heights in the hope that visiting his old haunt would stir more recollections.

As Howe steered the cruiser into the alleyway, Douglas peered eagerly out of either side. He got out and walked the length of the alley and back. He was still certain that he had dumped the body behind the Radio Shack. He seemed vaguely to remember returning to University Heights in the days thereafter to check it. His recollections were so vague that it was possible he dreamed it, but he vaguely remembered lifting the lid, peeking inside, and seeing the sleeping bag. He thought that this might have been on Thursday, the day after he got back from Washington, D.C. Howe pointed out that he could not possibly have seen the bag at that point, because the dumpster would probably have been emptied earlier in the week.

Douglas appeared upset to find the spot behind the Radio Shack empty. He scanned the apartments on the bluff above the center but could not identify the window in which he had seen the man with the red painting.

That afternoon Howe requested the Rhode Island state police to canvass the stores at University Heights to see what dumpsters matching Douglas's description might have been there on March 6. The following morning he received a call from a Lieutenant Wheeler, who delivered the welcome news that the Radio Shack had had a blue dumpster stationed out back the preceding spring. It had been supplied by the L.W. Fontaine Trucking Company of Attleboro, Massachusetts.

The refuse from that bin would have been dumped at the Attleboro Landfill, near the Rhode Island–Massachusetts border, on Wednesday, March 9.

Later that afternoon Howe called Al Dumonte, manager of the Attleboro Landfill, at his home. John Kivlan was intent upon keeping the reason for the search confidential, so Howe told Dumonte only that the state police were conducting a survey of landfills in southeastern Massachusetts and the Providence area to "determine the feasibility of unearthing a piece of evidence" thought to have been dumped there about fourteen months earlier.

Dumonte was dubious. Such a search would prove extremely difficult, he said. Still, the search could probably be restricted to an area three hundred feet by three hundred feet, if the state police were prepared to dig thirty-five feet deep. This was contingent, of course, on their locating the precise dumpster that Douglas had used. That now seemed to be the unit that was sitting behind Radio Shack on March 6.

WHILE Brian Howe was making quiet inquiries, the press had launched its own full-tilt search for the body. Certain details of the confession had leaked out, and by Saturday it was common knowledge that Douglas had stuffed the body into a child's sleeping bag and dropped it in a dumpster near a shopping center somewhere near the Rhode Island–Massachusetts border.

Throughout the weekend, reporters prowled every major shopping center near Providence and scavenged the four major landfills in northern Rhode Island and southern Massachusetts hoping to be a part of the big find. Birtwell and Estes of the *Herald* had hoped to insinuate themselves into the official search party. (Who, if not the vigilant *Herald*, should be there when the missing beauty was unearthed?) District Attorney Delahunt declined, on grounds that this might be a breach of good taste.

By Monday morning, however, Delahunt had waxed expansive. Encouraged by Brian Howe's inquiries into the Attleboro Landfill, he announced to the media, "It's possible, certainly, to find Ms. Benedict's body in that large an area." The district attorney announced that he had put crews from the Department of Public Works on standby to begin digging.

The optimism of the morning faded, however, when Howe did a little more checking with Fontaine. The dumpster that the company had supplied to Radio Shack during March of 1983 was indeed blue, but its front was not slanted. It was also much smaller than the one Douglas remembered. Only two yards across.

This sent the district attorney's office back to square one.

That afternoon Sharkey and Howe once again summoned Douglas over from the jail, hoping that the passage of a weekend had improved his memory.

Howe asked him if he was sure that University Heights was the right mall. Yes, Douglas said, he was positive.

Perhaps he was mistaken about the second recess, Howe suggested. Maybe the dumpster had been located around the corner on the small foot of the L. It was possible, Douglas allowed, but unlikely. He remembered seeing the large mechanical dumpster behind the Star Supermarket and looking up behind him to see the man in the window. This suggested that he had been standing between the bluff and the buildings. He had also recalled the dumpster being set out a bit from the back of the store. Yet, when he backed Robin's car up to it, he had plenty of space to maneuver. That ruled out the alleyway around the corner, which was very narrow.

When Howe began pressing him on color, Douglas began to quibble. It was not necessarily blue. It could have been black or purple. Even brown.

"I'm not trying to mislead you," Douglas pleaded. "I'll gladly have hypnosis if that will clarify it."

The subject of hypnosis had arisen periodically over the past three days. Kivlan and Howe did not set much store by hypnotism and were not encouraging this tack. Troy, however, seemed to like the idea.

The press and public were growing restless with the lack of results, and that threatened to create a backlash of public resentment against Douglas. Troy knew that he had to shift attention away from the body to Douglas's efforts to assist the Commonwealth in its search. On Wednesday, May 2, Troy leaked the confession to the *Boston Globe.*

Troy doubtless chose the *Globe* over the *Herald* because it offered the imprimatur of respectability, which could help Douglas in advance of sentencing. The *Globe* had lagged behind on the Douglas story, and it hoped to make up lost ground with a heavy blitz during the trial. The trial, of course, didn't materialize, so when Troy called, confession in hand, the paper's Dedham correspondent, Jerry Taylor, was happy to serve as the vehicle to Troy's ends.

Proceeding with characteristic cunning, Troy did not hand over to Taylor the full text of the confession—only those portions which were favorable to his client. His selective version did not reveal how many blows were landed, or in what room Robin had been killed, merely that Douglas, acting in self-defense, struck Robin only after she "hit him on his torso with the hammer and her fists." The details Troy doled out had the effect of portraying Robin as a heartless exploiter who tortured her poor victim at every turn. She sold him cocaine. She made him jealous by telling him about other men. She not only charged him $100 an hour for sexual services; she had even charged him for time he spent helping her move from her trick pads. She had been trying to gouge him for $5,000 the night he killed her.

When John and Shirley Benedict read the *Globe*'s front-page account on Thursday morning, they were furious that Troy—they had no doubt that it was Troy—had managed to arrange an account so wildly favorable to Douglas.

It had not taken the Benedicts long to regret having entered into a bargain with their daughter's killer. Douglas, they were convinced, was lying about many things, including what he had done with Robin's body. It was possible, they felt, that he had actually disposed of it in a fashion that would reflect unfavorably upon him—say, dismembered or incinerated it. Or he had preserved and hidden it somewhere and didn't want to give up the location of her shrine. Or he had dumped it in a river, from which it could never be recovered. Tom Troy, they felt, had concocted the entire story about the dumpster because it held out hopes that the body could be found, when, in fact, it could never be traced.

On Thursday morning after the *Globe*'s confession story, John Benedict announced to the *Herald* that he intended to speak to his daughter's killer "man-to-man, father-to-father." He went to Dedham and tried to get into the jail to see Douglas.

Douglas refused. Troy told the *Herald* that his client would not be speaking to the Benedicts until after sentencing.

Troy suspected that the Benedicts' motives in wanting to talk to Douglas were not entirely pure. He had heard that they had a book deal in the works, and suspected that they might be intending to sell whatever they got from Douglas to a prospective publisher.

Still, refusing the Benedicts permission to see Douglas was risky from a public relations standpoint. The spectacle of Douglas turning away a pair of grieving parents was not going to weigh in his favor during sentencing. Troy knew he would have to take some remedial measures to, as he later put it, "take away the sting."

The Benedicts' attorney had been calling for Douglas to take a lie detector test, using an expert of his own choice. Troy did not like or trust DiFruscia, whom he considered an outsider to the comfortable old Boston Irish cabal, and suspected that the "expert" he was suggesting might be a member of the Lawrence police, whom DiFruscia happened to represent. Troy sought out his own expert—not a polygraph operator but a hypnotist by the name of William Knox.

DR. KNOX was a tall man with a long face and intense stare that lent him the aspect of a medieval physician. For a time he had been minister of a Congregational church on the South Shore. After getting a doctorate in education from Calvin Coolidge College, a small, unaccredited school in Boston, he had taken up family counseling. His approach stressed getting to the root of "feelings." During the early seventies he had taken a course in hypnotism and later joined the Association of Clergyman Hypnotists. Dr. Knox considered his hypnotism a "ministry."

Troy, who had met Knox over a decade earlier when the two of them had taken a college psychology class, gave the hypnotist a call.

Knox knew little about the case. He did not read crime stories and so had missed the running melodrama in the Boston press. William Douglas's story, as related by Troy, nearly moved Dr. Knox to tears. The hypnotist had experienced his own problems with women. His first wife had had an aversion to the ministry, which drove him out of the pulpit. After that, his marriage fell apart, which drove him to the Combat Zone. He never picked up a prostitute, he claimed, because he didn't have the money. But he had seen enough of the Zone to know what it was like to be hooked by a Jezebel. Now, when he considered the plight of poor Douglas, he could only think, "There but for the grace of God, go I."

Knox agreed to meet Troy and Doyle at the jail in Dedham at around one-thirty on Friday afternoon. At that point no one but those three men knew about the hypnosis. Not even the district attorney was aware of what was in the offing. There was a chance that Douglas might suddenly reverse his testimony. If that happened, Troy preferred that it occur quietly in order to give him a chance to come up with the appropriate strategy.

Troy and Doyle met Knox in the street outside the jail, and, after exchanging greetings, the three men passed through the security trap and into the austere paneled office were Douglas had conferred with Doyle during the many weeks of pretrial hearings.

Douglas was brought to the room and directed to sit in a Breuer chair at the end of the table farthest from the door. Doyle set the tape recorder on the table close to Douglas.

"We're going to need to get a little background," Knox began in a deep, reassuring voice. "Perhaps we'll talk a little bit about some feelings or so in order to know just where we're coming from."

Knox intended to talk for a while to find out what he could about Douglas and try to put him at ease. This proved difficult. The room was noisy. The thin walls did not filter out the yelling of inmates or the clanging of the metal doors from the trap immediately below. The radiator hissed insistently.

After a bit of harmless chitchat about Douglas's wife and three children and home in the suburbs, Knox shifted the tack of his prehypnosis interview to the question of the girl.

KNOX.   Now, how did you first meet . . . is it Robin? Robin Benedict?
DOUGLAS.   Yes. . . . At a bar in the Combat Zone called Good Time Charlie's.

The hypnotist proceeded delicately.

KNOX.   Okay. And you went there [for] entertainment. Just an evening out, that kind of thing.

The subject seemed not offended in the least.

DOUGLAS.   No, I was looking to pick up a prostitute. . . . I remember that first night I met her in the bar. . . . I remember she came in the door and she went around the bar asking people to go out, and I noticed when she got to me, she skipped me and went by. [Robin later told him it was because she did not like fat men. Fat men sweat.] . . . She went all the way around the bar looking for a date again and then came back to me . . . and asked me, "Are you looking for some company?" And I said yes.

Douglas went on to tell how Robin had taken him to an apartment on Beacon Street, which she shared with three other working girls, and how he stayed for about half an hour. The next morning he went out of town for a few days on business. When he came back, he called her answering service and made another appointment to see her. After the third or fourth half-hour session, she suggested expanding their interludes to an hour. And soon they were going on dates to the movies, the observatory, the aquarium, and the swan boats in the Public Garden.

Douglas resented J.R. Rogers's claim that he was always "on the clock." The arrangement was much looser than that, he insisted. Sometimes he would pay her for four hours, and she would let him stay five or five and a half.

KNOX. Okay. And did you keep it . . . was it kind of a business, friendly business relationship? Or was it purely sex? Or did you get to get some feelings into it?

DOUGLAS. Well, a number of people have asked me if I ever loved Robin Benedict, and I firmly believe now I did not. Although the letters don't speak to that, but I don't think I firmly loved her. I like the word Mr. Troy used. "Infatuated" more than love.

KNOX. What were you infatuated about? The way she talked? The way she looked? The way she felt? The way she made love? . . .

DOUGLAS. Mainly, I guess, she said the right things at the right times relative to . . . pressure and tension at work. And I found [it] relaxing to be with her. And it was just as relaxing to walk down the Boston Commons as it was to have sex with her. . . . In fact, I would say that's a minimal part of the relationship. . . . There were times when I spent a whole day with her where we might have had sex for ten or fifteen minutes and then spent the rest of the day together playing tennis, canoeing, and other things.

Douglas explained that he felt Robin enjoyed his company more than that of some of her other johns because she found it more "interesting" than simply lying around in bed.

KNOX. Did you pay her for those hours you were playing tennis?

DOUGLAS. Yes.

KNOX. And walking in the park?

DOUGLAS. Yeah. . . .

KNOX. Okay. How were you paying Robin?

DOUGLAS. When I started, just out of my pocket, I had some money with me, you know. I'd always have some money either in my office for emergencies or some money on me in case something came up on the spur of the moment. . . . And I guess it wasn't too long after we started—she has, or she *had,* the skill to talk in a very sophisticated manner. . . . She did not at all appear to be a streetwalker, that type. She came across more as a professional. . . . She was very sophisticated about inquiring in a nonobtrusive manner about what I did, and she was very interested in my grants because I told her I had funding. . . . In fact, I showed her my CV [curriculum vitae] . . . and we talked about grants and how grants were funded. . . .

Douglas explained how he had briefed Robin on "several very exciting projects" and how she perked up when he arrived at the culture-model system for studying respiratory distress syndrome in the premature child. She had asked him, "Well, where are you going to get the human tissue?" He told her that he had an arrangement with an orderly at Harvard who would collect aborted fetuses and remove the lungs for tissue culture. Robin was "very interested" in how this fellow was paid. Douglas explained the work voucher system, and she suggested that this might be a good way to pay her.

"So to make a long story short," Douglas continued, "what she did is she sat down with me—and I paid her for this time—and I remember doing it in her apartment. She had a round table, and we were sitting at the table. And she . . . came up with this scheme for taking money from Tufts."

For the first time in any of his statements, Douglas had squarely credited Robin with being the genius behind the embezzlement.

DOUGLAS had recounted to Sharkey and Howe several days earlier how, during the late fall of 1982, Robin had grown increasingly paranoid. Much of her anxiety centered on cocaine. She would buy coke and sell it to customers, including himself. Then she would use his supply. She liked to put it on her gums and tongue, he said. (The night they took the wild ride through Natick, she had used so much on her tongue that she burned it and had to go to Mass General the following week to have the wound treated. It left a scar.)

Not only did the coke seem to make her paranoid, but she was also paranoid about using coke. She was so afraid of being caught, Douglas said, that she would ask him to check under her nose to make sure there was no telltale dusting of white powder.

Robin had also been afraid that people were stealing her money, and so she hid cash all over her trick pads. Douglas knew this, and during the second break-in he found $300 and took it to torment her. Robin also suspected that her friend Indian Debbie might somehow be in cahoots with Douglas. Her suspicions became so acute, Douglas said, that she had asked him to offer Debbie a ride home and tape her conversation just to make sure that Debbie wasn't spreading gossip about her.

(Whether she was reassured by Debbie's innocuous banter, he didn't say.)

Around Christmastime, Robin suddenly announced that she didn't want to see him anymore. At first she wouldn't tell him why. He finally got her to admit that she suspected that he was the one making the harassing calls and breaking into her apartment. Douglas feigned shock, telling her, "How could you think that I did that!" She said she could probably forgive him, but it would take a couple of weeks.

By New Year's Eve, Douglas had hoped that Robin had thawed sufficiently to go out with him. But this apparently was not the case. She told him she was going out with "a friend." Douglas assumed that this meant her pimp. By this time both Detective Dwyer and Arthur Rodman, whom he had met at one of Robin's pads, had told him that Robin had a black pimp. Douglas was consumed with curiosity about him. So, on New Year's Eve, he drove out to Natick and called her from a phone booth across the street from the apartment. When Robin answered, he told her that he had just been to the Combat Zone cavorting with another prostitute and that they had been doing coke together. Robin, he said, sounded upset when he told her about the coke. But he did not, apparently, succeed in making her jealous. "I've got to go," she told him. "We're leaving in a few minutes."

After hanging up the phone, Douglas drove into her parking lot and sat outside the house, hoping to catch a glimpse of J.R. He waited for a couple of hours in the cold, but nobody came out. He figured she must have seen him sitting there. Later she told him that her "friend" had been sick and that they just stayed at home.

Robin made tentative gestures of reconciliation after she got the job at the Danish Health Spa in Saugus. The first night Robin went to work there, she asked Douglas if he would come up to the spa and see her. When he arrived, she was all smiles and cheer. Then he went to see her a second time, and she was irritable again, telling him she didn't want him to come up and see her any more. When he called her a little later, she said she had stopped working at the club. He didn't believe her.

One morning early in January he drove up to Saugus and parked in the lot of the Kowloon Restaurant, the same restaurant where years earlier Robin, her family, and the Ramoses had celebrated Easter. The Kowloon was located on a bluff above the shopping center which housed the Danish Health Spa. Douglas climbed onto a rocky outcropping behind the restaurant, positioned himself among a clump of spindly trees, and watched through a pair of binoculars as Robin drove her car into the lot and went into the club. Just as he had guessed, she had been lying.

A few days later he mounted his perch a second time to spy on her. This time he happened to see a billboard advertising a company which installed garage doors. The owner's name was Schloss. Taking down the name and number, Douglas called the Board of Health and, pretending to be Mr. Schloss, registered a complaint about Bobbie Benedict. He gave them a description of Robin's car and the license plate number and said, "She's there now. You've got to do something about it." Then he went to a restaurant across the street from the shopping center, took a seat by the window, and watched the entrance of the Danish. Soon a strange man pulled into the lot and went over to look at Robin's car; then he went into the club. A little later Robin came out with her bag and left.

"NOW, BILL," Knox directed him gently but firmly, "let's get down closer to the time of the girl's death. How were you feeling about her, say, two or three weeks before, a month before the tragedy?"

Douglas picked up his narrative around the third week of February, giving his by-now standard story of how Robin thrust herself upon him in Plattsburgh, their wild ride through Natick, the Lynn hospital incident, the Sharon police incident, and their endless haggling over the $5,000 that he supposedly owed her.

Toward the end of the first week in March, Douglas told her, "I'm out of money," and she reportedly replied, "Well you can get money, you know you can get money. Don't give me that. You're just stalling."

So she came down to his house on the night of March 5 to collect what she insisted was owed her.

KNOX.   What happened?
DOUGLAS.   An altercation occurred, and I hit her with a hammer. . . .
KNOX.   Where'd you get the hammer? . . .
DOUGLAS.   I claim it was under her coat [when she came to] the door.
            . . . I know Mr. Doyle was talking about this and he said . . . "You
            know, you're more believable if the hammer was in [your] house."
KNOX.   [But] the truth of the matter is she brought the hammer in?
DOUGLAS.   Mm-hmm. . . .
KNOX.   When you grabbed her arm that was holding the hammer and
            pushed her down on the bed, how'd you feel?

This seemed to give Douglas pause.

DOUGLAS.   That's a good question. No one's ever asked me that. I guess it was
            a mixture of fear, because I was bleeding a great deal from the
            head. Fear and anger, I guess. . . . I sort of blocked that out of
            my mind. I don't like to think about that.

Knox did not relent.

KNOX.   . . . Try and turn yourself back now. You're not under hypnosis. You're just thinking aloud. You're just talking with friends. You're back there. She's on the bed. You're in control. You've got the hammer. . . .

DOUGLAS.   Right. . . . I don't know how I can forget this. I think part of the thing that precipitated [*sic*] besides the fear and anger was the pain, because when I pushed her down on the bed and had the hammer over her, she went and bit me on the leg.

Knox imagined that he knew the sting of a woman's wrath and winced at the thought of being bitten on the leg.

"So you have an intense pain in your thigh," he prodded sympathetically. "You've been hit on the forehead with the sledgehammer. You're bleeding. You're hurting. You're angry . . . aren't you?"

"Sure," Douglas replied.

"And scared," Knox persisted.

"Oh, terrified," Douglas hastened to add, "though probably not as terrified as when I realized what happened."

"You've got her," Knox pressed. "What are you waiting for?"

Douglas paused, then replied, "I have just blocked this out of my mind."

"Bill," Knox cajoled, "help me. This is why I'm here. I know you blocked some things; we all do. It's normal. But let's stay with it for a minute. . . . Here you are. You are in control. This woman's been doing you in for a year. Your weakness has let her take you over. You're no longer your own man. At last, after a year, you've got her down. You've got a hammer over her head. Right? You are now in charge."

"Yeah," Douglas replied, a little taken aback by this torrent of emotion, "but I don't think I thought of the year . . ."

Knox continued undeterred, ". . . Think now, what did you feel? Pain? Fear? Intense anger?"

Douglas hesitated, trapped and uncomfortable at having to articulate his feelings. Finally he said, "Would it help if I told you I was high on coke?"

"Yes," Knox replied. "Of course it would."

DOUGLAS.   So I don't know. I don't remember whether there was fear or not. I honestly don't. . . .

KNOX.   Then she . . . just went limp? Do you feel it? Do you see it right now?

DOUGLAS.   Yes. I just don't like to think about it.

KNOX.   I know. I know.

DOUGLAS.   Then I guess for the first time in my life I really knew what death was.

KNOX.   This was the first person you had seen die?

DOUGLAS.   No. No. No. I had seen my father die. . . . I saw him in the hospital the evening before he died and just after he died. . . . But I guess I've never actually seen anyone die.

KNOX.   And never caused it before?

Douglas.   Oh, no. Of course I never saw anyone actually die in front of me and I guess then I realized that death is final, because what I wanted to do is bring her back. You know, bring her back to life.

It had been an hour since the beginning of the interview, and now Knox set about preparing his subject for hypnosis.

"Close your eyes, Bill," he directed in a soft, melodic voice. "Please. Just close your eyes and just listen to my voice for a minute now. . . . Relax. Just keep calm. Quiet. Go into a kind of sleep."

Douglas closed his eyes. His neck muscles relaxed. His head fell back.

"You're . . . in a trance now," Knox crooned. "You're . . . in a deep twilight sleep. We're trying to recall every detail. You're driving south on 95. Where do you turn off next?"

In a low, expressionless tone, Douglas told how he had taken the Branch Avenue exit to his old neighborhood, turning into the darkened alley behind University Heights. About halfway down the alley, he parked the car and got out to examine the dumpsters. The first was a huge mechanical unit that was completely enclosed. Toward the middle of the alley there was a tall, brown one. He looked inside and saw several pasteboard boxes with square cardboard dividers. For some reason he did not specify, he decided against it, turned, walked past the car, and spotted another dumpster.

KNOX.   . . . Where was it from the first, big dumpster?

DOUGLAS.   . . . *There's a little indentation on the buildings where the building sort of indents in toward the shopping mall.*

Douglas's voice was becoming increasingly childlike, as if he was experiencing considerable discomfort.

KNOX.   What color was it?

There was a long pause, during which inmates' raucous laughter rose in the background.

KNOX.   Did you see the color? . . . Did you see the color, Bill?

There was no response.

KNOX.   [Stay] right with it now. What did ya do next?
DOUGLAS.   *[I remember] going up to it. Looking in it.*
KNOX.   Whadja see?
DOUGLAS.   *Half full of bags.*
KNOX.   Half full of plastic bags. Green ones?
DOUGLAS.   *Green and maybe a pink one. . . . I remember resting my hands on the bar. . . .*
KNOX.   Yeah. How high were the sides?
DOUGLAS.   *About the middle of my chest.*
KNOX.   Okay. Then whadja do?
DOUGLAS.   *I was looking in, clinging to the bar. Standing erect, my head bent over . . . looking in.*
KNOX.   What were you feeling?

The panic was rising in Douglas voice: *"I gotta get rid of the body!"* "Yes," Knox answered, as though he were soothing a child. "You see yourself doing that now? . . ."

DOUGLAS.   *I remember. I can't get that out of my mind, hanging on that bar . . . looking in there. And then I went back to the car. Now the car was facing the dumpster. I turned it around and backed it . . . up near the dumpster. I got out of the car and opened the hatchback. . . . And I remember checking, opening up the bag to see if the body was still there.*
KNOX.   Um, huh. Stay with it, Bill. You found the body. Stay with it.
DOUGLAS.   *I remember the head. The hair with matted blood. It's all I could look at was just the hair and the matted blood. I covered it back up. I didn't wanna look at it.* [Douglas sounded breathless and panicky.] *And I remember reaching under the head and under the legs and lifting the body up. I remember how heavy it was.*
KNOX.   You managed to get it up?
DOUGLAS.   *Not the way I would have wanted to.* [His voice was at once rueful and tender.] *. . . I had to really struggle to get it up. . . . I got it up. I rested the head against the bar . . . and then I just pushed with all my body to get the rest of it up.*

Douglas recalled that he finally got the body in a position that he could "gently push it in." Her head lay in the right-hand corner. He reached in and covered her with the comforter. Then he took two of the green garbage bags that he had lifted out and set on the back lid and put them on top of her.

DOUGLAS.   *. . . Then I just drove.*

Tom Troy, who had been listening quietly, was not yet satisfied with the dumpster account and began gesticulating to get Knox's attention. When that failed, he passed him a note that read, "Go over that again."

The hypnotist brought his subject back to the alleyway behind University Heights.

KNOX.   Would you please, Bill, concentrate again on the dumpster into which the body was placed. . . . Can you think anything else now about that dumpster? That seems to be important to everybody.

DOUGLAS.   *Dark. Dark color.*

KNOX.   Dark color. Dark?

DOUGLAS.   Dark. . . . I don't know if it was black, blue, brown. Dark.

KNOX.   Dark. Okay. But you don't remember any lettering?

DOUGLAS.   *. . . White letters maybe?*

KNOX.   . . . Bore right in on that. See if you can come up with those letters.

DOUGLAS.   *7-4-3 maybe.*

Troy and Doyle exchanged glances. Doyle wrote the numbers down.

KNOX.   Take your time. Just look.

DOUGLAS.   *Very angular. Very geometric. Lines of the dumpster.*

KNOX.   Geometric lines . . . comes up like a boat . . . landing boat. Is that what you mean?

DOUGLAS.   *I don't know what that means.*

KNOX.   Well, uh. Landing barge. A military landing barge.

DOUGLAS.   *Oh, yeah. . . .*

KNOX.   You see 7-4-3 . . . then a dash? . . . another number?

DOUGLAS.   *Threes and zeroes.*

KNOX.   Threes and zeroes. Yeah . . . okay. . . .

Douglas muttered something intently, but it was so low that it was lost to the listeners. Knox ignored the hushed message and pressed for the rest of the numbers.

KNOX.   Are you still able to see any more lettering . . . or numbers?

Again Douglas muttered something. Months later, when others listened to the tape, they could hear Douglas whispering, *"It's not me at the dumpster."* But again, Knox, Doyle, and Troy were too intent on the number to hear the provocative subtext.

KNOX.   Three. Would a 3-3-0-0 register?
DOUGLAS. *I gotta get that name to call.*

By now Knox was exhausted. He said, "We'll get it, Bill. I think we're gonna rest now, and when I count to five, you're gonna come outta this and we're gonna talk normally. All right?"

At the count of five, Douglas emerged from his trance.

Troy, who was naturally eager to put the best face on things, would later insist that he believed Douglas was hypnotized. Even the skeptical Doyle felt that Douglas had been speaking from the depths of his subconscious. The digits 7-4-3 had everyone excited. After delivering a cryptic "no comment" to reporters who had been scrupulously tipped off to this event, Troy and Doyle hurried from the jail to the district attorney's office, carrying the hypnosis tape.

It was one of the enduring ironies of the Douglas case that, in their eagerness to identify the dumpster, neither Troy nor Doyle nor Knox had listened closely enough to discern what Douglas had been mumbling sotto voce.

"It's not me at the dumpster," he said. He had said it three times.

That potentially explosive comment passed unnoticed in the current excitement over the numbers 7-4-3. Even John Kivlan and Brian Howe, who considered the hypnosis one more of Troy's publicity stunts, felt compelled to follow up on this new lead. Howe checked his notes and discovered that the dumpster on the far side of the indentation behind the Rhode Island Blood Center had a decal with white lettering indicating that it belonged to the James N. Viara Company of Seekonk, Massachusetts. The decal contained a phone number—"336-7742." Douglas had not only mentioned three of the numbers but also specified that there had been more than one 3.

The dumpster behind the blood center, in fact, matched Douglas's description inasmuch as it was dark brown and eight yards across. It was not, however, a rear loader. It had a completely open top and a door on the side. During his earlier round of checking, Howe had called Mrs. James Viara, wife of the owner, asking her if that dumpster had been in place behind the blood center on Sunday, March 6. Her records showed that it had. In light of these new revelations, Howe called again and asked her if she would mind rechecking her entries. In the meantime, Mrs. Viara gave him the name of Robert Mello, the driver who according to company records had picked up the trash from that dumpster between 5:00 and 5:30 A.M. on Monday, March 7.

Mello had quite a different story. He recalled that the dumpster he had emptied that Monday morning had been an eight-yard rear loader, just like the one Douglas had described. Mello could not recall anything unusual about the morning's pickup. His normal routine would have been to open the top covers, if they were closed. Then he would latch up the cable to the horizontal pins and tilt the trash into the back of his truck. Ordinarily, Mello said, he would not pay any attention to what was in the dumpster, especially in the early light of dawn.

Then Mrs. Viara called back to announce that she had been in error. Her records showed that there had indeed been a brown, eight-yard rear loader in place between early January and June of 1983. This, too, had the white lettering with the number 336-7742.

Howe had a gut feeling that this was *the* dumpster. It fit all the specifications. It was dark, sloped, and large and had white lettering on it. But if the Viara dumpster was the receptacle in question, that raised new problems.

Up until Douglas's session with the hypnotist, the district attorney's office had been operating on the assumption that Robin had been deposited in the Fontaine dumpster, the contents of which had been deposited in the Attleboro Landfill, where the dumping site could be narrowed down to a manageable area. Now that the presumption had shifted to the Viara dumpster, that premise had to be discarded. The Viaras routinely took their trash to Central Landfill in Johnston, Rhode Island.

Central Landfill, encompassing a hundred acres, was the largest dump in New England. Howe called Central's general manager, James Doorley, for information on the dump's operations and learned to his dismay that the landfill received refuse from four hundred trucks a day.

Like Attleboro, Central tried to route incoming trucks on some kind of predictable pattern. When bad weather set in, however, the dumping became more haphazard. In March the spring thaw caused the dirt roads which traversed the landfill to turn to mud. Under such conditions drivers had to abandon the pattern altogether and dump where the surface was reasonably stable. Doorley checked his records and found that from March 7 to March 12 rain fell every day. There was no telling where Robert Mello's load had gone that Monday morning a year ago.

Even if the dumping site could be narrowed down to a specific sector, the recovery work promised to be expensive. Excavating an area 9,000 feet square to a depth of thirty-five feet would take forty-five days and cost $125,000 to $150,000, a tab the Commonwealth was prepared to pick up if it was likely to produce results. But under the present circumstances, where it was impossible to isolate a probable location, a recovery team would have to search through all the new matter that had been dumped the preceding year. James Doorley figured conservatively that the entire landfill had been covered twice, adding a new layer of trash that was now between twenty-four and thirty feet deep. In Mr. Doorley's professional opinion, trying to locate a body in among those sprawling fields of refuse was simply "foolhardy."

BY NOW it was late Saturday afternoon. The sentencing hearing loomed large, and the district attorney's office found itself in a terribly awkward position. It would have been a triumph, of course, to walk into court on Monday morning with an announcement that the body had been found. That was now out of the question. What was worse, it was growing increasingly unlikely that the body would ever be found.

John Kivlan would insist testily to the media that the district attorney's office had not cut this deal with the understanding that Douglas could produce the body. Certain reporters had simply read that into the agreement. All that Douglas had promised, Kivlan would emphasize, was to tell *what happened.* That would shift the emphasis from the body to the confession. But the confession presented problems of its own. It was full of inconsistencies.

During the course of his rather exhaustive dumpster research, Brian Howe had come to the conclusion that Douglas had been telling the truth, at least about the way he had disposed of Robin Benedict's body. He seemed to possess too much detailed knowledge about the dumpster that was sitting behind the blood center on March 6 to have made it up. Since that receptacle had been replaced the following June, Douglas would have had to make a note of it the morning he disposed of the body. Another possibility, of course, was that he had visited University Heights sometime before June and taken down a description of the dumpster with an eye to fabricating a story. If so, it was possible that someone else had disposed of Robin the night she was killed and that Douglas had merely assisted in the cover-up.

No one at the district attorney's office had considered it necessary to listen to the hypnosis tape, so no one had heard Douglas whisper, *"It's not me at the dumpster."*

The rest of the confession, however, left Howe and other Gray House investigators feeling uneasy. Douglas had certainly delivered his lines with conviction. So much conviction, in fact, that Howe was sure that Douglas had concocted a story and then convinced himself it was true. Howe was certain that if Douglas had taken the polygraph test which the Benedicts were demanding, he would probably have passed it.

Nevertheless, one had only to compare the confession with the body of evidence to see that the account did not hold water. In the Plattsburgh episode, for instance, Douglas had consistently downplayed his own role, insisting that Robin had forced herself on him for two and a half days, then overbilled him for it. But Douglas's phone records showed that, throughout the weekend of February 18 and well into Monday, credit card calls and collect calls had been made from motels in the Saugus area to the Douglas home. This pattern suggested that Douglas and Robin had spent five days together holed up in motel rooms on the North Shore. If that was true, Douglas would have owed her at least $5,000.

More troubling, however, was Douglas's account of the fatal night. In the first place, he had recalled how Robin walked in with her jacket folded over her arm like a waiter's towel, the hammer hidden under it. This was difficult to imagine. If she had been gripping the hammer anywhere along its ten-inch handle, the implement would not have been obscured by a coat hanging towel-like from her arm. She could have been holding the hammer with one hand and hiding it under the coat hanging from the opposite arm, but this was a highly unnatural pose—one certain to arouse suspicion.

Douglas's account of the struggle was also hard to imagine. Robin had supposedly followed him into the bedroom and into the narrow passage between the bed and the closet. At the point when he bent down to open the door of the microscope case, she was standing to his left, between the closet and the bedroom door. As he was rising from his knees and turned to face her, she screamed and brought the hammer down. Here was an important discrepancy. During the first day of confession, he had claimed that he saw her holding the hammer midair. The following Monday, however, he insisted that he "didn't see a thing." And that was why he hadn't attempted to fend off the blow.

And then there was the matter of his head wound. The state police photo taken of Douglas on the night of the first search showed a scar, still rosy and inflamed, that ran down his forehead like an incision. The sledgehammer, however, had a broad, blunt end which was certainly capable of smashing, but not of cutting. Even if you assumed that the hammer had inflicted an incision wound, it was impossible to reconcile the way that Douglas said it had occurred with the simple laws of physics. Douglas claimed that when Robin brought the hammer down, he was sent sprawling onto the bed. The cut, however, was on his left side, which meant that Robin had to be swinging from the right—a blow which would have sent him hurtling away from the bed and into the closet.

Douglas would have had to climb out the closet and scramble onto the bed onto his back in order for his fight with Robin to proceed as he described. He had supposedly grabbed her wrist with one hand and the hammer with the other. Did he really mean to suggest that she had been hoisting the hammer with one hand? What was she doing with the other?

He wrestled her down, he claimed, and pinned her to the bed, but at the same moment was on his feet delivering blows with the hammer. The entire scenario sounded as if it had been fabricated by someone who had never been in an actual fight.

During the second day of confession, Douglas added another wrinkle. As Robin was hitting him, the phone rang. He reached for it, hoping to yell for help, but she pushed it away. In the fall the receiver came off the hook.

Asked who he thought might be calling the house so late, Douglas replied that he didn't know. It could have been a neighbor. Or his children. "I just never had the guts to ask them," he said. Finally, he conceded, "It could have been my wife."

It was not hard to conceive of Nancy Douglas driving aimlessly, trying to steer clear of the house, then calling home to see whether the coast was clear. It was also likely that if she heard her husband screaming, she hurried home to assist him. But did she come carrying a hammer? Nancy Douglas's role remained as elusive as ever.

John Kivlan had hoped that Douglas might inadvertently drop something that would implicate Nancy unequivocally in the events of March 5. If it could be established that Nancy was the one running around trying to dispose of the body, the Commonwealth might have her on obstruction of justice. (Even that was a long shot, because exactly what constitutes obstruction of justice had never been clearly defined under Massachusetts law.) All that Douglas would concede, however, was that Nancy had known about the killing as early as Sunday morning when she came to pick him up in Foxboro. That established her for certain as an accessory after the fact, but, as they all well knew, a wife couldn't be prosecuted under Massachusetts law for failing to turn her husband in.

The district attorney was now left with a handful of intimations that would probably not add up to an indictment. Kivlan could pursue his prerogative of going after Nancy's blood for enzyme analysis, but what now was the point? The blood on the evidence all appeared to be Robin's. If Robin's body could be found, her wounds might reveal that she had died in a way other than the one Douglas had described. Perhaps she had been ambushed from behind rather than hit from the front. Then William Douglas could be called on the carpet to give another account. But the secrets which the body could reveal lay out of reach.

During his prehypnosis chat with Dr. Knox, Douglas had said that for him the turning point in deciding to confess was a visit from his wife. She had purportedly admonished him, "You know, you may feel that you can go through a trial and watch the children up on the stand and then say, 'No, they won't testify.' And then . . . maybe they'd be put in jail. But I don't think you could really go through that."

Had that really been the extent of their conversations, or had the Douglases struck some kind of bargain? Perhaps it was Nancy who killed Robin but William Douglas who agreed to take the rap, an arrangement which allowed his wife to continue caring for the children. There was some justice in that. It was Bill, after all, whose sins had brought his loved ones to grief. After a decent interval Douglas would serve his term—with luck, a short one—and return home to Sandy Ridge Circle, and they would all start afresh. Assuming that they had made a pact of this sort, all they needed to do now was steadfastly maintain their silence. Nancy was untouchable.

If William Douglas was indeed innocent of the killing of Robin Benedict, it no longer mattered. The machinery which his confession had set in motion could not be stopped. In the preceding century when the murder of Francis Parkman had wrought such profound disturbances in public tranquillity, the Commonwealth's prosecutor had declared, "Someone must answer." A conviction was necessary to restore civil harmony and public trust. Even if, as some later claimed, the Commonwealth got the wrong man. Now, over 130 years later, when the press and general public were agitating for an answer to the question "What happened to Robin Benedict?" William Douglas had stepped forward to answer, "I am guilty." Without hard evidence to the contrary, the Commonwealth was in no position to reject his plea.

TOM TROY knew he had the district attorney over a barrel. That he had succeeded in luring his old friend Billy Delahunt into a plea bargain with the implied promise of a body seemed not to have troubled his conscience. That was the code of the tribe. Sometimes you scored one on your buddy; sometimes he scored one on you. If the combatants kept their perspective, the wounds incurred in a legal skirmish were no more serious than those incurred in a cutthroat game of poker. It would be only a matter of weeks before Delahunt and Troy would be downing beers together at J.J. Foley's.

For the present, however, the two had to maintain the stance of adversaries as they girded up for the final skirmish. Troy knew that John Kivlan was hell-bent on getting Douglas the maximum sentence. He had said so at the plea hearing. The defense attorney, however, drew encouragement from the fact that he would be going into court on Monday to plead clemency not for a hardened criminal but for a professional and family man who had no history of violence. Troy was hopeful that if he pushed the right emotional buttons, he could get Douglas six to ten, parole in four years. During the weekend before sentencing, therefore, Troy turned his prodigious tactical expertise toward one end—creating a final swell of public sympathy for William and Nancy Douglas.

The *Herald* had felt itself badly burned the preceding week when Troy had leaked details of the confession to the *Globe.* Troy now sought to mend fences by offering the tabloid a question-and-answer session with Nancy Douglas. This interview was to be carried out strictly on Troy's conditions, which did not include allowing a reporter anywhere near Mrs. Douglas. It was to be conducted strictly in writing.

In her subsequent replies "Nancy" ignored all the queries relating to Robin Benedict. Her vague, folksy answers were directed exclusively to the soft soaps. The resulting article, positioned prominently on Sunday's cover under the headline "Private Torment of Prof's Wife," was a sob story in the best tradition.

Asked to describe William Douglas's "best qualities" as a father and husband, Nancy replied, "Bill was everything I ever wanted as a husband and father. I wish he could have spent more time with me and the kids. But I knew how much his work meant to him and I understood it. I guess that is part of the reason I loved him. I still love him."

That same Sunday morning the *Globe,* which had also been given the opportunity to submit written questions, ran its own "Nancy speaks" story, in which Mrs. Douglas got off a few shots at those she considered to blame for her present torment:

> I don't know what I could have done differently. Maybe ask Bill to spend more time at home. But his work was so important. He was doing work on infantile diseases. Babies are so helpless and he was just trying to help babies. . . . Tufts University worked Bill so hard. There was always more and more work to do and Bill didn't know how to say "no." . . . Tufts has a lien on the house and there are three mortgages. We got a letter not too long ago from a Rhode Island lawyer saying the bank wanted to foreclose. I hope I can figure out how to pay the mortgage. . . .
>
> This has been hardest for the children, especially Johnny. When the police showed up with their summonses, or it was in the newspapers, Johnny seemed to take it personally. He's spent a lot of time by himself in his bedroom. He was always the quiet one—now even more so. Pamela seems to be alright. She's taking it the best. She seems determined not to let it affect her. . . .
>
> The children haven't seen Bill in over six months. It is important that a

father be there, but Bill wasn't. He'll miss so much being in jail. I know Bill must be punished for what he did. I only hope Judge Donahue doesn't forget how much we have been punished and will be punished.

Even as he positioned the Douglases as orphans of the storm, Troy was engaging in some aggressive damage control on another front. The Benedicts had somehow to be mollified before Monday morning, when, under the state's victims' rights act, they had the prerogative of giving testimony at the sentencing hearing. Troy was savvy enough to surmise that they were feeling burned by the plea bargain and that their statements to the court were likely to be a scream for vengeance. Now, as the hearing drew close, it would be in Douglas's interest to make some overtures of conciliation in hopes of softening their tone.

The Benedicts were, in fact, nearly sick with anger and frustration, and they were not precisely sure at whom to vent it—at the district attorney, William Douglas, or Tom Troy. On Friday afternoon a call from the media had alerted them to the fact that Douglas was being hypnotized. Tony DiFruscia hastily gathered up his clients in the Caddy limo and whisked them off to Dedham to see what they could find out. They arrived to find Troy surrounded by reporters, basking in the glow of another media coup. But neither Troy nor the district attorney's office would brief them as to what had happened at the jail.

DiFruscia was at his office the following morning when he received a call from Troy. Douglas, Troy told him, would like to meet with John Benedict that very day to "ask his forgiveness."

DiFruscia had his suspicions that Troy intended somehow to turn this seemingly gracious gesture to his client's advantage. When the Benedicts arrived at the jail, they would probably be greeted by TV cameras which Troy would have summoned to document the grieving parents on their way to reconciliation with their daughter's killer. DiFruscia did not intend to give Troy that advantage.

DiFruscia offered to relay Douglas's offer to the Benedicts but only if Troy agreed not to tip off the media. If Douglas wanted to ask the Benedicts' forgiveness, he said, he should meet them alone—without reporters and without attorneys. Troy apparently agreed, but within minutes after that conversation ended, DiFruscia received a call from a perplexed John Benedict, who had just received a call from a TV reporter asking him when he would be going to Dedham to meet with Douglas.

DiFruscia called Troy back and accused him of grandstanding; Troy called DiFruscia a "cute little bastard," and the negotiations to arrange a meeting between Douglas and the Benedicts broke down almost as soon as they started.

As badly as they wanted to meet with Douglas, the Benedicts agreed that DiFruscia had been right in thwarting Troy. At this point they stood to be robbed of the body. The confession, they were convinced, was a pack of lies. But there remained one satisfaction that was still within their reach: seeing Douglas get the maximum sentence. If they were now to be lured into appearing to give him their blessing, they might unwittingly assure his early release.

FOR THE REST of that weekend, the Benedicts and DiFruscia did a little strategizing of their own. Having decided to stay aloof from Douglas, they needed to determine the proper stance to take toward the district attorney's office. Had the stakes been lower, the Benedicts might well have gone public with their disappointment over the plea bargain. But with the final round approaching, they could not afford to alienate such a potentially powerful ally as John Kivlan. For all their past differences with him, the Benedicts considered Kivlan an essentially honest man. If they had been duped by the DA's office, it had not been Kivlan's doing, but the work of someone higher up. If Kivlan now intended to go into the sentencing hearing with guns blazing, there was no good purpose to be served in cutting him off at the legs. By late Sunday night John and Shirley Benedict had decided to suppress their grievances and walk into court the next day presenting a united front with the district attorney.

On Monday morning Douglas was brought over to the court as usual, in handcuffs. For once, however, he seemed to demonstrate emotion. His head was bowed. The quizzical stare was gone, and in its place was an expression approximating grief. Either Douglas had finally realized how potentially serious his present condition was or he had learned how to make a convincing show of contrition.

Judge Donahue announced that he would hear statements from all parties who had an interest in the sentencing.

"Are you ready, Mr. Kivlan?" he asked.

"Yes, Your Honor," Kivlan said, rising to his feet. He had forgone his customary grays and was wearing his navy blue "lucky suit."

The prosecutor began on a defensive note, announcing that he wanted to clarify a "misunderstanding" about the recovery of Robin Benedict's body.

"As Your Honor knows," he said, "that aspect of the agreement was, quite simply, that Douglas disclose to the Commonwealth . . . what he did with the body. There was no way of knowing, obviously, what he did with the body . . . until such time as he . . . made a statement to the state police. So it was understood by all, the Commonwealth as well as the Benedict family that . . . it was entirely possible he might have done something with the body that would have caused . . . no chance of recovering any remains."

Kivlan went on to report that Douglas had upheld his end of the bargaining by giving a lengthy account of what he had done with the body to Lieutenant Sharkey and Trooper Howe, whose own, independent investigation seemed to verify that he had, "in all probability," disposed of the body in a dumpster behind the Rhode Island Blood Bank at the University Heights Shopping Center, in Providence.

"It would appear," Kivlan announced grimly, "that it is near to impossible, if not impossible to recover Miss Benedict's remains."

That unpleasant business dispensed with, he moved more aggressively into the Commonwealth's sentencing recommendations.

"As Your Honor knows," he said, "manslaughter, by legal definition, is an intentional killing [that would be] murder but for the existence of . . . mitigating factors such as passion, provocation, or palliation of some kind. In this case, there is no question . . . that there was some passion . . . as one-sided as it may have been. No question about it. And the events that led up to the . . . confrontation the night of March 5 would indicate there was some provocation in the form of a dispute. . . . So there is mitigation. Yes, there is no question there is mitigation. . . .

"Now, according to his own account, he says that Robin brought the hammer to the house. I suggest to you, respectfully, that apart from the fact that through a year of investigation this defendant has demonstrated himself to be, if nothing else, a pathological liar, the weight of the evidence would show that the hammer was in the house . . . that his wife borrowed the hammer several months before, allegedly to do some work on the porch. But . . . even if you believe Douglas's account, at some point during the struggle, he either picked up the hammer or took the hammer from Robin [and] while that young girl, who weighed less than 120 pounds, was attempting to get off the bed . . . he took the hammer and smacked her over the head, by his own account, two or three times with such force to literally crush her skull and dislodge this brain tissue. . . . Manslaughter though it may be, it was about as close to a murder as one can get.

". . . Whatever this girl was, whether she was a prostitute or she wasn't a prostitute . . . she had a family. She was devoted to her family and her family was devoted to her. This was a human life. He had just brutally taken a human life. He took this girl's body and placed it in a . . . dumpster like it was a piece of trash. This body ended up in a landfill with garbage and debris. This family has been deprived, probably forever, of whatever remains there may exist of her. . . ."

"In addition to that," Kivlan continued, indignation giving his voice a harsher edge, "he took advantage and exploited for almost a year his successful disposition of that body to cause this family more anguish, more grief and to place blame wherever he could on innocent persons. He lied. He fabricated evidence. He hid behind his own children."

Kivlan's voice by now fairly dripped with contempt. He went on, "He got up here last week and attempted to suggest . . . that there is remorse. That the reason he confessed last week is because he wants to get it off his chest. I suggest to you, Your Honor, that were it not for . . . one of the most . . . exhaustive police investigations that ever occurred in the Commonwealth . . . he would have gotten away with it. . . . He pled at the last minute . . . because he knew the Commonwealth would prove, body or no body, that he killed Robin Benedict. It was a last-ditch attempt to obtain some consideration from this court as to the sentence.

"He deserves no consideration. He deserves eighteen to twenty, and not a day less. . . ."

It was now the Benedicts' turn to deliver the other half of the one-two punch.

"I have been informed by the Benedict family," Kivlan told Judge Donahue, "that they wish Mr. DiFruscia . . . to read a prepared statement to you."

John and Shirley Benedict had thought about delivering the statement themselves but had decided against it. There was a danger that they would break down, and they did not want to appear undignified before the court. There was an even more dangerous possibility that they might come off sounding angry. The last thing the Benedicts wanted was to have their plea dismissed as a cry for vengeance. So the Benedicts spent most of Sunday in conference with DiFruscia and his wife, Kathleen, a former textbook editor, framing what they hoped would be a subdued but passionate plea for justice.

Dispensing with his usual cockiness, DiFruscia approached the bench as though it were an altar and, in all humility, began to read.

"The Benedict family has asked me to acknowledge their sincere gratitude to all the members of the district attorney's office . . . who labored so arduously and meticulously in their investigation into the disappearance of their daughter Robin.

"Until the recent confession of Mr. Douglas detailing Robin's brutal killing, the Benedicts have lived with the nightmare of uncertainty as to what had happened to their daughter. . . . Mr. Douglas knew the Benedict family and knew of their concern for Robin when she was first known to be missing. He in fact communicated with them shortly after her disappearance. . . . Yet he cruelly let them believe that she was still alive. Even as the jury was being chosen days before his confession, he led his attorney to believe that Robin might walk through the door. Had Mr. Douglas come forward with the truth at the beginning, he would have saved the Benedict family and his own children this year of anguish and despair. . . .

"In reading Mr. Douglas' confession . . . one must wonder about the kind of man who has been able to live for more than a year with the knowledge that he committed such a heinous crime. The Benedicts also wonder about the kind of person his wife must be, a woman who was told by her husband of the killing the day after it occurred and who the very same night went off to attend a banquet.

"This is not a kind man. This is not a gentle man easily led astray by beautiful young women. This is a devious, mature man, an intelligent, calculating man who knew what he was doing and who must be held responsible for his actions. . . .

"Mr. Douglas . . . said, 'What I want to do is to apologize to the Benedict family. I know Mr. and Mrs. Benedict. They are fine people. They have raised a wonderful family unit.' Mr. Douglas is correct, but an apology is just not enough. To commit this man to anything less than the maximum penalty under the law would show disregard for a criminal justice system which is designed to protect the innocent and punish the guilty.

"A sentence of eighteen to twenty years is trivial in nature, Your Honor, when it is compared to the finality of death."

"MR. TROY," said Judge Donahue, "you are entitled to be heard. . . ."

Onlookers familiar with the old pugilist's style expected him to come out swinging. But now, as he rose to his feet, he seemed strangely subdued. The strain of the past few weeks and the pain of his diabetic toe had conspired to leave him tired and distracted. For the first five minutes or so, he rambled on with a passionless recitation of William Douglas's professional achievements.

Then, recovering his old fire, he plunged into the subject he loved best, the parable of a good man brought low by an evil woman.

"In the year 1982," he began, "Bill Douglas, in the early morning hours, left his scientific world at Tufts University on the edge of the Combat Zone. Yes, I say, this gentle, sensitive, educated man left the Alice in Wonderland world of academia and entered the world of sin and sex in Boston's Combat Zone. Yes, it was there that Samson met his Delilah. Her pleasant ways. The grace of a lady. Charm. Yes, her intelligence and her charming way made it okay and not quite so distasteful. And, yes, it made Bill Douglas a prisoner, just as he is now, a prisoner of sex, dope, and intrigue. . . . When the Combat Zone entered his Camelot of Sharon, he broke from the meek world he knew. He entered the world of the Combat Zone."

Troy's prose swelled in a riot of metaphor, culminating in the love letter—the "young fool" letter—which Douglas had written to Robin over a year before.

"Dearest Robin," he read meaningfully. "As you know, the truly wonderful times in my life this last year were those times I spent with you. You shared so much with me, your thoughts, our lives, and we had so many special, meaningful times together that can only happen between friends. I cherish those memories and look forward to the time when we are together again."

As Troy read, Douglas's head fell lower, bobbing slightly as though he was trying to control a heaving in his chest.

"You know I am sad that it happened but I have only myself to blame. I will change my ways. I will work hard on trying to act like an adult when I interact with you and not some love-struck teenager."

"Judge," Troy addressed Donahue, "this was a childlike infatuation that cost him his job, his family, and, yes, Robin Benedict's life. . . . Robin Benedict is dead, but for all practical purposes, so is Bill Douglas. Just a few days ago, Bill Douglas told this court, told the world, he had killed Robin Benedict. In effect, this courtroom became his confessional, Your Honor. He has repented. . . . I have heard his words, 'I hope the good Lord will forgive me.' "

Bill Douglas had to be punished, Troy conceded, but the punishment didn't have to be drastic. Had he been less prominent, or his case less publicized by "those people sitting there"—Troy gestured toward the press gallery—then there would be less pressure now to give him the maximum sentence. For a man of his background, twenty years at a minimum-security prison or five to ten at a maximum-security facility would suffice.

"Save some time for Bill Douglas," Troy implored, "so he can become a contributor once again to society."

Judge Donahue listened thoughtfully to the pleadings. But, in fact, he had already made up his mind.

Personally, Donahue was inclined to be sympathetic toward William Douglas. The judge had given careful consideration to Douglas's presentencing report, and from this he concluded that the defendant had attained a certain level of decency in his life. Before the Benedict episode, he had provided dutifully for his wife and family, and that carried a lot of weight with Donahue. The judge agreed with Troy that the man's basic sense of decency had simply been overwhelmed by infatuation.

Donahue was also impressed by Douglas's lengthy admissions. The judge was a devout Catholic who took confession very seriously. Granted, Douglas was a Protestant who probably did not appreciate all the spiritual significance of the rite. Still, Donahue reasoned, when a man confesses, he purges himself. Douglas's confession, he thought, had the "ring of sincerity."

Had his considerations stopped here, Judge Donahue would probably have been inclined to give the lighter sentence. But two more factors had to be considered: the nature and circumstances of the crime and the age of the victim.

In this case one had a man who took a large hammer and hit his victim so often and so hard that it broke her skull. Then he took measures to cover it up. That certainly exceeded the bounds of decency. Beyond that, the life he took was that of a twenty-one-year-old girl. It did not matter, in Donahue's estimation, what kind of life she had. Killing the young was so heinous that it deserved the harshest punishment the law allowed.

"Mr. Douglas," said the clerk, "kindly stand."

Douglas stood and lifted his head. His eyes appeared red and moist.

"The court, having accepted your plea of guilty," the clerk continued matter-of-factly, "sentences you to not less than eighteen nor more than twenty years at the Massachusetts Correctional Institution at Walpole and orders that you stand committed."

The effect of these words upon William Douglas was remarkable. His body, which had been hunched in a suggestion of abjection, snapped alert. His hangdog face contorted in a grimace. He looked to Troy, as though expecting him to challenge the bully. But court was promptly dismissed.

Troy appeared choleric as he made his way out of the courtroom, pausing to whisper to Kivlan, "You're a barracuda, kid."

Bailiffs hustled Douglas back to the jail to begin packing for the journey to Walpole.

The Benedicts, meanwhile, pushed their way without comment through an insistent throng of newsmen to the district attorney's office for a status report on the search for the body of their missing daughter.

Even now John and Shirley believed that the search would continue, and that assurance left them with the faint but enduring hope that they would find the body. Shirley still clung to the belief that when Robin was found, she would look much like her old self. Lifeless, perhaps, but still lovely.

When the Benedicts arrived at the conference room, they found not only Delahunt, Kivlan, and Howe but also the pathologist Dr. George Katsas. During the anxious days following the confession, Kivlan had conferred regularly with Katsas, relaying to him the rapidly changing scenarios of Robin's disposition in exchange for the pathologist's opinion on whether the body could be found.

Katsas learned through these conversations that the Benedicts hoped to unearth something they could recognize as their daughter. It saddened him to hear this. Katsas had seen a great deal of death over the years and, in the process, learned something about mourning. When members of a family lost a child, it was important for them to be able to look into the face of the dead and to recognize that this corpse was not, in fact, the loved one. Only by their grasping this central fact of death could the cycle of grieving be complete. If the loved one, as in Robin's case, was missing and presumed dead, it was more difficult to let her go. What this family needed then was to see the child and to give her a burial in order to put the past behind.

The diminutive Greek gentleman, his voice full of compassion, began explaining to the Benedicts the unfortunate facts of the matter. Even if searchers succeeded in locating her remains, which now seemed unlikely, they would find nothing which looked like Robin. Over a year had passed; at best, there would be teeth and bone. These remains, of course, were of considerable interest to a pathologist. By studying fracture lines in the skull, he could determine whether the wound had occurred the way Douglas said it had. He would also be able to tell if she had suffered other wounds besides. But they must not expect anything that looked like their daughter.

Katsas went on to explain how even these durable remnants—bones, teeth, and jewelry—might well have been destroyed or mangled beyond recognition in the landfill's compactor. There was also the possibility that dogs or other small animals had scattered the remains over a large area.

Blunt as it was, Dr. Katsas's analysis was a gentle precursor to the news which followed.

William Delahunt took over the briefing with an explanation of how impractical it would be to continue. If the Commonwealth were to dig up the landfill now, it would be taking on a project that could run into years and cost millions of dollars. With luck, they might recover some teeth, the zipper of the sleeping bag, or Robin's gold earrings. But there was always the possibility that Douglas had lied about what he did with the body. If that was so, the Commonwealth risked frittering away millions on a hoax. Justice, like most everything else, had a bottom line. The search for Robin Benedict, the district attorney announced, was being called off.

The Benedicts were silent. They had expected this news all along, but when it arrived, they were numbed nonetheless. The frustrating thing was that the decision was reasonable. They could offer the district attorney no good reason to continue searching.

Dr. Katsas asked if they would like the tiny paraffin blocks of brain tissue for burial. But they declined.

THAT FRIDAY evening a simple funeral mass was held for Robin Benedict at the Mt. Carmel Catholic Church in Methuen. It drew more than three hundred neighbors, friends, and curiosity seekers. William Delahunt attended. So did J.R. Rogers. Attired a little more garishly than usual, in a double-breasted silk suit, Rogers sat with the family.

In the place of a casket stood a pedestal on which sat the now-famous photo of Robin, head tilted, eyes twinkling at the assembly of mourners below her. Those eyes—joyous, secretive, provocative—had always had the power to arouse the ache of something missing: lost youth, spontaneous joy, realized ambitions. She had promised to fill the void and make the seeker complete. But those promises, like Robin herself, no longer had substance. All that was left of the dreams she had engendered was an impious glance—laughing eyes hinting at a secret which would never be revealed.

Ascending to the altar, Father Emile Guilmette reminded the crowd of mourners that the name Robin meant "bright flame." Nadine meant "hope." Benedict meant "one who is blessed."

"The tragedy," he said, "is that this bright flame was . . . dulled."

Some of these things which had been said about Robin Benedict, he continued, had been "harsh and insensitive. But tonight, in this place . . . at this mass, Robin will be called what truly was her name when she was baptized—a child of God."

Father Guilmette urged her family not to think too much about her final resting place. There was no point in longing for what one cannot have. It was not a good idea to dwell on the missing beauty.

EPILOGUE

DURING the months since William Douglas was sent to prison, the fortunes of many of the characters in this drama have changed, some slightly, others dramatically.

Karen Hitchcock and Ron Sanders—Both have left Tufts, Hitchcock to become an associate dean of basic science at a major midwestern university, Sanders to work in private industry. Douglas's lab has been disbanded. The New England Anti-Vivisection Society tried to interest other investigators in resuming the alternatives work but found no takers.

Stanley Spilman—Still working on his Ph.D.

Judge Robert Ford—Came under fire for allegedly using NEAVS funds to line the pockets and pension funds of family and friends. Resigned under a cloud of scandal.

John Kivlan—In 1985 won the Massachusetts lottery, becoming a millionaire. Continues to work in the Norfolk District Attorney's Office, where he has been elevated to the status of first assistant. Formerly known as "Johnny America," he is now more commonly referred to as "Lucky John" or "Diamond Jack Kivlan."

Paul Landry—Now working as a private eye.

William Dwyer—Transferred out of the Combat Zone in the spring of 1985 when the city of Boston—quietly and without explanation—disbanded the vice unit. (The word on the street was that the vice cops were doing so little that their presence was not needed; the explanation of vice cops was that the Zone was essentially dead and their work, therefore, done.)

Joe Murray—Indicted by the U.S. attorney's office in April 1986 for allegedly running guns to the Irish Republican Army. That year he pled guilty to arms charges as well as to attempting to import marijuana and federal tax evasion—for which he received a prison term of ten years.

J.R. Rogers—Stayed in touch with the Benedicts, who gradually saw less and less of him, because of what he described as pressing business interests in the South.

The working girls—After Good Time Charlie's closed in the summer of 1984—a casualty of police pressure and the Combat Zone's general decline—Robin Benedict's colleagues at the bar moved to a nearby club called the Mardi Gras. At length, the Mardi Gras, too, felt pressure to clean up the premises and threw the girls out.

Agatha Christie Crimestoppers—Betty Sanborn finally sold Bette Lou and got a job as an airport security guard. Miss Thawley is still investigating missing persons and trying to find a publisher for her treatise, "The Heart of Earhart."

John and Shirley Benedict—Sold the silver Toyota and rented Robin's dream house. Also sold their rights to a television producer, stipulating that the funds go to a charity for wayward girls. In the fall of 1984 the family filed and won a wrongful-death suit against William Douglas, giving them claim to any future income that he may receive. They intend to fight attempts to secure William Douglas an early parole.

The Douglases—During the months after William Douglas was sent to the maximum-security prison at Walpole, he proved a model prisoner—his only significant lapse was to have been caught running betting slips. In the summer of 1984 he pled guilty to larceny charges in Suffolk County. Judge Roger Donahue, presiding over this matter, gave him three to five years but decreed his sentences run concurrently so that the defendant not serve any more time. After doing less than a year at Walpole, Douglas was transferred to a more benign facility, in Gardner,

Massachusetts. After this move Nancy visited him only once. Sometime during the summer of 1986, Douglas received a letter from a woman who had read a feature story detailing his case. Forty-four-year-old Bonnie-Jean Smith, a recent divorcée, was a nurse of the same stolid ilk as Nancy Douglas, and she reportedly "felt sorry" for Douglas. In the wake of this development, William Douglas filed for divorce from his wife of twenty-three years. (The summons was witnessed by the probate judge and former NEAVS president Robert Ford.) In an uncontested agreement Douglas signed over to Nancy all his worldly goods as well as custody of John Douglas, their last remaining minor child. Nancy gave up her married name and became once again Nancy Boulton. She continues to live on Sandy Ridge Circle. On July 7, 1987, William Douglas and Bonnie-Jean Smith were married by a prison chaplain. Douglas has been imploring former professional colleagues for demonstrations of support, hoping to qualify for work release. As of this writing, he has enjoyed no success.

Robin Benedict—Robin Benedict is still missing. Her body has never been found.

ACKNOWLEDGMENTS

DURING the four years that I have spent working on this book, I have enjoyed the cooperation of many people whose contribution should be acknowledged. I could not have pieced together William Douglas's career at Tufts without the help of Karen Hitchcock, Ron Sanders, Tom Foxall, Jane Aghajanian, Diane Romeo, Lance Kisby, Stanley Spilman, Brian Toole, Richard Thorngren, and Henry Wilson. I would like to thank Ethel Thurston, Pegeen Fitzgerald, William Cave, and particularly Henry Spira for their help in elucidating Douglas's participation in the animal rights movement. Other colleagues who shed light on Douglas's professional rise and fall were Howard Berman, Darwin O. Chee, Sergey Fedoroff, William Grazaidei, H. Z. Liu, Worth Clinkscales, Robert Dell'Orco, Bud Patterson, Donald Merchant, William Momberger, Roland Nardone, Larry Davis, and Paul Thomas.

In researching Douglas's student years at Plattsburgh State and Brown University, I received invaluable assistance from Donald Catalfimo, Stephen Boyd, Frank Morisco, Ronald Bode, Barbara and John Pelkey, Mary Ann Riley, Ed Baker, Lillian Baker, John Curry, Robert Ellsworth, Stallard Waterhouse, Ken Miller, Richard Ellis, Elizabeth Leduc, Robert Ripley, James McAteer, Jim and Izola Hogan, Robert Bloodgood, Linda Malick, and Henry Holden.

Among those who were kind enough to share with me their private recollections of Douglas's years in Lake Placid were Nellie Cobane, Marjorie White, Bob and Pat La Hart, Roger Smart, Carol Stanclift, Bucky Hayes, Bill Beaney, Bev Reid, and Oldrich Blazka.

Special thanks to the ladies of the Berkeley Residence for their help in fleshing out the details of Douglas's employment there. I speak, in particular, of Cynthia Cajka and the Agatha Christie Crimestoppers: Mary Thawley, Betty Sanborn, Debbie Woodman, Pamela Anderson, and Cindy Segal.

I would also like to express my appreciation to Douglas's various defense attorneys who extended assistance to me along the way: Daniel O'Connell, Stephen Hrones, Richard Clayman, and Charles Balliro. Extravagant thanks to Tom Troy, Bill Doyle, Pat McCann, Bill Bolton, and Jimmy Rafferty.

Robin Benedict's brief life and times were made accessible through the reminiscences of Norm Salem, Sharyn and Richard Ramos, Danny Sanchez, Linda Fales, John Petralia, Edward Ratyna, Raymond Costict, and Raymond Clayborn. I would like to give particular thanks to Tony and Kathleen DiFruscia and, of course, to John and Shirley Benedict for their gracious hospitality and very valuable assistance.

Among those who helped me navigate the labyrinth of the Combat Zone were Dennis Schuetz, Betsy Ann Hill, Thomas D. Morehead, and Walter Penachio, whose friendship and protection were much appreciated. Thanks also to Pam McGrath, Cynthia Plowden, and many others for their insights into a life which was foreign and not a little frightening to me.

Special and heartfelt appreciation to the Norfolk district attorney William Delahunt. I would like to acknowledge the assistance of Mike McGorty, Don Gordon, Victor Savioli, Judith Cowin, Lou Sabadini, Tom Brennan, Peter Casey, Gerry Pudolsky, Peter Agnes, Rick Zebrasky, Bobby Murphy, James Sharkey, and Matt Connolly. Special thanks to Brian Howe and John Kivlan for the many hours they spent with me retracing the steps of their intricate and remarkable investigation.

Those other investigators who assisted me in my research were Paul Landry, Tom Neff, and William Anderson of the Massachusetts State Police; Christine Miller, Cornelius Dever, Kenneth Bowen, and Joseph Pirrello of the New York Police Department; and Ernie Porter, James Kearney, Alan Robillard, and Charles Perrotta of the FBI. Special thanks to members of the Boston Police Department: Eddie McNelley, John Ridlon, Mike Ingemi, Frank Sheehan, Mark Molloy, and particularly Bill Dwyer.

Others who provided valuable assistance were Roger Donahue, William Q. Sturner, George G. Katsas, Ronald Kaufman. Gerald Muldoon, Arthur Shabo, Steve Limon, Alex Nappen, Natalie Skvir, Robert Campbell, Tom Gasparro, James Testa, Charles Borstel, Andrew Palermo, Robert Mason, Marie Stephenson, Gloria James, John Vasapolli, Joseph Tabbi, Paul Moan, Henry Schultz, Bob Valukis, Sargent Nichols, John Conroy, Samuel Rao, Malcolm Weldon, Ed Willis, and Joe Brennan.

Thanks also to Albert Stunkard, James Heiman, Francis Cardillo, Ken Greenfield, Stephen Keefe, Mary Hickey, Paula Mills, Edith Alberino, Chuck Laurant, Gary Scheff, Susan Evans, Carrie Harris, Mark Pollack, Donald Bell, Robert Locke, Gil Lewis, John Roberts, Nan Elder, John Sedgwick, Jerome Wisefield, Electa Tritsch, Greer Hardwicke, Joe Swinyer, Bea Drutz, Helen Gollobin, Robert Johnson-Lally, Joseph Ligotti, Mary Miers, Michael Weinberg, Alan Goldberg, Ron Yard, Dave Fernandez, Ethel Person, and Manny Rich.

Many other reporters have, at one time or another, found themselves covering the Douglas case. A number of these have shared their time and material with me most generously. They are Shelly Murphy, Liz Holland, Andrea Estes, Norma Nathan, Michelle Caruso, and particularly the witty and insightful John Birtwell, all of the *Boston Herald;* Mike Frisby, Jerry Taylor, and Joe Harvey of the *Boston Globe;* Mike Matza and Jim Schuh of the *Boston Phoenix;* Carol Horner of the *Philadelphia Inquirer;* Mike Lawrence and Ron Sanders of WNEV, Channel 7; Marilyn Greenstein of WBZ, Channel 4; and Ron Gollobin of WCVB, Channel 5.

Special thanks to David Schneiderman and Jan Hoffman of the *Village Voice* for publishing the article upon which this book was based.

Thanks also to Charlie O'Brien, Don Forst, Doug Simmons, Kit Rachlis, Ellen Goodman, Alan Richman, Bella English, Leigh Montville, Joe Ruppucci, Jim MacLaughlin, Claude Marx, Ed Copp, James Dynko, Micki Siegel, Mike Wixon, Carol Bruce, Tom Ryder, John Foley, John Brady, Robert Parker, George Higgins, Mary Ellen Lyons, Jed and Kate Mattes, Eric Lazar, John Brockman, Katinka Matson, David Rosenthal, Chris Lortie, and David Hershey and to Renee Schwartz for special and much appreciated assistance.

Among those I would like to thank for their moral support, hospitality, and friendship, are Helen Rees, George Thomas, Elizabeth Bunker, Susan Orlean, Peter Sistrom, Charlotte and Bob Seeley, David Weinberg, Alma Bond, Katie Nelson, and Kathy Pohl.

I am deeply grateful to Esther Newberg, Victor Kovner, and Linda Healey, whose faith and enthusiasm sustained me through the difficult times. . . . and to Steven Levy, without whose love and judicious counsel I would never have made it to the finish.

Among those who—despite repeated invitations—declined to be interviewed were J. R. Rogers, Savitry Bisram, Bonnie-Jean Douglas, Stephen Boulton, Nancy Boulton-Douglas, Billy, Pamela, and John Douglas, and Dr. William H. J. Douglas.

There are many who requested anonymity and cannot, therefore, be acknowledged. I thank them just the same.

BIBLIOGRAPHY

Amory, Cleveland. *The Proper Bostonians.* New York: E. P. Dutton, 1947.

Bradbury, Savile. *The Evolution of the Microscope.* New York: Pergamon Press, 1967.

Cook, Louis A., ed. *History of Norfolk County, Massachusetts: 1622–1918.* New York and Chicago: S. J. Clarke, 1918.

Lewin, Lauri. *Naked Is the Best Disguise: My Life as a Stripper.* New York: William Morrow, 1984.

Lukas, J. Anthony. *Common Ground: A Turbulent Decade in the Lives of Three American Families.* New York: Alfred A. Knopf, 1985.

The Maintenance of High Ethical Standards in the Conduct of Research. Washington, D.C.: Executive Council of the Association of American Medical Colleges, June 24, 1982.

O'Donnell, Lawrence, Jr. *Deadly Force: The True Story of How a Badge Can Become a License to Kill.* New York: William Morrow, 1983.

Pauly, John E., ed. *The American Association of Anatomists: 1888–1987.* 1987 Centennial Volume. Philadelphia: Williams and Wilkinson, 1987.

Sedgwick, John. *Night Vision: Confessions of Gil Lewis, Private Eye.* New York: Simon and Schuster, 1982.

Sharon, Massachusetts: A History. Sharon American Revolution Bicentennial Committee, 1976.

Sullivan, Robert. *The Disappearance of Dr. Parkman.* Boston: Little, Brown, 1971.

Taylor, Robert. *Saranac: America's Magic Mountain.* Boston: Houghton Mifflin, 1986.

"William Dawes and His Ride with Paul Revere." Essay Read before the New England Historical Society, June 7, 1976.

Boston Magazine: "The Tortured Animal Advertising Machine," Craig Waters, April 1975; "The Politics of the Patriots," Jake Falla, Sept. 1979; "A Nieman Rates the *Globe,*" Jonathan Z. Larsen, Dec. 1980. "Rupert Buys Hub Rag: Wingo In, Forst Out," Greg O'Brien, May 1983; "Fallen Angel," Jeffrey Newman and Margery Eagan, Feb. 1984.

Boston Phoenix: "Banned in Boston Again?" Dave O'Brian, July 5, 1977; "Tales of Troy," Michael Matza, Oct. 24, 1978; "Give My Regards to Route One," Tom Davidson, May 10, 1983; "Days in Court: How Working Girls Handle the Morning Shift," Michael Matza, Dec. 27, 1983; "Nowhere Man. The Strange Case of Bucky Barrett," Jim Schuh, Dec. 24, 1985; "Cash on the Barrel? Feds Target Joe Murray in Valhalla Case," Jim Schuh, April 29, 1986.

Boston Globe: "Downtown Police Corruption Alleged," Richard J. Connolly, Nov. 9, 1976; "Prosecution or Reform?" Ken Hartnett, Nov. 9, 1976; "Police District 1 Area of Contrast by Day and Night," William Buchanan, Nov. 9, 1976; "Police Protected Mob Figures, Report Says," Nov. 9, 1976; "Harvard Athlete Is Stable after Combat Zone Melee," Alexander Hawes, Jr., Nov. 17, 1976; "The Zone Devoid of Combat as Police Replace Hookers," John F. Cullen, Nov. 19, 1976; "Police Report Shock Waves Rock diGrazia," David Farrell, Nov. 11, 1976; "Prostitutes Invade the Back Bay," John F. Cullen, Nov. 21, 1976; "Officials Say Concept of X-Rated Zone Failed, Plan Crackdown on Violations," Paul Feeney and Peter Mancusi, Nov. 30, 1976; "Cardinal, Licensing Official Assail Hub's Combat Zone," Dec. 20, 1976; "From Scollay Square Tattoo Parlors to Combat Zone Porno Films," Jonathan Kaufman, Dec. 27, 1984; "Raymond Clayborn: He'd Rather Use Quickness, Guile than Brute Force," Walter Haynes, Aug. 19, 1978; "Thomas Troy for the Defense," Nick King, Oct. 13, 1982; "Lab Fraud Case: Is There a Pattern?" Richard A. Knox, March 21, 1983; "Tufts Professor Resigns after University Probe," June 24, 1983; "Grand Jury to Hear Missing Woman Case," June 28, 1983; "Ex-Professor Subject of Funds Probe at Tufts," Michael Frisby, June 29, 1983; "Benedict's Lawyer Faults Coverage," Michael Frisby, July 22, 1983; "Petition Denied in Benedict Case," Diane Lewis, Aug. 16, 1983; "Ex-Professor's Children Appear before Jury," Aug. 17, 1983; "Ex-Tufts Teacher Denies Larceny," Diane Lewis and Michael Frisby," Oct. 13, 1983; "Murder Indictment Is Brought against ex-Tufts Professor," Stephanie Chavez, Oct. 29, 1983; "Douglas Lawyer Seeks Bail Hearing," Michael Frisby, Nov. 2, 1983; "Tufts Prof Denied Bail in Robin's Murder," Andrea Estes, Nov. 3, 1983; "Ex-Professor Again Denied Bail in Benedict Case," Joseph Harvey, Nov. 3, 1983; "Key Trial Issue: Is Victim Really Dead? Precedents Cited in Douglas Case; Lawyers Say It May Become Landmark," Michael Frisby, Nov. 6, 1983; "High Court: Douglas Children Can Testify in Murder Case," Michael Frisby, Jan. 10, 1984; "Lawyer Asks to Be Douglas' Counsel, Says Former Researcher Is Penniless," Feb. 15, 1984; "Supreme Court Paves Way for Douglas Children to Testify," Feb. 28, 1984; "Witness to Offer Alibi in Prostitute's Killing," Kevin Cullen, March 20, 1984; "How Robin Benedict Was Killed," Jerry Taylor, May 3, 1984; "Mrs. Douglas Tells of Family Hardships," Jerry Taylor, May 6, 1984; "Prosecutor Announces End to Benedict Search," Jerry Taylor, May 11, 1984; "The Big Grab," John Brady, May 5, 1985; "3 Sentenced in IRA Gunrunning Scheme," Ed Quill, July 1, 1987.

Boston Herald: "Her 'Nightmare Curse,' " Diane Breda, Jan. 6, 1980; "Distraught Dad Hunts Daughter," Shelly Murphy, March 15, 1983; " 'Missing' Woman Traced to Her Boston Apartment," Elizabeth Holland, March 17, 1983; "Prof #1 Suspect in Beauty Slaying," Andrea Estes and John Birtwell, June 29, 1983; "Secret Life of a Missing Beauty," Andrea Estes, June 30, 1983; "Prof in 6-Month Binge of Travel and Sex," Andrea Estes and John Birtwell; "Cops Find Lost Beauty's Car," Andrea Estes and John Birtwell, July 18, 1983; "Prof's Wife Linked to Missing Beauty," Andrea Estes and John Birtwell, July 19, 1983; "DA: Children May Be Key in Beauty Case," Andrea Estes and John Birtwell, July 20, 1983; "Prof's Kids at Courthouse," John Birtwell, Aug. 9, 1983; "Parents Plan Court Bid to Claim Robin's Belongings," Andrew Gully, Aug. 15, 1983; "Prof's Kids in Jury Ordeal," Andrea Estes and John Birtwell, Aug. 17, 1983; "Ousted Tufts Prof Tries to Sell Family Beach Lot," Andrea Estes and John Birtwell, Aug. 19, 1983; "No-Talk Children of Prof May Face Lockup," Andrea Estes, Aug. 24, 1983; "Prof's Shocking Confession: I Gave Robin Cash," Andrea Estes, Aug.

25, 1983; "Prof's Kids in Court but Don't Testify," August 31, 1983; "Prof Stole $50G for Romance, Court Says," Andrea Estes and John Birtwell, Oct. 13, 1983; "No-Bail Order 'Ridiculous': Attorney," Nov. 1, 1983; "Court Told of Beauty's Violent Death," Andrea Estes and John Birtwell, Nov. 1, 1983; "Douglas Settles Into Jail Life," John Birtwell, March 4, 1984; "Prof: "I'm Sorry I Killed Robin," Andrea Estes and John Birtwell, April 28, 1984; "Robin's Dad in Bid to See Prof," John Birtwell, May 4, 1984; "Douglas' Wife Reveals Private Torment," May 6, 1984; "Search for Robin Officially Ends," John Birtwell, May 11, 1984; "Robin Eulogized as 'Bright Flame,'" Joe Sciacca, May 12, 1984; "Douglas' Lawyer Doubts Movie Reality," Joe Heaney, Nov. 30, 1986.

New York Times: "Murder Charge against Tufts Professor Rocks Medical School," Dudley Clendinen, Nov. 20, 1983; "A Crusader for the Rights of Animals," David McKay Wilson, April 8, 1984; "About New York," William E. Geist, Jan. 8, 1986.

Philadelphia Inquirer: "2 Unlikely Characters Trapped in Tale of Love in Boston's Underside," Carol Horner, Dec. 27, 1983.

Lawrence Eagle-Tribune: "White Eagles Drum Corps Alive and Well in Methuen," April 1, 1976; "Missing Woman's Mother Running Out of Hope," Gwenn Friss, June 26, 1983; "Missing: The Case Intensifies," Russell Glitman, July 1, 1983; "Divers to Press On in Search for Woman," Russell Glitman, July 10, 1983; "Children to Testify before Grand Jury," Russell Glitman, Aug. 5, 1983; "Robin Benedict: Her Fateful Journey from Methuen to the Combat Zone," Russell Glitman, Aug. 21, 1983; "Robin Benedict Gets Noticed by Vice Squad," Russell Glitman, Aug. 22, 1983; "DiFruscia's Edge: Knowing the Angles," Gwenn Friss, March 19, 1984.

Lake Placid News: "History of Lake Placid PeeWee Association," Shirley Seney, April 3, 1975; "Cell Research Project Focuses on Breath of Life," Jan. 15, 1976; "Kinderhockey," Melissa Hale, Jan. 22, 1976.

Pawtuxet Valley Daily Times: "Announce Engagement," September 7, 1943; "Lois Graemiger Marries John Boulton at Church," Oct. 11, 1943; "Births," July 13, 1944; "William T. Boulton," Oct. 28, 1957; "Mrs. Boulton, P.T.A. Leader, Dies; Was 33," July 9, 1959; "Boulton Funeral," July 11, 1959.

Reverence for Life: "Revlon, Inc. and the Rockefeller University Announce Major Research Project," Feb. 1981; "An Historical Moment," May–June 1981; "Looking Back," May–June 1981; "Message from the President," May–June 1981; "NEAVS Sponsors Scientific Symposium," Sept.–Oct. 1982; "How the Mighty Have Fallen," March–April 1983.

Mississippi Press-Register: "Ray Costict's Source of Inspiration," Mike Wixon, Jan. 6, 1977; "He Knows about the Cruel Blows of Life and Football," Mike Wixon, Aug. 2, 1981;

Advances in Psychosomatic Medicine: "Psychiatric Observations on Obesity," M. L. Glucksman, 7:194, 1972; The Age: "How the Bunny Lobby Terrorised Revlon," Feb. 12, 1981; Berkshire Sampler: "The Best Little Cathouse in Connecticut," Steve Moore, Jan. 13, 1985. Brockton Enterprise: "Mystery Session Held in Benedict Slay Case," Gary Finkelstein, Dec. 2, 1983; Constabulary: "SP Foxboro," 1982; "The Robin Benedict Case," Tom Neff, 1983; Journal of Cell Biology: "Enzymatic Digestion of Desmosome and Hemidesmosome Plaques Performed on Ultrathin Sections," William H. J. Douglas, Robert C. Ripley, and Richard A. Ellis, 44:211, 1970; Journal of Cell Science: "Phosphatidate Phosphohydrolase Activity as a Marker for Surfactant Synthesis in Organotypic Cultures of Type II Alveolar Pneumonocytes,"

William H. J. Douglas, Sally K. Sommers-Smith, and John M. Johnston, 60:199, 1983; **Platts-burgh Press-Republican:** "Deaths and Funerals," March 8, 1961; "Accused Killer Wooed by PSUC," James Kinsella, Nov. 3, 1983; **Plattsburgh State Today:** "Biologist Wins '78 Teaching Excellence Award," May–June 1978; **Playboy:** "Sex in America: Boston," Ken Bode, May 1980; **Psychosomatic Medicine:** "Psychological Aspects of Reducing," Hilde Bruch, 14:337, 1952; "The Response of Obese Patients to Weight Reduction: A Clinical Evaluation of Behavior," M. L. Glucksman and J. Hirsch, 30:1, 1968; "The Response of Obese Patients to Weight Reduction," M. L. Glucksman, J. Hirsch, R. S. McCully, B. A. Barron, and J. L. Knittle, 30:359, 1968; **Salem News:** "New Russell Plaza Owners Seek to Evict Sauna Tenant," July 29, 1977. **Smithtown News:** "Wedding Bells," Aug. 29, 1963; **In Touch:** "New Methodology," William H. J. Douglas, May 1982; **Tufts Observer:** " 'Rocky Horror Show' Is True Punk Cinema," Bruce Newberg, Oct. 13, 1978; "Tufts Growth Threatens Chinatown," Barbara Kyle, March 23, 1979; **US:** "Murder in Boston," Micki Siegel, July 16, 1984; **WCVB:** "Chronicle" broadcast; **WBZ:** "Mysteries of the Supernatural."